Understanding Lawyers' Ethics in Canada

Understanding Lawyers' Ethics in Canada

Inspired by Monroe Freedman and Abbe Smith's Understanding Lawyers' Ethics

Alice Woolley

Understanding Lawyers' Ethics in Canada
© LexisNexis Canada Inc. 2011
March 2011

All rights reserved. No part of this publication may be reproduced, stored in any material form (including photocopying or storing it in any medium by electronic means and whether or not transiently or incidentally to some other use of this publication) without the written permission of the copyright holder except in accordance with the provisions of the Copyright Act. Applications for the copyright holder's written permission to reproduce any part of this publication should be addressed to the publisher.

Warning: The doing of an unauthorized act in relation to a copyrighted work may result in both a civil claim for damages and criminal prosecution.

Members of the LexisNexis Group Worldwide

Canada	LexisNexis Canada Inc., 123 Commerce Valley Dr. E. Suite 700, MARKHAM, Ontario
Australia	Butterworths, a Division of Reed International Books Australia Pty Ltd, CHATSWOOD, New South Wales
Austria	ARD Betriebsdienst and Verlag Orac, VIENNA
Czech Republic	Orac, sro, PRAGUE
France	Éditions du Juris-Classeur SA, PARIS
Hong Kong	Butterworths Asia (Hong Kong), HONG KONG
Hungary	Hvg Orac, BUDAPEST
India	Butterworths India, NEW DELHI
Ireland	Butterworths (Ireland) Ltd, DUBLIN
Italy	Giuffré, MILAN
Malaysia	Malayan Law Journal Sdn Bhd, KUALA LUMPUR
New Zealand	Butterworths of New Zealand, WELLINGTON
Poland	Wydawnictwa Prawnicze PWN, WARSAW
Singapore	Butterworths Asia, SINGAPORE
South Africa	Butterworth Publishers (Pty) Ltd, DURBAN
Switzerland	Stämpfli Verlag AG, BERNE
United Kingdom	Butterworths Tolley, a Division of Reed Elsevier (UK), LONDON, WC2A
USA	LexisNexis, DAYTON, Ohio

Library and Archives Canada Cataloguing in Publication

Woolley, Alice
 Understanding lawyers' ethics in Canada / Alice Woolley.

Includes bibliographical references and index.
ISBN 978-0-433-46330-6

 1. Legal ethics—Canada. I. Title.

KE339.W66 2011   174'.30971   C2011-900933-1
KF306.W66 2011

Printed and bound in Canada.

ABOUT THE AUTHOR

Alice Woolley is a Professor of Law at the Faculty of Law, University of Calgary. Prior to joining the Faculty in 2004, Professor Woolley practised law in Calgary, working primarily in the areas of energy regulation and civil litigation. Professor Woolley's academic interests are in the areas of lawyers' ethics, professional regulation and administrative law. She has published papers on billing, access to justice, character regulation, civility, ethics teaching and theoretical legal ethics. She is also the co-editor and co-author of the casebook *Lawyers' Ethics and Professional Regulation*, published by LexisNexis Canada. Professor Woolley received her B.A. and LL.B. from the University of Toronto, and her LL.M. from Yale Law School.

PREFACE

In the spring of 2009 Monroe Freedman asked if I would be interested in writing a Canadian version of his seminal American textbook, *Understanding Lawyers' Ethics*. While already familiar with his extensive and influential work on legal ethics, I had "met" Professor Freedman as co-bloggers at Legal Ethics Forum, where we had taken complimentary positions on a number of issues. His suggestion was instantly attractive; it would be impossible to overstate Professor Freedman's influence and importance in the field, and his commitment to the morality and ethics of zealous advocacy aligns with mine. The book, which he now co-authors with Abbe Smith, is an excellent introduction and overview to the field of legal ethics, that both explains the applicable law as well as analyzing and critiquing that law. More pragmatically, following an existing work's organization and structure made the somewhat overwhelming thought of writing a textbook less daunting.

Undertaking to write a Canadian version of *Understanding Lawyers' Ethics* was not, however, straightforward. The structure and content of the law governing lawyers in Canada is influenced by American law, and is similar in many important respects. Yet at the same time it does not follow from American law, is distinct in ways that matter and — most importantly — exists within a different constitutional, legal and cultural context. This meant that certain aspects of Professor Freedman's work, and particularly his reliance on American constitutionalism to justify zealous advocacy, did not translate into Canadian terms. Moreover, and perhaps because I am Canadian, my own understanding of the justification for zealous advocacy follows primarily from principles of democratic legitimacy, and the authority of law, rather than from the (admittedly related) principle of respect for individual autonomy. This meant that while I was likely to end up in many similar places to Professors Freedman and Smith, my journey there could not be the same.

I thus decided to approach this book as one inspired by Professors Freedman and Smith's book, and also by Professor Freedman's larger body of scholarship, but as a free standing work rather than as a Canadian version of theirs. I follow the structure of their book for the most part, borrow examples from them that I think are illustrative and helpful, rely on source materials that they relied upon and, where I take a distinct position from them I note the difference. In one or two places — for example, where I explain how a lawyer should present perjured testimony from a criminal accused — I modify text directly from their book and incorporate it here.

Professor Freedman has been continually helpful and encouraging as I undertook this task. He read every chapter of the book and provided me with comments and suggestions. While generously sharing with me his wisdom, insights and experience, he also gave me complete freedom to write the book as I saw fit, never suggesting that I change my position where it varied from his, or that I follow the American version more closely. I could not be more grateful for, and appreciative of, his mentorship.

Writing a Canadian textbook on lawyers' ethics inspired by an American book created one set of challenges. Writing that book as an Anglophone Albertan presented another. The practice of law in Québec is distinct substantively and organizationally; obtaining a proper understanding of those distinctions without French is essentially impossible — many publications of the Barreau du Québec are not available in English; and yet to write a textbook which essentially assumed Québec out of existence, or which described the situation in Québec inaccurately, was obviously wholly unsatisfactory.

I presented my problem to Gérald Tremblay, former President of the Barreau, and the Québec representative to the Federation of Law Societies. Mtre. Tremblay suggested that I approach a lawyer at his firm, Shaun Finn, who practises litigation and has a strong academic interest in the law, particularly in relation to class actions, a topic that he has been exploring in the context of obtaining an LL.M. at the Université Laval. Shaun generously agreed to read the entire text and did so, ensuring that I had properly interpreted the Barreau's Code of Conduct as well as providing important contextual information in relation to the *Civil Code of Québec* and other Québec laws, such as the *Code of Civil Procedure*. Again, I am extraordinarily grateful for his generosity to me, and to this project. His help exceeded his mandate, and there are several places where he added thoughts and analysis that made the book better than it would have been otherwise.

ACKNOWLEDGMENTS

As set out in the preface, this book would never have been written without Monroe Freedman's inspiration and encouragement. I am also, though, greatly indebted to many others who helped me work through the writing process. The University of Calgary supported this project with research leaves in the winter terms of 2010 and 2011, and with funded research assistance in the summer of 2010. LexisNexis also provided financial support to assist with the research and preparation of the manuscript.

Invaluable research and editorial support was provided by JD students Chad Conrad and Brynne Harding, both of whom were notable for their diligence, enthusiasm and willingness to be critical where necessary. University of Calgary colleagues Greg Hagen, Jennifer Koshan and Jonnette Watson-Hamilton were patient and willing sounding boards for many of the ideas developed here. Ethics colleagues Adam Dodek and Trevor Farrow provided excellent feedback on particular chapters, and Adam in particular engaged in many helpful e-mail exchanges with me about specific points of confusion or uncertainty in my analysis. Malcolm Mercer of the firm McCarthy Tétrault provided helpful comments and feedback on Chapter 8, "Conflicts of Interest". As he has done since first year law school, Jonathan Dawe clarified my thinking and analysis, here with respect to ethics in the context of criminal law.

More personally, my dear friend and colleague from practice Kate Morriset has spent much time over the years talking with me about the ethics of legal practice, particularly with respect to one's duty of candour in court and when counselling clients. My sister Frances Woolley has been of invaluable assistance here and in earlier articles in helping me to avoid or reduce errors in my economic analysis of the legal profession, and my sister Rachel Goddyn helped me work through ideas about what it means to be an effective advocate inside and outside of the law. My parents Lois and Peter Woolley have my greatest respect and affection for having taught me that every idea is worth discussing, and that there are some ideas worth fighting for.

Above all, though, I want to acknowledge the love and encouragement of Gerry and Emily, who bore with patience and good humour the practical burden of living with my intensity while writing this book. Moreover, Gerry's questioning of any and all received wisdom helped make my ideas better, and Emily's willingness to listen and to try and figure out these new and unfamiliar concepts helped me make sure my ideas were better expressed than they would otherwise have been.

And to my beloved John I say, "yes, this book is an 'iesta'."

AUTHOR'S NOTE

In order to retain gender neutrality, while avoiding using "they" as a singular pronoun, I have chosen to alternate between genders of lawyers and clients by chapter. In odd numbered chapters the lawyers are women and the clients are men. In even numbered chapters the lawyers are men and the clients are women. When discussing case law I of course use gendered pronouns based on the facts of the case.

TABLE OF CONTENTS

About the Author v
Preface vii
Acknowledgments ix
Author's Note xi
Table of Cases xxi

Chapter 1: The Sources and Context of Lawyers' Ethics
1. Introduction 1
2. Why do we Need to Understand Lawyers' Ethics? 1
3. Where do Lawyers' Legal and Ethical Duties Come From? ... 3
   - A. The Regulatory Structure of the Canadian Profession 4
   - B. Codes of Conduct as a Source of Lawyers' Legal and Ethical Duties 9
   - C. Law Society Discipline as a Source of Lawyers' Legal and Ethical Duties 12
   - D. Other Sources of Lawyers' Legal and Ethical Duties 13
   - E. The Purposes of the Rules Governing Lawyer Conduct 15
   - F. The Integrity Challenge 17

Chapter 2: In Defence of Zealous Advocacy
1. Introduction 21
2. Lawyers in Canadian Legal Culture 22
3. Substantive Legal Norms 25
   - A. Introduction 25
   - B. The Individual and the Law 26
   - C. Interpretation and the Law 31
   - D. Lawyers as Resolute Advocates 32
4. The Ethical Justification 33
   - A. Arguments Against Resolute Advocacy 33
     - i. The Postmodern Objection 34
     - ii. The Personal Morality Objection 36
     - iii. The Morality-of-Law Objection 38

    B.   In Defence of the Lawyer as Resolute Advocate 40

Chapter 3: The Lawyer-Client Relationship
1. Introduction 45
2. Client Selection 46
3. Lawyer-Client Decision Making and Client Counselling 52
    A.   Introduction 52
    B.   Lawyer-Client Decision Making 54
    C.   Client Counselling 59
    D.   Counselling and Unlawful Activity 61
4. Fees 64
5. Withdrawal 65
6. Conclusion 68

Chapter 4: The Practice of Advocacy
1. Introduction 69
2. Lawyer Competence: The Heart of Resolute Advocacy 71
3. Restraints on Zeal 75
    A.   Frivolous Arguments 75
    B.   The Rule Against Sharp Practice 81
    C.   Relevant Adverse Authority 85
4. Zeal in Context 87
    A.   Discovery 87
    B.   *Ex Parte* Applications 88
    C.   Investigating a Client's Case – Covert Investigations and Communicating with Witnesses 90
5. Lawyer Speech 93
    A.   Introduction 93
    B.   Public Statements 94
    C.   Criticism of Other Lawyers 96
    D.   Criticizing Judges and the Legal System 101
6. Conclusion 104

Chapter 5: Lawyer-Client Trust and Confidence
1. Introduction 107
2. When do Lawyers have a Duty not to Disclose? 109
    A.   The General Rule 109

	B.	There must be a Lawyer-Client Relationship for Information to be Confidential or Privileged	109
	C.	If the Lawyer-Client Communication does not Relate to the Giving or Receiving of Legal Advice, it will not be Privileged, but will still be Confidential	110
	D.	Criminal Communications are not Privileged, and are likely Excluded from the Duty of Confidentiality	112
	E.	Third Party Knowledge of Information usually Limits the Application of the Privilege, but does not normally Limit the Ethical Duty of Confidentiality	115
	F.	The Identity of the Client is generally Confidential, and is sometimes Privileged	117
	G.	If Information does not come from a Client, it is Confidential, but may not be Privileged	118
	H.	Information that is Real Property is Confidential, but not Privileged	119
	I.	When the Client is an Organization or Corporation, the Duty of Confidentiality is Owed to the Organization, not to Individuals within the Organization	119
	J.	Absolute Secrecy is Required for Information that is Confidential and Privileged	119
	K.	The Duty not to Disclose includes the Lawyer's Colleagues and Staff	120
	L.	The Duty of Confidentiality and the Privileged Status of Information Lasts Indefinitely	120
	M.	Consequences of Breaching the Duty	121
	N.	The Implied Undertaking Rule	124
3.	When are Lawyers either Permitted or Required to Disclose Confidential Information?		124
	A.	Introduction	124
	B.	The Lawyer's Ability to Disclose when Information is neither Confidential nor Privileged, or when the Information is Confidential but not Privileged	125
	C.	The General Duty to Comply with Valid Legal Orders that Require or Permit Disclosure of Confidential and Privileged Information	127
	D.	Information that is Confidential and Privileged may be Disclosed where the Client Waives Her Right to Confidentiality	127

	E.	When a Lawyer Acts for More than One Client on a Joint Retainer, Information Arising from that Retainer is not Confidential or Privileged between the Clients, but will be Confidential and Privileged Relative to Third Parties.............. 129
	F.	Information that is Confidential and Privileged may be Disclosed during Law Society Disciplinary Proceedings 130
	G.	Confidential and Privileged Information may be Disclosed to Another Lawyer to Obtain Legal Advice and may also be Disclosed to Allow the Lawyer to Defend Herself in Litigation.. 132
	H.	Where Confidential and Privileged Information is Necessary to Establish the Innocence of an Accused, the Court may Require the Lawyer to Disclose It........................... 133
	I.	Information that is Confidential and Privileged may be Disclosed to Prevent Serious, Clear and Imminent Threats to the Safety of an Identifiable Person or Group of People...... 136
	J.	Physical or "Real" Evidence of a Crime is not Privileged, and if Inculpatory must be Disclosed... 139
4.	What Duties does a Lawyer have to Protect the Client's Right to Confidentiality?.. 142
5.	What Duties do Lawyers have in Relation to the Confidentiality Claims of Others?... 143
6.	Can the Lawyer's Duty of Trust and Confidence be Justified?.......... 145
	A.	Justifying the General Duty 145
	B.	Some Specific Points 155
7.	Conclusion 157

Chapter 6: The Perjury Trilemma

1.	Introduction.. 159
2.	The Prohibition on Assisting Clients to Deceive the Court 163
3.	When does the Lawyer know that Testimony is (or will be) Deceptive?... 165
4.	The Lawyer's Duties where the Client Intends to Deceive, or has Deceived, a Court or Tribunal.. 167
5.	Assessing the Solutions to the Problem of Perjury 173
	A.	Introduction.. 173
	B.	The Solution of Withdrawal and Limited Disclosure 173
	C.	Disclosure... 176
	D.	Intentional Ignorance 177
	E.	Narrative Testimony 179

	F.	Continuing to Represent the Client as if the Testimony were Truthful.. 180
6.	Conclusion 182

Chapter 7: Examining Witnesses: Preparation of Witnesses and Cross-Examination

1.	Introduction... 185
2.	Preparing Witnesses... 185
	A.	Introduction... 185
	B.	The Law Governing Witness Preparation 187
	C.	Why is it Difficult to Prepare a Witness without Coaching? ... 190
	D.	The Skill of Effective Witness Preparation.............................. 197
	E.	Ethical and Effective Preparation of Witnesses 199
3.	Cross-Examination.. 201
	A.	Introduction... 201
	B.	The Law of Cross-Examination 204
	C.	Ethical Cross-Examination... 207

Chapter 8: Conflicts of Interest: Creating the Conditions for Loyalty and Confidentiality

1.	Introduction... 215
2.	Lawyer-Client Conflicts Defined 216
	A.	When will a Lawyer be considered to have Violated the "Fundamental Duty … To Act in the Best Interests of His or Her Client to the Exclusion of All Other Adverse Interests"?.. 217
		i.	Substantial Risk of Material and Adverse Effect on Representation.. 217
		ii.	Misuse of Confidential Information............................. 220
		iii.	Obtaining an Improper Advantage............................... 221
	B.	Who is a Client?.. 223
	C.	What Constitutes Informed Consent? 227
3.	Kinds of Conflicts of Interest 231
	A.	Conflicts Relating to the Lawyer's Own Interests 231
	B.	Conflicts between a Former Client and a New Client............ 232
	C.	Conflicts between Current Clients 233
	D.	Third Party and Multiple Role Conflicts................................. 235
4.	Why are Some Conflicts Forbidden? 236

5.	The Preventative Rationale		238
6.	The Appearances Rationale		241
7.	Lawyers' Specific Duties		242
	A.	Duties to Former Clients	243
		i. The General Principles	243
		ii. When is a New Matter Related to a Prior Retainer?	246
		iii. When will the Information Obtained in the Earlier Retainer be Confidential Enough to be Disqualifying?	249
		iv. Is the Restriction on Misuse of Confidential Information Limited to Retainers against the Former Client, or does it Apply More Generally?	251
		v. What Specific Rules Apply to Transfers of Lawyers between Firms?	252
		vi. The Problem of Tactical Applications to Disqualify	253
		vii. When Screening Devices will be Sufficient	254
		viii. When Acting Against a Former Client is Prohibited even though Confidential Information from that Client will not be Used to His Disadvantage	255
	B.	Duties to Current Clients	257
		i. General	257
		ii. Simultaneous Representation of Clients in a Dispute	258
		iii. Simultaneous Representation of Clients in a Conflict	259
		a. When is there a Conflict?	260
		b. Information that must be provided to Parties in a Joint Representation	261
		c. The Best Interests Requirement	262
		d. When a Dispute Arises	263
		e. High Risk Joint Retainers	263
		iv. Concurrent Representation of Clients	265
	C.	Lawyer-Client Conflicts	272
8.	Conclusion		276

Chapter 9: Lawyers' Ethics in the Context of Criminal Law

1.	Introduction		277
2.	Prosecutorial Ethics		277
	A.	Minister of Justice or Zealous Advocate?	277
	B.	Prosecutorial Discretion	284
		i. What is Prosecutorial Discretion?	284

		ii.	How is Prosecutorial Discretion to be Exercised? 288
		iii.	Oversight of Prosecutorial Discretion 291
	C.	Disclosure 297
3.	Defence Counsel Ethics 301
	A.	Defending the Guilty 301
	B.	Plea Bargaining 308
4.	Conclusion 311

Chapter 10: Zealous Advocacy and Access to Justice

1.	Introduction 313
2.	Barriers to Access to Lawyers 314
	A. Do I Need A Lawyer? 314
	B. How Do I Pay For One? 317
3.	Reducing the Barriers to Access 321
	A. Advertising and Solicitation 322
	B. *Pro Bono* 327
	C. Other Regulatory Measures 329
4.	Conclusion 331

Index 333

TABLE OF CASES

2475813 Nova Scotia Ltd. v. Green	226
A & B Auto Leasing & Car Rental Inc. v. Mississauga Auto Clinic Inc.	77
Achakzad v. Zemaryalai	224
Adams v. Law Society of Alberta	275
Adler Firestopping Ltd. v. Rea	86
Alberta Union of Provincial Employees v. United Nurses of Alberta	230
Alles v. Maurice	262
Allied Signal Inc. v. Dome Petroleum Inc.	244, 255
Anderson v. Bank of British Columbia	32
ATCO Gas and Pipelines Ltd. v. Sheard	250
Atland Containers Ltd. v. Macs Corp. Ltd. et al.	78
Attorney General v. Times Newspapers Ltd.	95
Baker v. Canada (Minister of Citizenship and Immigration)	28, 288
Bank of Montreal v. D'Angelo	82
Bank of Nova Scotia v. MacKinnon	82
Barrett v. Reynolds	229, 264
Bell v. Nash	224
Berry v. Law Society of New Brunswick	247
Biggs v. London Loan and Savings Co. of Canada	222, 274
Blackwell v. Dixon	83
Blank v. Canada (Minister of Justice)	108, 116, 147
Booth v. Huxter	228, 260
Bow Valley Energy Inc. v. San Diego Gas and Electric Co.	250
Bowman v. Rainy River (Town)	93
Boyd v. Boyd	273
British Columbia (Attorney General) v. Christie	3, 171
British Columbia (Ministry of Attorney General, Criminal Justice Branch) v. British Columbia (Commission of Inquiry into the Death of Frank Paul – Davies Commission)	293, 294
Brockton (Municipality) v. Frank Cowan Co.	236
Brookville Carriers Flatbed GP Inc. v. Blackjack Transport Ltd.	233, 237, 248, 255, 256
Brunswick News Inc. v. Langdon	89
Byers (Litigation Guardian of) v. Pentex Print Master Industries Inc.	77
Canada (Attorney General) v. Law Society of British Columbia	322
Canada (Minister of National Revenue) v. Reddy	111, 126
Canada (Minister of National Revenue) v. Singh	111, 126
Canada (Minister of National Revenue) v. Vlug	111, 126
Canada (Privacy Commissioner) v. Blood Tribe Department of Health	113, 127, 147
Canada Post Corp. v. Euclide Cormeir Plumbing and Heating Inc.	143
Canadian Pacific Railway Co. v. Aikins, MacAulay & Thorvaldson	249

Canadian Paraplegic Assn. (Newfoundland and Labrador) Inc. v. Sparcott
  Engineering Ltd. 89
Canadian Union of Public Employees v. New Brunswick Liquor Corp. 32
Cardinal v. Kent Institution 28
Carmichael v. Strathshore Industrial Park Ltd. 77
Carter v. Blake 57
Celanese Canada Inc. v. Murray Demolition Corp. 143, 145
Central Trust Co. v. Rafuse 74
Cewe Estate v. Mide Wilson 271
Chapates v. Petro Canada 253, 254
Chapters Inc. v. Davies, Ward & Beck 247
Chiefs of Ontario v. Ontario 230, 233, 256
CIBC Mellon Co. v. National Trust Co. 93
Committee for Justice and Liberty v. National Energy Board 242
Consulate Ventures Inc. v. Amico Contracting & Engineering (1992) Inc. 233, 248
Cooking Lake Enterprises Inc. v. Samson First Nation 93
Crevier v. Québec (Attorney General) 27
Crosby v. Guardian Insurance Co. of Canada 83, 84
Cunliffe v. Law Society of British Columbia 278
Cushing v. Hood 109, 125
Dabbs v. Sun Life 65
Davey v. Woolley, Hames, Dale & Dingwall 218, 230, 237, 262
De Beers Canada Inc. v. Shore Gold Inc. 237, 270
Delgamuukw v. British Columbia 69
Descôteaux v. Mierzwinski 107, 110, 112, 121, 127, 142
Diamond v. Kaufman 262
Dobbin v. Acrohelipro Global Services Inc. 225
Dreco Energy Services Ltd. v. Wenzel Downhole Tools Ltd. 227
Dunsmuir v. New Brunswick 27, 32, 42
Eldridge v. British Columbia (Attorney General) 31
Encorp Pacific (Canada) v. Rocky Mountain Return Centre Ltd. 89
Engle v. Carswell 226
Escott v. Collision Clinic Ltd. 225
Esso Resources Ltd. v. Stearns Catalytic Ltd. 88
Finney v. Barreau du Québec 5
First Property Holdings Inc. v. Beatty 220, 221, 237, 271
Forsyth v. Cross 224
Foster Wheeler Power Co. v. Société intermunicipale de gestion et d'élimination
  des déchets (SIGED) Inc. 109, 111, 141, 147
Frumasa v. Ungaro 74
Fullowka v. Pinkerton's of Canada Ltd. 78
G.H. Coulter v. Jens 250
Gainers Inc. v. Pocklington 226, 250
Galambos v. Perez 274
Garten v. Kruk 82
Geffen v. Goodman Estate 120
General Motors Acceptance Corp. of Canada v. Isaac Estate 86
General Motors of Canada Ltd. v. Canada 189

Case	Page
Girardet v. Crease & Co.	74
GMP Securities Ltd. v. Stikeman Elliott	237, 271
Goldberg v. Law Society of British Columbia	72, 73, 96, 99, 100, 101
Goodis v. Ontario (Minister of Correctional Services)	127
Grainger v. Hill et al.	78
Grand Anse Contracting Ltd. v. MacKinnon	264
Graybriar Investments Ltd. v. Davis & Company	74
Greater Vancouver Regional District v. Melville	256
Greater Vancouver Transportation Authority v. Canadian Federation of Students – British Columbia Component	27
Gualtieri v. Canada (Attorney General)	88
Guilford Industries Ltd. v. Hankinson Services Ltd. et al.	78
Gunn v. Washek	316
Hagblom v. Henderson	74
Heart (Town) v. School Board Ontario North East	93
Hill v. Church of Scientology	95, 99
Histed v. Law Society of Manitoba	102, 104
Interprovincial Pipeline Inc. v. Canada (Minister of National Revenue)	116
Jasmine Networks Inc. v. Marvell Semiconductor Inc.	144
Jellema v. American Bullion Minerals Ltd.	259, 262
Jorgensen v. San Jose Mines Ltd.	237, 259
Juman v. Doucette	108, 124
Kaila v. Khalsa Diwan Society	247
Kent v. Waldock	77
Kessiloff v. Law Society of Manitoba	103
Kilbreath v. Saskatchewan (Attorney General)	111, 126
King v. Arnett	262
Kostuch v. Alberta	285
Kovac v. Opus Building Corp.	259, 262
Krieger v. Law Society of Alberta	281, 284, 285, 286, 287, 288, 293, 299
Lafond v. Muskeg Lake Cree Nation	111
Lavallee, Rackel & Heintz v. Canada (Attorney General)	3, 107, 108, 127, 142
Law Society of Alberta v. Abbi	273
Law Society of Alberta v. Arkell	122
Law Society of Alberta v. Belzil	115, 122
Law Society of Alberta v. Bissett	122
Law Society of Alberta v. Breitman	88
Law Society of Alberta v. Clark	122, 273
Law Society of Alberta v. Engel	103
Law Society of Alberta v. Gelmon	81
Law Society of Alberta v. Gillis	81
Law Society of Alberta v. Harrison	73
Law Society of Alberta v. Merchant	88
Law Society of Alberta v. Michaels	73
Law Society of Alberta v. Miskuski	122
Law Society of Alberta v. Piragoff	283, 300
Law Society of Alberta v. Pozniak	97, 98, 99
Law Society of Alberta v. Stemp	327

Table of Cases xxiv

Law Society of Alberta v. Stephenson 118, 123
Law Society of Alberta v. Syed 72, 308
Law Society of Alberta v. Trawick 143, 144
Law Society of BC v. Trower 273
Law Society of British Columbia v. A lawyer 74
Law Society of British Columbia v. Christie 91
Law Society of British Columbia v. Ewachniuk 121
Law Society of British Columbia v. Goldberg 97
Law Society of British Columbia v. Hattori 261
Law Society of British Columbia v. MacAdam 123
Law Society of British Columbia v. Pierce 327
Law Society of British Columbia v. Siebenga 327
Law Society of Northwest Territories v. Crawford 96
Law Society of Saskatchewan v. Filyk 73
Law Society of Saskatchewan v. Kirkham 299
Law Society of Saskatchewan v. Merchant 131
Law Society of Saskatchewan v. Segal 164
Law Society of Upper Canada v. Amorim 121
Law Society of Upper Canada v. Ashebee 264
Law Society of Upper Canada v. Barnett 272, 322, 327
Law Society of Upper Canada v. Carter 97
Law Society of Upper Canada v. Clark 69
Law Society of Upper Canada v. Coady 102
Law Society of Upper Canada v. Daboll 273, 274
Law Society of Upper Canada v. De Teresi 56
Law Society of Upper Canada v. Freedman 121
Law Society of Upper Canada v. Frolick 264
Law Society of Upper Canada v. Grace 115, 122, 124
Law Society of Upper Canada v. Gray 121
Law Society of Upper Canada v. Hunter 218, 229, 230, 275, 276
Law Society of Upper Canada v. Joseph 123, 223, 275
Law Society of Upper Canada v. Kay 97, 98, 99
Law Society of Upper Canada v. Logan 222, 231, 273, 275
Law Society of Upper Canada v. Novak 222, 275
Law Society of Upper Canada v. Paletta 97, 98
Law Society of Upper Canada v. Roine 264, 275
Law Society of Upper Canada v. Ross 115, 123
Law Society of Upper Canada v. Tulk 97, 98
Law Society of Upper Canada v. Van Duffelen 275
Law Society of Yukon v. Kimmerly 103
Layden v. Canada (Minister of Human Resources and Social Development) 89
Little Sisters Book and Art Emporium v. Canada 28
Lotech Medical Systems Ltd. v. Kinetic Concept Inc. 270
Lougheed Enterprises v. Armbruster 85
M.D. v. Windsor-Essex Children's Aid Society 77
MacCulloch v. McInnes, Cooper and Robertson 74
MacDonald Estate v. Martin 120, 220, 241, 244, 246, 251, 252, 253, 254, 255
MacIntyre v. Dickie 88

MacMillan Bloedel Ltd. v. Freeman and Co.	91
Maranda v. Richer	111
Marchand v. Public General Hospital Society of Chatham	100
Martin v. Gray	220, 238
McGregor v. Crossland	86
McKenna v. Gammon Gold Inc.	226, 237
Merchant v. Law Society of Saskatchewan	15, 327
Metcalfe v. Metcalfe	129
Miazga v. Kvello Estate	292, 293, 296
Moffat v. Wetstein	273
Moose Mountain Buffalo Ranch v. Greene Farms Drilling Ltd.	82
Ms. R. v. W.A.	92
MTS Allstream Inc. v. Bell Mobility Inc.	89
Murphy Canada Exploration Ltd. v. Novagas Canada Ltd.	93
Nelles v. Ontario	292, 296
Nova Scotia Barristers' Society v. Langille	275
Nova Scotia Barristers' Society v. MacIsaac	74
Nova Scotia Barristers' Society v. Morgan	102, 103
Nova Scotia Barristers' Society v. Murrant	97, 98
Nova Scotia Real Estate Commission v. Lorway	110, 117
Ontario (Minister of the Attorney General) v. Ontario (Information and Privacy Commissioner)	111, 126
Order of the Oblates of Mary Immaculate v. Dohm, Jaffer and Jeraj	128
Philip Services Corp. (Receiver of) v. Ontario (Securities Commission)	108, 116, 129
Picha v. Lee Inquest (Coroner of)	295
Pritchard v. Ontario (Human Rights Commission)	111, 112, 129
Prosser v. Prosser	89
Quibell v. Quibell	238
R. Sherwin Enterprises Ltd. v. Municipal Contracting Services Ltd.	236, 258
R. v. Ahluwaia	282
R. v. Aldhelm-White	280
R. v. Arsenault	297
R. v. Bain	298
R. v. Bartle	29
R. v. Bear	279
R. v. Boucher	278, 280
R. v. Bouhsass	205
R. v. Brigham	55
R. v. Brissett	221, 251
R. v. Brown	134, 135, 138, 155
R. v. Campbell	110, 112, 113, 128, 170
R. v. Christie	30
R. v. Colpitts	180
R. v. Cook	279, 280, 281, 285, 300
R. v. Corbett	207
R. v. Cram	104
R. v. Cunningham	67, 68, 111, 128, 162, 168, 169, 170, 180
R. v. D.N.	285

R. v. Darrach	191, 192, 207
R. v. Delisle	302
R. v. Desmond	251
R. v. Dickson	191
R. v. DiPalma	56
R. v. Dixon	298
R. v. Downey	56
R. v. Dunbar	55
R. v. Ellard	205, 279
R. v. Felderhof	100, 280, 286
R. v. Gayle	280
R. v. Grabowski	298
R. v. Haneveld	285
R. v. Hanington	117
R. v. Hebert	28
R. v. Hector	309
R. v. Hillier	279, 280
R. v. Hobbs	128
R. v. I.B.B.	149, 177, 179, 306
R. v. Illes	298
R. v. J.(G.P.)	281
R. v. J.M.	310
R. v. J.P.B.	309
R. v. Jabarianha	207
R. v. Jackson	281
R. v. Jenkins	165, 169
R. v. Jewitt	292
R. v. Joanisse	55
R. v. Jolivet	285
R. v. Joseph	309
R. v. K.(M.)	289, 295, 296
R. v. K.(S.)	309
R. v. Kirkham	300
R. v. Kopyto	103, 104
R. v. La	297, 298
R. v. Lamoureaux	55
R. v. Laperrière	310
R. v. Latimer	290
R. v. Law Office of Simon Rosenfeld	111, 126
R. v. Lawlor	188, 190, 279
R. v. Leopold	138
R. v. Li	129, 305
R. v. Logiacco	278, 279
R. v. Lyttle	204, 206
R. v. M.(G.O.)	309
R. v. MacInnis	298
R. v. Malone	309
R. v. Manninen	29

Table of Cases

R. v. Martin 113
R. v. McClure 107, 120, 133, 134, 142, 147
R. v. McCrimmon 3, 29
R. v. McNeil 297
R. v. Messervey 309
R. v. Mitchell 86
R. v. Mohan 206
R. v. Moore 165, 166
R. v. Morgentaler 28
R. v. Muise 189
R. v. Murray 3, 108, 119, 132, 140, 141, 142
R. v. Neil 15, 16, 21, 33, 70, 217, 218, 227, 228, 234, 237, 238, 241,
                                     242, 257, 266, 267, 268, 269, 270, 271
R. v. Nelles 291
R. v. Ng 285
R. v. Nguyen 298
R. v. Nixon 287
R. v. Nome 298
R. v. Nova Scotia Pharmaceutical Society 27
R. v. O'Connor 292
R. v. O'Grady 298
R. v. Orbanski 29
R. v. Osolin 204
R. v. Paquette 280
R. v. Peruta 279
R. v. Pivonka 309
R. v. Polani 188, 190
R. v. Power 280, 285, 292
R. v. Puddick 277, 278
R. v. R.(A.J.) 56, 208
R. v. R.R. 279
R. v. Randell 285
R. v. Read 129
R. v. Regan 277, 278
R. v. Riche 279
R. v. Riley 286
R. v. Robinson 279
R. v. Rose 279, 280
R. v. Rosenfeld 113
R. v. Samra 56
R. v. Scotney 309
R. v. Seaboyer 206
R. v. Serfaty 111, 126
R. v. Silvini 218, 229, 237, 262
R. v. Sinclair 3, 29
R. v. Situ 280
R. v. Smith 56
R. v. Smythe 285

R. v. Snow 205, 206
R. v. Stinchcombe 297
R. v. Stockley 309
R. v. Swain 28, 55, 56, 57
R. v. T.(V.) 292
R. v. Taillefer 298
R. v. Therens 27
R. v. W.(B.A.) 205
R. v. Weibe 189
R. v. White and Sennet 56
R. v. Widdifield 218, 262
R. v. Willier 3, 29
R. v. Wojcik 279
R. v. Wood 298
R. v. Yarlasky 309
Rayner v. Enright 254
Re B.C. Motor Vehicle Act 28
Re Ford Motor Co. of Canada Ltd. v. Osler, Hoskin & Harcourt 244, 255
Re McAlevy 69
Re Ontario Crime Commission 164
Re Wirick 111, 126
Reagh v. Reagh 247, 253
Regular v. Law Society of Newfoundland and Labrador 218, 228, 275
Ribeiro v. Vancouver (City) 271
Richards v. Producers Pipelines Inc. 250
Robb Estate v. St. Joseph's Health Care Centre 93
Robertson v. Edmonton (City) Police Service 77
Robertson v. Slater Vecchio 255
Rocket v. Royal College of Dental Surgeons 322, 323, 324
Rogacki v. Belz et al. 95
Rogan v. Prud'homme 57
Roncarelli v. Duplessis 24, 26, 27
Rosenstein v. Plant 224
Rousseau v. The Queen 80
Saint John Shipbuilding Ltd. v. Bow Valley Husky (Bermuda) Ltd .. 237, 255, 258
Seigel v. Seigel 226, 254
Sherman v. Manley 56
Skogstad v. Law Society of British Columbia 130
Skye Properties Ltd. v. Wu 218, 237, 255, 258
Smith v. Hughes 85
Smith v. Jones 39, 112, 136, 137, 138, 139, 142, 147, 155, 156, 170
Society of British Columbia v. Eisbrenner 103
Society of Lloyd's v. Van Snick 86
Society of Upper Canada v. Ross 138
Sogelco International Inc. v. Pêcheries Cap Lumière Fisheries Ltd. 254
Spaulding v. Zimmerman 125, 126
Standard Life Assurance Co. v. Elliott 77
Stewart v. Canadian Broadcasting Corp. 56, 94, 117, 222, 223, 237, 273

Table of Cases

Strother v. 3464920 Canada Inc. 16, 33, 57, 117, 216, 218, 219, 221, 228, 238, 268, 269, 270, 272
Stucky v. Canada 292
Suhl v. Larose 128
Sutts, Strosberg LLP v. Atlas Cold Storage Holdings Inc. 65
Szarfer v. Chodos 121, 223, 275
Szebelledy v. Constitution Insurance Co. of Canada 236
TD Canada Trust v. Chapel Hill Pet Studio Inc. 82
Temple v. Riley 82
Terracap Investments Inc. v. 2811 Development Corp. 271
The Queen v. Husbands 189, 190
Tilley v. Hails et al. 143
Time Logistics Ltd. v. Haworth Ltd. 77
Toddglen Construction Ltd. v. Concord Adex Developments Corp. 237, 270
TransAmerica Life Insurance Co. of Canada v. Seward 91
TransCanada Pipelines Ltd. v. Nova Scotia (Attorney General) 246
Tsiopoulos v. Commercial Union Assurance Co. 78
United States of America v. Friedland 89
Unterreiner v. Wilson et al. 78
Vacation Brokers Inc. v. Gervasi 82
Verma v. Zimmer 263
Vriend v. Alberta 31
Walker v. Phantom Industries Inc. 259
Wallace v. Canadian Pacific Railway 271
Walsh v. 1124660 Ontario Ltd. 88
Waxman v. Waxman 229, 237, 238, 264
Werring v. British Columbia 285
Widrig v. Cox Downie 247
Wilder v. Ontario (Securities Commission) 14
Williamson v. Roberts & Griffin 226
Winter v. Phillips 247
Xpress View Inc. v. Daco Manufacturing Ltd. 82
Young v. Young 70, 75, 76, 77

Chapter 1

THE SOURCES AND CONTEXT OF LAWYERS' ETHICS

1. INTRODUCTION

This book explains the legal and ethical duties governing the conduct of Canadian lawyers. It seeks to provide an approachable and succinct overview of this complex and understudied body of Canadian law and, as well, to engage with that law critically. The book's central thesis is that the fundamental legal and ethical obligation of lawyers is to assist clients to pursue their goals under and through the law — to be zealous advocates within the constraints of legality. It argues that that obligation is justified in principle and in practice, and that lawyers' specific legal and ethical duties, as currently articulated, should be assessed based on the extent to which they foster or undermine lawyers' accomplishment of that fundamental obligation. In addition, however, the role of zealous advocate is a difficult one to play, one that can create challenges for the lawyer's ability to achieve a life well-lived. How lawyers can do so — how one can be a good lawyer and a good person — is a secondary question with which this book engages.

The remainder of this chapter provides some background and context for this discussion of lawyers' ethics. It gives an overview of sources of lawyers' legal and ethical duties, and explains the regulatory structure of the legal profession, including the role of self-regulation within that structure. It also considers in a preliminary way the principles and norms that underlie lawyer regulation. But first it will consider a basic question: why does understanding lawyers' ethics matter?

2. WHY DO WE NEED TO UNDERSTAND LAWYERS' ETHICS?

Understanding lawyers' legal and ethical obligations is essential for anyone seeking to practise law. Whoever your clients, wherever you practise, and in whatever area of law you choose to specialize, there are duties and restrictions imposed on you, the violation of which can result in adverse consequences for you or for your clients. These consequences may take the form of disciplinary action by a law society — which can range from a reprimand to fines, suspension and disbarment — but they may also take the form of cost sanctions imposed by a court of law; a civil action in damages for negligence, breach of fiduciary duty or breach of contract; or an application to remove the lawyer as counsel of record. Simple prudence and risk management suggest the benefits of a thorough familiarity with the rules governing lawyers' conduct.

Less prosaically — and considered more broadly — lawyers' *ethics* merits study because of its foundational importance both to the society within which lawyers practise, and to the lawyer herself. To understand why that is the case it is necessary to elaborate more generally what we mean when we talk about "lawyers' ethics". Lawyers' ethics as an area of study causes confusion, even in those who write about it with some frequency, because it can be reasonably understood as referring to many different things, things which relate and overlap but which are also importantly distinct.[1]

Lawyers' ethics incorporates the specific legal and ethical duties imposed on lawyers; that is, the many and various legal rules which determine how lawyers can and must behave. It also incorporates the resolution of moral quandaries faced by a lawyer when she has the freedom within or apart from the rules of professional conduct to choose between different courses of action. And, further, it incorporates the question of whether a person who does the things that lawyers do — whether what she is required to do or what she chooses to do on matters in her discretion — can consider herself to have lived a good life: "Can a good lawyer be a good person?"[2] Is the lawyer's role morally justified? And even if it is, is occupying that role something which can be integrated with a lawyer's other moral values and commitments?

In these different manifestations, lawyers' ethics raises profound questions going on the one hand, to the heart of what it means for a society to be free and democratic, governed by the rule of law, and on the other hand, to the heart of what morality and ethics requires of us, of what it means to lead a life well-lived.

Understanding what democracy means in practice in Canadian society requires not only understanding the rights and obligations imposed by the *Canadian Charter of Rights and Freedoms*,[3] through statutes, and under the common law, but also requires understanding how law is applied in practice; it requires understanding the systems and institutions which make laws

---

[1] In one Canadian article, for example, the authors stated, "[b]y definition, ethics involves making moral choices between what is right and wrong" (Margaret Ann Wilkinson, Christa Walker & Peter Mercer, "Do Codes of Ethics Actually Shape Legal Practice" (2000) 45 McGill L.J. 645 at 648). The article goes on to assume that the only "ethical choices" are those involving ethical deliberation by the lawyer. While this "definition" of ethics is true in those circumstances when lawyers' ethics requires lawyers to make moral choices, it does not account for those circumstances where lawyer's actions are properly determined by legal or constitutional obligations, rather than by the lawyer's own conscientious beliefs. Nor does it account for the extent to which matters properly falling within lawyer's ethics, such as competence, do not involve much in the way of moral conflict.

[2] Charles Fried, "The Lawyer as Friend: The Moral Foundations of the Lawyer-Client Relation" (1976) 85 Yale L.J. 1060 at 1060.

[3] Part I of the *Constitution Act, 1982*, being Schedule B to the *Canada Act 1982* (U.K.), 1982, c. 11.

manifest. That, in turn, requires understanding the obligations and constraints imposed on lawyers working within these systems and institutions. How lawyers represent clients, the extent of the right to counsel which Canadians enjoy (or, as it turns out, do not enjoy),[4] the substantive duties placed on lawyers to ensure the functioning of the legal system, and answers to other like questions, say a great deal about, for example, what we actually mean when we say that "[e]veryone has the right to life, liberty and security of the person and the right not to be deprived thereof except in accordance with the principles of fundamental justice."[5] Thus, that a person may confide to his lawyer that he has committed a crime and where he has hidden the gun, and can trust that the lawyer will not breach his confidences, is a very specific instantiation of that general principle.[6] So too, though, is the rule that a person who sends his lawyer to find videotapes of his commission of a crime cannot rely on the lawyer to suppress those videotapes.[7]

At the same time lawyers who fulfill their professional obligations, and respect the constraints placed upon them, must have a satisfactory answer to the question of whether, having done so, they have lived a life that is morally satisfactory. The lawyer who knows that her client "got away with murder" can legitimately ask whether holding that knowledge confidential is consistent with being a good person. One recent American author has claimed that the professional ethics of lawyers is fundamentally inconsistent with a well-lived life, and that lawyers as a group are best described as "tragic villains".[8] This book rejects that position, but agrees that the question of the sufficiency of a lawyer's moral life turns on understanding what lawyers are prohibited, required or permitted to do in their practising lives, and why.

3. WHERE DO LAWYERS' LEGAL AND ETHICAL DUTIES COME FROM?

Where do lawyers' legal and ethical duties come from? Most obviously, those duties can be found in the various codes of professional conduct enacted and enforced by the provincial law societies — that is, by the bodies that largely control the admission and regulation of all Canadian lawyers. The codes of conduct do not, however, provide a complete picture of lawyers' legal and ethical duties; the power of law societies to discipline

---

[4] *British Columbia (Attorney General) v. Christie*, [2007] S.C.J. No. 21, [2007] SCC 21 (S.C.C.); *R. v. Sinclair*, [2010] S.C.J. No. 35, 2010 SCC 35 (S.C.C.); *R. v. McCrimmon*, [2010] S.C.J. No. 36, 2010 SCC 36 (S.C.C.); *R. v. Willier*, [2010] S.C.J. No. 37, 2010 SCC 37 (S.C.C.).
[5] *Canadian Charter of Rights and Freedoms*, Part I of the *Constitution Act, 1982*, being Schedule B to the *Canada Act 1982* (U.K.), 1982, c. 11, s. 7.
[6] *Lavallee, Rackel & Heintz v. Canada (Attorney General)*, [2002] S.C.J. No. 61, [2002] 3 S.C.R. 209 (S.C.C.).
[7] *R. v. Murray*, [2000] O.J. No. 2182, 48 O.R. (3d) 544 (Ont. S.C.J.).
[8] Daniel Markovits, *A Modern Legal Ethics: Adversary Advocacy in a Democratic Age* (Princeton: Princeton University Press, 2008) at 243. See in response: Monroe Freedman & Abbe Smith "Misunderstanding Lawyers' Ethics" (2010) 108 Mich. L. Rev. 925.

lawyers for unethical conduct is not exhausted by the rules contained in the codes of conduct, and many rules are subject to light or no regulatory enforcement.[9] Further, positive and negative consequences for lawyer conduct — whether for the lawyer herself or for her client — can effectively be imposed by courts and other regulatory bodies, as well as by law societies. Consequently, while the codes of conduct are a fundamental statement of lawyers' legal and ethical duties,[10] they are not exhaustive. In addition to codes of conduct, the rules governing the conduct of Canadian lawyers can be found in specific disciplinary decisions made by the provincial law societies, regulatory requirements imposed on lawyers through other legal instruments such as securities legislation and rules of court, and judicial decisions of general application to all Canadian lawyers and relating to matters such as solicitor-client privilege and conflicts of interest.

This section provides an overview of the regulatory structure of the legal profession in Canada, and of the main sources of lawyers' legal and ethical duties.

A. The Regulatory Structure of the Canadian Profession

Canada is, arguably, the last bastion of unfettered self-regulation of the legal profession in the common law world. In the United States judges have always played a fundamental role in directly regulating lawyer conduct.[11] In the United Kingdom, Australia and New Zealand, significant non-lawyer involvement in the regulation of lawyer conduct has been statutorily imposed on the profession. In Canada, by contrast, the primary official jurisdiction for regulating lawyer conduct — defining what constitutes ethical and unethical conduct, and imposing sanctions on lawyers who violate those standards — is statutorily granted to the various provincial law societies, and in Québec to the Barreau du Québec.[12] Membership in one of these bodies is a precondition for the practice of law in Canada. As noted, other bodies, such as courts and securities commissions, set limits on lawyer

---

[9] See Gavin MacKenzie, "The Valentine's Card in the Operating Room: Codes of Ethics and the Failing Ideals of the Legal Profession" (1995) 33 Alta. L. Rev. 859 at 868; Harry Arthurs, Richard Weisman & Fredercik Zemans, "Canada" in Richard L. Abel & Philip S.C. Lewis, eds., *Lawyers in the Common Law World*, vol. 1 (Berkeley and Los Angeles: University of California Press, 1988) at 145-46.

[10] Beverley Smith has suggested that in Canada "a practicing lawyer's status as a professional person hinges on obedience to one or more of those codes" (*Professional Ethics for Lawyers and Judges*, looseleaf (Fredericton: Maritime Law Book, 2007) ch. 1, para. 26).

[11] In Canada judicial decisions help determine lawyers' ethical obligations. However, they do so indirectly through the principles that follow from the application of private law doctrines to lawyers (contract, tort and fiduciary obligations) and through the court's exercise of its inherent jurisdiction over its own processes. In the United States, judges are directly involved in disciplining lawyers for professional misconduct.

[12] The Barreau is moreover responsible for organizing, staffing and providing the course material and examinations used by the École du Barreau, a unique professional school that prepares its students for articling and, ultimately, admission to the Bar.

conduct, and impose consequences on lawyers who exceed those limits; the decisions of those bodies must be considered part of the rules of lawyer conduct.[13] Self-regulation remains, however, the "official model for the governance of the legal profession in Canada".[14]

The regulatory authority granted to the provincial law societies by the various provincial governments is of long standing.[15] The Law Society of Upper Canada was established by statute in 1797,[16] the Barreau du Québec in 1849 (although its predecessor was established in the late 1770s), the law societies of New Brunswick and Nova Scotia in 1825,[17] and the relative newcomers out west, Alberta and British Columbia, in 1898[18] and 1874[19] respectively. Today the law societies exercise statutory authority pursuant to legislation that generally grants them broad regulatory authority over the profession. The law societies are directed to regulate the profession in the public interest, and elected members of the profession are empowered to make decisions in relation to admission, practice standards and professional misconduct.

A typical mandate is that given to the Law Society of British Columbia pursuant to section 3 of the 1998 *Legal Profession Act*:

> It is the object and duty of the society
>
> > (a) to uphold and protect the public interest in the administration of justice by
> >
> > > (i) preserving and protecting the rights and freedoms of all persons,
> > >
> > > (ii) ensuring the independence, integrity and honour of its members, and
> > >
> > > (iii) establishing standards for the education, professional responsibility and competence of its members and applicants for membership, and

---

[13] This is also increasingly significant in countries outside of Canada; see, *e.g.*, *Sarbanes-Oxley Act*, 2002, PL 107-204, 116 Stat 745.

[14] Richard Devlin & Porter Heffernan, "The End(s) of Self-Regulation" (2008) 45(5) Alta. L. Rev. 169 at 170-71. The situation in Québec is somewhat more complicated. Under the *Professional Code*, R.S.Q. c. C-26, decisions made by the Barreau du Québec or the Chambres des notaires du Québec, are subject to review by the Professions Tribunal, which is composed of 11 members of the Québec Superior Court (s. 162). In addition, the government determines, in consultation with the Barreau, who will sit as chair on the Committee on Discipline, which adjudicates disciplinary decisions for the Barreau (s. 117). On the other hand, in its decision in *Finney v. Barreau du Québec*, [2004] S.C.J. No. 31 at para. 1, [2004] 2 S.C.R. 17 (S.C.C.), the Supreme Court referred to "our tradition of allowing the legal profession to regulate itself" in establishing the context for its consideration of whether, on the facts of that case, the Barreau could be held to be civilly liable to Finney with respect to its handling of disciplinary complaints.

[15] An overview of the history and structure of self-regulation in Canada is found in William H. Hurlburt, *The Self-Regulation of the Legal Profession in Canada and in England and Wales* (Edmonton: Alberta Law Reform Institute and the Law Society of Alberta, 2000).

[16] *Ibid.* at 15.

[17] *Ibid.* at 20-21.

[18] *Ibid.* at 25.

[19] *Ibid.* at 23.

(b) subject to paragraph (a),
  (i) to regulate the practice of law, and
  (ii) to uphold and protect the interests of its members.[20]

The *Act* goes on (1) to place primary decision-making power within the Law Society on "benchers" elected from the bar of British Columbia;[21] (2) to generally limit the practice of law in British Columbia to members of the Law Society;[22] (3) to empower the Law Society to make rules respecting the practice of law;[23] (4) to empower the Law Society to set standards for admission and to ensure that prospective members are of "good character";[24] and (5) to empower the Law Society to investigate lawyer misconduct, set rules of lawyer conduct, establish insurance against losses arising from lawyer misconduct, sanction misconduct and to otherwise exercise broad disciplinary powers over its membership.[25]

Also significant in the regulatory structure of the legal profession in Canada is the Federation of Law Societies, the national coordinating body of the 14 Canadian law societies. According to its own website, the Federation was traditionally a "low profile" organization in the regulation of the Canadian profession. Recently, however, it has become active in an attempt to increase consistency in regulation across Canada. The two main initiatives undertaken to this point are, first, the establishment of criteria for "Approved Law Degrees", which if adopted will be used to determine which common law schools will be points of entry to the Canadian profession.[26] Second, the Federation has drafted a Model Code of Conduct that it is proposing for adoption by all the Canadian law societies.

As indicated by s. 2(b)(ii) of the British Columbia legislation, some law societies are permitted to take into account the interests of the legal profession in their regulatory actions.[27] This is different from other jurisdictions, such as Australia, where statutes have been amended to take away that aspect of the law societies' regulatory authority.[28] The law societies do not, however, act as advocates for the interests of the legal

---

[20] S.B.C. 1998, c. 9, s. 3.
[21] *Ibid.*, ss. 4-8.
[22] *Ibid.*, s. 15.
[23] *Ibid.*, s. 11.
[24] *Ibid.*, ss. 19-22.
[25] *Ibid.*, ss. 26-48. In the other common law provinces and territories see: *Professional Code*, R.S.Q. c. C-26, s. 23; *Legal Profession Act*, R.S.A. 2000, c. L-8; *Legal Profession Act*, S.S. 1990-91, c. L-10.1; *Legal Profession Act*, C.C.S.M. c. L107; *Law Society Act*, R.S.O. 1990, c. L.8; *Law Society Act, 1996*, S.N.B. 1996, c. 89; *Legal Profession Act*, S.N.S. 2004, c. 28; *Law Society Act, 1999*, S.N.L. 1999, c. L-9.1; *Legal Profession Act*, R.S.P.E.I. 1988, c. L-6.1; *Legal Profession Act*, R.S.Y. 2002, c. 134; *Legal Profession Act*, R.S.N.W.T. 1988, c. L-2; *Legal Profession Act*, R.S.N.W.T. (Nu.) 1988, c. L-2.
[26] The approved law degrees requirement will not apply to the civil law schools in Québec.
[27] By contrast, see *Professional Code*, R.S.Q. c. C-26, s. 23.
[28] Duncan Webb, "Nefarious Conduct and the Fit and Proper Person Test" in Francesca Bartlett, Reid Mortensen & Kieran Tranter, eds., *Alternative Perspectives on Lawyers and Legal Ethics: Reimagining the Profession* (New York: Routledge, 2010) at 222.

profession. That role is distinct, and is played by the Canadian Bar Association ("CBA"), a private, voluntary organization to which lawyers may belong. The CBA has additionally played a significant role in the self-regulation of the legal profession. As detailed in the following section, the codes of conduct used by most Canadian law societies follow from model codes adopted by the CBA between 1920 and 1987. This role of the CBA has arguably been to some extent supplanted by the Federation of Law Societies' recent initiatives; whether the CBA's role in influencing the regulation of the legal profession grows or contracts in the future remains to be seen.

Is self-regulation of the legal profession a good thing? Proponents of self-regulation rely on arguments from "independence of the bar" to support their position. In a December 2009 debate over whether to abolish "life" benchers, for example, Toronto lawyer Clayton Ruby opposed the motion in part by invoking the spectre of challenges to self-regulation, and asserting the importance of self-regulation to independence of the bar: "Our independence is always at risk, and we are the guardians of that independence ... It is vitally important that we don't take steps to put it at risk. If the bar does not have that independence, we are nothing."[29]

It is not entirely clear, however, what is meant by independence of the bar. If it is independence from external regulation, then it is tautological as a justification for self-regulation: freedom from external regulation is important because freedom from external regulation is important. If it means independence from state coercion so as to permit lawyers to protect the rule of law, then it is not clear how self-regulation is necessary to ensure that lawyers can fulfill that role. If judges determined what constitutes ethical conduct by lawyers, or an independent regulator did so, it may be that lawyers' protection of the rule of law would be disrupted, but there exists little empirical evidence to bear out that concern. In countries which have moved away from self-regulation, or which like the United States have always had a more modified version of self-regulation than Canada, there is hardly evidence that the bar has been less independent than in Canada. Lawyers are not uniquely concerned with the rule of law. To put it slightly differently, in the event of a collapse of our constitutional rights or democratic norms, it seems most unlikely that self-regulation will be the one thing that maintains the rule of law. As noted by Richard Devlin and Porter Heffernan, "to confuse independence of the legal profession with self-regulation is a subtle, but indefensible legerdemain".[30]

Proponents also suggest that self-regulation can be understood as a form of social contract, in which lawyers are "delegated self-regulatory

---

[29] Tim Shufelt, "LSUC Votes to End Life Terms" *Law Times* (14 December 2009), online: <http://www.lawtimesnews.com/200912146005/Headline-News/LSUC-votes-to-end-life-terms>.
[30] Richard Devlin & Porter Heffernan, "The End(s) of Self-Regulation" (2008) 45(5) Alta. L. Rev. 169 at 192. Harry Arthurs also makes this point: H.W. Arthurs, "The Dead Parrot: Does Professional Self-Regulation Exhibit Vital Signs" (1995) 33 Alta. L. Rev. 800 at 801.

powers ... on terms that the profession will exercise those powers in the public interest."[31] That characterization seems reasonable, but leads to the legitimate follow up question, of whether the provincial law societies can claim to have acted in the public interest in discharging their regulatory mandates. There are undoubtedly great accomplishments of provincial law societies, such as their oversight of lawyer management of client funds and their establishment of assurance funds through which clients are compensated for lawyer malfeasance. In British Columbia, for example, a notorious case of lawyer mismanagement of client funds, which resulted in some $38 million in losses, was fully compensated for through a levy on British Columbia's lawyers by the Law Society of British Columbia.[32] Many members of the legal profession have devoted years of unpaid service to the regulatory functions discharged by the law societies. The law societies have recently engaged in numerous innovations with respect to ensuring competence in junior lawyers (in Ontario) and requiring mandatory continuing legal education (British Columbia and Saskatchewan in particular).

On the other hand, law societies have not acted with sufficient regulatory innovation and strength both in specific instances[33] and generally with respect to ensuring active and appropriate regulation of the legal profession. As Harry Arthurs has documented on numerous occasions, discipline for lawyer misconduct has usually been limited to instances of criminality,[34] and law societies have not always engaged actively with the question of what constitutes ethical conduct by lawyers. Indeed, it was as recently as 1998 that Arthurs could say of the Law Society of Upper Canada: "Canada's largest legal professional governing body has not yet attempted to develop and disseminate a *corpus juris* of legal ethics which probes, refines or illustrates either the statutory provisions under which it operates or its CBA-inspired code of professional conduct".[35]

---

[31] William H. Hurlburt, *The Self-Regulation of the Legal Profession in Canada and in England and Wales* (Edmonton: Alberta Law Reform Institute and the Law Society of Alberta, 2000) at 141-42.

[32] The Martin Wirick case, which is discussed at length in Chapter 12 of Philip Slayton, *Lawyers Gone Bad: Money, Sex and Madness in Canada's Legal Profession* (Toronto: Viking Canada, 2007). See with respect to the amounts paid in compensation. Gordon Turriff, "Self-Governance as a Necessary Condition of Constitutionally Mandated Lawyer Independence in British Columbia" (17 September 2009), online: <http://www.lawsociety.bc.ca/publications_forms/report-committees/docs/turriff-speech.pdf> at 18.

[33] Many of which are detailed by Slayton, *ibid.* and also by Richard Devlin & Porter Heffernan, "The End(s) of Self-Regulation" (2008) 45(5) Alta. L. Rev. 169.

[34] Harry Arthurs, Richard Weisman & Fredercik Zemans, "Canada" in Richard L. Abel & Philip S.C. Lewis, eds., *Lawyers in the Common Law World*, vol. 1 (Berkeley and Los Angeles: University of California Press, 1988) at 146. See also: H.W. Arthurs, "The Dead Parrot: Does Professional Self-Regulation Exhibit Vital Signs" (1995) 33 Alta. L. Rev. 800 at 804; H.W. Arthurs, "Why Canadian Law Schools Don't Teach Legal Ethics" in Kim Economides, ed., *Ethical Challenges to Legal Education and Conduct* (Oxford: Hart Publishing, 1998) 105 at 112-16; H.W. Arthurs, "Response to the Consultation Paper of the Task Force on the Canadian Common Law Degree", online: <http://www.ryerson.ca/law/ResponsetotheCanCommonLawDegreeConsultPaper.pdf>.

[35] "Why Canadian Law Schools Don't Teach Legal Ethics", *ibid.* at 111.

Ultimately there seems to be remarkably little public engagement in Canada with respect to the question of whether the legal profession should be self-regulating. Nor is there much engagement with the content of regulation, with the specific rules to which lawyers are subject. Which leads to the more fundamental point: far more important than the question of *who* regulates lawyers is the question of *how* and *in what way* lawyers are regulated. That is, the crucial question is whether the regulation of lawyers in Canada ensures that lawyers help Canadians to achieve their goals under and through the law. One aim of this book is to provide some basic materials to foster engagement with this question. Who lawyers are, what we do, and in what way, matters for the accomplishment of the norms and vision contained in our laws and our constitution; the public can — and should! — legitimately question whether the current regulatory model does enough to direct lawyers properly towards these ends.

B. Codes of Conduct as a Source of Lawyers' Legal and Ethical Duties

Until the Federation of Law Societies circulated its draft code in October 2009, the primary driving force behind codifying the ethical obligations of Canadian lawyers was the CBA. The achievement by the CBA of the first code of conduct shortly after the organization's creation in 1915 was notable. Although the American Bar Association published its first Code of Conduct in 1908, in Canada and in England there were no written codes of ethics. There was instead significant resistance to the attempt to codify lawyers' ethical obligations. A 1919 survey by Justice Riddell of "British Chiefs of Bench and Bar" evoked comments indicating the lack of need for such a code, and also its undesirability, with the Lord Justice Advocate of Scotland noting that "the application of the rules of strictly honourable conduct consorts very ill with any attempt to reduce the rules of honour to a written code",[36] and the Attorney-General of England noting that a code "could not be complete, because changing circumstances are bound to give rise to new questions from time to time".[37]

In Canada Justice Riddell led the opposition to the development of a code of conduct, noting the limited usefulness of a hortatory code, the risk of strict construction of more regulatory rules, and the difficulty in drafting stricter rules. He emphasized as well the difference between the legal and constitutional tradition in Canada and the United States: the "mind of the American lawyer naturally and instinctively inclines to written formulation of all precepts, all rules, all principles"; Canada should link itself instead to

---

[36] W. Wesley Pue, "'Becoming Ethical': Lawyers' Professional Ethics in Early Twentieth Century Canada" in Dale Gibson & W. Wesley Pue eds., *Glimpses of Canadian Legal History* (Winnipeg: Manitoba Legal Research Institute, 1991) Appendix A.
[37] *Ibid.*

the English tradition of "indefinite and indefinitely formulated principles upon which a British people should be governed".[38]

One objection raised by Justice Riddell is an interesting reflection of the long history of zealous advocacy in the Canadian profession. The objection, which led to a modification in the ultimate text, was to the rule that a lawyer's appearance in Court was tantamount to an assertion of the lawyer's own opinion that the case was properly brought.[39] Justice Riddell suggested that such a rule could have a chilling effect, leading to lawyers improperly judging their clients' cases:

> The client is entitled to the services of his lawyer to enforce any claim or defence which is not dishonest; the client is entitled to the full and candid opinion of his lawyer, but when that is given he is entitled to have his case put before the Court whatever may be the lawyer's opinion of the law. Neither Court nor client is at all concerned with the opinion of counsel — the client demands, the court enforces the law, as it is found to be — that is the duty of the Court, the right of the client.[40]

Despite these forces of opposition, the initiative to draft a Canadian code of conduct came to fruition in 1920, with the CBA's approval of the "Canons of Legal Ethics". For other leaders of the Canadian bar, the attractions of a code as part of a project of professionalism simply outweighed Justice Riddell's concerns. The Canons were a response to emerging populism and democracy, which "demanded that professions make good on their claims of superior expertise and high standards of professional conduct", a way of preserving the elitism of the bar in the face of such claims, and, more positively, a reflection of a "genuine commitment to the ideal of ethical legal practice".[41]

The 1920 CBA Canons of Legal Ethics set out 30 Canons with respect to a lawyer's duties to the state, the court, the client, her fellow lawyer and herself. The Canons are non-exhaustive, and are in large part hortatory as opposed to imposing clear legal obligations on the lawyer with respect to her dealings with any of these parties. In response to Justice Riddell's concern, the 1920 Canons expressly state that in defending a person accused of a crime a lawyer should not be understood to be stating a "personal opinion as to the guilt of the accused".[42] They further make it clear that a lawyer has a fundamental duty as an advocate, to "endeavor by all fair and honourable

---

[38] Justice Riddell, "Suggested Canons of Ethics" in Canadian Bar Association, "Report of the Committee on Legal Education and Ethics" (1919) 4 Report of the C.B.A. 129 at 138, cited in "Becoming Ethical", *ibid.* at 261-66.

[39] This rule was based on an American rule, which Justice Riddell interpreted broadly. Monroe Freedman suggested to me that Justice Riddell's interpretation of the American rule was incorrect.

[40] Justice Riddell, "Suggested Canons of Ethics" in Canadian Bar Association, "Report of the Committee on Legal Education and Ethics" (1919) 4 Report of the C.B.A. 129 at 140-41, cited in W. Wesley Pue, "'Becoming Ethical': Lawyers' Professional Ethics in Early Twentieth Century Canada" in Dale Gibson & W. Wesley Pue eds., *Glimpses of Canadian Legal History* (Winnipeg: Manitoba Legal Research Institute, 1991) at 264-65.

[41] "Becoming Ethical", *ibid.* at 269-70.

[42] 1920 Code, Canon 3, Rule 6, reproduced in "Becoming Ethical", Appendix B.

means to obtain for his client the benefit of any and every remedy and defence which is authorized by law".[43] The lawyer is to "discharge his duty to his client with firmness and without fear of judicial disfavour or public unpopularity".[44]

The 1920 Canons are, however, hardly an unambiguous statement in favour of zealous advocacy. The lawyer is given multiple duties as a "minister of justice, an officer of the Courts, his client's advocate, and a member of an ancient, honourable and learned profession".[45] His duties include the obligation to "promote the interests of the State, serve the cause of justice, maintain the authority and dignity of the Courts, be faithful to his clients, candid and courteous in his intercourse with his fellows and true to himself".[46] The lawyer is also subject to a variety of specific duties in this respect. He is precluded from assisting anyone to act contrary to law,[47] from stirring "up strife and litigation",[48] from making unjustified criticism of judges,[49] from acting in a way that involves "disloyalty to the state"[50] and, in general, is exhorted to "bear in mind that he can only maintain the high traditions of his profession by being in fact as well as in name a gentleman".[51] Other obligations in the 1920 Canons are ones we would recognize as similar to those imposed on lawyers today. The Canons require that the lawyer act with candor and fairness in legal proceedings,[52] treat adverse witnesses with fairness,[53] prohibit representation of conflicting interests[54] and grant the lawyer the right to "decline employment" for any particular client or cause.[55]

The 1920 Canons were adopted by the Law Societies of British Columbia, Alberta, Saskatchewan, Manitoba and Ontario in 1921, and remained the basic statement of lawyers' ethical duties until 1969, when the CBA created a committee to review the 1920 Canons and recommend changes. In 1974 a new Model Code of Conduct was adopted by the CBA. The 1974 Model Code was significantly revised in 1987.[56] In 2009 the CBA further significantly revised the chapter of the 1987 Model Code dealing with conflicts of interest.

---

[43] 1920 Code, Canon 3(5).
[44] 1920 Code, Canon 3(4).
[45] 1920 Code, Preamble.
[46] *Ibid.*
[47] 1920 Code, Canon 1(1).
[48] 1920 Code, Canon 1(4).
[49] 1920 Code, Canon 2(2).
[50] 1920 Code, Canon 5(5).
[51] 1920 Code, Canon 5(7).
[52] 1920 Code, Canon 2(1).
[53] 1920 Code, Canon 3(4).
[54] 1920 Code, Canon 3(2).
[55] 1920 Code, Canon 5(4).
[56] The 1987 Code added chapters on conflicts and public appearances and statements by lawyers, and also significantly amended the chapter dealing with advertising.

The 1987 CBA Code contains a combination of mandatory guidelines for professional conduct ("The lawyer shall not advise or represent both sides of a dispute"[57]) and exhortatory ethical precepts ("The lawyer should encourage public respect for and try to improve the administration of justice").[58] Further, even where its rules are mandatory guidelines, they are relatively brief and open-textured, leaving significant parts of the guidance given to lawyers to the commentaries following the rules, rather than codifying that guidance in the rules themselves. Because it trades significantly in generalities, the drafters of the CBA Code did not engage in some of the fierce debates, particularly in relation to the lawyer's duty of confidentiality, which roiled the ABA in the adoption of its 1983 Model Rules.

The 1987 Code of Conduct was adopted with only minor revisions by Newfoundland, Prince Edward Island, Yukon Territory and Northwest Territories. It was adopted in modified form by Saskatchewan, Manitoba, Ontario and Nova Scotia. British Columbia, New Brunswick and Alberta have codes of conduct that vary significantly from the CBA Code, particularly Alberta, which in 1995 adopted a more detailed, comprehensive and legislative set of rules to govern lawyer conduct.

As noted earlier, in October 2009 the Federation of Law Societies adopted a model Code of Conduct with the intention of creating a uniform code to apply to all Canadian lawyers. The Federation's Model Code does not represent a significant departure from the 1987 CBA Code, and does not involve a shift to a more legislative model of rules such as that found in Alberta or in the 1983 ABA Model Rules. The Federation of Law Societies' Model Code is currently under consideration for adoption by the various provincial law societies. Nationwide adoption does not at this time (2011) appear imminent, although the law societies appear to be making strong efforts to ensure that it is eventually adopted in some form.

In discussing lawyers' legal and ethical duties, I will attempt to synthesize the various approaches taken by the provincial law societies, the CBA and the Federation to the obligations of lawyers. I focus on the codes of conduct for the CBA, the Federation, New Brunswick, Québec, Ontario, Alberta and British Columbia to provide a comprehensive national perspective.

C. Law Society Discipline as a Source of Lawyers' Legal and Ethical Duties

As well as enacting the codes of conduct, law societies further articulate the duties of Canadian lawyers through issuing ethics opinions when requested to do so by lawyers. In addition, and more significantly, the law societies publish disciplinary decisions that describe particular facts that the law

---

[57] 1987 Code, Chapter V.
[58] 1987 Code, Chapter XIII.

societies consider sufficient to constitute either professional misconduct or "conduct unbecoming" a lawyer.

Ethics opinions from the law societies are not widely available, and have not yet been synthesized or published in a form that allows them to be considered systematically as a source of guidance in relation to lawyers' ethical duties.[59] I have thus not relied on those opinions in considering the content of Canadian lawyers' legal and ethical obligations.

Disciplinary decisions have, by contrast, been published by the various provincial law societies since 1994, and are available electronically through electronic databases such as Quicklaw (under the database, "Law Society Disciplinary Digests"). Those decisions provide helpful information about the content of lawyers' professional obligations and, in particular, about what the more abstract principles contained in the codes of conduct will mean when applied to particular fact situations. The decisions are not without flaws as a source of guidance — there are still relatively few available decisions on most ethical issues, not all the law societies routinely publish their decisions, and the analysis in the decisions is not always especially thorough. Nonetheless, in attempting to delineate the legal and ethical obligations of Canadian lawyers I have made extensive use of the disciplinary decisions published by the various law societies.

D. Other Sources of Lawyers' Legal and Ethical Duties

As noted at the outset, law society codes of conduct are not the only source of lawyers' legal and ethical duties. This is the case in the United States as well as here, but is especially significant here, if for no other reason than because, as outlined in sub-section B, with the exception of Alberta, the law societies in Canada have never adopted a comprehensive set of mandatory rules with which lawyers must comply.

The influence of the Canadian ethical codes is also limited by a number of additional factors.[60] First, as just noted Canadian law societies and the CBA do not have a synthesized body of ethics opinions giving guidance to lawyers on how the rules apply to specific situations, and have only published disciplinary decisions (and not all disciplinary decisions) since 1994. This limited availability of regulatory decisions renders the various codes of conduct somewhat abstract from practice because for many rules there are no decisions or available opinions to indicate what the rules actually mean when applied to a particular set of facts.

Second, the authority of law societies over lawyers is not limited to the codes of conduct, and is in fact legally distinct from the codes; the law

---

[59] Ethics opinions can be accessed for each province online, but are not on the general electronic databases such as QuickLaw, Westlaw or CanLII.
[60] With the growing interest in lawyers' ethics in the profession and as an academic discipline, some of these limitations may be addressed. These are fruitful areas for academic and professional collaboration.

societies have general statutory jurisdiction to regulate lawyers for "conduct unbecoming" or "professional misconduct", and do not clearly (or sometimes at all) link findings of professional misconduct by individual lawyers to provisions of the codes of conduct.

Third, there is no equivalent here to the American Law Institute's Restatement of the Law Governing Lawyers that provides guidance as to how ethics codes are interpreted in the United States.

Notably, in one study in which 180 Ontario lawyers were interviewed, only 16% of those lawyers mentioned referring to the code of conduct as a source of ethical guidance. Those who did so found the code to be helpful, but the failure of lawyers to use the code when faced with ethical problems indicates its more qualified significance in the Canadian law governing lawyers.[61]

What then are the other major sources of lawyers' legal and ethical duties? By far the most significant are judicial decisions which delineate the obligations of lawyers to their clients, to the courts, to the legal system and more generally. The rules of conduct in relation to conflicts of interest and lawyer-client privilege are in Canada largely the product of judicial decision-making. Case law also speaks, however, to the obligations of lawyers to opposing counsel and clients, to limits on filing frivolous and vexatious lawsuits, and to the scope and limits of cross-examination. Further, case law on fiduciary obligations, negligence, and the law of contract affects the duties owed by the lawyer to her client in a variety of ways.

Legal and ethical duties also arise from regulation and legislation that deal primarily with other subject matters, but which in the course of doing so affect the legal obligations of lawyers. The most important examples of these are the rules of court of the various superior courts of the provinces. Also notable, though, are statutes and regulations such as the federal and provincial evidence acts, securities legislation under which securities regulators will impose sanctions on lawyers who provide misleading or incomplete disclosure to the regulator,[62] and child welfare statutes which, in some provinces, impose obligations to report child abuse or neglect, even where the information in question is confidential or privileged.[63]

Finally, the obligations of lawyers must be understood in light of the rights enshrined in the Canadian constitution, and judicial interpretation of the extent (and limits) of those rights, in particular with respect to the duties of Crown counsel, the exercise of prosecutorial discretion, the right to counsel and solicitor-client privilege.

All of these sources will be relied upon here.

---

[61] Margaret Ann Wilkinson, Christa Walker & Peter Mercer, "Do Codes of Ethics Actually Shape Legal Practice" (2000) 45 McGill L.J. 645 at 648.

[62] See, *e.g.*, *Wilder v. Ontario (Securities Commission)*, [2001] O.J. No. 1017, 53 O.R. (3d) 519 (Ont. C.A.).

[63] See, *Child, Youth and Family Services Act*, S.N.L. 1998, c. C-12.1, s. 15.

E. The Purposes of the Rules Governing Lawyer Conduct

Why do we regulate lawyer conduct in the way that we do? What is the point in preventing a lawyer from acting for two current clients in unrelated matters where the representation of one client has an adverse effect on the legal interests of the other?[64] Why might we require a lawyer to keep her client's secrets even where potentially injuring another person's interests, yet in other circumstances require the lawyer to disclose her client's secrets? Why might we restrict lawyer advertising, prohibit or regulate particular types of fee arrangements or place limits on the types of actions that a lawyer can bring forward?

Socio-economic critics of the legal profession maintain that the regulations that exist are best understood as an assertion by lawyers of their own economic interests, that the best way to understand regulation of the legal profession is as an excellent example of "regulatory capture", in which the regulated in fact determine the content of regulation to ensure the maximization of their interests, economic or otherwise.[65] With respect to some initiatives undertaken by legal regulators, particularly historically, it seems difficult not to acknowledge that the regulation in question may have been as motivated by protection of the interests of lawyers as by protection of the public. This is especially so given the express mandate of the provincial law societies to regulate in the interests of the profession, as well as in the interests of the public, and given the transparent concern of legal regulators with maintaining the reputation of the legal profession.[66]

Socio-economic theories suffer, however, from several weaknesses. Even if one accepts that there is some truth to them, one is not left with much, analytically speaking: shrugging our shoulders in resignation at our collective human frailty does not do much to help a lawyer faced with an ethical problem. Further, the theories are in their own way simplistic about human motives and actions; people are capable of altruism, and when viewed broadly, taking into account judicial decisions as well as the codes of conduct, it is difficult to explain many of the rules that govern lawyers simply through the lens of lawyer self-interest.

The socio-economic theories also do not take into account the legitimate public interest economic reasons for regulating the market for legal services. As will be touched on at various points in this book, the market for legal services has numerous imperfections that warrant some regulation to ensure that consumers do not pay more than they should for legal services, and that the legal services they obtain are appropriate. In particular, because of market imperfections the forces of supply and demand

---

[64] *R. v. Neil*, [2002] S.C.J. No. 72, [2002] 3 S.C.R. 631 (S.C.C.).
[65] See in general Richard L. Abel, *American Lawyers* (New York: Oxford University Press, 1989) at 14-40. For a very moderate version of this sort of analysis see Duncan Webb, "Are Lawyers Regulatable?" (2008) 45(5) Alta. L. Rev. 233.
[66] See, *e.g.*, *Merchant v. Law Society of Saskatchewan*, [2009] S.J. No. 145, 2009 SKCA 33 (Sask. C.A.).

cannot be counted on to ensure that consumers get the services they need at a fair market price. These imperfections relate to the poor information available to consumers about the quality and appropriateness of legal services for resolving their problems, the vast difference between the services available (and needed) from different lawyers in distinct practice settings, the restrictions on entry and exit into the legal services market and, finally, the externalities that occasionally arise in the market. Regulation of lawyers helps to counter those market imperfections, and it does so in a way that cannot simply be reduced to an attempt to protect lawyer self-interest.

Finally, and most seriously in my view, socio-economic theories fail to take the law governing lawyers seriously as a matter of doctrinal law, as something which, when analyzed carefully and in terms of its own internal rationality, can be seen to fulfill important purposes related to the accomplishment of the rule of law and the administration of justice in a free and democratic society. The broader legal and philosophical underpinnings of this position are set out in Chapter 2; here it is simply worth noting that the legal and ethical duties imposed on lawyers, do not apparently reflect lawyers' own interests. Rather, they reflect a strong commitment to the principle that lawyers must be loyal advocates for their clients within the bounds of legality.

With respect to loyalty, the codes of conduct in particular impose on lawyers a paramount duty of loyalty to the client, in which the client determines what he wants to do, and the lawyer serves as the partisan representative of his interests within the legal system. This duty of loyalty pervades the law governing lawyers, and imposes on the lawyer the "fundamental duty ... to act in the best interests of his or her client to the exclusion of all other adverse interests"[67] and a duty of "commitment to the client's cause".[68] It is a duty that can be traced back to the 1920 Canons of Legal Ethics' requirement that the lawyer "should endeavor to obtain by all fair and honorable means to obtain for his client the benefit of any and every remedy and defence which is authorized by law"[69] and through to the more modern duties of the Federation of Law Societies Model Code which requires that lawyers provide competent service to clients,[70] that they be honest and candid with clients,[71] that they hold their clients' affairs in confidence[72] and that as advocates they represent their clients "resolutely and honourably".[73]

With respect to legality, lawyers' legal and ethical duties constrain them to act within the bounds of legality, to facilitate their clients in

---

[67] *Strother v. 3464920 Canada Inc.*, [2007] S.C.J. No. 24 at para. 1, [2007] 2 S.C.R. 177 (S.C.C.).
[68] *R. v. Neil*, [2002] S.C.J. No. 72 at para. 19, [2002] 3 S.C.R. 631 (S.C.C.).
[69] 1920 Code, Canon 3(5).
[70] FLS Model Rule 2.01(1).
[71] FLS Model Rule 2.02(2).
[72] FLS Model Rule 2.03(1).
[73] FLS Model Rule 4.01(1).

achieving full and equal rights under the law, but not to subvert the law or its administration. Again, these constraints are pervasive in the rules, date back to the 1920 Canons, and carry through to today. Thus, lawyers in 1920 were required to be candid and fair in their dealings with the Court,[74] were prohibited from putting forward inadmissible evidence[75] and were resolute advocates only "within the bounds of the law".[76] And in the Federation's Model Code lawyers must treat tribunals with "candour, fairness, courtesy and respect",[77] may not offer false evidence, misstate facts or law, fail to mention relevant adverse authority, dissuade a witness from giving evidence or permit a witness or party to be presented in a manner which is false or misleading.[78]

These purposes of lawyers' legal and ethical obligations exist in tension, and cannot always be reconciled satisfactorily. The justifiability of these purposes also needs to be explained in light of Canadian law more generally, and as a matter of principle — a task that, as noted, I take up in Chapter 2.

F. The Integrity Challenge

Since the enactment of the 1974 CBA Code, lawyers have been placed under a general obligation of "integrity" — to "carry on the practice of law and discharge all responsibilities ... honourably and with integrity".[79] In 1996, I published an article which suggested that this incorporation of personal integrity into the professional morality of Canadian lawyers was significant, and perhaps suggested that, in distinction from lawyers in the United States, the standard conception of the Canadian lawyer was less committed to the idea of the lawyer as a zealous advocate for the interests of her client. I speculated that here the standard conception was closer to the idea expressed by those philosophical legal ethicists who suggest that a lawyer's *professional* morality can never excuse violations of the obligations of *ordinary* morality; if a client proposes a course of conduct which is legal, but immoral, the ethical lawyer should decline to pursue that course of action. The moral autonomy of the client does not trump that of the lawyer.[80]

I am no longer convinced that this view of the standard conception of the Canadian lawyer accurately captures the nature of the Canadian lawyer's ethical obligations, largely because I do not think seeing the Canadian lawyer in this way sufficiently reflects the consistent weight given in the rules, and especially in judicial decisions, to the lawyer's duty of loyalty —

---

[74] 1920 Code, Canon 2(1).
[75] 1920 Code, Canon 2(3).
[76] 1920 Code, Canon 3(5).
[77] FLS Model Rule 4.01(1).
[78] FLS Mode Rule 4.01(2).
[79] CBA CPC, Rule 1.
[80] Alice Woolley, "Integrity in Zealousness: Comparing the Standard Conceptions of the Canadian and American Lawyer" (1996) 9 Can. J.L. & Jur. 61.

i.e., to the placement of paramount emphasis on the lawyer's professional obligation to her client. As discussed in Chapter 2, the role of the lawyer in Canadian legal culture is often described as one of zealous advocacy, and the legal principles that make zealous advocacy sensible are strongly reflected in Canadian legal doctrine. Further, as also discussed in Chapter 2, there are strong points of principle arising from the concept of democratic pluralism to suggest that the lawyer's role makes a unique moral claim that can trump the claims of personal morality when acting in that role.

Those shifts in my assessment do not, however, diminish the significance of integrity within the legal and ethical duties of lawyers, or suggest that requiring lawyers to act with integrity is impossible, or wrongheaded. This is for several reasons. First, the argument that the lawyer's role has a principled justification suggests a moral virtue in the lawyer's role. The lawyer who pursues that role can, therefore, make a claim to have acted morally — *i.e.*, with integrity — even if she is doing things that she finds problematic when assessed from a moral perspective apart from her role. Second, within the lawyer's role remain significant choices that can be made by the lawyer, and which she can make with an eye to her own sense of personal integrity. As will be discussed in Chapter 3, the most significant of these is client selection — the lawyer does not take on her role in the abstract; she takes on her role in relation to a particular client with a particular legal claim, and she remains largely unconstrained in her selection of for whom she will play that role. This, again, allows her to pursue her life with integrity. When a lawyer chooses a client, and takes on the role of that client's lawyer, she makes a promise to the client to represent his interests. That promise itself has moral significance, and the maintaining of that promise is a constituent part of her personal integrity.

Finally, integrity plays a crucial role in explaining the approach to be taken by the lawyer when professional morality and personal morality conflict. While the tension between professional and personal morality can be massaged and occasionally eliminated, many lawyers will face circumstances where the choice between their personal moral values and the obligations of their profession cannot be reduced, it can only be lived with, one way or another. The question for the lawyer is that which the CBA Code poses, but does not in this sense resolve: how in such circumstances does the lawyer maintain her personal integrity?

In *Understanding Lawyers' Ethics*,[81] Professor Freedman tells a story of a friend of his who expressed disappointment at not being able to serve in a jury, because the jury questionnaire asked whether the potential juror had objections to the death penalty; since the juror would answer "yes" he would be automatically disqualified from serving. Professor Freedman's friend was troubled by this rule, because he said that it meant that he could not serve on

---

[81] Monroe Freedman & Abbe Smith, *Understanding Lawyers' Ethics*, 4th ed. (New Providence, NJ: LexisNexis, 2010 at 9-10.

a jury, which also meant that he could not act to preserve human life. Professor Freedman countered that, in fact, the friend was simply making a moral choice: he was choosing the moral value of honesty in preference to the moral value of saving a life. The choice was not one dictated for him, it was one he made, and for which he had to take responsibility. That way of making decisions is, fundamentally, how integrity is maintained. As noted by Gerald Postema, where one has to compromise a principle to which one is committed — for Professor Freedman's friend, the principle of honesty — then the maintenance of integrity occurs through recognizing the nature of what one has done, and taking responsibility for it.[82]

In the end, that is the best that a lawyer faced with tension between her professional and personal moral obligations can do: she must choose how she acts, and take responsibility for her choices, including whatever perceived sacrifices she has made to her personal or professional values. In conscientiously making that effort, she will act with integrity.

---

[82] Gerald Postema, "Self-Image, Integrity and Professional Responsibility" in David Luban, ed., *The Good Lawyer* (Totowa, NJ: Rowman & Allanheld, 1984) at 309.

Chapter 2

IN DEFENCE OF ZEALOUS ADVOCACY

1. INTRODUCTION

Canadian lawyers play an adversarial role in asserting the interests of their clients, whether in or outside a traditional court of law. The lawyer's role is properly described as adversarial because the lawyer seeks to advance the legal interests of his clients even to the point of defeating the interests of others. Moreover, the lawyer seeks to advance his client's interests resolutely;[1] he may legitimately take advantage of any procedural or substantive legal rule to achieve what his client wants. The lawyer is constrained by legality, but nonetheless seeks to obtain legal advantages for his client regardless of the cost that obtaining those advantages may impose on other individuals or on the public generally.

Perhaps more traditionally, the lawyer's role is also considered adversarial because, in courtrooms or like settings, the lawyer may have an actual adversary, another lawyer representing the interests of the opposing party (or parties). Even in Québec, Canada's only civilian jurisdiction, the conduct of a legal matter is adversarial, not inquisitorial.[2]

The Law Society of Upper Canada's *Code of Professional Conduct* puts it this way:

> The lawyer has a duty to the client to raise fearlessly every issue, advance every argument, and ask every question, however distasteful, which the lawyer thinks will help the client's case and to endeavour to obtain for the client the benefit of every remedy and defence authorized by law. ...
>
> In adversary proceedings the lawyer's function as advocate is openly and necessarily partisan. Accordingly, the lawyer is not obliged (save as required by law or under these rules and subject to the duties of a prosecutor set out below) to assist an adversary or advance matters derogatory to the client's case.[3]

In practical terms this means that without entering into doubtful ethical territory a lawyer may advise a corporate client on technical interpretations

---

[1] In general Canadian Codes of Conduct refer to lawyers as "resolute" advocates. However, Canadian cases often refer to the lawyers duty as one of zealous advocacy — *R. v. Neil*, [2002] S.C.J. No. 72 at para. 19, [2002] 3 S.C.R. 631 (S.C.C.). I will use the words "resolute" and "zealous" interchangeably.

[2] This is why Québec is often properly described as a "mixed" regime.

[3] LSUC CPC Commentary to Rule 4.01.

of the *Income Tax Act*[4] to allow the client to reduce its tax payments to the greatest possible extent.[5] A lawyer may advise the client to sue the state in order to require the state to do specific things, even where the result will be a significant drain on the public fisc. A lawyer may use the evidence available to him to attack the credibility of a witness he believes to be truthful. A lawyer may assert a statute of limitations on behalf of a client to allow the client to defeat payment of a just debt. A lawyer may make legal arguments to a court that he believes would be contrary to the public interest if accepted. A lawyer may argue for interpretations of evidence that he believes to be spurious. A lawyer may — must — stay silent as an innocent man is convicted of a crime the lawyer knows his client committed. There are, of course, many things that a lawyer *cannot* do, as I will discuss in subsequent chapters of this book; the lawyer's role is zealous advocacy within the bounds of legality, not zeal unbounded. Nonetheless, the things that lawyers are permitted and even required to do in acting as a resolute advocate for a client are ethically significant, and require some explanation and justification.

In this chapter I argue that the lawyer's role as resolute advocate — as adversary — is central to Canadian legal culture, and is legally and ethically justified. Canadian legal culture conceives of the lawyer as resolute advocate for his client's interests, acting in opposition to the interests of others or the state. Further, the normative principles that underlie the lawyer as resolute advocate within the bounds of legality — the role of law in a pluralist society and the ability of law to be meaningfully interpreted — are deeply intertwined with substantive and procedural legal norms in Canada. The premises of resolute advocacy are premises of the legal system as a whole. Finally, I argue that while the ethical arguments against the lawyer as resolute advocate are sophisticated and merit serious attention, the ethical arguments for the lawyer as resolute advocate are ultimately more persuasive. In acting as loyal advocates for their clients' interests within the bounds of legality, lawyers do something good, something that fosters the freedom and democracy that underpin the Canadian system of laws.

2. LAWYERS IN CANADIAN LEGAL CULTURE

Observers of the legal profession consistently posit the standard conception of the Canadian lawyer as including a commitment to resolute advocacy. Trevor Farrow recently suggested that the dominant model of the lawyer's role is "to advance zealously the client's cause with all legal means; to be personally neutral vis-à-vis the result of the client's cause; and to leave the ultimate ethical, personal, economic, and social bases for the decision to

---

[4] R.S.C. 1985 (5th Supp.), c. 1.
[5] The competent lawyer would, of course, also have to take into account the effect of the general anti-avoidance rule and case law that has interpreted it.

proceed in the hands of the client."[6] Similarly, in 1995 Allan Hutchinson argued that the image of the lawyer as a hired-hand is traditional to the point that it has "remained largely static and unchanged for many decades."[7] And, finally, David Tanovich has asserted that "[t]here is no question that historically, the philosophy of lawyering in Canada has largely been driven by principles of partisanship, zealous advocacy, and morally unaccountable representation within the bounds of the law."[8] Each of these authors goes on to critique and ultimately reject the resolute advocacy model. Their arguments against resolute advocacy are addressed in section 4 of this chapter; for current purposes, however, those arguments serve simply to indicate the clear place in Canadian legal culture of the lawyer as a resolute advocate within the bounds of the law.

The perception of Canadian legal culture put forward by legal academics is also supported by historical examples of Canadian lawyers acting as resolute advocates, even in times when the general culture of Canada could be described as notable for "its reverence for law and order and authority".[9] A recent collection of essays, *The Promises and Perils of Law: Lawyers in Canadian History*[10] recounts the stories of Arthur Eugene O'Meara[11] and Lionel Cross,[12] who undertook the resolute representation of causes outside the legal mainstream. O'Meara spent years attempting to achieve greater justice for First Nations' clients in British Columbia through assertion of aboriginal title. Cross represented the rights of individuals outside the cultural mainstream, most notably in defending Ernest Victor Sterry, a member of the Rationalist Society ("a 'free thought' group of secularists, atheists and agnostics")[13] from a charge of blasphemous libel. Cross also advocated for the prosecution of KKK members who had persecuted a couple the KKK identified as interracial. Neither O'Meara nor Cross were especially successful in their efforts — while Cross was

---

[6] Trevor Farrow, "Sustainable Professionalism" (2008) 46 Osgoode Hall L.J. 51 at 63.
[7] Allan C. Hutchinson, "Calgary and Everything After: A Postmodern Re-Vision of Lawyering" (1995) 33 Alta. L. Rev. 768 at 770.
[8] David Tanovich, "Law's Ambition and the Reconstruction of Role Morality in Canada" (2005) 28 Dalhousie L.J. 267 at 271.
[9] Graham Parker, "Canadian Legal Culture" in Louis A. Knafla ed., *Law and Justice in a New Land* (Toronto: Carswell, 1986) at 24. Note as well Justice Riddell's objection to the draft of the 1920 CBA Canons of Ethics on the basis that they paid insufficient attention to the lawyer's role as advocate. Justice Riddell, "Suggested Canons of Ethics" in Canadian Bar Association, "Report of the Committee on Legal Education and Ethics" (1919) 4 Report of the C.B.A. 129 at 138, cited in W. Wesley Pue, "'Becoming Ethical': Lawyers' Professional Ethics in Early Twentieth Century Canada" in Dale Gibson & W. Wesley Pue eds., *Glimpses of Canadian Legal History* (Winnipeg: Manitoba Legal Research Institute, 1991) Appendix A.
[10] *The Promise and Perils of Law: Lawyers in Canadian History* (Toronto: Irwin Law, 2009).
[11] Hamar Foster, "If Your Life is a Leaf: Arthur Eugene O'Meara's Campaign for Aboriginal Justice" in W. Wesley Pue & Constance Backhouse, eds., *The Promise and Perils of Law: Lawyers in Canadian History* (Toronto: Irwin Law, 2009) at 225.
[12] Susan Lewthwaite, "Ethelbert Lionel Cross: Toronto's First Black Lawyer" in W. Wesley Pue & Constance Backhouse, eds., *The Promise and Perils of Law: Lawyers in Canadian History* (Toronto: Irwin Law, 2009) at 193.
[13] *Ibid.* at 200.

successful in ensuring the prosecution and conviction of the members of the KKK, Sterry was convicted and imprisoned; O'Meara met with repeated failures in his attempts to advance the cause of First Nations' peoples, even though the specific legal arguments he made were to be successful decades later. Yet over time, as the norms of Canadian legal culture shifted, lawyers taking on the resolute advocacy of outsider causes met, at least sometimes, with greater success than was achieved by O'Meara and Cross. One of the most famous examples is Frank Scott, the McGill professor who undertook various cases against government civil rights abuses during the Duplessis era in Québec, most notably his successful representation of Roncarelli in *Roncarelli v. Duplessis*,[14] discussed below.

This is not to suggest that Canadian lawyers as resolute advocates have always been on the side of outsiders, or have always worked to support the evolution of Canadian law towards greater substantive justice. Indeed, for every resolute advocate in support of the cause of an outsider, there has been an opposing lawyer working to maintain the status quo.

It is also not to suggest that resolute advocacy has always been greeted with enthusiasm by the public at large — O'Meara was the subject of a campaign of public persecution, and arguably Cross was as well. The point is simply to note that it is misleading, culturally speaking, to suggest that for Canadian lawyers "the highest duty of loyalty is owed to what is called the 'protection of the public interest' ... [which] perhaps not inaccurately may be taken to include the state and its systems, as well as its people".[15] Canadian lawyers owe a duty to the public interest, but Canadian legal culture expects them to fulfill that duty by acting as resolute advocates, even when their advocacy places them in an adversarial relationship with the legal status quo and with what the majority of the citizenry, the state, and its systems might identify as the "public interest".

That Canadian legal culture incorporates the conception of the lawyer as resolute advocate does not, of course, demonstrate that it *should* do so, except insofar as arguments against a deeply rooted cultural practice always have some serious work to do, particularly where that practice can make a claim to being supported by normative considerations. The remaining sections of this chapter will consider the question of whether Canadian lawyers should be resolute advocates or whether, in some way or another, their resolute advocacy for clients should be conceptually qualified.

---

[14] [1959] S.C.J. No. 1, [1959] S.C.R. 121 (S.C.C.).
[15] Beverley G. Smith, *Professional Conduct for Lawyers and Judges*, 2d ed., looseleaf (Fredericton: Maritime Law Book, 2002) at 17, describing the perspective of the CBA Code. Smith himself describes the duty as "amongst the highest, if not *the* highest duty" (at 18 [emphasis in original]).

3. SUBSTANTIVE LEGAL NORMS

A. Introduction

The argument in favour of lawyers as resolute advocates within the bounds of legality rests on three central premises. First, that people are free to determine their own conceptions of the good within and through a system of laws. That is, the power of the state should not be brought to bear against a person except where that power is justified by law, and the state should not be permitted to avoid its duly owed legal obligations to its citizenry.[16] Second, that the law is complex, and cannot be reduced to a "big book of legal rules" that any person of typical intellect can be guided by. As a consequence, for the freedom to determine one's conception of the good within the bounds of legality to be meaningful, people need help to ascertain what the law means for them, to ensure that it does not apply to them improperly, and to advocate for the accomplishment of their own conceptions of the good at points where the law does not provide a determinate answer. They must have the right to assistance from someone who has the legal expertise that they do not, to help them ensure that they can access what the law permits, enables and requires. Third, while the law is complicated and ambiguous, it is not radically indeterminate; it has meaning apart from the politics of those who read and apply it. Lawyers can ascertain what the law means in order to advise or assist a client in pursuing her choices about how to live, and to ensure the lawyer's own conduct remains within the bounds of legality.

None of these premises is uncontroversial,[17] and their conceptual validity is assessed in section 4 of this chapter. This section is more descriptive, and simply indicates the place of these principles in Canadian substantive law. Substantively and procedurally, Canadian law treats the individual as entitled to be self-determining under and through the law and, as well, treats the law as something complex and difficult, yet also as something meaningful and capable of reasonable interpretation. In addition, Canadian jurisprudence directly endorses the role of the lawyer as resolute advocate for the rights of his client.

---

[16] There are, of course, many things that constrain individual behaviour apart from legality and an individual's own personal conception of the good. We live in social structures, and our actions are constrained by ties with family, community, culture and many other things. The lawyer does not, though, claim moral justification for acting as an advocate for the individual against non-legal constraints on personal action. The premise underlying the lawyer as resolute advocate is not, therefore, unconstrained individual autonomy; it is autonomy, legally speaking. Why does individual autonomy in that sense matter? It matters insofar as autonomy is of value in and of itself and also insofar as, if law is a solution to the problem of pluralistic conceptions of the good, respect for individual freedom within the constraints of legality follows inherently from the concept of law itself.

[17] Except, perhaps, the argument that the law is complex and requires expertise to be understood, which I think is self-evident.

B. The Individual and the Law

The idea that the person is entitled to self-determination under and through the law permeates Canadian jurisprudence, and is enshrined in the *Civil Code of Québec*,[18] which is said to codify the *res communes* — or common law — of that province. As this sub-section will describe, the concept of the rule of law animates public law decision-making. The legal system embeds strong commitments to procedural fairness both in the traditional concept of adversarial trials but also more broadly through the modern regulatory state. In numerous ways the courts have recognized that legal (and in particular constitutional) duties owed by the state can be properly enforced through the courts.

Perhaps the most famous statement of the significance of the rule of law as a constraint on action against the individual except through the operation of law is *Roncarelli v. Duplessis*.[19] Duplessis was the Premier of Québec, and Roncarelli was the owner of a licensed establishment in Québec, which had been originally owned by his father and licensed continually for 34 years. There were no issues in relation to the operation of the establishment. However, Roncarelli was a Jehovah's Witness, and had supported Jehovah's Witnesses defending themselves from the campaign of public prosecution that was being used to try to prevent them from proselytizing their faith in Québec. In particular, he routinely posted bail for Jehovah's Witnesses who had been arrested for distributing copies of "Watchtower" and "Awake". When Roncarelli's conduct was brought to the attention of the Québec authorities, including Duplessis, his liquor licence was revoked, "'forever'… to warn others that they similarly would be stripped of provincial 'privileges' if they persisted in any activity directly or indirectly related to the Witnesses".[20] Roncarelli sought judicial review of the revocation, and was successful. The Supreme Court held that the actions against Roncarelli were illegal, and violated the fundamental principle that state action cannot be arbitrary, but must be an exercise of legal authority, duly granted and exercised in good faith:

> In public regulation of this sort there is no such thing as absolute and untrammelled "discretion", that is that action can be taken on any ground or for any reason that can be suggested to the mind of the administrator; no legislative Act can, without express language, be taken to contemplate an unlimited arbitrary power exercisable for any purpose, however capricious or irrelevant, regardless of the nature or purpose of the statute. Fraud and corruption in the Commission may not be mentioned in such statutes but they are always implied as exceptions. "Discretion" necessarily implies good faith in discharging public duty; there is always a perspective within which a statute is intended to operate; and any clear departure from its lines or objects is just as

---

[18] L.R.Q., c. C-1991.
[19] [1959] S.C.J. No. 1, [1959] S.C.R. 121 (S.C.C.).
[20] *Ibid.* at 133, *per* Rand J.

objectionable as fraud or corruption. Could an applicant be refused a permit because he had been born in another province, or because of the colour of his hair? The ordinary language of the legislature cannot be so distorted.[21]

Subsequent to *Roncarelli*, in its administrative law jurisprudence the Supreme Court has consistently emphasized the paramount significance of the rule of law, both in terms of the concept that all state action must be grounded in law, and in the sense of the court's constitutional obligation to ensure that state actors have complied with their legal obligations.[22] As the Court noted in *Dunsmuir v. New Brunswick*,

> By virtue of the rule of law principle, all exercises of public authority must find their source in law. All decision-making powers have legal limits, derived from the enabling statute itself, the common or civil law or the Constitution. Judicial review is the means by which the courts supervise those who exercise statutory powers, to ensure that they do not overstep their legal authority. The function of judicial review is therefore to ensure the legality, the reasonableness and the fairness of the administrative process and its outcomes.[23]

Also noteworthy in showing the significance of the rule of law to Canadian substantive law is the "prescribed by law" requirement of s. 1 of the *Canadian Charter of Rights and Freedoms*. The *Charter* prohibits government actions that violate substantive constitutional rights and that do not constitute "reasonable limits prescribed by law as can be demonstrably justified in a free and democratic society".[24] The "prescribed by law" aspect of s. 1 means that where rights-violating government action is not in some way legally authorized, then no appeal to reason, or to consistency with freedom and democracy, will be sufficient to justify it.[25] Statutes, regulation and the common law can create limits "prescribed by law"; however, any legal prescription must be both accessible to the public and intelligible (formulated with sufficient precision), in order to qualify.[26] Moreover, a mere government directive or guideline does not constitute a legal prescription,[27] and nor does action by government actors which exceeds the legislative authority they have been given. A decision, for example, by a customs official to distinguish between homosexual and heterosexual

---

[21] *Ibid.* at 140.
[22] See, for example, *Crevier v. Québec (Attorney General)*, [1981] S.C.J. No. 80, [1981] 2 S.C.R. 220 (S.C.C.).
[23] [2008] S.C.J. No. 9 at para. 28, 2008 SCC 9 (S.C.C.).
[24] *Canadian Charter of Rights and Freedoms*, Part I of the *Constitution Act, 1982*, being Schedule B to the *Canada Act 1982* (U.K.), 1982, c. 11, s. 1.
[25] *R. v. Therens*, [1985] S.C.J. No. 30, [1985] 1 S.C.R. 613 (S.C.C.); see generally Peter W. Hogg, *Constitutional Law of Canada*, looseleaf (Toronto: Carswell, 2007) Part 38.7.
[26] Hogg, *ibid.* See also *R. v. Nova Scotia Pharmaceutical Society*, [1992] S.C.J. No. 67, [1992] 2 S.C.R. 606 (S.C.C.).
[27] To be prescribed by law a directive "must establish a norm or standard of general application that has been enacted by a government entity pursuant to a rule-making authority". See: *Greater Vancouver Transportation Authority v. Canadian Federation of Students – British Columbia Component*, [2009] S.C.J. No. 31, 2009 SCC 31 (S.C.C.).

pornography in applying the law against importation of obscene materials was not authorized by the relevant statute and could not, as a result, be justified.[28]

The entire Canadian legal system is premised, therefore, on the idea that it is only through law that decisions affecting the rights, privileges or interests of individuals can be made. A decision without legal authority, of one sort of another, cannot stand. Not all legal authority has to satisfy the s. 1 "prescribed by law" standard — decisions that do not affect constitutional rights can arise from more informal guidelines and directives, for example. Nonetheless, as the administrative law cases demonstrate, even more generally legality must ground all state action that affects the rights, privileges or interests of the person.

The notion of the individual as entitled to self-determination under and through the law can also be seen in the commitment of the Canadian legal system to procedural fairness in all government decision-making that affects the rights, privileges and interests of the individual.[29] In administrative law terms this means that decisions must be made by "a fair and open procedure, appropriate to the decision being made and its statutory, institutional, and social context, with an opportunity for those affected by the decision to put forward their views and evidence fully and have them considered by the decision-maker".[30] More traditionally, what procedural fairness refers to is the judicial model of adversarial trial process. The determination of contested judicial proceedings, and of some administrative proceedings, occurs through an adversarial model, in which each person is entitled to present her case fully, both factually and legally, before a decision is made about how the law applies to her circumstances. The Court has stated this model is central to respect for personal autonomy and the dignity of the person.[31]

The extent of the commitment to procedural fairness in Canadian law can be demonstrated by considering in more detail one particular procedural doctrine — the case law on the constitutional right to counsel pursuant to s. 7 and s. 10(*b*) of the *Charter*. The case law on the right to counsel demonstrates the importance we give to the individual in relation to the power of the state, and in particular the dual significance of the individual as self-determining under the law and with entitlements created by law. The

---

[28] *Little Sisters Book and Art Emporium v. Canada*, [2000] S.C.J. No. 66, [2000] 2 S.C.R. 1120 (S.C.C.).
[29] *Cardinal v. Kent Institution*, [1985] S.C.J. No. 78, [1985] 2 S.C.R. 643 at 653 (S.C.C.).
[30] *Baker v. Canada (Minister of Citizenship and Immigration)*, [1999] S.C.J. No. 39 at para. 22, [1999] 2 S.C.R. 817 (S.C.C.).
[31] See in general, *R. v. Swain*, where the Supreme Court held that "the principles of fundamental justice contemplate an accusatorial and adversarial system of criminal justice which is founded on respect for the autonomy and dignity of human beings" ([1991] S.C.J. No. 32 at para. 35, [1991] 1 S.C.R. 933 (S.C.C.)). See also: *Re B.C. Motor Vehicle Act*, [1985] S.C.J. No. 73, [1985] 2 S.C.R. 486 at 503 (S.C.C.); *R. v. Hebert*, [1990] S.C.J. No. 64, [1990] 2 S.C.R. 151 at 195 (S.C.C.); *R. v. Morgentaler*, [1988] S.C.J. No. 1, [1988] 1 S.C.R. 30 at 171 (S.C.C.), *per* Wilson J.

cases on the right to counsel also begin to indicate the extent to which the courts directly recognize the role of counsel in mediating between the individual and the legal system.

The right to counsel under s. 10(*b*) of the *Charter* is triggered in any circumstance where an individual is "detained", a low threshold that includes such things as roadside screening to identify drunk drivers.[32] Violations of s. 10(*b*) rights may be saved under s. 1, and have been in roadside screening cases for example,[33] but at the same time the courts have been willing to find unjustified right to counsel violations in a broad variety of circumstances. In particular, the Supreme Court has held, consistent with the language of s. 10(*b*), that the right to counsel includes more than simply the right to be advised that you can speak to a lawyer; it also requires giving the individual a "reasonable" opportunity to exercise her rights.[34] This means that not only must an individual be advised of the existence of legal aid but must also, for example, be advised of the existence of 24-hour duty counsel when she expresses concern about being able to contact counsel outside of working hours.[35] Waivers of the right to counsel must be clear and unequivocal, with full knowledge about the rights being waived.[36] Finally, and significantly, the right to counsel is viewed as important by the Court because it allows the individual to exercise her legal rights fully, and to ensure that she is only convicted on a proper legal basis. Counsel can advise the client, for example, on whether there were grounds for detention or for a search and, most importantly, of her right to silence. In the absence of such advice from counsel, statements made to the police are improper, and may be excluded pursuant to s. 24(2).

Three features of this jurisprudence stand out. First, the right to counsel is easily triggered and not easily waived. Second, the right to counsel is intended to create some sort of barrier between the individual and the state by, for example, increasing the likelihood that the right to silence will be exercised. Third, the right to counsel is something the state does not simply permit, it is also something the state to some extent facilitates, and where the state fails to do so the constitutional right to counsel will be found to have been violated. Each of these features demonstrates the extent to which the Canadian legal system views the individual as entitled to be self-determining under the law (free from unwarranted state interference) and through the law (able to exercise her legal entitlements).[37]

---

[32] *R. v. Orbanski*, [2005] S.C.J. No. 37, 2005 SCC 37 (S.C.C.).
[33] *Ibid.*
[34] *R. v. Sinclair*, [2010] S.C.J. No. 35, 2010 SCC 35 (S.C.C.).
[35] *R. v. Manninen*, [1987] S.C.J. No. 41, [1987] 1 S.C.R. 1233 (S.C.C.); *R. v. Bartle*, [1994] S.C.J. No. 74, [1994] 3 S.C.R. 173 (S.C.C.).
[36] *Ibid.*
[37] The Supreme Court has moved to a significantly more limited protection of the right to counsel in its recent history: *R. v. Sinclair*, [2010] S.C.J. No. 35, 2010 SCC 35 (S.C.C.); *R. v. McCrimmon*, [2010] S.C.J. No. 36, 2010 SCC 36 (S.C.C.); *R. v. Willier*, [2010] S.C.J. No. 37,

One of the most notable examples of state facilitation of the individual right to access the law is the case of *New Brunswick (Minister of Health and Community Services v. G.(J.)*,[38] where the Supreme Court held that s. 7 of the *Charter* can give rise to a right to counsel outside of the criminal law context, where proceedings implicate an individual's security of the person, are serious and complex, and the person cannot present her case without the assistance of counsel. In that case, the appellant was attempting to regain custody of her children. The allegations were complex; a three day hearing had been scheduled, with fifteen affidavits, including two expert reports to be presented by the Crown, which was of course represented by counsel.[39] The Court held that it would take a person with "superior intelligence or education, communication skills, composure, and familiarity with the legal system in order to effectively present his or her case" and there was no evidence to suggest that the appellant had those qualities.[40] In those circumstances, a failure to provide counsel violated s. 7 of the *Charter*.

This point should not be overstated, however. Generally speaking the courts are more willing to protect against unwarranted state interference than to facilitate access to justice. Thus, in its more recent decision in *R. v. Christie*,[41] which denied a constitutional challenge to a British Columbia tax levied on legal services, the Supreme Court rejected the argument that there was a general constitutional right to legal services. It did so in part because it characterized the right claimed as generally as possible, as a claim for a "constitutionally mandated legal aid scheme,"[42] without engaging with the obvious point that the actual constitutional challenge was being brought against a tax on legal services. The tax was not a failure to facilitate access to legal services, it was a direct impediment to the ability of poverty lawyers such as Christie to represent their clients.[43] The Court, in other words, rejected the claim that there was a general right to counsel which would obligate the government to provide lawyers in all legal proceedings, but did not consider the point that, on the facts of the case, the British Columbia government had erected an actual barrier to legal services. The *Christie* decision is in my view both internally inconsistent and intellectually sloppy,

---

2010 SCC 37 (S.C.C.). It retains, however, at least a theoretical commitment to the ideas described here, even if it does not give them much practical heft.
[38] [1999] S.C.J. No. 47, [1999] 3 S.C.R. 46 (S.C.C.).
[39] *Ibid.* at para. 79.
[40] *Ibid.* at para. 80.
[41] [2007] S.C.J. No. 21, 2007 SCC 21 (S.C.C.).
[42] "[T]he logical result would be a constitutionally mandated legal aid scheme for virtually all legal proceedings, except where the state could show this is not necessary for effective access to justice." *Ibid.* at para. 13.
[43] Christie's story ends tragically. Unable to continue his practice on Vancouver's downtown East side because of the tax burdens placed on him (the government required him to remit taxes, even when his clients did not pay his fees, as often occurred), he decided to ride his bicycle across the country to raise awareness of the constitutional challenge and the issues of access to justice underlying it. Before his case could be heard by the Supreme Court, Christie was struck by a motorist and killed.

but it nonetheless indicates that the claim of the individual against government intrusion remains stronger, generally speaking, than does the claim to government action on behalf of the individual, even where necessary to exercise legal rights effectively.

That is true through the legal system more broadly; Canadian courts have consistently been far more willing to restrict state action than to mandate state action, particularly in the context of administrative decision-making. There are, though, sufficient cases where the courts have been willing to require the government to take action, to assert that Canadian law includes the idea of the individual as entitled to make positive claims against the government as well as negative ones. For example, in *Eldridge v. British Columbia (Attorney General)*,[44] the Supreme Court held that s. 15 of the *Charter* required that provincially funded health care provide sign language interpreters to patients who were hearing impaired. Those arguing to uphold the government's policy relied on the position that what was being provided was a government benefit, and argued that s. 15 "does not oblige governments to implement programs to alleviate disadvantages that exist independently of state action. Adverse effects only arise from benefit programs ... when those programs exacerbate the disparities between the group claiming a s. 15(1) violation and the general population".[45] The Court rejected this argument as "impoverished"[46] and held instead that the state was obliged to ensure that people with disabilities were equally able to take part in the benefit that it had provided.[47]

This brief overview of some legal doctrines and cases is not comprehensive, and does not fully capture the complexity of the rights and entitlements of the Canadian citizenry pursuant to law. It should indicate, however, the centrality to the Canadian system of laws of the premise that the power of the state should not be brought to bear against a person except where that power is justified by law, and that the state should not be permitted to avoid its duly owed legal obligations.

C. Interpretation and the Law

An additional premise that underlies the justification of the lawyer's role as resolute advocate is, as noted, that while the law is complex and cannot be reduced to a series of easily articulated rules, it is ultimately meaningful and susceptible to good faith interpretation. While not as pervasively reflected in the jurisprudence as the relationship between the individual and the law, this premise can also be clearly identified within Canadian jurisprudence. Most obviously, it can be seen in those cases where the Court has expressly articulated the nature of law in relation to the role of counsel, referring to the

---

[44] [1997] S.C.J. No. 86, [1997] 3 S.C.R. 624 (S.C.C.).
[45] *Ibid.* at para. 72.
[46] *Ibid.* at para. 73.
[47] See also *Vriend v. Alberta*, [1998] S.C.J. No. 29, [1998] 1 S.C.R. 493 (S.C.C.).

"complexity and difficulty" of the law, and the need for lawyers to assist lay people in making sense of it.[48]

It is also apparent in the leading case on substantive judicial review, *Dunsmuir v. New Brunswick*.[49] In that case the Supreme Court engaged directly with the question of the nature of the law's determinacy by articulating the basis on which courts should apply the standards of review to determine the legality of administrative decisions. The Court has two standards of review — correctness and reasonableness. Under correctness review, the Court decides the issue for itself, and then decides if, given the Court's analysis, the administrative decision maker can be considered to have erred. Under reasonableness review, the Court decides whether the decision falls within the "range of possible, acceptable outcomes"[50] available to the decision-maker given the nature of the matter to be decided. Deeply imbedded in this case, and in the other substantive judicial review cases from which it follows, is the idea that the meaning of law can be determined, that errors of law by administrative decision-makers can be made, and that even if an administrative decision-maker is properly charged with making a legal decision (such that deference is appropriately given), that deference runs out if the interpretation falls outside of the "range of possible, acceptable outcomes" open to the decision-maker. The idea of a "range of possible, acceptable outcomes" also, though, respects the idea that the law is not so determinate as to be nothing more than a set of rules. As was most clearly articulated by former Chief Justice Dickson in his famous 1979 decision, *Canadian Union of Public Employees v. New Brunswick Liquor Corp.*,[51] there are many questions of law which do not lend themselves to a single interpretation, but which can be reasonably interpreted in quite distinct ways; in those cases, as long as an interpretation is reasonable, it should stand.

The jurisprudence of the Court does not, therefore, treat the law as a set of rules to be identified, but nor does it view the law as wholly indeterminate and contingent. The law can be interpreted, and must be to ensure that the rule of law is maintained.

D. Lawyers as Resolute Advocates

Demonstrating that the Canadian legal system views the individual as self-determining through and under the law, and that it rests on an idea of the law as complex but subject to meaningful interpretation, is enough to show that the idea of the resolute advocate is embedded in doctrinal law. Because in a world of complex but interpretable laws, the ability of the individual to have the relationship with the state that the legal system envisions can only

---

[48] *Anderson v. Bank of British Columbia* (1876), 2 Ch. D. 644 at 649 (C.A.).
[49] [2008] S.C.J. No. 9, 2008 SCC 9 (S.C.C.).
[50] *Ibid.* at para. 47.
[51] [1979] S.C.J. No. 45, [1979] 2 S.C.R. 227 (S.C.C.).

meaningfully occur if she has the ability to retain counsel, who can then advise her about what the law means, about what entitlements she can claim under it and about how to resist its improper application to her. Otherwise her self-determination is illusory, and the notion of democratic compromise inherent in the law falls apart.

It is also worth noting, though, that the idea of the lawyer as resolute advocate is also, in itself, deeply embedded in Canadian law.

The judicial recognition of the lawyer as resolute advocate rests, at first, in the categorization of the lawyer as a fiduciary to her client, and then, more deeply, in the principle underlying all fiduciary obligations: the fiduciary must act in furtherance to the beneficiary's interests, not his own. This position is of long-standing in the common law, but was clearly affirmed in two relatively recent decisions on conflicts of interest,[52] where the Supreme Court was unambiguous in its assertion that the lawyer is a fiduciary who owes a strong duty of loyalty to his client. This includes, of course, the requirement that the lawyer not prefer his own interests to those of his client,[53] but also includes the requirement that the lawyer act as a zealous representative, committed to his client's cause and immune to the temptation to "soft-peddle" representation in order to serve other interests.[54] In both these cases, and elsewhere, the Supreme Court has cited with approval Lord Brougham's strong conception of the lawyer as committed advocate for his client's causes, without regard for the potential injury that representation will inflict on the "greater good".

4. THE ETHICAL JUSTIFICATION

The lawyer's role as a resolute advocate is thus both a long-standing feature of Canadian legal culture and one that flows from the norms of our legal system. Substantive legal doctrine in Canada validates the idea of the lawyer as resolute advocate but also rests on the concepts that make resolute advocacy sensible. This section considers (and rejects) the normative arguments against the lawyer as resolute advocate, and then outlines the broader normative foundations that justify resolute advocacy as a morally legitimate role for the lawyer.

A. Arguments Against Resolute Advocacy

For our purposes, the arguments against resolute advocacy can be categorized in three ways. The first, which is the category that appears most commonly in the Canadian literature, is what I will call the "postmodern objection". Postmodern objectors recognize the argument for resolute advocacy, but argue against any determinate moral obligation, of advocacy

---

[52] *R. v. Neil*, [2002] S.C.J. No. 72, [2002] 3 S.C.R. 631 (S.C.C.); *Strother v. 3464920 Canada Inc.*, [2007] S.C.J. No. 24, [2007] 2 S.C.R. 177 (S.C.C.).
[53] *Strother, ibid.*
[54] *R. v. Neil*, [2002] S.C.J. No. 72 at para. 19, [2002] 3 S.C.R. 631 (S.C.C.).

or otherwise, that governs lawyer decision-making in all circumstances. They argue instead for contextual- and dialogue-based decision-making that varies according to the circumstances in which the decision is made. The second category has dominated the anti-zeal literature in the United States, and can be described as the "personal morality" objection. The personal morality argument emphasizes the distinction between the lawyer's role in the legal system and morality, and argues for the primacy of moral obligations in all circumstances. The third category is the "morality of law" objection. The morality of law objection is premised on the argument that law instantiates and reflects morality, and argues for recasting lawyers' resolute advocacy in terms of law's underlying moral claims. I will consider each of these objections in turn.

i. The Postmodern Objection

Trevor Farrow's 2008 article "Sustainable Professionalism"[55] articulates a cogent postmodernist conception of the ethical lawyer.[56] Farrow's argument is that resolute advocacy can be justified in terms of principles, lawyer practices and concerns of policy. He suggests, however, that a singular emphasis on zealous advocacy over-simplifies the moral challenge that lawyers are required to resolve in practice. When a lawyer makes decisions there are many things that can make a legitimate claim on his attention, including the interests of the client, the lawyer's own moral and personal commitments, the concerns of the profession (in, for instance, fostering diversity) and, finally, what will best further the public interest and social responsibility. The ethic of the lawyer should not, therefore, be resolute advocacy; it should be "sustainable professionalism" in which the lawyer takes into account all of these inputs and engages in a dialogue, with himself and with others, to determine the right course of action. Ultimately,

> the goal is to foster deliberation both for the lawyer and between the client and the lawyer, in the spirit of enabling a sustained and engaged discussion that takes seriously a variety of potentially competing interests. This is not simply an exercise in client autonomy or an exercise in moral superiority. It is an exercise in real world, sustainable lawyering.[57]

There are several problems with postmodern perspectives on ethical questions. Most obviously, there is a fine line between postmodern ethics and no ethics at all. Farrow describes his approach, for example, as one of

---

[55] Trevor Farrow, "Sustainable Professionalism" (2008) 46 Osgoode Hall L.J. 51.
[56] I hasten to emphasize that Farrow does not identify his perspective as post-modern. I characterize it that way because (a) Farrow is not prepared to take a stand on ethical positions that are, in the end, fundamentally contradictory; (b) his emphasis on dialogue, discourse and individual decision-making is embedded in the postmodernist tradition; and (c) I see little foundational difference between his vision of the ethical lawyer and that earlier set out by Allan Hutchinson as a "Postmodern Re-Vision of Lawyering" (Allan Hutchinson, "Calgary and Everything After: A Postmodern Re-Vision of Lawyering" (1995) 33 Alta. L. Rev. 768).
[57] Trevor Farrow, "Sustainable Professionalism" (2008) 46 Osgoode Hall L.J. 51 at 100.

sustainable professionalism, and argues for sustainability as a value in itself. But the virtue of sustainability depends on that which is to be sustained — sustained suffering, for example, is not something to be valued or encouraged. For sustainable professionalism to be something worth achieving requires identifying the value of professionalism, not of sustainability — which, in the case of Farrow's article, requires identifying the moral value of each of the elements that he would have the lawyer factor into his decision-making.

That question, however, is one that Farrow avoids addressing. He does note the moral claim that different perspectives can make, but he is unprepared to take a stand on the relative merit of these claims, even though the claims are irreconcilable on their own terms. He does not, either, define those matters that can legitimately fall within the lawyer's balancing of his personal moral values, the client's goals and professional interests, or on what basis such a decision would be made. That makes sense in terms of Farrow's theoretical foundations, because the heart of postmodernism is to see ethical questions as not subject to determination based on universally applicable considerations. It leads, however, to the problem that postmodern lawyering ends up being entirely based on the personal moral assessments of the lawyer making the decision, informed perhaps by "discourse", but not subject to any sort of objective assessment. Allan Hutchinson, whose work predates and appears to significantly influence Farrow's, both acknowledges and celebrates this fact:

> [Postmodern lawyering] offers no magical guide as to what to do in any specific or conflict situation, because there is none to be given. It is for each person to arrive at an informed and conscientious decision in accordance with their own political and moral lights. The objective is not to chastise lawyers simply because they are corporate lawyers or represent rapists and bigots: it is to encourage each lawyer to take responsibility for the clients they take, and causes they fight for and the tactics they use. In doing so, however, the postmodern lawyer will ensure that these moral and political lights are always brought into play and are themselves open to debate and re-consideration. In the postmodern play-book, the goal is not an enforced and impersonal orthodoxy, but a respectful and responsible heterodoxy.[58]

Hutchinson's conclusion though, leads to further questions. Why, for example, should the heterodoxy of the postmodern lawyer be respectful and responsible? Are concepts of "respect" and "responsibility" not just as based in big ideas of morality as are, for example, personal autonomy, liberty and justice? And, if they are not, if all of the moral ideas are simply contingent things that we might or might not want to apply in any given circumstance, then why are the values that we should impose on heterodoxy respectfulness and responsibility, as opposed to other "contingent" values such as autonomy, liberty or democracy? Or, to return to Farrow's model, if we are

---

[58] Allan Hutchinson, "Calgary and Everything After: A Postmodern Re-Vision of Lawyering" (1995) 33 Alta. L. Rev. 768 at 781-82.

going to incorporate certain factors as relevant to the lawyer's decision, but make no evaluation of the relative claim each can make in a general sense, why do we try to identify any factors as relevant at all? Why not simply say to the lawyer "good luck with that" and move on?

In sum, the problem with postmodernist accounts of the lawyer is that they try to have their ethical cake and throw it to the pigs too. They want to impose values on the lawyer, but only in a sort-of-kind-of-maybe way, one that allows the lawyer — and us — to duck the difficult questions about what we, as a society, think the right thing is for lawyers to do. Or, more individually, they duck the questions about what for the individual lawyer is the right thing to do — which choices will properly merit moral acclaim and which will properly merit moral disapprobation?

ii. The Personal Morality Objection

Although similarly focused on the lawyer's exercise of individual judgment, the personal morality objection to zealous advocacy is not similarly reluctant to articulate what a lawyer seeking to be ethical should do. The personal morality objection starts from the premise that legality and morality are not co-terminus. There are some things that the law permits, and some that it even requires that are immoral. The law may permit a landlord to evict a tenant who has only technically violated the lease, and who has nowhere else to go. The landlord who makes that choice may nonetheless be categorized as acting immorally.[59] And so too, the personal morality objectors argue, should the lawyer who helps the landlord to accomplish that eviction.

A lawyer is a moral agent, and does not lose his moral agency by virtue of being a lawyer. The professional obligation to be a zealous advocate within the bounds of the law may require the lawyer to assist clients pursue actions that can be judged as immoral, but to the extent that it does so the professional obligation does not give the lawyer a moral excuse; it gives the lawyer a moral problem which he has to resolve, one way or another. David Luban, the best of those writing from the personal morality objection, argues that while a lawyer may operate under a "presumption in favor of professional obligation" that presumption can be rebutted and, in the end, "when professional and serious moral obligation conflict, moral obligation takes precedence."[60] Moreover, those moral obligations take precedence even where the lawyer may have to ignore legal requirements imposed on him as a lawyer: "When serious moral obligation conflicts with professional obligation, the lawyer must become a civil disobedient to

---

[59] This would, of course, depend on the totality of the facts and circumstances.
[60] David Luban, *Legal Ethics and Human Dignity* (New York: Cambridge University Press, 2007) at 63. See also: David Luban, *Lawyers and Justice: An Ethical Study* (Princeton, NJ: Princeton University Press, 1988); Gerald Postema "Moral Responsibility in Professional Ethics" (1980) 55 N.Y.U.L. Rev. 63; Richard Wasserstrom, "Lawyers as Professionals: Some Moral Issues" (1975) 5 Human Rights 1.

professional rules."[61] Luban acknowledges that a lawyer is unlikely to make that choice, but his point is to take apart the argument from zealous advocacy that would make that choice unnecessary.

The first difficulty with the personal morality objection is that it places an enormous trust in lawyer morality, while placing almost no trust at all in the morality of the laws and legal system within which lawyers work.[62] Yet individual lawyer morality both reflects and influences the laws and legal system, and cannot be so neatly separated from them.

The second and related difficulty with the personal morality objection is that, in contra-distinction to the postmodernist problem, it both does not account for the possibility of deep moral disagreement amongst people, nor acknowledge the extent to which the law exists as a way of allowing people with deep moral disagreements to live in peace together. The personal morality objection does not live in a morally simplistic universe, but it does assert the possibility of universal moral claims on the basis of which lawyers can reliably make ethical decisions. Moreover, it does not give much credit to the possibility that law, as a statement of our actual compromises and joint conclusions on how we will live together, has itself a claim to respect, even where it conflicts with an individual's deeply held moral commitments. It rejects the idea that the rule of law can itself make a moral claim.[63] It suggests, instead, that "the legal profession can properly regard itself as an oligarchy, whose duty is to nullify decisions made by the people's duly elected representatives".[64]

The philosopher Jeremy Waldron sets out the problem with both these assertions: that which reduces the significance of our moral disagreements, and that which disregards the achievement of the law. First, while not arguing against moral agreement *per se*, Waldron questions the extent to which moral consensus exists, even within our most basic moral concepts. On matters as apparently obvious as the moral prohibition on rape, serious moral disagreement is still possible with respect to specific issues such as marital rape, consent, mistaken but honest belief in consent, the age of consent and so on.[65] The function of law (and, Waldron argues, of political institutions which give rise to law) is to provide us with some way of

---

[61] *Ibid.*
[62] Monroe Freedman & Abbe Smith, *Understanding Lawyers' Ethics*, 4th ed. (New Providence, NJ: LexisNexis, 2010) at 47.
[63] Nigel Simmons, *Law as a Moral Idea* (Oxford: Oxford University Press, 2007) at 66:
> a government's compliance with the requirements of the rule of law is not best explained by considerations of instrumental efficacy. Rather, it must be explained by reference to a concern to maintain an intrinsically valuable form of moral association that is embodied in the rule of law ... non-hypocritical compliance with the rule of law can be motivated only by a concern for a particular form of moral association and not by a concern for instrumental efficacy.
[64] Monroe Freedman & Abbe Smith, *Understanding Lawyers' Ethics*, 4th ed. (New Providence, NJ: LexisNexis, 2010) at 47.
[65] Jeremy Waldron, *Law and Disagreement* (Oxford: Oxford University Press, 1999) at 105.

resolving these difficult questions, even when we disagree, and disagree strongly about the moral perspectives that different answers reflect. Without law, we are left with nothing but our original disagreement and the need to resolve that disagreement with whatever crude and potentially violent means are at our disposal.

What follows from Waldron's analysis is the identification of law as something in and of itself worthy of our attention and respect. A lawyer's own personal disagreement with what the law permits or requires speaks to that lawyer's own personal moral values, but the whole point of law is to provide both an actual settlement to controversies over the right way to live, and to allow people the freedom, under and through the law, to live as they like. To ignore the authority of the law based on a personal assessment that a different moral answer is required, is to undermine legality altogether.[66]

iii. The Morality-of-Law Objection

This response to the personal morality objection leads, though, to the morality of law objection to resolute advocacy. The morality-of-law objector looks to this point and says, "Yes! And the problem with resolute advocacy is that it also does not take the moral compromise of law seriously, but instead engages in legal trickery and tomfoolery, to obtain for clients results that the law does not properly permit." William Simon provides a uniquely rigorous articulation of the morality-of-law objection. Simon argues that lawyers are properly advocates for clients, but they are advocates within the context of ensuring that, in each case, the lawyer takes those "actions that, considering the relevant circumstances of the particular case, seem likely to promote justice".[67] Simon does not view justice as a moral value existing apart from the law; he views it as part and parcel of the legal system — justice is "legal merit". Similarly, in the Canadian context, David Tanovich has argued that the obligation of the lawyer is to pursue justice:

> Justice can be defined, for the purposes of the lawyering process, *as the correct resolution of legal disputes or problems in a fair, responsible, and non-discriminatory manner.* This approach to justice has both procedural and substantive elements. The procedural component is the right to a fair and non-discriminatory process that is capable of producing the result demanded by the law. The substantive component involves assessing the merit of the legal claim as seen through the lens of the law properly interpreted. A proper interpretation is one that gives effect to the purpose behind the legal provision and which ensures that the provision is consistent with other substantive legal norms such as

---

[66] *Ibid.* in general, but see in particular pp. 159-60.
[67] William H. Simon, *The Practice of Justice: A Theory of Lawyers' Ethics* (Cambridge, Mass.: Harvard University Press, 1998) at 138. Although this book comes later, it in large part sets out in more detail the arguments made by Simon a decade earlier in "Ethical Discretion in Lawyering" (1988) 101 Harv. L. Rev. 1083.

equality, fairness, and harm reduction. It is also one that pays special attention to our history of injustice.[68]

On its face, this re-working of resolute advocacy has much to recommend it. It can, arguably, be interpreted as simply a direction for lawyers to do their job well, to get the law right. It takes law seriously, and also provides lawyers with a way of making decisions that they are professionally competent to make.

The problem arises, though, when we unpack a little further what is meant by "legal merit" or by the invocation of substantive norms such as "equality, fairness and harm reduction" to guide our legal interpretation.[69] Consider this example:[70] A lawyer is acting for a mother in a child custody and support dispute. The mother is on welfare. The father is absent much of the time, and suffers from some issues related to mental illness that compromise his fitness as a parent. In a meeting between the lawyer and his client about a week before financial disclosure is required, the client tells her lawyer that she is also working as a prostitute to better financially support herself and her son; her sister is helping with childcare so the son can be looked after while his mother is working. The client tells the lawyer that he cannot disclose her extra work to the father, welfare authorities or the court.

What does legal merit require in a case such as this? It clearly does not permit the lawyer to provide false financial disclosure to the court or to the father. It also does not permit the lawyer to disclose the client's past welfare fraud. The law with respect to false representations and maintenance of these sorts of confidences is clear.[71] But does it permit the lawyer to avoid disclosure altogether by quickly negotiating a generous settlement with the father, one which is nonetheless less advantageous than the father would get if he had full information and went to court? The law permits this result — settlements are a legally recognized way of resolving legal disputes, and no fraud or misrepresentation is being used to achieve the settlement.[72] But is it consistent with legal merit? Does it achieve equality, fairness and the reduction of harm? There are good arguments for and against this course of action in terms of substantial legal merit, arguments which turn on an assessment of what is in the best interests of the child (which is the

---

[68] David Tanovich, "Law's Ambition and the Reconstruction of Role Morality in Canada" (2005) 28 Dal. L.J. 267 at 284. [Emphasis in original].
[69] Or why the relevant substantive norms are equality, fairness and harm reduction as opposed to, say, autonomy.
[70] Given to me by Brent Cotter.
[71] It is less clear whether the lawyer would be permitted to disclose the client's work in the event she is going to defraud welfare in the future. While most codes of professional conduct permit that disclosure, it is arguable that the law on privilege, as set out by the Supreme Court in *Smith v. Jones*, [1999] S.C.J. No. 15, [1999] 1 S.C.R. 455 (S.C.C.), precludes it. See Adam Dodek, "The Public Safety Exception to Solicitor-Client Privilege: *Smith v. Jones*" (2000) 34 U.B.C. L. Rev. 293.
[72] Note the distinction if there had been any false representations to the husband, as opposed to simply the welfare authorities.

applicable legal standard), what the purpose and form of the custody and support laws require, and so on.

But that means, I would suggest, that under our system of laws we have also reached the point where the decision as to what to do is properly given to the client — to the person allowed to be self-determining under and through the system of laws — not to the lawyer. If the law permits a course of action, and what constitutes legal merit is contentious, then the decision as to what should be done should be given to the person whose interests are at stake, not to the lawyer. The problem with the morality of law argument is that, in the end, it gives the lawyer the privilege of determining what can be done under and through the law, rather than leaving that privilege where it should be: with the person whose self-determination the law respects and facilitates.

B. In Defence of the Lawyer as Resolute Advocate

By now the basis for my argument in favour of the lawyer as resolute advocate should be clear. It turns on an assertion of law as something that can make an authoritative claim against our actions, not simply by virtue of the power of the state to enforce it, but because the law, in and of itself, is worthy of our respect and attention. It is worthy of our attention because it is through the law that we achieve a civil society, one in which our disagreements are resolved through politics and adjudication, not through riots, violence and discord: "People who have grievances against one another come to lawyers as an alternative to resorting to physical violence."[73] Whether the claim to authority that law makes is itself a moral claim, or not, is not one that I am attempting to resolve here.[74] But I am claiming that the law is authoritative, in terms of setting out our collective decisions on what we are forbidden from doing, what we are tolerated or permitted to do, and, finally, what we are encouraged to do or facilitated in doing.

Why does this lead to resolute advocacy? Resolute advocacy has two central features. First, it places decision-making about what is to be done in a legal representation with the client. The lawyer acts to facilitate the client's accomplishment of her ends within the legal system, but it is the client who determines those ends.[75] Second, resolute advocacy requires the lawyer to

---

[73] Monroe Freedman & Abbe Smith, *Understanding Lawyers' Ethics*, 4th ed. (New Providence, NJ: LexisNexis, 2010) at 22.

[74] Indeed, one could take a position much like that set out here even if one only, following Joseph Raz, thought that "practical respect [for the authority of law] might be thought of as a proper expression of loyalty to society", Joseph Raz, *The Authority of Law*, 2d ed. (Oxford: Oxford University Press, 2009) at 261. But see also the more vigorous claims made in Nigel Simmons, *Law as a Moral Idea* (Oxford: Oxford University Press, 2007).

[75] What this looks like, in practical terms, is discussed in Chapter 3.

interpret and work through the law to achieve the client's goals.[76] These features both follow from this authority claim for law. Because if law has the function of resolving disagreements between those to whom it applies, and of constraining, tolerating and encouraging conduct in those to whom it applies, then the decision about how to live within that legal framework lies with the person subject to it. If I am to decide not only how I am to live under and through the law, but also to decide how my neighbour lives under and through the law, then the law has ceased to achieve its essential function. It is not resolving disagreements between my neighbour and me; I am. And similarly for the relationship between the lawyer and the client: if the lawyer decides what the client may, must or should do, instead of simply assisting the client determine what the law permits or requires the client to do, the lawyer will have similarly usurped the law's function in resolving disagreement.

Further, to make the civil compromise of the law functional, the client must be given the means to access that civil compromise, in terms of knowing what the law means, of accessing the systems of dispute resolution that the law provides, and in terms of enforcing her legal rights and claims against others, including the state. Lawyers, in acting as resolute advocates within the bounds of the law, allow clients to achieve this access. This also means, though, that in representing a client a lawyer must engage in good faith interpretation of the law, and work within the systems of the law as they exist — if the lawyer burns documents that are properly producible in discoveries, for example, then the lawyer has not allowed the client to access the civic compromise of the law, he has helped the client to destroy it.

This leads to the other assertion that underlies the claim in favour of resolute advocacy, which is that the law is sufficiently complex that it requires the assistance of a lawyer, yet is also sufficiently capable of meaningful interpretation that the lawyer can provide assistance to the client. The first of these premises is self-evident.[77] The second is more difficult, and requires demonstrating that the law is something which precludes

---

[76] The lawyer's function is — at its heart — based in the law. The lawyer does not generally act to facilitate the client in accomplishment of her non-legal goals, and to the extent the lawyer does so it is not at all obvious that the norms of resolute advocacy properly apply to her conduct.

[77] To demonstrate this point I opened a copy of the *Income Tax Act* to a random page and found the following provision, which ably illustrates it:
> Where, otherwise than by virtue of a deemed disposition under paragraph 148(2)(*b*), an interest of a policyholder in a life insurance policy is disposed of by way of a gift (whether during the policyholder's lifetime or by the policyholder's will), by distribution from a corporation or by operation of law only to any person, or in any manner whatever to any person with whom the policyholder was not dealing at arm's length, the policyholder shall be deemed thereupon to become entitled to receive proceeds of the disposition equal to the value of the interest at the time of the disposition, and the person who acquires the interest by virtue of the disposition shall be deemed to acquire it at a cost equal to that value.

(*Income Tax Act*, R.S.C. 1985, c. 1, s. 148(7)).

certain interpretations as unreasonable, as falling outside the "range of possible, acceptable outcomes".[78]

Providing an explanation in favour of the meaningfulness of law sufficient to convince a sceptic is not possible in this context. Suffice it to say that if meaningfully interpreting the law is impossible, then we should all — lawyers, law students and legal academics — abandon the enterprise. If meaning in law cannot be engaged with, and at minimum some interpretations of the law rejected as unsustainable and bogus — as the equivalent of asserting a belief in fairies — then there is nothing that we have to offer anyone, whether it be clients, ourselves or the public interest in general. The debates of legal ethics are meaningless, and all that is left is determining what side to take in the power struggle within which we reside. I would suggest that if that is where the argument has gone, then it has gone so far as to disprove itself.

The functioning of the legal system itself, the absence of our collapse into armed conflict to resolve our disputes, means that, one way or another, we have managed to act for a very long time as if the law does say something meaningful that we can ascertain. The law may be open to a wide range of interpretations, but the boundaries of that range are ascertainable to the ordinarily competent lawyer. The role of the lawyer is, therefore, to act within that range on behalf of her client.

What, though, of the various examples given at the beginning of this chapter, and the suggestion that at the very least a lawyer who, for example, tries to make a truthful witness look like a liar, or invites a finder of fact to draw an inference from evidence the lawyer knows is untrue, has done something that is morally doubtful? The final point to be made in favour of resolute advocacy is that the morality of an action taken within a professional role is simply not assessed at the level of the act itself. What needs to be morally justified is, instead, the professional role. What has been offered here, is that sort of moral justification. The role of the lawyer is morally justified, because of the civil compromise that is law, and because of the necessity of the lawyer to achieving that civil compromise. What this means, is that any action that is required by the lawyer's role is also morally justified.

That does not make the life of the lawyer morally uncomplicated. The tension between personally felt moral obligation and professional role is real, and cannot be reduced simply by the assertion of the moral justification for the role. To use an example given by the philosopher Timothy Chappell, suppose the officer of a wrecked ship decides, when faced with a full lifeboat, that his obligations as an officer require him to actively prevent other survivors from climbing aboard. His actions help to contribute to the death of those survivors, but protect the lives of the people on board, which would otherwise have been endangered. Let's assume, as well, that the

---

[78] *Dunsmuir v. New Brunswick*, [2008] S.C.J. No. 9 at para. 47, 2008 SCC 9 (S.C.C.).

officer is correct in his assessment of what his role requires, and that a moral justification for the role of ship's officer can be given. As Chappell notes, it would nonetheless show a comprehensive failure to understand the situation to address the officer's subsequent remorse and guilt by saying "why are you so upset? You did what your role requires."[79] The existence of a role justification does not eliminate the moral complexity that the role brings with it. The task of the lawyer, as discussed with respect to integrity, in Chapter 1, is to learn to live with that moral complexity, as best as he or she can.

And as will be apparent throughout the remainder of this book, there are many ways in which a lawyer can manage this moral complexity, and reduce the moral tension that the role of the lawyer creates. While lawyers are constrained to act as resolute advocates for their clients, they have discretion when choosing their clients. Further, determining what a client wants — what are her ends, in fact — is in itself a complicated exercise, and a lawyer can legitimately engage in serious discussion with his client about what is an appropriate course of action within the constraints of the law. A mistake sometimes made by lawyers is to assume that they know what their client wants, and that their client wants every advantage the law permits.[80] Finally, the lawyer does in some circumstances have the opportunity to withdraw from representation.

These aspects of the lawyer's role — the challenge of respecting his own moral agency while zealously advocating for his client's within the bounds of legality — are taken up in the next chapter.

---

[79] Timothy Chappell, "Bernard Williams" *Stanford Encyclopedia of Philosophy*, online: <http://plato.stanford.edu/entries/williams-bernard/>.

[80] See generally Monroe Freedman & Abbe Smith, *Understanding Lawyers' Ethics*, 4th ed. (New Providence, NJ: LexisNexis, 2010) at 53-55; Katherine R. Kruse, "Beyond Cardboard Clients in Legal Ethics", (2010) 23 Geo. J. Legal Ethics 103.

Chapter 3

THE LAWYER-CLIENT RELATIONSHIP

1. INTRODUCTION

In the previous chapter I argued that the lawyer's fundamental ethical obligation is to be a resolute advocate for the interests of her client under and through the law. In making that argument I noted the moral complexity of the lawyer's role, and the tensions that can arise for the lawyer when her role appears to be — or is — at odds with what her own personal moral values suggest is the right thing to do in particular circumstances. A way to understand the tensions a lawyer may experience is as the natural consequence of the potential for conflict between the moral agency of the lawyer and the moral agency of the client. In particular, resolute advocacy requires the lawyer to further the moral agency of the client, to help the client execute his decisions about the right thing to do and how to live his life. But when the lawyer advocates, she does not cease to be a moral agent, with her own personal beliefs about what the right thing to do is in any given situation. And that view might be different from her client's.

Each of the topics discussed in this chapter — client selection, decision-making and counselling, fees, and withdrawal — raises in some way the question of how we can ensure that the lawyer fulfills her obligation to help the client execute his decisions about what to do, and the right way to live, while also recognizing that the lawyer will inevitably have her own beliefs about what should be done, and about the right way to live. It is when selecting clients that a lawyer can (and should) protect her own moral values. Proper client selection helps reduce the moral tension that the lawyer might otherwise experience when representing a client.

Client counselling and lawyer-client decision-making, on the other hand, are areas where there are temptations and opportunities for a lawyer to improperly override the client's decisions about what to do. The lawyer's obligations in both these areas must ensure that the lawyer respects the client's autonomy. At the same time, the obligations on the lawyer around client counselling and decision-making do not require the lawyer to pretend that her own moral values are other than they are.

With respect to fees, while not always explained in quite this way, the payment the lawyer receives for her work can be an important way in which her autonomy and dignity are respected; again, though, it is important to constrain the lawyer from improperly preferring her interests to those of her client.

Finally, the restrictions on lawyer withdrawal provide a general constraint on the lawyer's ability to prefer her own decisions to those of her client, while also recognizing that, in some circumstances, the lawyer cannot legitimately be required to continue to further her client's interests.

2. CLIENT SELECTION

Canadian lawyers enjoy a general right to decline to act in any case unless assigned to do so by a court.[1] That general right is, however, subject to some specific qualifications. There are situations in which a lawyer cannot take on a case: where the lawyer would be in an impermissible conflict;[2] where the lawyer would have to appear as a witness in the matter;[3] where the lawyer is not (and cannot affordably become) competent to take on the case;[4] and where the matter is "clearly without merit" or frivolous and vexatious.[5]

In addition, the lawyer may not select clients on a discriminatory basis — that is, the lawyer may not deny service or provide inferior service based on an individual's "ancestry, colour, perceived race, nationality, national origin, ethnic background or origin, language, religion, creed or religious belief, religious association or activities, age, sex, gender, physical characteristics, pregnancy, sexual orientation, marital or family status, source of income, political belief, association or activity, or physical or mental disability".[6]

Finally, most codes of conduct note the general duty on the profession to "make legal services available to the public in an efficient and convenient way". They suggest that a lawyer should be slow to exercise her right to decline representation where doing so would "make it very difficult for a person to obtain legal advice or representation".[8] Also, where a lawyer

---

[1] CBA MC Chapter XIV, Rule 6. FLS MC Rule 3.01; Que. CEA Rule 3.05.01, LSUC RPC Rule 3.01, NB CC Chapter 4, Rule 17, AB CPC Chapter 5, Rule 1. The BC PCH is silent with respect to the issue of client selection.

[2] See the discussion in Chapter 8 and also, for example, CBA MC Chapter V.

[3] See, for example, CBA MC Chapter IX, Commentary 5; FLS MC Rule 4.02; LSUC RPC Rule 4.02; Que. CEA Rule 3.05.06; NB CC Chapter 8, Rule 6; AB CPC Chapter 10, Rule 10; BC PCH Chapter 8, Rule 9.

[4] See, for example, CBA MC Chapter II, Commentary 3; FLS MC Rule 2.01(2), commentary; LSUC RPC Rule 2.01, commentary; Que. CEA Rule 3.01.01; NB CC Chapter 2, Rule 6; AB CPC Chapter 2, Rule 3; BC PCH Chapter 3, Rule 2.

[5] AB CPC Chapter 1, Rule 5. This may also be implicit in the rules of conduct in provinces that prohibit bringing forward matters which are frivolous or vexatious, such as the CBA MC Chapter IX, Commentary 2 and BC PCH Chapter 1, Rule 1.

[6] CBA MC Chapter XX; FLS MC Rule 5; LSUC RPC Rule 5.04(2); NB CC Chapter 21; AB CPC Chapter 1, Rule 9; BC PCH Chapter 3, Rule 4.1. Québec does not incorporate an anti-discrimination rule directly in the *Code of ethics of advocates*, although Que. CEA Rule 4.02.01 prohibits sexual harassment.

[7] FLS MC Rule 3.01.

[8] CBA MC Chapter XIV, Commentary 6. The AB CPC also suggests that lawyers should be cognizant of the fact that unpopular clients are more likely to find it difficult to find legal representation, and note that representing a client does not involve condoning the client's point of view. AB CPC Chapter 9, Rule 11, commentary. The Que. CEA states at Rule 2.04 that an

declines to act in a particular case she should assist the individual in finding representation elsewhere.[9]

This summary of the rules on client selection raises two questions. First, what follows from the constraints placed on client selection and, in particular, from the requirement that lawyers not discriminate when deciding whom to represent? Second, to the extent that the rules on client selection give lawyers a broad discretion in selecting clients, how should that discretion be exercised?

The most significant of the specific restrictions placed on client selection — the prohibition on conflicts, the requirement of competence, the rule against frivolous litigation — are simply the logical outcome of substantive obligations placed on the lawyer that are discussed separately in later chapters. Those restrictions are thus not explained further here. The prohibition on the lawyer acting in a case where she will be required to be a witness means basically what it says. The primary additional point to note is that the restriction does not operate where the lawyer's testimony is incidental to the action as a whole. A lawyer is not, for example, disqualified from acting in a case simply because the lawyer needs to file an affidavit about something that happened in the action, such as service of a document. Also, the rule generally applies only to testimony from the lawyer personally, not to testimony from a member of the lawyer's firm (although the lawyer may be restricted from, for example, conducting the examination of the firm member in court).

That leaves only the obligations related to access to justice and the rule against discrimination. The exhortation to foster access to justice is generally placed on the profession as a whole, not on individual lawyers.[10] To the extent it is placed on individual lawyers — the obligation to assist in finding alternative counsel — it is not an onerous requirement, and is satisfied by minimal acts such as referring the prospective client to a law society's lawyer referral service. The obligations related to access to justice are generally hortatory and do not meaningfully qualify the general discretion given to the lawyer to decline to act in any particular case.

The rule against discrimination is more complicated, and its meaning for lawyers selecting clients not entirely clear. In general, anti-discrimination laws in Canada prohibit discrimination which is either direct or arises as an "adverse effect" from a facially neutral statute. An example of direct discrimination would be a requirement that all firefighters be men. An

---

advocate may undertake the defence of a client "no matter what his personal opinion may be on the latter's guilt or liability".

[9] CBA MC Chapter XIV, Rule 6; FLS MC Rule 3.01; LSUC RPC Rule 3.01; AB CPC Chapter 1, Rule 5. Note that the NB CC, BC PCH and Que. CEA do not seem to impose any similar obligation on the lawyer.

[10] In the AB CPC, Chapter 1, Rule 4 states that the lawyer should facilitate and contribute to the legal profession's efforts to make legal services available to all, regardless of the ability to pay. The obligation is of the profession as a whole in the first instance, but the lawyer is placed under a specific obligation as well. See the discussion in Chapter 10.

example of adverse effect discrimination would be a workplace rule that employees not cover their heads, as applied to individuals whose religious beliefs require them to do so. In employment situations discrimination is permitted where it constitutes a *"bona fide* occupational requirement" — thus, for example, a requirement that daytime cleaning staff in a female locker room be women is discriminatory, but is unlikely to be unlawful.

As noted above, prohibited grounds for discrimination by lawyers include discrimination based on race, gender and disability, but may also include political beliefs or creed. How these rules apply in practice to lawyers' selection of clients is not clear; there are no published cases in which lawyers have been disciplined — under codes of conduct or under human rights statutes — for selecting clients on a discriminatory basis. The rules against discrimination in client selection do, however, have the capacity to complicate the ability of the lawyer to incorporate her own moral values in selecting clients. Consider these examples:

- A lawyer is approached by an individual charged with crimes related to hate speech because of the individual's publication of pamphlets stating that homosexuality is a "sickness" and that tolerance of gays and lesbians "violates the will of god". The lawyer declines the representation because she finds the pamphlets abhorrent. The accused person alleges that he has been discriminated against on the basis of his political and religious beliefs.

- A criminal defence lawyer refuses to take on sexual assault cases. The vast majority of people charged with sexual assault are men. A man whose retainer is declined by the lawyer argues that he has suffered adverse effect discrimination on the basis of his gender.

- A family law lawyer adopts a policy of only representing wives in divorces, and markets her practice on that basis. A man whose retainer is declined by the lawyer argues that he has been directly discriminated against on the basis of his gender.

- A criminal defence lawyer is consulted by a man who has been charged with drunk driving. The accused is a committed scientologist. The lawyer does not want to represent someone who is a scientologist, because the lawyer has an extremely negative view of scientologist beliefs. The accused argues that he has been discriminated against on the basis of his religious beliefs.

The last of these examples is the sort of decision that anti-discrimination rules as applied to client selection are obviously intended to prohibit. The prospective client's religious beliefs have nothing to do with the matter on which the lawyer is to be retained, and it seems appropriate to prohibit the lawyer from taking those beliefs into account in deciding whether to take the retainer. The example of the family law lawyer may also properly be prohibited as discriminatory; it may depend on the reason why the lawyer has restricted her practice to women only. If her reasons are based purely on marketing, then her restriction seems straightforwardly discriminatory.

On the other hand, if the family law lawyer's reasons are based on her moral commitment to the view that women are systemically disadvantaged on divorce, the situation is more difficult, and brings her situation closer to those of the first two examples, to which the application of anti-discriminatory statutes is problematic. While the decision is arguably discriminatory, the lawyer in each of those scenarios has moral beliefs of her own, and the representation proposed would, it seems, require her to compromise those beliefs in some way. The service the lawyer provides — resolute advocacy — requires her not simply to accept or accommodate the perspective of the client, but to advocate for it. Requiring the lawyer to do so in the face of her own conscientious beliefs seems hard to justify; a *bona fide* occupational requirement of resolute advocacy may be that the advocate not deeply object to the position she is being asked to take.

As noted, without case law applying and interpreting these rules, it is difficult to anticipate how they should guide a lawyer's conduct. There are two legal arguments that I think should be sufficient to prevent the anti-discrimination rules from improperly constraining the lawyer's right to decline representation where that representation would run against her own moral commitments.

First, the conflicts rules prevent lawyers from acting in circumstances where there is a conflict between the lawyer's personal interests and her duty to the client, which likely includes circumstances in which the lawyer's personal beliefs might consciously or unconsciously impair the effectiveness of her representation.[11]

Second, if the lawyer is personally uncomfortable, then her advocacy may be compromised, and if it is compromised, then she is (or may be) in breach of her professional duty of competence. A lawyer is not competent where her services are not "equal to that which lawyers generally would expect of a competent lawyer in a like situation".[12] If the lawyer's personal feelings or moral evaluation of the client undermine her advocacy, she would not meet this standard.

These arguments do not neutralize the rules against discrimination, but they do leave room within those rules to respect the lawyer's own significant moral commitments. Ultimately I would argue that, properly interpreted, the rules prohibiting discrimination are consistent with the broad discretion granted to lawyers with respect to client selection.

---

[11] See, *e.g.*, CBA MC Chapter IV, Rules 5 and 6. Rule 6, which says that the lawyer must comply with insurance policies, references AB CPC Chapter 6, Rule 9, which clearly prohibits a lawyer from acting in circumstances where her objectivity is impaired. The impairment can result from excessive commitment as well as from negativity to the client's goals.

[12] CBA MC Chapter II, Rule 2.

Which brings us to the second question: how should lawyers exercise that discretion? In answering that question, a preliminary observation must be emphasized. Lawyers exercise discretion in choosing clients with respect to individual clients but also — and in some ways more meaningfully — through choosing where they are going to practise law. Once a lawyer decides, for example, to work for the government, or to work in a large law firm, the lawyer has imposed meaningful *ex ante* constraints on the choice of clients in particular cases. Law firms will not necessarily permit an individual associate to refuse to act for firm clients, no matter how distasteful, and the reality of organizational practice is that organizations — whether law firms, government, corporations or otherwise — only offer certain types of client representation. Therefore, the question of client selection, and how it should be exercised, needs to be considered both at the point of individual client selection and at the point of choice of practice environment.

From one perspective, once the role of the lawyer as resolute advocate is defended on ethical grounds, it follows that no moral significance attaches to client selection. If the law exists as a compromise to the problem of pluralistic conceptions of morality, and if each of us is entitled to be self-determining under the law, then anyone who helps another person pursue his self-determination has done something that is morally justified, and can defend her actions on that basis. That is, I think, correct in terms of the lawyer's professional ethical life. A lawyer who acts as a resolute advocate can always assert that doing so was morally legitimate given the importance of law as a democratic compromise to the problem of pluralism.

At the same time, however, the right to choose for whom to act — the "general right to decline representation" — creates an opportunity for the lawyer to pursue her own moral values and conception of the good within the constraints of resolute advocacy. Once a lawyer chooses to be a resolute advocate for a particular client, and induces the client to rely on her as a resolute advocate, the lawyer's choices about how to represent that client are constrained by her client's own right of self-determination within and under the law. But to the extent the lawyer has chosen her client in accordance with her own moral values, that constraint may be experienced as a good thing, not a bad thing. A lawyer whose moral values favour the creation of wealth in a capitalist economy can choose to work in mergers and acquisitions, or securities, and can feel her life has been well lived through doing so. A lawyer who believes in the importance of procedural fairness in criminal cases can be a prosecutor or a criminal defence lawyer, to the same effect. These are just two examples. But by selecting clients in this way, the lawyer reduces the likelihood that the moral commitment that resolute advocacy requires will create an internal moral conflict in his working life.

Does that mean that a lawyer is also subject to criticism for her choice of clients? Perhaps, but not in the sense that there is an objective standard that the lawyer can be said to have violated. The objective moral standards are satisfied by the argument for the moral validity of resolute advocacy within and under a system of laws. The criticism against the lawyer who chooses clients in a way that does not accord with my own moral values — or even community moral values — is only ever a claim of disagreement, that "I would have made a different choice than the one that lawyer did."

The only more objective criticism that can be levelled against the lawyer with respect to client selection is the one raised by Allan Hutchinson, the criticism of the lawyer not because she has made a bad choice, but because she has either failed to recognize, or failed to engage with, the fact that client selection *is* a moral choice, and one for which the lawyer should take some sort of personal responsibility. "[L]awyers should appreciate that there is no position of no-decision: whatever decision they make will reflect and implicate a certain stand on the nature and extent of ethical obligations in the practice of law."[13]

What about the "cab rank rule", the principle said to govern English barristers, and to require that they accept clients in the order that they present themselves? The cab rank rule has two main arguments in its favour. First, it arguably facilitates access to justice by preventing lawyers from acting as gatekeepers to the legal system. Second, it prevents the lawyer from being overly identified with the client's cause; it facilitates the lawyer's independence of judgment. This stance of independence and neutrality to the client's position seems in some ways more consistent with the standard conception of the lawyer as resolute advocate than does active selection between clients, where the lawyer takes a moral position.

There are, though, a number of problems with the cab rank rule. Most obviously, lawyers cite it, but they do not follow it. Lawyers in cab rank jurisdictions *de facto* select clients in a variety of ways, whether by setting their fees at a certain level, or by specializing in particular areas of law, or by working in particular environments. A lawyer who truly followed the cab rank rule could, I think, make a plausible moral argument for why doing so is just and right. But lawyers who are not actually following the cab rank rule cannot then invoke that rule to pretend they have not, in fact, selected the type of clients they will represent. Also, unless the lawyer's commitment to a client's cause is such that her objectivity is impaired, it is not obvious why a general sense of the client's cause as worth pursuing will undermine representation. Indeed, for the reasons noted, it seems more likely that the reduction in the moral complexity which might otherwise arise will enhance the quality of the lawyer's advocacy, not impair it.

In asserting the moral significance of client selection I am not arguing that moral values are the only factor a lawyer may take into account in choosing where to work and whom to represent. A well-lived life does not arise simply through compliance with abstract moral commitments, but also

---

[13] Allan C. Hutchinson, "Taking It Personally: Legal Ethics and Client Selection" (1998) 1 *Legal Ethics* 168 at 179.

takes into account such things as earning a living for oneself and one's family, exercising one's skills and attributes effectively, working in an environment that is congenial, and achieving the right level of work-family balance. All of these factors can legitimately factor into the lawyer's choice of clients. It is not at all obvious, for example, that a person would lead a more ethical life as an uncomfortable and unhappy poverty lawyer than as an effective and fulfilled in-house counsel, even if she thinks poverty law is a more justifiable line of work, morally speaking.

Lawyers are not entirely unconstrained in how they select clients. Ensuring her own competence, avoiding conflicts, and not unlawfully discriminating, are real obligations that constrain how lawyers decide for whom to act. But within those constraints lawyers do have a broad discretion in deciding where to work, what cases to take, and in what areas to specialize. That discretion should be exercised carefully and thoughtfully. The path of least resistance (the "position of no-position" critiqued by Hutchinson) has its attractions, but will not contribute to a well-lived life overall.

3. LAWYER-CLIENT DECISION MAKING AND CLIENT COUNSELLING

A. Introduction

On October 3, 1984, 9-year-old Christine Jessop was sexually assaulted and murdered. Her next door neighbour, Guy Paul Morin, was charged with her murder, tried, acquitted, had his acquittal overturned on appeal, tried again, convicted and, in 1995, exonerated by DNA evidence. Not surprisingly perhaps, many factors contributed to Morin's wrongful conviction: lying jail house informants, dubious and over stated forensic evidence, prosecutorial tunnel vision, manipulated witnesses and poor decision-making by almost everyone involved in his prosecution. One factor, though, is of particular note here. Throughout the proceedings Morin maintained his innocence. But his lawyer at the first trial coupled the defence that Morin was not guilty with the defence that Morin was suffering from a mental illness such that, if he *was* guilty, he should nonetheless be acquitted by reason of his mental disorder. Morin strenuously objected to the offering of the insanity defence, and later swore an affidavit attesting that he only entered the defence because his lawyer placed him under "mental duress" by saying he (the lawyer) would withdraw unless Morin agreed to enter it.[14]

---

[14] See, Kirk Makin, "Insanity plea turned against Morin: Crown uses 1986 defence to argue against granting bail" *The Globe and Mail* (5 February 1993); "Trial by Jury" an episode of Ideas (12 January 1993), transcript available online: <http://www.cbc.ca/ideas/old-ideas/morin.html>: "Morin's lawyer (over Morin's strenuous objections) wanted the jury — in case they found him guilty — to say he ought to be locked up in a hospital instead of a jail because he was insane." Note that there was never an issue at any point as to Morin's mental competence to instruct counsel.

In the subsequent inquiry into how the justice system had failed Morin so badly, various parties raised the insanity defence as a factor, suggesting that the Inquiry should consider "the propriety of a defence lawyer raising a defence relating to the state of mind of the accused (such as insanity) absent proper instructions from the client".[15] The Commissioner noted that since Morin was acquitted at the first trial, the offering of the insanity defence could not be said to have been a direct factor in Morin's wrongful conviction. The Commissioner also suggested that the proffering of the defence was of "limited systemic interest" because changes in the law mean that no accused is now required to deal with a mental disorder defence during the body of a trial.[16] The Commissioner did, however, agree to consider the offering of the defence as relevant to the question of how the prosecution and police had viewed Morin. After doing so he concluded that the proffering of the insanity defence was indirectly important in Morin's wrongful conviction because it contributed significantly to the tunnel vision of prosecutors that undermined those prosecutors' handling of the case:

> The Commissioner found that John Scott, Leo McGuigan, Alex Smith and Susan MacLean wholeheartedly believed, throughout their involvement in the Guy Paul Morin proceedings, that Mr. Morin was guilty of the offence with which he was charged. Crown counsel at the first trial, believed that Mr. Morin was guilty prior to any knowledge that the alternative insanity defence would be raised. Accordingly, the insanity defence did not change their views, but they saw it as confirmation of what they already knew (or thought they knew). Mr. McGuigan and Mr. Smith, who came to the case after the insanity defence had been raised at the first trial, were affected by it in a similar way. *This was not unreasonable — the "insanity evidence," carefully scrutinized, may not have made Mr. Morin's guilt more likely, but the fact that such a defence would even be advanced had to impress itself on most anybody.*[17]

Given this conclusion by the Commissioner, I think it can fairly be stated that offering an insanity defence did not further Morin's interests in the long term. But even if it was the most prudent possible decision, and one

---

[15] Report from the Ontario Attorney General of the Kaufman Commission on Proceedings Involving Guy Paul Morin, "Chapter I: The Scope and Nature of the Inquiry" at 35, online: Ontario. Ministry of the Attorney General <http://www.attorneygeneral.jus.gov.on.ca/english/about/pubs/morin/morin_ch1.pdf>.

[16] *Ibid.*, at 35-36, online: Ontario. Ministry of the Attorney General <http://www.attorneygeneral.jus.gov.on.ca/english/about/pubs/morin/morin_ch1.pdf>.

[17] Report from the Ontario Attorney General of the Kaufman Commission on Proceedings Involving Guy Paul Morin, "Executive Summary" at 38 [emphasis added], online: Ontario. Ministry of the Attorney General <http://www.attorneygeneral.jus.gov.on.ca/english/about/pubs/morin/morin_esumm.pdf>. See also Kirk Makin, "Crown to seek Morin acquittal: DNA evidence ends Jessop neighbour's 10-year court ordeal" *The Globe and Mail* (23 January 1995) A1, A3. "He [a former Crown, Brian Gover] said the real key to what ultimately fuelled the passions of police and prosecutors was defence evidence of insanity led at Mr. Morin's first trial, when psychiatrists testified that Mr. Morin was schizophrenic ... 'That was a really strong dynamic in this case,' Mr. Gover said, 'It became very difficult for the Crown to walk away from proceedings against him. I see it as a spectre hanging over this case since his 1986 acquittal.'"

clearly in Morin's interests as his counsel identified them at the time, should counsel have offered such a defence when the client did not want to? Who should decide how a matter is conducted, the lawyer or the client? And what should go into that decision — if the client is to decide, what kind of information should the lawyer provide to the client before he does so? Is the lawyer's role simply to present the legal options available to the client? Or may the lawyer engage with the client on questions not just of what is legal, but also of what is right, given the circumstances?

This section considers these questions, both from the perspective of what is required by the law governing lawyers, and from the perspective of what, given the lawyer's role as a whole, the approach of a lawyer to client counselling and decision-making should be.

B. Lawyer-Client Decision Making

In the course of representing a client numerous decisions must be made. In civil litigation, decisions must be made about such issues as what to put in pleadings, how to structure a claim, what documents must be disclosed, how to approach examinations for discovery, whether or when to settle the claim, which witnesses to present at trial and what legal arguments are to be made. In criminal defence cases decisions must be made about how to plead, how to approach the preliminary inquiry, which witnesses to present (including the accused), how to approach cross-examination, whether *Canadian Charter of Rights and Freedoms*[18] applications are available or prudent, the approach to be taken to co-accused if any, whether to accept a plea agreement with the Crown, and so on. In negotiating an agreement decisions must be made about who should conduct the negotiations, what matters are crucial for the client and which can be conceded, and what legal form the agreement should take, amongst others.

In all of these contexts, the decisions to be made relate to what the client wants to accomplish, both in terms of the final result of the representation and in terms of how that result is to be achieved. They incorporate legal expertise but also things that have little to do with the law, such as the relationship between the parties, and interests of the client that are distinct from the legal issues (a desire of a parent, for example, to spare a child from testifying in court, or the desire of a business to preserve good relations with an important customer).

How are these decisions to be made, and by whom? The various codes of conduct give some direction on specific matters of lawyer-client decision-making but do not take a position on whether, in general, those decisions should be driven by the lawyer or the client. The codes state that the lawyer may not "waive or abandon the client's legal rights ... without the client's

---

[18] Part I of the *Constitution Act, 1982*, being Schedule B to the *Canada Act 1982* (U.K.), 1982, c. 11.

informed consent".[19] They also prevent the lawyer from disclosing confidential information without the client's consent[20] and prohibit the lawyer from entering into a plea agreement without instruction from the client.[21] They require that any proposed settlement be provided to the client for consideration.[22]

Some codes also clarify that where the client is an organization — either corporate or government — the lawyer must be certain that the instructions she receives originate properly from her client — that is, the corporation or the government — rather than from the interests of a person or faction within the organization.[23]

And, finally, the codes prohibit the lawyer from accepting any instructions that would result in the lawyer assisting the client in dishonest, criminal, fraudulent or dishonourable conduct, or would require the lawyer to violate her legal obligations, including her obligations under the code of conduct itself.[24]

In the context of litigation, case law provides additional guidance and clearly states that in judicial proceedings most decisions rest with the lawyer, not the client. In a variety of decisions courts have taken the position that while a client has the right to decide certain matters in a case — whether to testify,[25] how to plead,[26] whether to raise certain defences,[27] and whether to be tried by a judge or jury[28] — the general conduct of the litigation rests

---

[19] CBA MC Chapter IX, Commentary 7; FLS MC Rule 4.01(8); LSUC Rule 4.01(1). Interestingly, the NBCC imposes a materiality requirement: Chapter 8, Rule 8 prevents the lawyer from waiving "material equitable or legal rights" or the client. The BC PCH is silent on this point, as is the Que. CEA. In Alberta this point seems to be covered by AB CPC Chapter 9, Rule 5, discussed below.

[20] CBA MC Chapter IV, Rule 1; FLS MC Rule 2.03(1); LSUC RPC Rule 2.03(1); Que. CEA Rule 3.06.02 (this is a specific rule, but it seems to indicate the necessity for client consent); NB CC Chapter 5, Rule 1; AB CPC Chapter 7, Rules 7 and 8(e); BC PCH Chapter 5, Rule 1.

[21] CBA MC Chapter IX, Commentary 13; FLS MC Rule 4.01(8)(d); LSUC CPC Rule 4.01(9)(d); NB CC Chapter 8, Rule 15(a)(v) ; AB CPC Chapter 10, Rule 27; BC PCH Chapter 8, Rule 20. The Que. CEA does not speak to this point.

[22] CBA MC Chapter II, Commentary 7(j) and Chapter IX, Commentary 8; FLS MC Rule 2.02(1), commentary; LSUC RPC Rule 2.02(2); Que. CEA Rule 3.02.10; NB CC Chapter 3, Rule 4(j), Chapter 4, Rule 6 and Chapter 8, Rule 1; AB CPC Chapter 9, Rules 15 and 16; BC PCH Chapter 3, Rule 3(j).

[23] FLS MC Rule 2.03(3); LSUC RPC Rule 2.02(1.1); AB CPC Chapter 12, Rule 1 and commentary.

[24] CBA MC Chapter III, Commentary 7 and Chapter IX, Rule 2(b); FLS MC Rule 2.02(7) and 4.01(2)(b); LSUC RPC Rule 2.02(5) and 4.01(2)(b); Que. CEA Rule 2.00.01, 3.02.01 and 3.05.18 (these rules are different, but seem to embody the same principle); AB CPC Chapter 9, Rules 10 and 11; BC PCH Chapter 4, Rule 6 and Chapter 8, Rules 1(b), 7 and 8.

[25] *R. v. Brigham*, [1992] J.Q. no 2283, 79 C.C.C. (3d) 365 (Que. C.A.), *per* Fish J.A. (as he then was); *R. v. Dunbar*, [2003] B.C.J. No. 2767, 2003 BCCA 667 (B.C.C.A.); *R. v. Joanisse*, [1995] O.J. No. 2883, 102 C.C.C. (3d) 35 (Ont. C.A.).

[26] *R. v. Lamoureaux*, [1984] J.Q. no 289, 13 C.C.C. (3d) 101 (Que. C.A.).

[27] *R. v. Swain*, [1991] S.C.J. No. 32, 63 C.C.C. (3d) 481 (S.C.C.).

[28] This is the position that was recommended by New Approaches to Criminal Trials: The Report of the Chief Justice's Advisory Committee on Criminal Trials in the Superior Court of Justice, May 2006, cited in *Law Society of Upper Canada v. De Teresi*, [2009] O.J. No. 582 (Ont.

in the sole discretion of the lawyer.[29] This is the case in both criminal and civil matters, although most of the reported decisions deal with criminal cases.[30] According to 2005 Law Society of Upper Canada bar materials on criminal defence practice (which have been cited with approval by the courts) the lawyer may

> assume complete control and responsibility over the manner in which the defence will be conducted ... Defence counsel should decide which witnesses will be called, whether a witness should be cross-examined, and the form such cross-examination should take.[31]

The bar materials may overstate the case insofar as there is some (albeit inconsistent) judicial authority for the proposition that the decision as to what witnesses to call rests with an accused;[32] however, the materials are clearly consistent with the strong support in the case law for the position that the lawyer is not a "mere mouthpiece"[33] for her client, "is not merely to do the bidding of the accused"[34] and must exercise independent judgment about how the representation is to proceed. In 2006, the *Chief Justice's Advisory Committee on Criminal Trials in the Superior Court of Justice (Ontario)* stated that the position of defence counsel today is fundamentally unchanged from how it was described by G. Arthur Martin in 1969:

> In my view, basically, the proper relationship between counsel defending a criminal charge and his client is this — that counsel assumes total control and responsibility over the defence. It is, of course, for the client to decide whether to plead guilty or not guilty. ...
>
> Once the decision to plead not guilty has been made, it is for the defence counsel to decide how the case is to be conducted in accordance with his best judgment as to what is in the best interest of the client. ...
>
> Now, I don't suggest that whenever a client walks into your office to retain you, you commence by giving him a lecture as to what your function and role is because at that time he is probably a rather frightened and bewildered man and he is looking for help, not a law

---

S.C.J.). Chief Justice Dubin had also suggested that the accused be able to decide whether to have a preliminary inquiry, however the Criminal Justice Review rejected this position.

[29] *R. v. Downey*, [2002] O.J. No. 1524 (Ont. S.C.J.); *R. v. Samra*, [1998] O.J. No. 3755, 129 C.C.C. (3d) 144 (Ont. C.A.).

[30] *Sherman v. Manley*, [1978] O.J. No. 3342, 19 O.R. (2d) 531 (Ont. C.A.) (leave refused).

[31] Stephen Skurka & James Strigopoulos, "Professional Responsibility in Criminal Practice", 46th Bar Admission Course Criminal Procedure Reference Materials (Toronto: The Law Society of Upper Canada, 2005) at 17, cited in *Law Society of Upper Canada v. De Teresi*, [2009] O.J. No. 582 at para. 26 (Ont. S.C.J.).

[32] *R. v. Swain*, [1991] S.C.J. No. 32 at para. 36, 63 C.C.C. (3d) 481 (S.C.C.); *R. v. Smith*, [1997] O.J. No. 4797, 120 C.C.C. (3d) 500 (Ont. C.A.) but see *R. v. R.(A.J.)*, [1994] O.J. No. 2309, 94 C.C.C. (3d) 168 (Ont. C.A.); *R. v. White and Sennet*, [1997] O.J. No. 961 at para. 90 (Ont. C.A.).

[33] Arthur Maloney Q.C., "The Role of the Independent Bar", 1979 L.S.U.C. Special Lectures 49 at 61-62, cited in *Stewart v. Canadian Broadcasting Corp.*, [1997] O.J. No. 2271 at para. 143, 150 D.L.R. (4th) 24 (Ont. Gen. Div.).

[34] *R. v. DiPalma*, [2002] O.J. No. 2684 at para. 38 (Ont. C.A.).

lecture. But some time, quite early in the process, you should tactfully let him know that you are in charge.[35]

The courts have not uniformly endorsed the lawyer-centric approach in litigation. In his judgment in *R. v. Swain*, Lamer C.J.C. (as he then was) held that "the principles of fundamental justice must also require that an accused person have the right to control his or her own defence".[36] Further, the lawyer-centric approach does not apply universally to the lawyer-client relationship, as some of the provisions in the codes of conduct indicate — for example with respect to the settlement or the waiver of the client's rights. In addition, in any case where the relationship is governed by a retainer (contract), express or implied, the authority of the lawyer is also governed by the terms of that retainer, and a failure by the lawyer to obtain instructions from the client where required to do so could open the lawyer to an action for breach of contract.[37]

Finally, the lawyer-centric approach has no obvious application outside of the courtroom. The rationale for giving lawyers this sort of discretion, which tends to flow from the lawyer's stated duty to the courts to ensure the functioning of the judicial process, does not operate outside of the judicial context; in other circumstances the client should direct the lawyer as to how the representation is to be conducted, and the lawyer should implement any lawful instructions that the client gives.[38]

Indeed, even in the litigation context, as noted by Lamer C.J.C. (as he then was) in *R. v. Swain*, it seems strange to appoint lawyers to act as advocates for the interests of their clients, and to justify their doing so

---

[35] New Approaches to Criminal Trials: The Report of the Chief Justice's Advisory Committee on Criminal Trials in the Superior Court of Justice, May 2006 at paras. 127 and 136, online: Ontario Courts, Superior Court of Justice <http://www.ontariocourts.on.ca/scj/en/reports/ctr/index.htm#_Toc141087519>.

[36] *R. v. Swain*, [1991] S.C.J. No. 32 at para. 35, 63 C.C.C. (3d) 481 (S.C.C.).

[37] *Rogan v. Prud'homme*, [1924] M.J. No. 46, [1925] 1 D.L.R. 347 (Man. K.B.) (in that case retainer was viewed as broad enough to allow the lawyer to settle the claim; however, the court noted that where the retainer did not permit the lawyer to do so, an action for settling the claim without authority may lie against the lawyer if the settlement cannot be repudiated). See generally *Strother v. 3464920 Canada Inc.*, [2007] S.C.J. No. 24, [2007] 2 S.C.R. 177 (S.C.C.). Acting without instructions may also impair the ability of the lawyer to collect his fees: *Carter v. Blake* (1982), 41 A.R. 481 (N.W.T.C.A.) (fees relating to investigation by the lawyer were not allowed since the client had not agreed to the investigation).

[38] A client who has money to pay a lawyer also has some practical ability to assert control over the decision-making process. Obviously the client can fire the lawyer. In addition, though, the soft threat of losing the work may make the lawyer more accommodating. That point should not be overemphasized, however. First, even clients with money may be less sophisticated than their lawyers, and not realize that they are not being given much autonomy in making decisions. Second, switching lawyers is expensive, because there are sunk costs that have to be given up since the second lawyer will need to be paid to get to the point where the first lawyer already is. Third, in the criminal law context, factors other than money put the client in a vulnerable position. The socio-economic position of most criminal accused, the fact that at least some are in remand prior to trial, the fact that criminal clients are often "one-off" retainers, and the stresses and pressures of facing criminal prosecution make it difficult for that client to exercise meaningful control; the threat of withdrawal by counsel is more significant to the client than withdrawal by client is to the lawyer.

because of the client's autonomy and right to be self-determining under and through the law, but then to allow lawyers to make decisions without meaningful consultation with their clients. It is undoubtedly more work for a lawyer to obtain instructions from the client, and quite frustrating if the client is acting in a way that the lawyer sees as irrational, but to allow the lawyer to substitute her judgment for that of the client on any matter of substance simply substitutes the arbitrary authority of the lawyer for that of the state, which is neither an obvious improvement nor apparently justifiable. As argued by Michel Proulx and David Layton in their excellent book on legal ethics in criminal law practice, the lawyer-centric approach is "misguided paternalism ... [that] primarily reflect[s] the relative powerlessness of most criminal accused".[39]

Like Proulx and Layton, I would argue that regardless of the courts' comments, the only ethical approach for a lawyer in any case, whether a criminal trial, civil litigation, or otherwise, is to make decisions cooperatively, and in a way that does not "overwhelm the client's freedom of choice".[40] The lawyer is subject to the specific requirements of the codes of conduct (with respect to illegality, for example) but should otherwise "carry out any non-frivolous and otherwise ethical[41] course of action that is desired by the client".[42]

Think back to the case of Guy Paul Morin. Morin was innocent and sane. Yet through the Canadian judicial process both his innocence *and* his sanity were called into question. From his own point of view, is the wrongful impugning of his sanity that much better than the wrongful questioning of his innocence? Both violate his dignity in profound ways. Yet it was the advice and decisions *of his own lawyer* that helped put Morin in that position. This, I would argue, is the significant risk raised by the lawyer-centric approach.[43] Clients, and particularly highly vulnerable clients, should not be put in that position because lawyers and courts cling to the position that "lawyers know best".

Reaching decisions as to how to proceed is challenging. A client in remand, with drug addiction, a history of sexual abuse and perhaps a mild developmental disability, may have conflicting desires as to what he wants to result from his lawyer's representation, and may have difficulty even

---

[39] Michel Proulx & David Layton, *Ethics and Canadian Criminal Law* (Toronto: Irwin Law, 2001) at 132.
[40] *Ibid.* at 133.
[41] My only exception to this quotation is that I think it should be "otherwise lawful course of action" not "otherwise ethical course of action". Whether or not the client's conduct is ethical apart from legality is not relevant once the lawyer has agreed to represent the client.
[42] Michel Proulx & David Layton, *Ethics and Canadian Criminal* Law (Toronto: Irwin Law, 2001) at 134.
[43] Even if, as Kaufman notes, the structure of criminal trials now would prevent this particular manifestation of it. Report from the Ontario Attorney General of the Kaufman Commission on Proceedings Involving Guy Paul Morin, "Chapter I: The Scope and Nature of the Inquiry" at 35-36, online: Ontario. Ministry of the Attorney General <http://www.attorneygeneral.jus.gov.on.ca/english/about/pubs/morin/morin_ch1.pdf>.

articulating what he wants the lawyer to do. And the lawyer may be carrying myriad files, and with only a short period of time to try and figure out the best course of action. Neither I nor, I would venture, Proulx and Layton, are unrealistic about the reality of the challenges the lawyer faces, or of the role a lawyer can play in preventing their client from making a foolish and damaging decision. The crucial point is, simply, that the lawyer must approach the representation with an attitude that focuses on the client as a moral agent, with his own sense of how to proceed, rather than one in which the lawyer "tactfully" lets the client know that she is "in charge".[44] This attitude follows necessarily from the lawyer's role as zealous advocate, and no exception, even for litigation, can be justified.

C. Client Counselling

The observation that lawyers should respect clients' ability to make decisions about what should be done leads to the next issue respecting client counselling and advising: how can lawyers counsel clients in a way that enables those clients to make good decisions? And, secondarily, what place is there within client counselling for the lawyer to state her own point of view, particularly on non-legal questions?

The codes of conduct articulate some basic requirements for lawyer counselling. All advice given to clients must be honest and candid, and based on "sufficient knowledge of the relevant facts, an adequate consideration of the applicable law and the lawyer's own experience and expertise".[45] The lawyer should tell the client the facts and information on which the opinion is based, and should investigate where necessary, unless the client expressly directs otherwise, in which case the lawyer's opinion should be appropriately qualified.[46] The Alberta Code further suggests that while the lawyer has an obligation to ensure "economy and efficiency", the lawyer must obtain whatever information is necessary to provide a proper opinion; if the client cannot afford to pay the lawyer to obtain that information, then the lawyer must either withdraw or provide the information at no cost to the client.[47] Some of the codes emphasize that the lawyer needs to make sure that the client understands the information provided — the lawyer "should explain as well as advise".[48]

---

[44] New Approaches to Criminal Trials: The Report of the Chief Justice's Advisory Committee on Criminal Trials in the Superior Court of Justice, May 2006 at paras. 127 and 136, online: Ontario Courts, Superior Court of Justice <http://www.ontariocourts.on.ca/scj/en/reports/ctr/index.htm#_Toc141087519>.
[45] CBA MC Chapter III, Commentary 1; FLS MC Rule 2.02(2); LSUC RPC Rule 2.02(1); NB CC Chapter 4, Commentaries 1 and 2; AB CPC Chapter 9, Rules 1 and 2; BC PCH Chapter 3, Rule 3(k) and Canon 3(1).
[46] CBA MC Chapter III, Commentary 3; FLS MC Rule 2.01(1); LSUC RPC Rule 2.01(1); Que. CEA Rule 3.02.04 and 3.03.02; NB CC Chapter 4, Commentary 2; AB CPC Chapter 9, Rule 2.
[47] AB CPC Chapter 9, Rule 2.
[48] CBA MC Chapter III, Commentary 2; Que. CEA Rule 3.03.02; NB CC Chapter 4, Commentary 3; AB CPC Chapter 9, Rule 12.

The codes additionally place substantive requirements on lawyer advice. As well as being itself honest, the lawyer's advice may not encourage dishonesty, fraud, crime or illegal conduct by the client, and must not "instruct the client on how to violate the law and avoid punishment".[49] Further, the lawyer is directed to encourage the client to settle cases, where settlement can be done reasonably.[50] The codes do not, in general, restrict the matters on which the lawyer may advise the client, although they caution the lawyer not to exceed her competence, and also to be clear to the client when the advice the lawyer is giving does not relate to matters of law. Within those parameters, the lawyer may properly advise the client on non-legal matters, "such as the business, policy or social implications involved in a question".[51]

Can a lawyer advise a client on the morality of his conduct? As noted, allowing lawyers to provide moral counselling can reduce the moral tension of resolute advocacy. While the client ultimately gets to determine what to do, moral counselling allows the lawyer to be up front and authentic about her own perspective on things. In the end, her role as advocate is clear, but relative to the client she will have made no pretence as to her own point of view. The codes of conduct do not preclude lawyers providing such advice, and may even be said to contemplate it given their acknowledgement of the lawyer's role in advising on non-legal matters. A lawyer who wishes to counsel her client on whether the proposed course of action is not only legal, but also right, is free to do so.

Moreover, moral counselling may be crucial to the lawyer ascertaining what the client wants to do. While a client may want every advantage the law provides, lawyers are often too quick to assume that this is the case;[52] moral counselling can help ensure that such assumptions are not made inappropriately. In *Understanding Lawyers' Ethics*,[53] Professor Freedman tells a story of being asked to evict a tenant. On investigation Freedman found that the tenant was a Korean War widow with a young child. The only reason for the eviction was that the child had had difficulty turning off her bath water one evening, the tub had overflowed, and the ceiling below had

---

[49] CBA MC Chapter III, Commentary 7; FLS MC Rule 2.02(7); LSUC RPC Rule 2.02(5); NB CC Chapter 4, Rules 7 and 8; AB CPC Chapter 9, Rule 11; BC PCH Canon 3(5) and Chapter 3, Rule 6. For additional discussion of this issue see the following section and, as well, Chapter 4, Section 3, which discusses the ability of lawyers to make frivolous arguments in litigation, and the distinction between the wide latitude given to lawyers in that context and the more restrictive approach that is appropriate in the context of advising.

[50] CBA MC Chapter III, Commentary 6; FLS MC Rule 2.02(4); LSUC RPC Rule 2.02(2); NB CC Chapter 3, Commentary 4(j), Chapter 4, Commentary 6 and Chapter 8, Commentary 1; AB CPC Chapter 9, Rule 16; BC PCH Canon 3(3).

[51] CBA MC, Chapter III, Commentary 10; FLS MC Rule 2.01(2), commentary; LSUC RPC Rule 2.01(1), commentary; NB CC Chapter 4, Rule 14; AB CPC Chapter 9, Commentary G4.

[52] See Kate Kruse "Beyond Cardboard Clients in Legal Ethics" (2010) 23 Geo. J. Legal Ethics 103.

[53] Monroe Freedman & Abbe Smith, *Understanding Lawyers' Ethics*, 4th ed. (New Providence, NJ: LexisNexis, 2010) at 74.

been damaged. Otherwise there were no complaints about the tenant. Freedman told the client the circumstances and that if the client wanted to proceed with the eviction he would do so but that "I wasn't sure you'd want to, given the facts". After thinking it over, the client decided not to proceed with the eviction; in that case, what the law provides was not what the client wanted.

In addition, as noted by Rob Vischer, lawyers do, in fact, have personal moral values that inescapably influence the manner and content of the advice that they give. Vischer argues that it is better when counselling clients for the lawyer to be self-aware and up front about her own perspective on things, rather than having that perspective simply "out there", silently influencing the advice provided.[54] Clients need to know what lawyers think, but also why they might think as they do. Otherwise the clients may overvalue the advice the lawyer provides.

The important qualification to this analysis is that lawyers should be cautious with respect to their competence on matters of morality and, as well, should be careful not to ride roughshod over client interests. While the power dynamic between the lawyer and client varies considerably, there are circumstances in which the client will view the lawyer's statement of an "opinion" as determinative, or may be confused about whether the lawyer's advice is about the law or about morality. A lawyer must ensure that the nature of her advice on moral questions is understood to be distinct from her legal advice (as required by the codes of conduct).[55] She must also ensure that there is sufficient comfort and trust in the relationship to permit the client to reach his own conclusions without being improperly pushed towards the lawyer's own assessment of things.

D. Counselling and Unlawful Activity

As noted above, the codes of conduct prohibit lawyers from counselling clients in a way that will knowingly encourage illegal conduct, or that will instruct the client on how to violate the law and avoid punishment.[56] A significant issue raised by these provisions arises where lawyers are asked to provide legal advice to clients and suspect that the legal advice will be used by the client for an unlawful purpose. A client could ask the following questions:

> "If I do not report my income from tips on my tax return how likely is it that the government will find out?"
>
> "What countries do not have extradition treaties with Canada?"

---

[54] Robert K. Vischer, "Legal Advice as Moral Perspective" (2006) 19 Geo. J. Legal Ethics 225.
[55] CBA MC Chapter III, Commentary 10; FLS MC Rule 2.01(2), commentary; LSUC RPC Rule 2.01(1), commentary; NB CC Chapter 4, Rule 14; AB CPC Chapter 9, commentary G4.
[56] CBA MC Chapter III, Commentary 7; FLS MC Rule 2.02(7); LSUC RPC Rule 2.02(5); NB CC Chapter 4, Rules 7 and 8; AB CPC Chapter 9, Rule 11; BC PCH Canon 3(5) and Chapter 3, Rule 6.

"What are the fines for taking water from the river in excess of my water licence?"

"If I rob a bank with an automatic weapon will that result in a higher penalty than if I rob a bank with a knife?"

In each of these scenarios the client has asked the lawyer to share her legal knowledge, either with respect to what the law provides or with respect to how the law operates in practice. The client has not asked the lawyer to assist him in wrongdoing — by, for example, filing or preparing the false tax return, or driving the getaway car at the bank robbery — but has simply asked about the legal effect of particular decisions that the client may make. Can the lawyer provide the advice? Can he say, in effect, "I am a law book" and provide to the client that which, if the client was a lawyer, he could discover for himself?[57]

It is not obvious that providing the requested information is prohibited by the codes of conduct. The lawyer has not encouraged illegal activity, insofar as the lawyer has not suggested in any of these cases that the course of conduct proposed by the client is a good one. As stated in the commentary to the rule in the Alberta Code of Conduct:

> The mere provision of legal information must be distinguished from rendering legal advice or providing active assistance to a client. If a lawyer is reasonably satisfied on a balance of probabilities that the result of advice or assistance will be to involve the lawyer in a criminal or fraudulent act, then the advice or assistance should not be given. In contrast, merely providing legal information that could be used to commit a crime or fraud is not improper since everyone has a right to know and understand the law. Indeed, a lawyer has a positive obligation to provide such information or ensure that alternative competent legal advice is available to the client … Only if there is reason to believe beyond a reasonable doubt, based on familiarity with the client or information received from other reliable sources, that a client intends to use legal information to commit a crime should a lawyer decline to provide the information sought.[58]

It is also not obvious that providing the information should be considered to be unethical given the rationale for lawyers within the legal system as a whole. If lawyers exist to provide individuals with the information about what the law requires, permits or enables, then on what basis would we ever forbid lawyers from providing that information simply because clients may misuse it? If an individual decides that, for example, the benefit of withdrawing excess water from the river exceeds the cost of the fines payable for doing so, that suggests that the substantive law should

---

[57] Morroe Freedman & Abbe Smith, *Understanding Lawyers' Ethics*, 4th ed. (New Providence, NJ: LexisNexis, 2010) at 187.
[58] AB CPC Chapter 9, Rule 11, commentary.

be changed; it does not suggest that individuals should be kept in ignorance of the law.

On the other hand, if the point of lawyers is to allow individuals to pursue their own conceptions of the good within the bounds of legality, it does not seem logical to allow lawyers to counsel clients in ways that serve to encourage or permit clients to act outside the bounds of legality. Where the information in question is not about the content of the law, but about imperfections in the ability of the state to implement its laws — as is the case with the audit risk example — it is not clear that the client has any particular entitlement to that information from the lawyer.

Further, where the risk that the client will misuse the advice is substantially foreseeable, and the risk of harm to others from the client's conduct is high, the lawyer's justification "I am a law book" seems insufficient to shield the lawyer from accountability for the effect of the advice she has given. The information the lawyer has to allow her to assess how the advice is going to be used means that the lawyer's advice is not, on the facts, truly separated from the way in which it is going to be used. Moreover, the seriousness of the harm that may result simply outweighs the moral justification for the lawyer giving the advice. As noted, once the advice is being used for the *purpose of illegality* a justification for the lawyer's role based on allowing people to pursue their conceptions of the good *within the bounds of legality* does not do very much work, certainly not enough to permit the lawyer to participate, even if indirectly, in the infliction of serious harm on others.

In addition, on a purely pragmatic basis, a lawyer who provides legal advice that facilitates the commission of an unlawful act, particularly an unlawful act that involves harm to third parties, should be cognizant of the risk of legal liability she is incurring. The lawyer could be seen as owing (and as having violated) a standard of care to third parties harmed by the client's unlawful activities. As discussed in Chapter 5, where a lawyer is a "dupe" of a client committing a criminal act the discussions between the lawyer and the client are not privileged, and are arguably not confidential either.

In general while, as the Alberta Code of Conduct suggests, a lawyer should provide legal information to clients, she should not do so when the lawyer can reasonably foresee that the advice would significantly increase the likelihood of conduct that will result in death or serious injury to another person, including serious financial injury. When the harm is that serious, and that foreseeable, the lawyer is at risk of liability and, as well, cannot sufficiently separate the nature of the information being given (the content and application of the law) and the purpose for which it is being used (the infliction of serious harm on others).

4. FEES

Most of the time a lawyer works for pay. That fact does not denigrate what lawyers do. Legal services are not like sex; the moral quality of the act does not shift with payment. Rather, a lawyer's fee can be understood as a reflection of the value the lawyer provides in facilitating the moral agency of another and, in that way, as a recognition of the lawyer's own agency. The payment of money for legal services corresponds to the lawyer's promise to provide service to the client, and makes the relationship between the lawyer and client one of mutual obligation.[59]

In setting fees, though, lawyers can potentially take advantage of the significant imperfections in the market for legal services to charge more for services than is warranted.[60] They have better information than clients as to what services are required, and as to what services are worth. They can also potentially take advantage of the difficulty clients may have in assessing whether one lawyer is better than another, which can make it rational for a client to use price as a gauge for judging quality — *i.e.*, thinking that lawyers who cost more are better.

This possibility is moderated by regulation. Codes of conduct require that lawyers' fees be fair and reasonable, and indicate that the determination of what is fair and reasonable will depend on factors such as the time and effort spent, the difficulty and importance of the matter, the results obtained, the experience and ability of the lawyer, and similar factors.[61] The codes also deal with other matters, such as prohibiting hidden fees[62] and, in Alberta and Québec, requiring that all fee agreements be in writing.[63] Some law societies also provide fee mediation or arbitration services.

In addition, and more significantly, lawyers' fees are subject to the oversight of the courts, which have the power to "tax" lawyers' accounts. The taxation power allows courts to reduce fees where they are not fair and reasonable, taking into account the same factors that are indicated in the codes of conduct.[64] Although clients do not take advantage of the taxation power all that frequently — limitations periods are short, and not all clients are aware of its availability — courts are not reluctant to use the taxation power to reduce lawyers' accounts. In a random survey of 100 taxation cases published in Ontario in 2000, only 22% of the lawyer accounts were

---

[59] Peter Benson, "The Unity of Contract Law" in Peter Benson ed., *The Theory of Contract Law* (Cambridge: Cambridge Studies in Philosophy and Law, 2001) at 118-205.
[60] Alice Woolley, "Time for Change: unethical hourly billing in the Canadian profession and what should be done about it" (2004) 83 Can. Bar Rev. 858.
[61] See, for example, CBA MC Chapter XI, Commentary 1; FLS MC Rule 2.06(1) and commentary; LSUC RPC Rule 2.08; Que. CEA Rule 3.08.02; NB CC Chapter 9, Commentary 2; AB CPC Chapter 13, Rule 1; BC PCH Chapter 9, Rule 1 (fee must not be excessive).
[62] See, *e.g.*, CBA MC Chapter XI, Commentary 7 and Que. CEA Rule 3.08.05, which requires that an advocate "provide the client with all explanations necessary to the understanding of the invoice or statement of fees and the terms and conditions of payment".
[63] AB CPC Chapter 13, Rule 2; Que. CEA Rule 3.08.07.
[64] See, for example, Rules 10.2(1)-10.27 of the *Alberta Rules of Court*, Alta. Reg. 124/2010.

assessed as billed. All other accounts were reduced, and about 18% were reduced by more than 50%.[65]

Contingency fee agreements, particularly in the context of class actions,[66] are subject to specific additional regulation pursuant to the rules of court and other legislation. These regulatory regimes impose a variety of requirements on lawyers seeking to be retained on a contingency basis and, in some instances, allow the court to substitute a "fair and reasonable" amount for that agreed to by the parties.[67]

In setting fees with clients lawyers should be mindful of the full range of the regulatory requirements applicable and should adopt prudent billing practices, including written fee agreements, regular monthly billing, clear explanations about the basis for fees charged, and ensuring the level of the fees matches the value of the services provided.[68] Following these practices insulates lawyers from risks associated with judicial scrutiny of bills, is likely to improve the lawyer's relationship with the client and, at the same time, ensures that the lawyer is appropriately remunerated for the valuable services she has provided.

5. WITHDRAWAL

One of the reasons why client selection and the ability of the lawyer to establish a functional relationship with a client are so essential, is that the lawyer-client relationship is not terminable at will by the lawyer. A client may terminate a retainer at any time, but a lawyer owes an ethical duty not to withdraw from the representation except with good cause.[69]

In general, cause sufficient to *permit* the lawyer to withdraw will arise where there is a "serious loss of confidence" between the lawyer and the client.[70] The codes of conduct go on to suggest that circumstances sufficient

---

[65] R.M. Gramlow & R.B. Linton, *The Nature and Process for Assessing Solicitor and Client Bills* (Toronto: RWG Consulting, 2000).

[66] In class action settings a judge is called upon to approve and award class counsel fees after maintaining the proceedings on the merits, or authorizing them for settlement purposes. In such cases the Court must decide whether or not the fees sought are fair, reasonable and in the best interest of class members and make that determination based on a number of different criteria. *Dabbs v. Sun Life*, [1998] O.J. No. 1598 (Ont. Gen. Div.).

[67] In Ontario see *Contingency Fee Agreements*, O. Reg. 195/04, regulation pursuant to *Solicitors Act*, R.S.O. 1990, c. S.15. With respect to class actions see *Class Proceedings Act, 1992*, S.O. 1992, c. 6 and *Sutts, Strosberg LLP v. Atlas Cold Storage Holdings Inc.*, [2009] O.J. No. 4067, 2009 ONCA 690 (Ont. C.A.) (in which the Court substituted a much lower fee for that agreed to by the parties). In Alberta see R10.7 and R10.9 of the *Alberta Rules of Court*, Alta. Reg. 124/2010.

[68] I am not advocating value billing *per se*, but simply suggesting that lawyers be cognizant of the occasional disjunct between time and value in billing clients.

[69] CBA MC Chapter XII; FLS MC Rule 2.07(1); LSUC RPC Rule 2.09(1); Que. CEA Rule 3.03.04; NB CC Chapter 10; AB CPC Chapter 14; BC PCH Chapter 10.

[70] CBA MC Chapter XII, Commentary 5; FLS MC Rule 2.07(2) and commentary; LSUC RPC Rule 2.09(2) and (3) (although not referring to all of the specific examples of a serious loss of confidence); NB CC Chapter 10, Commentaries 2 and 4; AB CPC Chapter 14, Rule 1; BC PCH Chapter 10, Rules 2, 6 and 7.

to create a serious loss of confidence include deception of the lawyer by the client, a refusal by the client to follow advice (although the lawyer "should not use the threat of withdrawal as a device to force the client into making a hasty decision on a difficult question"),[71] the client acting in a way which is persistently unreasonable or uncooperative, or the client not paying fees that are owed.[72] British Columbia additionally gives the lawyer a residual right to withdraw in any circumstances where doing so would not be unfair to the client or be for an improper purpose.[73]

The codes vary with respect to when the lawyer is *required* to withdraw. The Canadian Bar Association ("CBA") Code provides that withdrawal is required where the client persists in instructing the lawyer to violate her duties to the court; the lawyer's continued representation of the client would cause the lawyer to violate the ethical rules (with respect to conflicts and competence, for example); or, the client is "guilty of dishonourable conduct in the proceedings or is taking a position solely to harass or maliciously injure another".[74] The FLS Code, by contrast, limits mandatory withdrawal to circumstances where the client persists in instructions that would require the lawyer to act contrary to professional ethics or the lawyer would not be competent.[75] This means that under the FLS Code, conduct requiring withdrawal could not simply be immoral ("dishonourable"), but would have to result in a violation of some specific ethical obligation placed on the lawyer.[76] The FLS Code's approach is superior. Once a lawyer has agreed to take on a case her reasons for withdrawal should be more concrete than a client's "dishonourable conduct".

The codes also require that when a lawyer withdraws she do so in a way that minimizes the expense and prejudice to the client. The codes place specific obligations on the lawyer to, for example, account for funds, cooperate with the successor lawyer and deliver papers to the client in an orderly and efficient manner (subject to any lien the solicitor has to enforce payment of her accounts). The codes emphasize that a lawyer should not enforce a lien for payment of fees and disbursements where doing so would materially prejudice the client in an uncompleted matter.[77]

What about lawyers working in organizational settings? Obviously for a lawyer employed as in-house counsel by a company or the government,

---

[71] CBA MC Chapter XII, Commentary 5.
[72] *Ibid.*
[73] BC PCH Chapter 10, Rule 3.
[74] CBA MC Chapter XII, Commentary 4. The LSUC RPC (Rule 2.09(7)), NB CC (Chapter 10, Commentary 3) and BC PCH (Chapter 10, Commentary 1) rules are similar.
[75] Similarly, the Que. CEA only mandates withdrawal when a "client induces an advocate to perform an illegal or fraudulent act", the lawyer advises the client that the act is illegal and the client persists in his intentions.
[76] FLS MC Rule 2.07(7). The AB CPC is similar: Chapter 14, Rule 2.
[77] CBA MC Chapter XII, Commentary 8-11; FLS MC Rules 2.07(8) and (9); LSUC RPC Rule 2.09(8); NB CC Chapter 10, Commentaries 5 and 6; AB CPC Chapter 14, Rules 3 and 4; BC PCH Chapter 10, Rule 8 (BC does not make the point about avoiding prejudice in enforcement of a lien). The Que. CEA does not speak to this issue.

withdrawal is not straightforward; effective withdrawal could mean resigning from her employment.[78] The codes of conduct do contemplate the possibility that resignation may be required, but only where the organization has engaged on a course of dishonest, fraudulent or criminal conduct, and attempts by the lawyer to bring the proposed action to the attention of those higher up within the organization have not resulted in any change.[79]

Lawyers acting in criminal cases are also subject to the jurisdiction of the court when seeking to withdraw from scheduled criminal proceedings; lawyers must request permission to withdraw, and that permission may be denied where the only reason offered is non-payment of fees.[80] In its 2010 decision in *R. v. Cunningham*,[81] the Supreme Court held that the inherent jurisdiction of the superior court to control its own processes, and to ensure the proper administration of justice, gives those courts the right to both remove counsel and to require them to continue.[82] Statutory courts have the same jurisdiction by way of implication from the statutory authority they are given over certain legal proceedings.[83]

The Court held that exercising jurisdiction to require counsel to continue in some cases is necessary to prevent delay that might prejudice the accused and the administration of justice.[84] The Court held that where counsel seeks to withdraw sufficiently in advance of proceedings, such that an adjournment would not be necessary, the court should permit withdrawal without requiring counsel to give reasons.

Where timing is at issue, and counsel states that the withdrawal is for ethical reasons, then "the court must accept counsel's answer at face value and not enquire further so as to avoid trenching on potential issues of solicitor-client privilege".[85] "Ethical reasons" include a request by the client that the lawyer violate ethical obligations or refusal of the accused to accept advice of counsel "on an important trial issue".[86] The court *must* grant a request to withdraw for ethical reasons.[87]

Where withdrawal is for non-payment of fees, permission to withdraw lies in the court's discretion; exercise of that discretion should take into account the feasibility of self-representation, the availability of alternative

---

[78] The AB CPC suggests that an organizational or government lawyer simply refuse to implement instructions that are improper. (Chapter 12, Rule 4, commentary.)
[79] CBA MC Chapter IV, Commentary 18; FLS MC Rule 2.02(8); LSUC RPC Rule 2.02(5.1); NB CC Chapter 10, Commentary 3; AB CPC Chapter 12, Rule 4.
[80] Some codes of conduct have codified the obligations reflected in the case law as it was prior to the Supreme Court's judgment in *R. v. Cunningham*, [2010] S.C.J. No. 10, 2010 SCC 10 (S.C.C.); those rules must be read in light of the decision in *Cunningham*. See: FLS MC Rule 2.07(4)-(6); LSUC RPC Rule 2.09(4)-(7).
[81] [2010] S.C.J. No. 10, 2010 SCC 10 (S.C.C.).
[82] *Ibid.* at para. 18.
[83] *Ibid.* at paras. 19-20.
[84] *Ibid.* at para. 22.
[85] *Ibid.* at para. 48.
[86] *Ibid.*
[87] *Ibid.* at para. 49.

representation, the impact of delay, the conduct of counsel, and the history of proceedings. Since none of these factors involves matters specific to the lawyer-client relationship, considering them will not breach privilege. Requiring counsel to continue without payment should only be used as a "last resort", where doing so is essential to avoiding prejudice to the accused or to the administration of justice.[88] Counsel required to continue to represent an accused may request that the court consider issuing a *Rowbotham* order, under which the government stays proceedings until legal aid is given to an accused. The Court in *Cunningham* was clear, though, that the issuance of a *Rowbotham* order was not related to a court's ability to refuse a counsel's request to withdraw from representation.

In sum, then, lawyers seeking to withdraw from retainers must have a reason for doing so; once a representation has been taken on it must be seen through to the end, so long as the client pays his bills and no ethical issues arise in the course of the representation.

6. CONCLUSION

The lawyer's promise to represent another person's interests resolutely is significant. It is a promise not to be undertaken lightly, and it potentially creates the opportunity for, on the one hand, an abuse of power by the lawyer or, on the other hand, a feeling in the lawyer that her own moral commitments have fallen by the wayside. The way the lawyer-client relationship operates — when it comes into existence, how decisions are made, the fees that clients pay and when the relationship ends — all affect, and are affected by, this dynamic. To the extent any unifying structure can be identified it is simply that the lawyer should enter the lawyer-client relationship with care, but once she has done so she should live up to the promise that she has made, not ceasing to be herself, open about her values and commitments, and ensuring that her client values the services she provides, but always with a focus on her role as advocate for that client. What that role requires in the context of litigation is picked up in the next chapter.

---

[88] *Ibid.* at para. 45.

Chapter 4

THE PRACTICE OF ADVOCACY

1. INTRODUCTION

In 1995 the lawyer Bruce Clark appeared at the British Columbia Court of Appeal at the opening of its hearing in the case of *Delgamuukw v. British Columbia*, and advised the judges that he was going to arrest them. The judges, he said, had assumed a "jurisdiction that was treasonable, fraudulent and genocidal", and deserved to be arrested for "those crimes".[1]

Twenty years earlier, in New Jersey, a lawyer

> sprang from his chair screaming, grabbed opposing counsel by the throat and began to choke him. The judge and the law clerk tried to separate the two men who were now locked in combat, and at one point all four persons — the judge, his law clerk and the other two attorneys — were rolling on the floor. The judge suffered minor injuries before the two combatants could be separated.[2]

Attempting to effect a citizen's arrest on the judiciary, or instigating a fist fight with opposing counsel, exceeds the bounds of resolute advocacy, and in both instances the lawyers were properly reprimanded for their misconduct.[3] There are some limits to lawyer zeal.

At the same time, however, the extent of the lawyer's duty of resolute advocacy in the context of litigation must not be underestimated. As stated in the various codes of conduct, lawyers acting as advocates must

> raise fearlessly every issue, advance every argument, and ask every question, however distasteful, which the lawyer thinks will help the client's case and ... endeavour to obtain for the client the benefit of every remedy and defence authorized by law.[4]

---

[1] Bruce Clark, *Justice in Paradise* (McGill-Queen's University Press, 2004) at 161.
[2] *In Re McAlevy*, 69 N.J. 349, 354 A. 2d 289, 290 (1976), quoted in Francis D. Doucette, *Advocacy and Chivalry*, Case and Comment 43 (July-August 1987), discussed in Monroe Freedman & Abbe Smith, *Understanding Lawyers' Ethics*, 4th ed. (New Providence, NJ: LexisNexis, 2010) at 81.
[3] *Law Society of Upper Canada v. Clark*, [1995] L.S.D.D. No. 199. Clark was subsequently disbarred for his conduct at a bail hearing in which he called the court a "'kangaroo court', spoke loudly and aggressively, flung papers which struck the court reporter on the arm and face, and assaulted a police officer by making contact with his leg or groin". He had also breached his undertaking to the judge to appear at a contempt hearing. [1999] L.S.D.D. No. 98 at para. 11.
[4] CBC MC Chapter IX; FLS MC Rule 4.01(1), commentary; LSUC RPC Rule 4.01(1); NB CC Chapter 8, Rule (b); AB CPC Chapter 10; BC PCH Canon 3(5). The Que. CEA has no similar rule, although it does generally require that the advocate establish a relationship of "mutual trust" (3.01.03) and that the advocate owes the client a duty of "loyalty, integrity, independence, impartiality, diligence and prudence" (3.00.01).

Or, as expressed by the Supreme Court of Canada, lawyers in litigation have the duty to "bring forward with courage even unpopular causes"[5] and must not "soft peddle" the client's case.[6]

In discussing the lawyer's obligation of zealous advocacy some central points require emphasis from the outset.

Most importantly, while discussions of the ethics of zeal usually focus on its limitations, the primary focus should not be on what is prohibited in advocating for clients, but rather on what is required to do so ethically and effectively. That may seem obvious — "zeal of course!" — but thinking about what, in fact, it means to be zealous is worth doing, and it is with that topic that the chapter begins.

Further, while lawyers' zeal has limits, those limits are not as significant as one might expect. The courts in particular have been hesitant to place direct constraints on how lawyers represent clients. To the extent that constraints on lawyer zeal exist, they are generally internal to the concept. That is, a lawyer's zeal is primarily constrained by the fact that certain types of advocacy are not in the client's interest, making the gains achieved by the client less stable or placing the client at risk of paying solicitor-client costs. The risks that zeal may pose for clients will be noted throughout the discussion in the chapter.

Finally, zeal operates in context. This chapter focuses on the lawyer's role as advocate in legal proceedings, but some of the issues it discusses also arise outside of courtroom advocacy. To the extent they do so, the proper resolution of those issues may not be the same outside of court as within it, and those distinctions are also noted here. In addition, even within the context of litigation, what zealous advocacy requires will vary depending on the specific task the lawyer is doing. What zeal requires may be different in, for example, an examination for discovery than during a trial,[7] and is required to be different when the lawyer brings forward an *ex parte* application.

This chapter discusses these issues. It begins, as noted, by emphasizing the paramount duty of lawyers to provide competent and effective representation that furthers their clients' interests. It then considers some specific issues within litigation ethics with respect to: frivolous arguments; taking advantage of obvious mistakes by other lawyers; examinations for discovery; the duty to provide the court with relevant adverse authority; *ex parte* applications; and, investigating a client's case. Finally, it considers issues related to lawyer speech: regulation by law societies and by the courts

---

[5] *Young v. Young*, [1993] S.C.J. No. 112 at para. 254, [1993] 4 S.C.R. 3 (S.C.C.), *per* McLachlin J. (as she then was).
[6] *R. v. Neil*, [2002] S.C.J. No. 72 at para. 19, 2002 SCC 70 (S.C.C.).
[7] Although as I will discuss, it is not that the obligations of the lawyer are different during an examination for discovery, but that the temptation and possibility for improper behaviour are greater in that context, and that what the lawyer will need to do to ensure that he has acted zealously within the bounds of legality will be different.

of public statements by lawyers during litigation, criticism of other lawyers, and criticism of judges and the legal system.[8]

2. LAWYER COMPETENCE: THE HEART OF RESOLUTE ADVOCACY

What does it mean to be a resolute advocate? Popular culture imagines the resolute advocate in court, devastating his opponent in pointed cross-examination, providing the evidence necessary to demonstrate the justice of his client's cause, and dazzling the judge and jury with elegant argument. When imagining lawyers in this way, popular culture draws a radically incomplete picture, not only because effective advocacy can come in many packages — zeal can be quiet as well as flashy — but also because it does not capture the effort and engagement that underlies what a lawyer does when he advocates for a client in court. Effective cross-examination, the necessary evidence, and elegant arguments, do not drop out of the sky into the lawyer's briefcase as he makes his way to the courthouse. They arise instead from the hard work, intelligence and experience of the lawyer before he ever gets to court. The heart of zealous advocacy is lawyer competence; a failure to be competent is unethical conduct. Indeed, it may be more significant unethical conduct — both because it occurs more frequently and because it is a more foundational breach — than the oft-invoked spectre of the lawyer who pursues his client's cause too far.

Many of the codes of conduct provide considerable guidance to lawyers as to the essential requirements of competent advocacy. Lawyers must have sufficient knowledge of the law; have sufficiently investigated the facts; and have the necessary skills to perform legal research and analysis, to apply the law to the facts, to write and draft effectively, to negotiate, to undertake alternative dispute resolution, to advocate and to problem solve. Lawyers must perform work conscientiously and diligently, applying "intellectual capacity, judgment and deliberation" to all functions the lawyer performs for his client.[9] The codes reinforce the position that competence is an ethical issue, and that a lawyer who does not have the necessary competence to take on a matter must either not do so or be "able to become competent without undue delay, risk or expense to the client".[10]

---

[8] Some of these issues and ethical principles — for example competence, the rule against sharp practice, and civility — have application beyond the context of litigation; the discussion of those concepts can therefore be applied more broadly. With respect to litigation, in particular, readers should also note Chapters 6, 7 and 9.

[9] CBA MC Chapter II; FLS MC Rule 2.01(1); LSUC RPC Rule 2.01(1); Que. CEA Rules 3.01.01 and 3.03.01; AB CPC Chapter 2, commentaries; NB CC Chapter 2, Rule 5; BC PCH Chapter 3, Rule 1. Interestingly, the CBA rules are less useful in this respect than the FLS rules. New Brunswick, the Law Society of Upper Canada and Alberta all set out guidelines similar to that of the FLS. British Columbia has a different approach again, but one which does not provide as much detail as the FLS. The least direction is given in the Que. CEA which simply states that the advocate must "display reasonable availability and diligence" (3.03.01).

[10] FLS MC Rule 2.01(1), commentary.

Lawyers have been subject to professional discipline for failing to provide competent representation in advocacy. In *Law Society of Alberta v. Syed*,[11] for example, the lawyer proposed a plea for a client in a sexual assault case where he had not determined whether his client was guilty. He had not interviewed the accused or explored potential defences. The lawyer did not look at the witness statements in a detailed fashion. As summarized in the decision:

> He did not confirm if the complainants were under the age of 14 years. He did not attempt to interview others present that night. In other words, he did not determine from his client, before offering the guilty plea to this one charge that the client was prepared to admit to more than consensual intercourse ...[12]

In essence, the lawyer appeared at the eve of trial knowing that he was unprepared to defend his client and suggesting a plea solely to get out of the dilemma his lack of preparation created. The lawyer agreed that his conduct in this respect was improper.

Syed is an illustrative case. It shows clearly the relationship between incompetence and a failure of zealous advocacy; the lawyer's lack of preparation and effort rendered him incapable of advocating on his client's behalf. It also shows why that behaviour is properly characterized as unethical. The potential consequences for a client in a criminal case involving a sexual assault allegation are serious, and putting the client's liberty and security of the person in jeopardy because the lawyer has failed to prepare adequately, violates that client's rights. The client did not have the resolute advocacy to which he was entitled because his lawyer was incompetent.

Goldberg v. Law Society of British Columbia[13] is a more recent example. In that case Goldberg had brought an application on behalf of various individuals arguing that they had received ineffective assistance of counsel in their criminal trials. Their first lawyer, Banks, had practiced law when no longer a member in good standing of the Law Society of British Columbia, when under considerable stress due to the death of his father, and in circumstances such that the Law Society continued to refuse to readmit him to practise. In bringing his application arguing that Banks' former clients had received ineffective assistance of counsel, Goldberg made a number of allegations against Banks which were unsubstantiated, and much of the orientation of the Law Society's disciplinary proceedings were directed at his having done so.[14]

The Law Society also found, however, that Goldberg was incompetent in his representation of his clients, and that this too was conduct deserving of

---

[11] [1994] L.S.D.D. No. 211.
[12] *Ibid.* at para. 9.
[13] [2009] B.C.J. No. 657, 2009 BCCA 147 (B.C.C.A.).
[14] See the discussion of this issue in Section 5.C. of this chapter.

sanction. The affidavits he filed in Court were irrelevant, rambling, repetitive and disorganized[15] and showed a "complete lack of knowledge of the law of evidence".[16] His facta were similarly "rambling and disorganized",[17] "presented almost completely without legal authority"[18] and were "stream of consciousness rendition[s] of the evidence".[19]

As noted by Prowse J.A. in her concurring reasons upholding the Law Society of British Columbia's disciplinary decision, Goldberg's incompetence in this respect raises a serious concern both for his clients and for the administration of justice. Banks, who was no longer a member of the Law Society of British Columbia, and whose own competence was therefore self-evidently at issue, had represented individuals in serious criminal cases, some involving murder charges. And now those individuals' *prima facie* non-frivolous argument that they had not received effective assistance of counsel from Banks had not been competently presented to the Court. Those clients remained in jail. Prowse J.A. suggested that

> the Law Society may consider it appropriate to review its records to ascertain whether there is a foundation therein for recommending a further investigation into this matter, with a view to determining whether there may have been a miscarriage of justice in relation to one or more of the Dunbar appellants.[20]

The ethical violation of Goldberg in relation to his clients was profound. Failed not once, but twice, those clients almost[21] certainly did not have the zealous advocacy to which they were entitled. And in both proceedings their liberty and security of the person were at issue. Goldberg needed to investigate the facts fully, present them properly in affidavits in compliance with the law of evidence, and focus his evidence and arguments on the legal points that need to be argued in a case alleging ineffective assistance of counsel. Goldberg may not have been successful given Banks' lack of cooperation, and his inability to access the law society record, but his clients would have had the legal representation to which they were entitled, at least once.[22]

---

[15] *Goldberg v. Law Society of British Columbia*, [2009] B.C.J. No. 657, 2009 BCCA 147 (B.C.C.A.), at para. 4, citing the original judicial proceeding on ineffective assistance of counsel, and at para. 38, citing the Law Society's decision.
[16] *Ibid.* at para. 38, citing the Law Society's decision.
[17] *Ibid.* at para. 4.
[18] *Ibid.*
[19] *Ibid.* at para. 38.
[20] *Ibid.* at para. 64.
[21] I qualify this point only because the Court was unprepared to find that they had received ineffective assistance of counsel in the first instance. I am troubled by this decision of the Court on the facts.
[22] Other cases in which lawyers have been disciplined for incompetent representation in litigation settings include *Law Society of Alberta v. Harrison*, [1994] L.S.D.D. No. 212 (lawyer avoided dealing with family law clients); *Law Society of Alberta v. Michaels*, [1996] L.S.D.D. No. 284 (missed limitation period); *Law Society of Saskatchewan v. Filyk*, [2008] L.S.D.D. No. 1 (delay arising from absence of diligence in dealings with own client and opposing counsel). Contra:

Solicitor negligence cases also provide guidance on the ethical obligation of competence that underlies zealous representation. Although negligence is often distinguished from incompetence with "mere negligence" being said to be insufficient to demonstrate incompetence,[23] legal doctrines arising from the law of negligence nonetheless indicate what zealous advocacy requires — or, as applied in specific cases, of what insufficiently zealous advocacy might look like. The standard of care to be met by lawyers is that of the "reasonably competent solicitor"[24] and includes the obligation to advise the client of risks in a course of action,[25] to research the law and understand the principles applicable to a client's case,[26] and to provide effective assistance of counsel.[27]

A particular example of the relationship between negligence law and the failure to provide resolute advocacy is *Hagblom v. Henderson*.[28] Henderson had acted for Hagblom in defence of a negligence claim. The defence was unsuccessful; the Court found in that proceeding that Hagblom had negligently constructed a chimney with the result that the house with the chimney was burnt to the ground. In his subsequent action against Henderson, Hagblom argued that Henderson had been negligent in his conduct of the defence. The Court of Appeal agreed and, in particular, they agreed that Henderson was negligent in failing to either consult or call an expert to testify with respect to aspects of Hagblom's construction of the chimney. The Court held that while a decision to call an expert can be a matter of judgment, there are circumstances in which calling an expert is essential. In this case it was impossible to defend Hagblom in the action without expert testimony, yet Henderson did not talk to any potential

---

Nova Scotia Barristers' Society v. MacIsaac, [2001] L.S.D.D. No. 1 (error on the law of probate may be negligence, but is not sufficient to demonstrate incompetence to the point of misconduct); *Law Society of British Columbia v. A lawyer*, [1999] L.S.D.D. No. 31 (failure to check that adjournment was arranged resulted in client being arrested on a bench warrant; single instance not sufficient incompetence to constitute misconduct).

[23] All of the codes of conduct make this distinction. Beverley Smith observes that civil negligence and "similar conduct resulting in professional misconduct are two distinct issues in the eyes of the legal profession". Beverley Smith, *Professional Conduct for Lawyers and Judges* (Fredericton: Maritime Law Book, 2002), ch. 2, para. 18.

[24] *Central Trust Co. v. Rafuse*, [1986] S.C.J. No. 52 at para. 58, [1986] 2 S.C.R. 147 (S.C.C.).

[25] *Graybriar Investments Ltd. v. Davis & Company*, [1990] B.C.J. No. 1239, 46 B.C.L.R. (2d) 164 (B.C.S.C.).

[26] *MacCulloch v. McInnes, Cooper and Robertson*, [2001] N.S.J. No. 16, 2001 NSCA 8 (N.S.C.A.).

[27] *Frumasa v. Ungaro*, [2005] O.J. No. 2412, 154 A.C.W.S. (3d) 1062 (Ont. S.C.J.), affd [2006] O.J. No. 686 (Ont. C.A.). Note that the decision dealt only with the applicability of a limitation period, and whether the alleged misconduct sounded in negligence or in breach of fiduciary duty. The Court held that ineffective assistance of counsel is negligence, but not a breach of fiduciary duty. A breach of fiduciary duty only arises where the lawyer acts in a conflict, violates confidentiality or fails to disclose relevant and material information — *i.e.*, "where the relationship of trust and loyalty between the lawyer and client has broken down". On the distinction between fiduciary obligations and the law of negligence in this context see also *Girardet v. Crease & Co.*, [1987] B.C.J. No. 240, [1987] 11 B.C.L.R. (2d) 361 (B.C.S.C.).

[28] [2003] S.J. No. 261, 2003 SKCA 40 (Sask. C.A.).

experts. Henderson's conduct did not meet the standard of the reasonably competent solicitor and he was, therefore, liable to Hagblom for damages.

This case is an example of what a failure to fulfill the duty of resolute advocacy looks like. Properly analyzing the plaintiff's allegations to determine the evidence that is necessary to present the defendant's case effectively, and locating that evidence if possible, is a precondition without which resolute advocacy cannot occur. No amount of cleverness in cross-examination, or rhetorical flourish in argument, can make up for the absence of that sort of basic preparation.

The word zeal, and even the word resolute, bring with them connotations of excitement, an image of the lawyer as superhero — or, to its critics, connotations of the lawyer as gangster, skirting the moral norms of society to achieve what the client wants. The reality is less dramatic, if not less ethically significant. Fulfilling the duty of zealous advocacy means hard work, intelligence and experience applied to the client's problem in order to achieve as successful a resolution as possible.

3. RESTRAINTS ON ZEAL

A. Frivolous Arguments

A zealous lawyer, with knowledge of the law and the skill to apply it, will understand the difference between arguments that have a reasonable likelihood of success in court and those that are "'doomed to failure', 'impossible to prove' or 'hopeless'".[29] Most of the time, therefore, the lawyer will not bring forward arguments that have no chance of succeeding, since doing so will not advance the client's interests. Sometimes, however, clients may wish to bring forward hopeless cases. They may believe that the law has taken the wrong direction; the frivolous argument may be the only argument they have; or the frivolous argument may simply be one they want to make. In general, a lawyer may make such arguments on his client's behalf although, as noted below, the lawyer has a clear ethical obligation to ensure that the client understands the risks associated with doing so.

Canadian lawyers are subject to few specific constraints in bringing forward arguments that might be characterized as frivolous. Although the Alberta and New Brunswick codes of conduct prohibit a lawyer from taking any step in litigation that is "clearly without merit",[30] and the Québec *Code of ethics of advocates*[31] permits a lawyer to withdraw where a client persists in continuing a "futile or vexatious proceeding",[32] most codes of conduct

---

[29] *Young v. Young*, [1990] B.C.J. No. 2254, 75 D.L.R. (4th) 46 (B.C.C.A.), affirmed on this point [1993] S.C.J. No. 112 at para. 251 ("the fact that an application has little merit is no basis for awarding solicitor-client costs" and para. 254, [1993] 4 S.C.R. 3 at 41 (S.C.C.).
[30] AB CPC Chapter 10, Rule 1; NB CC Chapter 8, Commentary 7.
[31] R.R.Q. 1981, c. B-1, r.1.
[32] Que. CEA Rule 3.03.04(d). Rule 4.02.01 also prohibits a lawyer from taking steps in a matter "when it is evident that such action is only intended to harm another person or to adopt an

only prohibit the lawyer from prosecuting proceedings that are motivated by malice or brought for the sole purpose of injuring another party.[33] Further, the Alberta code defines the standard of "clearly without merit" rigorously, noting in the commentary that a lawyer does not need to think a case will ultimately prevail to pursue it, and allowing the lawyer to take into account the possibility that more information may become available through discovery.[34]

In addition, and more significantly, courts have shown real reluctance to use the provisions of the rules of court that permit costs to be levied against lawyers personally[35] on the basis that lawyers have brought frivolous arguments or claims. In the leading case of *Young v. Young*,[36] the British Columbia Court of Appeal held that a cost order could only be made against the lawyer where the lawyer failed to advise his client that the case was "'irresistible', that the client's case is 'doomed to failure', 'impossible to prove' or 'hopeless'".[37] That is, costs may only be awarded against the lawyer personally where it is the lawyer who caused the case to be brought forward *and* where the case meets the high standard of hopelessness. The Court emphasized the importance of not creating a "chilling effect" on lawyer advocacy and, in particular, the problem for the lawyer of confidentiality obligations that may make it difficult for him to defend himself with an argument that the client had directed him to pursue the matter. McLachlin J. (as she then was) emphasized these latter points in her judgment affirming the British Columbia Court of Appeal's decision on this point:

> courts must be extremely cautious in awarding costs personally against a lawyer, given the duties upon a lawyer to guard confidentiality of instructions and to bring forward with courage even unpopular causes. A lawyer should not be placed in a situation where his or her fear of an adverse order of costs may conflict with these fundamental duties of his or her calling.[38]

Young has been followed in subsequent cases. Even where the proceedings were wholly unsuccessful, courts have not awarded costs against the lawyer personally. In *Byers (Litigation Guardian of) v. Pentex*

---

attitude contrary to the requirements of good faith" (4.02.01(a)). It should be noted that in Québec, in addition to the *Code of Ethics*, the *Civil Code* states that all persons must behave in good faith and may not abuse their rights. This underlying morality — which stems from canon law and the old Roman law — is a defining characteristic of the civilian legal tradition.

[33] CBA MC Chapter IX, Commentary 2(a). FLS MC Rule 4.01(2); LSUC RPC Rule 4.01(2).
[34] Note also that the Que. CEA only permits the advocate to withdraw; it does not require that the advocate do so.
[35] For example, LSUC RPC Rule 57.07.
[36] [1990] B.C.J. No. 2254, 75 D.L.R. (4th) 46 at 102 (B.C.C.A.), *per* Cumming J.A., affirmed on this point [1993] S.C.J. No. 112, [1993] 4 S.C.R. 3 (S.C.C.).
[37] *Young v. Young*, [1990] B.C.J. No. 2254, 75 D.L.R. (4th) 46 at 41 (B.C.C.A.).
[38] *Young v. Young*, [1993] S.C.J. No. 112 at para. 254, [1993] 4 S.C.R. 3 (S.C.C.).

Print Master Industries Inc.[39] the Court held that while the action was unsuccessful, there was no evidence that it was the lawyer who had insisted on pursuing the litigation. The Court also rejected the argument that if a lawyer advises his client that an action is hopeless, and the client nonetheless chooses to pursue the litigation, the lawyer has an obligation to withdraw from the representation.

In *Robertson v. Edmonton (City) Police Service*[40] the judge held that while the lawyer had shown bad judgment, he nonetheless had a *bona fide* belief in the merits of the litigation. Slatter J. (now J.A.) held that an award against the lawyer should only be made if "it is beyond doubt not only that the proceedings are devoid of merit, and that the solicitor knew or ought to have known them to be so, but also that the responsibility for continuing with the proceedings despite their lack of merit lies with the solicitor, rather than the client".[41] In other cases, lawyers have had costs awarded against them personally, but only in circumstances where the lawyer appears to have acted in bad faith or with an ulterior motive, such as commencing the litigation "as a weapon in his war against [an] insurer".[42]

The court's attitude to frivolous litigation thus provides wide latitude to lawyers to implement client instructions with respect to litigation strategy. That being said, because cost-shifting will almost always occur when litigation is unsuccessful, lawyers must advise clients of the risks and consequences associated with frivolous litigation. A client who brings litigation which has little or no chance of success takes on the significant risk of having a cost award made against her and, especially if the action is found to have been clearly without merit, to have an award of solicitor-client costs made against her.[43] These are costs that can run into the tens and even hundreds of thousands of dollars in the civil context. In addition, frivolous claims or defences are liable to be struck pursuant to the rules of court, and this may add to the risk of costs faced by the client. In extreme circumstances

---

[39] [2002] O.J. No. 1403 (Ont. S.C.J.), *per* Sachs J.
[40] [2005] A.J. No. 840, 2005 ABQB 499 (Alta. Q.B.).
[41] *Ibid.* at para. 18. See also *Kent v. Waldock*, [2000] B.C.J. No. 1144, 2000 BCCA 357 (B.C.C.A.) (costs awarded against lawyer for not providing full disclosure, but not for unmeritorious proceedings); *Time Logistics Ltd. v. Haworth Ltd.*, [2007] A.J. No. 1161, 2007 ABQB 633 (Alta. Q.B. (In Chambers)), *per* Master Laycock (costs not awarded against lawyer personally); *Carmichael v. Strathshore Industrial Park Ltd.*, [1999] O.J. No. 2182 (Ont. C.A.) (applies *Young* and refuses to award costs against lawyer personally).
[42] *Standard Life Assurance Co. v. Elliott*, [2007] O.J. No. 2031 at para. 30, 86 O.R. (3d) 221 (Ont. S.C.J.). See also: *A & B Auto Leasing & Car Rental Inc. v. Mississauga Auto Clinic Inc.*, [2009] O.J. No. 4670 (Ont. S.C.J.). For a discussion of the circumstances in which it is appropriate to award costs against a solicitor personally because of her conduct in relation to litigation see: *M.D. v. Windsor-Essex Children's Aid Society*, [2010] O.J. No. 2270 (Ont. S.C.J.). The lawyer in that case was required to pay costs for conduct that included filing inaccurate materials and attempting to make improper use of *ex parte* proceedings. It also appears that a number of the applications and motions she was pursuing were frivolous.
[43] Despite the statements made by McLachlin J. in *Young v. Young*, [1993] S.C.J. No. 112 at para. 251, a finding by a court that an argument has no or little merit may increase the likelihood of an award of solicitor-client costs. It may not on its own be sufficient, but it will be an aggravating circumstance.

a frivolous and vexatious claim could open the client to liability for the tort of abuse of process — where a court finds that the claim was made for a collateral or ulterior purpose.[44] The lawyer's duty of zealous advocacy thus requires that the lawyer set out these risks for his client in the clearest terms, and that he only bring forward borderline cases where his client fully comprehends the associated risks, and has voluntarily assumed them.

An additional point must be noted. The discussion to this point has only considered the ability of the lawyer to rely on frivolous arguments to pursue or defend a claim in court. The issue of frivolity may also come up in a non-litigation context. In particular, a client may request an opinion from a lawyer in order to subsequently argue in defence of a civil or criminal action that the client "acted on legal advice". The legal advice may allow the client to avoid adverse legal consequences that might otherwise arise. For example, a client engaged in aggressive tax planning can reduce the likelihood that she will have to pay penalties if she obtains in advance a legal opinion that the tax plan has a reasonable chance of success.[45] As the Supreme Court of Canada has recently held, this shield may be successful, at least for government clients, even if the advice turns out to be bad or wrong.[46]

Given that legal framework, in my view the ethical obligation of the lawyer when advising is to provide the client with an accurate and reasonable assessment of the law. The lawyer can — and must — make the best arguments available for the client, but cannot make arguments that are

---

[44] Although there would also have to be some evidence that the client had made some act or threat in furtherance of that collateral purpose. *Tsiopoulos v. Commercial Union Assurance Co.*, [1986] O.J. No. 1179, 57 O.R. (2d) 117, 32 D.L.R. (4th) 614 (Ont. H.C.J.); *Grainger v. Hill et al.* (1838), 4 Bing. (N.C.) 212, 132 E.R. 769; *Guilford Industries Ltd. v. Hankinson Services Ltd. et al.*, [1973] B.C.J. No. 666, 40 D.L.R. (3d) 398, [1974] 1 W.W.R. 141 (B.C.S.C.); *Atland Containers Ltd. v. Macs Corp. Ltd. et al.*, [1974] O.J. No. 2238, 7 O.R. (2d) 107, 54 D.L.R. (3d) 363, 17 C.P.R. (2d) 16 (Ont. H.C.J.); *Unterreiner v. Wilson et al.*, [1982] O.J. No. 3600, 40 O.R. (2d) 197, 142 D.L.R. (3d) 588, 24 C.C.L.T. 54 (Ont. H.C.J.), affd [1983] O.J. No. 3003, 41 O.R. (2d) 472, 146 D.L.R. (3d) 322 (Ont. C.A.).

[45] *Income Tax Act*, R.S.C. 1985 (5th Supp.), c. 1, s. 163(2); cases hold that a taxpayer is much less likely to be found to have been grossly negligent where the tax plan works. The most infamous context in which this issue has arisen is the American governments use of waterboarding and other "Enhanced Interrogation Techniques" in the pursuit of the war on terror. President Bush and other officials could only avoid the risk of future criminal prosecution if they had *ex ante* advice that such techniques were legal. The advice given to them that the techniques were legal has been described as "disingenuous", "absurd" and involving "kabbalistic textual manipulations". See David Luban, *Legal Ethics and Human Dignity* (New York: Cambridge University Press, 2007) at 163, 189. No debate has so animated legal ethics scholars in the U.S. over the last five years as the ethics of the "torture memos". As this discussion suggests, my position on that debate has been that the advice provided was a violation of the lawyers' ethical duties.

[46] *Fullowka v. Pinkerton's of Canada Ltd.*, [2010] S.C.J. No. 5, 2010 SCC 5 (S.C.C.). In that case an action against the government in negligence was unsuccessful in part because the government had relied on legal advice. The Court held that it was not relevant that the legal advice was wrong, and that it would only be "rarely" that liability in negligence would arise for a government actor following legal advice.

frivolous, or clearly without merit, in order to shield the client from subsequent legal consequences.

This characterization of the lawyer's ethical obligation in advising is consistent with the rules on advising set out in the preceding chapter,[47] but is also distinct from what the lawyer can do in court, where frivolity is permitted where pursued on the client's informed instruction. The reason for this is that when the lawyer goes to court the arguments that he makes are not determinative of the outcome; they are positions put forward to the court, for the court to decide. By contrast, when a lawyer is advising the client outside the litigation context, the arguments are determinative, both in terms of how the client will act and in terms of the future legal impact for the client. It is the content of the legal advice itself that creates the legal outcome. Moreover, if the lawyer provides advice that is fundamentally flawed, and he does so simply because *any* legal advice, no matter how bogus, will shield his client from future legal liability, doing so comes perilously close to fraud. It may also, in certain circumstances — such as the tax context — open the lawyer to independent legal liability.[48]

Advice provided by a lawyer even outside of litigation is not the equivalent of a judicial decision; the lawyer does not have an obligation to provide a balanced assessment of the situation (unless, of course, that is what the client has requested). The lawyer may make whatever arguments are non-frivolous and reasonably available to assist his client, including arguments to assist his client avoid future adverse legal consequences. In my view the limit to this wide discretion is simply that he may not make arguments that are frivolous or without merit, and in which he does not in good faith believe, to provide what is essentially an extra-legal shield for the legal consequences of his client's conduct. A useful standard to follow is that imposed by the *Income Tax Act*, which defines culpable conduct by third party advisors as arising where those advisors demonstrate a "wilful, reckless or wanton disregard of the law".[49]

A context related to litigation brings up one final issue with regard to frivolous arguments. The various codes of conduct prohibit lawyers from threatening to bring or withdraw criminal or like charges in order to obtain an advantage in civil litigation, and from advising their clients to do so:

> Apart from the substantive law on the subject, it is improper for the lawyer to advise, threaten or bring a criminal, quasi-criminal or disciplinary proceeding in order to secure some civil advantage for the client, or to advise, seek or procure the withdrawal of such a proceeding

---

[47] See Chapter 3, Section 3.
[48] See, *e.g.*, *Income Tax Act*, R.S.C. 1985 (5th Supp.), c. 1, s. 163.2(4).
[49] *Ibid.*, s. 163.2(1)(*c*).

in consideration of the payment of money, or transfer of property, to or for the benefit of the client.[50]

This rule relates to frivolous litigation insofar as at least part of the reason for the prohibition is to prevent abuse of the criminal process through the laying of dubious criminal charges, or to allow unmeritorious civil claims to get a firmer footing through fear of criminal charges. The rule also, however, appears "redundant or overbroad or both".[51] Consider two possible scenarios:

Scenario One

A lawyer for a company negotiating a takeover of another company threatens to report the target to the securities commission for reporting violations if they do not agree to his client's terms. He does so on the instruction of his client, even though the lawyer thinks it unlikely that the target has violated securities laws. The threat may nonetheless be effective because the target is in financial trouble, and the corporate officers are likely to be concerned about the impact of defending that sort of claim.

Scenario Two

A lawyer acts for a thirty-five year old man who was sexually abused by his hockey coach when he was twelve. The conduct is clearly criminal and tortious, but the lawyer is concerned about the possible impact of limitation periods on his client's claim. The client has never gone to the police, although the evidence that the assaults took place is strong. On his client's instructions, the lawyer presents an offer of settlement to the former hockey coach, including a provision which makes the settlement conditional on the client not reporting the assault to the police.

The conduct of the lawyer in the first scenario violates a number of ethical rules. It is an implicit (and perhaps explicit) misrepresentation to the opposing party that the acquiring company has reason to believe that the target has violated securities laws, and that it will report the target for doing so. It may also be in itself a crime — extortion or fraud — or an attempt to assist the client to commit those crimes. By contrast, the conduct of the lawyer (and of his client) in the second scenario is unlikely to be characterized as extortion under the *Criminal Code*.[52] The agreement to not pursue a criminal conviction also does not involve any misrepresentation or

---

[50] CBA MC Chapter III, Commentary 9; FLS MC Rule 2.02(5); LSUC RPC Rule 2.02(4); NB CC Chapter 4, Commentary 9; AB CPC Chapter 10, Rule 4; BC PCH Chapter 4, Rule 2. The Que. CEA contains no equivalent to this rule.
[51] Geoffrey C. Hazard, Jr. *et al.*, *The Law of Lawyering* §40.4 (3d ed. Supp. 2008). See generally: Ernest F. Lidge, "Client interests and a Lawyer's Duty to Expedite Litigation: Does Model Rule 3.2 Impose Any Independent Obligations" (2009) St. John's L. Rev. 307 at 345.
[52] R.S.C. 1985, c. C-46. See in general, *Rousseau v. The Queen*, [1985] S.C.J. No. 46, [1985] 2 S.C.R. 38 (S.C.C.).

dishonesty. The "wrong" that it arguably involves is that it stops the crime from being reported and, in a case like this one, there is a chance that the individual in question could exploit other young men. More abstractly, it eliminates the ability of the Crown to pursue wrongdoers criminally, which is a state interest not an interest of the individual victim; it may be wrong for an individual to deprive the state of its interest in that respect.

Yet while we might say the client in the second scenario has a moral duty to report the crime, he does not have any legal duty to do so. He commits no crime or illegal act either by not reporting the original wrong against him, or by accepting a civil settlement on the basis that he will not report it. This raises the serious problem that the effect of the ethical rule is to prevent the lawyer doing on his client's behalf that which the client would be permitted to do for himself. Indeed, the rule itself contemplates this result by beginning "Apart from the substantive law on the subject ..."

It is not self-evident, conceptually or in these examples, why the legal obligation of the lawyer should depart from the substantive law. To the contrary, such a result appears fundamentally inconsistent with the normative structure of the lawyer's role, as explained in Chapter 2. Ultimately, if the client does not wish to report the crime, and if he is legally free to make that choice, then should he not also be able to use that decision not to report to enforce his legitimate but technically compromised civil claim? And should he not be able to have a lawyer assist him to do so? There is a cost to society in the client's choice, but it is a cost the client is legally permitted to impose. As a consequence, I suggest that the Canadian law societies follow the lead of the American Bar Association and eliminate this rule.

Of course, unless and until the rules are amended, the lawyer faced with the second scenario cannot make such an offer on his client's behalf, and risks discipline by the law society should he do so.[53]

B. The Rule Against Sharp Practice

Lawyers' zeal in advocacy is constrained by the rule in the codes of conduct that prohibits "sharp practice":

> A lawyer must avoid sharp practice and must not take advantage of or act without fair warning upon slips, irregularities or mistakes on the part of other lawyers not going to the merits or involving the sacrifice of a client's rights.[54]

---

[53] See: *Law Society of Alberta v. Gillis*, [1998] L.S.D.D. No. 148 (lawyer reprimanded for using an offer of facilitating withdrawal of a criminal charge to obtain a civil settlement); *Law Society of Alberta v. Gelmon* [1998] L.S.D.D. No. 20 (lawyer fined $1,000 and ordered to pay over $3,000 in costs for using a threat of criminal proceedings to have ingredients returned to his client which the lawyer believed to have been stolen).

[54] CBA MC Chapter IX, Commentary 7; FLS MC Rule 6.02(2); LSUC RPC Rule 6.03(3); NB Chapter 8, Commentary 7; AB CPC Chapter 4, Rule 3; BC PCH Canon 4(3); The Que. CEA does not have an equivalent to the sharp practice rule, but s. 4.03.03 of the *Code of Ethics* prevents a lawyer from surprising, taking advantage of, or being disloyal toward a colleague.

Consistent with the point made at the beginning of the chapter, and as was the case with the restrictions on making frivolous arguments in court, the practical imperative for a lawyer to observe this constraint is not primarily the potential for personal costs or sanctions against a lawyer, but is rather effective advocacy for the client. While the rule does restrict lawyer's conduct, and a breach of the rule could result in discipline, the case law applying the rule generally arises in the context of adjudication of a client's legal position.[55] That is, a finding that the lawyer has engaged in "sharp practice" generally affects the legal situation of the client, not the lawyer.

The "sharp practice" rule has two essential elements. First, the mistake in question must be clear and obvious. If it is "questionable but ... may have involved a conscious exercise of judgment" it is a "mistake" that the opposing party *may* take advantage of.[56] Thus, a mathematical error is a clear and obvious mistake, but an interpretation of a legal rule that is less advantageous than the lawyer thinks could have been applied to the rule, is not. Second, the advantage that the client would receive from the mistake must be one to which the client has no legal right. The termination of a lawsuit because of a missed limitation period is an advantage to which the client has a legal right, but the failure of a lawsuit because the statement of claim has a typographical error in the name of the corporate defendant, is not.

This rule comes up most frequently in cases where a defendant in litigation has been noted in default without notice, and seeks to have the order noting in default set aside; the rule against sharp practice is cited by the courts as a basis for setting aside the order. In most cases, consistent with the rules in the codes of conduct, it appears that the defendant's "mistake" of failing to defend in a timely fashion was minor and had not deprived the plaintiff of its rights. Orders have been set aside where the delay was minimal;[57] the defendant had notified of her intention to defend and the parties had been discussing the claim;[58] the plaintiff was aware that the defendant had recently obtained new counsel;[59] or, where the statement of defence had been served but not filed.[60]

More substantively, in an action to enforce a settlement, the Ontario Superior Court relied on the principle underlying the sharp practice rule to refuse to allow a party to enforce as written a settlement with a known

---

[55] I did not find any disciplinary decisions in which a lawyer was disciplined for taking advantage of another lawyer's mistake.
[56] AB CPC Chapter 4, Rule 3, Commentary c. 3.
[57] *Moose Mountain Buffalo Ranch v. Greene Farms Drilling Ltd.*, [2009] A.J. No. 928, 2009 ABQB 489 (Alta. Q.B.), affd [2010] A.J. No. 172, 2010 ABCA 56 (Alta. C.A.).
[58] *Bank of Nova Scotia v. MacKinnon*, [1996] P.E.I.J. No. 105, 8 C.P.C. (4th) 271 (P.E.I.C.A.); *Bank of Montreal v. D'Angelo*, [2000] O.J. No. 5272, 103 A.C.W.S. (3d) 488 (Ont. S.C.J.); *Xpress View Inc. v. Daco Manufacturing Ltd.*, [2002] O.J. No. 4078, 36 C.C.E.L. (3d) 78 (Ont. S.C.J.); *Temple v. Riley*, [2001] N.S.J. No. 66, 2001 NSCA 36 (N.S.C.A.); *Garten v. Kruk*, [2009] O.J. No. 2143 (Ont. S.C.J.).
[59] *TD Canada Trust v. Chapel Hill Pet Studio Inc.*, [2008] O.J. No. 3901, 169 A.C.W.S. (3d) 978 (Ont. S.C.J.).
[60] *Vacation Brokers Inc. v. Gervasi*, [1999] O.J. No. 3071 (Ont. S.C.J.).

mistake.[61] In that case the party proposing the settlement had made a mathematical error that was known to the other side; the settlement was enforced but with the error corrected.

The most interesting case to apply the rule against sharp practice is *Crosby v. Guardian Insurance Co. of Canada*.[62] In that case Guardian was required to pay out on a surety bond for the benefit of minor applicants. It did not pay despite requests that it do so. An application was ultimately brought to enforce payment; Guardian agreed that it should pay, but argued that it should not have to pay interest, because the proper process for enforcing the bond had not been followed until that point, which constituted a failure to mitigate. The Court rejected Guardian's argument. It said that counsel for the children was unaware of the necessary requirements under the *Estates Act*.[63] Guardian and its counsel knew of the proper procedure, but did not advise counsel for the children as to what needed to be done; as a consequence, Guardian was required to pay the interest:

> I adopt the rule [from the Law Society of Upper Canada Code on sharp practice] and say that ***Guardian's solicitor's duty in the circumstances was to point out the necessity of an assignment under*** **The Estates Act**. This was a non-adversarial proceeding and the rights of children were affected adversely. There was no accretion on their accounts from interest. The failure to mitigate argument has no application to the facts. In these circumstances, the children should not be deprived of postjudgment interest and should be paid. It is regrettable that counsel for Guardian failed to act in accordance with his clear duty as set out in the Rules of Professional Conduct.[64]

If applied broadly, the court's interpretation of the duty of counsel in this case constitutes a notable addition to the constraints on lawyer advocacy; it may amount to requiring lawyers to correct mistakes in law by opposing counsel, a position that, while advocated for by some, has not generally been viewed as part of the law governing lawyers.[65] The interpretation of the sharp practice rule as having this effect is not necessarily wrong: if the mistake in law is sufficiently obvious to pass the first part of the test set out in the rule, taking advantage of the mistake almost certainly provides the opposing side a benefit to which it has no legal entitlement, thereby passing the second part of the test. That second point follows inexorably from the fact that the error in question is one of law: a benefit obtained through an error in law must necessarily be one to which there was no legal entitlement.

---

[61] *Blackwell v. Dixon*, [2009] O.J. No. 2968, 179 A.C.W.S. (3d) 318 (Ont. S.C.J.).
[62] [2001] O.J. No. 1120 (Ont. S.C.J.).
[63] R.S.O. 1990, c. E.21.
[64] *Crosby v. Guardian Insurance Co. of Canada*, [2001] O.J. No. 1120 at para. 18 (Ont. S.C.J.). [Emphasis added].
[65] William Simon, "Role Differentiation and Lawyers' Ethics: A Critique of Some Academic Perspective" (2010) 23(4) Geo. J. Legal Ethics 987.

Guardian does not necessarily warrant such broad application, however. The proceedings were "non-adversarial", the injured parties were minors, and the benefit sought by Guardian (non-payment of interest) was arguably an equitable remedy and not a legal one, such that an absence of "clean hands" could properly disqualify it from obtaining that remedy.[66] Which leads to the question of whether, apart from this case, the rule against sharp practice should apply to prohibit a lawyer from taking advantage of mistakes in law?

There is some reason to believe that it should. As noted, an obligation to correct obvious mistakes in law seems to fit *prima facie* within the terms of the rule. Further, the justification for the lawyer's role offered earlier in this book turns on a claim for the authority of law; permitting lawyers to take advantage of the equivalent of a legal spelling mistake does not fit particularly well with that justification. Also, as discussed in the following section, the lawyer would clearly have an obligation to correct a legal mistake of that type if the proceedings went to court; there seems to be no particular reason to have a different legal obligation on the lawyer simply because the parties are not yet in court. Indeed, as was suggested with respect to advising, the opposite may be the case. In court there are safeguards that may correct the mistake in law even if the lawyer fails to do so; outside of court those safeguards do not exist. Finally, where a party to a settlement discussion or negotiation knows that the other side has made a fundamental error in law, the agreement that results may be liable to be set aside on the basis of implied misrepresentation or mistake. That is, proceeding without revealing the mistake may simply not be in the client's interests, and she should be advised as such consistent with the lawyer's ethical duty of zealous advocacy.

Having said that, to the extent a requirement to correct mistakes of law by the opposing party exists, it is a narrow one. The mistake has to be the equivalent of the "mathematical error" referenced in the commentary to the rules, such as thinking a statute has been repealed when it has not. Mistakes about the interpretation of a law, or how it might apply to a set of facts, are not mistakes requiring correction by the opposing party. Even the type of mistake found to require correction in *Guardian* — not knowing that a particular process applies — would not, I think, typically trigger the duty; normally if a lawyer is ignorant of how to go about enforcing his client's rights, the lawyer on the other side is not obliged to tell him what to do.[67]

In addition, the rule against sharp practice could not properly broaden the obligations and rights of the client as they exist in the substantive law (that is, apart from the lawyer's ethical obligations). The sharp practice rule

---

[66] Or, in the civilian tradition, through application of the maxim *Nemo auditor propriam turpitudinem allegans*.
[67] This distinction is made largely because *Guardian* involved children; in a case which did not involve the interests of minors or other vulnerable parties, a lawyer is less likely to be placed under the same obligation to correct the ignorance of opposing counsel.

itself expressly prohibits the lawyer from altering the client's substantive legal position in order to correct a mistake. Thus, for example, under the law of contracts, where one party knows that the other side has made a mistake about the effect of a contract term, so long as the non-mistaken party did not induce it, the mistake does not affect the enforceability of the contract.[68] That lack of obligation to disclose under the substantive law of contracts cannot properly be altered by the lawyer's professional obligations pursuant to the sharp practice rule.

In sum, the sharp practice rule does impose some constraints on lawyer advocacy. The constraints are not broad, but they are material, particularly in the context of negotiations.

C. Relevant Adverse Authority

Another qualification of the lawyer's duty of resolute advocacy arises from the lawyer's ethical obligation with respect to the presentation of legal authority. Specifically, when lawyers go to court they must provide the judge with all relevant authority, even where adverse to their case, and even where the opposing party has failed to mention it. This obligation is imposed by the codes of conduct[69] and is affirmed as well in a number of judicial decisions. It raises three central questions with respect to its application. First, when is an authority sufficiently authoritative? Second, when is an authority sufficiently relevant? Finally, what duty does the lawyer have to identify or discover such authority if she is not already aware of it?

In its decision in *Lougheed Enterprises v. Armbruster*,[70] the British Columbia Court of Appeal addressed all of these points. It held that a decision is "authority" where it is one "decided within the judicial hierarchy"[71] of the province, in that instance the British Columbia Supreme Court, the British Columbia Court of Appeal or the Supreme Court of Canada. Decisions from other provinces, within the provincial court system, or from the federal courts, would not be authoritative in that sense.

A decision is relevant where it refers to any point of law on which the case in question might turn. Relevance does not include cases that have some resemblance to the case before the court on the facts; it "means cases which decide a point of law" on which the current case depends.[72]

With respect to the lawyer's obligation to discover the relevant law, while he does not have a duty to search out unreported cases, he does have

---

[68] *Smith v. Hughes* (1871), LR 6 QB 597.
[69] CBA MC Chapter IX, Principle 2(h); FLS MC Rule 4.01(2)(i); LSUC RPC Rule 4.01(2)(h); NB CC Chapter 8, Commentary 10(viii); AB CPC Chapter 10, Rule 18; BC PCH Chapter 8, Rule 1(f);. The Que. CEA is silent on this point perhaps because, strictly speaking, the doctrine of *stare decisis* does not apply in the context of Québec civil law and because it is assumed that the judge knows the law: *iuris novit curia*.
[70] [1992] B.C.J. No. 712, 63 B.C.L.R. (2d) 316 (B.C.C.A.).
[71] *Ibid.* at 324.
[72] *Ibid.*

an obligation to bring to the court's attention cases of which he has knowledge and, as well, he cannot "discharge this duty by not bothering to determine whether there is a relevant authority. In this context, ignorance is no excuse."[73] The Alberta Court of Appeal has similarly suggested that counsel has a duty to "look for and find" all relevant authority.[74]

The codes of conduct impose a somewhat more relaxed standard with respect to the lawyer's obligation to research and discover relevant authority; most suggest that a breach of the lawyer's obligation occurs only where the lawyer "deliberately" refrains from advising the court of relevant adverse authority. As a consequence, a lawyer will not be in breach of the code of conduct if he simply was unaware of a decision. In general, however, the higher standard imposed by the court should be understood as governing, provided that the lawyer's duty to find cases is reasonably construed. The lawyer has an obligation to act competently in preparing for a case, but cannot be expected to dig through every conceivable avenue of research "just in case" there are authorities unhelpful to the client's position.

The effect of violating the more stringent requirements of the court's adverse authority rule is not professional discipline for the lawyer, but rather a less favourable result for the client substantively or in terms of a requirement to pay costs on a solicitor-client basis. A lawyer could conceivably be ordered to pay costs personally, but the courts appear reluctant to reach that result.[75] As was the case with frivolous litigation, however, a lawyer should be primarily concerned with costs that may be imposed on a client as a result of the lawyer's actions.

Is the relevant adverse authority rule justifiable given the role of the lawyer as zealous advocate? The difficulty with the rule is that it requires the lawyer to take steps that are not in the client's interest, except insofar as it may be tactically better to address a relevant adverse authority up front rather than having to react to it later when it is raised by the judge or opposing counsel.[76] On the other hand, as was the case with respect to correcting mistakes in law, the role of the lawyer as resolute advocate is justified within and through the law itself. In that context, imposing some positive obligations on the lawyer to ensure the court knows of all relevant authority is coherent. Also, and importantly, the lawyer is not obliged to say that the authority is correct, and may indeed make whatever arguments he wishes to persuade the court that the authority is wrong and misguided. His

---

[73] *Ibid.* See also the commentary to AB CPC Chapter 10, Rule 18; *General Motors Acceptance Corp. of Canada v. Isaac Estate*, [1992] A.J. No. 1083, 7 Alta. L.R. (3d) 230 (Alta. Q.B.), *per* Master Funduk; *Adler Firestopping Ltd. v. Rea*, [2008] A.J. No. 124, 2008 ABQB 95 (Alta. Q.B.); *McGregor v. Crossland*, [1997] O.J. No. 2513, 72 A.C.W.S. (3d) 34 (Ont. Gen. Div.); *R. v. Mitchell*, [1994] A.J. No. 923, 162 A.R. 109 (Alta. C.A.); *Society of Lloyd's v. Van Snick*, [2000] N.S.J. No. 28, 182 N.S.R. (2d) 64 (N.S.S.C.).

[74] *R. v. Mitchell, ibid.* at para. 19.

[75] See in particular *General Motors Acceptance Corp. of Canada v. Isaac Estate*, [1992] A.J. No. 1083, 7 Alta. L.R. (3d) 230 (Alta. Q.B.), *per* Master Funduk.

[76] *Ibid.*

client is not silenced by this rule. The only thing the lawyer cannot do is pretend that the legal authority does not exist. This is in the end a relatively minor qualification, one that helps to ensure the coherence of the legal system.

The relevant adverse authority rule is thus justifiable as a matter of principle. It is nonetheless crucial that this obligation not be interpreted too expansively. Lawyers are not obliged to bring forward facts that the other side has omitted to bring to the court's attention. They are not obliged to make the other side's case for them. They are, simply, obliged to make sure that the court has before it all relevant legal authority, whether helpful or not.

4. ZEAL IN CONTEXT

A. Discovery

When a lawyer conducts an examination for discovery, or carries forward his client's rights and obligations under the rules of court with respect to the production of documents, his obligations as a zealous advocate are no different than they are in a court of law. Thus his obligations in conducting an examination for discovery should for the most part be identified through consideration of the rules of conduct in relation to such matters as cross-examination and preparation of witnesses, as discussed in Chapter 7.

Examinations for discovery give rise, however, to complexities that merit independent consideration. Specifically, the discovery process presents two challenges: first, the vast majority of civil litigation in Canada is resolved through or following the discovery process, and without going to trial. As a consequence, examinations for discovery are very important for establishing a client's case. Second, examinations for discovery occur under the shadow of judicial supervision, in the sense that an application to court is always theoretically available to address discovery abuse; however, that judicial supervision is indirect and often of limited effectiveness in practice. This means that discoveries include a high incentive for improper behaviour — because so much is at stake — and incorporate very few real controls over that improper behaviour at the moment it occurs.

Perhaps for this reason, some of the codes of conduct expressly note that lawyers have an obligation on examinations for discovery to explain clearly to the client the legal obligations imposed by the discovery process, and also emphasize the need for the lawyer not to abuse the discovery process through frivolous requests for information.[77] Further, in extreme cases the courts have been willing to impose cost sanctions on lawyers

---

[77] CBA MC Chapter IX, Commentary 15; LSUC RPC Rule 4.01(4). The FLS, New Brunswick and Alberta Rules have no specific provision dealing with discoveries. Presumably by "frivolous" the codes mean requests that would not fall within the terms of the applicable rules of court and jurisprudence.

personally for acting improperly in the course of examinations for discovery.[78]

Again, these rules and cases should not be understood as changing the obligations of lawyers as zealous advocates. They simply clarify that the absence of a judge does not allow the lawyer to exploit the discovery process.

A further point should be noted with respect to discoveries. Not only do discoveries provide an opportunity for the abuse of the lawyer's role, they also present a unique opportunity for the lawyer's skills as an advocate to be employed to his client's advantage. A lawyer who deals appropriately with improper conduct by opposing counsel, obtains as much relevant information as possible to further his client's cause and, finally, ensures that his client's case is not injured through the discovery process, will achieve more, most of the time, for his clients, than he will by representing clients effectively in court. Being able to navigate the discovery process in this way requires considerable skill, experience and, most of all, a great deal of preparation. Discoveries test the lawyer's ethical commitment to resolute advocacy.

B. *Ex Parte* Applications

In contrast to examinations for discovery, a lawyer's obligations when bringing an *ex parte* application do vary from those that apply in a contested proceeding. In particular, when the other party is not represented in court or chambers, the lawyer must provide full disclosure to the court not only of the relevant law, but also of the relevant facts. That this is the case is not surprising; *ex parte* orders are extraordinary remedies, and represent a marked departure from the procedural norms that inhere in our judicial process. They allow legal action to be taken against a party without that party being heard. Such a material departure from procedural norms necessarily qualifies the role of the lawyer who seeks such relief.

The modification in the lawyer's role is imposed expressly under some of the codes of conduct,[79] and has in at least one case resulted in law society discipline for the lawyer who failed to provide proper disclosure.[80] More

---

[78] *Walsh v. 1124660 Ontario Ltd.*, [2002] O.J. No. 4069, 116 A.C.W.S. (3d) 755 (Ont. S.C.J.); *MacIntyre v. Dickie*, [1996] O.J. No. 1336 (Ont. Gen. Div.). In addition, abusive discoveries have led the courts to impose restrictions that qualify the client's rights through the discovery process. In *Esso Resources Ltd. v. Stearns Catalytic Ltd.*, [1992] A.J. No. 1205, 20 Alta. L.R. (3d) 315 (Alta. Q.B.), the Court eliminated part of the answers provided by the corporate officer on the grounds that they were abusive, and said that the answers to be read into Court could be limited to the initial "yes" or "no" response that the officer had given; in *Gualtieri v. Canada (Attorney General)*, [2008] O.J. No. 698 at para. 26 (Ont. S.C.J.), the Court limited the amount of further discovery that could occur because counsel for the Crown had "taken their discovery beyond reasonable limits".

[79] CBA MC Chapter IX, Commentary 17; NB CC Chapter 8, Commentary 3(c); AB CPC Chapter 10, Rule 8. The LSUC RPC and FLS MC do not have rules on *ex parte* proceedings.

[80] See, for example, *Law Society of Alberta v. Merchant*, [2007] L.S.D.D. No. 178. See also *Law Society of Alberta v. Breitman*, [2002] L.S.D.D. No. 26 (lawyer not disciplined because

significantly, however, the obligation to provide proper disclosure in *ex parte* matters is imposed by the courts. Where an *ex parte* order is obtained without proper disclosure, the order is susceptible to being set aside with the party who obtained it being required to pay solicitor-client costs.

The duty of lawyers in this respect is set out most clearly in *United States of America v. Friedland*,[81] in which Justice Sharpe, then of the Ontario Superior Court, held that an applicant for an *ex parte* order must make full and frank disclosure:

> That party [applying for the order] is not entitled to present only its side of the case in the best possible light, as it would if the other side were present. Rather, it is incumbent on the moving party to make a balanced presentation of the facts in law. The moving party must state its own case fairly and must inform the Court of any points of fact or law known to it which favour the other side. The duty of full and frank disclosure is required to mitigate the obvious risk of injustice inherent in any situation where a Judge is asked to grant an order without hearing from the other side.[82]

Justice Sharpe went on to note that "mere imperfections" in an affidavit, or a failure to disclose "inconsequential facts", are not significant for the validity of the order granted.[83] On the facts Justice Sharpe set aside a Mareva Injunction, obtained by the United States to freeze Friedland's assets, on the basis of material non-disclosure on a wide-variety of relevant matters. He also ordered solicitor-client costs against the United States.

While, as noted, the obligation to provide proper disclosure on an *ex parte* application qualifies the lawyer's normal advocacy role, the lawyer's obligation to do so must also be understood, again, as a necessary component of his duty to protect his client's interests. A discovered failure to provide proper disclosure will, in most cases, hurt the client more than the lawyer. Thus, a lawyer providing proper advocacy for his client will ensure that

---

information not disclosed was found to be immaterial, although best practice would have resulted in its disclosure).

[81] [1996] O.J. No. 4399 (Ont. S.C.J.).
[82] *Ibid.* at para. 27.
[83] *Ibid.* at para. 31. See also: *Canadian Paraplegic Assn. (Newfoundland and Labrador) Inc. v. Sparcott Engineering Ltd.*, [1997] N.J. No. 122, 150 Nfld. & P.E.I.R. 203 (Nfld. C.A.) (order set aside and solicitor-client costs awarded); *Brunswick News Inc. v. Langdon*, [2007] N.B.J. No. 494, 2007 NBQB 424 (N.B.Q.B.) (although information should have been disclosed, counsel did not intend to mislead the Court, and the disclosure would not have changed the result; order maintained); *Encorp Pacific (Canada) v. Rocky Mountain Return Centre Ltd.*, [2005] B.C.J. No. 2634, 2005 BCSC 1700 (B.C.S.C.) (affirms existence of duty to disclose but finds that sufficient disclosure occurred); *Layden v. Canada (Minister of Human Resources and Social Development)*, [2008] F.C.J. No. 783, 2008 FC 619 (F.C.) (sets aside order granting leave to appeal because of absence of disclosure); *MTS Allstream Inc. v. Bell Mobility Inc.*, [2008] M.J. No. 137, 2008 MBQB 103 (Man. Q.B.) (Court refuses to even consider granting an interlocutory injunction on the merits in part because of the plaintiff's failure to provide full and frank disclosure when it obtained an *ex parte* injunction); *Prosser v. Prosser*, [1998] S.J. No. 875 (Sask. Q.B.) (order set aside because of failure to disclose).

sufficient disclosure is given such that the *ex parte* order will be sustainable once the other side is advised of its existence.

C. Investigating a Client's Case – Covert Investigations and Communicating with Witnesses

As noted, fulfilling his ethical obligation of zealous advocacy requires the lawyer to find out the evidence and facts necessary to establish his client's case. Doing so, however, raises secondary ethical issues, specifically in relation to communicating with witnesses and with lawyer involvement in the conduct of covert investigations. For example, in the 1960s Professor Freedman was involved in efforts on behalf of a fair housing group to enforce the District of Columbia's rules against racial discrimination in housing. The only way to make a case of discrimination was through "testers". An African-American couple would purport to be interested in buying or renting a house in a particular neighbourhood. They would claim to be married and to have two children and a particular income level. Immediately after they were told that no houses were available for sale or rent in the neighbourhood, a white couple purporting to have the same family and income would apply for a house. When the white couple was then shown two or three available houses, there would be persuasive evidence of racial discrimination. Without this investigation the case of racial discrimination would have been difficult, or perhaps impossible, to make out. Conducting the investigation therefore can be characterized as zealous advocacy, and in the circumstances seems like the type of conduct we would want lawyers to engage in within a free and democratic society. Yet it also required that Professor Freedman, through his investigators, act dishonestly, making material misrepresentations to the real estate brokers about who they were and what they were seeking. Such dishonesty and material misrepresentations, direct or indirect, violated (and would violate today) certain provisions of the codes of conduct governing American lawyers.[84]

While there is limited authority in Canada on the conduct of covert investigations, it appears likely that here, as in the United States, conducting investigations in a way that involves dishonesty or material misrepresentations by the lawyer, either directly or indirectly, is forbidden. All of the codes of conduct have prohibitions of one kind or another against lawyer dishonesty.[85] The codes of conduct do contemplate the lawyer's participation in a "test

---

[84] Monroe Freedman & Abbe Smith, *Understanding Lawyers' Ethics*, 4th ed. (New Providence, NJ: LexisNexis, 2010) at 115-16. As noted there, the legal status of these investigations is somewhat uncertain given that while provisions of the codes appear to prohibit some of what is done in the investigations, the fruits of the investigations are generally admissible in court.

[85] CBA MC Chapter I, Commentaries 4(g) and Chapter 3, Commentary 7; FLS MC Rule 1.01 and 2.02(7), commentary; LSUC RPC Rule 2.02(5); Que. CEA Rule 2.00.01 (requirement of honour and integrity); AB CPC Chapter 1, Rule 6 and Chapter 4, Commentary G2; BC PCH Chapter 2, Rule 1 (prohibition of dishonourable conduct).

case",[86] but that does not seem to permit the type of investigative activities undertaken by Freedman.

In one Canadian case, *MacMillan Bloedel Ltd. v. Freeman and Co.*,[87] lawyers went on a "public tour" of the pulp mill of MacMillan Bloedel, aspects of which were the subject matter of litigation by their client against MacMillan Bloedel. They had disclosed that they were lawyers, and appeared to the person conducting the tour to know more than one would expect an ordinary person to know about pulp mills. She therefore went to find the mill manager, who returned and spoke to the group of lawyers and answered questions. The lawyers were given a tour of the mill as well. The lawyers had not disclosed that they were acting for a party in litigation with MacMillan Bloedel. In a subsequent motion, the Court declined to remove the lawyers as solicitors for the plaintiff, holding that it was not "at all sure that a breach of ethics [had] been shown to have occurred"[88] and that, more importantly, it had not been established that there was real prejudice to the administration of justice resulting from the plaintiff's conduct. The information that was provided by the mill manager was information that would be given to any member of the public. Moreover, the manager would, if anything, have been more guarded than normal, given that he knew he was speaking with knowledgeable lawyers, and that the circumstances were somewhat unusual.

This case does suggest that lawyers may investigate. It does not, though, provide any assurance that a covert investigation would be permissible; the conduct of the lawyers in taking a public tour was not covert.[89]

Canadian lawyers may not have played, or play today, the same role as American lawyers in investigating unlawful activity. Nonetheless Canadian

---

[86] *Ibid.* and CBA MC Chapter III, Commentary 8; AB CPC Chapter 1, Rule 1.
[87] [1992] B.C.J. No. 2815, 78 B.C.L.R. (2d) 325 (B.C.S.C.).
[88] *Ibid.* at 335.
[89] See also *TransAmerica Life Insurance Co. of Canada v. Seward*, [1997] O.J. No. 2018 at para. 20, 33 O.R. (3d) 604 (Ont. Gen. Div.). In that case the Court did not find it inappropriate for a law firm to engage the forensic arm of KPMG to investigate activities by a person who was a witness in one litigation, and against whom a Statement of Claim had been filed but not served. The Court approved the opinion of the expert retained by the law firm that stated:
> The Rules of Professional Conduct and any other rule of conduct do not prohibit a lawyer from retaining an investigator on behalf of a client to interview a person who is either a witness in pending litigation in which this witness is not also a party or a potential defendant in possible future litigation that is in contemplation at the time of the interview.

In that case, though, there was no misrepresentation or deception in the interview, except insofar as it was videotaped without the person's consent and that had not been requested or authorized by the law firm. Also of interest is *Law Society of British Columbia v. Christie*, [2007] L.S.D.D. No. 68. In that case the lawyer was found guilty of professional misconduct for providing a fake court document in order to obtain production of documents. This conduct is, I think, properly prohibited by the rules, and I would not suggest that it be permissible under any amendment such as that proposed. The conduct of Christie was not so much investigative, as an attempt to avoid the judicial process that clearly applies to (and permits) the production of documentary evidence from parties to litigation.

regulators should consider following a course similar to that of the Oregon bar, which has amended its disciplinary rules to allow for covert investigations in limited circumstances. Oregon's rule, 8.4(b), permits lawyers "to advise clients or others about or to supervise lawful covert activity in the investigation of violations of civil or criminal law or constitutional rights".[90] It defines "covert activity" as "an effort to obtain information on unlawful activity through the use of misrepresentations or other subterfuge".[91] It limits that freedom, however, by requiring that the lawyer's conduct be "otherwise in compliance" with the rules of professional conduct and by requiring that the lawyer have a good faith belief that there is a reasonable possibility that unlawful activity has taken place or will take place in the foreseeable future.[92]

If undertaking such an amendment to the Canadian rules, it must be made clear that government lawyers do not have the ability to undertake covert investigations of this type other than through the usual legal channels available to government to engage in investigation of the citizenry. The type of "private investigation" undertaken by, for example, the Alberta energy regulator of interveners in a transmission line hearing, in which private investigators not only observed interveners but also participated in conference calls involving interveners and their legal counsel, was a significant violation of the norms of procedural fairness, and was only made worse to the extent it additionally involved lawyers for the Board.[93] In addition, to the extent legal mechanisms for investigation are available to counsel — such as an Anton Piller injunction — that mechanism should be employed rather than more covert means of discovering unlawful activity.[94]

Another issue for lawyers investigating a client's case is with respect to dealing with potential witnesses, whether represented or unrepresented. The various codes of conduct provide useful guidance to lawyers in this respect. In general, lawyers may seek information from any potential witness and, consistent with the obligation of zealous advocacy, should do so where the witness has information material to the proceeding.[95] The limits imposed on a lawyer speaking to a potential witness are that the lawyer may not do so

---

[90] Online: <http://www.osbar.org/_docs/rulesregs/orpc.pdf>.
[91] Ibid.
[92] Ibid.
[93] See, for example, Alice Woolley, "Enemies of the State? – The Alberta Energy and Utilities Board, Landowners, Spies, a 500 kV Transmission Line and Why Procedure Matters" (2008) 26(2) Journal of Energy and Natural Resources Law 234.
[94] For a case involving government investigations see also: *Ms. R. v. W.A.*, [2002] A.J. No. 250, 2002 ABQB 201 (Alta. Q.B.). R. and J. had been victims of sexual abuse by their parents (the parents were criminally convicted) and had commenced litigation against the Crown. In defending that litigation, the Crown hired private investigators to conduct surveillance of J. and to make various inquiries. The Court held that provided that J. filed a Statement of Claim with respect to the surveillance, it would be prepared to grant an injunction prohibiting the surveillance. The Court noted that surveillance may be acceptable in litigation, but that it could be enjoined where the plaintiff might suffer severe psychological harm as a consequence.
[95] CBA MC Chapter IX, Commentary 6; FLS MC Rule 4.03; LSUC RPC Rule 4.03(1); NB CC Chapter 8, Commentary 4; AB CPC Chapter 10, Rule 22; BC PCH Chapter 8, Rule 12.

where the witness is represented by counsel on the matter in question (unless the lawyer has obtained that counsel's consent);[96] the lawyer must disclose his interest to the potential witness; and the lawyer must not "subvert or suppress" the witness's evidence or try to prevent the witness from speaking to other people.[97]

Further, some of the codes provide that a lawyer may not speak to certain individuals within a corporation or organization where that corporation or organization is represented in the matter in question. In particular, the lawyer may not approach "a director, officer, or person likely involved in the decision-making process" with respect to the corporation or organization and, as well, may not approach an employee or agent "whose acts or omissions in connection with the matter may have exposed [the organization] to civil or criminal liability".[98] Courts have been clear that this rule prevents a party from speaking to current decision-makers in a corporation or organization; it does not, however, restrict contact with former employees,[99] even if those former employees were involved in decisions relevant to the litigation.[100] Former employees may not, however, be encouraged to violate their confidentiality obligations to the former employer.[101]

Having acknowledged these guidelines, which primarily relate to obligations of honesty and transparency, the lawyer's obligation to investigate the client's case remains of crucial importance in fulfilling her overarching duty of zealous advocacy on the client's behalf.

5. LAWYER SPEECH

A. Introduction

In the course of representing clients, lawyers from time to time make public statements with respect to cases on which they are acting, with respect to other lawyers, or with respect to judges and the justice system. Indeed, the lawyer's duty of zealous advocacy may require him to make such statements. Where his client is being convicted in the court of public opinion, such that

---

[96] CBA MC Chapter IX, Commentary 6; FLS MC Rule 6.02(6); LSUC RPC Rule 4.03(2); Que. CEA Rule 3.02.01(h); NB CC Chapter 8, Commentary 4(c); AB CPC Chapter 4, Rule 6; BC PCH Chapter 8, Rule 12.1.

[97] CBA MC Chapter IX, Commentary 6; FLS MC Rule 4.03; LSUC RPC Rule 4.03(1); Que. CEA Rule 3.02.01(f); NB CC Chapter 8, Commentary 4(b); AB CPC Chapter 10, Rule 22; BC PCH Chapter 8, Rules 12.2, 12.3 and 13.

[98] CBA MC Chapter IX, Commentary 6; FLS MC Rule 6.02(8); LSUC RPC Rule 4.03(3).

[99] *Robb Estate v. St. Joseph's Health Care Centre*, [1999] O.J. No. 734, 33 C.P.C. (4th) 147 (Ont. C.J.); *Heart (Town) v. School Board Ontario North East*, [2000] O.J. No. 3419, 99 A.C.W.S. (3d) 780 (Ont. S.C.J.).

[100] *Murphy Canada Exploration Ltd. v. Novagas Canada Ltd.*, [2009] A.J. No. 1102, 2009 ABQB 585 (Alta. Q.B.); *Cooking Lake Enterprises Inc. v. Samson First Nation*, [2000] A.J. No. 61, 2000 ABQB 32 (Alta. Q.B.); *Bowman v. Rainy River (Town)*, [2007] O.J. No. 1235, 156 A.C.W.S. (3d) 563 (Ont. S.C.J.); *CIBC Mellon Co. v. National Trust Co.*, [2000] O.J. No. 3480, 99 A.C.W.S. (3d) 863 (Ont. S.C.J.).

[101] *CIBC Mellon Co., ibid.*

the client's legal and other interests are being adversely affected, a lawyer has an obligation to make whatever statements are necessary to prevent or minimize that harm. Those comments may include, where appropriate, comments that point out issues with the conduct of other lawyers, or criticisms of judges or the justice system.

Courts and regulators have, however, a conflicted relationship with this aspect of the lawyer's role. While on the one hand regulators and courts recognize that lawyers have a duty to make public statements where necessary to protect their clients' interests, to bring forward misconduct by other lawyers, and to appropriately criticize the legal system where it fails to live up to its aspirations, there is also a strong feeling that lawyer statements should take a certain form, should meet a standard of "civility", failing which the lawyer making the statement is properly subject to professional discipline.

This section will set out the rules governing lawyer speech, and in particular the rules governing lawyers' statements about cases, statements about other lawyers, and statements about judges and the justice system. I will argue that some aspects of that regulatory structure have not paid sufficient attention to the paramount importance of the lawyer's role as resolute advocate.

B. Public Statements

Lawyers may make public statements about cases that are in the best interests of their clients[102] and, in some circumstances, may be required to make comments in order to effectively represent those clients.[103] A lawyer's comments must respect his client's confidentiality and must also fall within the scope of the retainer.[104] Prejudicial statements about the client that violate the terms of the retainer may be the basis for litigation against the lawyer.[105]

A lawyer's obligation to ensure that public statements are in his client's interests with respect to the subject matter of the retainer may carry on after the retainer ends. In *Stewart v. Canadian Broadcasting Corp.*,[106] discussed further in Chapter 8, a lawyer was found liable to his former client for making media statements which promoted the lawyer at the expense of the benefits his former representation was intended to obtain for the client. Edward Greenspan had represented Robert Stewart in the sentencing portion of his criminal trial and had, in the course of sentencing, attempted to lessen

---

[102] CBA MC Chapter XVIII, Commentary 1; FLS MC Rule 6.05; LSUC RPC Rule 6.06; NB CC Chapter 18, Commentary 2; AB CPC Chapter 5, Rule 8; BC PCH Chapter 8, Rule 23.
[103] CBA MC Chapter XVIII, Commentaries 11 and 12; FLS MC Rule 6.05, commentary; LSUC RPC Rule 6.06, commentary.
[104] CBA MC Chapter XVIII, Commentary 1.
[105] *Stewart v. Canadian Broadcasting Corp.*, [1997] O.J. No. 2271, 150 D.L.R. (4th) 24 (Ont. Gen. Div.).
[106] *Ibid.*

the public opprobrium experienced by Stewart because of the nature of the crime and because of the conduct of the defence in the guilt phase of the criminal trial. Some years later Greenspan produced an episode of the television show "Scales of Justice" which misrepresented aspects of Stewart's behaviour and had the potential to increase the public opprobrium that Greenspan had previously been retained to reduce. The Court held that Greenspan's participation in the episode was unnecessary, and was done to promote Greenspan's status as a lawyer, without regard for the negative impact on his former client. The Court thus held Greenspan to be liable for damages, albeit in a modest amount.

Two other restrictions on public statements by the lawyer are, first, that such statements are regulated by ordinary common law principles such as the tort of defamation[107] and, second, that they may not prejudice the legal proceedings in relation to which they are made. This latter restriction arises from the *sub judice* aspect of a court's contempt power, which permits a court to find a person in contempt where he makes a statement which creates, and was intended to create, a real risk of prejudice to the administration of justice and, in particular, with respect to prejudgment by the finder of fact.[108] The *sub judice* rule is codified in various forms in the codes of conduct. The New Brunswick Code prohibits a lawyer from making any statement that "may interfere with a fair trial or disposition";[109] the Alberta Code directs the lawyer to be aware of the *sub judice* rule;[110] and the British Columbia Code directs the lawyer not to comment publicly on the "validity, worth or probable outcome of a legal proceeding in which the lawyer acts".[111] Other codes simply reference the lawyer's general obligation not to interfere with the administration of justice.[112]

Some of the qualifications imposed by the codes on lawyers to ensure compliance with the *sub judice* rule seem unduly broad. The *sub judice* rule itself has very narrow application — there must be a real risk of prejudice to the administration of justice from the statement, not simply a possibility of such prejudice. By contrast, the rule in British Columbia, which prevents a lawyer from commenting on the validity or outcome of a legal proceeding, seems to prohibit almost all public comment on a proceeding, even if helpful for a client's case or interests. The New Brunswick Code adopts the low standard of "may interfere", which is, again, significantly more restrictive than the *sub judice* requirement of real prejudice. Given the lawyer's duty of zealous advocacy, and the recognized need in some instances for a lawyer to make a public statement to further the client's objectives, I think the

---

[107] See, *e.g.*, *Hill v. Church of Scientology*, [1995] S.C.J. No. 64, [1995] 2 S.C.R. 1130 (S.C.C.).
[108] See, generally, *Attorney General v. Times Newspapers Ltd.*, [1973] 3 All E.R. 54 (H.L.); *Rogacki v. Belz et al.*, [2003] O.J. No. 3809, 67 O.R. (3d) 330 (Ont. C.A.).
[109] NB CC Chapter 18, Commentary 8.
[110] AB CPC Chapter 5, Rule 8, Commentary 8.
[111] BC PCH Chapter 8, Rule 23.
[112] CBA MC Chapter XVIII, Commentary 4; FLS MC Rule 6.05; LSUC RPC Rule 6.06; Que. CEA Rule 2.01.01.

provisions of the code of conduct require narrow interpretation. A lawyer's paramount duty is to the interests of the client and, subject to the *sub judice* rule, that duty should direct his decision about what comments to make to the public.

It should be noted, however, that in at least one case a Law Society was prepared to take a stringent view of the restrictions on public statements made by a lawyer with respect to ongoing proceedings. In *Law Society of Northwest Territories v. Crawford*,[113] Crawford was found guilty of professional misconduct for a statement she had made to the media. Specifically, in defending a municipal councillor, Hellwig, from a legal claim made by another municipal councillor, Harper, Crawford said to the media: "In my opinion Mr. Harper's legal actions give most ordinary people the impression that he's trying to use the courts to intimidate the process of municipal government and control freedom of expression for elected representatives."[114] The Law Society of the Northwest Territories said that since these comments addressed the merits of the proceedings, they *prima facie* violated the lawyer's professional obligations. They found that they were not in the best interests of the client, the public or the profession, and that they reflected a lack of professional objectivity.[115]

In my view this case was wrongly decided. The Law Society imposed too rigid a standard on the speech of a lawyer, and on the tools that should sometimes be used to further a client's interests. The Law Society gave no meaningful consideration to the importance of Crawford's role as an advocate for her client. There was nothing in the statement that would undermine the judicial proceedings — what she said was qualified in a number of ways by such terms as "in my opinion" and "give most ordinary people the impression" — and the statement may have been important to the client's interests given the public and political nature of the dispute in question.

This case may give lawyers some reason to be cautious. On the other hand, it is also a single decision by a territorial Law Society. Ultimately, as noted in the codes of conduct, the lawyer's duty of resolute advocacy may require the lawyer to make public statements to advance his client's cause; that principle should guide his conduct.

C. Criticism of Other Lawyers

Earlier in this chapter I discussed the case of *Goldberg v. Law Society of British Columbia*, and the problem that arose from Goldberg's incompetent representation of his clients. As I noted there, however, the more significant concern from the point of view of the Law Society was with Goldberg's comments about Banks, the lawyer who had previously represented Goldberg's

---

[113] [2000] L.S.D.D. No. 3.
[114] *Ibid.* at para. 111.
[115] *Ibid.* at para. 113.

clients. Goldberg had, *inter alia*, accused Banks of drug and alcohol abuse, psychological problems, and dishonesty.[116] The Law Society found that these allegations were "unfounded"[117] and merited sanction.

In so holding the Law Society acted consistently with other disciplinary decisions, and also with the codes of conduct, which provide that public statements about misconduct by other lawyers may only be made if they are supported by factual evidence. The codes of conduct impose an obligation on lawyers to report other lawyers' serious misconduct,[118] and allow a lawyer to give a second opinion on advice that another lawyer has provided, but nonetheless prohibit one lawyer from making comments about another lawyer that are "ill-considered or uninformed".[119] The obligation is on the lawyer making the statement to demonstrate that it was well founded.[120] In addition, and more generally, codes of conduct impose duties of civility on counsel, requiring that the lawyer "at all times be courteous, civil, and act in good faith ... to all persons with whom the lawyer has dealings in the course of an action or proceeding".[121]

In disciplinary cases lawyers have been sanctioned for, *inter alia*, saying that a lawyer with whom the sanctioned lawyer used to have a personal relationship was "dangerous and out of control" and a "few bricks short of a load";[122] for writing a letter to another lawyer asking that lawyer not to write "rambling letters" and additionally accusing another lawyer of "fraud" with respect to her statements about settlement negotiations;[123] writing a letter to legal aid describing another lawyer as "biased, incompetent and a liar";[124] calling a lawyer "clueless";[125] making anti-Semitic comments about another lawyer;[126] and calling another lawyer "stupid" and telling her to "fuck off".[127]

The behaviour of these lawyers is not commendable. It does not appear to have advanced the interests of their clients in an obvious way, and it

---

[116] *Law Society of British Columbia v. Goldberg*, [2007] L.S.D.D. No. 162 at paras. 37-47.
[117] *Ibid.* at para. 48.
[118] Note that it is in general only serious misconduct that is to be reported. CBA MC Chapter XV, Commentary 1; FLS MC Rule 6.01(3) and commentary; LSUC RPC Rule 6.01(3) and commentary; Que. CEA 4.03.00.01 ("a derogatory act"); NB CC Chapter 5, Commentary 6; AB CPC Chapter 3, Rule 4; BC PCH Chapter 13, Rule 1.
[119] CBA MC Chapter XVI, Commentary 9; FLS MC Rule 6.02(3); LSUC RPC Rule 6.03(1), commentary; NB CC Chapter 5(a); AB CPC Chapter 4, Rule 2; BC PCH Chapter 11, Rule 13.
[120] *Law Society of British Columbia v. Goldberg*, [2007] L.S.D.D. No. 162 at paras. 37-47.
[121] CBA MC Chapter IX, Commentary 16; FLS MC Rule 4.01(5); LSUC RPC Rule 4.01(6); Que. CEA Rule 2.00.01; NB CC Chapter 3, Commentary 1; AB CPC Chapter 4, Commentary G2; BC PCH Canon 4(1).
[122] *Nova Scotia Barristers' Society v. Murrant*, [1995] L.S.D.D. No. 257.
[123] *Law Society of Upper Canada v. Kay*, [2006] L.S.D.D. No. 39 and [2006] L.S.D.D. No. 112.
[124] *Law Society of Upper Canada v. Carter*, [2005] L.S.D.D. No. 57.
[125] *Law Society of Alberta v. Pozniak*, [2002] L.S.D.D. No. 55.
[126] *Law Society of Upper Canada v. Paletta*, [1996] L.S.D.D. No. 99. Paletta's comments were a concern to the Law Society in significant part because they were viewed as discriminatory. That makes Paletta subject to discipline on *that* basis, but not because he was critical of the lawyer *per se*.
[127] *Law Society of Upper Canada v. Tulk*, [2009] L.S.D.D. No. 107.

certainly was not courteous. The question, though, is not whether the behaviour of the lawyers was commendable or courteous.[128] Nor is it whether these are lawyers with whom one would enjoy practicing or going out for a cup of coffee. And, most significantly, nor is it whether these lawyers could appropriately be shunned by their peers or subject to other informal social sanctions. The question is whether the behaviour was conduct worthy of sanction by the law society exercising its legislative authority. Answering "yes" to that question requires identifying the public interest that is served by sanctioning lawyers who make comments that are rude and unsubstantiated and, as well, requires ensuring that the benefit obtained by sanctioning lawyers in this way is not outweighed by any potential downside.[129]

Before answering the question of whether this was properly considered to be conduct worthy of sanction, a few additional points must be noted. First, in the majority of cases the comments made by the lawyer were not made to a broad audience. In one case the comments were made to another lawyer.[130] In three cases the comments were made only to the lawyer being criticized.[131] In one case the comment was made to a former client now represented by the new lawyer.[132]

Second, in at least some of the cases the problem with the comments was not with what the lawyer said, but rather with the manner of expression. Thus, the lawyer who was described as "clueless" had improperly imposed a trust condition in a real estate transaction that resulted in the transaction not closing in a timely fashion, and in the other side paying additional costs.[133] That lawyer could, I would argue, have been accurately described as "in error" or "mistaken" or, even, "ignorant of the law" without attracting regulatory sanction. Similarly, the lawyer who was described as "stupid" had not noted pleadings as closed when she could have. Again, that lawyer could have been accurately described as "in error" or as "not advancing the proceedings appropriately" without sanction.[134] And, while this is not clear from the facts, the lawyer who was described as "rambling" may perhaps have been accurately described as "failing to be concise" and the lawyer who was described as "fraudulent" may perhaps have been accurately described as "not providing entirely accurate information with respect to the

---

[128] It is the question insofar as the rules require courtesy; it is not at issue in the sense that it is the view of uncourteous behaviour as being conduct worthy of sanction that must be justified.
[129] For a general discussion of the civility movement see: Monroe Freedman, "Civility Runs Amok" (1995) 13 *Legal Times* 54; Alice Woolley, "Does Civility Matter?" (2008) 46(1) Osgoode Hall L.J. 175.
[130] *Nova Scotia Barristers' Society v. Murrant*, [1995] L.S.D.D. No. 257.
[131] *Law Society of Upper Canada v. Kay*, [2006] L.S.D.D. No. 39 and [2006] L.S.D.D. No. 112; *Law Society of Alberta v. Pozniak*, [2002] L.S.D.D. No. 55; *Law Society of Upper Canada v. Tulk*, [2009] L.S.D.D. No. 107 (although in *Tulk* the comments were made in a public place).
[132] *Law Society of Upper Canada v. Paletta*, [1996] L.S.D.D No. 99.
[133] *Law Society of Alberta v. Pozniak*, [2002] L.S.D.D. No. 55.
[134] *Law Society of Upper Canada v. Tulk*, [2009] L.S.D.D. No. 107.

state of settlement negotiations".[135] The point being, the lawyers in each of these cases may have been disciplined not so much for what they said, but for how they said it.

Third, with the exception of *Goldberg*, the comments made by the lawyer were made outside of the courtroom, such that the civil remedy of an action in defamation was potentially available to the lawyer about whom the comment was made. Lawyers who have been criticized unjustly by other lawyers have successfully used the law of defamation as a remedy.[136]

What these qualifications mean is that the justification offered for disciplining lawyers for criticizing other lawyers must explain why that discipline can justifiably be extended to comments that (a) are not widely reported, (b) may be substantially accurate and (c) could be dealt with under the law of defamation. In my view no such justification can be offered. The most coherent reason for regulation of lawyer criticism of other lawyers is that civility between lawyers enhances public respect for the legal profession:[137]

> Civility between counsel is not a trivial matter. Indeed it goes to the heart of professionalism and is essential to maintain the general reputation and integrity of the legal profession. Lawyers, on behalf of clients, must face adversity on a daily basis but this does not justify a descent into incivility. Indeed, quite the contrary. Professionals are expected to act professionally and must do so or they compromise the interests of not only their clients but society at large. Launching or exchanging insults is not professional behaviour.[138]

This justification for regulating civility to protect the profession's reputation, while coherent, seems hard to maintain. It is not at all clear that people distrust lawyers because lawyers are rude. The reputation of lawyers is complicated as well as troubled, and relates mostly neither to the conduct of specific lawyers, nor to specific abuses or misconduct, but simply to the fact that lawyers are lawyers. People dislike and distrust lawyers because lawyers advocate for clients, fight against state power and assert procedural claims in defeat of substantive rights.

Yet at the same time, lawyers are understood to play a valuable role in society, and to do good, because they advocate for clients, fight against state power and help people operate through the tangled thicket of legal procedure:

> People dislike us because we are guns for hire who manipulate the legal system, but they like us because we fight for our clients, protect their rights, and cut through bureaucratic red tape. When we fight zealously for our client, file lawsuits and cut through red tape we do good, but when fight zealously for our client, file lawsuits and manipulate the

---
[135] *Law Society of Upper Canada v. Kay*, [2006] L.S.D.D. No. 39 and [2006] L.S.D.D. No. 112.
[136] *Hill v. Church of Scientology*, [1995] S.C.J. No. 64, [1995] 2 S.C.R. 1130 (S.C.C.).
[137] This discussion draws from Alice Woolley, "Ethics as Regulation: A Comment on *Merchant v. Law Society of Saskatchewan*" (2009) 72 Sask. L. Rev. 279.
[138] *Law Society of Alberta v. Pozniak*, [2002] L.S.D.D. No. 55 at para. 17.

legal system, we do bad. We receive accolades and denunciations for doing the same thing.[139]

This means that, in general, attempts to foster the profession's reputation through sanctioning incivility are unlikely to meet with success. To the contrary emphasizing norms of civility between counsel may do as much harm as good — it may be seen as inhibiting the things which lawyers do that are valued.

Further, sanctioning lawyers for rudeness to other lawyers brings with it a very real downside. This is for two reasons. First, given that the profession is self-regulating, the major source of information about misconduct by lawyers is other lawyers; if law societies discipline lawyers every time an allegation against another lawyer is not well founded, or is poorly expressed, they create a major disincentive for reporting the misconduct of other lawyers, or of taking action to redress problems raised by the conduct of other lawyers. Consider again the *Goldberg* case. Will another lawyer, when faced with a case of a criminal accused whose lawyer had been in trouble with the law society at the time of the representation, not at least consider whether taking on the case might not be more trouble than it is worth? The *Goldberg* precedent tells him any claim he makes about the lawyer must be one that he can prove to be well founded or else he can be disciplined by the law society; this is a serious disincentive to taking the case, especially given that establishing detailed information about what the other lawyer has done may be difficult.

Second, the job of an advocate requires saying things that other people might find uncomfortable, and that some might find to be uncivil or rude. The difference between "ignorant" and "clueless" is, to a significant extent, in the eye of the beholder. A person could reasonably find the over the top and even light hearted use of "clueless" less offensive than the entirely serious "ignorant". Given the clear and paramount obligation of the lawyer to be a zealous advocate, there is a real risk that disciplining lawyers for not phrasing their criticisms of other lawyers appropriately will inhibit lawyers from fulfilling their most foundational ethical duty.

In general, lawyers should not be sanctioned when comments that are alleged to be uncivil about another lawyer are made in the context of representation of clients. It may be for this reason that on two occasions the Ontario Court of Appeal, while deploring the lack of civility of counsel in litigation, has declined to find any relationship between counsel's incivility and the fairness of the trial process. In both *R. v. Felderhof*[140] and *Marchand v. Public General Hospital Society of Chatham*[141] the Court declined

---

[139] Ronald D. Rotunda, "The Legal Profession and the Public Image of Lawyers" (1999) 23 J. Legal Prof. 51 at 61. For a discussion of the complex nature of lawyers' professional reputation see W. Bradley Wendel, "How I Learned to Stop Worrying and Love Lawyer-Bashing: Some Post-Conference Reflections" (2003) 54 S.C. Law Rev. 1027 at 1033-41.
[140] [2003] O.J. No. 4819, 235 D.L.R. (4th) 131 (Ont. C.A.).
[141] [2000] O.J. No. 4428, 51 O.R. (3d) 97 (Ont. C.A.).

counsel's request for relief due to a trial judge's alleged failure to control the incivility of opposing counsel.

There are some circumstances in which comments about another lawyer could properly lead to professional discipline. Where the comments violate other ethical obligations of the lawyer (such as the rules against discrimination, for example) discipline may be appropriate. In such cases, though, the real source of the discipline should be explained.

Lawyers may also run the risk of an action in defamation or, in some cases, of application of the court's *sub judice* contempt power. I am not arguing against the application of those legal remedies, both of which are attached to findings of real injury arising from the lawyer's statement. It could perhaps be argued further that some narrow scope for professional discipline for unfounded criticism of other lawyers exists where the doctrine of qualified privilege precludes an action in defamation. This seems conceptually problematic, though, given that the whole idea of a privilege is to protect the speaker from adverse legal consequences arising from the speech; applying professional discipline would undermine the point of having the privilege in the first place.[142]

Under the current regulatory regime lawyers are required to exercise some caution in criticizing other counsel. It is to be hoped, however, that lawyers do not let the actions of the law societies in this respect dampen their zeal for their clients, and that law societies become more cognizant of the serious problems that are raised by this type of regulatory action.

D. Criticizing Judges and the Legal System

Law societies and courts seem somewhat more hesitant to discipline or otherwise sanction lawyers for being critical of judges or the legal process, perhaps because the relationship between zealous advocacy and lawyer criticism of the legal system is more apparent than is the relationship between that advocacy and criticism of other lawyers.

The codes of conduct note that in general legal decisions are subject to public scrutiny and analysis by anyone, including lawyers, and that lawyers have a duty to seek to improve the administration of justice. Since, however, judges have only a limited ability to defend themselves, lawyers are directed to avoid criticism that "is petty, intemperate or unsupported by a *bona fide* belief in its real merit". In addition, lawyers are directed to avoid criticism in cases in which they were involved, where that criticism could be perceived

---

[142] Although note that in *Goldberg v. Law Society of British Columbia*, [2009] B.C.J. No. 657 at paras. 50-52, 2009 BCCA 147 (B.C.C.A.), the Court of Appeal expressly rejected the argument that the law of privilege shielded Goldberg from professional discipline. The Court said that the doctrine of privilege was a shield for the legal consequences of what an advocate might say, but that it could not shield an advocate from discipline in respect of how a court proceeding was brought forward. This seems reasonable with respect to disciplining Goldberg for incompetence; however, when the discipline itself is directed at what was *said*, not at what was *done*, the distinction becomes awfully fine.

as partisan rather than objective, and are directed to defend the judiciary from unwarranted criticism by others.[143]

Comments made by lawyers that have been found to violate these rules include describing a judge as a "bigot" in a letter to opposing counsel[144] and comments that judges are too political, have "ties to the Conservative Party" and that such political ties prevent judges from being "tree shakers".[145] In the latter case, *Nova Scotia Barristers' Society v. Morgan*,[146] the law society declined to discipline the lawyer because the comments were made in his capacity as a mayor, not as a lawyer.[147]

In approving the exercise of disciplinary authority by the Law Society of Manitoba in *Histed v. Law Society of Manitoba*[148] — the "bigot" case — the Manitoba Court of Appeal also expressed some caution about disciplining lawyers for this type of conduct. It noted that "lawyers must have the right to speak truth to power",[149] and that the "judiciary should be open to criticism".[150] It went on, however, to hold that the

> legal system must operate with some degree of civility and respect. Criticism must be within certain parameters. Lawyers are required by the *Code* to avoid the use of abusive or offensive statements, irresponsible allegations of partiality, criticisms that are petty or intemperate and communications that are abusive, offensive or inconsistent with the proper tone of professional communication.[151]

Any unfettered right to criticize the judiciary was lost through membership in the law society;[152] moreover, if the lawyer had reason to believe that the judge was, in fact, bigoted, then that should have been brought to the attention of the Judicial Council.[153]

Other disciplinary decisions have shown greater reluctance to sanction lawyers for this type of conduct.[154] As noted, in *Morgan* the Nova Scotia

---

[143] CBA MC Chapter XIII, Commentary 4; FLS MC Rule 4.06(1) and commentary; LSUC RPC Rule 4.06 and commentary; Que. CEA Rule 2.08; NB CC Chapter 20, Commentary 4; AB CPC Chapter 1, Rule 2 and commentary; BC PCH Canon 2.
[144] *Histed v. Law Society of Manitoba*, [2007] M.J. No. 460, 2007 MBCA 150 (Man. C.A.).
[145] *Nova Scotia Barristers' Society v. Morgan* (2010) NSBS 1 (CanLII), Complaint, paragraph 1(iii) and 1(v).
[146] *Ibid.*
[147] The Nova Scotia Barristers' Society did not clearly explain the basis for this distinction, which seems *prima facie* inconsistent with the general principle that lawyers can be disciplined for personal as well as professional misconduct. It may be that, as personal misconduct, the behaviour did not warrant discipline, but the NSBS simply does not explain its decision in this respect.
[148] [2007] M.J. No. 460, 2007 MBCA 150 (Man. C.A.).
[149] *Ibid.* at para. 71.
[150] *Ibid.* at para. 75.
[151] *Ibid.*
[152] *Ibid.* at para. 79.
[153] *Ibid.* at para. 77.
[154] There are also cases in which lawyers have been sanctioned for criticism of the judiciary, but the criticism was in the context either of broader professional misconduct, psychiatric instability or both. For example: *Law Society of Upper Canada v. Coady*, [2009] L.S.D.D. No. 61;

Barristers' Society drew a clear line between comments that were squarely within the lawyer's work as a lawyer and those that were not.[155]

In *Law Society of Alberta v. Engel*,[156] the disciplinary panel declined to sanction a lawyer who criticized an investigation into police misconduct as "purposefully flawed". The panel noted that the comments of the lawyer were well informed, that it had not been demonstrated that the comments by the lawyer were untrue, that the lawyer had an honest belief in the truth of the comments and that, in any event, the comments were neither "extreme or inflammatory" nor "abusive or offensive or unprofessional".[157]

Similarly, in *Law Society of Yukon v. Kimmerly*[158] the Law Society declined to discipline the lawyer acting as Minister of Justice who said that a judge had been "silly" and had brought the judiciary and courts into "disrespect" when the judge had placed a coat over the Territory's coat of arms that had been hung by the government in the courtroom. The Law Society said that

> It is the task of this Committee to balance the competing priorities; on the one hand the member's obligation to so conduct himself as to not harm the standing of the legal profession generally or bring the administration of justice into disrepute and on the other his freedom to make fair and reasonable comment in the exercise of his right to speak out.[159]

In that context the Committee found that the comments were not conduct deserving of censure.

Traditionally courts have also had the power to discipline lawyers for inappropriate comments about judges and the legal system through the contempt offence of "scandalizing the court". In the leading decision of *R. v. Kopyto*,[160] however, the Ontario Court of Appeal held that that offence as then understood was unconstitutional. Kopyto had been convicted of scandalizing the court for saying a judgment was "a mockery of justice. It stinks to high hell. It says it is okay to break the law and you are immune so long as someone above you said to do it."[161] He had also said that there was no useful recourse to "this charade of the courts in this country which are warped in favour of protecting the police".[162] While Justice Cory described these comments as

---

Kessiloff v. Law Society of Manitoba, [1919] S.C.J. No. 35, [1919] 3 W.W.R. 150 (S.C.C.); *Law Society of British Columbia v. Eisbrenner*, [2003] L.S.D.D. No. 61.
[155] *Nova Scotia Barristers' Society v. Morgan* (2010) NSBS 1 (CanLII).
[156] [2008] L.S.D.D. No. 173.
[157] *Ibid.* at para. 71.
[158] [1988] L.S.D.D. No. 1. Note that in that case the lawyer was, like Morgan, arguably not acting in his capacity as a "lawyer". That aspect of the situation was not commented on by the panel.
[159] *Ibid.* at 5.
[160] [1987] O.J. No. 1052, 62 O.R. (2d) 449 (Ont. C.A.).
[161] *Ibid.* at para. 7.
[162] *Ibid.*

... in the poorest possible taste. It was no more than the whining of an unhappy loser. It was unreasonable, unprofessional and unworthy of even the most marginal and most recent member of the profession. It was, in a word, disgraceful.[163]

he nonetheless vacated Kopyto's conviction for having made them. Cory held that courts are properly subject to "comment and criticism" and are not "fragile flowers that will wither in the hot heat of controversy".[164] As a consequence, the only sort of conviction for contempt that could be upheld would be of the nature of *sub judice* — that is, statements which "demonstrate a clear and present danger to the administration of justice"[165] in an ongoing proceeding. Houlden J.A. would have gone further and eliminated entirely the idea of an offence of scandalizing the court, while Dubin J.A. would have narrowed the offence, found Kopyto not guilty of it, and maintained its constitutionality.

Subsequent to *Kopyto* a lawyer has been convicted of contempt for statements in court; however, the case had the rather extraordinary facts of the lawyer urging those in attendance at court to attack a sheriff arresting the lawyer's client, while at the same time the lawyer shouted out allegations of misdeeds and corruption about the judge.[166] The lawyer was found to have been suffering from a mental disorder at the time.

The conservative approach taken in most of the cases in this area should be followed in all cases in which a lawyer has criticized the judge or legal system. Unless a lawyer has created a real risk of prejudice to the administration of justice in an ongoing proceeding, contempt and disciplinary proceedings against that lawyer are inappropriate. On this basis I would argue that *Histed*[167] was wrongly decided. Describing a judge as a bigot in private correspondence may well be in the "poorest possible taste". However, it may also be understood as a short hand way of explaining the nature of the lawyer's concern with the selection of a particular judge to handle a racially sensitive civil proceeding. Since the comments were made only to another lawyer, it is difficult to see what prejudice to the administration of justice could arise from them being made; without such a risk of prejudice, discipline for making the statements is overbroad and, again, creates the risk of inappropriately suppressing the lawyer's zealous advocacy.

6. CONCLUSION

Zealous advocacy requires that lawyers provide competent and effective representation of a client's legal interests, knowing the law and how to apply

---

[163] *Ibid.* at para. 21.
[164] *Ibid.* at para. 33.
[165] *Ibid.* at para. 85.
[166] *R. v. Cram*, [1994] B.C.J. No. 2258, 99 B.C.L.R. (2d) 127 (B.C.S.C.).
[167] *Histed v. Law Society of Manitoba*, [2007] M.J. No. 460, 2007 MBCA 150 (Man. C.A.).

it, investigating the client's case and employing their skills to obtain the best possible outcome in each case. Fulfilling that ethical duty challenges the lawyer's skills and intellect. It also requires nuanced understanding of the way advocacy operates in particular contexts, such as examinations for discovery, and of the constraints on zeal that arise from time to time, such as in *ex parte* applications or with respect to the provision of relevant adverse authority. The pervasive ethic of advocacy also poses challenges to regulators faced with lawyers who have a poor grasp of good manners and whose behaviour makes the life of everyone in the legal profession more unpleasant than it needs to be. In the end, though, the paramount importance of the lawyer's duty to his client remains clear, and the lawyer's constant orientation should be towards ensuring that duty is fulfilled.

Chapter 5

LAWYER-CLIENT TRUST AND CONFIDENCE

1. INTRODUCTION

Under Canadian law clients enjoy a "right to confidentiality" when they speak to their lawyers.[1] It is a "personal and extra-patrimonial"[2] substantive right of the client that places Canadian lawyers under a near absolute[3] obligation to keep their clients' secrets.

The significance of the lawyer's obligation of trust and confidence under Canadian law is only matched by its complexity. The lawyer's duty of trust and confidence has dual foundations; it is based in the common law, finding expression there in the doctrine of solicitor-client privilege, but is also based in the lawyer's independent ethical duty of confidentiality.

The common law privilege and the lawyer's ethical duty of confidentiality grew up together. The lawyer's ethical duty arises from the doctrine of privilege,[4] and the original concept of privilege reflected lawyers' ethics: "The basis for the early rule was the oath and honour of the solicitor, as a professional man and gentleman, to keep his client's secret. ... [T]he early privilege belonged solely to the solicitor, and the client benefited from it only incidentally."[5]

The duties continue to share conceptual foundations today. The law of privilege in Canada is not only a rule of evidence, or restricted to court control of litigation; it is like its ethical counterpart in arising from a substantive right of confidentiality held by the client.[6] Both are justified in

---

[1] *Descôteaux v. Mierzwinski*, [1982] S.C.J. No. 43, [1982] 1 S.C.R. 860 at 870 (S.C.C.).
[2] *Ibid.* Extra-patrimonial means something that has no quantifiable economic value.
[3] "[S]olicitor-client privilege must be as close to absolute as possible to ensure public confidence and retain relevance": *R. v. McClure*, [2001] S.C.J. No. 13 at para. 35, 2001 SCC 14 (S.C.C.); *Lavallee, Rackel & Heintz v. Canada (Attorney General)*, [2002] S.C.J. No. 61 at para. 36, [2002] 3 S.C.R. 209 at 241, 2002 SCC 61 (S.C.C.).
[4] David A. Green, "Lawyers as 'Tattletales': A Challenge to the Broad Application of the Attorney-Client Privilege and Rule 1.6, Confidentiality of Information" (2004) 20 Ga. St. U. L. Rev. 617 at 626.
[5] John Sopinka, Sydney N. Lederman & Alan W. Bryant, *The Law of Evidence in Canada*, 2d ed. (Toronto: Butterworths, 1999) at 728. The honour doctrine is also discussed extensively in: Adam Dodek, "Reconceiving Solicitor-Client Privilege" (2010) 35 Queen's L.J. 493.
[6] This may be distinct from the approach to privilege in the United States — see, for example, Fred C. Zacharias, "Harmonizing Confidentiality and Privilege" (1999) 41 S. Tex. L. Rev. 69 at 73, referring to attorney-client privilege rules as "products of lawsuits", as only applying "when one client attempts to prevent the other side's access to potentially probative evidence in litigation" (at 74). It may also explain the extent to which the solicitor-client privilege in the United States is narrower than in Canada — for example, in Canada the privilege survives

terms of their necessity to the lawyer-client relationship, and the importance of that relationship to the administration of justice. There is no principled distinction between the privilege and the ethical duty.

At the same time, however, privilege and confidentiality are doctrinally distinct. Information may fall within the lawyer's duty of confidentiality but not be privileged. An exception to privilege may remove information from the protection of the privilege but, if there is no matching exception to the duty of confidentiality, the information will remain within the lawyer's ethical duty of confidentiality.

Further and to add to the complexity arising from the interaction between confidentiality and privilege, the lawyer's duty of trust and confidence is also affected by other legal rules or principles such as the law of fiduciary obligations (particularly conflicts of interest), the distinct litigation privilege,[7] and obligations arising from rules of court[8] and various statutes such as the *Income Tax Act*[9] and the *Criminal Code*.[10]

The goal of this chapter is to clarify and analyze the lawyer's obligation of trust and confidence. It starts by explaining the applicable doctrine, focusing in particular on what the various sources — codes of conduct, discipline decisions, civil liability cases and privilege cases — mean for lawyers in their relationships with clients. It considers four questions in relation to the lawyer's duties: (1) When do lawyers have a duty not to disclose? (2) When are lawyers either permitted or required to disclose confidential information? (3) What duties do lawyers have to protect their clients' rights in relation to confidentiality and privilege? (4) What obligations do lawyers have in relation to the confidentiality claims of others? In each case the similarities and differences between the requirements of the duty of confidentiality, and the rules of privilege, will be noted.

My goal throughout is to direct the discussion towards the question most likely to concern lawyers faced with a confidentiality issue: what am I supposed to do?[11]

---

limited disclosure to third parties: *Philip Services Corp. (Receiver of) v. Ontario (Securities Commission)*, [2005] O.J. No. 4418, 77 O.R. (3d) 209 (Ont. Div. Ct.), which it does not in the United States.

[7] Litigation privilege and solicitor-client privilege "often co-exist and one is sometimes mistakenly called by the other's name, but they are not coterminous in space, time or meaning": *Blank v. Canada (Minister of Justice)*, [2006] S.C.J. No. 39 at para. 1, [2006] 2 S.C.R. 319 (S.C.C.).

[8] For example, the lawyer's implied undertaking not to disclose information obtained through pre-trial discovery except in the litigation in question: *Juman v. Doucette*, [2008] S.C.J. No. 8, 2008 SCC 8 (S.C.C.).

[9] R.S.C. 1985 (5th Supp.), c. 1.

[10] R.S.C. 1985, c. C-46, s. 23. Most notably the provisions in relation to law office searches as amended by the Supreme Court of Canada: *Lavallee, Rackel & Heintz v. Canada (Attorney General)*, [2002] S.C.J. No. 61, [2002] 3 S.C.R. 209, 2002 SCC 61 (S.C.C.) and the provisions related to obstruction of justice: *R. v. Murray*, [2000] O.J. No. 2182, 144 C.C.C. (3d) 289 (Ont. S.C.J.).

[11] It must be noted, though, that every case turns on its own facts; the rules of conduct identified here are general, and should be applied carefully to specific circumstances that may raise

Following the doctrinal analysis the chapter then turns to the question of principle: can the approach to lawyer-client confidentiality in Canadian law be justified?

2. WHEN DO LAWYERS HAVE A DUTY NOT TO DISCLOSE?

A. The General Rule

Lawyers have an obligation not to disclose information concerning a client's business and affairs acquired "in the course of the professional relationship".[12]

B. There must be a Lawyer-Client Relationship for Information to be Confidential or Privileged

A lawyer-client relationship is necessary for the duty of confidentiality to arise, or for the law of privilege to apply. Information that the lawyer learns in some other capacity, even as a trusted advisor, will not be subject to the duty. In *Cushing v. Hood*[13] an action against a lawyer for violating the duty of confidentiality was unsuccessful because it was found that the lawyer, Hood, did not have a lawyer-client relationship with the plaintiff, Cushing. Cushing was the wife of Hood's employee. She told Hood that she was thinking of leaving her employment, and Hood told her that she should make sure to give notice to her employer. Cushing ignored Hood's advice, and Hood told Cushing's former employer the advice he had given her about

---

multiple issues for consideration. For example, a single fact situation may raise questions of whether the information relates to the giving or receiving of legal advice, whether the information is producible under legal order, and whether third party knowledge of the information is sufficient to eliminate privilege.

[12] CBA MC Chapter IV, Rule 1; FLS MC Rule 2.03(1); LSUC RPC Rule 2.03(1); NB CC Chapter 5; AB CPC Chapter 7; BC PRH Chapter 5, Rule 1. The duty of professional secrecy in Québec essentially matches this position, but is quite complicated. The positive duty is set out in the *Professional Act Code*, R.S.Q. c. C-26, s. 60.4, and *An Act Respecting the Barreau du Québec*, R.S.Q. c. B-1, s. 131. The Que. CEA itself does not articulate the positive duty of professional secrecy. It instead lists the various restrictions on misuse of information that is secret (to benefit the lawyer — 3.06.01 — or to benefit another client — 3.06.02), the requirement that the advocate's colleagues maintain professional secrecy (3.06.03), some exceptions (future harm — 3.06.01.01 — and to obtain advice — 3.06.04), and requirements of minimal disclosure (3.06.01.02, 3.06.01.03 and 3.06.01.05). See in general, *Foster Wheeler Power Co. v. Société intermunicipale de gestion et d'élimination des déchets (SIGED) Inc.*, [2004] S.C.J. No. 18 at paras. 18-29, [2004] 1 S.C.R. 456, 2004 SCC 18 (S.C.C.). In that case the Court stated, at para. 29:

> Professional secrecy includes an obligation of confidentiality, which, in areas where it applies, imposes a duty of discretion on lawyers and creates a correlative right to their silence on the part of their clients. In relation to third parties, professional secrecy includes an immunity from disclosure that protects the content of information against compelled disclosure, even in judicial proceedings, subject to any other applicable legal rules or principles.

[13] [2008] N.S.J. No. 201, 2008 NSCA 47 (N.S.C.A.), affg [2007] N.S.J. No. 147, 2007 NSSC 97 (N.S.S.C.).

giving notice. The trial court found that this was not a breach of confidentiality because there was no lawyer-client relationship; Hood had simply been consulted "off the cuff" for his "two cents worth" regarding the proper way to conduct business in a small town.[14]

In a similar decision in the context of privilege, the Nova Scotia Supreme Court held that documents obtained by a law firm in the course of the firm's lawyers acting as real estate agents were producible. Since the lawyers only provided real estate agent services, there was no lawyer-client relationship created and no privilege attached to the documents.[15]

The requirement of a lawyer-client relationship does not mean that the lawyer and client must have a formal retainer; the relationship can be more casual, and includes prospective clients. This is set out in the various codes of conduct[16] and also in the case law. In *Descôteaux v. Mierzwinski*,[17] for example, the Supreme Court of Canada considered the validity of a law office search to obtain a legal aid application that, it was alleged, contained fraudulent statements. The Crown argued that the document was not privileged, because at the time of the application no solicitor-client relationship had yet been established. The Supreme Court disagreed, holding that the duty of confidentiality arose at the point the client filled in the application for legal aid, even though no consultation with the lawyer had yet taken place.[18]

C. If the Lawyer-Client Communication does not Relate to the Giving or Receiving of Legal Advice, it will not be Privileged, but will still be Confidential

Once a lawyer-client relationship is established, the boundaries of the lawyer's duty not to disclose diverge. The ethical duty of confidentiality applies to any information received by the lawyer during a lawyer-client relationship. The solicitor-client privilege, by contrast, only applies to information that relates to the giving or receiving of legal advice.

In *R. v. Campbell*,[19] in which the Court held that solicitor-client privilege applies to advice given by government lawyers, it also held that the privilege does not attach where the government lawyer is acting in a non-

---

[14] *Ibid.* at para. 1.
[15] *Nova Scotia Real Estate Commission v. Lorway*, [2009] N.S.J. No. 527 (N.S.S.C.).
[16] CBA MC Chapter IV, Commentary 5, 11 and 12; FLS MC Rule 2.03(1); AB CPC Chapter 7, Commentary G1. The New Brunswick and British Columbia codes do not speak to this issue.
[17] [1982] S.C.J. No. 43, [1982] 1 S.C.R. 860 (S.C.C.).
[18] *Ibid.* The Court went on to hold, however, that the application document fell outside of the privilege because it was a criminal communication. This aspect of the case is discussed below. The low standard for establishing the relationship necessary to create an obligation of confidentiality can have implications for lawyers with respect to conflicts of interest, as discussed in Chapter 8. In general lawyers should be careful not to obtain information unless intending to establish a lawyer-client relationship with an individual, as they will be required to keep information obtained confidential, which can preclude representing other clients where the information is relevant to that other retainer. See the discussion in Chapter 8, Section 2.B.
[19] [1999] S.C.J. No. 16, [1999] 1 S.C.R. 565 (S.C.C.).

legal capacity, advising for example on matters of policy or business. The Court held that "[w]hether or not solicitor-client privilege attaches ... depends on the nature of the relationship, the subject matter of the advice and the circumstances in which it is sought and rendered."[20] In *Maranda v. Richer*[21] the Court held that information on the payment of legal fees may fall within the privilege, but it acknowledged that not everything arising within a lawyer-client relationship is privileged.[22] Indeed, in its recent decision in *R. v. Cunningham*,[23] the Supreme Court held that fee information is not privileged unless it is "relevant to the merits of the case, or disclosure of such information may cause prejudice to the client".[24] In numerous lower court decisions the privilege has been held not to apply to accounting information.[25]

Solicitor-client privilege has in general been held to exclude the ability of clients to use their lawyers to play "hide the pea" with information that is not actually related to the giving or receiving of legal advice.[26] In *Foster Wheeler Power Co. v. Société intermunicipale de gestion et d'élimination des déchets (SIGED) Inc.*,[27] which addressed the civil law doctrine of professional secrecy, the Court explained the distinction between information which related to the giving of legal advice and that which did not through the example of a lawyer giving advice to a client while the client was driving and had an accident; the Supreme Court held that professional secrecy would prevent the lawyer from testifying as to the advice he was giving, but would not preclude the lawyer from testifying about his observations of the accident.[28]

This example also indicates, though, that the standard for finding that communications do not relate to giving legal advice will be a high one. That the court used the lawyer's observation of an act as an example of a matter not related to the giving of legal advice — that is, something that would not

---

[20] *Ibid.* at para. 56.
[21] [2003] S.C.J. No. 69 at para. 49, [2003] 3 S.C.R. 193, 2003 SCC 67 (S.C.C.).
[22] *Ibid.* at para. 30. A similar point was made by the Court in *Pritchard v. Ontario (Human Rights Commission)*, [2004] S.C.J. No. 16, [2004] 1 S.C.R. 809, 2004 SCC 31 (S.C.C.), where the Court held that information provided by the in-house counsel to the Human Rights Commission was privileged, but that it does not apply to advice given by those lawyers outside of the realm of their legal responsibilities.
[23] [2010] S.C.J. No. 10, 2010 SCC 10 (S.C.C.).
[24] *Ibid.* at para. 30.
[25] *Canada (Minister of National Revenue) v. Reddy*, [2006] F.C.J. No. 348, 2006 FC 277 (F.C.T.D.); *R. v. Serfaty*, [2004] O.J. No. 1952 (Ont. S.C.J.); *Canada (Minister of National Revenue) v. Singh*, [2005] F.C.J. No. 1907, 2005 FC 1538 (F.C.T.D.); *Kilbreath v. Saskatchewan (Attorney General)*, [2004] S.J. No. 770, 2004 SKQB 489 (Sask. Q.B.); *R. v. Law Office of Simon Rosenfeld*, [2003] O.J. No. 5821 (Ont. S.C.J.); *Re Wirick*, [2005] B.C.J. No. 2878, 2005 BCSC 1821 (B.C.S.C.); *Canada (Minister of National Revenue) v. Vlug*, [2006] F.C.J. No. 142 (F.C.A.); *Ontario (Minister of the Attorney General) v. Ontario (Information and Privacy Commissioner)*, [2007] O.J. No. 2769 (Ont. Div. Ct.).
[26] *Lafond v. Muskeg Lake Cree Nation*, [2008] F.C.J. No. 1766 at para. 16, 2008 FC 1369 (F.C.T.D.).
[27] [2004] S.C.J. No. 18, [2004] 1 S.C.R. 456, 2004 SCC 18 (S.C.C.).
[28] *Ibid.* at para. 39.

be privileged in any context[29] — suggests that the definition of "legal advice" is likely to be broad. Further, in the cases where the Court has suggested that advice in a non-legal capacity will not attract the privilege, *R. v. Campbell*[30] and *Pritchard v. Ontario (Human Rights Commission)*,[31] the lawyers were government lawyers. For lawyers in private practice, who are found to have a lawyer-client relationship with the individual in question, it is likely that all private communications with that client will be privileged, whether or not clearly "law" related.[32] This position is supported by the fact that the qualification on the extent of the privilege in these cases was *obiter*. When the matter has been squarely raised on the facts, the Court has taken a liberal approach to defining what constitutes communications relating to giving legal advice.[33] This position is also supported by the Court's discussion of the rationale for privilege, which emphasizes the importance of a client being able to make full and frank disclosure to his lawyer, which necessarily requires allowing the client some latitude as to what may or may not be relevant to obtaining that advice.[34]

Thus, in addition to not voluntarily disclosing any information arising from a lawyer-client relationship, a lawyer should resist compelled production of that information, even if it relates only tangentially to the legal services provided, since it may nonetheless still be privileged.

D. Criminal Communications are not Privileged, and are likely Excluded from the Duty of Confidentiality

Solicitor-client privilege does not apply to communications that are "criminal", and such communications are also likely excluded from the ethical duty of confidentiality.[35] Communications can be criminal where either the communication itself is criminal, or where the lawyer's advice is being, or was, sought to further a criminal scheme.

The exclusion of communication that is itself criminal is relatively straightforward, focusing on acts such as fraud. In *Descôteaux v. Mierzwinski*, where the prospective client had allegedly filed a false financial information form when claiming legal aid, the communication was excluded from the privilege under this exception. In that case the communication itself was the crime, and so could not be privileged.

The exclusion of communications where the lawyer's advice is being used to further a criminal scheme is more complicated. It includes obvious

---

[29] Just like a spouse observing an act of murder by his or her spouse falls outside the spousal privilege because it is an observation, not a communication.
[30] [1999] S.C.J. No. 16, [1999] 1 S.C.R. 565 (S.C.C.).
[31] [2004] S.C.J. No. 16, [2004] 1 S.C.R. 809, 2004 SCC 31 (S.C.C.).
[32] Unless of course the court views the client as simply trying to play hide the pea.
[33] *E.g.*, *Descôteaux v. Mierzwinski*, [1982] S.C.J. No. 43, [1982] 1 S.C.R. 860 (S.C.C.).
[34] *Smith v. Jones*, [1999] S.C.J. No. 15, [1999] 1 S.C.R. 455 (S.C.C.).
[35] As I discuss below, the uncertainty with the ethical duty is because the codes themselves do not address this point at all.

cases such as a lawyer and a client having a conversation about how best to use the lawyer's trust accounts for the purposes of money laundering.[36] Beyond that, however, its application is less clear. Specifically, it is not uncommon for clients to consult lawyers about the legality of their actions; yet doing so does not constitute a criminal communication even if the actions were or could be unlawful. Further, lawyers may advise clients that conduct is legal but turn out to be wrong, so that, in retrospect, the conversation between the lawyer and client was one that furthered an unlawful purpose. The Supreme Court has held that the criminal communications exclusion also does not apply to situations of this type.

In *R. v. Campbell*[37] the Court considered disclosure of information in relation to a police "reverse sting" operation. The accused were seeking a stay of proceedings because of the unlawful police conduct, and sought disclosure of the legal opinion on which the police claimed to rely. The Supreme Court agreed that the conduct of the police was unlawful. It also allowed disclosure of the legal opinion on the basis that the police had waived privilege by relying on the opinion in defence of their conduct.[38] The Court held, however, that the opinion was privileged even though the conduct turned out to be unlawful. Where a person seeks advice about the legality of conduct before the conduct takes place, and it later turns out that the conduct was criminal, the legal advice received remains privileged.[39] The criminal communication exclusion only arises where the "client is knowingly pursuing a criminal purpose"[40] and the lawyer is a "dupe" or "conspirator"[41] in the furtherance of that purpose. The Court has subsequently suggested that the scope of the exclusion from protection of communications in furtherance of a crime is "extremely limited".[42]

What if the client simply indicates to the lawyer that he intends to commit a crime, but does not ask the lawyer for advice or assistance in how to do it? This also does not seem to fall within the criminal communications exclusion, since it does not involve the lawyer's assistance — the lawyer is neither dupe nor conspirator; she is simply aware of the client's unlawful intentions. The lawyer's ability to disclose that information is determined,

---

[36] *R. v. Rosenfeld*, [2009] O.J. No. 1478, 2009 ONCA 307 (Ont. C.A.). Rosenfeld was convicted of money laundering. An undercover RCMP officer, who had been given Rosenfeld's name by an informant as a potential money launderer, had approached Rosenfeld. After discussions Rosenfeld agreed to launder drug proceeds for the officer. Early on in their conversations, Rosenfeld had the officer pay him a $1 fee which, he said, would make all of the conversations with the officer privileged. His conduct and abuse of his role as a lawyer was held by the Court of Appeal to be an aggravating factor in sentencing.
[37] [1999] S.C.J. No. 16, [1999] 1 S.C.R. 565 (S.C.C.).
[38] *Ibid.* at para. 71.
[39] *Ibid.* at para. 56.
[40] *Ibid.* at para. 57.
[41] *Ibid.* at para. 63.
[42] *Canada (Privacy Commissioner) v. Blood Tribe Department of Health*, [2008] S.C.J. No. 45 at para. 10, 2008 SCC 44 (S.C.C.). Although that may not be the case for litigation privilege. See *R. v. Martin*, [2008] O.J. No. 1596 (Ont. S.C.J.).

instead, by the future harm exception to confidentiality and privilege, discussed below.

What about where the question posed by the client is facially neutral, but is also the sort of question that a client is unlikely to pose except to further an unlawful purpose? What if, for example, a client asks a lawyer for a list of countries that do not have an extradition treaty with Canada.[43] The client does not add, "and I want to know so I can go there and not be forced to come back here to be convicted". If the client wants the information in order to flee justice, the client will by doing so commit obstruction of justice, and the lawyer's legal advice will assist the client to commit that unlawful act. On the other hand, the lawyer has no knowledge of this, and has simply provided the client with information available to the lawyer as a legal expert which the client would otherwise have difficulty acquiring — that is, the lawyer has acted in a classically lawyerly way.

That may be the case, and the ethics of the lawyer providing advice to a client in this type of situation was discussed in Chapter 3. I think it is almost certain, however, that the advice provided by the lawyer in that instance would be excluded from the duty of confidentiality and privilege if the client later disappeared, and the lawyer was asked where he was. The lawyer in that instance was a dupe, whose advice was knowingly sought by the client to further a criminal purpose, obstruction of justice. That the lawyer was ignorant as to the client's criminal purpose at the time the advice was given is, in this context at least, irrelevant. Thus, even if the lawyer can ethically give the advice, if she finds out that the client has used the advice to commit a crime, the lawyer may be justified in disclosing the communications with the client.

What if the lawyer discovers that she has been assisting a client to commit an unlawful act without knowing it, but the client has now admitted to the lawyer that the conduct was unlawful? For example, what if the client used the lawyer's services to commit a massive financial fraud, and now admits to the lawyer what he was doing? The communications that were made in order to obtain the lawyer's help in the commission of the fraud are not privileged due to the criminal communications exclusion. However, the admission that the fraud occurred is likely still privileged. That admission is, indeed, the very typical and clearly privileged situation in which a client seeks advice from a lawyer about the implications of his unlawful conduct. The lawyer in this example thus has the difficulty that she may be permitted, and need, to disclose the communications that furthered the client's fraud, but she cannot do so through disclosing the client's admission of the fraud.

The final complexity in the criminal communications exclusion is that the ethical codes are silent as to its application to the lawyer's ethical duty of confidentiality. In my view the ethical duty of confidentiality should be

---

[43] Monroe Freedman & Abbe Smith, *Understanding Lawyers' Ethics*, 4th ed. (New Providence, NJ: LexisNexis, 2010) at 87.

interpreted as excluding criminal communications. The exclusion is very narrow; it simply releases the lawyer from the obligation of confidentiality where a client has knowingly used the lawyer's services to achieve a criminal end. Since the ethical codes allow the lawyer to disclose confidential information to defend herself from allegations of wrongdoing, it seems logical to assume that she could disclose information to distance herself from the accomplishment of an unlawful scheme to which she has, whether wittingly or unwittingly, contributed. Indeed, the justification seems greater here where the disclosure could foster the effective administration of justice rather than simply protecting the lawyer's own interests.

In sum, then, where communications are themselves criminal, or where the lawyer is being used as a dupe or conspirator to provide active assistance in furtherance of a crime, the information is neither confidential nor privileged, and may be disclosed.

E. Third Party Knowledge of Information usually Limits the Application of the Privilege, but does not normally Limit the Ethical Duty of Confidentiality

The ethical duty of confidentiality applies even if third parties are also aware of the communications between the lawyer and the client, and lawyers have been disciplined for breaching confidentiality with respect to information known to third parties.

For example, in *Law Society of Upper Canada v. Grace*,[44] the lawyer Grace had acted for I.D. in various matters in relation to a Mental Health Review Board proceeding. I.D.'s common law husband was then charged with assaulting her. The husband's lawyer subpoenaed Grace for the husband's show cause hearing, and Grace testified about what happened at I.D.'s Mental Health Review Board proceeding. Grace argued that doing so did not violate confidentiality because the information was filed in a proceeding. The Law Society rejected this position because Mental Health Review Board proceedings are not matters of public record, even if known to third parties. For this and other misconduct Grace was disbarred.[45]

By contrast, the privilege usually ceases to apply whenever a third party is aware of the communication. Thus, for privilege to apply to legal advice, that advice will only have been given to the client. For privilege to

---

[44] [1991] L.S.D.D. No. 115.
[45] See also *Law Society of Alberta v. Belzil*, [2008] L.S.D.D. No. 167 (lawyer used information that was confidential in relation to one party to advise another party; the other party already knew about the advice, but the lawyer's conduct was nonetheless held to violate her confidentiality obligation (as well as being a conflict); *Law Society of Upper Canada v. Ross*, [2010] L.S.D.D. No. 10 (even though another person was present when the client advised the lawyer that she intended to remove her child from the jurisdiction in violation of a court order, that fact did not permit the lawyer to disclose the information).

apply to information provided by the client to the lawyer, only the lawyer and client will know what information the client provided to the lawyer.[46]

This distinction is correct, but is also qualified in important ways. Through the concept of limited waiver, the law of privilege permits third parties to in some circumstances have knowledge of the advice provided by the lawyer without eliminating the privilege.[47] A client may, for example, provide its auditor with legal advice it has been given about certain issues in order to permit the auditor to prepare financial statements without losing the privilege over that advice.

In the context of litigation, information known to third parties that is not covered by solicitor-client privilege may nonetheless be kept confidential by virtue of the litigation privilege. Litigation privilege is distinct from solicitor-client privilege; as noted by the Supreme Court, "[t]hey often co-exist and one is sometimes mistakenly called by the other's name, but they are not coterminous in space, time or meaning."[48] The litigation privilege does not relate to the solicitor-client relationship, and can arise prior to the client contacting a lawyer. It exists to allow litigants "to prepare their contending positions in private, without adversarial interference and without fear of premature disclosure".[49] It shields from disclosure any information prepared for the dominant purpose of preparing for litigation.[50] Expert reports and client records of symptoms — information that would otherwise not be privileged — may be shielded from disclosure for the duration of the litigation by the litigation privilege. The litigation privilege is not indefinite; it expires with the litigation with which it was associated.[51]

Through the doctrine of limited waiver, and through the application of litigation privilege, information may thus be both confidential and privileged even though it is known to third parties.

At the same time, neither confidentiality nor privilege will apply to prevent disclosure of information that is truly in the public domain. While it is clear that a third party knowing information does not eliminate the lawyer's ethical duty of confidentiality,[52] information that is unequivocally in the public domain does not fall within the scope of the duty. In a case

---

[46] If the information was independently given to others, it may be producible from those others, but will not be producible from the lawyer unless someone else was present when the information was given to the lawyer. This is, to eliminate the privilege the third party needs to be privy to the lawyer-client communication, not just to the information that was communicated.

[47] *Philip Services Corp. (Receiver of) v. Ontario (Securities Commission)*, [2005] O.J. No. 4418, 77 O.R. (3d) 209 (Ont. Div. Ct.); *Interprovincial Pipeline Inc. v. Canada (Minister of National Revenue)*, [1995] F.C.J. No. 1384 (F.C.T.D.).

[48] *Blank v. Canada (Minister of Justice)*, [2006] S.C.J. No. 39 at para. 1, [2006] 2 S.C.R. 319 (S.C.C.).

[49] *Ibid.* at para. 27.

[50] *Ibid.* at para. 43.

[51] *Ibid.* at para. 8.

[52] CBA MC Chapter IV, Commentary 2; FLS MC Rule 2.03(1), commentary; LSUC RPC Rule 2.03(1), commentary; NB CC Chapter 5, Commentary 2; AB CPC Chapter 7, Rule 1; BC PRH Chapter 5, Rule 1.

dealing with conflicts of interest, *Strother v. 3464920 Canada Inc.*,[53] the Supreme Court of Canada held that once a tax ruling obtained for a client became public, the lawyer and law firm had no duty of confidentiality with respect to that ruling, and were in fact contractually obliged to disclose its existence to another client whom they were advising on the issue the tax ruling addressed. In the case of *Stewart v. Canadian Broadcasting Corp.*,[54] in which Edward Greenspan participated in a television broadcast with respect to a former client, the Court found that Greenspan had not violated his obligation of confidentiality because, *inter alia*, the information had been "known to the public for years".[55]

Discipline of lawyers for breaches of confidentiality has also not extended to the point of covering information that is "public" in the sense of being widely known. While some codes of conduct suggest that the obligation of confidentiality extends even to information in the public domain,[56] most suggest more circumspectly that the duty of confidentiality, "may not apply to facts that are public knowledge".[57] Further, those codes of conduct that extend the duty of confidentiality to information in the public domain are inconsistent with the position of the Supreme Court in *Strother* that public information is not covered by the duty, and may be required to be disclosed by the lawyer in certain circumstances.

In sum, then, information communicated in a lawyer-client relationship that is truly in the public domain is neither confidential nor privileged. Information communicated in the lawyer-client relationship that is known to third parties is still confidential, and may be privileged through the application of the doctrine of limited waiver or litigation privilege.

F. The Identity of the Client is generally Confidential, and is sometimes Privileged

The lawyer's duty of confidentiality generally includes the identity of the client and the fact of a retainer.[58] Under the law of privilege, identity is normally only confidential where the identity and the fact of the representation disclose something material about the client.[59]

---

[53] [2007] S.C.J. No. 24, 2007 SCC 24 (S.C.C.).
[54] [1997] O.J. No. 2271, 150 D.L.R. (4th) 24 (Ont. Gen. Div.).
[55] *Ibid.* at para. 212.
[56] AB CPC Chapter 7, Rule 1.
[57] CBA MC Chapter IV, Commentary 10; FLS MC Rule 2.03(1), commentary; LSUC RPC Rule 2.03(1), commentary.
[58] CBA MC Chapter IV, Commentary 4; FLS MC Rule 2.03(1), commentary; LSUC RPC Rule 2.03(1), commentary; NB CC Chapter 5, Commentary 3; AB CPC Chapter 7, Rule 2; BC PRH Chapter 5, Rule 3.
[59] In *R. v. Hanington*, [2006] A.J. No. 750, 2006 ABQB 378 (Alta. Q.B.) the Court expressed some concern about a decision to publish in the newspaper the names of individuals who may want to assert a privilege claim in documents held by Hanington which were being sought by the RCMP, although it did not outright condemn the decision to do so. In *Nova Scotia Real Estate Commission v. Lorway*, [2009] N.S.J. No. 527, 2009 NSSC 266 (N.S.S.C.) the Court

Again, however, this difference should not be overstated. The examples given in the commentary to the codes of conduct tend to emphasize situations of the type that would also invoke the privilege, indicating that a family or criminal law specialist should not state that they represent someone because doing so will indicate to the public that the person has legal troubles in relation to his family or conduct.[60] In other contexts — where the fact of the representation either says nothing in particular (where, for example, a law firm acts for a corporation on a wide variety of matters on a regular basis) or says something that is already widely known — it is unlikely that the lawyer stating that information will or should be considered to have violated confidentiality. This view is also supported by the fact that some codes, such as the Canadian Bar Association ("CBA") Code, indicate that the lawyer "generally" has a duty of confidentiality in relation to client identity, implying that the lawyer does not always have such a duty. This means that the scope of the confidentiality and privilege on this issue are not really that different, and that a lawyer is only restricted from noting the identity of a client where doing so will indicate something about the nature of the retainer. As a matter of prudence, however, a lawyer should not normally disclose the identity of a client without that client's consent.

G. If Information does not come from a Client, it is Confidential, but may not be Privileged

Under the codes of conduct it is clear that the lawyer's obligation of confidentiality applies irrespective of where information came from.[61] Law societies have been willing to discipline lawyers for breaching confidentiality even where the lawyer received the information from someone other than the client. In *Law Society of Alberta v. Stephenson*[62] a lawyer was fined $1,000 for disclosing information he knew about a former client who was a complainant in a criminal matter involving his current client; the disclosure was found to be a breach of confidence even though at the time of the prior representation of his former client he had learned about the information from the police, not from his former client.

Conversely, under the law of privilege, information learned from third parties will only be confidential if it falls within the litigation privilege; the solicitor-client privilege only includes information provided by the client.

---

held that names of clients are not privileged unless publication of the name goes to the essence of the legal advice provided.
[60] See, for example, AB CPC Chapter 7, Rule 2, commentary.
[61] CBA MC Chapter IV, Commentary 2; FLS MC Rule 2.03(1), commentary; LSUC RPC Rule 2.03(1), commentary; NB CC Chapter 5, Commentary 2; AB CPC Chapter 7, Rule 1; BC PRH Chapter 5, Rule 1.
[62] [1999] L.S.D.D. No. 82.

H. Information that is Real Property is Confidential, but not Privileged

The ethical duty of confidentiality applies to client property.[63] The privilege does not apply to client property, except for "property" such as memoranda provided to the lawyer for the purpose of obtaining legal advice. Both the privilege and the ethical duty of confidentiality prohibit disclosure of information given to the lawyer *about* property; if a client told a lawyer that he had thrown a gun under a bush in the park, the gun would not be privileged, but the client's statement to the lawyer about the gun would be.[64]

I. When the Client is an Organization or Corporation, the Duty of Confidentiality is Owed to the Organization, not to Individuals within the Organization

In representing organizations, the lawyer's duty of confidentiality — either ethically or under the law of solicitor-client privilege — is owed to the organization, rather than to individuals within the organization.

When a lawyer learns of proposed wrongdoing by an organizational client, the lawyer's duties in relation to external third parties are the same as for an individual client: the lawyer may not disclose an organizational intention of wrongdoing unless some exception or exclusion from the lawyer's duty not to disclose arises. Some of the codes of conduct note, however, that a lawyer apprised of wrongdoing by *individuals* within an organization does have a duty to bring that potential wrongdoing to the attention of individuals higher up the organization.[65] This is not an exception to the lawyer's duty not to disclose, since the lawyer is not disclosing the information outside of the organization; it does, however, clarify how the duty not to disclose operates within an organizational context.

J. Absolute Secrecy is Required for Information that is Confidential and Privileged

Once the duty not to disclose information is established, there is no room for lawyer indiscretion or casualness with respect to that information. This is set out in the codes of conduct, which prohibit a lawyer from engaging in

---

[63] CBA MC Chapter VIII, Commentary 5; FLS MC Rule 2.05(1), commentary; LSUC RPC Rule 2.07(1), commentary; NB CC Chapter 5, Commentary 1 and Chapter 7, Commentary 3; AB CPC Chapter 7, Rule 3. It should be noted, though, that important exceptions to this rule apply where the property is evidence of a crime.

[64] And if the client gave the lawyer the gun, not only would the gun not be privileged but the lawyer would also be required to disclose it as an exception to confidentiality (because doing so is required by law). See *R. v. Murray*, [2000] O.J. No. 2182, 144 C.C.C. (3d) 289 (Ont. S.C.J.).

[65] CBA MC Chapter IV, Commentary 18; FLS MC Rule 2.02(8); LSUC RPC Rule 2.03(3), commentary. If doing so does not stop the proposed wrongdoing, then the obligation of the lawyer is to withdraw, which in the case of in-house counsel would require resignation.

"indiscreet shop talk"[66] but can also be inferred from the consistent statement in the case law that the confidentiality of the lawyer under solicitor-client privilege should be as "absolute as possible".[67] A lawyer is unlikely to face any negative consequences if no harm arises from, for example, talking about a case with her intimate partner. However, the effect of this rule is that if harm arises from a lawyer sharing confidential information it will be no defence for the lawyer to claim that her indiscretion was *de minimus*.

K. The Duty not to Disclose includes the Lawyer's Colleagues and Staff

The duty of confidentiality extends to the law firm or organization within which a lawyer works and includes the requirement that the lawyer ensure that those who work for her keep the information confidential. This is set out in the codes of conduct with respect to confidentiality[68] and, as well, in the case law and codes of conduct dealing with conflicts of interest, which generally restrict law firms from acting against a party where any lawyer in the firm has confidential information about that party which may be relevant to the new retainer.[69]

Although not addressed directly in the case law on privilege,[70] this broad scope of the duty also applies to the solicitor-client privilege. Sharing information with others in a law firm does not breach the privilege, but rather binds those others to the same duty of secrecy.

L. The Duty of Confidentiality and the Privileged Status of Information Lasts Indefinitely

The lawyer's ethical duty of confidentiality and the solicitor-client privilege survive termination of the retainer and even the death of the client. Obligations arising from litigation privilege end with the termination of the litigation in question.[71]

---

[66] CBA MC Chapter IV, Commentary 9; FLS MC Rule 2.03(1), commentary; LSUC RPC Rule 2.03(1), commentary; NB CC Chapter 5, Commentary 6; AB CPC, Chapter 7, Rule 1, commentary; BC PRH Chapter 5, Rule 8.
[67] *R. v. McClure*, [2001] S.C.J. No. 13 at para. 35, 2001 SCC 14 (S.C.C.).
[68] CBA MC Chapter IV, Commentary 13; FLS MC Rule 2.03(1), commentary; LSUC RPC Rule 2.03(1), commentary; NB CC Chapter 5, Commentary 7; AB CPC Chapter 7, Rule 4; BC PRH Chapter 5, Rule 2.
[69] *MacDonald Estate v. Martin*, [1990] S.C.J. No. 41, [1990] 3 S.C.R. 1235 (S.C.C.).
[70] It is made clear in the law on conflicts of interest.
[71] *Geffen v. Goodman Estate*, [1991] S.C.J. No. 53, [1991] 2 S.C.R. 353 (S.C.C.): "the confidentiality of communications between solicitor and client survives the death of the client and enures to his or her next of kin, heirs, or successors in title". The Court in *Geffen* noted the exceptions that arise in the context of wills litigation. In the codes of conduct see: CBA MC Chapter IV, Commentary 6; FLS MC Rule 2.03(1), commentary; LSUC RPC Rule 2.03(1), commentary; NB CC Chapter 5, Commentary 4; AB CPC Chapter 7, Rule 5 and commentary; BC PRH Chapter 5, Rule 4.

M. Consequences of Breaching the Duty

Where a lawyer discloses information that is confidential and privileged she faces a number of potential consequences. She may be subject to civil liability in lawsuits brought by the client for damages resulting from the breach. The Supreme Court has alluded to this possibility in general terms, noting in *Descôteaux v. Mierzwinski* that "a lawyer who communicates a confidential communication to others without his client's authorization could be sued by his client for damages".[72] In the case of *Szarfer v. Chodos*,[73] a claim against a lawyer for breach of fiduciary duty was successful because of the lawyer's misuse of confidential information to commence an affair with the client's wife.

Lawsuits for breach of confidence appear to be rare, however.[74] More common is law society discipline. Lawyers have been subject to sanctions ranging from reprimands through fines to permission to resign from the law society for disclosing confidential and privileged information, with the sanction generally depending on the circumstances surrounding the breach.

Interestingly, the discipline cases appear to follow identifiable patterns. Lawyers who breach confidences tend to have done so out of anger or frustration at the client or a related third party; because of some confusion about the nature of their obligations; or in order to obtain an advantage for another client or themselves.

Angry lawyers have sent letters to clients listing the things they view the client as having done wrong, and then copied those letters to opposing counsel.[75] In one case a lawyer facing a lawsuit from a former client's husband told the husband that he would "embarrass and humiliate" the husband and would "raise the fact that he had previously acted for [the wife] who had divulged her personal life to him".[76] That lawyer was given permission to resign by the Law Society.

---

[72] [1982] S.C.J. No. 43, [1982] 1 S.C.R. 860 at 871 (S.C.C.).

[73] [1986] O.J. No. 256, 54 O.R. (2d) 663 (Ont. H.C.J.), affd [1988] O.J. No. 1861, 66 O.R. (2d) 350 (Ont. C.A.).

[74] As discussed in the chapter on conflicts of interest (Chapter 8), legal action with respect to the misuse of confidential information tend to be prophylactic more than responsive. Former clients bring actions to remove lawyers from cases where there is a potential for lawyers to misuse confidential information; they far less often bring actions against lawyers for harm arising from the misuse of confidential information.

[75] *Law Society of Upper Canada v. Freedman*, [2005] L.S.D.D. No. 20 (alleged in letter copied to opposing counsel that clients had fired him, kept changing their minds about what to do and had falsely accused him of not following instructions; lawyer reprimanded and ordered to pay costs); *Law Society of British Columbia v. Ewachniuk*, [1995] L.S.D.D. No. 255 (in personal injury matter copied ICBC on a letter to client, in which he asserted that she had in fact settled her claim and owed him his contingency fee; since the client had new counsel and was negotiating with ICBC this was potentially quite prejudicial to her interests; he was fined); *Law Society of Upper Canada v. Gray*, [1995] L.S.D.D. No. 220 (when former client in matrimonial matter made a complaint to the Law Society he copied his response to the Law Society, which contained otherwise confidential information, to counsel for the husband; he was suspended for 60 days).

[76] *Law Society of Upper Canada v. Amorim*, [1998] L.S.D.D. No. 112 at para. 10.

Lawyers have become confused about their confidentiality obligations, and breached them, in a variety of circumstances. One lawyer disclosed confidential information where the client's affairs were taken over by a trustee in bankruptcy under the mistaken impression that the trustee could waive the client's right to confidentiality.[77] Another lawyer improperly discussed a client's affairs with the client's daughter when the client was under a guardianship order. The disclosure was improper because the daughter was not the client's trustee or guardian, and could not waive the client's right to confidentiality.[78] Finally, a lawyer improperly disclosed information from one party to another in litigation because confused over who could give instructions on the matter — the lawyer had previously received instructions from more than one party associated with litigation.[79] In such cases, unless the lawyer has otherwise acted improperly, the sanctions tend to be very minor, if any are even imposed.

The most troubling and significant lapses arise, however, from lawyers who breach obligations of confidentiality to former clients in order to benefit current clients or themselves. For example, in *Law Society of Alberta v. Bissett*,[80] a lawyer knew that a former client had filed a false statutory declaration. The circumstances of the former client doing so were somewhat explicable, arising from unanticipated changes in circumstances. As noted by the Law Society, "while the statutory declaration signed by Mr. W. may have been false, any concern [the Member] had as to its truth was alleviated in discussions with the counsel who had prepared the document".[81] Subsequently the lawyer acted for a criminal accused in a case in which the former client was a witness for the Crown. The lawyer used the false statutory declaration to discredit the credibility of his former client and to secure an acquittal for his current client. The lawyer asserted that he had spoken to his partners and no one had seen any issue with his cross-examination of his former client, although he acknowledged that he had neither consulted the Code of Professional Conduct nor spoken with the Law Society to determine his obligations. He seems only to have been sensitive to issues in relation to a possible conflict of interest.[82]

---

[77] *Law Society of Alberta v. Clark*, [1998] L.S.D.D. No. 152.
[78] *Law Society of Alberta v. Miskuski*, [1999] L.S.D.D. No. 60.
[79] *Law Society of Alberta v. Belzil*, [2008] L.S.D.D. No. 167. Because the lawyer in this case had also acted in a conflict of interest, the sanction was higher — a $10,000 fine.
[80] [1999] L.S.D.D. No. 74.
[81] *Ibid.* at para. 9.
[82] See also *Law Society of Alberta v. Arkell*, [1995] L.S.D.D. No. 289 (lawyer advised other lawyer in his firm who was acting for creditor of client's husband of the existence of a joint bank account from which the lawyer's own client (the wife) was trying to obtain overdue support payments); *Law Society of Upper Canada v. Grace*, [1991] L.S.D.D. No. 115 (Former client alleged victim of assault by common law husband; lawyer testifies under subpoena from husband that he had been her counsel in Mental Health Review Board matters in which her capacity to take an oath had been questioned and a judge had questioned her behaviour as bizarre. On the Crown raising his ethical duties, the lawyer indicated that all of the information was in the public record; this was incorrect as Mental Health Review Board proceedings are not

Two other disciplinary decisions are of note. The first, *Law Society of British Columbia v. MacAdam*,[83] demonstrates that even though disclosure may seem to a lawyer like the "right" thing to do, morally speaking, it can open the lawyer up to professional consequences. In *MacAdam* the lawyer was asked to prepare a custody agreement that would permit former clients to look after the child of a current client. He advised the current client that giving the former clients custody was a bad idea because he had evidence of their instability, drug trafficking, drug abuse and violence. The former clients complained to the Law Society. Due to his disclosure, and some other misconduct issues, the lawyer was fined, required to apologize and reprimanded.

This case is interesting because it does not fit easily into any exception to the lawyer's confidentiality obligation. Yet at the same time, a lawyer who knows that the disclosure of confidential information may avoid endangering a child's safety and welfare will certainly be tempted to disclose. This case may suggest that the future harm exceptions to confidentiality, discussed below, have been too narrowly focussed on the criminality of the conduct to be prevented by the disclosure. If the lawyer in this case has information that the child would be endangered by staying with his former clients, the lawyer ought to be permitted to disclose that information.

The second case, *Law Society of Upper Canada v. Ross*[84] does not involve a breach of confidentiality but, rather, a situation where the lawyer, Ross properly retained confidentiality of a client's information, but ended up being disciplined for misleading the Court. Ross's client had advised the lawyer that she intended to leave Canada and return to Hungary with her child while custody proceedings were ongoing. The Law Society agreed with Ross that this was information that he could not disclose. However, it found that once he had the information, and could not disclose it, he had an obligation to withdraw from the record. He could not, as he did, adjourn a custody application to a future date knowing that by the time the application took place she would be gone. The lawyer did not need to disclose the reasons for his withdrawal, but he did need to withdraw rather than participate in a deception on the court.[85]

---

in the public record); *Law Society of Upper Canada v. Joseph*, [2003] L.S.D.D. No. 34 (lawyer using confidential information about client's vulnerability to commence a sexual relationship with her); *Law Society of Alberta v. Stephenson*, [1999] L.S.D.D. No. 82 (lawyer gave information about a complainant learned during his representation of her to the police in order to help a current client against whom the former client was the complainant).

[83] [1997] L.S.D.D. No. 55.
[84] [2010] L.S.D.D. No. 10.
[85] The problem of lawyers forced to choose between the obligation of confidentiality and the duty not to mislead the court is discussed further in Chapter 6 in relation to the perjury trilemma. *Law Society of Upper Canada v. Ross*, though, does not raise quite the same issues as in the perjury trilemma not only because this was not a case of a client exercising a right to testify, but also because in a civil context the right to counsel and the right against self-incrimination do not operate in the same way, with the result that there is no justification in civil cases for misleading the court. Further, withdrawal in the preliminary stage of a civil proceeding, where

What about circumstances where information is confidential but is not privileged? As noted below, a lawyer who discloses that information because legally required to do so cannot be subject to legal consequences. However, a breach of confidentiality where not required by law can lead to law society discipline even if the information was not privileged.[86]

N. The Implied Undertaking Rule

Before turning to the exceptions to the lawyer's duty not to disclose, one additional aspect of that duty should be noted. For the most part the lawyer's duty not to disclose focuses on the lawyer's own client, on the information learned in the course of representing that client and/or in the course of preparing for litigation. Lawyers do, however, also have duties in relation to information of third parties in some circumstances. Specifically, the process of pre-trial discovery places lawyers (and their clients) under an implied undertaking not to disclose information learned through that process except in the proceedings in which it was disclosed. Even where the information in question may reveal criminal wrongdoing, it may only be disclosed to the police or a non-party after a court order permitting the disclosure has been obtained. The only exception to this requirement is where the information reveals a situation of immediate and serious danger.[87]

3. WHEN ARE LAWYERS EITHER PERMITTED OR REQUIRED TO DISCLOSE CONFIDENTIAL INFORMATION?

A. Introduction

The legal exceptions to confidentiality and privilege are varied, and this section does not purport to discuss them all. It will highlight some of the most significant and interesting exceptions and, as well, indicate some of what a lawyer should be considering when applying the legal principles to her particular circumstances. In particular, in any situation the lawyer needs to consider (a) Do I have a duty not to disclose? (b) Does this legal rule provide a valid exception to that duty? (c) Is the exception one that is

---

the lawyer's reason could include such matters as non-payment of fees, will not result in *de facto* disclosure of a client's confidences as it can in the context of withdrawal in the middle of a criminal trial. In short, any justification for misleading the court to protect confidentiality and the client's right to counsel does not arise here. Instead the decision points to the importance for lawyers of recognizing that there can be circumstances where violating confidentiality is not permitted, but the lawyer must nonetheless qualify how, if at all, the client is represented in court.

[86] For example, *Law Society of Upper Canada v. Grace*, [1991] L.S.D.D. No. 115. Mental Health Review Board proceedings would not be privileged, but the lawyer was nonetheless disciplined for using his confidential knowledge of what took place there to testify about his former client.

[87] *Juman v. Doucette*, [2008] S.C.J. No. 8 at paras. 1-4, 2008 SCC 8 (S.C.C.).

permissive or mandatory? (d) Is a court or other legal order required prior to disclosure?

B. The Lawyer's Ability to Disclose when Information is neither Confidential nor Privileged, or when the Information is Confidential but not Privileged

Where information is neither privileged nor confidential, the lawyer is as free to disclose that information as is a non-lawyer who has been given information. This includes where no lawyer-client relationship exists, where the communications are criminal in nature, where the information is truly in the public domain, and information about the identity of a client, where identity is not in itself revelatory of anything substantive.

This does not mean, however, that the lawyer necessarily *should* disclose the information, but only that the professional duty of confidentiality does not answer that question. To illustrate, when the lawyer in *Cushing v. Hood*[88] disclosed to Cushing's former employer that he had advised her not to resign without notice, we can question whether he should have done so, but the question will not be posed to him *qua* lawyer, but only *qua* ordinary person who had to judge the moral weight of keeping confidences against the weight of other moral obligations.

Where information is confidential but not privileged, the lawyer must not disclose the information unless there is a legal requirement that she do so, or another applicable exception to the ethical duty of confidentiality applies. The exceptions to the duty of confidentiality, such as client waiver and the prevention of future harm, are discussed below. Legal requirements to disclose confidential information may arise under rules of court, other legislation or court order. Unlike legislation or judicial rules requiring disclosure of privileged information, no special rules or standards apply to the interpretation or enactment of legal rules requiring disclosure of confidential but not privileged information. The legislation or court order may simply require disclosure of the confidential but not privileged information, and then the lawyer must comply with that direction. All the ethical codes subject the lawyer's duty of confidentiality to the requirement that the lawyer comply with legal orders.[89]

An example of the lawyer's duties of disclosure when information is confidential but not privileged, is a famous American case, *Spaulding v. Zimmerman*.[90] In *Spaulding* the plaintiff sued the defendant for losses arising from an automobile accident. The defendant obtained a medical examination

---

[88] [2008] N.S.J. No. 201, 2008 NSCA 47 (N.S.C.A.), affg [2007] N.S.J. No. 147, 2007 NSSC 97 (N.S.S.C.).
[89] CBA MC Chapter IV, Commentary 17; FLS MC Rule 2.03; LSUC RPC Rule 2.03(2); NB CC Chapter 5, Commentary 8(1); AB CPC Chapter 7, Rule 8(1); BC PRH Chapter 5, Rule 13. *An Act respecting the Barreau du Québec*, R.S.Q. c. B-1, s. 131(2).
[90] 263 Minn. 346 (1962).

of the plaintiff that disclosed that the plaintiff had a potentially fatal aortic aneurysm caused by the accident. The aneurysm had not been caught by the plaintiff's own physician. The medical report was a document produced by a third party, and was not privileged. It was also producible under the applicable rules of court if requested by the plaintiff.[91] The medical report was, however, confidential as information arising from the lawyer-client relationship between the defendant and his lawyer.

Thus, if the procedure for obtaining the medical report under the rules of court was invoked, the lawyer would have to produce the report. Otherwise, unless an exception to confidentiality applied — such as client consent — the lawyer could not produce it. In *Spaulding* the medical report was not produced, and the settlement negotiated between the plaintiff and defendant was vacated when the report later became known to the plaintiff. The reasons for non-disclosure in *Spaulding* are not entirely clear; it is not certain that the defendant's lawyer asked the defendant whether he could disclose the document, and nor is it known why the plaintiff's lawyer did not seek disclosure of the report. Nonetheless, the case demonstrates an important ethical principle: where information is confidential but not privileged, that information may not be produced unless the legal rules requiring production are invoked, or some exception to confidentiality applies. That that is the case is exactly why *Spaulding* is famous — it shows clearly the potential for tension between the demands of the lawyer's professional morality (non-disclosure) and those of ordinary morality (disclosure).[92]

Another, albeit less dramatic, example in which legislation or court order will obligate production of confidential but not privileged information, is with respect to accounting or other information that does not relate to the provision of legal advice.[93] Thus in *Canada (Minister of National Revenue) v. Singh*,[94] the government was seeking information on whether annuitants of a Registered Retirement Savings Plan (RRSPs) were engaged in a scheme to extract funds from the RRSPs without payment of tax. The funds were

---

[91] And would be producible under the rules of court in every Canadian jurisdiction. See, for example, *Alberta Rules of Court*, Alta. Reg. 124/2010, Rule 5.44(3).

[92] It also shows the potential for professional principles to be adjusted where too much at odds with personal morality. The result of *Spaulding v. Zimmerman* was revision of most American codes of conduct, including that of the ABA, to permit disclosure of any information necessary to prevent death or serious bodily harm, not just information necessary to prevent a crime causing death or serious bodily harm. Most Canadian codes have not yet followed suit.

[93] *Canada (Minister of National Revenue) v. Reddy*, [2006] F.C.J. No. 348, 2006 FC 277 (F.C.T.D.); *R. v. Serfaty*, [2004] O.J. No. 1952 (Ont. S.C.J.); *Canada (Minister of National Revenue) v. Singh*, [2005] F.C.J. No. 1907 (F.C.T.D.); *Kilbreath v. Saskatchewan (Attorney General)*, [2004] S.J. No. 770, 2004 SKQB 489 (Sask. Q.B.); *R. v. Law Office of Simon Rosenfeld*, [2003] O.J. No. 5821 (Ont. S.C.J.); *Re Wirick*, [2005] B.C.J. No. 2878, 2005 BCSC 1821 (B.C.S.C.); *Canada (Minister of National Revenue) v. Vlug*, [2006] F.C.J. No. 142 (F.C.A.); *Ontario (Minister of the Attorney General) v. Ontario (Information and Privacy Commissioner)*, [2007] O.J. No. 2769 (Ont. Div. Ct.).

[94] [2005] F.C.J. No. 1907 (F.C.T.D.).

paid through the solicitor's trust account. The Court held that this information was not privileged; it was "a straight commercial relationship using the law firm's trust accounts to receive and transfer funds",[95] and information about those transfers was producible under the applicable legislative provisions.

C. The General Duty to Comply with Valid Legal Orders that Require or Permit Disclosure of Confidential and Privileged Information

As noted, the ethical codes subject the lawyer's duty of confidentiality to the requirement that the lawyer comply with legal orders.[96] The Supreme Court has also held that the solicitor-client privilege may be limited by legislation or common law. The Supreme Court has emphasized that any legal limitation on privilege must be strictly construed; the incursion on privilege must be expressly contemplated for by the legislation,[97] and the only incursions that are permitted are those that are "absolutely necessary" to the accomplishment of the legislative purpose.[98] Moreover, since the privilege is a principle of fundamental justice, and protected by s. 7 of the *Canadian Charter of Rights and Freedoms*,[99] any limitation in circumstances where the life, liberty or security of the person of the client are at stake must be justified pursuant to s. 1.[100] Given the strict view of privilege adopted by the case law, such justification will be difficult to establish.

D. Information that is Confidential and Privileged may be Disclosed where the Client Waives Her Right to Confidentiality

The various codes of conduct permit disclosure where the client has expressly or by implication waived the lawyer's duty of confidentiality.[101]

---

[95] *Ibid.* at para. 10.
[96] CBA MC Chapter IV, Commentary 17; FLS MC Rule 2.03; LSUC RPC Rule 2.03(2); NB CC Chapter 5, Commentary 8(1); AB CPC Chapter 7, Rule 8(1); BC PRH Chapter 5, Rule 13. *An Act respecting the Barreau du Québec*, R.S.Q. c. B-1, s. 131(2). This would of course also apply to information that is confidential but not privileged.
[97] *Canada (Privacy Commissioner) v. Blood Tribe Department of Health*, [2008] S.C.J. No. 45, 2008 SCC 44 (S.C.C.).
[98] *Descôteaux v. Mierzwinski*, [1982] S.C.J. No. 43, [1982] 1 S.C.R. 860 (S.C.C.); *Goodis v. Ontario (Minister of Correctional Services)*, [2006] S.C.J. No. 31, [2006] 2 S.C.R. 32, 2006 SCC 31 (S.C.C.).
[99] Part I of the *Constitution Act, 1982*, being Schedule B to the *Canada Act 1982* (U.K.), 1982, c. 11.
[100] *Lavallee, Rackel & Heintz v. Canada (Attorney General)*, [2002] S.C.J. No. 61, [2002] 3 S.C.R. 209, 2002 SCC 61 (S.C.C.).
[101] CBA MC Chapter 4, Commentary 1; FLS MC Rule 2.03(1), commentary; LSUC RPC Rule 2.03(1), commentary; NB CC Chapter 5, Commentary 9(1); AB CPC Chapter 7, Rule 8(3) and commentary; BC PRH Chapter 5, Rule 11(a). *An Act respecting the Barreau du Québec*, R.S.Q. c. B-1, s. 131(2).

Case law similarly permits disclosure of privileged information with client consent, either express or implied. Express waiver must be clear, and in Alberta the commentary to the exception suggests in particular that where the lawyer intends to use the confidential information for her own benefit — to write a memoir, for example — the lawyer needs to ensure that the client understands the effect and implications of the waiver. Codes of conduct also direct the lawyer to try to obtain waivers to confidentiality where doing so is necessary to fulfill other ethical duties of the lawyer, most significantly, not misleading the court or other counsel. In such circumstances, if the lawyer cannot obtain a waiver permitting disclosure, the lawyer is required to withdraw.[102]

Implied waiver must be invoked with caution. It generally operates only where the waiver seems to follow logically from the fact of the representation — that is, where it is necessary to make the representation functional or where some act of the client communicates waiver by implication. With respect to the first type of implied waiver, the commentaries to the rules suggest that such waivers permit the lawyer to file pleadings and take other steps necessary to run the lawyer's office or bring forward the client's legal interests.[103] The Alberta commentary also suggests that this sort of implied waiver is sufficient to permit the lawyer to make disclosure as necessary to safeguard the client's health and property in the event that the client becomes incapacitated.

With respect to the second type of implied waiver — waiver communicated by the act of a client — the most common act of a client that will be used to imply waiver of confidentiality and privilege, is where a client places the legal advice provided by a lawyer at issue in a proceeding. Thus in *R. v. Campbell*,[104] where the police claimed that their decision to use a reverse sting, which it turned out was illegal, had been based on legal advice provided by the Department of Justice, the Supreme Court held that the police had waived the confidentiality of that advice.[105]

In *R. v. Hobbs*,[106] Hobbs had been convicted at trial and commenced an appeal based on ineffective assistance of counsel. In particular, he claimed that he had instructed his counsel to make a s. 8 argument and counsel had decided not to do so. Hobbs' trial lawyer sought to introduce an affidavit in response to the client's argument attesting to the advice that he had given his client at trial. The Court of Appeal held that he should be allowed to do so: "A client who puts in issue the advice received from his or her solicitor risks being found to have waived the privilege with respect to

---

[102] If permission for withdrawal is required, the lawyer must state that withdrawal is for "ethical reasons". *R. v. Cunningham*, [2010] S.C.J. No. 10 at para. 49, 2010 SCC 10 (S.C.C.).
[103] AB CPC Chapter 7, Rule 8(3) commentary.
[104] [1999] S.C.J. No. 16, [1999] 1 S.C.R. 565 (S.C.C.).
[105] See also *Suhl v. Larose*, [2006] B.C.J. No. 1913 (B.C.S.C.); *Order of the Oblates of Mary Immaculate v. Dohm, Jaffer and Jeraj*, [2007] B.C.J. No. 2067, 2007 BCSC 1412 (B.C.S.C.).
[106] [2009] N.S.J. No. 409, 2009 NSCA 90 (N.S.C.A.).

those communications."[107] The Court was of the view that the lawyer should be "permitted to respond to the allegations about his competence"[108] arising from the appeal. The right of response is, however, limited to the specific allegations of incompetence; there is no general waiver of the solicitor-client privilege as a result of the argument of ineffective assistance.

The courts are clear that inadvertent disclosure does not constitute a waiver,[109] and also that limited disclosure — for example to a client's auditors — will not constitute a waiver of the totality of the privilege.[110] The duties of opposing counsel when receiving inadvertent disclosure are discussed below in Section 5.

E. When a Lawyer Acts for More than One Client on a Joint Retainer, Information Arising from that Retainer is not Confidential or Privileged between the Clients, but will be Confidential and Privileged Relative to Third Parties

When a lawyer acts for more than one client on a joint basis, then no confidentiality or privilege exists between those clients, and the lawyer has a duty to disclose information received from one to the other. The codes of conduct make this clear with respect to confidentiality,[111] and it has been noted as an applicable exception by case law dealing with solicitor-client privilege. In the case of *Pritchard v. Ontario (Human Rights Commission)*,[112] the Supreme Court described this as the "common interest" exception to privilege and as applying to parties who have a "common goal or [are] seeking a common outcome".[113] The Court described this as a narrow exception.

In some circumstances a lawyer may undertake a joint representation and discover subsequently that one client does not wish to provide information to the other. In those circumstances, unless the client will consent to the disclosure to the other client, the lawyer must withdraw. A notable but hypothetical example of this situation is where a husband and wife ask the lawyer to prepare joint wills. The wife tells the lawyer privately that she does not agree with the husband's proposed division of the estate. The wife also tells the lawyer that she had a child prior to meeting her husband whom she gave up for adoption, and that she would like to make

---

[107] *Ibid.* at para. 14.
[108] *Ibid.* at para. 11. See also *R. v. Read*, [1993] B.C.J. No. 2162, 36 BCAC 64 (B.C.C.A.); *R. v. Li*, [1993] B.C.J. No. 2312, 36 BCAC 181 (B.C.C.A.).
[109] *Metcalfe v. Metcalfe*, [2001] M.J. No. 115 (Man. C.A.).
[110] *Philip Services Corp. (Receiver of) v. Ontario (Securities Commission)*, [2005] O.J. No. 4418, 77 O.R. (3d) 209 (Ont. Div. Ct.).
[111] CBA MC Chapter V, Commentary 6; (FLS Rule on conflicts not yet drafted); LSUC RPC Rule 2.04(6); NB CC Chapter 5, Commentary 8(d); AB CPC Chapter 7, Rule 8(d); BC PRH Chapter 6, Rule 4.
[112] [2004] S.C.J. No. 16, [2004] 1 S.C.R. 809, 2004 SCC 31 (S.C.C.).
[113] *Ibid.* at para. 24.

some provision for that child in her estate. She asks the lawyer not to tell her husband, and says that she is prepared to go along with her husband's wishes.[114] The academic writing on this topic divides on the appropriate response for the lawyer in this situation — some suggest that the lawyer should continue acting without disclosure, while others suggest that the lawyer should try to persuade the wife to disclose her reservations and the existence of the child, and should withdraw if she refuses to do so.[115] Whether the lawyer can continue the joint representation given the conflicting interests of the husband and wife is the central ethical issue in this hypothetical; however the point here is to note the clear rule in the Canadian context that given the joint retainer rule, information in such retainers is not confidential and privileged between the parties. Thus if the lawyer chooses to honour the wife's request of non-disclosure, the lawyer must withdraw from the representation.

F. Information that is Confidential and Privileged may be Disclosed during Law Society Disciplinary Proceedings

A lawyer will be required to disclose confidential information if subject to disciplinary proceedings by the law society.[116] In such proceedings, the privilege may also be breached for the limited purpose of facilitating the law society's investigation and discipline of a lawyer. The law society has an obligation to protect the client's interests; however, the client cannot assert the privilege to prevent the law society from using the information when proceeding against the lawyer, and the lawyer may not rely on the privilege to avoid testifying. Two appellate decisions confirm the validity of this legislative incursion, and suggest its broad scope.

In *Skogstad v. Law Society of British Columbia*,[117] the lawyer was being investigated with respect to complaints made by non-clients about his handling of a charitable trust on behalf of his client. The client had not cooperated in the investigation while he was alive, and had died before the investigation was completed. The lawyer refused to answer questions posed

---

[114] The original version of this hypothetical is by Thomas Shaffer. Thomas L. Shaffer, "The Legal Ethics of Radical Individualism" (1987) 65 Tex. L. Rev. 963 at 968. It is revised to add the out of wedlock twist by David Luban in *Legal Ethics and Human Dignity* (New York: Cambridge University Press, 2007) at 328-29.
[115] With respect to his less inflammatory example Shaffer suggests that the lawyer acts well by opening up the question for the family of the "truth of what it is". (Shaffer, *ibid*. at 979). David Luban argues that this is all very well provided that the family is equal to that truth; if the result of the lawyer's probing is that the family collapses the lawyer cannot necessarily be said to have done well. If the truth remains hidden the husband may die deceived and the wife may die without leaving money to her child, "[b]ut they live and love together, and they do not die alone". (Luban, *ibid*. at 329).
[116] CBA Chapter IV, Rule 4 (this rule, like that of the LSUC, does not make the principle explicit in the same way other rules do; however, I think it is intended to have the same effect); FLS Rule 2.03(1)(c); NB Chapter 5, Rule 8(a); LSUC Rule 2.03(4); AB CPC Chapter 7, Rule 8(a); BC PRH Chapter 13, Rule 3(b).
[117] [2007] B.C.J. No. 1197 (B.C.C.A.).

by the Law Society on the basis of solicitor-client privilege. The British Columbia Court of Appeal accepted the Law Society's position that regulation of the legal profession requires the Law Society to have "access to confidential, and occasionally, privileged information, such as client instructions".[118] The Court held that this was the case whether the investigation was instigated at the complaint of a client or a non-client, and emphasized the provisions of the Law Society's governing legislation that require it not to disclose publicly the privileged information.

In the case of *Law Society of Saskatchewan v. Merchant*,[119] the Saskatchewan Court of Appeal upheld a decision by the Law Society that Merchant was required to provide a client's privileged information, even over that client's objections, in response to a complaint by a third party. The third party, Wolfe, alleged that Merchant had violated a court order. In that case Merchant had acted for Hunter in a child support matter against Wolfe. He had also acted for Hunter in respect of claims by Hunter against the government in the residential schools litigation. Wolfe obtained a court order that permitted her to obtain funds received by Hunter in settlement of the residential schools litigation to offset her child support claim, with the court order binding on the Merchant Law Group as well as on Hunter. The aspect of the court order binding the Merchant Law Group was later vacated; however, in the meantime it was alleged that funds for Hunter's residential schools claim had been paid to the Merchant Law Group and distributed to Hunter, rather than being paid to Wolfe in compliance with the court order.

The Saskatchewan Court of Appeal held that the Law Society was entitled to consider the documents in relation to Merchant's representation of Hunter, even though Hunter did not consent to disclosure. The Court of Appeal noted the principle recognized by the Supreme Court of Canada that privilege could be abrogated by "appropriate statutory language".[120] It held that the Law Society had sufficient legislative authority to permit it to pierce the privilege here and that, importantly, it had only sought to breach the privilege here to the extent absolutely necessary.[121]

---

[118] *Ibid.* at para. 8.
[119] [2008] S.J. No. 623, 2008 SKCA 128 (Sask. C.A.), leave refused [2008] S.C.C.A. No. 538 (S.C.C.).
[120] *Ibid.* at para. 42.
[121] *Ibid.* at paras. 56-58.

G. Confidential and Privileged Information may be Disclosed to Another Lawyer to Obtain Legal Advice and may also be Disclosed to Allow the Lawyer to Defend Herself in Litigation

Even without a waiver, lawyers may disclose confidential and privileged information in order to obtain legal advice about their conduct of a matter.[122] The information so disclosed remains confidential and privileged relative to anyone else; the consulted lawyer is bound not to disclose it to the same extent as the first lawyer.

In addition, and more significantly, lawyers may disclose confidential and privileged information in order to defend disputes arising from their representation of the client, or in relation to the collection of fees. This rule is directly incorporated into the various codes of conduct,[123] and indirectly recognized in the case law. For example, in *R. v. Murray*,[124] Murray was accused of obstructing justice by not disclosing in a timely fashion videotapes depicting his then client, Paul Bernardo, and Bernardo's wife Karla Homolka, assaulting various young women. In defending himself from the charges Murray disclosed the instructions that Bernardo had given him with respect to the videotapes, including the fact that Bernardo had directed Murray to where they were hidden, and had not wanted to disclose the tapes. Murray's disclosure of this information was not discussed in the decision, and appears to have been assumed to have been acceptable in the circumstances, presumably as necessary to permit Murray to defend himself from the allegations made against him.

To allow this disclosure without explanation or justification is problematic. Self-interested exceptions such as these have the potential to harm the client significantly. At minimum, courts and law societies must be prepared to explain the basis for permitting the lawyer to breach the privilege in any circumstance where the client has not herself placed the lawyer's conduct at issue, and thereby impliedly waived privilege and confidentiality.

Further, the breadth of disclosure permitted for self-interested reasons such as collection of fees seems doctrinally inconsistent with the near-absolute nature of the duty of confidentiality generally asserted by the Court. Giving lawyers the discretion to disclose whatever confidential information they see fit simply to collect fees, or because their reputation may be hurt by an allegation of ineffective assistance of counsel, is a significant intrusion into the client's right to confidentiality. It may be that it results in a just

---

[122] FLS MC Rule 2.03(6); AB CPC Chapter 7, Rule 8(e.1). Not all codes expressly contemplate this possibility; however, given that whomever the lawyer consults will also be subject to a duty of confidentiality, it seems reasonable to infer the ability for lawyers to disclose on that basis.

[123] CBA MC Chapter V, Rule 4; FLS MC Rule 2.03(4) and (5); NB CC Chapter 5, Commentary 9(b); LSUC RPC Rule 2.03(4) and (5); AB CBC Chapter 7, Rule 8(f).

[124] [2000] O.J. No. 2182, 48 O.R. (3d) 544 (Ont. S.C.J.).

outcome for the lawyer. But in no other context do we breach confidentiality and privilege simply because, in that instance, doing so would lead to more justice. The whole point of an across the board right to confidentiality for clients, in which confidentiality is protected regardless of the circumstances of a particular case, is to avoid the weighing of confidentiality versus justice on a case by case basis. Doing so only where it benefits lawyers requires explanation. And any explanation that extends the lawyer's ability to disclose beyond that provided by the doctrine of implied waiver may be hard to come by.

H. Where Confidential and Privileged Information is Necessary to Establish the Innocence of an Accused, the Court may Require the Lawyer to Disclose It

A lawyer may be required to provide privileged information to a third party criminal accused if the accused obtains a court order applying the "innocence at stake" exception. The innocence at stake exception is notable as an exception arising not from statute, but from the operation of the common law. It is rarely invoked successfully (indeed, I am unaware of any case in which a criminal accused has done so) but has nonetheless been clearly recognized by the Supreme Court.

The doctrine may be invoked where a criminal accused can only establish his innocence through information that would otherwise be privileged and non-disclosable. The Court has held that in those circumstances, where there is a competing claim to fundamental justice in the form of a risk of wrongful conviction, the privilege may be pierced. The Court established, however, a very high threshold for such disclosure.

In the case of *R. v. McClure*,[125] McClure was charged with a variety of sexual offences in relation to minors. One of the minors, J.C., had commenced a civil action against McClure prior to filing a police complaint. McClure sought access to J.C.'s lawyer's file in the civil action, and was granted such access by the trial judge on the basis that "the accused should be entitled to question the motive of the appellant at the trial of the accused in an attempt to show that the appellant's complaint in the criminal proceeding was made merely to bolster the civil action against the accused and the North York School Board".[126] The Supreme Court reversed, holding that while disclosure of privileged communications to prevent the possibility of a wrongful conviction was possible, such disclosure was not warranted on the facts.

The Court held that before even considering the application of the "innocence at stake" test, the accused "must establish that the information he is seeking in the solicitor-client file is not available from any other

---

[125] [2001] S.C.J. No. 13, 2001 SCC 14 (S.C.C.).
[126] *Ibid.* at para. 12.

source" *and* that "he is otherwise unable to raise a reasonable doubt as to his guilt".[127] If that threshold is established then a two-stage test must be satisfied. First, the accused must "provide some evidentiary basis upon which to conclude that there exists a communication that could raise a reasonable doubt as to his guilt".[128] This requires more than "mere speculation" about what the file contains, although it does not have to be precise knowledge.[129] It could be simply "a description of a possible communication".[130] Second, the trial judge must look at the file to determine "whether, in fact, there exists a communication that is likely to raise a reasonable doubt as to the accused's guilt".[131] This means something which goes directly to one of the elements of the offence. It cannot go, for example, to "ancillary attacks on the Crown's case", such as impugning the credibility of a Crown witness, as was sought by McClure.[132] If this second test is satisfied then the judge should order production "but only of the portion of [the] solicitor-client file that is necessary to raise the defence claimed."[133]

The Court considered the "innocence at stake" exception again in the case of *R. v. Brown*.[134] In that case Brown was charged with murder. Robertson told the police that her boyfriend Benson had confessed to the murder to her and to his lawyers. Although the police investigated Benson's conduct, he was never charged. Instead charges were brought against Brown based on information from a jailhouse informant. Brown sought access to the files of Benson's lawyer. The Supreme Court of Canada denied access because Brown had other ways to get the information related to Benson's confession into court. It also suggested that it was not at all obvious that the Crown would be able to prove Brown's guilt beyond a reasonable doubt on the case as presented, which further made the piercing of the privilege unnecessary at that point in time.

In the course of so concluding, however, the Court made some observations about the operation of the "innocence at stake" rule. First it held that a *McClure* disclosure order could include oral communications as well as written communications — that is, it could be used to compel a lawyer to testify. Second, disclosure should be made only to the accused, and not to the Crown. The Crown will only gain access to the information to the extent the accused chooses to use it. Third, the Court held that s. 7 of the *Charter*[135] gives both direct and derivative use immunity to a person whose information is used pursuant to a *McClure* order: "the privilege holder's

---

[127] *Ibid.* at para. 48.
[128] *Ibid.* at para. 50.
[129] *Ibid.* at para. 53.
[130] *Ibid.* at para. 54.
[131] *Ibid.* at para. 57.
[132] *Ibid.* at para. 58.
[133] *Ibid.* at para. 51.
[134] [2002] S.C.J. No. 35, 2002 SCC 32 (S.C.C.).
[135] *Canadian Charter of Rights and Freedoms*, Part I of the *Constitution Act, 1982* being Schedule B to the *Canada Act 1982* (U.K.), 1982, c. 11.

communications and any evidence derived therefrom cannot be used in a subsequent case against the privilege holder."[136]

The "innocence at stake" exception demonstrates one of the challenges of the distinction between the lawyer's ethical duty of confidentiality and the solicitor-client privilege. Specifically, there may be circumstances where a lawyer knows that her client committed a crime of which another person has been convicted. Under the current ethical rules, a lawyer in that situation cannot disclose the existence of such information, even to trigger counsel for the accused bringing an application under the "innocence at stake" exception. The lawyer may be compelled to produce the information if there is a successful application to invoke the "innocence at stake" exception, but cannot voluntarily disclose that the information exists. As often as not this will mean that even if the "innocence at stake" exception could be invoked, the accused will not even be aware that the information exists and that he could bring a court application to obtain it.

In an infamous American case Alton Logan was convicted of murdering a security guard during an armed robbery of a McDonald's restaurant.[137] The real perpetrator of the murder had admitted his factual guilt to his lawyers, but did not permit those lawyers to disclose the admission; he was in jail, but faced the death penalty had his confession come to light. Alton Logan spent 26 years in jail for those murders. When the real perpetrator died his lawyers, with consent he had given before his death, came forward with their client's confession. Logan was released.

The decision by those lawyers was unexceptional in terms of their ethical duties. And, as they pointed out, and as discussed below, without the obligation of confidentiality it is not at all certain that their client would ever have confessed to the crime. Further, given the absence of an "innocence at stake" exception in the United States, the reality is that bringing forward the confession would likely have resulted in their client's execution. Having a client's own lawyers be the causal agent in their client's execution seems wholly inconsistent with the trust and fidelity of the lawyer-client relationship.

The existence of the "innocence at stake" exception does suggest, however, a more nuanced resolution of the problem raised by the Alton Logan case. If a lawyer indicated to counsel for an innocent accused that he had information that might be producible under the "innocence at stake" exception, a court could then determine whether the exception was satisfied and allow disclosure under the circumstances that that exception permits — that is, to a minimal extent and with use and derivative use immunity being provided to the privilege holder. This still violates the client's right to confidentiality, and the merits of doing so are legitimately debatable; however, given the points of principle made by the Supreme Court in the

---

[136] *R. v. Brown*, [2002] S.C.J. No. 35 at para. 100, 2002 SCC 32 (S.C.C.).
[137] For an introduction to the Alton Logan case, including interviews with the lawyers who did not disclose, see "26-Year Secret Kept Innocent Man In Prison" (25 May 2008), online: 60 Minutes <http://www.cbsnews.com/stories/2008/03/06/60minutes/main3914719.shtml>.

"innocence at stake" context, it seems more consistent to allow this sort of limited disclosure than not to do so. To put it slightly differently, whatever is appropriate at the level of principle, at the level of doctrinal consistency it seems incoherent to permit an exception to privilege in order to serve other interests of fundamental justice, but not to modify the lawyer's ethical duty of confidentiality so as to actually ensure that those interests of fundamental justice will be protected.

I. Information that is Confidential and Privileged may be Disclosed to Prevent Serious, Clear and Imminent Threats to the Safety of an Identifiable Person or Group of People

Probably the most confusing exception to the lawyer's duty of confidentiality concerns whether a lawyer has a duty to voluntarily disclose information in order to prevent an imminent threat to the safety of another person (or group of people). The duty is confused in two ways: first, it is not clear when the duty arises — what type of threat to public safety is necessary. Second, it is not clear whether the lawyer's duty to disclose such information is mandatory or permissive. This is an area where the lack of congruity between the lawyer's ethical duty of confidentiality and the duty of confidentiality arising under solicitor-client privilege is especially confusing. It is also an area where the lack of congruity is especially unnecessary. If there is a risk to public safety that justifies overriding the client's interest in maintaining secrecy then that justification should operate equally against the privilege and against the ethical duty. The Court and the law societies need to address this issue and clarify to lawyers what their duty to disclose is, and when it arises.

What is clear from the case law is that where there is a clear, serious and imminent threat to the public safety of an identifiable person or group of people, then the duty of confidentiality with respect to the information should be "set aside".[138] In *Smith v. Jones*,[139] the Supreme Court considered an application by a psychologist to disclose the report he had prepared on a criminal accused at the request of accused's counsel. When meeting with the psychologist the accused had talked about his plan to commit serious and violent criminal acts against prostitutes in Vancouver. The psychologist then learned that the report he had prepared was not going to be disclosed because the accused had agreed to a plea with the Crown and so there would be no trial. He brought an application seeking the right to disclose the information. The Court held that he could disclose his report.

Writing for the majority, Justice Cory held that the solicitor-client privilege was of central importance, but could be set aside "where the facts

---

[138] *Smith v. Jones*, [1999] S.C.J. No. 15 at para. 85, [1999] 1 S.C.R. 455 (S.C.C.).
[139] [1999] S.C.J. No. 15, [1999] 1 S.C.R. 455 (S.C.C.).

raise real concerns that an identifiable individual or group is in imminent danger of death or serious bodily harm. The facts must be carefully considered to determine whether the three factors of seriousness, clarity, and imminence indicate that the privilege cannot be maintained."[140] The Court defined seriousness as including serious physical harm or death, and serious psychological harm. It qualified imminence by noting that imminent did not necessarily mean immediate — the harm could be imminent even if not becoming manifest for a period of time. The Supreme Court held that the privilege was set aside on the facts because the nature of the threat was sufficiently serious, clear and imminent.

What the Court did not address, though, was whether in such circumstances the person holding the information should be required or simply permitted to disclose it. In his judgment Cory J. discussed the American "duty to warn" cases but when talking about the consequence of the ruling on the facts simply referred to the privilege as being "displaced" or "set aside". The judgment never stated clearly whether or not a privilege holder must disclose the information; as noted by Adam Dodek, the Court employed the language of duty, but created a rule of discretion.[141] The Court may have been hesitant to state that lawyers or doctors have a duty to disclose the information because of the potential for civil liability for them if they do not do so (as exists in the United States); however, the failure to clearly state what lawyers should do simply adds uncertainty to the additional risk that civil liability might pose.

The ethical codes provide no better guidance on this issue. The Canadian Bar Association incorporates the *Smith v. Jones*[142] standard for disclosure — "an imminent risk to an identifiable person or group of death or serious bodily harm, including serious psychological harm that would substantially interfere with health and well being" — and makes the duty to disclose mandatory.[143] The Law Society of Upper Canada incorporates the *Smith v. Jones* standard for disclosure but makes disclosure optional ("may disclose").[144] Other law societies have not responded to *Smith v. Jones*, and instead retain the prior position that lawyers have an obligation of mandatory disclosure where a client threatens to commit a crime involving bodily harm or death, and the option of disclosure when a client threatens to commit any other crime.[145] In the jurisdictions that have not addressed the Supreme Court's decision, the overlap with *Smith v. Jones* is especially confusing: in light of that case it is not clear that a lawyer could lawfully disclose a client's intention to commit a crime that did not satisfy the *Smith v. Jones*

---

[140] *Ibid.* at para. 85.
[141] Adam Dodek, "The Public Safety Exception to Solicitor-Client Privilege: *Smith v. Jones*" (2000) 34 U.B.C. L. Rev. 293 at paras. 73-75.
[142] [1999] S.C.J. No. 15, [1999] 1 S.C.R. 455 (S.C.C.).
[143] CBA MC Chapter IV, Rule 2.
[144] LSUC RPC Rule 2.03(3); Que. CEA Rule 3.06.01.01; *An Act respecting the Barreau du Québec*, R.S.Q. c. B-1, s. 131(3).
[145] NB CC Chapter 8(b) and 9(c); AB CPC Rule 8(c); BC PRH Chapter 5, Rule 12.

standard, and nor is it apparent that the lawyer's duty should be limited to crimes, or that it should be mandatory rather than permissive.[146]

Additional confusion is created by the fact that some codes of conduct have rules addressing the question of public safety in particular circumstances. In some jurisdictions lawyers are placed under an obligation to disclose if they believe a dangerous situation is likely to develop at a court facility,[147] and in New Brunswick lawyers have an obligation to disclose threats to national security.[148] It is not clear how these circumstances relate to the standard established by *Smith v. Jones* and, in particular, whether it is necessary in the circumstances contemplated by those rules to additionally satisfy the clear, imminent and serious danger standard established by that case.

No subsequent case law clarifies the issue, either with respect to the nature of the lawyer's duty or when it arises. In one disciplinary decision the Law Society of Upper Canada considered the scope of the doctrine. In *Law Society of Upper Canada v. Ross*,[149] discussed earlier, the Court considered the conduct of a lawyer whose client had advised him that she intended to take her child to Hungary in the middle of custody proceedings. The lawyer was disciplined for misleading the court in his subsequent conduct; however, the panel found that he could not have disclosed the information from his client, despite the future harm exception. The panel noted that the governing Law Society of Upper Canada rule on disclosure of future harm was permissive and that it was "highly qualified". Further, the panel suggested that there was "no evidence" that the standard was met on the facts of the case.

Another final and quite troubling aspect of this area is that in *Smith v. Jones* the Court did not — and this is distinct from its dealing with the innocence at stake doctrine — provide any restrictions on how the disclosed information could be used going forward against the privilege holder. With respect to the accused in *Smith v. Jones* himself, the medical report disclosed was used not simply to take prophylactic measures to protect the women targeted, but as a basis for withdrawing the plea agreement and having the accused labelled a dangerous offender.[150] The Supreme Court refused leave to appeal this result.[151] This decision was made prior to the decision in *R. v. Brown*,[152] and if the issue arises again a different result may be given, but until that time that outcome adds significant negative consequences for the lawyer's client in the event a lawyer chooses to disclose risks to the public.

---

[146] This point is made clearly in Adam Dodek, "The Public Safety Exception to Solicitor-Client Privilege: *Smith v. Jones*" (2000) 34 U.B.C. L. Rev. 293 at para. 42.
[147] CBA MC Chapter IV, Rule 3; FLS MC 4.06(3); LSUC RPC Rule 4.06(3); NB CC Chapter 5, Commentary 11.
[148] Chapter 5, Commentary 8(c).
[149] [2010] L.S.D.D. No. 10.
[150] *R. v. Leopold*, [2001] S.C.C.A. No. 551 (S.C.C.).
[151] *Ibid.*
[152] [2002] S.C.J. No. 35, 2002 SCC 32 (S.C.C.).

Until the state of law with respect to public safety exceptions is clarified, the prudent course of conduct for a lawyer who is given information by a client that satisfies the exception in *Smith v. Jones* depends on the nature of the information and the rules that apply to the lawyer:

- If the threat is serious and an emergency, the lawyer should immediately disclose the information necessary to deal with the threat. An example of this would be if a client advised the lawyer that he had planted a bomb in a school; the lawyer should call the police and tell them what the client has done.[153]
- If the threat is not an emergency but is a serious and clear threat to public safety, the lawyer should obtain direction through a court order as to whether disclosure is permitted or required. Obtaining advice from counsel, or from the law society, may also be effective, although not as authoritative.
- Where the lawyer works in a jurisdiction with a *mandatory* public safety exception based on crime causing violence, or one of the other specific duties of disclosure such as a threat to a court facility or national security, and circumstances involving that mandatory duty have arisen then
    - if the information also satisfies the test in *Smith v. Jones*, the lawyer should proceed as above;
    - if the information does not satisfy the test in *Smith v. Jones*, the lawyer should not disclose but should seek clarification from the law society as to his ethical obligations.
- If circumstances arise where the lawyer could disclose under a permissive exception of the applicable code of professional conduct, but the circumstances do not satisfy the test in *Smith v. Jones*, the lawyer should not disclose.

These suggestions attempt to describe the lawyer's obligations given the current confused state of the law in this area. How the public safety confusion *should* be resolved is discussed below.

J. Physical or "Real" Evidence of a Crime is not Privileged, and if Inculpatory must be Disclosed

The final exception to the lawyer's duty of confidentiality arises where the client[154] gives the lawyer physical evidence of a crime. As noted, physical evidence generally falls outside of the solicitor-client privilege; however, it is subject to the ethical duty of confidentiality. Moreover, information surrounding the property — such as where it came from, and what it is — is

---

[153] A criminal defence lawyer who I spoke with when preparing this book had such an incident happen.
[154] Or, presumably, a third party.

both privileged and confidential. Most codes of conduct do not create an express exception to permit disclosure of physical evidence. The exception is Alberta, where the Code of Conduct prohibits a lawyer from participating in the concealment of property having evidentiary value in a criminal proceeding.[155] Lawyers nonetheless have a duty of disclosure with respect to physical evidence of a crime.

In the case of *R. v. Murray*,[156] noted earlier, Murray was charged with obstruction of justice in relation to his failure to disclose videotapes of his client Paul Bernardo and Bernardo's wife Karla Homolka assaulting a number of women. The Court held, first, that the videotapes were not privileged. Communication in relation to the tapes would be, but the tapes themselves were not. This meant that Murray had no ability to conceal the tapes that was greater than that of any other citizen. If the tapes were exculpatory then Murray would not necessarily need to disclose them — no obstruction of justice would necessarily result from non-disclosure of exculpatory evidence — and would certainly be justified in delaying disclosure until the trial of the matter. But since the tapes were "overwhelmingly inculpatory"[157] Murray was left with only three "legally justifiable options":

(a) Immediately turn over the tapes to the prosecution, either directly or anonymously;
(b) Deposit them with the trial judge; or
(c) Disclose their existence to the prosecution and prepare to do battle to retain them.[158]

Murray was nonetheless acquitted because the Court held that he lacked the *mens rea* to commit the offence. There was reasonable doubt about his intention to permanently conceal the tapes and as to whether he believed that he was entitled to delay disclosure. The Court noted that while his ethical duty was to produce the tapes, and while Murray made no attempt to discover that duty, "had he done careful research he might have remained confused".[159] Further, while Murray's strategy for using the videotapes to discredit Homolka was dubious, the judge was not prepared to determine conclusively that Murray did not intend to use the tapes in that way.

In discussing the *Murray* case, Michael Code has suggested that the obligations of counsel presented with inculpatory physical evidence are (or at least should be) as follows:

review the material immediately and refuse to accept instructions from the client not to review the material; advise the client that accepting such instructions and not reviewing the material is unethical; advise the client that if the material, once reviewed, turns out to be substantially or predominantly incriminatory, it is illegal and unethical for counsel to

---

[155] Chapter 10, Rule 20. See also FLS MC Rule 2.05(6), commentary.
[156] [2000] O.J. No. 2182, 48 O.R. (3d) 544 (Ont. S.C.J.).
[157] *Ibid.* at para. 117.
[158] *Ibid.* at para. 124.
[159] *Ibid.* at para. 149.

conceal it from the authorities; and finally, if the exculpatory uses of the material are not plain and obvious, or are not clearly the predominant uses of the material, counsel must consult immediately with a panel of senior lawyers convened by the relevant Law Society.[160]

Fulfilling these obligations does not require that a lawyer search for inculpatory evidence about which she only has information, or that she produce evidence which she has seen but of which she does not have control or custody.

For example, in the famous American "Lake Pleasant Bodies Case", lawyers were told by their client that he had committed two murders other than those on which they were representing him. The bodies of the victims of those crimes had not been found; the lawyers went and took photographs of the bodies. Ultimately they disclosed the information about the additional murders in presenting an insanity defence for their client; however, both lawyers were publicly castigated for failing to disclose the information earlier. It is clear, however, that under their ethical duties they were bound not to disclose. The photographs of the bodies were solicitor work product and privileged. The information about the location of the bodies was privileged. The lawyer's observation of the bodies could be argued to fall outside of the privilege (along the lines of the lawyer witnessing the car accident as envisioned by the Court in *Foster Wheeler*); however that information was both wholly derived from privileged information and, in any event, was confidential. The lawyers presented with such information carry a difficult burden, particularly where, as happened in the case, the parent of one of the victims asks one of the lawyers directly if he knows anything about his child's whereabouts. But that burden is theirs to carry under their professional duty not to disclose their client's secrets.

In the event a lawyer is required to disclose physical evidence, she must take steps to protect the information in relation to the property that remains privileged. In the *Murray* case the evidence was notable for not only being evidence of a crime, but for being clear evidence that the crime was committed by Murray's client. Thus, while Murray should not have disclosed Bernardo's instructions about how to deal with the tapes without Bernardo's consent, it was only of minor consequence that he did so; the authorities did not need that additional information to link the videotapes to Bernardo. A handgun, by contrast, may be evidence of a crime, but does not necessarily link any particular person to that crime. A counsel turning over a handgun should retain other counsel to assist in doing so, and should be sure to protect the privileged information about where the handgun was found, and from whom the lawyer received it.

The *Murray* case provides guidance to lawyers about their obligations when given physical evidence of a crime by their clients. It is essential,

---

[160] Michael Code, "Ethics and Criminal Law Practice" in Alice Woolley *et al.*, eds., *Lawyers' Ethics and Professional Regulation* (Toronto: LexisNexis Canada, 2008) at 392-93.

however, that codes of conduct be revised to provide clarity and guidance to lawyers on this point. The rule in Alberta, which on its face appears to require disclosure of any physical evidence of a crime, whether exculpatory or inculpatory, is too broad. However, it should be possible to draft a rule that incorporates the obligations set out here. No lawyer who makes a good faith effort to discover her obligations should be left "confused."[161]

4. WHAT DUTIES DOES A LAWYER HAVE TO PROTECT THE CLIENT'S RIGHT TO CONFIDENTIALITY?

The lawyer has a duty to protect the client's right to confidentiality. That means two things: first, the lawyer has an obligation to resist incursions into the client's confidentiality and, second, to the extent disclosure is permitted or required, the lawyer must provide as little disclosure as possible.

The first of these duties follows from the lawyer's duty of loyalty, and her obligation to implement the client's instructions in a representation. It primarily consists of advancing privilege claims in court and ensuring that documents are properly sealed if seized prior to adjudication of privilege claims. The lawyer's duty to protect client interests has been specifically noted by the Supreme Court in the context of law office searches. The Supreme Court has held that where a client whose privilege may be affected by the execution of the search warrant cannot be contacted, then "the lawyer who has custody of the documents seized, or another lawyer appointed either by the Law Society or the court, should examine the documents to determine whether a claim of privilege should be asserted".[162]

The second duty, of minimal disclosure, follows from Supreme Court jurisprudence, where the Court has often noted that disclosure should be as limited as possible.[163] It is also expressly provided for in some ethical codes,[164] and may be implicitly contemplated by the others, insofar as they only allow disclosure where authorized by law. Lawyers should be especially mindful of this requirement if exercising the permission to disclose to defend an action, or to collect fees from a client.

---

[161] *R. v. Murray*, [2000] O.J. No. 2182 at para. 149, 48 O.R. (3d) 544 (Ont. S.C.J.).
[162] *Lavallee, Rackel & Heintz v. Canada (Attorney General)*, [2002] S.C.J. No. 61, [2002] 3 S.C.R. 209 at 251, 2002 SCC 61 (S.C.C.). LSUC RPC Rule 2.07, commentary, directs the lawyer to be alert to privilege issues where there is an attempt to seize client property; BC PRH Chapter 5, Rule 14 also directs the lawyer to assert privilege where there is a search pursuant to the *Criminal Code*, R.S.C. 1985, c. C-46, *Income Tax Act*, R.S.C. 1985 (5th Supp.), c. 1 or like provisions.
[163] For example, *Smith v. Jones*, [1999] S.C.J. No. 15 at para. 86, [1999] 1 S.C.R. 455 (S.C.C.), although the dissent and majority disagreed on what minimum disclosure meant on the facts of that case. Also *Descôteaux v. Mierzwinski*, [1982] S.C.J. No. 43, [1982] 1 S.C.R. 860 at 891 (S.C.C.); *R. v. McClure*, [2001] S.C.J. No. 13, 2001 SCC 14 (S.C.C.).
[164] LSUC RPC Rule 2.03(5), which allows disclosure to collect fees, states that the lawyer "shall not disclose more information than is required"; NB CC Chapter 5, Commentary 10; AB CPC, Chapter 7, Rule 9.

5. WHAT DUTIES DO LAWYERS HAVE IN RELATION TO THE CONFIDENTIALITY CLAIMS OF OTHERS?

Lawyers not only represent clients who have a right to confidentiality, they also act in matters in which other parties have rights to confidentiality. A lawyer may challenge the confidentiality and privilege claims asserted by others; however, the lawyer also has a duty not to subvert the confidentiality and privilege claims of others. This is reflected in the implied undertaking rule, discussed above in Section 2.N. but also in the rule that requires a lawyer who inadvertently becomes aware of confidential and privileged information to return that information to its source without looking at it.[165]

Where lawyers have received and improperly reviewed confidential information from the opposing party, courts have been prepared to remove those counsel from the record. In *Celanese Canada Inc. v. Murray Demolition Corp.*[166] the Supreme Court removed counsel where they had received privileged information through an Anton Piller injunction, had improperly handled that information, reviewing it and making notes on it, and then had destroyed the information rather than returning it. As summarized by the Court, the "disclosure of solicitor-client confidences came about not by egregious misconduct, but through a combination of carelessness, overzealousness, a lack of appreciation of the potential dangers of an Anton Piller order and a failure to focus on its limited purpose, namely the *preservation* of relevant evidence."[167] The Court held that the test for whether counsel should be removed properly requires consideration of how the documents came into the possession of opposing counsel, what they did once they recognized the documents were privileged, how extensive was their review of the materials, the prejudicial nature of the communications, the stage of the litigation and the effectiveness of other means to remedy the prejudice.[168]

A lawyer may also be disciplined by a law society for improper use of inadvertently disclosed information. In *Law Society of Alberta v. Trawick*,[169] lawyers were reprimanded for their handling of documents that were confidential in the hands of a third party, which they had not been given permission to view, and that they had both viewed and then attempted to obtain by other means. The lawyers were acting for a client involved in corporate litigation; one of the parties on the other side had been involved in

---

[165] Not all of the ethical codes deal with this issue. See, though, AB CPC Chapter 4, Rule 8; BC PRH Chapter 5, Rule 15.
[166] [2006] S.C.J. No. 35, [2006] 2 S.C.R. 189, 2006 SCC 36 (S.C.C.).
[167] *Ibid.* at para. 31 [emphasis in original].
[168] See also *Canada Post Corp. v. Euclide Cormeir Plumbing and Heating Inc.*, [2007] N.B.J. No. 364 (N.B.Q.B.), affd [2008] N.B.J. No. 300 (N.B.C.A.) (counsel not removed; party receiving the disclosure was blameless, the material might have been produced in any event and other means could be used to protect the privilege); *Tilley v. Hails et al.*, [1993] O.J. No. 333, 12 O.R. (3d) 306 (Ont. Gen. Div.) (party required to return confidential information it had received inadvertently).
[169] [2002] L.S.D.D. No. 59.

a divorce proceeding. The lawyers contacted the party's ex-wife and asked to view the documents from the divorce proceeding. Because she had signed a confidentiality agreement, the ex-wife gave them permission only to review those documents that were in the public record. The junior lawyer was inadvertently given the confidential documents to review. He nonetheless reviewed and copied some of those documents, being of the view that they were not in fact legitimately confidential. Eventually the lawyers realized that this was incorrect, and that they had documents that they should not have had in light of the limited consent they had been given by the ex-wife; specifically, documents related to the divorce proceeding that were not in the public record. However, they were also of the view that some of the documents were legitimately producible by the other side in their litigation, and brought an application to have them produced.

Not only was the application unsuccessful, but the court found that the lawyers had engaged in professional misconduct in relation to their handling of the documents. The judge prohibited the lawyers' client from using any information contained in the documents, even if not privileged, unless the matters in the documents were brought into issue by the other side. He ordered that the lawyers pay costs of the motion personally. That decision was upheld on appeal.[170] In a separate proceeding the Law Society agreed that the lawyers had engaged in professional misconduct; they were reprimanded and ordered to pay the costs of the disciplinary proceeding.[171]

It is likely that a less harsh outcome would occur if the disclosure received by the lawyers was truly inadvertent, particularly if the information was confidential but not privileged. For example, in an interesting American case, *Jasmine Networks Inc. v. Marvell Semiconductor Inc.*,[172] a lawyer from

---

[170] [2001] A.J. No. 1317 at paras. 7-9, 2001 ABCA 248 (Alta. C.A.). The Court of Appeal stated: In any event, we regard producibility of the documents by the respondent company as something of a red herring. The appellant lawyers got documents which they soon learned were beyond their request, were beyond the permission of their beneficial owner, or were the fruit of innocence or neglect by a legal assistant in the absence of the counsel who owned the documents. It was plain that the beneficial owner had refused to extend consent to this class of documents. The plain duty of the recipient counsel was to seal them up, not read them further, take no copies, take no notes, and return any copies or notes already taken. At the very highest, the appellant lawyers could have sealed everything up and got the court's direction. They did none of those things. They hid the problem for months, then tried ex post facto to get the beneficial owner's consent (despite a contract preventing that), then tried to get the court to make orders which would give them other copies of the documents another way. ... The chambers judge found that these counsel were guilty of enough misconduct to justify an order that they pay costs of the resulting motions personally. In our view, that conclusion and penalty were amply justified, even moderate.

[171] *Law Society of Alberta v. Trawick*, [2002] L.S.D.D. No. 59.

[172] *Jasmine Networks Inc. v. Marvell Semiconductor Inc.* (Calif. CA, Sixth Appellate District), April 8, 2004, online: <http://www.courtinfo.ca.gov/opinions/revpub/H023991.PDF>. The (non) resolution of the matter was discussed at Legal Ethics Forum, online at: <http://www.legalethicsforum.com/blog/2009/06/jasmine-v-marvell-the-forgot-to-hang-up-and-left-incriminating-voicemail-with-the-opposing-lawyer-ca.html>; Mike McKee, "Marvell May

Jasmine received a voice mail from the general counsel for Marvell during negotiations for Marvell to purchase some intellectual property and a group of Jasmine's engineers. The counsel for Marvell was on speaker phone, along with another in-house counsel and executives in the company. After leaving a message for counsel for Jasmine, the Marvell lawyer forgot to hang up the phone; he and his client allegedly proceeded to discuss a scheme under which they had or were going to steal Jasmine's trade secrets and its key employees. After investigating matters and finding other evidence that allegedly showed a theft, Jasmine brought an action against Marvell alleging trade secret misappropriation and related claims. Jasmine sought to be able to rely on the phone call in the litigation on the basis that, as a criminal communication, it was not privileged. Although the California appellate court agreed that the communication was criminal and therefore not privileged, that decision was under appeal and never finally resolved, as the underlying litigation was dismissed for lack of standing.[173] However, I would argue that production of the phone call in such a case would be legitimate. The lawyer did not act inappropriately in listening to the phone call in the first instance and, as it turned out, the phone conversation was not privileged because it was a criminal communication.

This then raises, though, the difficult question of whether a lawyer who has received inadvertent disclosure should review that disclosure to see if it is, in fact, privileged and confidential. The codes of conduct that address this issue clearly do not contemplate the lawyer doing so. Further, cases such as *Celanese*[174] cast significant doubt on the ability of the lawyer to take this step, raising the possibility that if the lawyer does review the information, and it turns out that it *is* privileged, the lawyer may be prevented from acting for the client further, or even subject to disciplinary proceedings.

On the whole, it seems likely that while inadvertent review of information that is claimed to be privileged will allow a lawyer to challenge the privilege claim in the event that the claim is ill-founded, a lawyer is nonetheless not permitted to review information "just in case" it is not as privileged as it first appears.

6. CAN THE LAWYER'S DUTY OF TRUST AND CONFIDENCE BE JUSTIFIED?

A. Justifying the General Duty

Whatever the confusion and complexity in determining the boundaries of the application of the lawyer's duty of confidentiality, it is nonetheless clear in

---

Have Lost Battle to Suppress Voice Mail in Trade Secrets Case" (24 April 2008), online: Law.com <http://www.law.com/jsp/article.jsp?id=1209001761648>.

[173] Zusha Elinson, "IP Suit Against Marvell Semiconductor Dismissed for Lack of Standing" (4 June 2009), online: Law.com <http://www.law.com/jsp/article.jsp?id=1202431206629>.

[174] *Celanese Canada Inc. v. Murray Demolition Corp.*, [2006] S.C.J. No. 35, [2006] 2 S.C.R. 189, 2006 SCC 36 (S.C.C.).

Canadian law that lawyers have a strong ethical duty not to disclose information about their client, even when doing so might be viewed as in some way in the public interest. Without the consent of their clients, lawyers may not disclose information to ensure that criminals get punished, may not disclose information to prevent future harm unless that harm is serious and imminent, and may not disclose information to ensure that a court is not misled. Individuals and organizations alike enjoy the right to confidentiality, and lawyers are bound to respect it or risk civil liability, removal from representation or professional discipline.

The obvious question this raises, however, is whether this broad and near-absolute duty of confidentiality is justified, or whether it should be qualified in some way. Should the exceptions to prevent future harm be extended? Should the self-interest exceptions be limited? Should the strong professional duty not attach to organizations or to civil actions? Or, at its most extreme, should the professional duty be eliminated altogether? Marvin Frankel, for example, argued that since the search for truth was the paramount purpose of the legal system, a strong duty of confidentiality could not be justified. He argued for "a pervasive broadening of the [lawyer's] duty to reveal the truth, even when it hurts".[175] Specifically, Frankel suggested that lawyers should rectify falsehoods arising from a client's testimony even where doing so requires breaching confidentiality. Further even if a client did not testify, but has revealed facts to the lawyer that would have a substantial effect on the determination of a material issue in litigation, he argued that the lawyer should give the information to the court, even where doing so is adverse to the client's interests and contrary to the client's instructions.

Frankel's argument is utilitarian. That is, he argues that the lawyer's obligation of confidentiality has a negative impact, and that that negative impact outweighs any benefits to which the lawyer's obligation may give rise. Interestingly, utilitarian arguments are also what proponents suggest justifies the doctrine of confidentiality and privilege. In particular, in its jurisprudence, the Supreme Court returns repeatedly to the idea that the lawyer's duty of confidentiality is justified because that duty results in good effects or, more negatively, that the absence of the duty would have very bad ones.

The argument made by the Court runs like this: (1) Without assurance that their secrets will not be disclosed, clients are less likely to provide full and frank disclosure to their lawyers; (2) Without such disclosure, lawyers cannot properly advise their clients; (3) Unless lawyers can properly advise their clients, the legal system cannot function; and (4) The functioning of the legal system outweighs any costs incurred by the duty of confidentiality:

> Clients seeking advice must be able to speak freely to their lawyers secure in the knowledge that what they say will not be divulged without

---

[175] Monroe Freedman & Abbe Smith, *Understanding Lawyers' Ethics*, 4th ed. (New Providence, NJ: LexisNexis, 2010) at 135.

their consent. It cannot be forgotten that the privilege is that of the client, not the lawyer. The privilege is essential if sound legal advice is to be given in every field. It has a deep significance in almost every situation where legal advice is sought whether it be with regard to corporate and commercial transactions, to family relationships, to civil litigation or to criminal charges. Family secrets, company secrets, personal foibles and indiscretions all must on occasion be revealed to the lawyer by the client. Without this privilege clients could never be candid and furnish all the relevant information that must be provided to lawyers if they are to properly advise their clients. It is an element that is both integral and extremely important to the functioning of the legal system. It is because of the fundamental importance of the privilege that the onus properly rests upon those seeking to set aside the privilege to justify taking such a significant step.[176]

What we have, then, is a utilitarian fight. Confidentiality and privilege are either justified because they create a social good, or they should be eliminated because they create a social bad. Which of these positions is most convincing? In my view, while the Supreme Court is too quick to assume the self-evident truth of its position, the utilitarian argument in favour of the confidentiality is somewhat more persuasive than the utilitarian argument against it. Ultimately, though, the utilitarian framing of the debate is insufficient. To think about the merits of lawyers having a duty not to disclose requires returning to the fundamental argument set out in Chapter 2; since confidentiality is a central attribute of the lawyer's loyal representation of the interests of her client, it needs to be justified (or critiqued) through consideration of its relationship to why we have loyal representation in the first place.

The rest of this section sets out, first, the utilitarian debate. It then considers the "human dignity" alternative to utilitarianism, arguing that the argument from human dignity does not help resolve the problem, since it asks (and answers) the wrong question. The section concludes by arguing that the duty of confidentiality should be maintained because of its relationship to the role of the lawyer in a democratic system of laws.

The utilitarian critics of the duty of confidentiality make two arguments. They argue that the empirical premises asserted by utilitarian proponents like the Supreme Court of Canada are fundamentally flawed, or they argue that even if the premises are correct, the privilege creates consequences that are negative overall. Jeremy Bentham, for example, argued that the premise that confidentiality was necessary to ensure that

---

[176] *Smith v. Jones*, [1999] S.C.J. No. 15 at para. 46, [1999] 1 S.C.R. 455 (S.C.C.). See also: *Canada (Privacy Commissioner) v. Blood Tribe Department of Health*, [2008] S.C.J. No. 45 at para. 9, 2008 SCC 44 (S.C.C.); *Blank v. Canada (Minister of Justice)*, [2006] S.C.J. No. 39 at para. 26, [2006] 2 S.C.R. 319 at 330 (S.C.C.); *Foster Wheeler Power Co. v. Société intermunicipale de gestion et d'élimination des déchets (SIGED) Inc.*, [2004] S.C.J. No. 18, [2004] 1 S.C.R. 456 at 476-77, 2004 SCC 18 (S.C.C.); *R. v. McClure*, [2001] S.C.J. No. 13 at para. 33, 2001 SCC 14 (S.C.C.).

clients make full and frank disclosure did not account for the point that if a criminal accused was innocent, the duty of confidentiality would not be necessary for that individual to make fulsome disclosure to his lawyer — if he is innocent, he has nothing to hide. The only people who are helped to make full and frank disclosure by the lawyer's duty of confidentiality are people who have something to hide, and those people, who are guilty, do not deserve our protection.[177] In other words, confidentiality is not necessary for full and frank disclosure in the only cases where such disclosure is necessary to help the legal system work well. And the circumstances in which the duty is necessary for full and frank disclosure are the precise circumstances where the duty injures the functioning of the legal system, rather than assisting it.

The problem with Bentham's point, however, was squarely addressed by Monroe Freedman in *Legal Ethics in an Adversary System*,[178] in which he noted that Bentham assumes that the client knows he is innocent, and also knows which facts will tend to be exculpatory and which inculpatory. A woman who killed her husband after years of abuse might not appreciate the availability of the defence of self-defence, and might not tell her lawyer about the abuse fearing that doing so would simply incriminate her further by giving her motive. That is, she would assume that what is in fact exculpatory evidence is inculpatory, and dangerous to disclose. Further, the blanket categories of "innocent" and "guilty" seem unduly simplistic. A person could be innocent of a charge of murder, but guilty of some other more minor crime, such as robbery. If the person fears that the admission of robbery will implicate them in the more serious crime, will disclosure be forthcoming?[179] The idea that full and frank disclosure will occur wherever a client is innocent seems difficult to maintain. Finally, it takes no account of the operation of confidentiality in circumstances where the client is not trying to avoid the consequences of illegal action, but is rather trying to determine whether conduct is, or is not, lawful.

Other critics of the utilitarian justification for the privilege, such as Adam Dodek, attack the full and frank disclosure point differently. Relying on a handful of small scale studies on the effect of confidentiality and privilege, they argue that there is simply no empirically demonstrable correlation between the obligation and client disclosure. To the extent disclosure to lawyers occurs, that is not because of the duty of confidentiality. Clients are simply unaware of, or misunderstand, the nature

---

[177] Jeremy Bentham, "Rationale of Judicial Evidence" in *The Works of Jeremy Bentham, 1748–1832* (London: Hunt and Clarke, 1827) v, at Book IX, Part IV, 302–4.

[178] Monroe Freedman, *Legal Ethics in an Adversary System* (Indianapolis, Ind., Bobbs-Merrill, 1975) at 4–5.

[179] It was once thought that these were the facts in relation to the wrongful conviction of Donald Marshall for the murder of Sandy Seale, as at one time it was suggested that Marshall and Seale had robbed the person who killed Seale. Marshall denied this allegation. It is not hard to imagine, though, a case in which an individual could end up with that problem — of being guilty of a lesser charge the admission of which would increase the probability of a wrongful conviction of a much more serious offence.

of the lawyer's duty, and do not rely on it in determining what, or what not, to say when talking to their lawyers. Further, full and frank disclosure is not necessary for lawyers to present a client's case, since lawyers do so without such disclosure on a regular basis.[180]

The problem with this criticism, however, is that the empirical evidence on which it relies as to the effect of the lawyer's duty of confidentiality is simply too weak to support such unequivocal conclusions. Susan Martyn summarized the direct empirical evidence in a 2003 article and stated that only "[t]wo small scale surveys" have been done on the question.[181] Notably the author of one of the studies relied upon by critics, Professor Fred C. Zacharias, acknowledged that his study was "somewhat unscientific"[182] and warned against "overreliance"[183] on the data in assessing the merits of the lawyer's duty.

Further, Dodek's point that lawyers act for clients without frank disclosure may be correct in the sense that lawyers often do so, but it is far from obvious that the outcomes of that fact are happy. In one Canadian case,[184] the lawyer's apparently strategic refusal to obtain information from his client resulted in that lawyer pushing the client to enter a plea of guilty without realizing that the client maintained his innocence, and had done so consistently. It also compounded the lawyer's failure to appreciate the significant weaknesses in the Crown's case. As noted by the judge who expunged the client's plea,

> [i]f you don't discuss the facts with the client until the morning of the trial, then how do you prepare for trial? ... It isn't enough to discuss what it means to be a party to an offence or to discuss the difference in law ... There must be a discussion of the facts, in the context of the elements of the offences, that the client is prepared to admit. The client must also be informed and this means to have full disclosure and his counsel's frank assessment of the import of that disclosure.[185]

In the end, given the limited empirical data, we are to some extent stuck with our intuitions as to the effect of confidentiality on clients' willingness to disclose, and with our experience as lawyers in determining the importance of such disclosure to functional lawyer advocacy. While

---

[180] Adam M. Dodek, "Reconceiving Solicitor-Client Privilege" (2010) 35 Queen's L.J. 493. See also: Adam Dodek, "Doing Our Duty: The Case for a Duty of Disclosure to Prevent Death or Serious Harm" (2001) 50 U.N.B.L.J. 215 at 222–23, where he notes the lack of empirical support for an absolute doctrine of privilege; Wayne Renke, "Case Comment: Secrets and Lives – The Public Safety Exception to Solicitor-Client Privilege: *Smith v. Jones*" (1999) 37 Alta. L. Rev. 1045 at 1064–65 where he criticizes the dissenting judgment of Justice Major for its assertion of predictions of what is likely to occur without empirical evidence.

[181] Susan Martyn, "In Defense of Client-Lawyer Confidentiality ... and Its Exceptions" (2003) 81 Neb. L. Rev. 1320.

[182] Fred Zacharias, "Rethinking Confidentiality" (1989) 74 Iowa L. Rev. 351 at 396.

[183] *Ibid.*

[184] *R. v. I.B.B.*, [2009] S.J. No. 378, 2009 SKPC 76 (Sask. Prov. Ct.), discussed further in Chapter 9.

[185] *Ibid.* at para. 65.

intuitions should not be clung to when they are demonstrated to be false,[186] they should not be ignored. We can ask ourselves this question: "would I be more or less willing to be honest and candid with someone if I knew, beyond a shadow of a doubt, that they would not repeat what I said unless I told them that they could?" To the extent most of us answer "yes" to that question, then the empirical foundations of the utilitarian argument retain some force, even if less solid and scientific than the Court's statement of them might suggest.

This, though, does not answer Frankel's broader point, that even if full and frank disclosure is more likely when confidentiality is protected, and even if such disclosure is important for lawyers to function well, the overall effect of the duty not to disclose is nonetheless bad. As explained by David Luban in response to Freedman's battered spouse example, the full and frank disclosure justification for the privilege does not address the point that the number of innocent people who would be convicted if the confidentiality were eliminated would almost certainly be significantly outnumbered by the increase in convictions of the guilty — that is, the elimination of confidentiality would tend to increase the overall accuracy of judicial decision making, which creates a utilitarian justification for doing so.[187]

The problem with Luban's response to Freedman is that even if it is empirically true, it does not account for the possibility that from a societal perspective we almost certainly place different weighting on those outcomes, which must be taken into account in any utilitarian analysis. Assume that we as a society put 1000 units of negative utility on a single wrongful conviction that would arise from the elimination of the privilege, and one unit of positive utility on the conviction of a guilty person who would have otherwise gone free. If those assumptions are correct, then the utilitarian justification for a change in the current legal regime would have to show that 1000 times more guilty people would be convicted than innocent ones as a result of the change. Or, to reference Frankel's argument, what he fails to take into account is that, as a society, we may value some failures of truth more significantly than others; a failure of truth that results in the conviction of the innocent may simply matter much more to us than a failure of the truth that results in the acquittal of the guilty. And in utilitarian terms, different weighing of preferences must be taken into account in determining the appropriate social policy.

On the whole, I think the utilitarian analysis of the privilege, whether in individual cases or more generally, provides strong if not irrefutable

---

[186] See, for example, Alice Woolley, "Tending the Bar: The Good Character Requirement for Law Society Admission" (2007) 30 Dal. L.J. 27; Alice Woolley & Jocelyn Stacey, "The Psychology of Good Character: the past, present and future of good character regulation in Canada" in Kieran Tranter *et al.*, eds., *Re-affirming Legal Ethics* (New York: Routledge, 2010) at 165.
[187] David Luban, *Lawyers and Justice: An Ethical Study* (Princeton: Princeton University Press, 1988) at 191-92. See also *Lawyers' Ethics and Human Dignity* (New York: Cambridge University Press, 2007).

support for the doctrine. It may not have the persuasive force suggested by the Supreme Court's rhetoric, but its foundations remain legitimate.

In any event, and importantly, utilitarian justifications are not the only — or even the most important — justification for the privilege. Utilitarianism always, and only, considers the justification for decisions based on their consequences. But ethical and legal principles are as often as not best understood non-consequentially, in terms of the underlying rights and interests that they protect. Confidentiality and privilege can, and should, be justified in this way.

The most common non-consequentialist justification for the privilege is that it protects the human dignity of clients.[188] David Luban argues, for example, that keeping secrets is a moral principle, generally speaking, albeit one that can be outweighed by competing moral values. It is not that telling secrets you have promised to keep is ethically good, but that, despite the moral weight of keeping promises of confidentiality, there are circumstances in which breaking that promise is the right thing to do. And, for Luban, the question that must be answered is why we would make keeping secrets the paramount moral value, as we do through the lawyer's duty of trust and confidence — *i.e.*, a moral value that is not weighed against counter-vailing moral arguments in each case?

He argues that the answer to that question is that secret keeping should only be the paramount moral value in those circumstances in which it follows from other moral values that can clearly be accepted as paramount — that is, in criminal defence work. Confidentiality arises in criminal defence work as an essential component of the accused's human dignity. Because to protect the accused's dignitary interests in criminal cases we give the accused both a right against self-incrimination and a right to counsel. Without a duty of confidentiality, the client would be forced to choose between these rights — if he chose the right to counsel, and told counsel the truth, then counsel might reveal that truth to someone else. But if he chose the right against self-incrimination, he could not have counsel, because counsel might incriminate him when he disclosed information to the lawyer. Luban suggests that this justifies the paramount obligation of confidentiality in criminal defence work, but argues that in other legal contexts, such as civil litigation, where there is no right against self-incrimination, or in corporate or organizational representation, where the client has no dignity interest to protect, the duty should not be paramount. It can be an ethical duty — just as it is in everyday life — but it should have no special weight as against other moral values.

The weakness of this non-consequentialist justification, though, is that it frames the debate in ordinary moral terms — what is the right thing to do, all things considered? But the whole point of a system of laws, and of the

---

[188] David Luban, *ibid.*, and Adam Dodek make this argument. Adam Dodek, "Reconceiving Solicitor-Client Privilege" (2010) 35(2) Queen's L.J. 493 at 519-28.

role of lawyers within the system of laws, is to allow us to achieve a democratic compromise about what we will (or will not) require of each other, including in some circumstances what we will and will not require each other to disclose. Lawyers help achieve that compromise, as discussed in Chapter 2. What this means is that the non-consequentialist assessment of the lawyer's duty of confidentiality and privilege must proceed not on the basis of whether that duty is compatible with ordinary moral intuitions, but on the basis of whether it fosters the lawyer's representation of the client within a democratic system of laws and, as well, whether it in some way undermines the pre-existing determinations of the legal system in relation to secret-keeping. That is, is confidentiality necessary to allow individuals to determine their conception of the good within a system of laws? Is it consistent with the compromises on secret keeping that the system of laws reflects?[189]

To answer these questions requires returning to the nature of the duty of confidentiality set out in prior sections of this chapter. When looked at as a whole, the duty of confidentiality protects three things from disclosure. First, and most importantly, it protects from disclosure the legal advice provided by the lawyer. This is always the case unless the client himself puts the legal advice at issue in some way.

Second, it protects from disclosure the information provided to the lawyer to obtain that advice *in the form in which it was given to the lawyer*. To the extent that information is itself producible in another way, it is, in and of itself, not protected from disclosure by the confidentiality or privilege. For example, if I created a memorandum for a lawyer summarizing all of the health impacts that I had suffered following a car accident, that memorandum would not be producible. However, in an examination for discovery I would have to answer any generally relevant question posed by opposing counsel about those health impacts. That will, or at least should, result in disclosure of all the facts that the memorandum contains. And to the extent that it does not do so, then non-disclosure is not a result of the privilege, but of whatever factors resulted in the information not being disclosed (*e.g.*, that the examining lawyer did not ask the right questions). The privilege prevents the non-disclosure from being rectified in that case, but does not itself create the non-disclosure.

Third, the privilege protects from disclosure information given to the lawyer by the client that the client will not be required to disclose through the operation of the law. In the criminal context facts are kept hidden from the state to a much more significant extent than in civil proceedings — there

---

[189] This is not a circular argument. I am not arguing that because the privilege is a rule of law, it is a democratic compromise that it is justified on that basis. I think that is a reasonable position — and is one reason why I tend to think reform of the privilege should be legislative not judicial. But my question is, rather, whether the confidentiality undermines *other* legal positions on the disclosure of information. Does it undermine disclosure in civil cases? Investigations of corporate wrongdoing? Regulatory enforcement of the payment of taxes?

is no right to discovery against a criminal accused, and no obligation on an accused to testify. In criminal cases lawyers will have information disclosed to them by clients in the course of the lawyer-client relationship that will not be produced in any other way, and the doctrine of privilege means that it will not be produced by the lawyer.

Similarly, outside of litigation, information held by one person will not necessarily be produced to another; in the context of contract negotiations, for example, parties may, within the bounds of the duties imposed by the private law of torts, contracts and fiduciary duties, keep information from each other. Again, the result of the client's right to confidentiality and privilege is that the lawyer will have information disclosed to her by clients in the course of the lawyer-client relationship, that information will not be produced in any other way, and the doctrine of privilege means that it will not be produced by the lawyer.

Each of these outcomes can be justified as part of the lawyer's role in a democratic system of laws. With respect to the non-disclosure of legal advice, in a perfect world the individual would not need legal advice. What the law permits, provides or prohibits in relation to his conception of the good would be something that he could determine for himself. And were he to do so then his assessment would be private to him; he would be under no obligation to tell anyone what his review of the law in relation to his own situation revealed.

The world is not perfect, however, and people do need legal advice to determine what the law provides, permits or prohibits. It seems reasonable, though, to treat that advice when given by a lawyer in the same way that it would be treated if the person gave it to himself — as private and not compellable. To do otherwise is to undermine the very thing that having lawyers provides — assisting people to pursue their conceptions of the good within the system of laws. Not because without confidentiality full and frank disclosure would not occur. And not because people have the right to be free from self-incrimination. But because confidentiality simply neutralizes the difference between figuring out the law for yourself, and having someone telling you what it means.

With respect to the information provided to the lawyer that is producible in some other way, the client's right to confidentiality makes the production of information less efficient, but it does not preclude it. And to the extent the gathering of information needs to be made more efficient, that can be addressed in ways that do not limit the client's right to confidentiality when seeking legal advice — that is, by facilitating the other ways of obtaining the evidence. Thus, for example, instead of requiring that taxpayers provide to the government the memorandum provided to their counsel seeking advice on the likely outcome of particular transactions, the government can simply require the corporation to identify any transaction over a monetary amount which the corporation thinks falls within the government's audit scope. In a self-reporting tax system, such a requirement is not incoherent. Similar disclosure requirements can be — and are — created to ensure corporate compliance with regulatory requirements such as those set out by the securities regulations.

With respect to the information provided to the lawyer that is not producible in some other way, then the same point follows as is the case for legal advice: if the client has the right not to disclose that information under law, and the lawyer exists to allow the client to pursue his conception of the good within the law, it is perverse to make the cost of going to a lawyer a change in the client's underlying legal entitlements, in this case non-disclosure.

The difficult issue, and where the objection of critics like Luban arises, is where a client is not legally required to disclose information, but is also in a sense not legally entitled to keep the information secret, and keeping the information secret is wrongful both morally and in terms of the norms underlying the law. Information in this category would be information about wrongful conduct by a client, past or future, and also where the client is taking advantages of weaknesses in the enforcement mechanisms in the law in order to keep information secret. The analysis in the previous paragraphs suggests why the lawyer keeping this information secret is justified — since the client is not legally required to disclose the information, and since the client should not be made worse off by consulting a lawyer, the lawyer should not disclose the information. Having said that, this seems like a somewhat weak basis for the client to claim the lawyer's loyalty and advocacy: "I'm a wrongdoer who the law isn't able to catch, so you have to keep quiet."

This does not mean, though, that the lawyer's duties change. The foundation of the lawyer's obligation does justify this result, even if less strongly than in other contexts. What it does mean is that it is at precisely this point that principled exceptions to the duties of confidentiality can be appropriately articulated. The criminal communications exclusion, the future harm exception and the innocence at stake exception make sense in part because they operate at the point where the client's claim to the lawyer's silence is the weakest.

As was the case with the justification for the lawyer's role, this justification for confidentiality does not reduce the moral complexity of the obligation that lawyers have. A lawyer who knows that an innocent man is in jail, that she could establish the man's innocence, and yet has to stand by and watch that injustice and suffering continue, bears an irreducible moral burden. The burden is not of the magnitude of the suffering of the man in jail, but nor is it something that can be remedied by coming up with a rock solid justification for the privilege. No matter how well justified the rule that creates it, the lawyer must carry that moral burden. Nor, however, is the cost for lawyers something which means the privilege should be abolished. Our broader legal system has established a process and system for adjudicating cases, for imposing obligations of disclosure, and for establishing zones of privacy within which each of us gets to live. The law permits me to keep my longings to myself, and my consultation of a lawyer about whether the law can help me to realize them should not change that legal compromise.

B. Some Specific Points

That the general duty of confidentiality is justified, however, does not mean that the precise shape of the legal doctrine that exists in Canada is perfect, or that every specific issue should be resolved in favour of the duty. What it means is simply that the duty, and its exceptions, should be thought about in terms of their justifications: given the function of the lawyer's duty not to disclose within our democratic legal system, is a change to the duty required or permitted, and what should that change be? This section considers and makes recommendations with respect to three particular issues arising from the client's right to confidentiality: (1) the public safety exception; (2) the exceptions for lawyer self-interest; and (3) confidentiality for organizations and corporations.

As noted, the public safety exception in Canada is currently in a state of confusion. In my view that confusion should be resolved in accordance with Chapter IV, Rule 2 of the CBA Model Code: lawyers should be required to disclose any threat that satisfies the test set out in *Smith v. Jones*,[190] but should not be permitted to disclose information on the basis of public safety in other circumstances. In particular, lawyers should not be permitted to disclose simply because a client has stated a criminal intention. Further, however, and following the principles of *R. v. Brown*[191] with respect to the doctrine of innocence at stake, when lawyers make the disclosure to protect the public safety, the privilege holder should normally be entitled to use and derivative use immunity for that information.

The basis for a mandatory exception of this type is tricky. Our desires to do wrong to others are amongst the things that we are not required to disclose under law, and even third parties who know of the wicked intentions of others are generally not legally culpable for failing to avert the execution of those intentions. In a situation where the law generally permits a client to be silent, and even permits silence in third parties who become aware of the information, the default position should be that lawyers who are advised of the wicked intentions of others should also not disclose them. On the other hand, it is at this point that, as noted, the client's claim against the lawyer is weakest and, as well, the law does not uniformly permit or encourage silence. While a client may exercise a right to silence and a right to counsel, a client may also be interrogated by the police and asked questions about what he or she is intending to do. We allow the state to investigate threats of which they become aware. In addition, in some situations positive duties of disclosure are placed on third parties with

---

[190] [1999] S.C.J. No. 15, [1999] 1 S.C.R. 455 (S.C.C.).
[191] [2002] S.C.J. No. 35, 2002 SCC 32 (S.C.C.).

respect to harms to others — people who become aware of child abuse, for example, generally have a positive duty to advise the authorities that that abuse is occurring.[192]

This suggests that where the threat is clear enough, and serious enough, and imminent enough, disclosure can be justified as consistent with other legal obligations. And if disclosure is justified because of the severity of the threat, then the discretion as to whether to make the disclosure should not reside with the lawyer. The fundamental point here is that the duties placed on the lawyer with respect to confidentiality reflect societal determinations of the answer to the moral question of when disclosure is justified; that suggests that, generally speaking, the determination of the appropriate response should not be left with the individual lawyer. The lawyer has to determine whether the standard has been met, but should not determine what happens when it is met.

The fact that this exception reflects a departure from the general position in law as to what should be disclosed suggests, though, that more protection should be given to the privilege holder. The purpose of the exception is not to "get" the client; it is to protect the public. The difficulty with this position is if, for some reason, using the privileged information against the client is the only way to protect the public. Presumably the use of the privileged information against the accused in *Smith v. Jones* to have him branded a dangerous offender was justified on this basis — for an individual that dangerous the only way to protect the public is indefinite incarceration. In a case with those facts, however, a court should need to identify an additional basis for overriding use and derivative use immunities, *e.g.*, because the public safety cannot be protected in any other way. Subject to that qualification for exceptional cases, the immunities should be offered whenever a privilege holder's confidences are breached on grounds of public safety.

With respect to the self-interest exceptions, these seem both unnecessarily broad and unjustifiable in light of the strong justification for the duty of confidentiality. Under the doctrine of implied waiver, a lawyer is already entitled to breach confidentiality where a client has put the advice given by the lawyer in issue. Provided this is interpreted expansively enough to include allegations that the lawyer has not done work sufficient to justify the fee charged, so that the lawyer can indicate, in general terms, what the lawyer has done, there seems to be no reason to have any further exception simply to allow lawyers to defend claims more effectively. If the right to confidentiality is as important as lawyers and judges say it is, then it makes no sense to allow that right to bend uniquely to lawyers' own convenience.

---

[192] See, for example, *Child and Family Services Act*, R.S.O. 1990, c. C.11, s. 72; that section excepts privileged information. Other provinces do not: *e.g.*, *Child, Youth and Family Services Act*, S.N.L. 1998, c. C-12.1, s. 15.

With respect to corporations and organizations, a number of academic critics, including David Luban and Adam Dodek, have suggested that the right to confidentiality should not apply. They argue that corporations and organizations are unlikely to be deterred from seeking legal advice by the absence of confidentiality, since such legal advice is essential to the functioning of their operations. Moreover, they suggest that since corporations and organizations have no personal existence, and thus have no dignity or underlying moral right that the privilege protects, it follows that those entities have no right to the privilege. Or, to put it in terms of the argument in the previous section, corporations and organizations have no personal conception of the good to pursue within a system of laws.

There are a number of problems with these arguments. In the first place, it is not obvious that corporations will seek legal advice if they cannot do so on a confidential basis. They may, but the assertion that they will is largely speculative. Second, while it is true that corporations and organizations have no dignity, the argument made for confidentiality here does not rest on the notion of dignity in particular; to the extent corporations and organizations have no personal conception of the good, that would not simply disentitle those organizations to confidentiality, but also to either legal advice or the freedom to act within a system of laws. Since corporations are, conceptually, understandable as vehicles to allow individuals to act in furtherance of their conception of the good, this latter point seems too radical. It ignores the fact that our legal system as a whole permits corporations to act as persons in relation to the law — that is, as entitled to pursue a conception of the good within what the law permits, requires or provides.[193] And, as such, corporations should also be entitled to confidentiality when they seek legal advice from lawyers in order that they may do so.

7. CONCLUSION

The centrality and significance of the lawyer's duty to keep her client's secrets cannot be overstated. Without reasoned justification — that is, the careful application of one of the exceptions or exclusions from that duty — lawyers must not disclose what they learn from their clients, or what they have advised.

---

[193] Whether the law should treat corporations this way is a different question. See, *e.g.*: <http://worthwhile.typepad.com/worthwhile_canadian_initi/2011/02/im-a-corporation-and-sos-my-wife.html#more>.

Chapter 6

THE PERJURY TRILEMMA

1. INTRODUCTION

What do you do if you discover that your client wants to tell a lie? What do you do if you discover that your client has told a lie? The answer depends on the interaction of a number of the lawyers' professional obligations and, in some circumstances, on obligations from ordinary morality:

1. Does the information fall within the lawyer's legal duty to respect a client's confidences?
2. How certain is the lawyer that the client is lying?
3. Does the client have a right to counsel?
4. Is the lie to a court, such that the lie is both a crime by the client (perjury) and a violation of the lawyer's ethical obligation of candour to the court?
5. Is the lie to another party to whom the client (and/or the lawyer) has a legal duty of candour? Does the lie place the lawyer at risk of civil liability in tort or otherwise?
6. Does the lie injure anyone?
7. Do the circumstances justify (or prohibit) withdrawal from the representation?
8. Do the circumstances justify (or prohibit) disclosure of the lie?
9. If the lawyer is to disclose the lie, to whom should the disclosure be made?

Generally speaking, where a client states her *intention* to deceive another person in connection with the subject matter of a representation, the lawyer should try to stop her from doing so, and if the lawyer cannot persuade her to stop he should withdraw from the representation. Where a client wants to deceive another party in the course of a contract negotiation, for example,[1] the client may be intending to make a misrepresentation that will undermine the validity of the contract, as well as to commit the tort of negligent (or

---

[1] I do not think all deceptions in this context would require the lawyer to withdraw, or would prohibit the lawyer from participating — *e.g.*, "we won't sell for anything less than a million" when the client is in fact willing to sell for as little as $500,000 is a negotiating tactic, where the participants in the negotiation understand the statement as just what it is, a strategy not a representation. The ethics of the lawyer's participation in the deception turn, there, on such factors as the listener's entitlement to the information, and how they would understand what is being said. See, in general, Monroe Freedman "In Praise of Overzealous Representation: Lying to Judges, Deceiving Third Parties and Other Ethical Conduct" (2006) 34 Hofstra L. Rev. 771.

perhaps fraudulent) misrepresentation. In that case the client has only a limited right to counsel; the lawyer may be risking liability to the client or, perhaps, the third party; and the conduct may involve the lawyer in an act that will injure another party. While the duty of confidentiality prevents disclosure of the client's intention, if the lawyer cannot persuade the client not to go ahead with the deception, the lawyer's justified and prudent course of action is withdrawal.

Similarly, when a client advises that she *has* deceived another person in connection with the subject matter of the lawyer's representation, the lawyer should endeavour to have the client correct the deception, and if the client is not willing to do so the lawyer should withdraw. A corporate client who has deceived securities regulators or shareholders, for example, has violated its legal duties of candour to those entities. The client has only a limited right to counsel. Further, the client's acts create a risk to the lawyer of civil and, in the worst case, of criminal liability. The duty of confidentiality may, depending on the requirements of the applicable securities legislation, and the application of the criminal communications exclusion, prevent disclosure of the deception, but the continued participation by the lawyer in the deception cannot be justified.

The codes of conduct governing lawyers' conduct codify these general principles with respect to deception. In the clearest example, the Alberta Code of Professional Conduct prevents the lawyer from misleading the court, another lawyer, or the opposing party to a negotiation, and requires that a lawyer correct any misconceptions created by himself or his client in the court, another lawyer, or opposing parties to a negotiation. The lawyer's duty is subject to confidentiality, but if the client will not consent to the lawyer correcting the misapprehension created, then the lawyer must withdraw.[2]

Like all general principles, however, the interesting questions arise at the margins — when does the duty not arise or when should it be qualified in some way? What if a lawyer's client, a celebrity athlete, has been involved in a domestic altercation in which his wife pursued him with a golf club, breaking his car window and causing a car accident, but the client wants to protect his wife by making a public statement denying categorically that any incident of domestic violence took place (since his assessment is that, overall, he was the wrongdoer in the situation)? What if he tells the lawyer the truth, but asks for advice about the legality of lying in his public statement? Can the lawyer not only advise the client about the legality of

---

[2] AB CPC Chapter 4, Rule 2 (other lawyers); Chapter 10, Rule 15 (the court); Chapter 11, Rule 2 (other parties to negotiations). The commentary to the rules defines misconception broadly:

> The concept of "misleading" includes creating a misconception through oral or written statements, other communications, actions or conduct, failure to act, or silence. A lawyer may have provided technically accurate information that is rendered misleading by the withholding of other information; in such a case, there is an obligation to correct the situation. In paragraph (c) of Rule #2, the concept of an inaccurate representation is not limited to one that would be actionable at law.

lying, but also help him construct the statement so as to make it as invulnerable as possible? Or should the lawyer resign, perhaps disclosing what the client has said?

My interpretation of the ethical rules as applied to that hypothetical is that unless the public statement can be characterized as an unlawful act, the client's desire to make it would not require the lawyer to withdraw, and certainly would not justify disclosure. The lie is not made to any parties to whom the lawyer owes a duty to ensure that the client makes accurate statements — in Alberta, another lawyer, a court or in negotiations. The more effort the lawyer makes to help the client construct the lie so as to avoid illegality, the less ethically compromised the lawyer will be. Thus the lawyer could, legally and ethically, help the client construct the statement carefully so as to avoid risks of civil or criminal liability for making it.[3] In other words, the client can lie, and the lawyer can help him to do it consistent with the lawyer's ethical obligations.

What if judges in a jurisdiction routinely ask, as apparently do some judges in Brooklyn, whether the lawyer's client is guilty of the offence — "Come on, let's move this along. Did he do it or didn't he?"[4] Can the lawyer legitimately say, "I have no doubt that my client is not guilty of the offence with which he is charged" even if the lawyer knows the client is factually guilty? Like Monroe Freedman, who addressed this particular issue in a 2006 article in the *Hofstra Law Review*,[5] I would suggest that while perhaps inconsistent with the obligations imposed by the various codes of conduct,[6] the most ethical course of conduct for the lawyer in that scenario would be to make the deceptive statement. The statement is technically accurate — the lawyer is simply stating that until the client's guilt has been established in a court of law, he cannot yet be considered guilty of the offence by the lawyer or anyone else — and the court has no entitlement to any information beyond that which the lawyer has provided.[7] Any less deceptive answer, such as "I cannot answer that question" or "that question is a most improper one" will have the tendency to suggest to the judge, albeit implicitly, that the answer to the question of whether the client is guilty is "yes". Or, through making the judge feel criticized, simply prejudice the judge against the lawyer's client. The client has a right against self-incrimination, a right to counsel and a right to confidentiality, all of which will be compromised by the less deceptive answers. The lawyer's deceptive act is ethically justified.

---

[3] And of course would want to do so — given that the legality of the act is what permits the lawyer to assist the client in doing it.
[4] Monroe Freedman, "In Praise of Overzealous Representation: Lying to Judges, Deceiving Third Parties and Other Ethical Conduct" (2006) 34 Hofstra L. Rev. 771 at 773.
[5] Ibid.
[6] Because of how misleading is defined. I think, though, that this example illustrates some weaknesses with an acontextual application of that definition.
[7] Monroe Freedman, "In Praise of Overzealous Representation: Lying to Judges, Deceiving Third Parties and Other Ethical Conduct" (2006) 34 Hofstra L. Rev. 771 at 774.

This chapter addresses a specific and significant aspect of the lawyer's duties with respect to the lying client: the client who has lied, or intends to lie, to a court or tribunal. Most significantly, it addresses the situation of the criminal accused who has lied, or intends to lie, in her criminal trial. The position in Canadian law is that in all contexts, civil or criminal, the lawyer whose client intends to lie to a court or tribunal must first attempt to dissuade the client from doing so. If the lawyer learns that the client has already lied to the court or tribunal, then the lawyer must try to persuade the client to correct the misapprehension. If the lawyer fails to dissuade (or persuade) the client, then the lawyer must withdraw from the representation. If judicial permission to withdraw is required, then the lawyer must advise the court that he is withdrawing from the representation for "ethical reasons".[8] Unless the client consents, the lawyer may not advise anyone of the information that the client has provided about the false testimony, even if the client has already provided perjurious testimony to the court with the lawyer's unwitting assistance.[9]

In providing this general answer to the problem of intended or completed perjury, Canadian law necessarily chooses between three competing, and in these circumstances irreconcilable, legal principles that are at play when a criminal accused wants to lie or has lied in her criminal trial — that is, on the "perjury trilemma":

1. The right to confidentiality. The lawyer has a duty not to disclose confidential and privileged information, which includes information about intended or completed perjury provided in the context of a lawyer-client relationship.
2. The right to counsel. A criminal accused requires the competent assistance of counsel. Competent assistance is not provided if the lawyer withdraws in the middle of a scheduled criminal proceeding, or if the client cannot speak candidly with the lawyer about how to proceed.[10]

---

[8] *R. v. Cunningham*, [2010] S.C.J. No. 10 at para. 48, 2010 SCC 10 (S.C.C.).
[9] A number of Canadian commentators claim that lawyers can advise the court where they learn after the fact that the client has committed perjury. In my view, with the exception of the New Brunswick Code of Conduct, this position is simply not supported by the provisions of the codes of conduct, and is inconsistent with the strict approach to solicitor-client privilege taken by the Supreme Court of Canada. I will explain this position in detail later in this chapter. A clear summary of the lawyer's duties with respect to false testimony is found in the BC PCH, Chapter 8, Rules 2-5.
[10] This point requires some care. Given the provisions of the rules of professional conduct, and the likely result of a court case on lawyer participation in perjury, it is almost certain that a court would hold that the right to counsel does not extend to the right to have counsel participate in deception of a court or tribunal. So, in that sense, the right to counsel is not jeopardized by the Canadian solution to the perjury trilemma. That argument, though, is too circular. The point I am making is that considered *ex ante*, does the withdrawal of counsel mid-trial jeopardize the client's receipt of competent legal advice? I argue that in principle it does, although I acknowledge that in a positivist sense the position of the courts means that it does not.

3. The obligation of candour to the court. A lawyer must not lie or misrepresent the facts to a court in judicial proceedings; he must not participate in the presentation of perjured testimony.

In circumstances of anticipated or completed perjury it is impossible for a lawyer to fulfill all of these obligations; whatever the lawyer's response, whether to withdraw, to disclose, to attempt to avoid knowledge of the deception, or to carry on with representation as usual, the lawyer will choose one duty over the others. The question thus becomes: which of these duties or rights should be sacrificed?

This chapter will outline in more detail the law governing Canadian lawyers with respect to both intended and completed client perjury. It will set out the basic prohibition on the presentation of false testimony to a court or tribunal, the standard that must be met before a lawyer should consider a client's testimony to be "false", and the requirements imposed by the Canadian law governing lawyers when a lawyer realizes that his client intends to lie or has lied to a court or tribunal. The discussion to this point will discuss all advocacy contexts, both civil and criminal, since, as noted, in Canadian law no distinction is drawn between the duties of the lawyer in civil and criminal representation.

The chapter will then consider the merits of various solutions to the perjury trilemma in criminal cases, including the Canadian approach of withdrawal and non-disclosure; disclosure; conducting the representation so that the perjury problem never arises; presenting the testimony in narrative form; and, finally, simply continuing to act for the client and presenting the testimony in the ordinary way. The thesis developed will be that the Canadian approach to lying clients is appropriate in the civil context. However, in the context of criminal proceedings the better (albeit still unsatisfactory) approach is for the lawyer to continue to represent the client in the ordinary fashion, even where perjury is anticipated or has occurred.

2. THE PROHIBITION ON ASSISTING CLIENTS TO DECEIVE THE COURT

The codes of conduct universally prohibit lawyers from deceiving the court, or assisting a client to do so. The rules contain a general prohibition against a lawyer knowingly assisting the client in dishonesty, fraud or illegal conduct.[11] More specifically, in the context of advocacy the rules state that the lawyer must not "knowingly attempt to deceive or participate in the deception of a tribunal" through offering false evidence or otherwise.[12] They

---

[11] CBA MC Chapter IX, Commentary 2(b); FLS MC Rule 2.02(7) and 4.01(2)(b); NB CC Chapter 8, Commentary 10(ii) and 10(v); LSUC RPC Rule 2.02(5) and Rule 4.01(2)(b); AB CBC Chapter 1, Rule 3; Chapter 9, Rule 11; BC PCH Chapter 4, Rule 6; Chapter 8, Rule 1(b).
[12] CBA MC Chapter IX, Commentary 2(e); FLS MC Rule 4.01(2)(e); NB CC Chapter 8, Commentary 10(v); Que. CEA Rule 3.02.01(c); LSUC RPC Rule 4.01(2)(e); AB CPC Chapter 10, Rule 14; BC PCH Canon 2(3).

prohibit the lawyer from knowingly presenting a witness or party in a false or misleading way, or allowing a person to impersonate another.[13] And they prohibit knowingly asserting the truth of a fact before a tribunal when "its truth cannot reasonably be supported by the evidence or as a matter of which notice may be taken by the tribunal".[14]

The codes of conduct also impose generalized limitations on advocacy for any criminal accused who has admitted to the lawyer the "factual and mental elements" of the offence with which she is charged. In those circumstances the lawyer may not present any evidence that appears false given the general admission that the accused has made or suggest an "affirmative case inconsistent with such admissions".[15]

In *Law Society of Saskatchewan v. Segal*,[16] a civil case, a lawyer was disciplined when his client gave false evidence in an examination for discovery. The lawyer argued that since he had advised the client to tell the truth, the client's failure to do so could not be a basis for disciplining the lawyer; the obligation to discover the inaccuracy in the client's testimony rested with the opposing party. The Law Society of Saskatchewan disagreed, holding that the lawyer may not knowingly participate in a client's deception of the other side, even if the participation is only passive:

> The Hearing Committee observes that when any counsel is presented with a situation as that which arose at AC's discovery, he should request an adjournment. At that point counsel should privately advise the client of the error and, more to the point, that the error must be corrected. If the client refuses, the lawyer should withdraw.
>
> The Hearing Committee would also allow that there may be situations where the realities of the pressures of an Examination for Discovery might be such that the lawyer does not stop the discovery and correct the mistake. However, the obligation would remain and that any counsel in such a situation would be obliged, within a reasonable time, to bring to the attention of opposite counsel the incorrectness of the client's response. Failure to take action within a reasonable time must, by definition, constitute conduct unbecoming a lawyer.[17]

The Law Society reprimanded Segal.

In *Re Ontario Crime Commission*,[18] also a civil case, the Ontario Court of Appeal discussed a filed affidavit that falsified what had taken place in prior proceedings. The Court held that counsel had acted improperly in filing the false affidavit, and that the instructions of a client in this regard are

---

[13] CBA MC Chapter IX, Commentary 2(j); FLS MC Rule 4.01(2)(k); NB CC Chapter 8, Commentary 10(x); LSUC RPC Rule 4.01(2)(j).
[14] The CBA does not have a like provision. FLS MC Rule 4.01(2)(g); NB CC Chapter 8, Commentary 10(vii); LSUC RPC Rule 4.01(2)(g); AB CPC Chapter 10, Rule 17.
[15] CBA MC Chapter IX, Commentary 11; FLS MC Rule 4.01(1), commentary; LSUC RPC Rule 4.01(1), commentary; NB CC Chapter 8, Commentary 14; AB CPC Chapter 10, Rule 14, commentary. The general effect of this rule is discussed in Chapter 9, Section 3.A.
[16] [1999] L.S.D.D. No. 9.
[17] *Ibid.* at paras. 30-31.
[18] [1962] O.J. No. 678, [1963] 1 O.R. 391 (Ont. C.A.).

irrelevant. A lawyer's silence in the face of the provision of false information is "at the very least, a gross neglect of duty".[19] The Court ordered that the lawyer "personally pay the costs of all other parties".[20]

In criminal cases the courts have also indicated clearly that a lawyer may not participate in the presentation of perjurious testimony,[21] and various commentators have confirmed this position. Austin Cooper, a renowned criminal defence lawyer, said that a lawyer may not lead evidence that he knows is false: "The client may view the refusal as a breach of counsel's fiduciary duty. However, the court and the Law Society demand that the prohibition be observed."[22]

3. WHEN DOES THE LAWYER KNOW THAT TESTIMONY IS (OR WILL BE) DECEPTIVE?

A crucial question raised by the lawyer's duty not to present deceptive testimony is, how certain does the lawyer need to be that the testimony is deceptive before deciding that the testimony presents an ethical issue? Where a client advises the lawyer, "I am going to testify that I was at my mother's house, and that is a lie, because I was really at my boyfriend's house" then the analysis is straightforward: the lawyer knows the testimony is a lie, and cannot assist the client to present it. But what if the client simply tells inconsistent stories, advising at different times that she was at her mother's, that she was at a friend's, or that she went for a walk on her own? Can the lawyer present evidence attesting to any of those versions of events? Or what if the client's story is simply dubious, and the lawyer strongly believes that it is made up? Or what if the lawyer erred in preparing the client, and indicated exactly what was necessary to satisfy the defence of provocation, and the client now tells the lawyer a version of the facts that satisfies the test of provocation, such that the lawyer thinks the client has made up the testimony in response to the lawyer's advice?

The limited Canadian authority that speaks to this issue requires a high standard of certainty before the lawyer views testimony as false; it is only where the lawyer has a clear basis for viewing the testimony as false that the duty not to present it arises. Under the Alberta Code of Conduct it states that the duty not to present testimony arises only where the lawyer knows that the testimony is false "based on personal knowledge or the client's own

---

[19] *Ibid.* at para. 20.
[20] *Ibid.*
[21] *R. v. Jenkins*, [2001] O.J. No. 760, 152 C.C.C. (3d) 426 (Ont. S.C.J.); *R. v. Moore*, [2002] S.J. No. 124, [2002] 7 W.W.R. 424 (Sask. C.A.). Both of these cases deal with issues that arise with respect to client perjury — in the first case about whether it permits withdrawal; in the second case about when the lawyer has sufficient information to determine that the client is going to perjure himself (the Court held that the lawyer did not have sufficient information).
[22] Austin Cooper, "The 'good' criminal law barrister" (2004) 23 Advocates' Soc. J. No. 2, 7-12, para. 9. See also Gary Oakes, "BC Chief Justice uses Home Page to Explain Law, Slam Story" *The Lawyers Weekly* 21:47 (19 April 2002), where the Chief Justice is quoted as saying, "if the lawyer knows the client will lie on the stand he or she must withdraw from the case".

admission".[23] The British Columbia Professional Conduct Handbook states that "mere inconsistency" in testimony does not demonstrate falsity, although once inconsistency exists the lawyer has a duty to investigate to determine whether the testimony is true.[24] Where falsity has not been established after the investigation, then "the lawyer is entitled to proceed, leaving it to the court or tribunal to assess the truth or otherwise of the client's or witness's statement or testimony".[25]

In their discussion of the perjury issue in *Ethics and Canadian Criminal Law*,[26] Michel Proulx and David Layton also argue for a high degree of certainty of deception in the lawyer before he treats his client as a liar; they emphasize that the lawyer "should not jump to rash conclusions about a story's falsity or the client's nefarious intention. The role of counsel in the adversary system is to act as the accused's advocate, not to assume the role of judge".[27] They suggest that the limits on representation only arise where the lawyer draws an "irresistible conclusion of falsity from available information".[28] The lawyer cannot avoid that conclusion through intentional ignorance, and has a duty to check information that the client provides; however the lawyer may also present evidence even if he personally feels that it is not credible.

The one Canadian case on point clearly affirms the high standard of certainty that a lawyer must have before he understands himself as having conflicting duties to the client and to the court. In *R. v. Moore*,[29] Moore was convicted of sexual assault against a former girlfriend and appealed his conviction on the basis of ineffective assistance of counsel. Moore's employer was a former police officer and had strongly advised Moore to take a polygraph test. His lawyer had advised him not to do so, on the basis that the results of the polygraph test could limit the conduct of the defence. Moore nonetheless took the test and failed. His lawyer then told Moore that, as a consequence, he could not testify, even though he had never admitted his guilt to his lawyer. The lawyer later testified in Moore's appeal of his conviction that "I didn't feel that I would be — that that would be proper for me to do ... That's the — when you talk about ethics, that's the ethics and morals that I practice by."[30] The Court held that the lawyer had erred in not permitting Moore to testify. Polygraph tests are not reliable, and Moore's failure of the test was insufficient for his lawyer to treat Moore's evidence as potentially perjurious. Moore had a constitutional right to testify, and that

---

[23] AB CPC Chapter 10, Rule 14, commentary.
[24] BC PCH, Chapter 8, Rule 6.
[25] *Ibid.*
[26] Michel Proulx & David Layton, *Ethics and Canadian Criminal Law* (Toronto: Irwin Law, 2001).
[27] *Ibid.* at 370.
[28] *Ibid.*
[29] [2002] S.J. No. 124, 2002 SKCA 30 (Sask. C.A.).
[30] *Ibid.* at para. 25.

right was improperly denied through the misinformation given to him by his lawyer:

> In some instances counsel may face a difficult task in balancing these duties [to the client and court]. In this case we are all of the opinion that Mr. Lindgren subordinated his duty to his client to his own ethical decision that he would not call Mr. Moore to testify in light of his "failed" polygraph examination. In hindsight it might have been preferable for him to have withdrawn.
>
> Given the jurisprudence on the reliability of polygraph examinations, the decision taken and the advice given to Mr. Moore involved insufficient regard to his duty to Mr. Moore in the special circumstances of this case. A self-imposed constraint on one's ability to advise a client, particularly at the crucial stage — the close of the prosecution's case — does not relieve an advocate of his duty to give effective assistance to his client on the crucial question whether to testify on his own behalf.[31]

This case provides clear support for the strong standard articulated by Proulx and Layton, with which I agree: unless the conclusion that the testimony is false is "irresistible", the lawyer may participate in the presentation of that testimony to the court. A lawyer must investigate, and cannot simply duck knowledge of falsity, but the falsity must be clear before the lawyer limits representation of the client because of it.

4. THE LAWYER'S DUTIES WHERE THE CLIENT INTENDS TO DECEIVE, OR HAS DECEIVED, A COURT OR TRIBUNAL

In circumstances of anticipated perjury, where a lawyer draws an irresistible conclusion that his client intends to deceive a court or tribunal, the first obligation of that lawyer is to try to dissuade the client from doing so. Lying to the court is generally poor strategy, as well as being illegal and unethical. Given his duty of zealous advocacy for his client's interests, the lawyer has a paramount obligation to try to prevent the client from doing something that will injure her case, including lying in court. Even before addressing the lawyer's own ethical concerns, this should motivate the lawyer to be as clear and persuasive as possible in dissuading the client intent on committing perjury. The client is unlikely to be impressed or persuaded by lawyerly moralizing; however, Proulx and Layton provide a helpful checklist of the information which should be given to a criminal accused set on committing perjury:[32]

1. perjury is a crime;

---

[31] *Ibid.* at paras. 53-54.
[32] I have some reservations with this list in light of the perjury trilemma; I think it could undermine the relationship of trust and confidence between the lawyer and client. However, given the obligations imposed on counsel in Canadian law it seems a reasonable guideline for lawyers to follow.

2. the prosecution will likely attack the perjured testimony, using cross-examination, reply evidence, and/or argument to the trier of fact (concrete examples should be provided if at all possible);
3. the perjury may well be discovered by the trier of fact, leading or contributing to the client's conviction;
4. once revealed, the bogus defence may cause the court to impose a harsher sentence than would otherwise be the case ...[33]
5. the client's falsehood may also lead authorities to lay a separate charge of perjury, with the attendant risk of an additional conviction and punishment; and
6. defence counsel has an ethical duty not to mislead the court, and this duty may operate to permit or mandate remedial measures if the client does not change his or her mind.[34]

In civil cases the information given to the client should indicate the ways in which the misrepresentation may undermine the client's likelihood of success on the substance of the case, even if the case is otherwise meritorious, and that the misrepresentation may lead to solicitor-client costs being levied against the client.

In circumstances of completed perjury, where a lawyer draws an irresistible conclusion that the client *has* deceived a court, the first obligation of the lawyer is to try to persuade the client to correct the deception. Under the codes of conduct the lawyer has a duty to correct misleading information provided to the court or tribunal, even if the misleading information was provided inadvertently.[35] The lawyer must thus try to persuade the client to consent to correction of the deception, emphasizing with the client the consequences and risks associated with perjury as indicated above and, as well, the ability to manage and decrease prejudice to the client through voluntary pre-emptive disclosure.

Where the lawyer is unable to dissuade the client from giving misleading testimony, or to persuade the client to correct deception of the court, then the lawyer has an obligation to withdraw from the representation.[36] If reasons for the withdrawal must be given to the court, then the lawyer must indicate that the withdrawal is for "ethical reasons".[37] The court is required to permit the lawyer to withdraw in those circumstances.[38] Although in some cases counsel have indicated to the court more specific information about the reasons for withdrawal — "the information which the accused had conveyed to [his lawyer] was such that it was fundamentally inconsistent with the very essence of the case which had been advanced to

---

[33] Proulx and Layton note that the case law on this issue is unclear.
[34] Michel Proulx & David Layton, *Ethics and Canadian Criminal Law* (Toronto: Irwin Law, 2001) at 372-73.
[35] CBA MC Chapter IX, Commentary 3; FLS MC Rule 4.01(4); NB CC Chapter 8, Commentary 11; LSUC RPC Rule 4.01(5); AB CPC Chapter 1, Rule 15.
[36] *Ibid.* See also the discussion of withdrawal, in Chapter 3, Section 5.
[37] *R. v. Cunningham*, [2010] S.C.J. No. 10 at para. 48, 2010 SCC 10 (S.C.C.).
[38] *Ibid.*

the jury on behalf of the accused"[39] — doing so is improper because of the lawyer's obligation of confidentiality.[40] A lawyer may not directly[41] indicate to the court, the tribunal, or to any other party the client's anticipated or completed deception.

The view that confidentiality generally forbids specific disclosure requires further elaboration, particularly as a number of Canadian commentators have suggested that where the perjury is "completed" — that is, the client has provided the misleading information to the court — the lawyer has, or should have, an obligation to correct the misapprehension even if the client does not agree to do so.[42] In my view this assessment is incorrect under the law governing lawyers. Instead, the lawyer's duty of confidentiality ordinarily[43] prohibits any disclosure of an intended *or* completed perjury.[44]

With the exception of the New Brunswick Code of Conduct, which permits the lawyer to disclose false testimony intentionally provided to the court (either directly or by indicating to the court that the testimony may not be relied upon),[45] the codes of conduct make disclosure of a client's misleading testimony subject to the duty of confidentiality.[46] While not universally clear on this point, the implication of the rules appears to be that disclosure cannot be made unless the information is not confidential, or some exception to confidentiality applies.

---

[39] *R. v. Jenkins*, [2001] O.J. No. 760 at para. 25, 152 C.C.C. (3d) 426 (Ont. S.C.J.); David Layton, "*R. v. Jenkins*: Client Perjury and Disclosure by Defence Counsel" (2001) 5 Crim. Rep. 259.

[40] *R. v. Cunningham*, [2010] S.C.J. No. 10, 2010 SCC 10 (S.C.C.).

[41] Saying that withdrawal is for "ethical reasons" may indirectly indicate the perjury to the court.

[42] See, *e.g.*, Gavin Mackenzie, *Lawyers and Ethics: Professional Responsibility and Discipline*, 3d ed. (Toronto: Thompson Carswell, 2001) at 7-13-7-14; Proulx and Layton acknowledge that the codes of conduct generally prohibit disclosure, but suggest that once the perjury is completed the "balance shifts somewhat in favour of disclosure" (Michel Proulx & David Layton, *Ethics and Canadian Criminal Law* (Toronto: Irwin Law, 2001) at 401).

[43] This analysis is generic; there may be exceptional circumstances in which disclosure of the intended or completed perjury is justified. For example, if the perjury is intended to remove an order limiting a client's access to a child so that the client may sexually abuse the child, the future harm exception would apply and disclosure would be warranted. That disclosure is justified not, though, because of the fact of the perjury *per se*, but because of the surrounding circumstances and what the perjury is intended to accomplish.

[44] Except, of course, that the lawyer is required to state that the lawyer is withdrawing for "ethical reasons". *R. v. Cunningham*, [2010] S.C.J. No. 10 at para. 48, 2010 SCC 10 (S.C.C.).

[45] NB CC Chapter 8, Commentary 12. I am not sure whether this rule is a valid exception to the doctrine of privilege, particularly in criminal cases where constitutional rights are at stake.

[46] CBA MC Chapter IX, Commentary 3; FLS MC Rule 4.01(4); LSUC RPC Rule 4.01(5); AB CPC Chapter 10, Rule 15. The commentary to Alberta's Rule 15 makes the requirement of client consent prior to disclosure absolutely clear: "Briefly, if correction of the misrepresentation requires disclosure of confidential information, the lawyer must seek the client's consent to such disclosure. If the client withholds consent, the lawyer is obliged to withdraw." BC PCH Chapter 8, Rule 4 prohibits the lawyer from advising the court that withdrawal was because of a "client's insistence on offering false testimony". The rules do not speak to disclosure of an intended perjury in particular. This is because an intended perjury does not yet engage the lawyer's duty of candour to the court — or, more accurately, there has as yet been no violation of that duty of candour.

Is information of intended or completed perjury confidential? Does it fall within any applicable exception to confidentiality?

With respect to an intended perjury, the communication to the lawyer that the client intends to provide false evidence falls within the protection of the solicitor-client privilege and the lawyer's ethical duty of confidentiality. The client is seeking legal advice, both with respect to the underlying action and with respect to the advisability of providing false evidence; the information provided arguably goes to the heart of the lawyer's mandate, which requires advising and representing the client through the trial process. In addition, the communication is not excluded from the privilege as a "criminal communication". While the client states her intention to commit a crime, she is not duping the lawyer into assisting her to do so (indeed, she is being up front about her criminal intentions), and since the lawyer refuses to participate in the perjury, the discussion between the lawyer and client is not a conspiracy or other inherently criminal communication. As discussed in Chapter 5, the criminal communications exclusion is "extremely limited".[47]

Further, no exception to the privilege will ordinarily apply. The public safety exception does not permit disclosure of an act simply because it is criminal; the crime must create a clear, imminent and serious threat to public safety.[48] Under the public safety exception the perjury may only be disclosed where it is intended to accomplish a danger to public safety, such as obtaining access to a child the accused tends to abuse. Finally, the statement by the Supreme Court in *R. v. Cunningham*,[49] where the Court directed judges not to ask counsel any further questions where counsel states that withdrawal is for "ethical reasons",[50] affirms the view that information about the nature of those ethical reasons, including prospective client perjury, should be viewed as falling within the lawyer's duty of confidentiality.

Lawyers should also not disclose a completed perjury. Again, the information falls within the privilege and within the ethical duty of confidentiality because the client is still seeking legal advice, either with respect to the consequences of the perjury itself, or with respect to the consequences of the perjury for the underlying legal action. The information also is not excluded from the privilege as a criminal communication; since the crime has already been committed without the lawyer's knowledge (although with his unwitting assistance) the communication about the consequences of committing the crime are not themselves criminal nor are they made to obtain the lawyer's assistance in the commission of a crime.[51]

---

[47] *R. v. Campbell*, [1999] S.C.J. No. 16 at para. 63, [1999] 1 S.C.R. 565 (S.C.C.).
[48] *Smith v. Jones*, [1999] S.C.J. No. 15, [1999] 1 S.C.R. 455 (S.C.C.).
[49] [2010] S.C.J. No. 10, 2010 SCC 10 (S.C.C.).
[50] *Ibid.* at para. 48.
[51] Like the example of financial fraud discussed in Chapter 5, Section 2.D., the communication here is about a crime the lawyer may have assisted the client to commit, which is different from a communication about a crime for which assistance is sought. The distinction between these communications is required because of the "extremely limited" nature of the criminal communication exclusion.

And since the crime has already been committed, no serious, clear or imminent threat to the public safety from the perjury is likely to arise.[52]

The prohibition on disclosure applies not only to disclosure to the court or tribunal, but also to disclosure to successor counsel. The lawyer's duty of confidentiality, and the scope of the solicitor-client privilege, is near-absolute, and applies to anyone with respect to whom the client has not consented that the lawyer disclose information.[53]

In sum, then, a lawyer should try to persuade a client to tell the truth, or to correct deceptions that have occurred, even if inadvertent. If the client cannot be persuaded to do the right thing, then the lawyer must withdraw, advising the court or tribunal that the withdrawal is for "ethical reasons" if court permission to withdraw is required. Beyond that, the lawyer may not disclose the client's intended or completed misrepresentation to the court or to anyone else, unless for some particular reason an exception to the duty of confidentiality applies.

The remaining sections will consider the merits of this and other approaches to the problem of the client who lies to the court or tribunal in a criminal trial. Before doing so, however, the circumstances of civil litigation, or where someone other than the accused gives the deceptive testimony, need to be addressed. In my view, the approach of the Canadian law governing lawyers to false or misleading evidence in those contexts is appropriate.

In the context of civil litigation, the right to counsel does not have the same force or application as in a criminal trial; the Supreme Court has suggested that civil litigants normally do not enjoy a constitutional right to counsel.[54] That means that the lawyer withdrawing from representation where the client has or intends to commit perjury does not have the same constitutional impact; in the context of civil litigation there is no constitutional reason why the client who wishes to deceive the court should have the benefit of counsel while doing so. The client still has a right to confidentiality that will (and does) prevent direct disclosure of the client's deception. In the civil litigation context, though, where there is no liberty or security of the person interest at stake, the indirect disclosure[55] that may result from the lawyer withdrawing mid-trial, has less force when measured against the importance of not deceiving the court. Further, in civil litigation contexts a lawyer may not have to provide reasons for withdrawal in the same way that she does in a criminal context, with the result that the indirect disclosure problem may not even arise.

---

[52] Although see footnote 43.
[53] With the exception of New Brunswick.
[54] *British Columbia (Attorney General) v. Christie*, [2007] S.C.J. No. 21, 2007 SCC 21 (S.C.C.).
[55] As discussed below, the problem with withdrawal for ethical reasons is that it signals to the court something is wrong, and if occurring contemporaneously with the client's testimony, it may well signal that what is wrong is that the client lied.

With respect to evidence from a party other than the accused in a criminal trial, the distinction is more complicated. If the knowledge that the evidence is false comes from the person testifying, that person has no right against self-incrimination in this context, no right to counsel and no right to confidentiality relative to the accused's lawyer. A lawyer may not present evidence he knows is false offered by a party whose rights are not implicated, and who can make no particular claim to the lawyer's attention.

Monroe Freedman and Abbe Smith argue for the ability of the lawyer to present perjured testimony by someone very close to an accused, such as the parents or spouse of the accused.[56] For the reasons just indicated, however, I am not convinced by this position. Even though they are people close to the accused, the spouse or parents of the accused do not have rights implicated in the accused's proceeding that would warrant the lawyer participating in their presentation of false evidence to the court.

What if the lawyer knows that the evidence provided by the third parties is false as a result of disclosures given by the accused? In that instance, the right to confidentiality is at play (since the information that the testimony is false comes from the client), and the relationship between the lawyer and the client, including the right to counsel, is at issue. If the lawyer does not present the evidence as instructed by the client, or withdraws from the representation, the client does not have assistance of counsel or may directly or indirectly have her confidences disclosed.

Nonetheless, the prohibition on the presentation of that evidence, or withdrawal if the evidence has been presented unknowingly and the client will not consent to correcting it, is justified. The courts have consistently treated the right of the accused to testify in her own defence as of unique importance; as discussed in Chapter 3, even in the lawyer-centric approach that the Canadian law governing lawyers takes to lawyer-client decision-making, the decision about whether to testify is viewed as the client's to make. Further, if lawyers could present any evidence without concern for its falsity, the process of criminal adjudication would break down. The identification of the perjury trilemma does not diminish the significance of the duty of candour to the court; it simply notes that in some situations respecting the duty of candour involves defeating other important duties. That is the case here as well, but I think that the duty of candour is paramount in this instance. It is only in truly exceptional circumstances — that is, where the accused herself seeks to testify but has advised the lawyer in confidence that the testimony is false — that violations of the duty of candour to the court may be justified.

In sum, the normal duty of the lawyer is to decline to present evidence to the court that is false, or to refuse to continue to act in litigation where a client will not permit the lawyer to rectify the presentation of false evidence.

---

[56] Monroe Freedman & Abbe Smith, *Understanding Lawyers' Ethics*, 4th ed. (New Providence, NJ: LexisNexis, 2010) at 166-67.

That normal duty is justified by the duty of candour even though it may undermine the ability of a client to be represented by counsel, or strain the lawyer-client relationship of trust and confidence. The only question, which is addressed in the following sections, is whether in the singular circumstance of an accused testifying falsely in a criminal trial, the duty of candour should be outweighed by other considerations.

5. ASSESSING THE SOLUTIONS TO THE PROBLEM OF PERJURY

A. Introduction

The presentation of perjured evidence by a criminal accused presents a trilemma for the lawyer representing that accused. The lawyer has an obligation of candour to the court, but the client requires the competent representation of counsel, and the lawyer has a duty of confidentiality to the client. The client's intended or completed perjury places these duties in conflict, and unless the lawyer can dissuade the client from lying, or persuade the client to correct deceptions she has created, any path forward for the lawyer will require that he compromise one or the other of them. As the previous sections outlined, the law governing lawyers has provided an answer to the question of how these competing legal principles should be resolved. This section will analyze the merits of that approach, and of other approaches that could be taken to responding to the perjury trilemma. In doing so, the main purpose will be simply to highlight what each solution means for the conflicting legal entitlements of the client and obligations of the lawyer. I take a position on which resolution of those conflicting legal entitlements and obligations is the most desirable; however, the main point is to emphasize that whatever solution is adopted, important legal principles will be compromised. The only questions are: which ones, to what extent, and with what impact?

B. The Solution of Withdrawal and Limited Disclosure

By requiring lawyers to withdraw from representation of a criminal accused intent on deceiving the court, the Canadian approach helps ensure candour towards the court. A lawyer will not knowingly participate in such deception and, if it occurs, the court may be given some signal that the testimony was not reliable, through the fact of the lawyer's withdrawal for ethical reasons, especially if that withdrawal occurs during or immediately following the testimony. It also incents a client to be truthful in the first place; knowing that the lawyer will be forced to withdraw if the client does not testify truthfully will help motivate the client to do so.

The protection of candour towards the court is, however, somewhat undermined by the limits on the lawyer's disclosure for the reasons for withdrawal, particularly to successor counsel. If the first lawyer withdraws the client will know not to tell a subsequent lawyer about the deceitful testimony, and that second lawyer will unknowingly participate in presenting the false testimony to the court.[57] That lawyer will also not have any further opportunity to try to dissuade the client from testifying that way.

Further, even if the first lawyer withdraws and a new lawyer is not retained, once the perjury is completed the court cannot entirely discount the testimony, since it does not have actual confirmation that the testimony is false. A judge may feel compelled to simply carry on and consider that testimony as if it at least might be truthful, even if the withdrawal of the lawyer provides some indication that it is not. Otherwise the judge is determining credibility on an improper basis, improper both because the judge would ultimately only have speculative reasons for believing that the lawyer has withdrawn because of a perjury problem, and because through the Supreme Court's prohibition on the lawyer revealing the basis for the lawyer's withdrawal, the Court has implicitly signalled that judges should not take those reasons into account in making their decisions.

The effectiveness of the withdrawal and non-disclosure approach in ensuring candour to the court is, therefore, somewhat mixed, although certainly orientated towards that goal. While a judge may not discount testimony simply because of the lawyer's withdrawal for ethical reasons right around the time of the testimony, the judge will be more inclined towards scepticism, and less likely to be "taken in" by the client's testimony. Even if successor counsel brings forward the evidence, the judge's scepticism will have been triggered.

This means, necessarily, that the approach of withdrawal and limited disclosure provides only limited protection of the trust and confidentiality of the lawyer-client relationship. The approach does not require total abandonment of the duty of confidentiality, since specific information about the perjury is not disclosed; however, enough is disclosed to reveal important secrets about the lawyer-client relationship — specifically, that the lawyer and client have had an ethical conflict. The duty of confidentiality is thus not fully respected. Further, the client is highly unlikely to approach the lawyer (or a successor lawyer) with the same or any level of trust after this experience. This is most obviously the case with successor counsel, who will not be told by the client about the intended or completed perjury, or perhaps about other matters of importance, since the client can no longer trust that the information she presents will not be revealed, or will not lead to adverse consequences in her relationship with the lawyer. Further, even if the client decides not to proceed with the perjury, being told by her lawyer that the lawyer will withdraw unless the client behaves in a particular way may create an overall sense in the client that the lawyer is not truly aligned with her interests.

---

[57] The lawyer may suspect that the client's testimony is not truthful, but likely would not have sufficient knowledge to trigger the duties that caused the first lawyer to withdraw.

The Canadian approach also places clients in the situation that they are worse off in the conduct of their trials simply as a consequence of being candid with their own lawyers. In the American version of this book Professors Freedman and Smith posit an innocent accused who was placed near the scene by an eye witness close to the time the crime took place. The witness is in fact truthful and accurate, but not especially credible as she is elderly and her eyesight is poor. The accused is concerned that if he admits that he was near the scene at the time the crime took place, his chance of being convicted increases significantly; he decides to lie about that fact.[58] If he tells the lawyer about the lie, he will lose his lawyer and, if the trial is imminent, will have a red flag placed over his testimony by the act of his lawyer's withdrawal for ethical reasons. Or, if the lie has already been told, he will have the consequences either of withdrawal for ethical reasons or having to consent to the lawyer's disclosure of the lie, which will almost certainly cause significant prejudice to his defence, even though he is innocent. These outcomes are imposed even though the client himself has no legal obligation to disclose to the court his own wrongdoing;[59] by telling his lawyer, and having his lawyer respond, the client's legal position in effect changes, even though nothing has happened to warrant that change beyond the act of disclosure itself.

This approach also has the potential to undermine the accused's right to counsel, since the lawyer's withdrawal may leave the client unrepresented. If the client can obtain successor counsel this issue is ameliorated; however, the client's newly learned reluctance to be candid with that new counsel might undermine the effectiveness of the representation received. The client may not only keep secret her intention to lie, she might also keep secret other information, simply because she does not know whether it is important, or what the effect of disclosing the information to her lawyer will be.

The solution offered to the perjury trilemma in Canada is not unreasonable, in the sense that it tries to protect an important value — candour to the court — and also attempts to minimize the prejudice to the accused by limiting disclosure by the lawyer and inquiries by the court into the lawyer's reasons for withdrawal. The problem, though, is that even with that limit the price for candour is a high one, and one that we would not impose on individuals who could effectively represent themselves in court. The requirement that lawyers withdraw for "ethical reasons" in situations of intended or completed perjury undermines the ability of a lawyer to establish a relationship of trust with his client; it requires the lawyer to compromise the duty of confidentiality; and, it impedes the client's representation by counsel.

---

[58] Monroe Freedman & Abbe Smith, *Understanding Lawyers' Ethics*, 4th ed. (New Providence, NJ: LexisNexis, 2010) at 156-57.

[59] Although to be fair he also has no right to engage in that wrongdoing or to be protected in acting wrongfully.

C. Disclosure

If the law were to shift to the New Brunswick rules, and require or permit disclosure of completed perjury, or require disclosure of intended perjury, the protection of candour to the court would be improved from what is offered under current Canadian law. Not only would completed perjury be rectified, but intended perjury would be better controlled by the significant hammer given to the lawyer who can now advise the client that, if the client insists on deceiving the court, the lawyer will withdraw, disclose the perjury to the court, or both. The lawyer will also be able to advise successor counsel of the intended or completed perjury, thereby eliminating that avenue for the client to work around the restrictions on lawyers participating in deception of the court.

A disclosure obligation would, however, violate or undermine the right to confidentiality, the right to counsel and, indirectly, the right against self-incrimination. It would mean that a client, who has no obligation to disclose malfeasance to the state, would have that disclosure made by her lawyer, the person charged with protecting her interests under the law; instead of protecting her interests the lawyer would change the client's legal situation for the worse. It would prejudice the trial against the accused even if, as in the example posited by Freedman and Smith, the accused is innocent of the crime with which she is charged. The client's near-absolute right to confidentiality would be abandoned. And the client would lose the benefit of counsel given that, even if the lawyer were to continue to represent her, the trust and confidence necessary to allow that relationship to function effectively would be gone.

Ultimately, it is hard to see how disclosure of the client's intended or completed perjury could be justified given the general structure of our legal system and the right to silence that it provides to individuals with respect to their own wrongdoing. The police cannot knock on your door and require you to advise them as to the bad things that you have done. The court cannot compel a criminal accused to admit the ways in which she has acted wrongfully. When a person consults a lawyer to find out what the law says about the bad things they have done, we do not generally permit the lawyer to disclose those bad things to the state. This is the case despite the fact that in each of those instances the law would capture more wrongdoers if the disclosure took place. If we do not permit or require disclosure in those circumstances, there seems no logical basis to permit or require it here; however worthy of moral condemnation, the crime of perjury seems insufficiently serious to justify a requirement that lawyers reveal its occurrence.[60]

---

[60] Unless, as noted elsewhere, the perjury is part of a scheme to do an act which will cause clear, serious and imminent threat to another — *e.g.*, lying to the court to obtain access to a child whom the client intends to abuse.

D. Intentional Ignorance

A way to "avoid" the perjury problem is through intentional ignorance. Intentional ignorance can take a variety of forms. One form is to advise the client at the beginning of the representation that there is some information that the lawyer does not want to know, or that if confidential information is provided it may limit the lawyer's representation. The problem with intentional ignorance, however, is that it does little for any of the legal obligations at play: it does not increase candour to the court, it undermines trust and confidence in the lawyer-client relationship, and it impinges on the right to counsel by making the lawyer less effective in advocacy because not necessarily having all of the information required to properly represent the client. It forces the client to determine the information that is relevant and can be safely disclosed; given the fact that the client's ignorance of the law is one of the bases for the lawyer-client relationship in the first place, this seems unlikely to permit the client to obtain proper legal representation.

It makes candour to the court less likely because it means that the lawyer cannot explain to the client the risks associated with providing deceptive testimony, and may implicitly give the client the message that deceptive testimony might be a good idea — why else would the lawyer be trying to make it easier for the client to present such testimony? Finally, it disrupts the relationship of trust and confidence because creating barriers to disclosure rather than developing a relationship in which disclosure seems safe. Most criminal accused do not start from a default position of trust with their lawyers; they perceive their lawyers as part of the criminal justice system, not as apart from it, and establishing the trust that will encourage disclosure is not easy to do. Starting the conversation with a warning not to say too much makes the development of that trust even less likely.

A striking example of the problem of intentional ignorance is found in the case *R. v. I.B.B.*[61] I.B.B. was charged with offences related to a home invasion. He made a videotaped statement to the police in which he maintained his innocence. His co-accused also maintained that I.B.B. was innocent. I.B.B. had been identified through a photo line-up; however, there were some flaws related to that identification.[62]

When he met with his lawyer, Nolin, Nolin directed I.B.B. to provide no information about what had happened:

> I reviewed the disclosure with him and I explained to him that there are two types of lawyers, in my dealings, being a criminal defence lawyer. One type is the lawyer that wants to know everything you did and feels that complete and honest and forthright disclosure up front is the only way that they can represent you or the second type, which I placed myself in that category, that at this stage, I don't want to know what you've done or haven't done. I'm going to go through the disclosure.

---

[61] [2009] S.J. No. 378, 2009 SKPC 76 (Sask. Prov. Ct.).
[62] *Ibid.* at para. 67.

I'm going to let you know what the Crown is saying about you at this stage.[63]

Nolin took no notes of his meetings with I.B.B. He further stated that "he didn't ask I.B.B. for his account, he said, because he was simply waiting to see if the witnesses showed up at trial".[64] Nolin further made no application for a bail hearing for I.B.B., with the result that I.B.B. was in remand for four months while the matter was being dealt with.

Despite his total lack of information, Nolin pushed I.B.B. to plead guilty to the offence. He "emphasized throughout, the very high risk of jail and penitentiary time".[65] I.B.B. agreed to plead guilty, and did so. A pre-sentencing report was prepared. The report indicated that I.B.B. maintained his innocence. Nolin then withdrew from the representation because of the conflict created by the pre-sentencing report in light of the client's earlier plea.

A lawyer, Kozakavich, who represented Nolin's co-accused, then reviewed I.B.B.'s file. Kozakavich became aware of the weaknesses with the Crown's case, noted above, and testified on I.B.B.'s behalf in seeking to have the guilty plea expunged.

The Court expunged I.B.B.'s plea. In so doing, the Court emphasized in particular the problems with Nolin's approach of not speaking to his client about the case:

> There are two main systemic concerns with Mr. Nolin's approach to receiving I.B.B.'s side of the story:
>
> (i) If you don't discuss the facts with the client until the morning of the trial, then how do you prepare for trial? According to Mr. Nolin he was only waiting to see if the witnesses appeared. It wasn't until the morning of the trial that the facts were discussed and then it was with a view to pleading guilty, not defending the matter, yet I.B.B.'s instructions had been a denial of responsibility to that point.
>
> (ii) Having given that initial instruction to his client that he didn't want to discuss his side of the story with him and having persisted in this for 4 1/2 months; there is considerable concern that such an approach invites a cynical rather than an open and honest discussion of the essential elements of the offence with a view to acceptance of responsibility by means of a guilty plea. It isn't enough to discuss what it means to be a party to an offence or to discuss the difference in law between aggravated assault and assault causing bodily harm. There must be a discussion of the facts, in the context of the elements of the offences, that the client is prepared to admit. The client must also be informed and this means to have full disclosure

---

[63] *Ibid.* at para. 20.
[64] *Ibid.* at para. 23.
[65] *Ibid.*

and his counsel's frank assessment of the import of that disclosure.

Before leaving these concerns, it's important to stress that, generally speaking, I am not criticizing an approach by counsel, to delay discussion of the facts with a client to a more suitable time, perhaps when all of the available disclosure is in the hands of counsel and immediate concerns such as bail have been addressed. Rather the concern is that delaying a discussion of the facts to the morning of the trial, in circumstances such as these, may impact upon the fairness of the proceedings.[66]

Thus, in *I.B.B.*, the result of Nolin's intentional ignorance was ignorance of his client's innocence, and the entering of a plea which the client should never have entered. The law governing lawyers should not be structured so as to encourage the "second type" of advocacy identified by Nolin.

Roy Cohn has suggested that lawyers adopt a more subtle form of intentional ignorance, one which will avoid the problem that arose in *I.B.B.*:

> Before a client could get three words out, any lawyer with half a brain would say, "You probably don't know whether you're guilty or not, because you don't know the elements of the crime you're charged with.
>
> [Then, to avoid hearing what I'm not supposed to hear, I ask the client:] "If someone was going to get up on the stand and lie about you, who would it be? And what would they lie about?" And if the client's got any brains, he'll know what I'm talking about.[67]

The idea of the Cohn solution is that the client will disclose the information, but because the lawyer and client structure the conversation around the idea that the other person is the one who would lie, not the client, the lawyer remains "ignorant" of the extent to which any information being provided by the client is not truthful.

The Cohn solution entirely ignores the duty of candour. It provides no opportunity for the lawyer to urge the client to be truthful with the court. It may in fact encourage the client to lie, providing a wink and a nudge from the lawyer to suggest that lying is tactically desirable. It may develop trust and confidence, and ensure the right to counsel, but it simply avoids the ethical problem rather than providing any solution to it.

As attractive as intentional ignorance may be, it provides no legitimate solution to the perjury trilemma. It simply obscures the moral problem client perjury creates.

E. Narrative Testimony

An alternative that has been proposed to the perjury problem is to allow a client who intends to commit perjury to testify in narrative form, without the

---

[66] *Ibid.* at para. 65.
[67] David Berreby, "The Cohn/Dershowitz Debate" June 7, 1982 Nat'l. L.J. at 15.

lawyer asking any questions beyond "you may now tell your story to the court". This solution, like intentional ignorance, cleans the lawyer's hands, insofar as the lawyer is distanced from the deception of the court. It is, however, an unsatisfactory solution to the perjury trilemma. It only increases candour to the court in a complex way. If a judge or jury views the use of narrative as indicating that the testimony cannot be relied upon, then candour to the court is increased. In that case, however, the violation of the client's confidentiality is equivalent to full disclosure. If the judge or jury does not view the narrative testimony as indicating that the testimony cannot be relied upon, but simply assesses credibility in the ordinary way, then candour to the court has not been increased. In the first instance the narrative solution suffers from the same problems as full disclosure, violating the client's right to confidentiality and the right to be free from self-incrimination. In the second instance the narrative solution suffers from the same problem as intentional ignorance in that it does nothing to increase candour to the court. It is important to note in this respect that under the Supreme Court's judgment in *R. v. Colpitts*, a trial judge is required to present an accused's testimony to the jury, even if the accused's lawyer makes no reference to the testimony in closing argument.[68] This might make it more likely that a jury presented with testimony in narrative form will take that testimony into account in its deliberations.

The solution of narrative testimony appears to have little to recommend it; it simply creates confusion without ensuring a better outcome with respect to any of the important principles at play.

F. Continuing to Represent the Client as if the Testimony were Truthful

The final alternative to the perjury trilemma is for the lawyer to present the evidence as if it were truthful, examining the client in the ordinary course and making due reference to the testimony in closing argument to persuade the judge or jury of the client's innocence. Under this approach, at the initial client interview, the lawyer impresses upon the client that it is essential that the lawyer know everything there is to know about the client's case. The lawyer also assures the client that he will maintain her confidences and secrets in strict confidence.

If the lawyer learns through those confidences that the client is contemplating perjury, the lawyer will make continuing, good faith efforts to dissuade the client from that course, emphasizing the points set out by Proulx and Layton. If withdrawal can occur without prejudice to the client,[69] — if, for example, the trial is some time away — then the lawyer may

---

[68] *R. v. Colpitts*, [1965] S.C.J. No. 48, [1965] S.C.R. 739 (S.C.C.). See the discussion in Michel Proulx & David Layton, *Ethics in Canadian Criminal Law* (Toronto: Irwin Law, 2001) at 387.

[69] Taking into account the criteria for permitting withdrawal by counsel set out in *R. v. Cunningham*, [2010] S.C.J. No. 10, 2010 SCC 10 (S.C.C.).

withdraw. The lawyer should continue to use his relationship of trust and confidence with the client, "up to the very hour of the client's ... testimony",[70] to dissuade the client from committing the perjury.

The client, faced with the threat of prison, may or may not be impressed with the fact that perjury is immoral and illegal, but may well be persuaded by the negative consequences associated with perjury as an independent crime, as something likely to be demonstrated on cross-examination by the Crown, as undermining other more plausible bases for defending the client against the charges, and as potentially leading to an increased sentence. Some American sources suggest that lawyers are frequently successful in dissuading client perjury.[71]

Where the client who has contemplated perjury rejects the lawyer's advice and decides to proceed to trial, to take the stand, and to give false testimony, the lawyer should go forward in the ordinary way. That is, the lawyer should examine the client in a normal manner and should rely on the client's testimony in closing argument to the extent sound tactics justify doing so. The lawyer should not assist the client in constructing the fabricated story so as to resist cross-examination, but in the course of attempting to dissuade the client from committing the perjury may provide information to the client about the type of questions that the Crown will ask.

This solution does not increase candour to the court, and clearly involves the lawyer in the client's deception. The lawyer's hands are dirty. It also takes away some of the lawyer's power to encourage client candour, because the lawyer will not be able to advise the client that lying in testimony will result in the lawyer's withdrawal from the representation. On the other hand, it retains the lawyer's relationship of trust and confidence with the client which, in the end, may be more effective for dissuading the client from committing perjury than a threat would be. It contributes to the ability of the lawyer to represent the client effectively, because enhancing the client's certainty that, in fact, the lawyer can be counted on to fulfill his duty of confidentiality and protect the client's interests. It means that the client is not in a worse position as a result of having a lawyer than of not having a lawyer, insofar as the lawyer will not be required to disclose that which the client would not be required to disclose if unrepresented. It also creates consistency between the situation of perjury and other intended or completed crimes by the client of which a lawyer becomes aware; unless the crime is such that it creates a clear, serious and imminent risk to the safety of others, it will not be disclosed. Finally, while it does not increase candour to the court, it leaves in place the usual safeguards against dishonest testimony,

---

[70] James Exum, "The Perjurious Criminal Defendant: A Solution to His Lawyer's Dilemma" (1980) VI Soc. Resp. 16 at 20.

[71] "[E]xperienced defense lawyers have pointed out time and again, that, permitted to ... counsel ... their criminal clients up to the very hour of the client's proposed testimony, they almost always were successful in persuading the client not to take the stand to testify falsely." Exum, *ibid*. Exum is the former Chief Judge of the North Carolina Supreme Court.

namely effective cross-examination by the Crown and the ability of the judge or jury to assess the credibility of the witness.

This solution is not satisfactory, and may not be more reasonable than the current Canadian approach of withdrawal and non-disclosure. In my view, however, it is more consistent with the general approach to the duties of the lawyer when aware of a client's criminal activities, and protects the values that, in the context of criminal representation, should be paramount: that the client receive fair and effective representation, and that the client's confidences be respected, particularly where disclosure of those confidences will *de facto* violate the client's right against self-incrimination.

6. CONCLUSION

Not all lies are created equal. In his 2006 *Hofstra Law Review* article Monroe Freedman discussed the topic of lying in general, and the difficulty that lying can create for general moral analysis of wrongdoing, noting some famous examples of "lies" that could only with difficulty be characterized as wrong:

> In Genesis, for example, when Sarah learns that God will give her a child, Sarah laughs, saying that *both* she and Abraham are too old to conceive a child. When God relates this to Abraham, however, He says only that Sarah had said that *she* was too old to conceive. Recognizing that God has told less than the whole truth, rabbinical authorities have understood God's equivocation to have been justified by the overriding importance of maintaining peace between husband and wife. ...
>
> Further, when Jesus is asked when the Day of Judgment will come, he replies, "But of that day and that hour knoweth no man, no, not the angels which are in heaven, neither the Son, but the Father." Catholic theologians have reasoned that Jesus could not have been speaking the truth because, as the Son of God, He must have known the answer to the question. What then are we to make of his statement?
>
> One response to that question is St. Thomas Aquinas' doctrine of mental reservation, which is a form of morally justifiable equivocation. That is, there are circumstances in which "[i]t is licit to hide the truth prudently by some sort of dissimulation." In the case of Jesus' denial of knowledge of the Day of Judgment, for example, His justifiable mental reservation is that the Son has no knowledge *that the questioner is entitled to know.*
>
> That reasoning has produced a variety of illustrative situations. A simple one is a husband who tells a door-to-door salesman, contrary to fact, that his wife is not at home, when the husband means, in his own mind, "She is not at home *to you.*"
>
> A more important illustration is of the priest who is asked whether a penitent has confessed certain self-incriminatory information to the priest. For the priest to answer simply that he cannot reveal what he has been told under the sacred seal of the confessional, could be taken to imply that there has indeed been an incriminating confession. In such a

case, the priest can properly deny that any admission has been made. The justification, again, is that the questioner has no right to a truthful answer, and the priest may therefore make use of a mental reservation such as, "The penitent has not made any such admission to me *outside the confessional, and, therefore, he has made no admission that I can reveal to you.*"[72]

When a client lies during the course of a court trial or a tribunal hearing the lie is generally morally unambiguous: it violates a legal obligation in order to obtain an advantage to which the client is not entitled, insofar as that advantage is obtained as a result of the deception. Where the client is a criminal accused the lies that the client may tell to a court or tribunal remain morally unambiguous: the lies of the client are both immoral and illegal. The suggestion made here, though, is that to the extent a lawyer participates in the client's deception, then, provided the lawyer has done everything that he can to prevent the lie, the lawyer's own deception is *not* morally unambiguous, and may even be justifiable. The lie acts to protect other principles of fundamental importance to the legal system. It preserves the relationship of trust and confidence between the lawyer and client, and the criminal accused retains her right to counsel. It does not increase candour to the court, but it leaves in place other safeguards against dishonest testimony. In the end, asking the lawyer to participate in the client's deception is unsatisfactory, but nonetheless the best alternative, all things considered.

---

[72] Footnotes omitted. Monroe Freedman, "In Praise of Overzealous Representation: Lying to Judges, Deceiving Third Parties and Other Ethical Conduct" (2006) 34 Hofstra L. Rev. 771 at 775-76.

Chapter 7

EXAMINING WITNESSES: PREPARATION OF WITNESSES AND CROSS-EXAMINATION

1. INTRODUCTION

This chapter discusses the examination of witnesses in adjudicative proceedings. It considers first the ethical issue that arises in relation to the lawyer's presentation of witnesses to support her client's case: how can the lawyer prepare witnesses to ensure they are effective, without engaging in coaching of witnesses to improperly influence what they say? It then turns to the ethical issues that arise in relation to cross-examination and, in particular, the ethical issue of whether a lawyer should cross-examine a truthful witness to make that witness's testimony appear unworthy of belief.

2. PREPARING WITNESSES

A. Introduction

What the lawyer needs to do in preparing witnesses is relatively clear: she needs to ensure that the evidence presented to the court by her witnesses is truthful and not misleading, while at the same time acting as a competent advocate to present that evidence effectively. That is, while respecting the need for accuracy she must prevent her client's case from being undermined because a witness fails to disclose relevant information, is inarticulate, misunderstands a question, tends to ramble or volunteer unhelpful information, is bullied by opposing counsel in cross-examination, or is otherwise likely to present the facts of the case in a way that is not compelling or credible. The lawyer does not have to provide all relevant evidence to the decision-maker, but the evidence that is provided cannot be false or misleading, and must be presented effectively.

    The lawyer can thus straightforwardly identify her task in relation to the presentation of evidence through witnesses; accomplishing this task is, however, an act of some difficulty. Witnesses are not objects to be manipulated; they are people with motivations, weaknesses, biases, feelings, intelligence (or not), and the tendency to respond to the circumstances in which they find themselves.

Consider this picture of two boxes. Can you identify the dimensions of the unshaded part of the box?

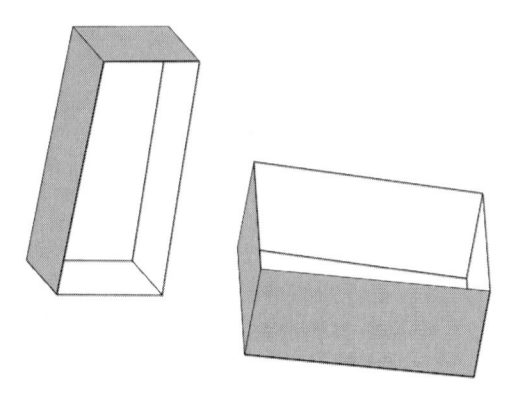

This picture is based on a drawing of two tabletops by the psychologist and artist Roger Shepard.[1] Almost everyone who looks at it thinks that the dimensions of the unshaded parts are quite different, with the one on the left having a ratio of length to width of 3:1, and the one on the right having a ratio of length to width of 1.5:1 (that is, that the box on the right is almost square, whereas the box on the left is a clear rectangle). In fact, the boxes have identical dimensions, and the only difference between them is the inherent fallibility in the perception of the viewer.

Witnesses are viewers of boxes, capable of misperception and confusion about what they see or know, particularly where motivated to see the world in different ways. The ethical challenge for the lawyer is to ensure that she has found out everything she needs to know to present the case competently, and has provided the witness with enough direction so that the witness can present the evidence effectively, without doing the equivalent of shifting the witness's perception of reality by moving around the boxes. Or, to express it slightly differently, the lawyer's ethical challenge is to figure out the actual dimensions of the boxes even though the witness may not be relied upon to tell the lawyer the answer accurately.

The problem of perception is heightened when the issue is not what the witness sees, but what the witness saw on some earlier occasion. The inaccuracy and malleability of human perception is matched or exceeded by the inaccuracy and malleability of human memory, and the capacity for people to subjectively believe things that, it turns out, are objectively false.

This is the problem that this section of the chapter will discuss. It begins by outlining the content of the lawyer's ethical obligations in preparing and presenting witnesses pursuant to the codes of conduct and applicable case law. It then considers further the complexity of fulfilling

---

[1] This version was created by my niece, Jaime Luchuck. The original picture of the tabletops was created by Roger Shepard, *Mind Sights: Original Visual Illusions, Ambiguities and Other Anomolies* (W.H. Freeman & Co. Ltd., 1990) at 47 and 127-28.

those obligations given certain types of testimony and witnesses that the lawyer may encounter, and given the psychology of human memory. The third sub-section describes some of the usual advice given to lawyers in Canada about how to prepare witnesses, and suggests that while the advice given is sound in strategic terms, it pays insufficient attention to the ethical context of witness preparation. The final sub-section provides some guidance and guidelines for lawyers to follow in order to ensure that they prepare witnesses both effectively and ethically.

B. The Law Governing Witness Preparation

Rules and case law provide that the lawyer must present evidence to the court that is truthful and not misleading.[2] The lawyer does not have an obligation to present to the court or tribunal all evidence that might be relevant to the determination of the issue presented by the case. Inherent in the concept of an adversarial system of adjudication is the idea that a lawyer need present only the evidence favourable to her client, leaving the presentation of unfavourable evidence to the opposing party. As stated by the Alberta Code of Professional Conduct, a lawyer is "not required to inform the court of facts that should have been brought forth by opposing counsel".[3] The evidence that the lawyer does present cannot, however, be false or misleading.

In addition, the lawyer has a duty to competently prepare a case, investigating the facts, interviewing potential witnesses, and preparing them to testify, so that the case is presented persuasively, consistent with the rules of civil procedure and evidence.[4] A lawyer acts both negligently and incompetently if she fails to prepare witnesses for the rigours of an adversarial proceeding.

With respect to how the lawyer should achieve these goals, the codes of conduct and case law require that a lawyer not "coach" a witness. The codes of conduct reflect this principle by prohibiting lawyer conversations with witnesses in circumstances where there is a heightened risk that such conversations could result in coaching.[5] All of the codes of conduct prohibit a lawyer from having a conversation with a witness under cross-examination by opposing counsel. The Law Society of Upper Canada Rules additionally require that the lawyer not speak to a witness during an examination-in-chief

---

[2] CBA MC Chapter IX, Commentary 2(e) and Commentary 3; FLS MC Rule 4.01(2)(e) and Rule 4.01(4); NB CC Chapter 8, Commentary 10(v) and Commentary 11; Que. CEA 3.02.01(c); LSUC RPC Rule 4.01(2)(e) and 4.01(5); AB CPC Chapter 10, Rule 14 and Rule 15; BC PCH Canon 2(3). See discussion in Chapter 6, Sections 2 and 4.

[3] AB, Chapter 10, Rule 14, commentary. See also CBA MC Chapter IX, Commentary 17; FLS Rule 4.01(1), commentary; NB Chapter 8, Commentary 4(a); LSUC Rule 4.01(1), commentary.

[4] See in general, Chapter 4, Section 2. The governing rules on competence are, FLS Model Code Rule 2.01(1); CBA MC Chapter II; Que. CEA Rules 3.01.01 and 3.03.01; LSUC Rule 2.01(1); Alberta Chapter 2, commentaries; NB Chapter 2, Rule 5; BC Chapter 3, Rule 1.

[5] CBA MC Chapter IX, Commentary 18; FLS Rule 4.04(2); AB Chapter 10, Rule 25(b); NB Chapter 8, Commentary 5.

about matters not yet covered by that examination, not talk to a witness prior to cross-examination about matters that were covered during the examination-in-chief, and not talk to a witness between cross-examination and re-examination.[6]

The Alberta Code of Conduct discusses the issue of coaching expressly. Chapter 10, Rule 24 prohibits the lawyer from counselling a witness to give evidence that is "untruthful or misleading", and the commentary to the Rule states further:

> While a lawyer may legitimately suggest alternative ways of presenting evidence so that it is better understood, it is improper to direct or encourage a witness to misstate or misrepresent the facts. An advocate's role is not to change or distort the evidence, but to assist the witness in bringing forth the evidence in a manner that ensures fair and accurate comprehension by the court and opposing parties.[7]

Case law also prohibits coaching, but indicates that judges generally will not interfere *ex ante* with counsel's preparation of witnesses, and will instead give latitude to lawyers as to the appropriate method for preparing a witness. In *R. v. Polani*,[8] the lawyer for the accused sought an order prohibiting the Crown from discussing defence allegations with the person who swore the affidavit to obtain a wiretap. The Court refused to grant the order on the basis that it was not proper to interfere with the Crown's conduct of its case. The Court held that it could rely on the Crown not to coach or improperly prepare its witnesses:

> Here the court would not be surprised were the Crown to tell the affiant, "You will be cross-examined generally in respect to the issues of errors and omissions in your affidavit material," but would rely on the Crown, acting neutrally as he is duty bound to do in his role as Crown, and by the Canons of Legal Ethics to serve the cause of justice, not in any way to coach or lead the witness in areas he knows will be canvassed by the defence through notices provided ... [about the content of the motion]. The Crown must face this task knowing that there is a risk they may end up being a witness and therefore no longer able to act as counsel.[9]

In *R. v. Lawlor*[10] the Newfoundland Trial Court permitted a lawyer to talk to a witness between cross-examination and re-examination. The Court held that rules against discussion with witnesses are directed at ensuring that witnesses are not coached about how to respond to cross-examination. However, a discussion post cross-examination is really just intended to find out if re-examination is necessary or a good strategy, and that requires conversation between the lawyer and the client. The Court was thus willing to leave this matter to the discretion of the lawyer, without asserting the

---

[6] LSUC Rule 4.04. This would not, presumably, apply to conversations directed at ensuring that a witness correct untruthful or misleading testimony.
[7] AB Chapter 10, Rule 24, commentary.
[8] [2006] B.C.J. No. 915, 2006 BCPC 166 (B.C. Prov. Ct.).
[9] [2006] B.C.J. No. 915 at para. 13, 2006 BCPC 166 (B.C. Prov. Ct.).
[10] [1999] N.J. No. 83 (Nfld. T.D.).

necessity of a prophylactic rule designed to decrease the risk that coaching will occur.

Courts have also been willing to allow lawyers to provide witnesses with copies of evidence given in prior proceedings so long as the lawyer does not give the evidence to the witness in order to coach him. In *R. v. Muise*,[11] the Nova Scotia Court of Appeal held that it was acceptable for witnesses to have read statements given at the preliminary inquiry.

On the other hand, the courts are clear that coaching a witness is unacceptable, and will warrant sanction if it occurs. Thus in *R. v. Muise* the Court also held that coaching by counsel would

> be grounds for judicial censure and would seriously affect the weight of such evidence and indeed, depending on particular circumstances, might make such evidence inadmissible as not being the witness' own independent recollection of the facts being testified to. Such is not the case here and I would reject this ground of appeal.[12]

The Court in *Muise* noted the decision of the Ontario County Court in *The Queen v. Husbands*,[13] in which the County Court had held that while it was proper to provide witness statements to a witness for the purpose of refreshing the witness's memory, it would be improper to read witness statements to witnesses gathered together, to place pressure on a witness to refresh his memory or to pressure a witness to "adhere to a statement even if he no longer believed it to be true".[14]

Courts have been willing to allow counsel to pursue a line of cross-examination relevant to determining whether coaching of a witness occurred.[15] They have also been willing to find that a lawyer coached a witness, and impose sanctions of costs, when the testimony given by the witness leads inexorably to the conclusion that the witness was coached. In *General Motors of Canada Ltd. v. Canada*[16] a witness for the Minister of National Revenue was testifying in an examination for discovery with respect to whether the Minister had made certain assumptions in assessing the taxpayer.[17] In response to almost every question the witness stated, "the services were taxable".[18] Tax Court Judge Campbell concluded that the Crown lawyer had cued and coached the witness to give that response. As a consequence of this and other misconduct, which Campbell T.C.J.

---

[11] [1974] N.S.J. No. 298 (N.S.S.C.A.D.).
[12] *Ibid.* at para. 38.
[13] [1973] O.J. No. 1340, 24 C.R.N.S. 188 (Ont. Co. Ct.).
[14] Cited in *R. v. Muise*, [1974] N.S.J. No. 298 at para. 35 (N.S.C.A.).
[15] *R. v. Weibe*, [2006] O.J. No. 544 (Ont. C.A.), although in that case the questions did not relate to discussions between the lawyer and client. It would be more complicated with lawyer-client communications because of privilege.
[16] [2008] T.C.J. No. 80, 2008 TCC 117 (T.C.C.).
[17] Whether or not the Minister made assumptions is relevant to the allocation of the burden of proof in tax proceedings.
[18] *General Motors of Canada Ltd. v. Canada*, [2008] T.C.J. No. 80 at para. 72, 2008 TCC 117 (T.C.C.).

characterized as "intrinsically appalling",[19] he made an elevated award of costs against the Crown.

In light of this authority, what constraints are placed on witness preparation? First, lawyers must not have conversations with witnesses in circumstances in which coaching will be hard to avoid. This includes conversations during cross-examination, but may also include,[20] as reflected by the Ontario rules, conversations during other types of examinations. Whenever a witness is under examination the lawyer must be careful about the type of questions and conversation that the lawyer has with that witness.

Second, lawyers must not be too directive in preparing witnesses for certain types of cross-examination. As indicated by *Polani*, a lawyer may indicate to the witness the type of questions that are likely to be asked during cross-examination, but should not suggest to the witness specific responses to those questions.

Third, lawyers should not place pressure, either directly or indirectly, on a witness to give certain types of testimony. This includes the scenarios contemplated in *Husbands*, where a witness is pressured through contact with other witnesses, or the witness is made to feel that he cannot change or qualify the information he has otherwise provided.

Finally, and most obviously, the lawyer should not tell the witness what to say in answer to a question. The lawyer must not give the witness a script or provide the witness with the substantive content of the answer.

These rules and the guidance from the case law prohibit some of the more egregious ways in which lawyers can act improperly in preparing witnesses. They do not, however, provide either positive direction to lawyers as to what an ethical but effective witness preparation will include, or indicate some of the more subtle ways in which lawyers may inadvertently coach witnesses in the course of preparing them for trial.

C. Why is it Difficult to Prepare a Witness without Coaching?

By now the ethical issue in preparing witnesses should be clear: how do you prepare a witness to be effective while not coaching the witness as to what to say? That general statement of the problem may not fully communicate why drawing the line between coaching and preparation is so difficult. Why can the lawyer not simply ask the witness some questions, ask the witness to answer the questions truthfully and fully, and assume that the information that results is truthful and accurate? As long as the lawyer does not provide direction to the client similar to that given by the lawyer in the film and book *Anatomy of a Murder*

---

[19] *Ibid.* at para. 73.
[20] Although note *R. v. Lawlor*, [1999] N.J. No. 83 (Nfld. T.D.), discussed earlier.

If the facts are as you have stated them, you have no legal defense, and you will probably be convicted and given a lengthy prison sentence. On the other hand, if you acted in a blind rage, there is a possibility of getting you off. Think it over, and we'll talk about it tomorrow.[21]

the lawyer can feel some confidence that she has stayed on the right side of the preparation/coaching divide.

Despite this apparent simplicity, there are a number of reasons why it is challenging to avoid coaching a witness. Three of the most important are, first, that often the "facts" that the lawyer needs to elicit are difficult to distinguish from legal concepts, so that it is hard to provide the witness with enough information to find out what the lawyer needs to know, while at the same time not prompting the witness simply to provide the answer that best suits the legal case that the client is trying to make. Second, witnesses have varying levels of sophistication, intelligence, speaking ability, confidence and willingness to testify; that means that preparation must be variable, and what will be necessary to ensure preparation but not coaching in one case might be quite different from what is necessary to ensure preparation but not coaching in another. Finally, the psychology of human memory and perception is complicated and malleable; in every case there is a risk that through the act of preparing the witness the lawyer will, in fact, manipulate the witness's recollection.

With respect to the intersection of facts and law, the challenge arises most obviously where the witness testifies to his mental state or intention. In general, the mental state or intention relevant to a lawsuit is with respect to some underlying legal concept — did you intend to make a gift, enter a contract, use different language than that which the signed contract contains and so on.

For example, in establishing a defence to sexual assault, the accused may testify that the complainant consented or that he had an honest but mistaken belief in consent. If the accused simply testifies as to facts that suggest the complainant consented, that may fail to raise the defence of honest but mistaken belief in consent.[22] However, in many cases that the accused believed the complainant was consenting may be implicit in his

---

[21] Paraphrased in Monroe Freedman & Abbe Smith, *Understanding Lawyers' Ethics*, 4th ed. (New Providence, NJ: LexisNexis, 2010) at 202. As Freedman and Smith note, this "lecture" is a difficult example to use to analyze the conduct of lawyers in real cases, because the lawyer in the book is portrayed as having absolute certainty that the initial story provided by the client is true, and is giving the lecture to persuade the client to say something that is untrue and exculpatory. In real life, both the lawyer's and the client's state of mind would be much less clear.

[22] See *R. v. Dickson*, [1994] S.C.J. No. 9, [1994] 1 S.C.R. 153 (S.C.C.). In that case the accused sought to introduce evidence of the complainant's sexual history but was not permitted to do so because the evidence spoke only to honest but mistaken belief in consent, and at the *voir dire* into admission of the evidence the accused argued consent, but not honest but mistaken belief in consent. This demonstrates the severability of those defences, and the need for the accused to testify to both aspects. See also *R. v. Darrach*, [2000] S.C.J. No. 46, [2000] 2 S.C.R. 443 (S.C.C.).

testimony as to her actual consent. The preparation challenge for the lawyer is to obtain explicit testimony about the accused's belief in consent — "some evidence of what he believed at the time of the alleged assault"[23] — without creating it; if the lawyer fails to elicit this testimony the defence will not be raised, and the accused may be convicted, even though he had a legitimate defence. But if the lawyer pushes the witness too hard, he may obtain testimony about a belief the accused never had.

Or consider this example:

> Jack and Frank have a contract to allow Jack to purchase Frank's business. The contract is drafted by their lawyers to both reflect the substantive terms of the agreement between them, and also to maximize the beneficial tax consequences of the agreement for each party. Unfortunately, the result of a term of the contract is that losses associated with the business in the taxation year immediately prior to the purchase cannot be deducted by either Jack or Frank. The only way to solve the tax problem created by the contract is to seek rectification of its terms. The test for rectification requires that the parties show that the written contract does not reflect their actual prior agreement. That is, they may have wanted to have a different tax result, but they may have had no particular intention other than that the clause say what it does. Yet to obtain a rectification order they will need to testify that they intended the terms of the contract to be those that give the better tax result.

The challenge for the lawyers in this example will be to obtain testimony that is truthful and not misleading about events in the past, events which, at the time, the witnesses would simply not have conceptualized in terms relevant to the matter as it stands now. The challenge is complicated on these facts because, since the witnesses are also clients, the lawyers have an obligation to explain to the clients the nature of the legal problem and what can be done to solve it. The lawyers need to discharge that obligation while also not simply coaching Jack and Frank to say what is most helpful to obtain a rectification order without regard to the accuracy of that testimony.

The second issue, the variability of witnesses, does not require much further explanation, although it can perhaps be usefully illustrated. In my time as a lawyer I acted as junior counsel for corporations or advocacy groups in the context of utility rate proceedings. In utility rate proceedings many witnesses, whether for the utility or for intervenors, have been involved in such proceedings numerous times, have extensive knowledge of the factual context and legal framework within which utility rates are set, and need little in the way of preparation from the lawyer to be effective. With that sort of witness the lawyer is unlikely to inadvertently coach the witness as to the appropriate answer to give. There the ethical challenge is

---

[23] *R. v. Darrach*, [2000] S.C.J. No. 46 at para. 59, [2000] 2 S.C.R. 443 (S.C.C.).

instead ensuring that the testimony is truthful and not misleading, given that the witness's own knowledge and sophistication may make it difficult for the lawyer to assess the testimony's accuracy.[24]

By contrast, in ordinary civil litigation — even corporate litigation — many witnesses have never testified before, do not necessarily appreciate the information or knowledge they have that is relevant to the proceeding, may be concerned about the effect of testifying on their careers, and may require extensive preparation to navigate the rigours of an adversary proceeding. In that situation, the challenge for the lawyer is the usual one of preparing but not coaching, but requires taking into account issues such as the seniority and motivations of the employee, his intelligence, his litigation experience and his legal sophistication. An additional consideration in the corporate setting is the extent to which in-house counsel have been involved in sounding out and perhaps even preparing potential witnesses prior to (or even simultaneously with) the involvement of external counsel — *i.e.*, the outside counsel must ensure that coaching has not occurred under the auspices of in-house counsel.

In general, then, the lawyer's approach to ensuring that the witness has been prepared but not coached must vary with the witness. A significant part of the lawyer's challenge is to ensure that preparation is appropriate for this witness, in this proceeding.

The third issue, the malleability of human memory, is the most significant. Even though people believe they can remember events clearly and accurately, they cannot. Psychologists talk about the *"illusion of memory*: the disconnect between how we think memory works, and how it actually works".[25] Most people think that memory works like a video camera that accurately records what we see, and allows us to bring it out to look at again. It does not. We often do not recall things at all, and what we do recall may or may not resemble what actually happened — what we in fact read, or witnessed or experienced.[26]

In 2002, a couple named Leslie Meltzer and Tyce Palmaffy saw a man riding a bicycle, who was then attacked and stabbed by another man. Leslie called 911, but was put on hold for approximately one minute. In describing to the 911 operator what had happened, Leslie and Tyce had different recollections on a number of points — they disagreed on the pants the assailant was wearing, his shirt, his height and his race. The only points on which they agreed were the assailant's age, and that he had used a knife in the attack.[27]

---

[24] I should emphasize that I did not identify issues of this type; it was simply obvious that the circumstances were such that it could have been an issue.
[25] Christopher Chabris & Daniel Simons, *The Invisible Gorilla: And Other Ways Our Intuitions Deceive Us* (New York: Random House Inc., 2010) at 45.
[26] See generally, Daniel L. Schacter, *The Seven Sins of Memory: How the Mind Forgets and Remembers* (Boston: Houghton Mifflin, 2001).
[27] *Ibid.* at 51-52. Interestingly, over time the memories of Leslie and Tyce diverged even more significantly: at 74-75.

Even when recalling an experience that was vivid or profound, our memories are not accurate. In 1986, the day after the space shuttle *Challenger* exploded, two psychologists asked their undergraduate psychology class to write out what they had been doing when they heard about the explosion, and to answer a set of detailed questions about the incident. Two and a half years later, they asked the students to fill out a similar questionnaire about the incident. The students' answers had changed radically, "incorporating elements that plausibly fit with how they could have learned about the events, but that never actually happened",[28] based on their earlier answers. During the later survey, however, the students were confident as to the accuracy of their later memories. They believed that what they now remembered was entirely accurate. A similar experiment was conducted after 9/11, in which students were asked on September 12 to record their memories of the previous day, and of another personal incident. Students were then asked about those memories 1, 6 or 32 weeks later. The responses given in the later tests indicated growing inaccuracies in what the students could recall. Whether with respect to the memory of 9/11, or with respect to the other personal memory, as time passed the students could recall events less well, and included more inaccurate details in their memories. The only difference was that the students tended to have a disproportionate sense of the accuracy of their memories of 9/11 and to have a more realistic sense of their inability to recall the more ordinary incident.[29]

The "problem" of memory is illustrated by the inadequacies of the video recorder analogy. People are not video recorders, and they never merely "play back" what they see or experience. Instead, they filter what they have seen through their preconceptions, expectations, temperament, emotional experiences and desires. They remember what is, but only as seen through what they needed it to be. It's not that people lie; its that what they subjectively recall simply does not reflect the truth, objectively speaking.[30]

An interesting illustration of the tendency for one's subjective position to affect one's memory is the Bobby Knight "choking" incident. Bobby Knight was the long time basketball coach at Indiana University who had a "national reputation for a volatile temper, crass behavior, and a disdainful attitude".[31] Knight was ultimately fired following an interaction with an undergraduate student in which Knight grabbed the student's arm and

---

[28] *Ibid.* at 72-73.
[29] *Ibid.* at 76-76.
[30] Dillard S. Gardner, "The Perception and Memory of Witnesses", (1933) 18 Cornell L.Q. 391; *cf.* Daniel L. Schacter, *The Seven Sins of Memory: How the Mind Forgets and Remembers* (Boston: Houghton Mifflin, 2001) at 88-137 (discussing misattribution and suggestibility). "When misattribution combines with ... suggestibility ... people can develop detailed and strongly held recollections of complex events that never occurred. ... [S]uch recollections have been linked with deeply troubling events in the therapist's office, the courtroom, and the preschool." *Ibid.* at 111.
[31] Christopher Chabris & Daniel Simons, *The Invisible Gorilla: And Other Ways Our Intuitions Deceive Us* (New York: Random House Inc., 2010) at 43.

lectured him. In 1997 Knight was angry with a player, Neil Reed, who did not call out a teammate's name when passing the ball. Knight approached Reed, grabbed "him by the front of the neck with one hand for several seconds"[32] and pushed him backward. This incident was recorded on videotape. It also was discussed in an article about Knight in *Sports Illustrated* just before he was fired. In that article Reed described the incident as follows:

> At that point coach thrust right at me, just came right at me, wasn't far away enough to where I couldn't see it coming, was close enough to come at me and reach and put his hand around my throat. He came at me with two hands but grabbed me with one hand. People came in and separated us like we were in a school yard to fight ... He had me by the throat for I would probably say that little situation lasted about 5 seconds. I grabbed his wrist and started walking back and by this time people, coaches Dan Dakich, Felling grabbed coach Knight and pulled him away.[33]

Dakich denied this incident, as did another player who was there. Bobby Knight said "I might have grabbed him by the back of the neck. I might have grabbed the guy and moved him over. I mean if you choke a guy, I would think he would need hospitalization."[34]

In other words, every participant in the incident had an inaccurate memory of what happened, when assessed against the objective evidence contained in the video recording. Reed recalled others intervening when they had not; Knight had no recollection of choking Reed, even though on an ordinary understanding grabbing someone by the front of the throat will likely be described that way. Further, as suggested by Christopher Chabris and Daniel Simons, who discuss this incident in their book *The Invisible Gorilla: And Other Ways Our Intuitions Deceive Us*,[35] the reason for the difference in recollection was the relationship between what happened and the situation of each of the people recollecting it. As the authors note, for Reed this was an extraordinary experience, a "jarring and unusual event, one that he stored in his memory as 'coach choked me'"[36] and one he filled out with details consistent with a traumatic experience — other people interfering and pulling Knight away. For Knight, by contrast, the event was nothing out of the ordinary, and he remembered it in just that way, taking away the aspects of his memory that would certainly strike an ordinary observer as unusual (as, indeed, "choking" a player).

Distortions in memory can also result from interest or prejudice. A classic example of prejudice is the study in which subjects were shown an illustration of a scene on a subway car, including an African-American man

---

[32] *Ibid.* at 48.
[33] *Ibid.* at 44.
[34] *Ibid.* at 45.
[35] *Ibid.*
[36] *Ibid.* at 50.

wearing a jacket and tie, and a white man dressed in work clothes and holding a razor in his hand. In an experiment in which people serially described the picture to each other (as in the game "telephone"), the razor "tended to migrate" from the white man's hand to that of the African-American man.[37]

Perhaps because of its relationship to the subjectivity of our experiences, memory can be manipulated, both by direct suggestion and through playing on our desires, wishes and weaknesses. Simply changing the word used when asking a question will affect how an experience is recalled in response to that question. Thus in one experiment when subjects were asked to recall a car accident, when the question was phrased in terms of one car "contacting" the other, the speed averaged 31.8 miles per hour. The speed of the car increased in the witnesses' memory, however, as the verb was modified: "hit" (34.0 mph), "bumped" (38.1 mph), "collided" (39.3 mph), and "smashed" (40.8 mph).[38] In another experiment, when subjects were rewarded for giving particular answers (in that case, estimating the number of dots on a page) answers changed. Specifically, when subjects were rewarded for giving a higher estimate of dots, subjects produced more overestimates. Once overestimates ceased to lead to any sort of reward, overestimation disappeared.[39]

Some studies have even suggested that through manipulation and suggestion, memories can be created out of whole cloth. In the "lost in the mall" study, a teenager named Chris was asked by his older brother Jim to try to remember the time Chris was lost in a shopping mall when he was five. Chris initially recalled nothing, but after a few days produced a detailed recollection of the incident. According to Jim and other family members, Chris was never lost in a shopping mall.[40]

In sum, remembering is nothing at all like playing back a videotape. Rather, it is a process of active, creative reconstruction, which begins at the moment of perception. Moreover, this reconstructive process is significantly affected by the form of the questions asked and by what we understand to be in our own interest — even though, on a conscious level, we are responding as honestly as we can.

---

[37] Elizabeth Loftus, *Memory* (Reading, MA: Addison-Wesley, 1980), referring to an experiment reported in Gordon W. Allport & Leo J. Postman, "The Basic Psychology of Rumor" in Eleanor E. Maccoby *et al.*, eds., *Readings in Social Psychology* (New York: Holt, 1958).

[38] Elizabeth Loftus, "Reconstructing Memory: The Incredible Eyewitness" 8 *Psychology Today* (December 1974) 117 at 119. In addition, twice as many witnesses reported seeing nonexistent broken glass on the ground when the questioner used the word "smashed" instead of "hit".

[39] M.D. Vernon, *The Psychology of Memory* (Baltimore: Penguin Books Inc., 1962) at 206-207.

[40] Elizabeth Loftus & Jacqueline E. Pickrell, "The Formation of False Memories" (1995) 25 Psychiatric Annals 720. In a subsequent study with twenty-four participants, Loftus demonstrated that after several probing interviews, approximately one-fourth of the participants falsely remembered being lost as a child in a shopping mall or similar place. See also Ira E. Hyman *et al.*, "False Memories of Childhood Experiences" (1995) 9 Applied Cognitive Psychology 181; Ira Hyman & James Billings, "Individual Differences and the Creation of False Childhood Memories" (1998) 6 Memory 1.

What this means, when combined with the disjunct between law and facts, and the variability in the skill and sophistication of witnesses, is that the art of preparing a witness without coaching, of fulfilling the duty to zealously advocate while presenting only evidence that is truthful and not misleading, requires considerable sensitivity and skill in the lawyer.

D. The Skill of Effective Witness Preparation

Most Canadian writing about witness preparation approaches the issue from the perspective of advocacy guidance for litigation lawyers. Those writers generally acknowledge the need for preparation not to undermine the truthfulness or accuracy of a witness's testimony; the main focus is, however, on using preparation to ensure the most effective presentation of the client's case. In general, the task of ensuring truthful and accurate testimony is not seen as especially complicated:

> A witness must be briefed so that counsel will know what he will say and how he will say it. It is well known that counsel must not change the content of a witness's testimony. However, it is appropriate to assist a witness in the way he gives his evidence. The line is not a fine one. There is nothing confusing about whether counsel is improving clarity or changing content.[41]

In his book *On Trial: Advocacy Skills, Law and Practice*,[42] Geoffrey Adair takes a more nuanced approach. Adair suggests that witness preparation has four basic stages. First, the witness should do some "preliminary preparation". This involves the witness reviewing independently all documents or prior statements that relate to his testimony. It may also involve, for example, taking the witness to where the incident being testified about took place. Adair suggests a witness to a motor vehicle accident should be taken to the scene and asked to indicate where the cars were at the time of the accident. If there is an issue as to where the cars were relative to a set of lights, then the measurements from the location can be taken and given to the witness, rather than leaving "everything to the notoriously unreliable ability of witnesses to estimate distances".[43] Adair says that a witness should not, however, be given every possible document that relates to the case, because doing so may encourage the witness to "tailor his or her evidence to fit the existing documentation".[44]

The second stage in the witness preparation is meeting with counsel. Adair suggests that information be elicited from the witnesses using two techniques. First the witness should be examined using questions similar to those that would be used in an examination-in-chief — that is, open ended

---

[41] Robert B. White, *The Art of Trial* (Aurora: Canada Law Book, 1993) at 86.
[42] Geoffrey Adair, *On Trial: Advocacy Skills, Law and Practice*, 2d ed. (Toronto: LexisNexis, 2004); See also John A. Olah & Colin Piercey, *The Art and Science of Advocacy*, looseleaf (Toronto: Carswell, 1995) at 7-14–7-21.
[43] Geoffrey Adair, *On Trial: Advocacy Skills, Law and Practice*, 2d ed. (Toronto: LexisNexis, 2004) at 101.
[44] *Ibid.* at 102.

questions. Second, the witness should be examined using questions similar to those that would be used during a cross-examination. Cross-examination style questioning can be used in particular to probe areas likely to affect the witness's credibility. In sum, Adair suggests that

> There is no substitute, during the entire process, for a repetitive, often forceful, hammering away at the witness to dredge out all necessary evidence and refine it with appropriate words to create impact, all with a view to bringing out the story of the witness in chief to maximum effect with a minimum of intervention by counsel conducting the direct examination.[45]

The third stage in preparation is "polishing the witness". This stage is directed towards making the witness's presentation as effective as possible, and reducing some of the intimidation of the adversarial process. For the most part the preparation at this point does not go to the substance of the witness's testimony; exceptions include the suggestion that witnesses be directed to make responses work better for the transcript (such as suggesting that a witness say that he can only lift his arm "parallel with the ground" rather than "this high").[46] Adair advises that witnesses be told of the ethical responsibilities of witnesses and counsel, which are identified as counsel not speaking to the witness, and the witness not speaking to anyone, while the testimony is ongoing.[47] Adair emphasizes that the witness's testimony should not be polished by simply handing him a list of pointers; polishing should instead be part of the ongoing process of preparation:

> For example, if, in the course of rehearsing the story the witness says that he heard a noise from "up the street", the lesson to provide for-the-record evidence is much more effectively delivered if counsel works with the witness to rephrase the answer in the desirable way rather than lecturing on the necessity of properly answering.[48]

The final stage is preparing the witness for cross-examination. Adair notes the importance of instructing the witness in such basic cross-examination strategy as only answering questions as they are asked. With respect to matters of credibility he suggests that the lawyer "stress the importance of answering any such questions truthfully without regard to how the answers may make the witness look."[49] Adair also suggests that the witness be advised of documentary evidence or other testimony that contradicts the witness's. He suggests that the witness be "instructed to stand firm upon his evidence if that is the truth" and that the lawyer must not inadvertently "violate any order excluding witnesses."[50]

---

[45] *Ibid.* at 103.
[46] *Ibid.* at 104.
[47] Adair also identifies the specific circumstances in which counsel may and may not speak with a witness (at 106).
[48] *Ibid.* at 106.
[49] *Ibid.* at 107.
[50] *Ibid.* at 108.

I have focused on the advice given by Adair because he seems more sensitive to the ethical issues related to preparation than are other Canadian writers on the topic. The attitude of writers such as Robert White, quoted earlier for his suggestion that respecting the line between coaching and preparation is straightforward, reflects a somewhat simplistic and naïve attitude to the relationship between what counsel says to a witness, and the nature of the evidence that the witness will provide. Admonishing the witness to be truthful, and stopping short of telling the witness what to say, does not eliminate the opportunity for lawyers, whether consciously or unconsciously, to manipulate the substance of the witness's recollection of events.

Even Adair does not, however, emphasize these points much beyond the most obvious ways in which a lawyer can coach a witness. Adair notes the clear prohibitions such as having conversations when the witness is under examination or providing documentation other than that which the witness was involved in preparing where it may shape the witness's testimony in inappropriate ways. Adair does not consider more subtle forms of coaching such as how the routine act of "hammering away at the witness"[51] may result in the witness's testimony being created as well as shaped. The point in the preparation where the lawyer turns from a direct type of examination of the witness to one that is closer to a cross-examination may also significantly affect the tendency of the preparation to create rather than collect information from the witness. If the lawyer begins cross-examination too early the witness may be more likely to pick up on cues from the questions and recall events in ways that the questions suggest are correct.

Adair also does not observe the effect that taking the witness back to the scene may have on the substance of the witness's testimony. The fact may be that the witness simply has no reliable recollection of where the motor vehicle was at the time of the accident; taking the witness to the scene may not refresh the witness's memory, but may rather encourage the witness to create a recollection that seems plausible given what he is seeing at that later time.

E. Ethical and Effective Preparation of Witnesses

The identification of the reasons why ethical witness preparation is more complicated than writers about preparation normally recognize does not translate into straightforward modifications of the advice that those writers give. Knowing that memory is unreliable and malleable does not, for example, lead to obvious additions, deletions or modifications to Adair's four stages of preparation. Rather, the issues identified with respect to preparing witnesses suggest the need for a continual awareness by the

---

[51] *Ibid.* at 103.

lawyer of the potential to slip from preparation to coaching. The line between those things is indeed a "fine one",[52] and the possibility of inadvertently encouraging a witness to perceive the past in a particular way is always present. Whatever approach a lawyer takes to preparing a witness requires vigilance and awareness of the ethical problems that may arise.

A few practical and more concrete points can be suggested, however.

First, a lawyer should be sure to avoid the more egregious forms of coaching captured in the rules and case law — conversations at high risk times such as during cross-examination, excessively directive preparation, pressuring witnesses to give particular testimony or scripting what the witness says.

Second, a lawyer should be cautious in her expectations of what a witness is capable of remembering. A limited recollection of events that happened months, or especially years, previously is normal, and pushing the witness to remember more in those circumstances increases the likelihood of created memory.

Third, Adair's suggested method of beginning with a direct type of examination and moving into a cross-examination style is a good one, but the lawyer must be cautious not to shift to asking leading questions too soon during preparation. Leading questions are more likely to lead the witness to shift to what the questions suggest was true, rather than what the witness independently recalls to be the case.

Fourth, putting some time into the preparation prior to meeting the witness, particularly with respect to the questions that will be asked, is worth doing. Ensuring that questions do not inadvertently employ trigger words (for example, "smashed" in relation to a motor vehicle accident) is more easily accomplished beforehand than at the time.

Fifth, as suggested by Adair, reliance on contemporaneous information — such as documents prepared or received by the witness — increases the likelihood of accurate information being provided by the witness later. The creation of contemporaneous information — speaking to a witness as soon as possible after the incident, encouraging a personal injury plaintiff to keep a record of his injuries — is therefore a desirable litigation strategy. Further, where such information exists it can be used to help refresh the witness's memory. If Neil Reed or Bobby Knight had been shown the choking incident video their recollections would — obviously — have been far more accurate. A lawyer should, though, also be careful with the possibility of creating evidence through reconstruction of events at "the scene". While that strategy may be very helpful in some cases, in others it may be an invitation to the reconstruction of memory, particularly if the lawyer asks questions that encourage the witness to do so.

Finally, lawyers need to independently investigate where appropriate, so that they can help avoid errors clients may make through the vagaries of

---

[52] Robert B. White, *The Art of Trial* (Aurora: Canada Law Book, 1993) at 86.

memory. In one famous case of innocently misleading testimony, John Dean testified before the Senate Watergate hearings that he had met with Herbert Kalmbach at the Mayflower hotel.[53] He stuck to this testimony, even when shown evidence that Kalmbach was not staying at that hotel. It turned out that he had met with Kalmbach at the Mayflower Doughnut Coffee Shop in the Statler Hilton, where Kalmbach was staying. If a lawyer representing Dean (or the client for whom Dean was testifying) discovered, for example, that there is a Mayflower restaurant in another hotel, and that that hotel was where the person with whom the witness met was staying, the lawyer can better help the witness achieve accurate recollection of where a meeting took place and, hopefully, of what happened there.

None of this is intended to soften the lawyer's zealous advocacy for her client's interests. Indeed, there are times when this type of more nuanced preparation may protect or foster those interests; John Dean was truthful, but had he been under cross-examination, and it had been shown clearly that his recollection about the Mayflower hotel was simply implausible, his credibility would have been negatively impacted. As often as not it is in everyone's interests, including the client's, that a witness's testimony be introduced accurately in the first instance.

It is also not intended to suggest that a lawyer can ever achieve a perfect balance between obtaining truthful and not misleading evidence, and presenting the client's case as effectively as possible. If the world divided into liars and truth tellers, and if all of us knew when we were accurate about what happened in the past, then achieving that perfect balance would be as straightforward as writers like White suggest. But the world does not divide that simply, and all of us can look at boxes and sometimes see a rectangle and sometimes see a square. The ethical obligation of the lawyer is, simply, to be aware of the complexity and risks that preparation of witnesses in the real world involves, and to try and achieve the best balance possible between truthful and effective advocacy.

3. CROSS-EXAMINATION

A. Introduction

In the previous section it was noted that the central ethical problem of witness preparation arises from the human frailty of witnesses: the weaknesses in their capacity for accurate perception and the malleability of their memories. With respect to cross-examination, the central ethical problem for lawyers also arises from human frailty. In the case of cross-examination, however, it is not the frailty of witnesses, but rather that of the triers of fact who assess those witnesses' credibility. Triers of fact are required to determine whether witnesses are truthful, and what aspects of a witness's

---

[53] Dean's testimony was discussed in Monroe H. Freedman, *Lawyers' Ethics in an Adversary System* (Indianapolis: Bobbs-Merrill, 1975) at 66.

testimony can or should be relied upon in determining what happened. But to make that assessment triers of fact are given no window through which to see the truth of what occurred, or the honesty of the witness; they instead assess credibility based on their general impression of the witness, the plausibility of the testimony and other factors that indirectly indicate veracity or plausibility. As a consequence, triers of fact can be misled, and can make significant errors in determining whose evidence can be relied upon, and to what extent. Triers of fact may, for example, be misled by a witness's hesitancy, past misconduct or inconsistent statements to disbelieve a witness who is truthful. Or they may be misled by a witness's confidence, politeness and apparently blameless past life to believe a witness who is testifying dishonestly or inaccurately.

In January 1985, Jennifer Thompson gave eye witness testimony identifying Ronald Cotton as the man who had broken into her house and raped her.[54] Thompson was a confident and compelling witness, her testimony strong enough to convince a jury to convict Cotton then, and again two years later after another prisoner, Bobby Poole, who looked a lot like Cotton, had confessed to the crime. Thompson stated during the second trial with respect to Poole that "I have never seen him in my life. I have no idea who he is."[55] In 1995 DNA evidence showed that Cotton was innocent, and that Poole was the man who had raped Jennifer Thompson. Thompson was devastated, and now speaks — with Cotton — on the need for reform to the criminal justice system.[56] The problem that her testimony demonstrates remains with us, however: witnesses who speak with confidence and certainty are far more likely to be believed, regardless of whether their testimony is accurate.

Of course Thompson believed that she was testifying accurately. One would think that it might be easier to determine the difference between truthful testimony and testimony that was deliberately dishonest — that is, between a truth and a lie. One would be wrong. In fact, determining the difference between truth and lies is notoriously difficult; in experiments listeners have no greater accuracy in detecting lies than would arise from flipping a coin:

> Despite decades of research effort to maximize the accuracy of deception judgments, detection rates rarely budge. Professionals' judgments, interactants' judgments, judgments of high-stakes lies, judgments of unsanctioned lies, judgments made by long-term acquaintances — all reveal detection rates within a few points of 50%. We wonder if it is premature to abort the quest for 90% lie detection and accept the conclusion implied by the first 384 research samples — that to people

---

[54] Christopher Chabris & Daniel Simons, *The Invisible Gorilla: And Other Ways Our Intuitions Deceive Us* (New York: Crown Publishers, 2010) at 109-11.
[55] *Ibid.*
[56] *Ibid.* at 114.

who must judge deception in real time with no special aids, many lies are undetectable.[57]

Judges and juries do not of course simply watch film of a person speaking; they are given many "special aids" for lie detection, including the benefit of cross-examination that may identify inaccuracies or lies in a witness's testimony. This likely heightens the ability of judges and juries to assess accuracy — certainly our adversary system is premised on the notion that cross-examination enhances the ability of triers of fact to determine the truth.

It is, though, unlikely that the aids of the adversary system perfect the perceptions of judges or juries, or remove the possibility for errors similar to those made when people watch a film of a person speaking. In particular, the adversary system does not eliminate problems such as those that arise from the fact that, when a person most wants to be believed they are most likely to appear deceptive,[58] or from our over-valuing of confidence. Nor does it eliminate problems that arise from mistaken assumptions that people have about how other people are likely to behave, or how we can accurately judge the behaviour of others. It does not, for example, eliminate our tendency to believe that "character" can be identified and can predict conduct across circumstances, even though character cannot be reliably identified and does not predict future conduct in any straightforward way.[59]

Moreover, in circumstances where, in fact, the witness is testifying truthfully and accurately, the rigours of cross-examination may make the trier of fact's assessment of credibility less accurate than would be that of the person watching a film of the witness's initial testimony. The cross-examination may make the witness appear hesitant, inconsistent or incoherent — that is, not believable — even when the witness has actually told the truth.

In short, when a lawyer cross-examines a witness, she has the capacity to make a trier of fact disbelieve a witness who is truthful. Is it ethical for a lawyer to do so? This is the question considered by this section. It begins by considering the role of cross-examination in the adversary system. It notes the ways in which lawyers may challenge the credibility of witnesses through cross-examination but also the constraints imposed on lawyers' cross-examination of witnesses by the law of evidence and the rules of professional conduct. Based on this analysis, it will identify the characteristics of ethical cross-examination, concluding that, in some circumstances, the

---

[57] Charles F. Bond Jr. & Bella M. DePaulo, "Accuracy of Deception Judgments" (2006) 10(3) Personality and Social Psychology Review 214 at 231.
[58] *Ibid.* at 226: "People who are afraid of being disbelieved may come to resemble the stereotypic liar."
[59] See, in general, Alice Woolley & Jocelyn Stacey, "The Psychology of Good Character: the past, present and future of good character regulation in Canada" in Kieran Tranter *et al.*, eds., *Reaffirming Legal Ethics: Taking Stock and New Ideas* (New York: Routledge, 2010) at 165-87; Alice Woolley, "Tending the Bar: The Good Character Requirement for Law Society Admission" (2007) 30 Dal. L.J. 27.

lawyer's role does require that the lawyer make a witness appear dishonest even when the lawyer knows the witness has testified truthfully.

B. The Law of Cross-Examination

The Supreme Court of Canada has asserted unambiguously the importance of cross-examination in the adversary system, describing it as a "faithful friend in the pursuit of justice and an indispensable ally in the search for truth".[60] The Court views cross-examination as essential for determining the accuracy of the evidence before the Court:

> There can be no question of the importance of cross-examination. It is of essential importance in determining whether a witness is credible. Even with the most honest witness cross-examination can provide the means to explore the frailties of the testimony. For example, it can demonstrate a witness's weakness of sight or hearing. It can establish that the existing weather conditions may have limited the ability of a witness to observe, or that medication taken by the witness would have distorted vision or hearing. Its importance cannot be denied. It is the ultimate means of demonstrating truth and of testing veracity. Cross-examination must be permitted so that an accused can make full answer and defence. The opportunity to cross-examine witnesses is fundamental to providing a fair trial to an accused. This is an old and well-established principle that is closely linked to the presumption of innocence.[61]

The courts give "wide latitude" to lawyers in conducting a cross-examination.[62] Cross-examination is not restricted to matters raised in an examination-in-chief, but can touch on any matter that is relevant and admissible in the proceeding.[63]

Cross-examination can be loosely identified as comprising two types, which I shall describe as "process" cross-examination and "substantive" cross-examination. In a process cross-examination the lawyer challenges the credibility of the witness's testimony by focusing on the manner of the witness's testimony — its consistency, the witness's narrative ability or the witness's confidence. That is, the lawyer does not focus on substantive facts about the witness, or that arise from the witness's testimony, but rather on the ways in which the witness's presentation of the evidence suggests that the evidence is not worthy of belief.[64] In general, the purpose of a process cross-examination is to undermine the credibility of the witness and his testimony.

In a substantive cross-examination, a lawyer focuses on the substance of what the witness has done or said, or on what other people have done or

---

[60] *R. v. Lyttle*, [2004] S.C.J. No. 8 at para. 1, [2004] 1 S.C.R. 193, 2004 SCC 5 (S.C.C.).
[61] *R. v. Osolin*, [1993] S.C.J. No. 135 at para. 157, [1993] 4 S.C.R. 595 (S.C.C.), *per* Cory J.
[62] *R. v. Lyttle*, [2004] S.C.J. No. 8 at para. 50, [2004] 1 S.C.R. 193, 2004 SCC 5 (S.C.C.).
[63] Alan W. Bryant, Sidney N. Lederman & Michelle K. Fuerst, *Sopinka and Lederman: The Law of Evidence in Canada*, 3d ed. (Toronto: LexisNexis Canada, 2009) at 1137.
[64] See generally, *Sopinka and Lederman, ibid.*, at 1147-48.

said, in order to challenge the witness's character and credibility, to suggest that the witness's version of events is incomplete or inaccurate, or to confirm additional facts that the witness had not mentioned during the examination-in-chief. A substantive cross-examination would include cross-examining on the witness's past criminal record or character, on facts that contradict the evidence that the witness has provided or on additional facts of which the witness has knowledge. As an example of substantive cross-examination, in the second trial of Guy-Paul Morin, the mother of the victim, Janet Jessop, testified that she had thrown out the clock that she had looked at on returning home on the day of the murder because it was faulty. In cross-examination counsel for Morin forced Jessop to concede that this testimony was inaccurate through showing her a videotape of her kitchen at a later time in which the clock was visible on the wall. It is not clear whether in other respects Jessop's testimony was accurate, but on this point the cross-examination clearly established that her testimony was substantively in error.[65]

The law of evidence and the codes of conduct place constraints on both types of cross-examination. The codes of conduct and the case law prohibit the lawyer from acting in a way that is "sarcastic, personally abusive and derisive".[66] The lawyer must not "needlessly abuse, hector or harass" a witness, and should be courteous and civil.[67] In Québec, the Ethics Code requires that the advocate's behaviour be characterized by objectivity, moderation and dignity at all times.[68] As stated more specifically by the Alberta Code of Conduct, "professional ethics preclude actions by a lawyer having no substantial purpose other than to intimidate, harass or embarrass a witness."[69] These constraints go less to the type of questions that a lawyer may ask than they do to the manner in which the lawyer asks them. The lawyer may point out inconsistencies, ways in which the testimony is inarticulate or the witness's apparent nervousness or hesitation. But the lawyer cannot do so in a manner that will demean or belittle the witness.

---

[65] Report from the Ontario Attorney General of the Kaufman Commission on Proceedings Involving Guy Paul Morin, "Executive Summary" at 24, online: Ontario. Ministry of the Attorney General <http://www.attorneygeneral.jus.gov.on.ca/english/about/pubs/morin/morin_esumm.pdf>.

[66] R. v. Bouhsass, [2002] O.J. No. 4177, 169 C.C.C. (3d) 444 (Ont. C.A.). See also R. v. W.(B.A.), [1992] S.C.J. No. 106, [1992] 3 S.C.R. 811 (S.C.C.); R. v. Ellard, [2003] B.C.J. No. 231, 172 C.C.C. (3d) 28 (B.C.C.A.).

[67] CBA MC Chapter IX, Commentary 2(k) and Commentary 16; FLS MC Rule 4.01(2)(m) and 4.01(5); NB CC Chapter 8, Commentary 5(a) and Commentary 10(xi); LSUC RPC Rule 4.01(2)(k) and 4.01(6); AB CPC Chapter 19, Rule 21; BC PCH Canon 3(4). Note also that Ontario Rule 53.01(2), *Rules of Civil Procedure*, R.R.O. 1990, Reg. 194 gives judges the power to protect witnesses from "undue harassment or embarrassment" and to disallow questions that are "vexatious or irrelevant to any matter that may be properly inquired into".

[68] Que. CEA Rule 2.03.

[69] AB CPC Chapter 19, Rule 21, commentary. In *R. v. Snow*, [2004] O.J. No. 4309 at para. 25, 73 O.R. (3d) 40 (Ont. C.A.), the Court held that the trial judge was "entitled to intervene to cut off editorializing and argumentative questions".

As well, within the wide latitude lawyers are given about what they may ask, there are a number of constraints imposed by the law of evidence on the questions that lawyers may put to a witness. Most obviously, in cross-examining a witness a lawyer may only raise evidentiary points that are relevant and admissible.[70] The lawyer will be given the opportunity to establish relevance through the questions, rather than having to establish relevance from the outset, but relevance to either credibility or a substantive issue raised by the case is required.

In addition to the requirements of relevance and admissibility, a lawyer may not ask a question unless the lawyer has a good faith basis for doing so. The lawyer's information may be "incomplete or uncertain" and may only be something that the lawyer can prove through the process of cross-examination;[71] however, the lawyer may not "put suggestions to the witness recklessly or that he or she knows to be false".[72]

There are also restrictions placed on particular avenues of cross-examination, some of the more notable of which are mentioned here. Most of these restrictions arise out of the general principle that evidence should not be admitted into a proceeding where its prejudicial effect outweighs its probative value.[73] Thus, the character of a criminal accused may not be raised in cross-examination unless the accused has put his character in issue. As summarized in *Sopinka and Lederman, The Law of Evidence in Canada*:

> An ordinary witness is subject to wide cross-examination on the issue of credibility, including cross-examination as to previous convictions and specific acts of misconduct, a bad reputation and disposition. To expose the accused to such cross-examination would be unfair because of the tendency of juries to give such evidence undue weight on the issue of guilt. On the other hand, it would be unfair to the Crown to confer complete immunity on the accused from such questioning, particularly where an accused is relying on an unblemished character which he or she does not possess. The principles respecting the admissibility of evidence of the accused's bad character attempt to balance these concerns.[74]

---

[70] See, for example, *R. v. Snow*, [2004] O.J. No. 4309 at para. 25, 73 O.R. (3d) 40 (Ont. C.A.), in which the Court held that the trial judge "was entitled to curtail questions by defence counsel that were irrelevant, prolix and repetitive". See also Alan W. Bryant, Sidney N. Lederman & Michelle K. Fuerst, *Sopinka and Lederman: The Law of Evidence in Canada*, 3d ed. (Toronto: LexisNexis Canada, 2009) at 1137.

[71] *R. v. Lyttle*, [2004] S.C.J. No. 8 at para. 47, [2004] 1 S.C.R. 193, 2004 SCC 5 (S.C.C.).

[72] *Ibid.* at para. 48. This principle has been codified in a number of the codes of conduct, although not all (for example, the LSUC). See: CBA MC Chapter IX, Commentary 2(g); FLS MC Rule 4.01(2)(h); NB CC Commentary 10(xiii); AB CPC Chapter 10, Rule 21, commentary; BC PCH Chapter 8, Rule 1(e.1).

[73] *R. v. Mohan*, [1994] S.C.J. No. 36, [1994] 2 S.C.R. 9 at 21 (S.C.C.); *R. v. Seaboyer*, [1991] S.C.J. No. 62, [1991] 2 S.C.R. 577 (S.C.C.).

[74] Alan W. Bryant, Sidney N. Lederman & Michelle K. Fuerst, *Sopinka and Lederman: The Law of Evidence in Canada*, 3d ed. (Toronto: LexisNexis Canada, 2009) at 660.

Similarly, while s. 12 of the Canada *Evidence Act*[75] allows cross-examination on the criminal record of a witness, the Supreme Court has given judges the ability to limit cross-examination where the prejudicial effect of such questions outweighs their probative value.[76]

The Supreme Court has also held that witnesses may not be examined as to their knowledge of s. 13 of the *Canadian Charter of Rights and Freedoms*.[77] Section 13 grants testimonial immunity to witnesses who are compelled to testify in a proceeding from use of that testimony against them in subsequent proceedings. In *R. v. Jabarianha*,[78] the Supreme Court held that witnesses could not be asked about their knowledge of s. 13 in an attempt to impugn their credibility, since the prejudicial effect of that question significantly outweighed its probative value. The only circumstance in which a question about s. 13 would be permissible is where the Crown had some basis for asserting that the witness is engaged in a plot to deceive.

Finally, cross-examination of complainants in sexual assault cases with respect to their sexual history is generally prohibited by s. 276 of the *Criminal Code*.[79] Past sexual activity is only admissible if the accused satisfies the judge in a *voir dire*[80] that the evidence is relevant, relates to a specific instance of sexual activity, has a probative effect that outweighs its prejudicial value, and is relevant to a specific issue in the trial.[81]

This list of restrictions is not exhaustive; it does, though, indicate the extent to which courts will constrain lawyer cross-examination that has the potential to undermine the fairness and accuracy of the trial process.

In sum, cross-examination is essential and important to the adversary process, and lawyers are given wide latitude to challenge both the manner and substance of a witness's testimony. Cross-examination is also, though, subject to constraints. Lawyers may not cross-examine witnesses in a way that is abusive or offensive, and may only ask questions that are relevant, admissible, based on a good faith belief and which are not specifically precluded by the law of evidence.

C. Ethical Cross-Examination

Given that brief summary, what does ethical cross-examination require? Most obviously, it requires that the lawyer stay within the constraints that the ethical rules and the law of evidence impose. The conduct of a cross-examination must be done in a way that respects the dignity of the witness,

---

[75] R.S.C. 1985, c. C-5.
[76] *R. v. Corbett*, [1988] S.C.J. No. 40, [1988] 1 S.C.R. 670 (S.C.C.).
[77] Part I of the *Constitution Act, 1982*, being Schedule B to the *Canada Act 1982* (U.K.), 1982, c. 11.
[78] [2001] S.C.J. No. 72, [2001] 3 S.C.R. 430 (S.C.C.).
[79] R.S.C. 1985, c. C-46.
[80] A hearing on a specific issue during a trial.
[81] The constitutional validity of s. 276 was established in *R. v. Darrach*, [2000] S.C.J. No. 46, 148 C.C.C. (3d) 97 (S.C.C.).

no matter what the lawyer's assessment of the witness's morality or honesty. Even a criminal charged with the most heinous crime should not be asked questions like whether the witness "wanted the jury to believe that one too"[82] or "gee, I guess everybody would react the way you did"[83] or comments such as "let's try and be honest".[84] "No counsel can abuse any witness."[85] The judge can control that sort of cross-examination, but the functioning of the legal system also depends on lawyers understanding and respecting those limits independently.

Not all improper cross-examination can be easily controlled by the trial judge given the "wide latitude" which lawyers have to ask questions. Because, for example, relevancy can be established through a line of questions, a judge will (or at least should) give lawyers the opportunity to pursue a line of questioning without first establishing relevance. If lawyers do not have any good faith basis for asking the questions, and are simply casting dust in the air to obscure the significance of unhelpful facts, by the time that becomes apparent it may be too late to repair the harm that arises. Similarly, since a lawyer need only have a "good faith" basis for pursuing a line of questions, and judges rely on the representations of lawyers as to whether such a basis exists, it is the ethics and judgment of the lawyer that will determine whether or not the limit is respected.

Even when a lawyer scrupulously observes the constraints imposed on cross-examination by the law of evidence and the ethical rules, however, cross-examination may have effects that are dubious given our general sense of what the legal system should accomplish — that is, the production of legally just results in each case. This would not be the case if judges and juries were without human weakness, incapable of distraction or mistake, free from normal human misconceptions, and always able to judge honesty accurately. But they are not, and lawyers may take advantage of those weaknesses to obtain a better result for their clients than would otherwise be available.

For example, lawyers may, as noted, cross-examine any witness on his character in order to challenge that witness's credibility (except for a criminal accused who has not put his character in issue). The lawyer may raise past criminal convictions or other misconduct in order to suggest that the witness is not worthy of belief. This is the case despite the fact that the evidence of behavioural psychology is, overwhelmingly, that judgments we make based on "character" are rarely reliable, simply because the intersection between personality and circumstances in determining how people behave is so complicated. Dishonesty in one situation does not necessarily indicate that a person will be dishonest in another, quite different, situation. That an alleged victim of sexual assault was a petty thief does not mean that he is lying

---

[82] *R. v. R.(A.J.)*, [1994] O.J. No. 2309 at para. 25, 94 C.C.C. (3d) 168 (Ont. C.A.).
[83] *Ibid.*
[84] *Ibid.* at para. 28.
[85] *Ibid.* at para. 27.

about the assault. Yet people deeply believe that character does predict behaviour, and that dishonesty in one situation *does* indicate a likelihood of dishonesty in another situation.[86] As a consequence, a lawyer may effectively challenge a witness's credibility through challenging the witness's character, even though there is no necessary empirical basis for the conclusion that the trier of fact will draw, and it may well be erroneous. The law of evidence controls this problem to some extent through the prohibition on cross-examining a criminal accused on his character, but it does not do so sufficiently to prevent all instances in which cross-examination may have this effect.

Further, lawyers may raise facts that are admissible and relevant, and which influence the trier of fact's assessment of the situation, but whose effect on the trier of fact may exceed their actual relevance. The fact that a witness is old, or has poor eyesight, may lead the trier of fact to discredit even accurate parts of that witness's testimony. This is less of an issue in Canada, where far fewer trials involve a jury, but it remains a potentially effective strategy in some cases. Also effective may be highlighting the problems with the manner in which a witness testifies, even though not actually relevant to the witness's honesty. For example, undermining a witness's apparent confidence may increase the likelihood that a witness will be disbelieved, even though confidence does not reliably correlate to testimonial accuracy.

Can cross-examination that has this effect on the functioning of a trial be ethically justified? Can a lawyer who has reason to believe that a witness is testifying truthfully bring up evidence of past criminal activity in order to invite the false inference that the witness is lying? What if the lawyer does not know that the witness is truthful, but nonetheless suspects that the past evidence of criminal activity is not relevant to that question?

In circumstances where the lawyer does not know whether or not the witness is truthful, and thus does not know that cross-examination will produce inaccurate adjudication by the trier of fact, the answer is yes, the lawyer may cross-examine in that way, even if inaccurate adjudication results. In that instance the lawyer has no intention to mislead or abuse the system. The lawyer's conduct falls within what the law permits and does not involve any apparent immorality, since the lawyer has not harassed the witness or asked questions without a good faith basis for doing so. Any negative consequences that follow from the lawyer's actions are unintended, to some extent unpredictable (since the lawyer cannot anticipate what errors might be made, or whether they are, in fact, errors), and arise from the weaknesses in the system itself, not from what the lawyer has done. Our legal system relies on triers of fact being able to make accurate adjudications

---

[86] See, in general, Alice Woolley & Jocelyn Stacey, "The Psychology of Good Character: the past, present and future of good character regulation in Canada" in Kieran Tranter *et al.*, eds., *Reaffirming Legal Ethics* (New York: Routledge, 2010) at 165; Alice Woolley, "Tending the Bar: The Good Character Requirement for Law Society Admission" (2007) 30 Dal. L.J. 27.

of credibility and of what has taken place; to the extent triers of fact cannot do so, that is a matter outside the lawyer's control or responsibility.

What, though, of the lawyer who has reason to believe that a witness is testifying truthfully and accurately? What if the lawyer knows, further, that cross-examination will tend to make the witness appear untruthful or inaccurate because demonstrating issues with the manner in which the witness is testifying, issues with the witness's character and credibility, or issues with some aspects of the witness's testimony? Imagine Morin had not been innocent, and had told his lawyer that he was at the Jessop's house at 4:25 p.m., and Christine's mother and brother were not yet home? In that instance the cross-examination of Janet Jessop on the clock, while factual and correct, would have the effect of making her look dishonest and inaccurate. This will be the case even though the lawyer knows, in this hypothetical, that on the actual matter of importance Jessop's testimony is correct.[87] This example is the opposite of the facts, and on the real facts the cross-examination of Jessop was an important part of Morin's lawyer's attempt to defend his innocent client. But the hypothetical nonetheless shows the ethical question that cross-examination raises, even where that cross-examination falls squarely within the bounds of legality: is it ethical for a lawyer to knowingly make an honest witness appear dishonest?

Many of the arguments that support the position that it is ethical to make a truthful witness appear dishonest when the lawyer does not know whether the witness is truthful apply here as well. In this case the lawyer's actual actions also seem to accord with morality and law. The lawyer conforms to the law of evidence, does not harass or abuse the witness and only pursues questions for which he has a good faith basis. The lawyer acts honestly.

It is also not always the case that making a truthful witness appear dishonest undermines the outcomes of the legal system. Monroe Freedman and Abbe Smith present the example of the suspect wrongfully accused of murder, who is nonetheless accurately placed near the scene of the crime by an eyewitness.[88] The eyewitness is elderly, and has poor vision, but the lawyer knows that the witness's testimony is both honest and liable to increase the likelihood of the lawyer's client being wrongfully convicted. The lawyer can impugn the witness's testimony by cross-examining her on

---

[87] It is interesting to consider why Jessop's testimony was inaccurate. I would guess that she did not intend to do Morin an injustice and, further, that she did not even realize that her testimony was inaccurate. But her daughter had been murdered, and she believed that Morin was guilty. This led her, I would guess, to simply incorporate into her memory things she desperately wanted to believe to be true, things that would explain what had happened to Christine, and would result in the person who had hurt her little girl being brought to justice. If the testimony had been largely accurate, and Morin guilty (which of course he wasn't), discrediting her testimony through cross-examination would have simply been additional hurt to add to the worst kind of hurt a person can suffer, the loss of a child.

[88] Monroe Freedman & Abbe Smith, *Understanding Lawyers' Ethics*, 4th ed. (New Providence, NJ: LexisNexis, 2010) at 156-57, 211-12.

her bad eyesight. Doing so will make an honest woman appear dishonest; it will also help avoid an injustice.

The problem, though, is that the lawyer's knowledge of the witness's accuracy does change the ethical quality of the act of cross-examining that witness. Despite the example of the innocent accused and the accurate witness whose testimony will lead to wrongful conviction, the more likely situation is that making a truthful witness appear dishonest will decrease the validity of the results reached by the court. It will lead to errors and the application of law to "facts" that did not happen, or at least did not happen in quite that way. When the lawyer knows that is the case, while her actions appear on their face to be lawful and moral, she knows that that appearance is deceiving, and that the truth-seeking function of the adjudicative process is being undermined by cross-examination, not enhanced by it.

She also knows that she inflicts an injury on the witness, the injury of being disbelieved despite being truthful. While that may seem like a small thing to someone else, it will not seem like a small thing to that witness, particularly where the witness's rights or interests depend on her being perceived as truthful by the court. The effect on the witness can be traumatic, particularly if the trial judge makes caustic or negative comments about the witness's credibility. A lawyer who knowingly inflicts that cost on another person is in a different position, ethically speaking, than the lawyer who does not know that her cross-examination will have that effect.

Most of the time lawyers do not have certain knowledge of the truthfulness of a witness. The standard of knowledge required is high as was the case with the presentation of perjured testimony discussed in Chapter 6. In litigated cases the facts are messy enough that ordinarily a lawyer will not achieve that standard. The lawyer in most cases will be able to leave the determination of what happened to the trier of fact. In some cases, though, lawyers do have that knowledge.

What is the ethical course of action for those lawyers? The first thing the lawyer should do is speak to her client. It may be that the client's only chance for success requires discrediting a truthful witness. But it may also be that the client does not wish to do so, or recognizes the ethical problems with that course of action and does not want to take it. As discussed with respect to client counselling in Chapter 3, lawyers should not assume that clients wish to act unethically or even to avail themselves of every legal advantage.

If the client wants to proceed with the cross-examination, then in my view the lawyer's role as resolute advocate within the bounds of legality requires that the lawyer undertake the cross-examination. Ultimately, the law of evidence and the codes of conduct establish the constraints on cross-examination. They represent the legal compromise of moral claims in which clients may participate, even if doing so seems immoral to the lawyer or seems to take advantage of weaknesses in the system. In general, as I have argued in a number of contexts, having a lawyer should not make a client worse off than if he could represent himself. In the middle of a proceeding, where withdrawal from the representation is not a realistic option, where the law clearly permits the line of cross-examination to be pursued, and where the client instructs the lawyer to pursue it, then ethical representation of that client requires the lawyer to cross-examine the witness in that way, even if doing so will make a truthful person appear unworthy of belief.

The best hope for lawyers wanting to avoid these situations where personal and professional morality conflict, and one must be sacrificed to the other, is for the law of evidence to develop in a way that makes it improper for the lawyer to ask questions which will lead to an error by the trier of fact. In the United States, discussion of the problem of cross-examination of truthful witnesses almost always turns to the specific example of cross-examination of a sexual assault victim on her sexual history, where the accused has admitted guilt to the lawyer. In Canada, because of the stringent limitations on the use of sexual history evidence, lawyers normally cannot pursue the types of questions that are identified as especially problematic in the American context. Here the moral difficulty for lawyers has, to that extent, been eliminated.

One can question the compromise of the rape shield laws. While they protect victims from lines of inquiry that are almost certain to be distressing, they also have the tendency to prevent the accused from narrating all of the information likely to be relevant to his story. While a past sexual act of the complainant may not be relevant to whether she consented from her point of view, it is much more likely to be relevant to whether she consented from the point of view of the accused. Excluding that evidence may, in some cases, create a strong sense in the accused that the case has not been fully presented.

What relevance does this have to the question here? It points to the reason why the scope and extent of cross-examination is something that does not get determined on a case-by-case basis, based on the lawyer's exercise of her personal discretion. The identification of what is proper cross-examination, both in terms of how it is done and the type of questions that are asked, needs to take into account broader analysis of how to ensure the most effective adjudication of legal cases. Decisions must factor in fairness to all parties (and third parties) and the broader legal goals that a democratic society seeks to achieve. It is not clear that, as a society, we have yet engaged sufficiently with serious questions about the effectiveness of our system of adjudication — the extent to which we rely on triers of fact to distinguish truth from lies and the weight we place on evidence of "character". But those are questions that a democratic society can legitimately claim the right to answer, not to have answered by a lawyer's personal determination of the right way to proceed.

None of this lessens the significance of the ethical challenge that a lawyer cross-examining a truthful witness faces. And nor does it change the answer to how the lawyer should respond to that dilemma, professionally speaking. A lawyer should cross-examine witnesses within the rules established by the law of evidence and the codes of conduct, even if it sometimes requires making a truthful witness appear dishonest. Doing so imposes a moral cost on the lawyer, but that cost is irreducible given the significance and moral justification of the lawyer's role.

Chapter 8

CONFLICTS OF INTEREST: CREATING THE CONDITIONS FOR LOYALTY AND CONFIDENTIALITY

1. INTRODUCTION

Perhaps no area of the law governing lawyers consumes more lawyer time, creates more confusion and frustration, or causes lawyers more difficulty in their practices, than the rules governing conflicts of interest.[1]

Conflicting interests are ubiquitous in the lawyer-client relationship. The fact that, for example, the client pays the lawyer means that to at least that extent the lawyer's and client's interests are not aligned: the lawyer wants to earn more; the client to pay less. Lawyers may also have a personal stake in such decisions as whether to settle a case or to carry it through to trial. Different clients represented by the same lawyer may be adversarial in any number of ways — as economic competitors or as individuals who personally dislike each other. Such divergent interests are neither inherently immoral nor obviously problematic. Even in the most intimate and caring relationships between people — such as in a happy marriage — the interests of the parties will be imperfectly aligned, and may conflict. The existence of different needs or desires, or even of conflicting needs or desires, does not necessarily mean that one party to a relationship has acted, or is likely to act, in contravention of the duties he owes to the other.

Yet in a relationship premised on a duty of loyalty, and on the maintenance of confidentiality, conflicts between the wants and desires of the parties, or between the duties that the parties owe to one another or to others, may in some circumstances create the potential for improper conflict, create the appearance that improper conduct will occur or, in a worst case scenario, may lead to improper conduct in fact. While, to continue the marriage analogy, it may be that a spouse's obsession with career success will not necessarily lead to abandonment of his obligations to his partner and

---

[1] Two Canadian books have been written on conflicts of interest. Paul M. Perell's first-rate book on the topic, *Conflicts of Interest in the Legal Profession* (Toronto and Vancouver: Butterworths, 1998) is unfortunately somewhat dated given subsequent Supreme Court decisions. M. Deborah McNair's *Conflicts of Interest: Principles of the Legal Profession*, looseleaf (Aurora: Canada Law Book, 2005) provides some interesting information on the topic, particularly with respect to conflicts in specific areas of representation.

children, it certainly creates the risk of that outcome, and it may lead his partner and children to view his behaviour in that way. That interest or desire could be seen, in the context of a marriage, as an improper conflict with the interests of the others in the family, and even with the duties that he owes to those other family members, especially his children.

How, in the context of the lawyer-client relationship, do we draw the line between ordinary course conflicts and those that are improper? The line is neither obvious nor intuitive. And the complexity of the rules governing conflicts of interest, the difficulty of applying those rules to particular fact situations, and the significant disagreement amongst some members of the bar and the judiciary as to how those lines should be drawn,[2] reflects that fact.

The purpose of this chapter is to set out the foundations, principles and rules of the law of conflicts. It will:

- Identify the general principles that govern conflicts of interest and, in particular, the principles used to identify conflicts, to identify clients and to establish client consent to a conflict.
- Identify the kinds of conflicts with which a lawyer may be confronted.
- Set out the relationship between the law on conflicts of interest and lawyers' duties of loyalty and confidentiality.
- Note in particular the focus of the law on the potential for, or appearance of, a conflict, rather than on demonstrated violations of the lawyer's duties.
- Review:
  - The duties of the lawyer and law firm when acting against a former client of the lawyer or the firm;
  - The duties of the lawyer and law firm when acting for two or more current clients whose interests may be at some point or are presently in conflict; and
  - The duties of the lawyer when the lawyer's own interests may conflict with the duties owed by the lawyer to the client.

2. LAWYER-CLIENT CONFLICTS DEFINED

A conflict of interest arises where a lawyer violates his or her "fundamental duty ... to act in the best interest of his or her client to the exclusion of all other adverse interests, except those duly disclosed by the lawyer and willingly accepted by the client."[3] This general statement of principle raises, however, three important additional questions:

---

[2] See in particular, CBA Task Force on Conflicts of Interest, *Conflicts of Interest: Final Report, Recommendations and Toolkit* (Ottawa: Canadian Bar Association, 2008).
[3] *Strother v. 3464920 Canada Inc.*, [2007] S.C.J. No. 24 at para. 1, 2007 SCC 24 (S.C.C.). In my view this statement overstates the nature of the lawyer's obligation. It is only those adverse

- When will a lawyer be considered to have violated the "fundamental duty ... to act in the best interests of his or her client to the exclusion of all other adverse interests"?
- Who is a client?
- What constitutes informed consent by the client?

This section addresses these questions, which are relevant across the law of conflicts of interest. The rules governing conflicts are complex, contextual and nuanced, and the rules that apply to specific sorts of conflicts are addressed later in the chapter. Nonetheless, the answers to these general questions are always relevant to the analysis of whether a lawyer has violated his fundamental duty to act in the best interests of his client to the exclusion of all other adverse interests.

A. When will a Lawyer be considered to have Violated the "Fundamental Duty ... To Act in the Best Interests of His or Her Client to the Exclusion of All Other Adverse Interests"?

The law governing lawyers sets out three general principles that establish when a lawyer will be in an improper conflict of interest. A lawyer will be in an improper conflict of interest where:

i. A lawyer's duties to another client, a former client or a third person, create a substantial risk of a material and adverse effect on the representation of a client;

ii. A lawyer acting in a matter creates a possible risk that confidential information obtained from a client will be used to that client's disadvantage;

iii. The lawyer uses the lawyer-client relationship to obtain an improper advantage or benefit for himself.

This section considers the nature and extent of each of these principles.

i. Substantial Risk of Material and Adverse Effect on Representation

The first principle defining prohibited conflicts comes from the United States *Restatement of the Law Governing Lawyers*[4] as adopted by the Supreme Court of Canada in its 2002 decision in *R. v. Neil*:

---

interests identified pursuant to the tests set out in the subsequent section — *i.e.*, that create a substantial risk of a material and adverse effect on the lawyer's representation; that create a risk of misuse of confidential information or that create a risk of improper advantage taking by the lawyer — that are sufficiently adverse to constitute a conflict. Mere adversity is not, based on consideration of the totality of the jurisprudence, sufficient to create a conflict of interest.

[4] Restatement Third, The Law Governing Lawyers (2000), §121, vol. 2, at 244-45.

I adopt, in this respect, the notion of a "conflict" in s. 121 of the *Restatement Third, The Law Governing Lawyers* (2000), vol. 2, at pp. 244-45, as a "substantial risk that the lawyer's representation of the client would be materially and adversely affected by the lawyer's own interests or by the lawyer's duties to another current client, a former client, or a third person".[5]

It is clear from the Canadian cases that to establish a conflict it does not normally need to be demonstrated that, in fact, the representation of a client will be adversely affected; the possibility of an adverse effect is sufficient, provided that the possibility is more than "mere speculation".[6] In the Restatement itself it says that to be a substantial risk it must be "more than a mere possibility" but need not be "immediate, actual, and apparent".[7] Indeed, the Restatement suggests that a risk can be substantial even if it is "potential or contingent", and despite the fact that it is neither "certain or even probable" that impairment of the representation will occur.[8] The question is one of appearances — whether the "reasonably well-informed and objective lay person" could view the lawyer's representation of the client as compromised.[9]

An actual effect on the lawyer-client relationship will only need to be established if the person asserting the conflict is seeking a legal remedy that requires that the relationship was actually impaired, rather than only potentially or apparently impaired. Thus, where a person is appealing a criminal conviction on the basis of ineffective assistance of counsel, and the grounds for the argument is that the accused's lawyer was in a conflict of interest, the appellant must demonstrate that, in fact, the conflict led to some impairment of effective representation.[10] This is also true in a lawsuit for

---

[5] *R. v. Neil*, [2002] S.C.J. No. 72 at para. 31, [2002] 3 S.C.R. 631, 2002 SCC 70 (S.C.C.). The Court's judgment on this point is consistent with the oft-cited earlier decision of the Ontario Court of Appeal, *per* Wilson J. (as she then was) in *Davey v. Woolley, Hames, Dale & Dingwall*, [1982] O.J. No. 3158, 35 O.R. (2d) 599 (Ont. C.A.). This definition has been adopted in CBA MC Chapter V, Commentary 1; Chapter 6, Rule 1; and FLS MC MC Rule 2.04, commentary. Other law societies use similar but somewhat more general definitions. The Law Society of Upper Canada rules define a conflict as something "likely to affect adversely a lawyer's judgment on behalf of, or loyalty to, a client or prospective client" (Rule 2.04(1)(a)) (see similarly NB CC Definitions and Chapter 6, Rule 1; BC PCH Chapter 6, Rule 1); the Alberta CPC requires that the lawyer's judgment be free from "compromising influences" (Chapter 6, Statement of Principle). In disciplinary decisions law societies have emphasized that the lawyer must be able to provide "objective, disinterested, professional advice" (*Law Society of Upper Canada v. Hunter*, [2007] L.S.D.D. No. 8 at para. 43) and defined a conflicting interest as something which "would, or likely would, adversely affect the lawyer's judgment or advice on behalf of or loyalty to his client" (*Regular v. Law Society of Newfoundland and Labrador*, [2010] N.J. No. 165, 2010 NLTD 90 (N.L.T.D.) (citing the Law Society of Newfoundland and Labrador's Code of Professional Conduct at para. 66).
[6] *Strother v. 3464920 Canada Inc.*, [2007] S.C.J. No. 24 at para. 61, 2007 SCC 24 (S.C.C.).
[7] Restatement of the Law Governing Lawyers ss. 121-135 (2000), Commentary c(iii).
[8] *Ibid*.
[9] *Skye Properties Ltd. v. Wu*, [2003] O.J. No. 3481 at para. 60, 43 C.P.C. (5th) 118 (Ont. S.C.J.), affd [2004] O.J. No. 3948 (Ont. C.A.).
[10] *R. v. Silvini*, [1991] O.J. No. 1931, 5 O.R. (3d) 545 (Ont. C.A.); *R. v. Widdifield*, [1995] O.J. No. 2383, 25 O.R. (3d) 161 (Ont. C.A.).

breach of contract, tort or breach of fiduciary duty. If a lawyer is being sued on the basis that the lawyer was acting when in an improper conflict, it will be necessary for the client to establish not only that the lawyer breached her duties (which include avoiding a conflict situation), but also that damages flowed from that breach — that is, that the failure to avoid the conflict in fact harmed the lawyer-client relationship.[11] As discussed further in Section 1.A.iii, with respect to lawyers taking an improper advantage of clients, in these sorts of cases the issue is not really one of conflict of interest, it is one of a breach of the lawyer's legal duties such as effective assistance and loyalty; however, since the breach of duty apparently flows from a conflict of interest, the cases are considered in this chapter.[12]

To determine whether a lawyer-client relationship may be, or has been, materially or adversely affected, some attention must be paid to the nature of the relationship between the lawyer and client. In *Strother v. 3464920 Canada Inc.*,[13] Strother was found to have violated his duty of loyal advocacy for his client, and to have breached his contract, as a result of his conflicting financial interest in a competitor of the client.[14] In her dissenting judgment, McLachlin C.J.C. held that Strother's investment in the competitor had no effect on the lawyer-client relationship as defined by the retainer between the lawyer and the client. On that basis she would have found that Strother did not violate his duties to the client. By contrast, in his judgment for the majority, Binnie J. stated that the lawyer's fiduciary duties "may include obligations that go beyond what the parties expressly bargained for".[15] On the facts, though, he also disagreed with McLachlin C.J.C. on the scope of the retainer undertaken by Strother, and found that Strother had violated his contractual duty as well as his fiduciary duty. In other words, on the facts as Binnie J. saw them, his resolution of the case was not inconsistent with what McLachlin C.J.C. held was necessary to establish a conflict. As a result, it is not entirely clear that, as a matter of principle, the judgments diverged significantly on the relevance of the retainer to the identification of the conflict.

In my view, the best interpretation of the Supreme Court's judgment in *Strother* is that while the lawyer's duty of loyalty to the client exists

---

[11] *Strother v. 3464920 Canada Inc.*, [2007] S.C.J. No. 24, 2007 SCC 24 (S.C.C.).
[12] As Professor Freedman emphasized to me in our conversation about this chapter, however, this fact is one of the reasons why the law on conflicts of interest is so confused. Many conflicts cases are really not conflicts of cases at all, they are breach of duty cases, and considering them within conflicts may obscure how we consider true conflicts cases — *i.e.*, cases where the harm is as yet potential and apparent. Further, in those cases the legal issue is not *why* the lawyer breached the duties to the client (however interesting that question may be in some other sense); the legal issue is the lawyer's breach of duties to the client.
[13] [2007] S.C.J. No. 24, 2007 SCC 24 (S.C.C.).
[14] As earlier noted, this means that *Strother* is really not a conflicts case at all; it is a case about breach of loyalty and breach of contract; the conflict is what caused the breach, but it is not itself the breach of duty. Had *Strother* invested in the competitor, and provided ardent and effective legal advice to the client, the investment would be meaningless, legally speaking.
[15] *Strother v. 3464920 Canada Inc.*, [2007] S.C.J. No. 24 at para. 34, 2007 SCC 24 (S.C.C.).

independently of the lawyer-client retainer — because the duty also protects the administration of justice — the nature of the retainer must be taken into account in determining whether a conflict exists. While the majority judgment clearly establishes that the duties of the lawyer go beyond what the parties expressly bargained for, McLachlin C.J.C. is also certainly correct when she states that the "duty of loyalty is not a duty in the air".[16] Specifically, the retainer, whether express or implied, must be considered to determine whether there is a plausible risk that the lawyer's representation of the client would be materially and adversely affected. A representation that a lawyer has not undertaken cannot be materially and adversely affected by the lawyer's own interests or duties to other parties, and without such an effect, neither the lawyer-client relationship, nor the administration of justice, is compromised.

ii. Misuse of Confidential Information

A lawyer may not act in a matter where the representation creates a risk that confidential information obtained from a client will be used to that client's disadvantage. This principle arises from the Supreme Court's first significant conflicts judgment, *MacDonald Estate v. Martin*.[17] The Court in *MacDonald Estate* held that "[n]othing is more important to the preservation of this relationship than the confidentiality of information passing between a solicitor and his or her client."[18] A lawyer will be in a conflict of interest where he received "confidential information attributable to a solicitor and client relationship relevant to the matter at hand" and there is a "risk that it will be used to the prejudice of the client."[19]

Under the law of conflicts of interest, confidential information may be defined more narrowly than it is by the lawyer's duty of confidentiality. In a

---

[16] *Ibid.* at para. 135, *per* McLachlin C.J.C.
[17] Also known as *Martin v. Gray*, [1990] S.C.J. No. 41, [1990] 3 S.C.R. 1235 (S.C.C.). The facts and holdings in this case are discussed in Section 7.A. below, dealing with the duties owed by lawyers to former clients.
[18] *Ibid.* at para. 15.
[19] *Ibid.* at para. 45. The code of conduct rules dealing with confidential information are discussed in more detail in relation to the rules applying to former client conflicts but see, in general, CBA MC Chapter V, Commentary 12; FLS MC Rule 2.04(5)(c); Que. CEA Rule 3.06.02 and 3.06.09; LSUC RPC Rule 2.04(4)(c); Alberta CPC Chapter 6, Rule 3(b); BC PCH Chapter 6, Rule 7. It should be noted, though, that the prohibition against acting where there is a risk of misuse of confidential information also applies with respect to current client-current client conflicts. In *First Property Holdings Inc. v. Beatty*, [2003] O.J. No. 2943, 66 O.R. (3d) 97 (Ont. S.C.J.) where the fact that the law firm had confidential information arising from doing securities filings for Iatra Life Sciences Corporation, prevented it from acting in litigation for another client against Iatra where the information obtained to make Iatra's filings was relevant to the litigation (and, arguably, had already been inappropriately obtained from the law clerk who did the filing and included in the statement of claim). This point is captured under the confidentiality rules of the codes of conduct: CBA MC Chapter IV, Commentary 7; FLS MC Rule 2.03(1), commentary and Rule 2.03(2); NB CC Chapter 5, Commentary 5; LSUC RPC Rule 2.03(1), commentary; AB CPC Chapter 7, Rule 6(b).

number of cases, and in some codes of conduct,[20] it is suggested that if the information would be otherwise available to the lawyer, then possession and use of that information, even to the client's disadvantage, will not create a conflict of interest. Having said that, the use of information obtained from a client to the disadvantage of that client may be an aggravating factor in a "substantial risk" conflict — that is, it may be seen as evidence of the possibility of a material and adverse effect on representation — even if the information is arguably public in nature.[21]

Conflicts arising from the possibility for the misuse of confidential information may overlap with conflicts arising from the substantial risk of material and adverse effect on client representation; they do not necessarily do so, however. A representation of one client may be adversely affected by the representation of another client even without the risk of misuse of confidential information. In *Strother*, Strother's personal financial interest in the business of one client led to his failure to fulfill his contractual and fiduciary duties to another client; at no point was it suggested that Strother misused confidential information from the adversely affected client, or that the conflict of interest related to his holding of confidential information from the adversely affected client.

Further, even if the use of confidential information has no impact on the matter on which the lawyer was formerly retained by the client, a lawyer may be prohibited from using confidential information to that client's disadvantage. In *R. v. Brissett*[22] a lawyer was disqualified in acting on a matter where he would be cross-examining a former client on the basis of confidential information he had previously obtained about the client, even though there was no suggestion that the cross-examination would negatively affect the results achieved in the matter on which the former client had been represented.

iii. Obtaining an Improper Advantage

The final principle establishing prohibited conflicts of interest — that a lawyer must not obtain an improper advantage from the lawyer-client relationship — is distinct from the other principles discussed, not because it incorporates different ideas, but rather because in these cases the conflict of interest of the lawyer leads to an actual breach of the lawyer's duties to the client. Where a lawyer places himself in a position where there is a substantial risk that the representation will be impaired, or confidential information misused, the lawyer is in a conflict of interest whether or not he in fact breaches his duties to the client. However, in some cases the lawyer is

---

[20] CBA MC Chapter V, Commentary 33; FLS MC Rule 2.014(17) (dealing with transfers of lawyers between firms); LSUC RPC Rule 2.0591); AB CPC Chapter 6, Rule 3(a), Commentary 3.2.
[21] *First Property Holdings Inc. v. Beatty*, [2003] O.J. No. 2943, 66 O.R. (3d) 97 (Ont. S.C.J.).
[22] [2005] O.J. No. 343 (Ont. S.C.J.).

in a conflict position, and then apparently because of the conflict, goes on to breach the duties to the client, usually in order to obtain an advantage for himself at his client's expense. In these cases the client has a cause of action, and the lawyer is subject to professional discipline, because the lawyer has breached his duties of zealous advocacy or confidentiality or both; the conflict is relevant, but mostly as a causal or aggravating factor.

This means that, arguably, these cases are not properly dealt with as conflicts of interest cases at all, but should instead be treated as either breach of confidentiality or breach of the duty of zealous advocacy cases. The cases do, however, indicate points of importance about what constitutes a conflict, and indicate the bad effects (for lawyers and clients) that will arise if conflicts of interest are not properly addressed before a breach of the lawyer's duty arises. They tend, overall, to say more about conflicts than they do about either the duty of confidentiality or the duty of zealous advocacy. The cases are, therefore, dealt with here, but it must be noted that the lawyers in these cases were not just in circumstances of an improper conflict of interest; they were in an improper conflict of interest *and* violated their fiduciary duties to their clients. When regulating conflicts of interests, courts and law societies must distinguish between true conflict of interest cases (where there is only a risk of a breach of duty by the lawyer) and breach of duty cases arising from a conflict, since the issues they present, and the consequences they warrant, are not the same.

A well known example of a case where a lawyer was required to pay damages for breaching his duty of loyalty because of his conflicting personal interests, is *Stewart v. Canadian Broadcasting Corp.*[23] In *Stewart* the lawyer was found to have violated his fiduciary obligations to his former client where, in order to promote his own interests,[24] the lawyer participated in a television show about his former client's criminal conviction. The impropriety of the advantage taken by the lawyer in that case arose from the fact that the broadcast increased personal opprobrium suffered by the client, yet a significant part of the lawyer's original representation of that client had been to decrease the personal opprobrium the client had suffered. In other words, the problem was that the lawyer "undercut the benefits and protections he had provided as counsel",[25] and did so to serve his own ends.

---

[23] [1997] O.J. No. 2271 (Ont. H.C.J.).
[24] *Ibid.* at para. 320.
[25] *Ibid.* See also, cases in which the lawyer enters into a business or payment transaction with the client and the client does not have independent legal advice: *Law Society of Upper Canada v. Logan*, [2005] L.S.D.D. No. 39 (lawyer has client take a mortgage on her house as security for fees; charges 24% interest on fees owing); *Law Society of Upper Canada v. Novak*, [1999] L.S.D.D. No. 88 (sold client 1.3% interest in 4-day-old company for $50,000; shares now worthless); *Biggs v. London Loan and Savings Co. of Canada*, [1933] S.C.J. No. 17, [1933] S.C.R. 257 (S.C.C.) (lawyer acted for both mortgagor and mortgagee in transaction; he received a significant bonus but the transaction was "highly improvident and one which was fraught with disaster" for both clients (at 266)).

In *Szarfer v. Chodos*,[26] the lawyer had a sexual relationship with a client's wife. In doing so the lawyer violated his fiduciary duty to his client, and took an improper advantage of the representation, because he used confidential information obtained from the client about the problems in the client's marriage in order to commence the affair.[27] The violation of the lawyer's fiduciary duty arose, in other words, from a conflict relating to the possibility of misusing confidential information. Similarly, in *Law Society of Upper Canada v. Joseph*[28] the lawyer had a sexual relationship with his client. The lawyer referred the case to another lawyer. However, the Law Society found that he had taken improper advantage of his client because her vulnerabilities had been disclosed to him confidentially in the course of the lawyer-client relationship:

> In the instant case, the client disclosed to the member confidential information, relevant to her representation, which revealed her personal vulnerability and dependence. In these circumstances, the member was under a fiduciary duty to refrain from initiating a sexual relationship with her.[29]

As illustrated by these examples, breach of duty cases tend to arise from circumstances in which the lawyer's own needs, interests and desires create a risk that he will undermine the representation of the client (*Stewart*) or will misuse confidential information (*Szarfer* and *Joseph*). These cases are thus particularly important for identifying the circumstances in which the lawyer's own interests may be in an improper conflict with the client's. When a lawyer wants or needs something that may undermine the representation of the client, or result in the misuse of confidential information, the lawyer should withdraw and also take steps to make sure that the misuse of information does not occur. If he does not, and he breaches his duties to the client, then he will be guilty of professional misconduct, and civilly liable, for that breach of duty.

B. Who is a Client?

All three of the principles that define conflicts of interest presuppose a lawyer-client relationship. In most cases the existence of such a relationship will be obvious; the lawyer will have been formally retained, and the obligation to avoid improper conflicts of interest will arise accordingly. The analysis becomes more complicated, however, where the lawyer was never officially retained by the client, or where the party asserting the conflict has a relationship to a client, rather than being a client itself.

A person can be a "client" even if never formally retaining the lawyer; a client is simply a person who "might reasonably feel entitled to look to the

---

[26] [1986] O.J. No. 256, 54 O.R. (2d) 663 (Ont. H.C.J.).
[27] *Ibid.*
[28] [2003] L.S.D.D. No. 34.
[29] *Ibid.* at para. 20.

lawyer for guidance or advice".[30] Whether a person can properly be considered to be a client "is to be determined having regard to all the circumstances."[31] Courts have been willing to impose a lawyer-client relationship, and have removed counsel to avoid conflicts of interest, in circumstances where individuals have simply phoned a lawyer and received some introductory advice, even if no account was ever rendered or retainer entered into. In *Forsyth v. Cross*,[32] a law firm was disqualified in acting for the wife in a matrimonial case where a lawyer in the firm had had an earlier phone conversation with the husband's mother. In the phone call with the husband's mother the lawyer was provided with specific information about the dispute. The lawyer in that case had also opened a file, and had drafted a letter to the husband, although no account had been rendered.

In *Achakzad v. Zemaryalai*[33] the mother in a child custody case had had two phone conversations with a lawyer who specialized in cases involving wrongful removal of a child. One conversation was 12 minutes long; the other was 20 minutes long. The mother had been unable to afford to retain the lawyer, who would not accept a legal aid certificate, and so the representation had not progressed further. The father then retained the lawyer. The mother applied for the lawyer to be disqualified. The Court disqualified the lawyer. It noted corroborating evidence of phone records proving the length of the phone calls, an affidavit filed by the solicitor who had referred the mother to the lawyer, and the mother's testimony which indicated that she had provided the lawyer with confidential information. The Court noted the inconsistencies in the affidavit filed by the lawyer's clerk, which claimed on the one hand that the lawyer had no recollection of the phone conversation, and on the other hand stated categorically both that the mother's affidavit was "replete with misrepresentations, falsehoods and exaggerations" and that no confidential information had passed.[34] The Court found that the best assessment of the evidence was that confidential information had passed, and that the wife had "reposed her trust" in the lawyer.[35] For that reason, the lawyer was disqualified.[36]

---

[30] CBA MC definitions and Chapter VI, Commentary 7. The FLS Code defines a client as a person who has consulted the lawyer and whom the lawyer agrees to represent, or the client reasonably believes that the lawyer has so agreed. FLS MC 2.04, definitions. The LSUC RPC definitions section commentary notes that a lawyer-client relationship may not always be formally established. AB CPC Chapter 7, Commentary G1; Chapter 6, Rule 3, Commentary 1 is similar; BC PCH Chapter 6, Rule 7.1 defines client as any person to whom the lawyer owes a duty of confidentiality, but only for the purpose of that rule. NB CC defines client as a person to whom the lawyer has or is providing legal services (Definitions).

[31] CBA MC, *ibid.*

[32] [2009] S.J. No. 321, 2009 SKQB 184 (Sask. Q.B.). See also *Bell v. Nash*, [1993] B.C.J. No. 1873, 83 B.C.L.R. (2d) 155 (B.C.C.A.).

[33] [2010] O.J. No. 431, 2010 ONCJ 24 (Ont. C.J.).

[34] *Ibid.* at para. 11.

[35] *Ibid.* at para. 34.

[36] See also *Rosenstein v. Plant*, [2010] O.J. No. 302, 2010 ONSC 502 (Ont. S.C.J.), in which a lawyer was disqualified on the basis of conversations he'd had with the husband on a casual basis about the husband's circumstances. The husband was also a family law lawyer, and had

By contrast, in *Escott v. Collision Clinic Ltd.*[37] the Court declined to find a solicitor-client relationship when the individual asserting the conflict had simply spoken to the lawyer at a Christmas party. The plaintiff in the litigation, Sheena Escott, was the sister of a former partner of the lawyer for the defendant, Barrie Heywood. She claimed that at the then law firm's Christmas party she had spoken with Heywood about her wrongful dismissal claim against Collision Clinic. She said that she had told him about the issues, and had expressed her opinion on the merits. She said that she had expected confidentiality with respect to the conversation. Heywood said that he had no recollection of the conversation. He noted that he had not opened any files for Escott, nor billed her for any services. His evidence was that she had attended the party as a caterer, not as a guest. The Court held that there was no solicitor-client relationship between them. Escott's expectation of confidentiality was not sufficient to create a solicitor-client relationship, and certainly was not sufficient to warrant depriving the Collision Clinic of its choice of counsel.

In some cases courts have been willing to impose a lawyer-client relationship, and have removed counsel to avoid conflicting interests, where the party asserting the conflict was a "near client" of the lawyer. A near client is someone related to the actual client of the lawyer, and to whom the lawyer can be said to have some duties that may create an improper conflict of interest if the lawyer then acts against that near client. In *Dobbin v. Acrohelipro Global Services Inc.*[38] the Stewart McKelvey firm was disqualified from acting in wrongful dismissal litigation against Vector Aerospace because it represented the Bank of Nova Scotia in negotiating a credit facility with Vector. In the course of the negotiations Vector had provided the Bank with disclosure regarding the "claims by the employees, including Vector's strategy in dealing with the claims" that was passed on to the lawyers.[39] The Bank had offered to retain alternative counsel on the negotiations since the law firm had already been retained by the employees in the wrongful dismissal matter, but Vector did not want the Bank to do so because it did not want delay. Vector took the position with the Bank, though, that "continuing discussions would not be considered to be a waiver of Vector's concerns regarding the conflict of interest issue".[40] The Court held that the law firm could not continue to act for the employees against

---

had conversations on the street and while waiting to appear in court with the lawyer now seeking to represent the wife. In my view a court needs to be careful about disqualification in such circumstances; spouses of lawyers may end up peculiarly disadvantaged in obtaining counsel if casual conversations between lawyers about their personal problems can create disqualifying conflicts. The result may have been justified on these facts, but should not be extended without caution.

[37] [1996] N.J. No. 135, 141 Nfld. & P.E.I.R. 16 (Nfld. T.D.).
[38] [2005] N.J. No. 124, 246 Nfld. & P.E.I.R. 177 (Nfld. C.A.), aff'g [2004] N.J. No. 323, 240 Nfld. & P.E.I.R. 313 (N.L.T.D.).
[39] *Ibid.* at para. 5.
[40] *Ibid.* at para. 6.

Vector. It held that "Vector was a person involved in or associated with Stewart McKelvey's client, the Bank, and that this association had a relationship to the matter of the employees' claim for damages, so as to engage the conflict of interest rule".[41] The Court held that in general a "near client relationship will engage a conflict of interest concern only where the information relates to the particular matter at issue between the parties, or involves a situation where the lawyer might be tempted or appear to be tempted to breach the rule relating to confidential information".[42]

This case should not be interpreted too broadly. Had the firm taken steps to shield the information, a different result would be warranted. Vector knew of the conflict when it provided the information. The employees had established a lawyer-client relationship with the firm, and had no part in creating the conflict. To deprive them of their choice of counsel required extraordinary circumstances.[43]

That analysis is supported by the fact that in other cases courts have been reluctant to disqualify a law firm on the basis of duties to "near clients". High level employees and shareholders of clients,[44] unit holders in a condominium board client,[45] a fiancé of the client,[46] subsidiaries of clients[47] and even sole shareholders of clients,[48] have been held not to be entitled to assert a disqualifying conflict of interest against a law firm. And in one case the customer of a bank represented by the law firm was not able to assert a conflict of interest for the law firm because the bank's customer had not demonstrated that the law firm held confidential information in relation to it. The Alberta Court of Appeal held that the presumption that law firms have confidential information from clients in relation to a matter does not apply to near clients, and the near client has the burden of demonstrating that the law firm had confidential information that should disqualify it from acting

---

[41] *Ibid.* at para. 52.
[42] *Ibid.* at para. 53.
[43] For another case with unusual facts, and a similar and a quite problematic result, see *Williamson v. Roberts & Griffin*, [1997] B.C.J. No. 2248, 39 B.C.L.R. (3d) 216 (B.C.C.A.). In that case Williamson had represented the Regional District of Comox-Strathcona on some matters related to litigation. Comox ended up in litigation against its legal advisors, but not Williamson or his firm. Comox's new lawyers interviewed Wiliamson with the idea that he would be examined for discovery. They told him that he was on their team, and he agreed to speak with them. He was then added as a defendant in the lawsuit. It was found that the communications he made to the lawyers for the District were intended to be confidential, and that they could not act against him in the litigation. This result seems to me to be deeply problematic. Whatever representations made by the new lawyers for Comox, Williamson must have understood that he was not identical in interest to their client, and that if he disclosed information that might disclose a cause of action against him that that would not be confidential. If it was not confidential, then on what basis should the lawyers be precluded from acting against him? And as a non-client he cannot make any reasonable claim to a duty of loyalty from the lawyers.
[44] *Gainers Inc. v. Pocklington*, [1995] A.J. No. 438, 29 Alta. L.R. (3d) 323 (Alta. C.A.).
[45] *2475813 Nova Scotia Ltd. v. Green*, [2000] N.S.J. No. 254, 186 N.S.R. (2d) 374 (N.S.S.C.).
[46] *Seigel v. Seigel*, [2008] O.J. No. 5680, 60 R.F.L. (6th) 143 (Ont. S.C.J.).
[47] *McKenna v. Gammon Gold Inc.*, [2009] O.J. No. 39 (Ont. S.C.J.).
[48] *Engle v. Carswell*, [2006] N.W.T.J. No. 7, 2006 NWTSC 3 (N.W.T.S.C.).

against the near client. The Court held that the bank's client had not discharged that burden on the facts of the case.[49]

Overall, though, these cases do show that lawyers and law firms may have troubles with conflicts of interest even with respect to individuals who do not fit obviously within the traditional lawyer-client relationship.

C. What Constitutes Informed Consent?

Not all conflicts of interest can be cured by informed consent from a client.[50] And in some circumstances a conflict may be permissible even if the client does not provide informed consent.[51] However, informed consent is the most common and effective way for a lawyer or law firm to resist an allegation that it has acted in circumstances of an improper conflict of interest. The various codes of conduct allow informed consent to cure many types of conflicts of interest,[52] and the courts have also acknowledged the importance and significance of informed consent in circumstances that would otherwise constitute a conflict of interest. In *R. v. Neil*,[53] for example, the Supreme Court stated that the rule against acting for one current client against another current client in an unrelated matter does not apply where "both clients consent after receiving full disclosure (and preferably independent legal advice)".[54]

What constitutes sufficiently informed consent? The codes of conduct provide that the client must have been given information about all matters likely to be relevant to evaluating the conflict.[55] Consent should be in writing or, if not in writing, should be recorded in a letter from the lawyer provided to the parties.[56] Consent must be voluntary.[57] Independent legal advice does not generally need to be given to the client for consent to be valid,[58] although the client's receipt of such advice may be desirable, and in

---

[49] *Dreco Energy Services Ltd. v. Wenzel Downhole Tools Ltd.*, [2006] A.J. No. 85, 2006 ABCA 39 (Alta. C.A.).
[50] Most notably, as discussed below, when the parties are in an actual dispute. A lawyer can never represent both sides to a dispute, regardless of consent.
[51] As discussed below, a law firm may act against a former client of the firm if it has taken appropriate safeguards to prevent the disclosure of confidential information with respect to that client.
[52] See, for example, CBA MC Chapter V, Rule 1; FLS MC Rule 2.04(2); NB CC Chapter 6, Rule 1(b); Que. CEA Rule 3.06.08; LSUC RPC Rule 2.04(3); AB CPC Chapter 6, Rule 2; BC PCH Chapter 6, Rules 3 and 4.
[53] [2002] S.C.J. No. 72, [2002] 3 S.C.R. 631, 2002 SCC 70 (S.C.C.).
[54] *Ibid.* at para. 29.
[55] CBA MC Chapter V, Commentary 5; AB CPC, definition of "disclosure".
[56] FLS MC, definition of "consent"; LSUC RPC Rule 1.02, definition of "consent"; AB CPC Chapter 6, Rule 2, Commentary 2.2.
[57] AB CPC, definition of "consent".
[58] CBA MC Chapter V, Commentary 7; FLS MC Rule 2.04(2), commentary; LSUC RPC Rule 2.04(3), commentary.

circumstances of more serious conflicts, such as a business transaction between the lawyer and client, will be required.[59]

The case law is generally consistent with the codes about what is necessary for consent to be sufficient to cure a conflict. The cases similarly suggest, for example, that consent should be in writing. In *Booth v. Huxter*[60] the Court considered a determination in a Coroner's Inquiry that the same lawyer could not act for both the Police Services Board and police officers because the legal positions offered by the parties appeared to contain an inherent conflict. The Court upheld the Coroner's decision, and while noting that the police officers did not seem to object to the joint representation, it nonetheless held that signed and informed waivers were necessary to establish consent sufficient to cure the apparent conflict.

The writing requirement is not rigid, however. In *Regular v. Law Society of Newfoundland and Labrador*[61] the Court upheld a waiver as valid even though it was not in writing. In that case Regular had had a long-standing extra-marital relationship with a woman who had been his client, and who he represented a second time a number of years into the relationship. The Court accepted the Law Society's determination that commencing a sexual relationship with the client in the first instance was a conflict of interest;[62] however, it held that representing the client in the second instance was only doubtfully a conflict and, in any event, was consented to by the client. The Court found that the client had "full disclosure and ... full knowledge"[63] with respect to the conflict, and it was not relevant that her waiver of the conflict was not written or signed.

In *Neil* and in *Strother* the Supreme Court held that in some circumstances consent not only does not need to be in writing, but might simply be inferred from the nature of the retainer and the circumstances. In *Neil* the Court suggested that where a law firm represents institutional clients frequently engaged in litigation, such as a bank, it may be possible to imply consent by that client to the law firm acting against it in an unrelated matter.[64] In *Strother*, the Court suggested that where a client consults a lawyer with a specialty, the client can be taken to have consented "to a degree of overlapping representation inherent in such practices".[65] Implied

---

[59] For example, CBA MC Chapter VI, Rules 2 and 3; FLS MC Rule 2.04(28) and (29); NB CC Chapter 11, Rule 1; LSUC RPC Rule 2.06(2); AB CPC Chapter 6, Rule 9, commentary; BC PCH Chapter 7, Rule 3 (requiring independent representation).
[60] [1994] O.J. No. 52, 16 O.R. (3d) 528 (Ont. Div. Ct.).
[61] [2010] N.J. No. 165, 2010 NLTD 90 (N.L.T.D.).
[62] As an aside, the tendency for law societies to analyze sexual relations with clients solely in terms of conflicts of interest is unsatisfactory. Even if the representation is unimpaired in the first instance, the sexual relationship itself may be an abuse of the relationship of trust and confidence between lawyer and client — *i.e.*, the sexual relationship may be wrong, even if there is no "conflict" with the retainer.
[63] [2010] N.J. No. 165 at para. 77, 2010 NLTD 90 (N.L.T.D.).
[64] *R. v. Neil*, [2002] S.C.J. No. 72 at para. 28, [2002] 3 S.C.R. 631, 2002 SCC 70 (S.C.C.).
[65] *Strother v. 3464920 Canada Inc.*, [2007] S.C.J. No. 24 at para. 55, 2007 SCC 24 (S.C.C.).

consent will be the exception, though, and in general express consent should be obtained in conflict situations.

Also consistent with the code requirements, the case law is clear that the failure to provide proper information to the client, or the client's ignorance of a material fact, will vitiate consent. In *R. v. Silvini* the Court held that a criminal accused could not waive a conflict arising from joint representation of a co-accused when he did not appreciate that the joint representation would preclude him from calling the co-accused as a witness.[66] In *Barrett v. Reynolds*[67] the lawyer was found to have acted improperly in a joint representation of parties to a real estate transaction where he did not fully advise the vendors of the implications of also representing the purchasers in the transaction.

In *Law Society of Upper Canada v. Hunter*,[68] the lawyer had an extra-marital affair with a client that lasted several years. He eventually decided to terminate the relationship. He met with the client in a coffee shop and showed her the conflicts provisions of the Law Society of Upper Canada's Code of Conduct. He had her initial the pages, and then had her sign an acknowledgment that he had complied with the rules. As soon as she had signed the documents, he told her that during the time he had been with her he had also had relationships with other women, and that he was terminating the relationship with her to repair his marriage. He then attempted to obtain further confirmation from her that the relationship had been appropriate. He phoned and e-mailed her on several occasions, and even went to her home, without prior notice, at around 9:30 p.m. one evening to obtain confirmation from her as to her consent. The consent given in the coffee shop was found by the Law Society to have been insufficient. The acknowledgment was facially inaccurate, as the lawyer had not, in fact, complied with the Law Society's rules in his conduct of the relationship with his client. He did not allow her to make an informed decision and, in his conduct at the coffee shop and after, he pursued his own interests with little regard to hers.

---

[66] *R. v. Silvini*, [1991] O.J. No. 1931, 5 O.R. (3d) 545 (Ont. C.A.).
[67] [1998] N.S.J. No. 344, 170 N.S.R. (2d) 201 (N.S.C.A.). See also *Waxman v. Waxman*, [2004] O.J. No. 1765 at paras. 646-50, 186 O.A.C. 201 (Ont. C.A.).
[68] [2007] L.S.D.D. No. 8. As noted in the earlier footnote (62), one can question whether the wrongful conduct by Hunter is properly described as a conflict. In my view the problem with his decision to have sex with a vulnerable client was not primarily the effect on his representation of the client. The primary problem was his decision to act for his own benefit in a fiduciary relationship, where his duty was to foster the interests of the client, and that client's interests almost certainly did not involve having an extra-marital relationship with her lawyer. It is not in every case that a sexual relationship would be a violation of the lawyer's duties, but the existence of a violation does not depend on the relationship impairing the lawyer's ability to represent the client effectively. That being said, most cases do treat sexual relationship cases primarily in terms of their impact on the representation or the extent to which they involved misuse of confidential information.

Hunter also indicates the additional requirement that consent is to be obtained in a timely fashion. Consent obtained after the conflict has already begun, arguably to the prejudice of the client, has no effect.[69]

Consent can be obtained in advance of a conflict of interest arising, provided that the consent is sufficiently broad to cover the later conflict, and no change of circumstances has occurred so as to render the initial consent invalid. In *Alberta Union of Provincial Employees v. United Nurses of Alberta*,[70] the Court refused to disqualify a firm acting for the United Nurses of Alberta at a Labour Relations Board proceeding opposed by the Alberta Union of Provincial Employees. The Alberta Union of Provincial Employees was also a client of the law firm; however, it had consented to the conflict as part of its retainer agreement. The retainer agreement advised the Union that the law firm would only act for them insofar as it did not jeopardize the firm's representation of the United Nurses of Alberta, and that if the legal interests of the two conflicted it would represent the United Nurses. The Court, upholding the Labour Relations Board decision, found that the consent was sufficient even though it was generic, rather than directed at a specific problem, and even though there was no independent legal advice for the Union of Provincial Employees. The Union of Provincial Employees was a sophisticated litigant and was aware of the "risk or eventuality of adversity, and [was] prepared to enter into [that retainer] agreement [nonetheless]".[71] The Court held that withdrawal of consent was not relevant; allowing consent to be withdrawn would undermine "the essential nature of the retainer agreement".[72] The Court did recognize that in some circumstances consent in advance would not be sufficient; if the law firm had confidential information that it might be using to the disadvantage of the client in the proceeding that would not be excused by a previously given consent that did not address the specific conflict that had now arisen.

An example of that latter situation — where a subsequent event vitiates an earlier consent — arose in the case of *Chiefs of Ontario v. Ontario*.[73] In that case the Blake Cassels and Graydon firm had acted as general counsel for the Mnjikaning First Nation for a number of years. In 2000 it sought to act for the Chiefs of Ontario in an action in which the Nation was involved. The Nation consented to Blakes acting after receiving advice from independent counsel. The consent was "*pro forma*, oral, and never reduced to writing".[74] It was also based in significant part on the fact that, at that time, the parties were acting "in the same interest" in the litigation.[75] In 2003, however, the Statement of Claim in the action was amended to allege

---

[69] See also *Davey v. Woolley, Hames, Dale & Dingwall*, [1982] O.J. No. 3158, 35 O.R. (2d) 599 (Ont. C.A.).
[70] [2009] A.J. No. 48, 2009 ABCA 33 (Alta. C.A.).
[71] *Ibid.* at para. 35.
[72] *Ibid.* at para. 37.
[73] [2003] O.J. No. 580, 63 O.R. (3d) 335 (Ont. S.C.J.).
[74] *Ibid.* at para. 72.
[75] *Ibid.* at para. 74.

that the Nation had taken bribes. The allegations related to matters on which, as general counsel, Blakes had advised the Nation. The allegations also placed the Chiefs and the Nation in clear opposition to each other. The Court found that, in those circumstances, Blakes could not continue to act for the Chiefs, and that the consent earlier given by the Nation was of no effect. The Court held that given the nature of the allegations now being made against Blakes' former client, and the relationship of those allegations to the matters on which Blakes had represented the client, only the "clearest consent" would be sufficient.[76] That type of consent had not been obtained here.

Finally, the disciplinary decision in *Law Society of Upper Canada v. Logan*[77] illustrates the requirement that, consistent with the codes, in some circumstances independent legal advice is necessary for consent to be valid. In that case Logan represented a client in a matrimonial case who had no money to pay Logan's fees. Logan had his client take out a mortgage on her house as security for later payment of his fees. He charged her interest of 24% on her outstanding fees. The disciplinary panel found this rate of interest to be "grossly excessive" but also found that the transaction created an improper conflict of interest with the client. The conflict could conceivably have been cured by consent, but only if the client received independent legal advice. "The obligation imposed upon the member to require that the client receive independent legal advice is of fundamental importance."[78]

3. KINDS OF CONFLICTS OF INTEREST

The principles identified in the previous section identify when conflicts of interest will be considered to be improper. Identifying the principles in the abstract does not, though, indicate the circumstances in which such conflicts of interest tend to arise. This section briefly identifies the kinds of conflicts that most typically arise for lawyers in practice, given the principles that define such conflicts. The specific obligations of the lawyer in relation to avoiding and managing these different types of conflicts will be discussed in the final section of the chapter.

A. Conflicts Relating to the Lawyer's Own Interests

As noted at the outset of this chapter, a lawyer's own interests may not be aligned with the interests of a client. The economic relationship between the lawyer and the client places their interests in conflict. But beyond that a lawyer may not like a client, may not think that the client's case is worthy from a public policy perspective or might have desires in relation to the conduct of the litigation that conflict with the client's. For reasons quite

---

[76] *Ibid.* at para. 72.
[77] [2005] L.S.D.D. No. 39 at para. 28.
[78] *Ibid.* at para. 34.

unrelated to the merits of the client's case, or the client's own interests, the lawyer may wish to proceed to trial instead of settling, or may wish to settle instead of proceeding to trial. Those reasons may range from a dislike of the adversariality of judicial proceedings, to a desire to do something in the lawyer's personal life that conflicts with the trial, or to a desire to raise the lawyer's profile in the community by arguing a high profile case in court. This absence of alignment in the interests of the lawyer and the client is something to which the lawyer should be sensitive. Lawyers should examine the advice that they give to clients, and consider whether their advice has been tainted by motivations other than pursuit of the client's interests. Though lawyers must be sensitive in this way, the absence of alignment in their interests does not necessarily place a lawyer in an improper conflict of interest with her client.

Improper conflicts of interest will arise when the lawyer's own interests are such that they create a substantial risk of a material and adverse effect on the lawyer's representation of a client, or where they create the risk that confidential information obtained from a client will be used to the client's disadvantage. The lawyer's own interests or circumstances typically create an improper conflict in circumstances where the lawyer has business dealings with the client, where the lawyer has sexual relations with the client, where the lawyer receives a gift from the client, or where the lawyer has specific personal circumstances — such as a financial stake in another party to the representation, or a personal relationship with another party to the representation — that create a clear and tangible risk that the lawyer will not represent the client properly, or will misuse the client's confidential information, to the lawyer's own advantage.[79]

B. Conflicts between a Former Client and a New Client

No general rule prohibits lawyers from acting against former clients. A lawyer who, for example, defends a client from a petty theft charge today, would normally be free to act for that former client's spouse in matrimonial litigation against the former client some years later. Representing a new client in a matter that is adverse to the legal interests of a former client is, though, restricted in some significant ways as a result of the principles defining improper conflicts.

When representing a former client a lawyer will have received confidential information in relation to that client and, in particular, in relation to the matter on which the lawyer represented her. If confidential

---

[79] As noted, it may be that by the time these things have happened — *e.g.*, a sexual relationship — there has been a breach of duty in addition to a conflict indicating a potential risk of a breach of duty. The conflict will usually exist at the point where the lawyer *wants* to have a sexual relationship, and there is the potential for misuse of confidential information to bring about that relationship. Once the lawyer misuses the confidential information, there is additionally a breach of the lawyer's duty of confidentiality.

information from the former retainer is relevant to the current retainer, then one of two improper results is inevitable. Either the lawyer will use the information, and violate his duty of confidentiality to the former client, or the lawyer will not use the information and violate his duty of zealous advocacy to his new client. The lawyer's duties to the clients necessarily conflict, and the lawyer cannot continue to act for the new client.

Even where acting for a new client against a former client does not create a risk of the misuse of confidential information, the lawyer may be prohibited from acting. In particular, the lawyer may not act for the new client if the representation would have the effect of "attacking or undermining" the legal work done for the former client by the lawyer.[80] A lawyer is prohibited from "effectively changing sides by taking an adversarial position against a former client with respect to a matter that was central to the previous retainer".[81]

This rule follows from the substantial risk principle. While the representation in the earlier matter has concluded, the representation of the new client against the former client will either have a material and adverse effect on the advice earlier provided to the former client or, conceivably, will undermine the representation of the new client given that the lawyer may be committed to the results earlier achieved. Either way, an improper conflict exists.

C. Conflicts between Current Clients

Three types of conflicts typically arise between current clients. First, two or more current clients may be in an actual dispute with each other. Even if one party does not name another in a statement of claim (the most obvious type of legal "dispute"), the legal interests of the parties may be such that the successful achievement of the legal goals of one party can only be achieved at the expense of the other party. When parties are in a dispute, a lawyer may not act for them both, even if the parties consent.[82]

Second, two or more current clients can have interests in a matter or related matters[83] that either are in conflict, or may develop into a conflict. A husband and wife writing joint wills, the vendor and purchaser of property, or co-accused in a criminal trial, have legal interests that may be capable of mutually beneficial resolution, but may not be. A lawyer or law firm can

---

[80] *Brookville Carriers Flatbed GP Inc. v. Blackjack Transport Ltd.*, [2008] N.S.J. No. 94 at para. 51, 2008 NSCA 22 (N.S.C.A.).
[81] *Ibid.* See also *Chiefs of Ontario v. Ontario*, [2003] O.J. No. 580, 63 O.R. (3d) 335 (Ont. S.C.J.); *Consulate Ventures Inc. v. Amico Contracting & Engineering (1992) Inc.*, [2010] O.J. No. 4996, 2010 ONCA 788.
[82] How a lawyer can distinguish between a "conflict" and a "dispute" is discussed below in Section 7.B.ii.
[83] Where, for example, two parties have separately filed lawsuits arising out of closely related facts against a single defendant, and are represented by the same lawyer.

jointly[84] represent such clients only in limited circumstances; such joint representation places significant obligations on the lawyer in relation to disclosure, confidentiality, consent and taking appropriate steps if the potential or actual conflict ripens into a dispute.

Third, a lawyer may concurrently represent two or more clients. A concurrent representation is distinct from simultaneous (joint) representation because it does not involve joint planning with the parties, joint instruction of the lawyer and the sharing of confidential information between the clients. The lawyer or law firm represents both clients, but does not represent them together. It is premised on the notion that the matters on which the two clients are distinct, even if related in some way. For example, a lawyer may act for Bob in bringing a civil claim for damages arising from a wrongful dismissal, and for Frank in bringing a civil claim for damages arising from a motor vehicle accident. That would be a concurrent representation in unrelated matters. Normally such representation raises no conflicts issues for the lawyer. However, if the defendant in Frank's case is Bob — so that the lawyer is both prosecuting a claim for Bob and suing Bob — then the lawyer may be prohibited from acting unless the parties consent. In general, a lawyer may not concurrently represent two clients, even in unrelated matters, where the legal interests of one client are "directly adverse to the immediate interests of another current client."[85]

What if the lawyer acts for Bob as plaintiff in a motor vehicle case, and for Frank as defendant in a motor vehicle case in which the legal arguments that are necessary for Bob to succeed will be injurious to Frank's defence? That is, what if Frank and Bob are not in conflict, but their legal positions are? Is that sufficient to say that Bob's interests are "directly adverse to the immediate interests" of Frank?

It is not clear, at this time, whether a lawyer would be prohibited from acting for Bob and Frank in circumstances of a positional conflict. In general the possibility that the representation of clients will require the lawyer to adopt conflicting legal positions will not create a disqualifying conflict of interest, particularly as with lawyers within the same firm representing different clients, the fact of such competing legal positions may be both unknown and unforeseeable.[86] On the other hand, as noted by Paul Perrell (now Justice Perrell), a client whose matter fails because of a legal argument

---

[84] The terms joint/jointly are used here interchangeably with simultaneous/simultaneously. Both are used to imply representing the clients in some way together, while concurrent means simply representing the clients at the same time, but not together.

[85] *R. v. Neil*, [2002] S.C.J. No. 72 at para. 29, [2002] 3 S.C.R. 631, 2002 SCC 70 (S.C.C.). As discussed below, there is some uncertainty still as to the nature of the adverse effect necessary to trigger the bright line rule. As written, and as applied in some subsequent cases, it seems that an adverse effect on any legal interest of the client will be sufficient to create a disqualifying conflict. However, on the facts of *Neil*, it may make more sense only to disqualify the lawyer where there is an adverse effect on the matter on which the lawyer or lawyer firm is representing the client in question.

[86] See Paul M. Perrell, *Conflicts of Interest in the Legal Profession* (Toronto and Vancouver: Butterworths, 1998) at 47-48.

successfully pursued by her own lawyer (or her lawyer's firm) in another matter may be "disappointed or suspicious that the lawyer did not do his or her best because of a disposition or pressure to favour the other client".[87] That sort of perception of an adverse impact on client representation may well be the foundation of a finding of a conflict of interest, given the general principle against a lawyer being in a position where there is a substantial risk of a material and adverse effect on representation of a client. This would depend on the circumstances, but it seems reasonable to suppose that if, for example, a lawyer or law firm is arguing a legal position at the Supreme Court of Canada it may be considered a conflict of interest to simultaneously take a contrary position before a trial court.[88]

D. Third Party and Multiple Role Conflicts

Clients may have multiple roles within the matter on which the lawyer is acting. A client may, for example, be simultaneously an employee of a corporation, shareholder of the corporation, and a member of the corporate board of directors. A client may be the beneficiary of a will and the executor of the will. When lawyers represent clients with distinct roles in relation to the matter in question, the lawyer is, in essence, in a situation of joint representation. And, like with joint representation, the alignment of interest between the clients (or in this case, between the client's dual roles) may develop into a conflict or dispute. As noted, for example, a client may be both beneficiary and executor of a will. The client may want to challenge the will in her capacity as beneficiary. In her capacity as executor, however, she is legally obligated to respond to that challenge consistently with her responsibilities to the estate and to the other beneficiaries of the estate. The management of this type of joint representation is more complicated than where the lawyer represents two clients, particularly where one of the "roles" of the client involves duties to other parties, as would be the case with the client's role as executor or board member in these examples. The lawyer cannot simply rely on the consent of the client to permit the joint representation since that consent may not be consistent with the client's fulfillment of her duties in one of the roles. Usually if a conflict develops the client will need advice from a different lawyer with respect to each role.[89]

    Where a lawyer represents a client with multiple roles, therefore, the lawyer must be aware of the possibility that those roles may conflict, and discuss with the client what would happen in that instance, and the requirement for the client to have dual representation if a conflict develops.

---

[87] *Ibid.* at 47.
[88] For a straightforward discussion of the American position on this issue see Noreen L. Slank, "Positional Conflicts: Is it ethical to simultaneously represent clients with opposing legal positions?" (2002) Mich. B.J. 14, online: <http://www.michbar.org/journal/pdf/pdf4article427.pdf>.
[89] This seems very cumbersome; it may simply be that in that circumstance the client herself cannot properly discharge both roles, and needs to resign from one.

As indicated by the discussion of lawyer's obligations to "near clients", conflicts may also arise from the relationship between lawyers and third parties who are related to clients. Lawyers may have obligations not to act against third parties where they have received information from those parties through a client, or in connection with representation of a client.

Special issues also arise where a third party pays the lawyer's fees, such as an insurance company (the most common example) or the client's employer. The lawyer may be acting for both the insurance company and the insured, and in that instance issues around joint representation arise. Also, though, the contract between the insurance company and the insured may give the insurance company significant authority to direct litigation even where it is the insured who is the lawyer's actual client. The interests of the insurance company and the insured may not be in alignment, and conflicts may arise if that misalignment creates a substantial risk of a material and adverse effect on the lawyer's representation of one of the clients, or of misuse of confidential information. While courts have generally been deferential to the contractual rights of insurance companies in this respect, courts have also required that insured have independent counsel where there is "a reasonable apprehension of conflict of interest on the part of counsel appointed by the insurer".[90]

In addition, courts have seen representation of an insurance company as imposing duties on the law firm relative to the insured; in one case a court disqualified a law firm from acting for a third party in litigation against an insured where it had previously given advice to an insurance company about coverage of the insured in matters related to the litigation.[91] The concern of the Court was with respect to confidential information that would have been provided to the law firm about the insured, which might now be used against the insured in the subsequent litigation.

4. WHY ARE SOME CONFLICTS FORBIDDEN?

In the introduction to this chapter I suggested that the lawyer's duties of loyalty and confidentiality required that some conflicts of interest be prohibited. Linking conflicts of interest to loyalty and confidentiality assumes that those values are relevant to the lawyer-client relationship. That assumption has been explored more fully in Chapters 2 and 5; it bears repeating briefly here. The moral justification for lawyers arises from the concept of law as a democratic settlement of moral controversies over the right way to live. Within the boundaries of what the law requires, permits or

---

[90] *Brockton (Municipality) v. Frank Cowan Co.*, [2002] O.J. No. 20 at para. 43, 57 O.R. (3d) 447 (Ont. C.A.). The Court noted that the appointment of independent counsel was unusual. For an example of a case where independent counsel was required see: *Szebelledy v. Constitution Insurance Co. of Canada*, [1985] O.J. No. 1639 (Ont. Div. Ct.).

[91] *R. Sherwin Enterprises Ltd. v. Municipal Contracting Services Ltd.*, [1994] O.J. No. 2233, 20 O.R. (3d) 692 (Ont. Gen. Div.). That the insurance company had denied coverage to the insured was viewed as irrelevant.

enables, individuals are free to pursue their own conception of the good. For individuals to exercise this freedom sometimes requires that they be able to access a lawyer who can tell them what they might not be able to discover for themselves; that is, whether the law in fact permits, requires or enables them to pursue the course of action they have chosen. That lawyer must, if he is to provide competent assistance to the client, act with the client's interests in mind — with loyalty and zeal in pursuit of the client's cause. Further, the client should be no worse off from consulting a lawyer than she would be representing herself, and as a consequence, her confidences should be no more exposed than if she had no lawyer; hence the lawyer's duty of confidentiality.

The significance of loyalty and confidentiality to the lawyer-client relationship means that lawyers should not place themselves in a position where their ability to act in loyal pursuit of their client's interests, or to maintain confidences, is at risk of being compromised. The law prohibiting conflicts of interest that create a substantial risk of a material and adverse effect on representation of the client, or that create a risk that confidential information will be misused, helps ensure that the lawyer-client relationship is not compromised in that way.

The courts have recognized the relationship between conflicts of interest and the general duty of loyalty. Most notably, in *R. v. Neil*,[92] the Supreme Court identified loyalty as "the defining principle" of the legal world,[93] "essential to the integrity of the administration of justice"[94] and requiring that the lawyer be "free from conflicting interests".[95] Both before and after the Supreme Court's decision in *Neil*, lower courts have recognized the lawyer's duty of loyalty, and the relationship between ensuring loyalty and prohibiting conflicting interests.[96] Courts have also noted the risk that a

---

[92] [2002] S.C.J. No. 72, [2002] 3 S.C.R. 631, 2002 SCC 70 (S.C.C.).
[93] *Ibid.* at para. 12.
[94] *Ibid.*
[95] *Ibid.* at para. 13.
[96] For a discussion of the evolution of the duty of loyalty in the case law see Richard F. Devlin & Victoria Rees, "Beyond Conflicts of Interest to the Duty of Loyalty: From *Martin v. Gray* to *R. v. Neil*" (2005) 84 Can. Bar Rev. 433. Cases noting the duty of loyalty include: *Davey v. Woolley, Hames, Dale & Dingwall*, [1982] O.J. No. 3158, 35 O.R. (2d) 599 (Ont. C.A.); *R. v. Silvini*, [1991] O.J. No. 1931, 5 O.R. (3d) 545 (Ont. C.A.); *Stewart v. Canadian Broadcasting Corp.*, [1997] O.J. No. 2271 (Ont. C.J.); *Saint John Shipbuilding Ltd. v. Bow Valley Husky (Bermuda) Ltd.*, [2002] N.B.J. No. 205, 2002 NBCA 41 (N.B.C.A.); *First Property Holdings Inc. v. Beatty*, [2003] O.J. No. 2943, 66 O.R. (3d) 97 (Ont. S.C.J.); *Skye Properties Ltd. v. Wu*, [2003] O.J. No. 3481, 43 C.P.C. (5th) 118 (Ont. Div. Ct.), affd [2004] O.J. No. 3948 (Ont. C.A.); *Waxman v. Waxman*, [2004] O.J. No. 1765, 186 O.A.C. 201 (Ont. C.A.); *Jorgensen v. San Jose Mines Ltd.*, [2004] B.C.J. No. 1562, 2004 BCCA 400 (B.C.C.A.); *GMP Securities Ltd. v. Stikeman Elliott*, [2004] O.J. No. 3276 (Ont. S.C.J.); *Toddglen Construction Ltd. v. Concord Adex Developments Corp.*, [2004] O.J. No. 1788 (Ont. S.C.J.); *De Beers Canada Inc. v. Shore Gold Inc.*, [2006] S.J. No. 210, 2006 SKQB 101 (Sask. Q.B.); *Brookville Carriers Flatbed GP Inc. v. Blackjack Transport Ltd.*, [2008] N.S.J. No. 94, 2008 NSCA 22 (N.S.C.A.); *McKenna v. Gammon Gold Inc.*, [2009] O.J. No. 39 (Ont. S.C.J.); *First Property Holdings Inc. v. Beatty*, [2003] O.J. No. 2943 (Ont. S.C.J.); *Stewart v. Canadian Broadcasting Corp.*, [1997] O.J. No. 271 (Ont. C.A.).

conflict of interest will impair a lawyer's zealous advocacy[97] and, as is clear from the extensive case law on misuse of confidential information, they have been especially concerned about the relationship between certain conflicts of interest and risks to the client's right to confidentiality.

How far the duty of loyalty extends has yet to be fully determined. Richard Devlin and Victoria Rees have suggested that "a more comprehensive and vigorous understanding of the duty of loyalty" needs to be developed following the Court's judgment in *Neil*.[98] The Supreme Court's own division in *Strother v. 3464920 Canada Inc.*,[99] noted earlier, in which Justice Binnie emphasized the free standing obligation of loyalty owed by the lawyer, and Chief Justice McLachlin asserted that the duty of loyalty had no meaning except as identified through the specific agreement entered into between the lawyer and client, suggests that the contours of loyalty have yet to be determined. While Justice Binnie was writing for the majority, the fact that he did not in that case impose any obligation of loyalty beyond what he found that the lawyer had (implicitly) agreed to do for the client, means that it is not clear how far the independent duty of loyalty reaches. It is unlikely that it can (or should) be uncoupled from the nature of the representation undertaken by the lawyer.

Regardless of the outcome of that dispute, however, it is clear that the duty to act in loyal pursuit of his client's legal interests, and the duty of confidentiality, properly underpin the law on conflicts of interest.

5. THE PREVENTATIVE RATIONALE

In some of the cases discussed in this chapter, lawyers have actually breached duties that they owed to their clients, and they have done so — or been motivated to do so — because of a conflict of interest. Strother, for example, invested in a competitor of a client and, as a consequence, did not provide the legal advice to the client that he was required to provide.

Those cases do not, though, represent the heart of the law on conflicts of interest and, as noted, are arguably not really conflicts cases at all. The main thrust of the law on conflicts of interest is not to remedy a violation of the lawyer's duties; it is to *prevent* a lawyer from violating his duties. That is, the focus is not on whether the lawyer actually breached confidentiality, or represented a client in a way that was inadequate, but is rather on whether the circumstances are such that there is an undue incentive for the lawyer to do either of those things. Similarly, the conflicts of interest rules in the codes of conduct do not merely prohibit violation of lawyers' duties to clients;

---

[97] *Waxman v. Waxman*, [2004] O.J. No. 1765, 186 O.A.C. 201 (Ont. C.A.) and *Quibell v. Quibell*, [2010] S.J. No. 110, 2010 SKQB 83 (Sask. Q.B.).

[98] Richard F. Devlin & Victoria Rees, "Beyond Conflicts of Interest to the Duty of Loyalty: From *Martin v. Gray* to *R. v. Neil*" (2005) 84 Can. Bar Rev. 433 at 450.

[99] [2007] S.C.J. No. 24, 2007 SCC 24 (S.C.C.).

rather, they direct the lawyer not to place himself in circumstances that create a substantial risk that such a violation will occur.

In imposing a legal duty in order to prevent other legal wrongs, the law on conflicts of interest falls within regulatory norms. Regulation often — even normally — operates by imposing requirements and restrictions in order to ensure the occurrence of substantive outcomes. Those requirements and restrictions are legal duties, but they are not themselves the point; rather, they are legal duties used to create a desired outcome. For example, an oil and gas company cannot drill a natural gas well without a licence. The licence granted will impose restrictions on how the company drills the well in order to ensure the appropriate exploitation of the resource and the protection of the environment. Any breach of the terms of that licence will result in the company being sanctioned. The point of the regulation in that case is not, however, to protect licences *per se*. The licence itself is not inherently good, and breach of the terms of the licence is not inherently bad.[100] Rather, the point is that the system of licensing and sanctions for breach of the licence, operate together to ensure substantive ends, in that case the protection of the environment and the proper exploitation of the resource.

Regulation is used for this purpose in circumstances where those substantive ends will not otherwise be accomplished. In particular, we use regulatory mechanisms to accomplish substantive ends in circumstances where market forces will not work to create the ends because of some sort of market failure, or because the ends are not ones that markets can create. In the case of licensing for natural gas wells, we license because without a licensing system we cannot ensure that the environment will be protected, or that the resource will be properly exploited. Imperfections in the market for natural gas — in that case that the party developing the well does not bear the costs of environmental harm or inadequate exploitation, and so will not otherwise factor that cost into its drilling and production decisions — mean that otherwise the ends will not be achieved.

The law on conflicts of interest is another example of this sort of regulatory system — like the licence, it is a system of regulatory rules designed to accomplish substantive ends, and it exists because the market for legal services will not otherwise ensure that those ends are achieved. In particular, in the case of conflicts of interest, the point of the regulatory norm is to ensure that lawyers act consistently with their duties of loyal representation and confidentiality. That a lawyer is in a conflict is not necessarily in itself an ethical problem — there is nothing wicked about, for example, having two clients whose interests are currently aligned but may conflict. The conflict is nonetheless regulated, and the avoiding of conflicts made a legal duty, because doing so helps to avoid ethical problems such as breach of loyalty or confidentiality.

---

[100] Except in the sense of indicating an absence of respect for rule of law.

Further, it is regulated because it is only through regulation that the ethical problems will be avoided. The forces of supply and demand will not, in this case, operate to incent lawyers to avoid the conflicts that cause the problems, or to act properly regardless of the conflict. The market for legal services in general suffers from the problem that lawyers know more than clients about what is necessary to resolve a legal problem, and clients' lack of information makes it difficult for them to make rational choices about which lawyers to hire, about when a lawyer will be of benefit, and about how much to pay for legal services. In the case of conflicts of interest, there is an additional specific information problem, insofar as a client will not necessarily know when a conflict has arisen, and may not know the risk that the conflict presents for her relationship with her lawyer. As a result, the client will not be able to bargain with the lawyer to ensure that the conflict is avoided.

In addition, in some circumstances the client will have limited economic bargaining power in relation to the conflict. Where the client is a former client, she no longer has bargaining power relative to the lawyer; unless she offers a financial payment to the lawyer to avoid the conflict; she simply has to wait and accept the risk that the conflict may result in the breach of her confidential information. And even then it may be difficult for her to prove that confidentiality has been breached because, again, she lacks information about what the lawyer is doing or has done in the relationship with the new client. When a client is a current client her economic power may also be limited; the cost of shifting lawyers is high,[101] and the threat of retaining new counsel in the event of a conflict may be accurately perceived by the lawyer to be an empty one. Those existing clients may be stuck with living with a conflict were the conflict not to be forbidden.

The law of conflicts of interest addresses this market problem. It requires that the client be given information about the conflicts and, moreover, it gives the client bargaining power in relation to the lawyer, because without the client's consent the lawyer cannot continue to act. The conflicts rules essentially mean that the onus is on the lawyer to negotiate and address the risk of harm that the conflict creates.

Do the rules and requirements around conflicts of interest place undue emphasis on prevention of harm to clients? Would it be more coherent to emphasize actual violations by lawyers or, at least, to be less restrictive of lawyer's activities in circumstances where the concern is merely prevention of harm?

While the question of where the precise line should be drawn can be reasonably disputed — and has been the subject of recent and vigorous

---

[101] Clients have a sunk costs problem — if they shift lawyers they will not recoup what they have already spent, and will further not be able to gain any advantage from that expenditure, since the information will not be in the hands of the new lawyer, except inefficiently (through transfer of materials from one lawyer to another).

controversy within the Canadian legal profession[102] — in my view the Canadian courts have been correct both to emphasize the prevention of harm to clients, and to be quite rigorous in their identification of the circumstances in which harm may arise. As noted, the market for legal services is unlikely to ensure that clients are protected from the risks associated with conflicts of interest. Further, again emphasizing the market rationale, the current conflicts rules do not, for the most part, outright prohibit lawyers from acting in conflict situations. They simply require that lawyers negotiate and communicate properly with clients before doing so. They essentially shift the costs of dealing with conflicts to lawyers, and the bargaining power to clients. Given that it is clients' rights that are at stake, that the risk is one that lawyers can avoid and often clients cannot, and given that lawyers have better information than clients in this respect, that shift seems defensible.

Further, the risk to clients of actual violations of the lawyers' duties are real; courts are not being paranoid in the cases when they have disqualified lawyers, or unduly sensitive to the interests of clients. As noted at the outset, there are many respects in which the interests of lawyers and clients are misaligned. The conflicts of interest cases simply address the circumstances where that misalignment is such that the risk of the lawyer acting improperly has become material — where the risk of harm is "substantial", even if still only possible and contingent. Of course in individual cases one could argue whether the result reached was the right one but, as the discussion in the final section will indicate, in most cases the courts appear to be sensitive to the interests of both lawyers and clients, to be sensitive to the risk that lawyers are being removed for tactical reasons, and motivated to permit lawyers to act where the lawyers have demonstrably attempted to address the conflict in a pro-active way.

6. THE APPEARANCES RATIONALE

A significant aspect of the law in relation to conflicts of interest is ensuring "public confidence" in the integrity of the administration of justice.[103] The focus in many cases is on how the public would view the circumstances of the lawyer: would the "public represented by the reasonably informed person ... be satisfied that no use of confidential information would occur."[104] More generally, the Supreme Court suggested in *Neil* that "[u]nless a litigant is assured of the undivided loyalty of the lawyer, neither the public nor the litigant will have confidence that the legal system, which may appear to them to be a hostile and hideously complicated environment, is a reliable

---

[102] See in particular, CBA Task Force on Conflicts of Interest, *Conflicts of Interest: Final Report, Recommendations and Toolkit* (Ottawa: Canadian Bar Association, 2008).
[103] *R. v. Neil*, [2002] S.C.J. No. 72 at para. 12, [2002] 3 S.C.R. 631, 2002 SCC 70 (S.C.C.); *MacDonald Estate v. Martin*, [1990] S.C.J. No. 41 at para. 15, [1990] 3 S.C.R. 1235 (S.C.C.).
[104] *MacDonald Estate, ibid.* at para. 44.

and trustworthy means of resolving their disputes and controversies."[105] A significant focus of the conflicts jurisprudence is thus on the appearance that the lawyer is in an improper conflict, such that the integrity of the administration of justice is threatened, rather than on determining whether, in fact, the lawyer is in an improper conflict of interest.

In general, focusing on appearances is problematic in legal ethics. Concerns with what lawyers wear, or generally on the popularity or reputation of the legal profession, tend to confuse rather than clarify the proper scope and nature of the lawyer's ethical obligations. That something looks bad does not, in and of itself, explain why it *is* bad; the concern of legal ethics needs to be with realities not appearances.

The concern with appearances is somewhat different, however, where a concern with appearances is not an amorphous and general concern with "how the profession appears", but is rather attached to a specific and justifiable ethical obligation, and is in fact a method for ensuring the appropriate scope for enforcement of that obligation. The focus on appearances in the conflicts jurisprudence is that latter sort of concern. Specifically, in the cases the courts use the idea of appearance, and of the reasonably informed member of the public, as a method for applying the rules that delineate when a lawyer is in a conflict of interest. The reasonably informed member of the public is not relevant in the abstract; he is relevant as a way of determining whether there is a substantial risk of a material and adverse effect on the lawyer's representation of the client, or that confidential information will be misused. The reasonably informed member of the public is, in other words, much like the reasonable man on the Clapham Omnibus, who can help determine when a harm has been negligently imposed, or like the reasonable person who helps determine whether an adjudicator should be disqualified for bias.[106] That sort of heuristic for thinking sensibly about when a lawyer might be in a conflict position is useful, and does not reflect an inappropriate concern with appearances over realities.

7. LAWYERS' SPECIFIC DUTIES

This section focuses on the specific rules and case law that delineate lawyers' duties with respect to acting against former clients, in acting for more than one current client where the interests of those clients are or may be in conflict, and in acting in circumstances where the lawyer's own interests may conflict with those of his client.

---

[105] *R. v. Neil*, [2002] S.C.J. No. 72 at para. 12, [2002] 3 S.C.R. 631, 2002 SCC 70 (S.C.C.).
[106] *Committee for Justice and Liberty v. National Energy Board*, [1976] S.C.J. No. 118, [1978] 1 S.C.R. 369 (S.C.C.).

A. Duties to Former Clients

i. *The General Principles*

A lawyer may not act against a former client in a matter that is the same or related to the matter on which the lawyer was formerly retained for that client.[107] The point of the prohibition is primarily to ensure lawyers do not act in circumstances where there is a heightened risk that confidential information obtained from a client will be used to the client's disadvantage. Where two matters are the same or related, it is far more likely that the lawyer will have confidential information from the first retainer that is relevant to the subsequent retainer, and acting against the former client in the subsequent retainer will create the risk that the information may be used to the former client's disadvantage.[108]

The secondary reason for the prohibition is that lawyers are prohibited from acting in circumstances where there is a risk that doing so will involve attacking or undermining the benefit that had been obtained by the former client from the lawyer's advice. The lawyer is prohibited from "attacking the legal work done [for the client] during the retainer, or from undermining the client's position on a matter that was central to the retainer."[109]

A lawyer may act against the former client if the former client gives informed consent to the lawyer doing so.[110]

The prohibition against acting against a former client applies to lawyers who practise in the same firm as one another,[111] law firm being defined to include circumstances where lawyers hold themselves out as practising law in association with each other, as well as partnerships that are legally formalized.[112] However, to the extent law firm conflicts arise from concerns about misuse of confidential information, they may be "cured" by the use of screening devices to ensure that the lawyer who has the confidential information has no participation whatsoever in the new representation, and

---

[107] CBA MC Chapter V, Commentary 12; FLS MC 2.04(5); Que. CEA Rule 3.06.02; LSUC RPC 2.04(4); NB CC Chapter 6, Commentary 4; AB CPC Chapter 6, Rules 3(b) and (c); BC PCH Chapter 6, Rule 7.

[108] Or, conversely, the risk that the lawyer will not use the information, and thereby not act with zeal in relation to his new client.

[109] FLS MC Rule 2.04(5), commentary; LSUC RPC Rule 2.04(4), commentary. See also CBA MC Chapter V, Commentary 12; AB CPC Rule 3(b).

[110] CBA MC Chapter V, Commentary 12; FLS MC 2.04(5); LSUC RPC 2.04(4); AB CPC Chapter 6, Rules 3(b) and (c); BC PCH Chapter 6, Rule 7.

[111] CBA MC Chapter V, Commentary 14; FLS MC Rule 2.04(6); NB CC Chapter 6, Commentary 4, footnote 6; Que. CEA Rule 3.06.09; LSUC RPC Rule 2.04(5); AB CPC Rule 3(c); BC PCH Chapter 6, Rule 7.4.

[112] CBA MC Chapter V, Commentary 15; FLS MC, definitions, "law firm"; NB CC, definitions, "firm"; LSUC RPC Rule 1.02, definitions, "law firm"; AB CPC, definitions, "firm"; BC PCH Chapter 6, Rules 6.1 and 6.2.

the information held by that lawyer cannot be accessed by the lawyers acting against the firm's former client.[113]

According to Guidelines published by the Canadian Bar Association ("CBA") in 1993, law firms should, along with prohibiting discussions about the matter between the screened lawyer and other members of the firm, physically segregate files of the current client, circulate a written policy to everyone in the firm about the screening devices, and provide appropriate undertakings to affected parties about what is being done.[114] Screening devices generally need to be erected prior to the commencement of the new litigation,[115] and in some jurisdictions must be approved by the court in order to be effective.[116] In other jurisdictions court approval is not required, but may in some circumstances be obtained by a law firm for the purposes of achieving greater certainty.[117]

Neither lawyers nor law firms are prohibited from acting against a former client in a "fresh and independent matter wholly unrelated to any work the lawyer has previously done for that person".[118]

These principles are, as indicated by the footnotes, contained in all of the provincial codes of conduct. They also flow from, and are further developed in, numerous cases, beginning with the foundational case in this area, *MacDonald Estate v. Martin*.[119] In *MacDonald Estate*, Kristin Dangerfield had been an articling student and associate at the Winnipeg law firm of A. Kerr Twaddle, who acted from 1983 for the defendant Martin, in litigation brought by Gray. Dangerfield was actively involved in the litigation, and received confidential information from Martin. In 1985 Twaddle was appointed to the bench, and Dangerfield joined the firm of Scarth, Dooley. She did not continue to represent Martin, who obtained new counsel. In 1987, Scarth, Dooley was absorbed into Thompson, Dorfman, Sweatman ("TDS"), which had acted for Gray from the outset of the litigation against Martin. Martin sought to disqualify TDS from continuing

---

[113] CBA MC Chapter V, Commentary 14; FLS MC 2.04(6); Que. CEA Rule 3.06.09; LSUC RPC 2.05(5); AB CPC Chapter 6, Rules 3(b) and (c), and Commentary 3.3; BC PCH Rule 7.4.

[114] See FLS MC 2.04(6) and 2.04(26); LSUC RPC Rule 2.05, commentary, reproducing guidelines from the CBA MC Task Force, *Conflict of Interest Disqualification: Martin v. Gray and Screening Methods* (February 1993).

[115] This is the position taken in various cases, as discussed below (see, *inter alia, Re Ford Motor Co. of Canada Ltd. v. Osler, Hoskin & Harcourt*, [1996] O.J. No. 31, 131 D.L.R. (4th) 419 at 441-42 (Ont. Gen. Div.): "the screening mechanism must be put in place when the conflict arises".). Note, though, *Allied Signal Inc. v. Dome Petroleum Inc.*, [1997] A.J. No. 193 (Alta. C.A.) (although in that case the concern may have been that the application for disqualification was merely tactical) and CBA MC Chapter V, Commentary 36. The CBA MC 2008 Task Force took real exception to the court requirement that screening devices be in place at the time the conflict arises.

[116] AB CPC, Chapter 6, Rule 3(c), Commentary 3.3. In practice Alberta lawyers do not generally seek court approval unless an issue appears likely to arise.

[117] FLS MC Rule 2.04(25) (relating to transferring lawyers); LSUC RPC Rule 2.05(9) (relating to transferring lawyers); BC PCH Chapter 6, Rule 7.8.

[118] CBA MC Chapter V, Commentary 13.

[119] [1990] S.C.J. No. 41, [1990] 3 S.C.R. 1235 (S.C.C.).

to act for Gray. Dangerfield and members of TDS swore affidavits to the effect that no discussions about the case had occurred, or would occur in the future.

The Supreme Court of Canada held that TDS must be disqualified. Justice Sopinka, writing for the majority, held that a lawyer or law firm must be disqualified from acting against a former client if there is a risk that confidential information will be used to the prejudice of that client. He held further that there is a rebuttable presumption that where one member of a law firm has confidential information with respect to a client, all members of the law firm do so. Therefore, in order to resist disqualification a law firm must establish that no one in the firm has confidential information that has a "substantial relationship"[120] to the matter on which the law firm is acting against the former client. If the law firm or a lawyer within the firm formerly acted for the client on a matter that relates to the matter on which the law firm is now acting against the former client, then it will be presumed that confidential information relevant to the current retainer is possessed. The presumption can be rebutted, but in rebutting the presumption no "specifics of the privileged communication" may be revealed.[121]

If the presumption that the lawyer and law firm have confidential information cannot be rebutted, then to continue acting the law firm must establish that there is no risk that the confidential information will be used against the former client. That means that the lawyer who has the confidential information can never act personally against the former client:

> A lawyer who has relevant confidential information cannot act against his client or former client. In such a case the disqualification is automatic. No assurances or undertakings not to use the information will avail. The lawyer cannot compartmentalize his or her mind so as to screen out what has been gleaned from the client and what was acquired elsewhere. Furthermore, there would be a danger that the lawyer would avoid use of information acquired legitimately because it might be perceived to have come from the client. This would prevent the lawyer from adequately representing the new client. Moreover, the former client would feel at a disadvantage. Questions put in cross-examination about personal matters, for example, would create the uneasy feeling that they had their genesis in the previous relationship.[122]

If lawyers in the firm other than the lawyer who holds the confidential information are acting against the former client, then the law firm must establish that it has taken institutional measures to prevent the communication of the confidential information from the lawyer who has it to the other lawyers now acting against the former client. The Court left the development of those mechanisms to the Canadian Bar Association and the

---

[120] *Ibid.* at para. 46.
[121] *Ibid.*
[122] *Ibid.* at para. 47.

provincial regulators; however, it held that "undertakings and conclusory statements in affidavits without more are not acceptable".[123]

On the facts, therefore, TDS was disqualified. Dangerfield clearly had confidential information relevant to the matter on which the firm was acting against Martin. The only basis on which the firm could rebut the presumption that other members of TDS shared that information were the undertakings that she and members of the firm had filed. Those were insufficient to rebut the presumption.

In his concurring minority reasons, Justice Cory would have made the presumption of shared information irrebuttable. In his view, once it was demonstrated that one member of a law firm had confidential information relevant to the matter on which the firm was acting against a former client, that law firm must be disqualified. He took exception in particular to Justice Sopinka's assertion of the "virtual disappearance of the sole practitioner and the tendency to larger and larger firms".[124] As Justice Cory pointed out, the majority of Canadian lawyers in private practice do not work in large law firms. In Justice Cory's view, it was not appropriate to allow firms to act against clients on the premise that they could prevent the sharing of confidential information between lawyers in the firm.

ii. When is a New Matter Related to a Prior Retainer?

As noted, *MacDonald Estate* and the codes of conduct contemplate the possibility that a lawyer may act against a former client when the new matter is unrelated to the prior retainer. Subsequent case law confirms *MacDonald Estate* on this point, and gives some indication of when a new retainer will be considered sufficiently unrelated to the prior retainer.

In *TransCanada Pipelines Ltd. v. Nova Scotia (Attorney General)*,[125] a lawyer, Dickson, had acted for the province of Nova Scotia in negotiating an oil and gas accord with the federal government. Subsequently Nova Scotia and TransCanada Pipelines Ltd. ended up in litigation with respect to a memorandum of agreement into which they had entered. TransCanada was represented in the litigation by a member of Dickson's firm. Nova Scotia sought to disqualify the firm on the basis of Dickson's prior representation of the province in negotiating the oil and gas accord with the federal government. The Court disagreed. It held that while the definition of "sufficiently related" should not be very narrow, it should also not be "extremely broad".[126] In this case there were substantial differences between

---

[123] *Ibid.* at para. 50.
[124] *Ibid.* at para. 14. And whatever the relative legal merits of the judgments, on this point Justice Cory was clearly correct; large law firms are influential, but there are far more Canadian lawyers working in other practice settings than there are working for large law firms. Large law firms dominate the areas they specialize in — law involving corporations — but not the legal services market as a whole.
[125] [1999] N.S.J. No. 409, 180 N.S.R. (2d) 355 (N.S.S.C.).
[126] *Ibid.* at para. 47.

the matters on which Dickson and his firm were acting for and against the government; to disqualify the firm would be, in effect, to say that anyone who had acted for the government could never act against it.

In its somewhat later decision in *Reagh v. Reagh*[127] the Nova Scotia Supreme Court put the matter bluntly:

> There are people who believe that once a lawyer has acted for a client that he or she cannot thereafter, at any time, act against them. Similarly, there are some people who believe that, once a law firm has acted for them, that the same law firm, no matter what changes in personnel occur, has no right to take action against them, or further still, that all former members of that firm, or lawyers associated with them, have no right to act against them. That is flawed and unreasonable thinking. It may be that the parties will feel hurt by the fact that someone they used before is suing them, or on the other side of the coin — may be responding to suit they have started. It may be a public relations matter for the legal profession, but, the ethical guidelines for lawyers recognize that clients may retain different lawyers, and different law firms, to act for them for different matters, and similarly, it is not improper for a lawyer to take on a matter against a former client in an unrelated matter, provided that the former client is protected from disclosure or misuse of related confidential information. Binding a lawyer, or firm, to not act against a client requires a continuing contract ...[128]

A more borderline case, where the court had to consider whether a matter was related, and ultimately decided that it was, was *Chapters Inc. v. Davies, Ward & Beck*.[129] In that case Davies had acted for SmithBooks in acquisition of the Coles book chain, to form Chapters books. It had been retained on competition law matters, and had received confidential information about the two companies. The retainer ended in 1995. In 2000, Davies was retained by Trilogy, who was seeking to purchase shares of Chapters in order to merge Chapters and Indigo Books. Davies established a firewall with the lawyer who had acted in the 1995 matter, but ultimately decided that it was unnecessary and, in fact, the lawyer who had originally acted on the competition matter during the SmithBooks acquisition was now acting directly for Trilogy with respect to the competition issues raised by the purchase of the shares in Chapters.

---

[127] [2005] N.S.J. No. 560, 2005 NSSC 365 (N.S.S.C.). The facts of *Reagh* were that Parker had represented a husband and wife in various matters. He had been law partners with Gillis, although they had maintained separate offices. That partnership terminated in 2003, and Gillis started practicing with Schumacher. Schumacher was then retained by the husband in a divorce proceeding. The court not surprisingly found no disqualifying conflict arising from Parker's original representation.

[128] *Ibid.* at para. 29. See also: *Widrig v. Cox Downie*, [1992] N.S.J. No. 298, 114 N.S.R. (2d) 320 (N.S.T.D.); *Winter v. Phillips*, [1987] A.J. No. 1114, 47 D.L.R. (4th) 309 (Alta. Q.B.); *Berry v. Law Society of New Brunswick*, [1989] N.B.J. No. 829, 100 N.B.R. (2d) 245 (N.B.Q.B.); *Kaila v. Khalsa Diwan Society*, [2004] B.C.J. No. 830, 2004 BCCA 236 (B.C.C.A.).

[129] [2001] O.J. No. 206, 52 O.R. (3d) 566 (Ont. C.A.).

Chapters brought an application to court to prevent Davies from acting in the new matter. Notably, there was no litigation before the court to which to attach the motion, but the court held that it could consider it nonetheless; it was sufficient that it was "very much a legally regulated dispute".[130] The Court also rejected Davies' argument that no preclusion should arise because the matters were not sufficiently related. The Court held that whether the matters are sufficiently related depends on the confidentiality issue itself. If there is a possibility that confidential information will be misused, then the matters are sufficiently related:

> In the end, the client must demonstrate that the possibility of relevant confidential information having been acquired is realistic not just theoretical. For the court to find that the retainers are sufficiently related it must conclude that in all the circumstances it is reasonably possible that the lawyer acquired confidential information pursuant to the first retainer that could be relevant to the current matter.[131]

Here the Court held that the matters were sufficiently related. In the original matter significant confidential information was communicated about the nature of the businesses that subsequently became Chapters, and about what would happen over the next ten years. It could not be said that the nature of the industry and business has so changed that the earlier information "cannot possible be relevant".[132]

Finally, in a case that did not deal with confidential information, but rather addressed the question of acting against former clients more generally, *Brookville Carriers Flatbed GP Inc. v. Blackjack Transport Ltd.*[133] the Nova Scotia Court of Appeal defined "related matters". The Court held the matters were related where the subsequent matter "involves the lawyer taking an adversarial position against the former client with respect to the legal work which the lawyer performed for the former client or a matter central to the earlier retainer".[134]

In sum, for a conflict to disqualify a lawyer or law firm from acting against a former client, the subject matter of the new retainer must be sufficiently related to the legal work undertaken by the lawyer in that prior retainer. The primary indicator of that relationship is whether confidential information from the prior retainer is likely to be relevant to the former retainer. If it is, then acting in the subsequent matter is prohibited unless the former client consents.

---

[130] *Ibid.* at para. 25.
[131] *Ibid.* at para. 30.
[132] *Ibid.* at paras. 34 and 35, the Court noting the firm's submission and rejecting it.
[133] [2008] N.S.J. No. 94, 2008 NSCA 22 (N.S.C.A.).
[134] *Ibid.* at para. 17. See also *Consulate Ventures Inc. v. Amico Contracting & Engineering (1992) Inc.*, [2010] O.J. No. 4996 at para. 15, 2010 ONCA 788 (Ont. C.A.), where the Court stated that the determination of whether two matters are the same or related should be based on a "functional approach which asks the question, from a reasonable client's perspective, what was the matter on which that client retained the lawyer and what is the matter on which that same lawyer now proposes to act against his former client?".

iii. When will the Information Obtained in the Earlier Retainer be Confidential Enough to be Disqualifying?

Case law and codes of conduct take into account the nature of the information held by the lawyer in the analysis of whether a law firm should be disqualified. In the rules governing transferring lawyers, for example, some of the codes of conduct suggest that the rules protecting confidential information only apply to information that is not in the public domain.[135] In Alberta, the Code provides that while all confidential information is protected from disclosure under the duty of confidentiality, there is less need for disqualification on the basis of a conflict where the relevant information the lawyer knows is generic, rather than unique to that client:

> "*Confidential information*" means all information concerning a client's business, interests and affairs acquired in the course of the lawyer/client relationship (see Chapter 7, Confidentiality). A lawyer's knowledge of personal characteristics or corporate policies that are notably unusual or unique to a client will bar an adverse representation if such knowledge could potentially be used to the client's disadvantage. An example is the knowledge that a client will not under any circumstances proceed to trial or appear as a witness. However, a lawyer's awareness that a client has a characteristic common to many people (such as a general aversion to testifying) or a fairly typical corporate policy (such as a propensity to settle rather than proceed to litigation) will not generally preclude the lawyer from acting against that client.[136]

In *Canadian Pacific Railway Co. v. Aikins, MacAulay & Thorvaldson*[137] the Manitoba Court of Appeal declined to disqualify a law firm from acting against Canadian Pacific in a matter at the Canadian Transportation Agency. A lawyer at the Aikins firm, Smith, had been a senior legal officer at Canadian Pacific from 1983-1994, and was involved in legal, strategic and operating issues concerning Canadian Pacific over time. Those years were not directly implicated in the Transportation Agency proceedings; however, Canadian Pacific invoked them as relevant, and Aikins sought production of documents in relation to those years. Canadian Pacific then sought to have Aikins disqualified because of Smith's prior employment with Canadian Pacific. Canadian Pacific succeeded at motions court, but the Manitoba Court of Appeal overturned the result because the information held by Smith was not sufficient to warrant disqualification. Canadian Pacific never made clear allegations regarding the information with which they were concerned. Smith would clearly have had extensive information about Canadian Pacific in general terms, but it was not clear that he had information relevant to the matter at issue, which substantially dealt with years after Smith was at Canadian Pacific. That Smith had some knowledge was not enough;

---

[135] CBA MC Chapter V, Commentary 33; FLS MC Rule 2.04(17); LSUC RPC 2.05(1).
[136] AB CPC Chapter 6, Commentary 3.2.
[137] [1998] M.J. No. 77, 157 D.L.R. (4th) 473 (Man. C.A.).

Canadian Pacific had to allege something specific that was relevant to the matter on which Aikins was acting: "I recognize that CPR is entitled to protection against the use of privileged communication by a lawyer previously in its employ, but it must surely provide some information as to the nature of the communication which it seeks to protect and as to its relevance to the lawsuit in question."[138]

Courts have also refused to disqualify counsel in circumstances where the information, even if confidential generally, was not confidential relative to the party for whom the lawyer is now acting. In other words, where the lawyer has confidential information from a former client, but that information is not confidential relative to the lawyer's new client, the court may permit the lawyer to continue to act. In *Richards v. Producers Pipelines Inc.*,[139] the law firm had acted for the company, but was now acting for the former Chief Executive Officer of the company in a wrongful dismissal matter. The company sought to disqualify the law firm. The Court refused to do so because any information the firm had obtained in representing the company it had obtained from the CEO, with the result that "[i]t cannot, by definition, be confidential information as between the parties since it has always been in the possession of or available to all of them."[140]

This case is consistent with the Alberta Court of Appeal's decision in *Gainers Inc. v. Pocklington*,[141] where Pocklington attempted to disqualify McLennan Ross from acting for Gainers based on his "near client" status as Gainer's former Chief Executive Officer. Along with other reasons, the Court of Apepal rejected the application because none of the information provided by Pocklington was confidential relative to Gainers.

A different approach is taken in joint retainer cases. Where the lawyer has acted for parties in a joint retainer, even though the information the lawyer has is not confidential as between those parties, the court has still refused to permit the lawyer to act for one party and against the other with respect to matters arising from the joint retainer.[142] This may be because in the case of joint retainers, the issue is not simply confidential information, but also the prohibition against attacking or undermining the work previously done by the lawyer in acting for the client. Outside of the joint retainer context, it appears that if the information is truly public, or not

---

[138] *Ibid.* at para. 30. It may have had some relevance to the Court that Smith left Canadian Pacific because they closed their office in Winnipeg, rather than leaving for strategic or opportunistic reasons. In addition, the Court expressly noted that Canadian Pacific had not raised the conflicts issue in a timely fashion. For a contrasting judgment — in terms of facts — see *ATCO Gas and Pipelines Ltd. v. Sheard*, [2003] A.J. No. 235 at para. 25, 2003 ABCA 61 (Alta. C.A.) — where the Court disqualified a former general counsel of ATCO from acting in a rate proceeding where he would clearly have had information about proceedings "identical" to those in which he now sought to act against ATCO.

[139] [1996] S.J. No. 132 (Sask. C.A.).

[140] *Ibid.* at para. 22.

[141] [1995] A.J. No. 438, 29 Alta. L.R. (3d) 323 (Alta. C.A.).

[142] *G.H. Coulter v. Jens*, [1992] S.J. No. 321 (Sask. C.A.); *Bow Valley Energy Inc. v. San Diego Gas and Electric Co.*, [1996] A.J. No. 269, 38 Alta. L.R. (3d) 116 (Alta. C.A.).

confidential vis-à-vis the subsequent client, then the lawyer will not be prohibited from acting.

iv. Is the Restriction on Misuse of Confidential Information Limited to Retainers against the Former Client, or does it Apply More Generally?

Where the information that the lawyer has is confidential relative to a former client, then that information may prevent the lawyer not only from acting against the former client, but also from acting in a matter where the lawyer would have to cross-examine the former client. In *R. v. Brissett*,[143] a lawyer, McComb, had acted for Cunningham in a criminal case in which charges were stayed prior to trial. McComb and Bernstein then acted for Brissett who was charged with the murder of Ranglin, and with the attempted murder of Cunningham. Cunningham was an important witness for the Crown against Brissett. During cross-examination of Cunningham by Bernstein at the preliminary inquiry, the matter of Cunningham's prior criminal conviction was raised, and the following exchange took place:

> Bernstein: Who was your lawyer for that one?
>
> Cunningham [indicating co-counsel for the defence]: That man right there with the glasses was my lawyer.
>
> Bernstein: This man?
>
> Cunningham: Yeah.
>
> Bernstein: Mr. McComb?
>
> Cunningham: Yeah.[144]

Prior to this exchange, McComb had no recollection of having acted for Cunningham. The Court nonetheless required that Brissett obtain new counsel, because it was improper for a lawyer and his colleague to cross-examine a former client on matters related to the former retainer, in this case the prior criminal convictions. The cross-examination raised the possibility of the misuse of confidential information, even though the prior representation was itself distinct from the matter here, and Cunningham was not in fact a party to the new matter.[145]

---

[143] [2005] O.J. No. 343 (Ont. S.C.J.).
[144] *Ibid.* at para. 12.
[145] In *R. v. Desmond*, [2010] O.J. No. 2142 at para. 40, 2010 ONSC 2945 (Ont. S.C.J.), the Court refused to disqualify the lawyer who would have to cross-examine a former client. In that case, though, the lawyer had only acted for the former client on a consent bail hearing, and the main basis for the decision was that the nature of the representation made it inappropriate to draw the inference from *MacDonald Estate* regarding the disclosure of confidential information. The accused did "not confirm that confidential information creating a conflict of interest was disclosed".

v. What Specific Rules Apply to Transfers of Lawyers between Firms?

The case of *MacDonald Estate v. Martin*[146] dealt with the particular issue of transferring lawyers. Many of the provincial law societies, and the Canadian Bar Association, have subsequently written rules dealing with the issue of how transfers between firms should be handled. The details of those rules are not addressed here, since most simply give specific articulation to the general principles set out in the case; however two points are of note. First, the rules make it clear that the issues of confidential information on transfers between law firms apply to non-lawyer employees, as well as to lawyers. Second, some of the rules take the position that where a lawyer was at a law firm that acted for a client on a related matter, but the lawyer did not himself or herself act for the client, then that lawyer does not fall within the restrictions of *MacDonald Estate v. Martin*.[147]

The first of these positions is clearly consistent with the judgment of Justice Sopinka. If law firm employees have confidential information in relation to a matter, then the former client must be protected from disclosure of that information as well. The risks may be less significant than with lawyers, but it is nonetheless appropriate that they be dealt with.

The second position is more problematic. Justice Sopinka held that there is a rebuttable presumption that confidences are shared within a law firm, and that the presumption cannot be rebutted merely through affidavits and undertakings. When a lawyer leaves a firm, what will that lawyer have to prove that he does not have confidential information on a matter, other than an affidavit swearing that he never worked on the file, or discussed it with anyone? In my view, where a lawyer transfers from a firm acting against a client of the lawyer's former firm, a law firm may be prudent to implement screening mechanisms in relation to the lawyer and the new firm's retainer against his former client, even if the lawyer did not work on the file. The necessity of those mechanisms depends on the circumstances (Were they in the same department? In the same city? Working on that client but on different matters?) but certainly a firm should not assume them to be unnecessary simply because the transferring lawyer says that he had no connection with the representation of the client on the related matter at his former firm.

Conversely, courts should be careful not to engage in too many levels of imputation in disqualifying law firms from acting for clients. To impute knowledge to a lawyer in one law firm, and then impute knowledge from that lawyer to other lawyers in the new firm, seems to move from the possible to the merely speculative, which is inconsistent with the case law, and does not give sufficient attention to the real costs to clients in having their law firm disqualified. In general, I would argue that an affidavit and

---

[146] [1990] S.C.J. No. 41, [1990] 3 S.C.R. 1235 (S.C.C.).
[147] See, for example, CBA MC Chapter V, Commentary 32.

plausible supporting circumstances — for example, having worked in a department of the firm unrelated to the matter of the retainer — should be sufficient to rebut the presumption of shared confidential information where a transferring lawyer did not work on the file.[148]

vi. The Problem of Tactical Applications to Disqualify

One problem raised by the conflicts rules set out in *MacDonald Estate* is the incentive created for opportunistic or tactical disqualification applications; that is, where the former client does not consent, and in fact seeks disqualification of opposing counsel, not because of any real concern with the misuse of confidential information, but because depriving the other side of its counsel offers a litigation advantage.

On the one hand, the mere existence of tactical reasons or motivation does not make a legitimate assertion of a disqualifying conflict illegitimate; usually a disqualification application will have some strategic aspect to it. In *MacDonald Estate* itself it may well be that the motivation for objecting to TDS continuing was the strategic advantage obtained by disqualifying Gray's longstanding counsel; however, that motivation (if it existed) did not change the impropriety of how the conflict raised by Dangerfield joining the firm was handled, nor make TDS's continued representation of Gray appropriate.

On the other hand, where an application is primarily strategic, and provides little substantive basis for the alleged conflict, there is a potential for abuse, and for imposing unwarranted costs on the party whose lawyer is disqualified, or even who has to spend the time and money necessary to resist the tactical application. The challenge for the court, therefore, is to identify those applications for disqualification that are merely strategic, without ignoring real conflicts simply because the party seeking disqualification may have strategic motivations.

Courts try to make these distinctions. The judgments often note as significant the timing of the application, whether the party registered its objection to the conflict immediately, and other like factors that may indicate that the party does not truly object to the conflict of interest it is asserting. Those factors will usually not be sufficient, in and of themselves, to prevent a court from disqualifying a lawyer; however, when the allegation of a conflict is substantively weak, those facts will make a court more likely to refuse disqualification. In Québec, this process of identification could arguably be grounded in new Article 4.2 of the *Code of Civil Procedure*,[149] which provides that "the parties must ensure that the proceedings they choose are proportionate, in terms of the costs and time required, to the

---

[148] For an example of a sensible judicial example of this see *Reagh v. Reagh*, [2005] N.S.J. No. 560, 2005 NSSC 365 (N.S.S.C.); *Chapates v. Petro Canada*, [2004] N.S.J. No. 75, 2004 NSSC 52 (N.S.S.C.).
[149] R.S.Q. c. C-25.

nature and ultimate purpose of the action or application and to the complexity of the dispute".

In *Chapates v. Petro Canada*,[150] the plaintiff was suing for soil and water damage to a residential property purchased from the defendant Webber. Webber retained a firm to represent him. Piercey was a member of the firm, but not involved in the litigation. The case was in abeyance for a number of years, and during that time Piercey left the firm. The plaintiff was no longer able to have the same lawyer and, after some delay, retained Piercey. Webber then sought to have Piercey disqualified based on Piercey's former employment at the firm representing Webber. The court refused. It held that in the circumstances the administration of justice would be "brought into greater disrepute by the removal of the plaintiff's counsel in a case which has been ongoing for almost twelve years and where in excess of one year was spent by the [(plaintiff)] respondent trying to find a new lawyer who would represent him on a lengthy and complex trial".[151] The Court also suggested that "[a] reasonably informed member of the public viewing this application might conclude that the removal of the plaintiff's solicitor was simply an attempt to dissuade the plaintiff (respondent) from continuing with his action."[152]

The judgment in *Chapates* is arguably inconsistent with *MacDonald Estate* in terms of the application of the law; the imputation of knowledge to Piercey from his former firm seems sufficient to at least create a potential conflict. On the other hand, that sort of double imputation is, as noted earlier, a weak basis for asserting a conflict. That weak basis for asserting a conflict, when coupled with apparently strategic motivations, justifies the court's decision.[153]

vii. When Screening Devices will be Sufficient

An important aspect of the decision in *MacDonald Estate* was the recognition by Sopinka J. — which Cory J. rejected — that screening devices may be sufficient to cure a conflict of interest that arises where one lawyer in a firm possesses confidential information from a prior retainer relevant to another lawyer in the firm's current retainer. In subsequent cases courts have recognized the legitimacy of screening devices. Further, courts have generally not scrutinized the specific screening devices used by lawyers. Provided that the screening device is in place in time, and includes some attempt to prevent the communication of confidential information, the

---

[150] [2004] N.S.J. No. 75, 2004 NSSC 52 (N.S.S.C.).
[151] *Ibid.* at para. 36.
[152] *Ibid.* at para. 37.
[153] For other judgments in which the court has refused to disqualify lawyers, either because the argument was facially weak, or because the motivation appeared largely strategic, see: *Sogelco International Inc. v. Pêcheries Cap Lumière Fisheries Ltd.*, [2004] N.B.J. No. 424 (N.B.C.A.); *Rayner v. Enright*, [1993] S.J. No. 654, 115 Sask. R. 159 (Sask. Q.B.); *Seigel v. Seigel*, [2008] O.J. No. 5680 (Ont. S.C.J.).

court appears to be satisfied by its sufficiency. In cases where the screening device was found to be insufficient, the problem was that it was not in place in a timely fashion, not that the specific type of device used was inadequate as a means of protecting the confidential information.[154] It seems that in general a timely and good faith effort to prevent the sharing of confidential information will be sufficient.

viii. When Acting Against a Former Client is Prohibited even though Confidential Information from that Client will not be Used to His Disadvantage

The emphasis in *MacDonald Estate*, and in most of the subsequent cases, is on the issue of preventing misuse of confidential information. The cases focus on determining when matters are related, when information is truly confidential, when screening devices are sufficient and so on. Perhaps the most significant post-*MacDonald* cases are, however, the cases holding that the prohibition on acting against former clients is not limited to the potential for misuse of confidential information, but can also apply where the representation implicates the lawyer's general duty to be a loyal advocate.

The most important decision in this respect is the 2008 judgment of the Nova Scotia Court of Appeal in *Brookville Carriers Flatbed GP Inc. v. Blackjack Transport Ltd.*[155] in which Justice Cromwell (as he then was) concluded that lawyers have a "duty not to act against a former client in a related matter whether or not confidential information is at risk".[156] A matter is related where it "involves the lawyer taking an adversarial position against the former client with respect to the legal work which the lawyer performed for the former client or a matter central to the earlier retainer".[157]

The facts of *Brookville* involved a lawsuit brought by a company against its former employees alleging dishonesty over a period of time. The former employees and the company had previously been sued on the basis of allegations that the employees had taken bribes. Both the employees and the company were represented in the first action by Stewart, McKelvey, Stirling

---

[154] *Saint John Shipbuilding Ltd. v. Bow Valley Husky (Bermuda) Ltd.*, [2002] N.B.J. No. 205, 2002 NBCA 41 (N.B.C.A.) (screening device not in place in time); *Skye Properties Ltd. v. Wu*, [2003] O.J. No. 3481, 43 C.P.C. (4th) 118 (Ont. Div. Ct.) (screening device not in place in time; they had to be in place prior to the firms physically integrating their offices); *Re Ford Motor Co. of Canada Ltd. v. Osler, Hoskin & Harcourt*, [1996] O.J. No. 31, 131 D.L.R. (4th) 419 (Ont. Gen. Div.) ("the screening mechanism must be put in place when the conflict arises" (at 441-42)); *Robertson v. Slater Vecchio*, [2008] B.C.J. No. 1353, 2008 BCCA 306 (B.C.C.A.) (substantial compliance with law society Guidelines re screening devices was sufficient, even though some steps were not followed. The Court stated that you cannot treat the guidelines as "mandatory rules that must be met in every case and in every detail"; *Allied Signal Inc. v. Dome Petroleum Inc.*, [1997] A.J. No. 193 (Alta. C.A.) (screening device was not in place in a timely manner but Court held that it was sufficient on the facts, which included a concern about strategic behaviour motivating the application).

[155] [2008] N.S.J. No. 94, 2008 NSCA 22 (N.S.C.A.).

[156] *Ibid.* at para. 17.

[157] *Ibid.*

and Scales; in the second action the company was also represented by Stewart, McKelvey. The first action had been dismissed, and it was found as a fact at the initial hearing into the application to disqualify Stewart, McKelvey, that no relevant confidential information had been obtained from the employees in the first action. As noted, however, Justice Cromwell held that that fact was not determinative, and that Stewart McKelvey should nonetheless be disqualified.

He noted that while there is no general duty not to act against a former client, it is improper for a lawyer to act in a subsequent proceeding that attacks or undermines "the legal work which the lawyer did for the former client".[158] The lawyer may not act so as to be "effectively changing sides by taking an adversarial position against a former client with respect to a matter that was central to the previous retainer".[159]

A different result, but with a similar position on the law, was reached by the British Columbia Court of Appeal in *Greater Vancouver Regional District v. Melville*.[160] In that case a lawyer had given a legal opinion to the City of Vancouver regarding the validity and enforceability of land expropriations by the City in the 1970s. In 2006 the lawyer commenced an action on behalf of the respondents arguing that the 1971 expropriation of their property was invalid. The City sought to have the lawyer disqualified. The Court agreed that a lawyer "may owe a former client a continuing fiduciary duty of loyalty"[161] but that whether that duty is violated depends on the "particular positions taken by the lawyer in their subsequent actions".[162] On the facts of the case, the lawyer could not be disqualified because it was not "seeking to take advantage of the appellants by exposing their legal affairs to the public ... or taking a position that attacks, or contradicts in any way, the advice he previously gave".[163] The lawyer had received confidential information from the City; however, none of that information was relevant to the application now being brought by the respondents.

In general the court's concern in the cases with lawyers who seek to act against former clients is to ensure that confidential information received from those clients is not used to those clients' disadvantage. *Brockville* and *Melville* also show that the court is concerned with the duty of loyal advocacy and the risk that lawyers may act in a way that undermines, even if *ex post*, that

---

[158] *Ibid.* at para. 51.
[159] *Ibid.* Although confidential information may have been involved, a similar emphasis was apparent in the judgment of the Ontario Court in *Chiefs of Ontario v. Ontario*, [2003] O.J. No. 580 at para. 146, 63 O.R. (3d) 335 (Ont. S.C.J.), where the Court held, that there
are some things that a law firm cannot do. A law firm cannot act for a client under a million dollar five year confidential retainer as general counsel and then, without explicit consent, attack the client for alleged breach of fiduciary duty, deception, and bribe-taking in respect of closely related matters.
[160] [2007] B.C.J. No. 1750 (B.C.C.A.).
[161] *Ibid.* at para. 17.
[162] *Ibid.* at para. 18.
[163] *Ibid.* at para. 23.

which their representation of the former client was intended to achieve. The duty of loyal advocacy plays an even more significant role with respect to conflicts between current clients, as I will discuss in the following sub-section.

B. Duties to Current Clients

i. *General*

There are three central principles with respect to conflicts between current clients of a lawyer:

1. A lawyer may not simultaneously represent opposing sides to a dispute.[164]
2. A lawyer may not simultaneously represent parties in a single matter, or related matters, where the interests of those parties conflict, or potentially conflict, unless the parties give informed consent to the representation,[165] including consent to the particular requirements of joint representation, and the lawyer determines that the joint representation is in the clients' best interests.[166]
3. Unless all parties give informed consent, a lawyer may not act concurrently for one client in a matter that is directly adverse to the "immediate interests of another current client" even if the matters on which the clients are represented are unrelated.[167]

The nature and extent of each of these duties are discussed separately in the following sub-sections. They are duties that arguably exceed the duties that a lawyer owes to former clients. When representing two or more

---

[164] CBA MC Chapter V, Rule 1; FLS MC Rule 2.04(1); NB CC Chapter 6, Commentary 1(c); Que. CEA Rules 3.06.06 and 3.06.07; LSUC RPC Rule 2.04(2); AB CPC Chapter 6, Rule 1; BC PCH Chapter 6, Rules 1 and 2.

[165] CBA MC Chapter V, Rule 1; FLS MC Rule 2.04(2); NB CC Chapter 6, Commentary 1(b); Que. CEA Rules 3.06.06 and 3.06.07; LSUC RPC Rule 2.04(6); AB CPC Chapter 6, Rule 2; BC PCH Chapter 6, Rule 4.

[166] Only Alberta expressly refers to the "best interests" test. However, other jurisdictions do suggest that a lawyer should not act where it is likely that a dispute will arise, or the interests, rights and obligations of the parties will diverge, or where one party is more vulnerable or less sophisticated than the other, which amounts to the same thing. See FLS MC Rule 2.04(4); Que. CEA Rule 3.06.07(2); LSUC RPC Rule 2.04(8); CBA MC Chapter V, Commentary 6. The Alberta rules direct the lawyer to consider the complexity of the transaction, whether there are terms remaining to be negotiated, the cost and availability of alternative counsel, any particular knowledge of the lawyer, the likelihood of a conflict becoming a dispute, the effect of a dispute on the parties, whether past history makes the lawyer likely to be perceived as favouring one side over the other, and the ability of the clients to provide informed consent to the conflict. AB CPC, Chapter 6, Commentary 2.1.

[167] *R. v. Neil*, [2002] S.C.J. No. 72 at para. 29, [2002] 3 S.C.R. 631, 2002 SCC 70 (S.C.C.); CBA MC Chapter V, Rule 2; (The CBA MC Rule is arguably not consistent with *Neil*, as discussed below). FLS MC Rule 2.04(3); AB CPC Chapter 6, Rule 3(a); BC PCH Rule 6.3 prohibits a lawyer from acting against a current client unless both clients consent, the matters are substantially unrelated and the lawyer has no confidential information that could be used by one client against the other. This Rule predates *Neil*, however, and also may be inconsistent with *Neil*, although in this case by being more restrictive (since it requires both consent *and* that there be no confidential information).

current clients the lawyer retains the same obligations with respect to ensuring protection of confidentiality that underlie the former client conflicts cases; with current clients, however, there is an additional requirement that the lawyer not act for one current client where doing so may undermine the lawyer's loyal pursuit of another client's interests. This is most notably the case with respect to the third principle, dealing with concurrent representation of clients whose interests are directly adverse, which does not require any risk of misuse of confidential information, or that the lawyer be attacking work previously done for the client, for the lawyer to be prohibited from acting. The rule generally prohibits the lawyer from acting in a manner contrary to the legal interests of a current client, unless the client consents.

This means that, in some cases, it may be relevant to consider when identifying the lawyer's duties whether a client is a "current" or "former" client. Most codes of conduct do not address this point directly; however, the Alberta Code provides useful direction in this regard. The Alberta Code suggests that a client is a current client if the lawyer is currently acting for the client, or if there is a reasonable basis for viewing the lawyer as owing an ongoing duty of loyalty to the client. The Code directs the lawyer to assess this question taking into account such factors as the duration of the relationship, the terms of the past retainer or retainers, and the length of time since the last representation was concluded.[168]

ii. Simultaneous Representation of Clients in a Dispute

The rule that lawyers may not simultaneously represent opposing sides to a dispute is relatively straightforward. Lawyers generally only end up off-side this rule where, for some reason, they do not realize that they (or their firms) are acting for parties on opposing sides of a dispute. These circumstances include where law firms merge and different lawyers at the newly merged firm represent adversaries in a dispute;[169] where the law firm acted for an insurance company and did not realize that this made the lawyer effectively counsel for the insured, and the lawyer was now acting against the insured in a related matter;[170] where the dispute arises unexpectedly from a court order

---

[168] AB CPC Chapter 6, Commentary 3.1.
[169] *Saint John Shipbuilding Ltd. v. Bow Valley Husky (Bermuda) Ltd.*, [2002] N.B.J. No. 205, 2002 NBCA 41 (N.B.C.A.); *Skye Properties Ltd. v. Wu*, [2003] O.J. No. 3481, 43 C.P.C. (5th) 18 (Ont. Div. Ct.).
[170] *R. Sherwin Enterprises Ltd. v. Municipal Contracting Services Ltd.*, [1994] O.J. No. 2233, 20 O.R. (3d) 692 (Ont. Gen. Div.). McCarthy Tétrault acted for the respondent on the conflicts matter in litigation commenced by a plaintiff against the respondent and the applicant. The respondent had cross-claimed against the applicant. McCarthy Tétrault had advised the applicant's insurer on whether the insurance would provide coverage to the applicant on the subject matter of the litigation. The insurance company had denied coverage. However, the Court found that that essentially amounted to acting "for" the applicant on the subject matter of the litigation in which it was now acting against the applicant. This case could alternatively be viewed as a former client case.

consolidating two actions;[171] and, most commonly, where the lawyer acts for multiple parties in a corporate action and does not, for whatever reason, realize that the parties are in a dispute, and not merely in a conflict or potential conflict.[172]

The Alberta Code of Conduct provides guidance to lawyers on the difference between a mere conflict and a dispute, which can be referred to when a lawyer represents clients in circumstances that started as a mere conflict, but have deteriorated to the point where the lawyer may be at risk of violating the absolute prohibition on representing both sides to a dispute. The Code suggests that lawyers take into account the

- degree of hostility, aggression and "posturing";
- importance of the matters not yet resolved;
- intransigence of one or more of the parties; and
- whether one or more of the parties wishes the lawyer to assume the role of advocate with respect to that party's position.[173]

The Code concludes by stating, "[w]hen in doubt, a lawyer should cease acting".

iii. *Simultaneous Representation of Clients in a Conflict*

Joint representation in circumstances of an actual or potential conflict between the lawyer's clients is more complicated. As noted above, the basic rule in all of the codes of conduct, and in the case law, is that a lawyer may not act simultaneously for clients in circumstances of an actual or potential conflict unless the clients give informed consent, and the lawyer determines that doing so is in the clients' best interests, taking into account such factors as the likelihood of an actual dispute developing between the parties.[174] Lawyers thus need to be able to (1) identify when jointly represented clients have a conflict or potential conflict; (2) provide those clients with the information necessary to give informed consent to the joint representation, and to ensure that the clients know the special rules that apply to joint representation; (3) make an independent assessment of whether the representation is in the interests of all the clients; (4) manage the situation appropriately if the conflict develops into a dispute; and, (5) be cognizant of the types of joint representation most likely to lead to trouble. This section addresses these responsibilities.

---

[171] *Walker v. Phantom Industries Inc.*, [2006] O.J. No. 4731 (Ont. S.C.J.).
[172] *Kovac v. Opus Building Corp.*, [2010] A.J. No. 228, 2010 ABQB 36 (Alta. Q.B.); *Jellema v. American Bullion Minerals Ltd.*, [2007] B.C.J. No. 1717 (B.C.S.C.); *Jorgensen v. San Jose Mines Ltd.*, [2004] B.C.J. No. 1562, 2004 BCCA 400 (B.C.C.A.).
[173] AB CPC Chapter 6, Commentary 1.1.
[174] CBA MC Chapter V, Rule 1; FLS MC Rule 2.04(2); NB CC Chapter 6, Commentary 1(b); LSUC RPC Rule 2.04(6); AB CPC Chapter 6, Rule 2; BC PCH Chapter 6, Rule 4. See also footnote 166, which discusses the necessity of the lawyer's assessment of the client's interests by the lawyer.

a. When is there a Conflict?

An actual or potential conflict in a joint representation arises where the clients' interests are misaligned such that there is a substantial risk that the lawyer's or law firm's representation of one or both of those clients may be materially and adversely affected. More specifically, as explained in the Alberta Code:

> "Conflict" means the situation existing when the parties in question are *prima facie* differing in interest but there is no dispute among the parties in fact. Examples include vendor and purchaser, mortgagor and mortgagee, insured and insurer, estranged spouses, and lessor and lessee. "Potential conflict" means the situation existing when the parties in question are *prima facie* aligned in interest and there is no dispute among the parties in fact, but the relationship or circumstances are such that there is a possibility of differences developing. Examples are co-plaintiffs; co-defendants; co-insured; shareholders entering into a unanimous shareholder agreement; spouses granting a mortgage to secure a loan; common guarantors; beneficiaries under a will; and a trustee in bankruptcy or court-appointed receiver/manager and the secured creditor who had the trustee or receiver/manager appointed.[175]

In *Booth v. Huxter*,[176] which I discussed earlier with respect to informed consent, the Ontario Divisional Court upheld a decision by the Coroner requiring that police officers and the Police Services Board have separate counsel at an inquiry into a police shooting. The rationale for the decision was that the police officers were denying that systemic issues had contributed to the shooting, but the Police Services Board had a legal duty to deal with systemic issues if they were established. The Court found that it was open for the Coroner to find a potential but disqualifying conflict in these circumstances, since the Police Services Board might want or need to explore issues contrary to the position of the officers in cross-examination or argument.

Conflicts that make joint representation problematic may also arise where the lawyer acts for a single person or entity, but that person occupies multiple roles, and the satisfaction of the duties of one role may conflict with the representation of the interests of the party in its other role. Where, for example, an individual is both the beneficiary and executor of a will, his duties as an executor may conflict with his interests as a beneficiary. In those circumstances a lawyer must treat the representation in the same way that he would if he were acting for two clients, with the additional complication that, in that instance, the lawyer cannot rely on informed consent, since the duties of the client as executor are owed to third parties. In that case, where the conflict is actual, and not merely potential, the lawyer

---

[175] AB CPC Chapter 6, Rule 2, commentary.
[176] [1994] O.J. No. 52, 16 O.R. (3d) 528 (Ont. Div. Ct.).

will need to ensure separate representation for the client in his role as executor and in his role as beneficiary.[177]

b. *Information that must be provided to Parties in a Joint Representation*

When jointly representing parties whose interests conflict, lawyers need to provide those clients with the disclosure sufficient to allow the clients to give informed consent to the conflict — that is, the lawyer must disclose all facts relevant to the client's determination of whether the representation in circumstances of a conflict is desirable.[178] Lawyers have, however, additional disclosure obligations in circumstances of a joint retainer.[179] This includes facts that might be of specific importance to the parties in deciding on the joint retainer, such as whether one of the clients has a long-standing relationship with the lawyer.[180] Also, lawyers must disclose to the clients that no information is confidential as between the clients jointly represented; information disclosed by one client will be disclosed to the other client or clients.[181] They must disclose that if a dispute develops, or joint representation otherwise ceases to be possible, the lawyer may have to withdraw and new counsel obtained by all parties.[182]

---

[177] See, for example, AB CPC Chapter 6, Rule 2, Commentary 2.4.
[178] And, of course, comply with all other rules around informed consent, such as those with respect to independent legal advice and memorializing the consent in writing.
[179] For an example of a disciplinary decision arising out of a lawyer's failure to make proper disclosure in a joint representation see *Law Society of British Columbia v. Hattori*, [2009] L.S.D.D. No. 23.
[180] Most codes expressly require this, and it seems like sound practice in order to prevent later discovery of that fact colouring a client or court's perception of whether the lawyer had properly acted in the best interests of all parties. See CBA MC Chapter V, Commentary 6; FLS MC Rule 2.04(8); NB CC Chapter 67, Commentary 2; LSUC RPC Rule 2.04(7).
[181] CBA MC Chapter V, Commentary 6; FLS MC Rule 2.04(7); NB CC Chapter 6, Commentary 2; LSUC RPC 2.04(6)(b); AB CPC Chapter 6, Rule 2, Commentary 2.2; BC PCH Chapter 6, Rule 4(b). It may also be possible, in some circumstances, for different lawyers within a firm to act for different clients in a single matter, without sharing confidential information, so long as the clients consent and appropriate safeguards are in place to protect confidential information from being disclosed. This is contemplated by FLS MC Rule 2.04(4); AB CPC Chapter 6, Rule 2, Commentary 2.2. This type of representation — concurrent representation in a single matter or related matters — is not permissible if the clients are in an actual dispute, and should only be used if the clients are sophisticated and more or less equals in terms of power within their relationship, if the clients clearly understand the benefits and risks associated with that representation, and the lawyers involved determine that the parties' interests can be properly represented, with neither side being improperly preferred.
[182] A lawyer will have to withdraw unless all parties consent to the lawyer continuing to act for one party. Some jurisdictions suggest that the clients can consent to this prior to the conflict developing; however, I think the Alberta rules correctly suggest that such consent is not valid since it could not have been made with proper information about the changing circumstances. CBA MC Chapter V, Commentary 8; FLS MC Rule 2.04(7); NB CC Chapter 6, Commentary 2; LSUC RPC Rule 2.04(7); AB CPC Chapter 6, Rule 2, Commentary 2.2; BC PCH Chapter 6, Rules 5 and 6.

c. The Best Interests Requirement

If lawyers obtain the client's informed consent to the representation, they must still assess whether the joint representation is in the interests of the parties.[183] Informed consent will not justify acting for clients in circumstances where the clients' interests cannot be properly represented by a single lawyer. The lawyer who represents clients whose interests cannot in fact be jointly represented effectively risks injuring the clients' interests, disqualification, discipline, or civil liability. The lawyer is independently required to determine whether joint representation is possible. In situations where, for example, it is alleged that a corporation, or some of the shareholders, have acted oppressively towards other shareholders, it is not possible for a lawyer to effectively represent both the corporation and one group of shareholders. Joint representation would not permit the lawyer to properly advise the corporation about its duties, particularly relative to those shareholders alleging that oppression has occurred.[184]

Issues preventing effective advocacy for all parties in a conflict situation may also arise where a lawyer seeks to jointly represent co-accused. In *R. v. Silvini*,[185] the lawyer acted for co-accused in a joint proceeding where the defence of one accused required the testimony and cross-examination of the other accused. This required, in turn, that the one accused be able to compel his co-accused, which meant that an application had to be made to sever the proceedings. No lawyer could effectively identify and pursue the interests of each co-accused in the application to sever; the Court thus found that the accused had not received effective assistance of counsel, and awarded him a new trial.[186]

In *Davey v. Woolley, Hames, Dale & Dingwall*,[187] joint representation was problematic because the firm had not received proper consent from the clients. However, in finding the firm civilly liable, the Ontario Court of Appeal also emphasized factors that made it difficult for the firm to effectively represent both parties. Most obviously, a senior member of the law firm had a financial interest in the transaction, which created the possibility and appearance that the law firm would not act resolutely for all parties. Further, although the parties had negotiated the substance of the agreement before retaining counsel, there were still a significant number of issues left to be resolved, and with respect to which legal advice was necessary. The Court noted the various factors identified by the firm as

---

[183] See in general, footnote 166.
[184] *Diamond v. Kaufman*, [1984] O.J. No. 452, 45 C.P.C. 23 (Ont. H.C.J.); *King v. Arnett*, [2006] A.J. No. 1361, 2006 ABQB 639 (Alta. Q.B.); *Kovac v. Opus Building Corp.*, [2010] A.J. No. 622, 2010 ABQB 366 (Alta. Q.B.); *Jellema v. American Bullion Minerals Ltd.*, [2007] B.C.J. No. 1717 (B.C.S.C.); *Alles v. Maurice*, [1992] O.J. No. 331, 5 B.L.R. (2d) 154 (Ont. Gen. Div.).
[185] [1991] O.J. No. 1931, 5 O.R. (3d) 545 (Ont. C.A.).
[186] For a different outcome, see *R. v. Widdifield*, [1995] O.J. No. 2383, 25 O.R. (3d) 161 (Ont. C.A.). Joint representation of criminal accused is possible, provided that they can be effectively represented jointly.
[187] [1982] O.J. No. 3158, 35 O.R. (2d) 599 (Ont. C.A.).

protecting the interests of the various parties, but concluded that the client was nonetheless required to conscientiously determine whether the representation was in the best interests, taking into account current and future circumstances.

d. When a Dispute Arises

Even if joint representation appears possible at the outset, it may cease to be possible during the course of a representation, whether because a dispute has arisen between the parties, or because the circumstances have changed such that effective representation of all sides is no longer possible. In *Verma v. Zimmer*[188] the lawyer discovered that one client was taking a secret profit relative to the other client. The lawyer did not disclose and did not withdraw from representation. The Court held that the lawyer could not continue to act for both parties in those circumstances. The lawyer had a number of choices in how to handle the situation, such as dissuading the client from taking the secret profit, withdrawing from the representation, or disclosing the intention to take the profit (since the information was not confidential between the parties). The one thing the lawyer could not do was continue to act in the interests of one of the parties in preference to those of the other.

In some circumstances, where a dispute has arisen during a joint representation, it can be resolved without the lawyer's involvement. If that is the case, and the parties are sophisticated, it may be possible for the lawyer to let the clients resolve the dispute amongst themselves, and then come back for joint representation when they have done so.[189] The availability of this approach depends on the nature of the dispute, the sophistication of the parties and whether, in fact, effective representation of all parties after the dispute is resolved is possible. If joint representation is not possible because of the dispute then, unless the clients consent to the lawyer continuing to act for one party, the lawyer should withdraw from the matter entirely.

e. High Risk Joint Retainers

The types of conflicts or potential conflicts that cause the most problems for lawyers in joint representation situations arise where lawyers are acting for borrowers and lenders, or for multiple parties in a real estate transaction. Codes of conduct have specific provisions dealing with these situations,[190] and a review of law society disciplinary decisions reveals that by far the

---

[188] [1994] A.J. No. 816, 24 Alta. L.R. (3d) 240 (Alta. C.A.).

[189] Some of the codes of conduct expressly contemplate this possibility. See, for example CB Chapter 5, Commentary 8; NB CC Chapter 6, Commentary 3; LSUC RPC Rule 2.04(9).

[190] Some codes of conduct have extensive specific rules around acting for borrowers and lenders. See, for example, CBA MC Chapter V, Commentary 10 and 11; FLS MC Rules 2.04(12)-(15); Que. CEA Rule 3.06.07(3); NB CC, Schedule B; LSUC RPC Rules 2.04(6.1), (8.1) and (8.2); AB CPC, Chapter 6, Commentary 2.1 and "Memorandum re: Multiple Representation"; BC PCH Chapter 6, Rule 10 and Appendix 3.

most common context for discipline of lawyers who have acted in joint retainers is lending or real estate transactions.[191]

These transactions cause problems for lawyers because the nature of the clients involved makes joint retention of counsel financially attractive — and perhaps essential — and the significant misalignment in interests can make it difficult to represent all parties effectively. In addition, the legal fees associated with these transactions may be low, which does not justify lawyers providing less than competent service, but which can make it more challenging for lawyers to respond appropriately when the file goes sideways. In general, lawyers can materially reduce the risk of civil liability or disciplinary proceedings by avoiding these type of joint retainers or, at minimum, by being cognizant of the risks that go along with undertaking them. Most importantly, lawyers need to be sensitive to the point where a conflict becomes a dispute or where, even if not a dispute, joint representation in the best interests of both parties has become impossible.

In *Barrett v. Reynolds*,[192] for example, a lawyer acted for the vendors, purchasers and bank in a real estate transaction. The bank had approved the purchasers' financing conditional on their sale of their own home. The bank told the vendors that financing had been arranged, and did not disclose the condition. The lawyer also did not disclose the condition to the vendors. The condition was not satisfied, and the deal fell through. The vendors ultimately sued the lawyer, who was held to be liable to the vendors in damages. The lawyer had not satisfied his disclosure obligations in relation to the transaction; in addition, however, he had not recognized that once the condition was imposed there was a conflict between the parties that made it impossible for him to act for all of them effectively.

Ultimately, if a lawyer acts for multiple parties in a joint representation, even with properly informed consent, the lawyer risks civil liability if the lawyer does not act in the best interests of the parties or, particularly, if the lawyer prefers the interests of one party to those of another.[193] Informed consent does not change the fundamental nature of the lawyer's duties to act competently and resolutely in furtherance of the interests of all parties. If the lawyer cannot do so, or ceases to be able to do so, the lawyer should withdraw.

---

[191] See, for example, *Law Society of Upper Canada v. Frolick*, [1998] L.S.D.D. No. 163; *Law Society of Upper Canada v. Ashebee*, [1996] L.S.D.D. No. 197; *Law Society of Upper Canada v. Roine*, [1996] L.S.D.D. No. 95. There are many other cases in the Law Society Disciplinary Digest on QuickLaw that deal with these types of transactions.

[192] [1998] N.S.J. No. 344, 170 N.S.R. (2d) 201 (N.S.C.A.).

[193] See, in addition to the cases already noted, *Waxman v. Waxman*, [2004] O.J. No. 1765, 186 O.A.C. 201 (Ont. C.A.). For a case where the lawyer was not liable, see *Grand Anse Contracting Ltd. v. MacKinnon*, [1993] N.S.J. No. 101, 121 N.S.R. (2d) 423 (N.S.T.D.).

iv. Concurrent Representation of Clients

Simultaneous representation (and compliance with the rules governing simultaneous representation) is required where a lawyer or law firm represents multiple clients on a single or closely related matter.[194] Such representation presupposes some direct connection between those clients — the sharing of confidential information and, usually, some shared instructions from those clients to their jointly retained counsel.

In circumstances of concurrent representation, that direct connection between clients does not exist. A lawyer, or law firm, will represent two clients at the same time, but without those clients dealing directly with each other, or sharing information with each other. The matters may be loosely related or unrelated, but are not the same.[195] An example of a situation of concurrent representation would be where an intellectual property lawyer represents two companies bringing forward independent patent applications for new types of bitumen (oil sands) extraction technology. The lawyer represents both clients concurrently, but those clients otherwise have no connection with each other.

As with simultaneous representation, concurrent representation raises issues of improper conflicts of interest when the interests of the concurrently represented clients conflict or potentially conflict. This is most likely to arise where the matters on which the lawyer or law firm are concurrently representing the clients are related — if, on the above example, the extraction technology developed by the clients was similar, such that success on one of the above patent applications might preclude the acceptance of the other. The ability of one client to achieve its legal goals may rest on the other client failing to achieve its legal goals; in that case the interests of the clients conflict, and it is difficult to see how a lawyer could loyally and confidentially pursue the legal goals of each at the same time.

---

[194] Assuming, of course, that representation is permitted at all. That the matters on which parties are jointly represented are a single matter or closely related matters is largely assumed by the rules, and is implied by the extent to which the rules direct lawyers to represent clients in accordance with joint representation's requirements of sharing information when it is a single matter (see, *e.g.*, CBA MC Chapter V, Commentary 6) and by the definitions of conflict and potential conflict, which only refer to conflicts arising in circumstances of single or closely related matters (see, *e.g.*, AB CPC Chapter 6, Rule 2, commentary). It also follows necessarily from the lawyer's duty of confidentiality. In a single or closely related matter the lawyer will normally have confidential information from one client that relates to the matter on which the lawyer acts for the other client. In order to prevent a breach of duty by the lawyer, that information must be shared between the clients with their mutual consent. As a rule of thumb, if the lawyer has relevant confidential information from one client that is relevant to the circumstances of another, concurrent representation will not be possible. At most a law firm may be able to act concurrently for both clients without sharing confidential information, in accordance with the requirements noted above in footnote 181.

[195] If they are the same then, as noted, the lawyer or law firm can only represent the clients in accordance with the rules governing simultaneous representation.

In its 2002 decision in *R. v. Neil*,[196] the Supreme Court of Canada addressed the question of conflicts of interests in concurrent representation. It held that a lawyer and law firm may not concurrently represent two clients whose interests are directly adverse, even in unrelated matters, unless those clients consent and the concurrent representation is in the clients' best interests:

> The general prohibition [of conflicts of interest] is undoubtedly a major inconvenience to large law partnerships and especially to national firms with their proliferating offices in major centres across Canada. Conflict searches in the firm's records may belatedly turn up files in another office a lawyer may not have been aware of. Indeed, he or she may not even be acquainted with the partner on the other side of the country who is in charge of the file. Conflict search procedures are often inefficient. Nevertheless it is the firm not just the individual lawyer, that owes a fiduciary duty to its clients, and a bright line is required. The bright line is provided by the general rule that a lawyer may not represent one client whose interests are directly adverse to the immediate interests of another current client — *even if the two mandates are unrelated* — unless both clients consent after receiving full disclosure (and preferably independent legal advice), and the lawyer reasonably believes that he or she is able to represent each client without adversely affecting the other.[197]

In articulating this "bright line rule" the Supreme Court in *Neil* did two things of importance. First, it suggested that a conflict of interest could arise even if the matters in which the interests of the clients did not align were unrelated. Second, it suggested that a conflict arises where the interests of one client are "directly adverse to the immediate interests of another current client" without apparently requiring that that adversity in interest create a substantial risk of a material and adverse effect on the lawyer's or law firm's representation of one or both of the clients. Both these aspects of *Neil*, and particularly the second, have been controversial and have caused analytical problems. They are discussed in this section.

In *R. v. Neil* the Ventrakaman firm had acted for Neil in various matters related to his paralegal business. It was also acting for him with respect to criminal charges arising from his conduct of the paralegal business. During the course of the firm's criminal representation of Neil, Lazin, a lawyer at the Ventrakaman firm, was acting on two other matters, one related to the Neil matter and one that was not. In the related matter, Lazin was effectively (although not formally) retained by Neil's assistant, Helen Lambert, in relation to the criminal charges. Lambert's defence was to blame all criminal conduct on Neil. In order to gather information necessary to mount that defence, Lazin attended a meeting between Neil and other members of the Ventrakaman firm. Doing so was an obvious violation of

---

[196] [2002] S.C.J. No. 72, 2002 SCC 70 (S.C.C.).
[197] *R. v. Neil*, [2002] S.C.J. No. 72 at para. 29, 2002 SCC 70 (S.C.C.).

Lazin's ethical duties to Neil as a member of the firm that was representing Neil in the criminal trial; Lazin was deliberately attempting to extract confidential information from Neil to use to Neil's disadvantage in the criminal proceeding.

In the matter not directly related to the firm's representation of Neil, Lazin acted in the divorce proceedings of Darren Doblanko. Doblanko's legal problems arose in part from actions alleged to have been taken by Neil in his paralegal practice. In particular, Neil had filed various documents on behalf of Doblanko's estranged wife that were false. Lazin suggested that Doblanko provide the false documents to the police and, in particular, that he provide the documents to the police officer responsible for the various criminal proceedings being brought against Neil. The Court used the "bright line rule" as the basis for finding that Lazin's actions in the Doblanko matter were improper. Since the representation of Doblanko was unrelated to the representation of Neil, the bright line rule was arguably necessary to explain why the conduct of Lazin was improper.

The problem with this reasoning is that while the Doblanko representation was unrelated to the representation of Neil, the conduct of Lazin that was problematic was not really in respect of the Doblanko representation. Nothing Lazin did to further Doblanko's interests was injurious to Neil, since providing the information to the police officer did not further Doblanko's interests, and was not done in order to further Doblanko's interests. At most it was an incidental effect of the Doblanko retainer.[198] The representation that drove the disclosure was, instead, Lazin's representation of Lambert; it was to benefit Helen Lambert that Lazin disclosed the information in the way that he did. Thus, the conduct of Lazin that was problematic was in relation to a related matter — the Lambert representation — and was also in relation to the very matter on which the firm was representing Neil. The injurious conduct was taking an action based on information obtained during the Doblanko representation in a manner that was injurious to Neil's interests *on the very matter for which the Ventrakaman firm had been retained.*

---

[198] It may have been done by reason of the order of the court — *i.e.*, as a necessary consequence of representing Doblanko at all. In his reasons Binnie emphasizes that once Lazin was representing Doblanko he was inevitably highlighting further instances of Neil's misconduct, which was contrary to Neil's legal interests. Again, however, doing so was not inherently part of the Doblanko retainer, which was directed at regularizing Doblanko's divorce. The point and purpose of that retainer was in no way to impair Neil's legal interests. Further, since Lazin was motivated throughout by advancing Lambert's defence, it is difficult to separate his actions on behalf of Doblanko from his actions on behalf of Lambert, who was the party truly benefiting from the further evidence of Neil's malfeasance. Finally, even if one accepts this point, it does not change the fact that the legal interests affected were the ones Ventrakaman was supposed to protect, not Neil's legal interests writ large, yet the bright line rule is said to prevent any representation which injures the client's interests, seemingly whether or not they were the interests the firm was committed to represent. That broad formulation is not required by the facts of *Neil*.

On the facts of *Neil*, therefore, it is hard to see the bright line rule, in its broad formulation, as essential to the decision. The problem was not that Lazin sought to further Doblanko's interests; the problem was that he used that retainer as an opportunity to injure the specific legal interests the firm was committed to represent.

As a consequence, it is not clear what exactly the bright line prohibits. Does it simply prohibit the type of conduct engaged in by Lazin, in which his retainer in an unrelated matter led him to take steps that materially and adversely affected the Ventrakaman firm's representation of Neil? Or would it be sufficient to demonstrate that, in some way or another, the representation of one client was adverse to the interests of another client, as the bright line rule on its face suggests? Would it, for example, prohibit a law firm from acting for Big Co. in a corporate transaction to take over Small Co. while another lawyer at the law firm was acting for Small Co. to defend a wrongful dismissal case? Further, what type of interests does the bright line rule protect? Is it only the legal interests of the client, or are other interests — such as economic interests — also protected? The facts of *Neil*, and the test it articulated, do not provide a coherent way to answer that question.

In 2007 the Supreme Court had the opportunity to revisit these questions in its decision in *Strother v. 3464920 Canada Inc.*[199] The main issue in *Strother* was Strother's breach of his fiduciary duties to one client as a result of his personal financial interest in another client. The Court also considered, however, the separate question of whether it violated the bright line rule for a lawyer — Strother — to provide tax advice that would give one client an economic advantage over another client to whom he had also provided tax advice. The Court held that the bright line rule in *Neil* does not prohibit a law firm from acting for one client where doing so will create a non-legal disadvantage for another client. Binnie J. for the majority stated that:

> the conflict of interest principles do not generally preclude a law firm or lawyer from acting concurrently for different clients who are in the same line of business, or who compete with each other for business. There was no *legal* dispute between Monarch and Sentinel ...
>
> The clients' respective "interests" that require the protection of the duty of loyalty have to do with the practice of law, not commercial prosperity. Here the alleged "adversity" between concurrent clients relates to business matters.[200]

Binnie J. did suggest that, in some circumstances, commercial matters between clients could be relevant; the focus is on whether there is a "real risk of impairment"[201] to the ability of the lawyer to represent the client's interests.

---

[199] [2007] S.C.J. No. 24, 2007 SCC 24 (S.C.C.).
[200] *Ibid.* at paras. 54-55 [emphasis in original].
[201] *Ibid.* at para. 55.

Again, though, while the bright line rule is not *obiter* to the Court's decision in *Strother* — since the Court applied the rule directly in reaching its decision — the judgment does not give much in the way of guidance about how far the rule reaches, or as to what exactly it prohibits. It does indicate that mere economic conflicts are insufficient; however, it does not make it clear whether in a case such as the Big Co./Small Co. example, in which a law firm wants to represent Big Co. in taking over Small Co., and to represent Small Co. in defending a wrongful dismissal case, the law firm should be prohibited from the representation. On its face the bright line rule cuts a wide swathe through concurrent representation of clients in unrelated matters unless the clients consent; however, the Supreme Court cases themselves give little guidance as to what limits or contours might, in closer cases, be part of the bright line rule.

Most codes of conduct that have incorporated the bright line rule have done so on its own terms, simply referencing the Supreme Court's language.[202] The new CBA model rules do not do so, however, instead suggesting that a bright line rule conflict should only be disqualifying where it is demonstrated that there is a substantial risk that the lawyer's representation of the clients will be materially and adversely affected.[203] The justification for the CBA's new rule is, in essence, that the bright line test as written has never been applied by the Supreme Court; the bright line test is not in the best interests of the public or of the profession; and, the reference in *Neil* to the substantial risk test justifies interpreting the bright line rule in light of that articulation of what it is that makes a conflict of interest disqualifying. Further, the CBA can rely on the comments made by Binnie J. in *Strother* to the effect that the significant question is whether the lawyer's representation of the clients will be adversely affected.

It is clearly the case that where the representation of clients in unrelated matters creates a substantial risk that the representation of one or the other will be materially and adversely affected, the lawyer is in a conflict position, and must obtain consent from the clients before continuing to act. On its face, though, the bright line rule seems to preclude the necessity of inquiring into whether a substantial risk of a material and adverse effect is present. The rule may be directed at identifying when a substantial risk is present; however, that does not necessarily mean that, within the rule, there is a secondary requirement that the complaining client also demonstrate a substantial risk. If that requirement existed, then the bright line rule would not be necessary; the question would be, simply, whether a substantial risk existed. The bright line rule seems designed, in part, to eliminate the need for case by case inquiries into whether there is a substantial risk of

---

[202] FLS MC Rule 2.04(3); AB CPC Chapter 6, Rule 3(a); BC PCH Chapter 6, Rule 6.3. A number of jurisdictions, including Ontario and New Brunswick, have not dealt with the bright line rule.
[203] CBA MC Chapter V, Rule 2.

impairment to the lawyer-client relationship. Indeed, in his judgment in *Strother* Binnie J. made a similar point, stating that

> [t]his is not to say that in *Neil* the Court advocated the resolution of conflict issues on a case-by-case basis through a general balancing of interests, the outcome of which would be difficult to predict in advance ... The "bright line" rule is the product of the balancing of interests not the gateway to further internal balancing.[204]

Cases applying the bright line rule subsequent to *Neil* do not entirely resolve this question. They do, though, suggest a few points of note. First, it is clear that in some cases the courts have been willing to simply apply the bright line rule from *Neil* to disqualify counsel, even though it is not demonstrated that there is a substantial risk that the representation of the clients will be materially and adversely affected.

In *Lotech Medical Systems Ltd. v. Kinetic Concept Inc.*[205] a law firm was prohibited from acting in litigation on intellectual property matters against a client for whom it had acted on unrelated patent matters. The firm was disqualified even though it was agreed that the case "[did] not involve or raise any concern regarding the possession or use of confidential information",[206] it seems likely that the firm's conduct of the unrelated patent matters was unaffected, and the client against whom the law firm was acting retained many law firms in the Ottawa area, and could have transferred its unrelated work to one of those firms.

In *De Beers Canada Inc. v. Shore Gold Inc.*,[207] a law firm was disqualified for acting for De Beers in an action against Cameco alleging that Cameco had violated its joint venture agreement with De Beers. The basis for the disqualification was that the law firm was concurrently acting for Cameco in defending ongoing wrongful death actions. The two matters were wholly unrelated, but the law firm was nonetheless disqualified: "While their mandates are unrelated, the interests of De Beers are directly adverse to the interests of Cameco as those words are used in the 'bright line' rule."[208]

In *Toddglen Construction Ltd. v. Concord Adex Developments Corp.*[209] a law firm was disqualified in acting for Concord in defending litigation brought by Toddglen when the firm had performed corporate work for Toddglen. The firm was disqualified even though the corporate work for Toddglen "generated only a few thousand dollars per year in legal fees".[210]

In both *De Beers* and *Toddglen* the courts seemed particularly troubled by the fact that the law firm appeared willing to cast aside the current client

---

[204] *Strother v. 3464920 Canada Inc.*, [2007] S.C.J. No. 24 at para. 51, 2007 SCC 24 (S.C.C.).
[205] [2008] F.C.J. No. 1595, 2008 FC 1195 (F.C.T.D.).
[206] *Ibid.* at para. 28.
[207] [2006] S.J. No. 210, 2006 SKQB 101 (Sask. Q.B.).
[208] *Ibid.* at para. 15.
[209] [2004] O.J. No. 1788 (Ont. S.C.J.).
[210] *Ibid.* at para. 25.

in order to pursue more lucrative work that was contrary to that client's interests.[211]

Second, though, the case law also indicates that the courts have a clear sense of the equities of the situation, and are not blindly following the bright line rule to disqualify all law firms who are technically off side its requirements. Where law firms are disqualified there is often some reason beyond the bright line test to justify the disqualification[212] and, in a few cases the courts have resisted applications for removal where removal seems unnecessary in light of the totality of the circumstances.[213] Those cases do not disavow the bright line rule, and often invoke it, but they suggest some hesitation in the courts about removing counsel where doing so seems inequitable.

In one case in which a lawyer was disqualified, the court actually relied upon the CBA's test in applying the bright line rule. In *Wallace v. Canadian Pacific Railway*[214] the law firm was disqualified in acting in a class action against Canadian Pacific when it had acted extensively for the company, acting on at least six matters, billing some $70,000 and having three open files. The matters were unrelated. In disqualifying the law firm the judge said that the *Neil* test prohibited a lawyer from acting unless the lawyer could demonstrate that there was "no substantial risk that the lawyer's representation of the current client would be materially and adversely affected by the new unrelated matter".[215] On the facts the Court held that the law firm had not discharged that burden:

> the McKercher Firm's decision to act against CN in a $1.75 billion lawsuit that claims aggravated and punitive damages, while still representing CN, understandably led to a sense of betrayal which damaged the solicitor-client relationship such that the McKercher Firm's ability to represent CN effectively was substantially and irrevocably impaired.[216]

It should be noted that as applied by the Saskatchewan Court of Queen's Bench the substantial risk test does not seem to qualify the bright line rule significantly. The impairment of representation rests only on the client's sense of betrayal arising from the lawyer's violation of the bright line rule; in any case where the bright line rule has been violated that sense of betrayal

---

[211] See also *Terracap Investments Inc. v. 2811 Development Corp.*, [2010] O.J. No. 798, 2010 ONSC 1183 (Ont. S.C.J.).

[212] See, for example, *Cewe Estate v. Mide Wilson*, [2009] B.C.J. No. 1445, 2009 BCSC 975 (B.C.S.C.) (law firm disqualified but matters not wholly unrelated); *GMP Securities Ltd. v. Stikeman Elliott*, [2004] O.J. No. 3276 (Ont. S.C.J.) (law firm disqualified but matters not wholly unrelated); *First Property Holdings Inc. v. Beatty*, [2003] O.J. No. 2943, 66 O.R. (3d) 97 (Ont. S.C.J.) (law firm disqualified but matters not wholly unrelated).

[213] See, for example, *Ribeiro v. Vancouver (City)*, [2002] B.C.J. No. 2843, 2002 BCCA 678 (B.C.C.A.) (lawyers not disqualified because doing so would be manifestly unjust even if a bright line conflict might exist).

[214] [2009] S.J. No. 549, 2009 SKQB 369 (Sask. Q.B.) (under appeal).

[215] *Ibid.* at para. 31.

[216] *Ibid.* at para. 48.

is likely to arise. The judgment seems to undermine completely the narrowing of the bright line rule that the CBA was trying to achieve.

Overall, the case law post-*Neil* suggests that lawyers and law firms risk disqualification or other negative consequences if they fail to obtain client consent to act in the circumstances of bright line rule violations; that is, they are at risk even if the adverse legal effect of a client's case is not on the lawyer or law firm's own representation of another client. The cases also suggest, though, that this area of law will continue to evolve, and that courts will not apply the bright line test rigidly and unthinkingly. Over time the emphasis is likely, as the CBA has suggested, to be on the effect of the violation of the rule on a firms' ability to represent both clients effectively. That effect will simply be relatively easy to demonstrate once a bright line rule violation has occurred.

C. Lawyer-Client Conflicts

The principles used to identify conflicts of interest may be most straightforward when applied to the relationship between the lawyer and the client. There are no mediating bright line rules to consider, screening devices to implement, or the shifting circumstances that can arise where the lawyer navigates conflicts between clients. If the circumstances of the lawyer-client relationship are such that there is a substantial risk that the lawyer's representation will be materially and adversely affected, that the lawyer may misuse confidential information, or that the lawyer will take improper advantage of the client, then the lawyer may not act, and will be liable to the client (and subject to discipline at the law society) if he has acted in those circumstances, unless the client has given informed consent to the representation. As stated by the Québec *Code of ethics of advocates*, an advocate "shall subordinate to the interests of the client his personal interests".[217]

Thus, in *Strother v. 3464920 Canada Inc.*,[218] Strother was held liable because he had taken a financial interest in one client that resulted in him failing to fulfill his legal duties to another client. Strother's representation of one client was materially and adversely affected because of his financial interest in the other client.

In *Law Society of Upper Canada v. Barnett*,[219] a lawyer was suspended for one month because, amongst other things, he entered into an agreement with a credit card company whereby the company would finance clients using the lawyer and his firm. That was not in and of itself a problem; however, as part of his agreement with the credit card company Barnett agreed to notify the company if anything said by the client raised the risk of

---

[217] R.R.Q. 1981, c. B-1, r.1, Rule 3.06.05.01.
[218] [2007] S.C.J. No. 24, 2007 SCC 24 (S.C.C.).
[219] [1997] L.S.D.D. No. 94.

non-payment. This created a risk of improper disclosure of confidential information.[220]

In *Moffat v. Wetstein*[221] the Court held that a lawyer could not act in litigation against an accounting firm alleging wrongdoing, because the lawyer had been a partner at the accounting firm for at least part of the time covered by the allegations. Although the lawyer was not alleged to have been involved in the wrongdoing, he would be financially affected if a judgment were made against the firm. That was sufficient to preclude his acting against the firm.[222]

In *Stewart v. Canadian Broadcasting Corp.*,[223] noted earlier as an example of an improper advantage being taken by the lawyer, Edward Greenspan was found to have violated his fiduciary duties to his client when he participated in a television program about the client's case, the program made factual errors in respect to the former client, the purpose of participating in the program was to further the lawyer's own interests, and doing so was directly contrary to the legal benefits he had previously sought for the client. In particular, the television broadcast increased the public opprobrium towards Stewart that Greenspan had previously worked to ameliorate. Greenspan "favoured his financial interests over the plaintiff's interests ... put his own self promotion before the plaintiff's interests ... and undercut the benefits and protections he had provided as counsel, and therefore, increased the adverse public effect on the plaintiff of his crime, trial and sentencing".[224]

Perhaps the most egregious examples of conflicts that may have affected — or been perceived to affect — a lawyer's representation of a client, arose in the cases of *Law Society of Upper Canada v. Daboll*[225] and *Law Society of Alberta v. Abbi*.[226] In both cases lawyers were acting for husbands in matrimonial cases, and began intimate relationships with the wife on the other side of the dispute. In *Abbi* the relationship turned intimate

---

[220] In *Law Society of Alberta v. Clark*, [1998] L.S.D.D. No. 152, a lawyer was disciplined in part for improperly disclosing information about a client to the client's trustee in bankruptcy in order to improve the lawyer's chance of recovering the legal fees owed by the client. Lawyers have also been disciplined for suing clients for non payment of fees, or placing a lien on the client's home, while ostensibly still representing the client: *Boyd v. Boyd*, [2008] O.J. No. 180, 54 R.F.L. (6th) 460 (Ont. S.C.J.) and *Law Society of Upper Canada v. Logan*, [2005] L.S.D.D. No. 39.

[221] [1996] O.J. No. 1966, 29 O.R. (3d) 371 (Ont. Gen. Div.).

[222] In *Moffat v. Wetstein*, the application to disqualify was brought against a law firm that the lawyer was no longer working at. It was not successful, but the Court made it clear that the lawyer himself would be disqualified from acting, and the firm would be if he still worked there. See also *Law Society of BC v. Trower* [1999] L.S.D.D. No. 55, where a lawyer was held to be in a conflict with a client where the lawyer was in a financial dispute with another lawyer about which of them was entitled to fees owed by the client. The financial dispute meant that the lawyer did not properly advise the client about whether the fees claimed were reasonable.

[223] [1997] O.J. No. 2271 (Ont. Gen. Div.).

[224] *Ibid.* at para. 320.

[225] [2006] L.S.D.D. No. 82.

[226] [1995] L.S.D.D. No. 291.

after the representation was concluded; however, in *Daboll* the relationship began while the representation of the husband was ongoing. The lawyer did not withdraw and, at one point, gave advice to the wife with respect to her dealings with her husband. Perhaps unsurprisingly, the lawyer in *Daboll* acknowledged that he had been in a conflict position. The disciplinary panel described the conflict as "patent, blatant and self-evident".[227]

The Supreme Court has, though, made it clear that where the conflict between a lawyer and client is truly unrelated to a retainer, it will not constitute an improper conflict of interest. In the rather odd case of *Galambos v. Perez*,[228] Perez was an employee of a law firm. She made unsolicited cash advances to the law firm amounting to $200,000. The law firm then declared bankruptcy, and Perez became an unsecured creditor to the law firm. She sued the law firm, relying in part on the fact that the firm had done legal work for her and that, as a result, they were in a conflict position relative to the cash advances she had provided. The Supreme Court disagreed. The matters on which the firm had represented Perez were minor, and had no relationship to the cash advances provided. There was neither an actual conflict nor a reasonable apprehension of a conflict in the circumstances.

The most common circumstances of improper conflicts of interest between lawyers and clients arise when lawyers have either sexual relations or business dealings with their clients. Such interactions are fraught with difficulty and risk, to both the client and the lawyer, and are addressed independently in the codes of conduct.

The codes of conduct often have extensive — and sometimes highly complicated — rules relating to business dealings with clients.[229] The essence of those rules is, however, relatively straightforward: unless the lawyer can show that a business relationship was advantageous to the client, that the client clearly understood the conflict and consented to it, and that the client had independent legal advice, the lawyer has a major problem and is at significant risk of civil liability and profession discipline.

These principles were established by the Supreme Court in its early judgment in *Biggs v. London Loan and Savings Co. of Canada*.[230] In that case the lawyer had extracted a commission when he acted for both the mortgagor and mortgagee in a loan transaction. The transaction was described by the Court as "highly improvident and one which was fraught with disaster to both Biggs and the Loan Company, and advantageous only to himself".[231] The Court held that where a lawyer and client enter into a business transaction, the onus is on the lawyer to demonstrate that the

---

[227] *Law Society of Upper Canada v. Daboll*, [2006] L.S.D.D. No. 82 at para. 12.
[228] [2009] S.C.J. No. 48, [2009] 3 S.C.R. 247 (S.C.C.).
[229] See for example, CBA MC Chapter VI; FLS MC Rules 2.04(29)-(39); LSUC RPC Rule 2.06; AB CPC Chapter 6, Rule 9 and commentary.
[230] [1933] S.C.J. No. 17, [1933] S.C.R. 257 (S.C.C.).
[231] *Ibid.* at 266.

transaction was "fair and just and in no way disadvantageous"[232] for the client. Moreover, the lawyer must show that he behaved with the "utmost frankness and good faith"[233] and that he made full disclosure of "all material facts within his knowledge in relation to the transaction".[234] Where a lawyer cannot satisfy these requirements he will be liable to the client for the losses the client suffers.

A more recent disciplinary decision, *Law Society of Upper Canada v. Novak*[235] reinforces this perception. In that case the lawyer sold the client an interest in a company. The sale involved the client purchasing a 1.3% interest in a four-day-old company for $50,000; the company was subsequently worthless. The Law Society found that this was conduct worthy of sanction, mostly because the transaction was so disadvantageous to the client. In addition, the lawyer did not ensure that the client received independent legal advice.[236]

When entering into a business relationship with a client, it is prudent for the lawyer to ensure that the client not only has independent legal advice, but is also independently represented with respect to that transaction. When a client receives independent legal advice the client is simply advised on the desirability of having the lawyer act in the transaction; with independent legal representation the client is independently represented in the transaction itself. While having the lawyer act on the transaction may save on legal costs in the short run, it makes it less obvious that the client's interests are being represented, and also makes it more difficult for the lawyer to ensure that the transaction is appropriate for both parties.

With sexual relationships, the codes of conduct provide less direction. Such relations are not prohibited outright in any jurisdiction; however, it is clear from the disciplinary decisions that any sexual relationship that involves taking advantage of a vulnerable client is prohibited, and may not be cured even by the lawyer finding new counsel for the client.[237] This approach is appropriate. While no problem may arise when a lawyer at a large firm has a sexual relationship with the in-house counsel of a corporate client, a lawyer who has a sexual relationship with a client in a matrimonial or criminal law matter can rightly be seen as taking advantage of a client who is not only vulnerable in general, but even more vulnerable in relation

---

[232] *Ibid.* at 261.
[233] *Ibid.*
[234] *Ibid.*
[235] [1999] L.S.D.D. No. 88.
[236] See also: *Law Society of Upper Canada v. Roine*, [1996] L.S.D.D. No. 95; *Nova Scotia Barristers' Society v. Langille*, [2002] L.S.D.D. No. 8; *Law Society of Upper Canada v. Logan*, [2005] L.S.D.D. No. 39; *Law Society of Upper Canada v. Van Duffelen*, [2005] L.S.D.D. No. 78.
[237] *Szarfer v. Chodos*, [1986] O.J. No. 256, 54 O.R. (2d) 663 (Ont. H.C.J.); *Law Society of Upper Canada v. Hunter*, [2007] L.S.D.D. No. 8; *Regular v. Law Society of Newfoundland and Labrador*, [2010] N.J. No. 165, 2010 NLTD 90 (N.L.T.D.); *Law Society of Upper Canada v. Joseph*, [2003] L.S.D.D. No. 34; *Adams v. Law Society of Alberta*, [2000] A.J. No. 1031, 2000 ABCA 240 (Alta. C.A.).

to the person whom she has entrusted with helping her navigate the complex legal difficulties in which she has found herself. Further, as the Law Society of Upper Canada noted in its decision in *Law Society of Upper Canada v. Hunter*,[238] a client who has started sleeping with her lawyer may not ask difficult questions that she should be asking, and may have a more difficult time determining whether the legal services she is receiving, or has received, were appropriate.

A lawyer may act for an individual with whom she has a pre-existing sexual relationship — a husband can act for his wife, for example. In that instance the determination that the lawyer must make is whether the personal relationship is such that it might impair his objectivity. As noted by the Alberta Code of Conduct, circumstances that can lead the lawyer to favour the interests of the client unduly may impair the ability of the lawyer to provide proper advice just as much as do circumstances that lead the lawyer to undervalue those interests.[239]

8. CONCLUSION

An academic article once claimed that lawyers' ethics are similar to the ethics one learns in kindergarten.[240] Even a cursory review of the law governing conflicts of interest demonstrates the problems with this description. In order to avoid improper conflicts of interest lawyers need to be aware of the obligations that arise when acting against former clients, when acting simultaneously for multiple clients in a single matter or related matters, when acting concurrently for clients whose legal interests are directly adverse, or when in a situation where the lawyer's and client's interests conflict. Lawyers need to be vigilant to ensure that improper conflicts have been identified, that the necessary disclosure has been made and consent obtained, and that they remain alert to shifts in their obligations as the circumstances of the clients change.

This is not to suggest that the law of conflicts is unduly complex or opaque, but simply that it is complicated, and important, and lawyers need to ensure a proper understanding of it to represent their clients, and manage their practices, effectively.

---

[238] *Ibid.*
[239] AB CPC Chapter 6, Rule 8 and commentary.
[240] Susan N. Turner, "Raising the Bar: Maximizing Civility in Alberta Courtrooms" (2003) 41 Alta. L. Rev. 547 at 557.

Chapter 9

LAWYERS' ETHICS IN THE CONTEXT OF CRIMINAL LAW

1. INTRODUCTION

Lawyers working in criminal cases have generally the same ethical obligations as other lawyers. They must, for example, provide competent representation to clients, maintain confidences, and avoid improper conflicts of interest. At the same time, criminal law practice raises some distinct ethical issues, and presents some distinct ethical challenges.

Most significantly, criminal prosecutors have different ethical obligations than other lawyers. This is true generally, insofar as criminal prosecutors are required to be "ministers of justice"[1] rather than simply advocating for conviction. It is also true specifically given criminal prosecutors' unique responsibilities in relation to prosecutorial discretion and to disclosure, responsibilities that prosecutors must discharge ethically. Criminal defence lawyers have the same ethical obligations as other lawyers; however, being a criminal defence lawyer presents some unique challenges for ethical conduct.

This chapter considers ethical issues specific to criminal law practice.[2] It will begin with prosecutorial ethics: the Crown prosecutors' role as "minister of justice", prosecutorial discretion, and Crown disclosure. It will then consider some issues specific to criminal defence practice: defending the guilty client and plea bargaining.

2. PROSECUTORIAL ETHICS

A. Minister of Justice or Zealous Advocate?

The lawyer's role requires pursuing the interests of the client within the bounds of legality. With private sector clients, this usually means attempting to achieve a positive outcome — a "victory" — exemplified by triumph in court, success in negotiations, or the identification of solutions to a client's legal problem. In private sector representation, victory for the client often

---

[1] *R. v. Puddick* (1865), 175 E.R. 662; *R. v. Regan*, [2002] S.C.J. No. 14 at para. 137, [2002] 1 S.C.R. 297, 2002 SCC 12 (S.C.C.), *per* Binnie J. (dissenting, but not on this point).
[2] I am indebted to the exceptional work of Michel Proulx and David Layton in this area: *Ethics and Canadian Criminal Law* (Toronto: Irwin Law, 2001). I would also refer readers to the discussion in Chapter 6 of the Perjury Trilemma, and the ethical issues related to the presentation of perjured testimony by the lawyer's own client in a criminal trial. The discussion here of representing clients who have admitted guilt, and presenting a plea for a client who maintains innocence, are closely related to the perjury trilemma.

necessitates defeat for someone else. For the criminal prosecutor, however, the situation is quite different. The interests of the client do not orientate towards victory in that sense; the client — the Crown — wants justice to be done, even if that requires "failing" to achieve the conviction of a person accused of a crime.

This is, arguably, not a difference in the lawyer's ethical role, but simply a difference in the interests of the client that determine how that role is fulfilled. The courts and ethical rules do, however, articulate the difference in the aims of the Crown as one which shifts the nature of the lawyer's role. A crown prosecutor is not simply an advocate, she is both advocate and "minister of justice".[3] As famously stated by Justice Rand when explaining the impropriety of an inflammatory jury address by a Crown:

> It cannot be over-emphasized that the purpose of a criminal prosecution is not to obtain a conviction, it is to lay before a jury what the Crown considers to be credible evidence relevant to what is alleged to be a crime. Counsel have a duty to see that all available legal proof of the facts is presented: it should be done firmly and pressed to its legitimate strength but it must also be done fairly. The role of prosecutor excludes any notion of winning or losing; his function is a matter of public duty than which in civil life there can be none charged with greater personal responsibility. It is to be efficiently performed with an ingrained sense of the dignity, the seriousness and the justness of judicial proceedings.[4]

Courts have subsequently noted the importance of Crown counsel being "of absolute integrity"[5] and fulfilling their "duty to be fair".[6] The *Federal Prosecution Service Deskbook*[7] directs Crown prosecutors to conduct themselves with "fairness, moderation and dignity" and to ensure that litigation does "not become a personal contest of skill or professional pre-eminence".[8] Law society codes of conduct define the prosecutorial function as requiring that a Crown prosecutor act "not to seek a conviction, but to present before the trial court all available credible evidence relevant to the alleged crime in order that justice may be done through a fair trial on the merits."[9]

What follows from this? Does the judicial and regulatory invocation of justice, fairness, dignity and moderation, and the exclusion of adversarial

---

[3] *R. v. Puddick* (1865), 175 E.R. 662; *R. v. Regan*, [2002] S.C.J. No. 14 at para. 137, [2002] 1 S.C.R. 297, 2002 SCC 12 (S.C.C.), *per* Binnie J. (dissenting, but not on this point).
[4] *R. v. Boucher*, [1954] S.C.J. No. 54, [1955] S.C.R. 16, 110 C.C.C. 263 at 270 (S.C.C.).
[5] *R. v. Logiacco*, [1984] O.J. No. 15, 11 C.C.C. (3d) 374 at 379 (Ont. C.A.).
[6] *Cunliffe v. Law Society of British Columbia*, [1984] B.C.J. No. 1514 at para. 41, 13 C.C.C. (3d) 560 (B.C.C.A.).
[7] Department of Justice Canada, *The Federal Prosecution Service Deskbook* (Ottawa: Department of Justice, 2000).
[8] *Ibid.*, s. 9.3.
[9] CBC MC Chapter 9, Commentary 9. See also FLS MC Rule 4.01(3) and commentary; NB CC Chapter 8, Commentary 13(a)(ii) and (iii); LSUC RPC Rule 4.01(3) and commentary; AB CPC Chapter 10, Rule 28(a) and (b); BC PCH Chapter 8, Rule 18 and Canon 1(2).

contest in respect to the role of the Crown prosecutor, have any practical meaning, or is it simply a form of rhetorical aspiration?

The specific requirements and decisions of the law governing Crown prosecutors demonstrate that this shift in obligation is more than mere rhetoric. Most significantly, while permitting a Crown prosecutor to "vigorously pursue a legitimate result to the best of its ability",[10] the case law clearly requires Crown prosecutors to exercise only "controlled zeal"[11] in representation. Crown cross-examination of witnesses, introduction of evidence, presentation of argument, and general trial conduct, must be consistent with ensuring a fair trial for the accused. Where prosecutors exceed the bounds of controlled zeal at trial, and the trial judge does not control their conduct, appellate courts take exception. In particular, appellate courts have ordered new trials where Crown counsel were sarcastic, demeaning, irrelevant or belligerent in cross-examination;[12] attempted to introduce inadmissible evidence when examining a witness;[13] queried an accused about the credibility of another witness;[14] had discussions with their own witness between cross and re-examination;[15] suggested a nefarious aspect to an accused's exercise of his right to silence;[16] expressed a personal opinion on the guilt of the accused;[17] asserted that the process of criminal justice

---

[10] *R. v. Cook*, [1997] S.C.J. No. 22 at para. 21, [1997] 1 S.C.R. 1113 (S.C.C.).
[11] Proulx & Layton, *Ethics and Canadian Criminal Law* (Toronto: Irwin Law, 2001) at 647.
[12] *R. v. Logiacco*, [1984] O.J. No. 15, 11 C.C.C. (3d) 374 (Ont. C.A.); *R. v. Riche*, [1996] N.J. No. 293 (Nfld. C.A.); *R. v. Rose*, [2001] O.J. No. 1150, 153 C.C.C. (3d) 225 (Ont. C.A.); *R. v. R.R.*, [2007] O.J. No. 1121 (Ont. S.C.J.) (cross-examination not found to be improper because impropriety could not be derived from the transcript on its own); *R. v. Wojcik*, [2002] M.J. No. 243, 2002 MBCA 82 (Man. C.A.); *R. v. Robinson*, [2001] O.J. No. 1072 at para. 35, 153 C.C.C. (3d) 398 (Ont. C.A.) (the cross-examination had many "questions ... laced with sarcasm and framed in a manner that made it apparent that Crown counsel personally held the appellant in utter contempt ... [and] an attempt at character assassination"). Robinson subsequently committed an extremely violent sexual assault for which he was convicted: *R. v. Robinson*, [2006] O.J. No. 3882, 212 C.C.C. (3d) 439 (Ont. C.A.)).
[13] *R. v. Hillier*, [1994] N.J. No. 51, 115 Nfld. & P.E.I.R. 27 (Nfld. C.A.) (Crown asked accused "Where's your brother spending time these days?" in order to bring out the fact that the accused's brother had been convicted with perjury in the same matter on which accused was being tried for perjury).
[14] *R. v. Bear*, [2008] S.J. No. 815 at para. 24, 2008 SKCA 172 (Sask. C.A.) ("Requiring an accused to explain inconsistencies between his testimony and that of a Crown witness is said to offend the presumption of innocence. It also unfairly requires the accused to argue his case in the context of his testimony"); *R. v. Ellard*, [2003] B.C.J. No. 231, 2003 BCCA 68 (B.C.C.A.); *R. v. Wojcik*, [2002] M.J. No. 243, 2002 MBCA 82 (Man. C.A.).
[15] *R. v. Peruta*, [1992] J.Q. no 1886, 78 C.C.C. (3d) 350 (Que. C.A.). Note that this can be acceptable in some contexts: *R. v. Lawlor*, [1999] N.J. No. 83 (Nfld. T.D.).
[16] *R. v. Wojcik*, [2002] M.J. No. 243 at para. 17, 2002 MBCA 82 (Man. C.A.).
[17] *R. v. Peruta*, [1992] J.Q. no 1886, 78 C.C.C. (3d) 350 (Que. C.A.).

means that only a guilty person would be brought to trial;[18] or asked leading questions of their own witnesses.[19]

The *Federal Prosecution Service Deskbook* similarly directs Crown counsel specifically not to express "personal opinions on the guilt or innocence of the accused",[20] to restrict cross-examination to "relevant and proper questions"[21] and to avoid "inflammatory remarks".[22]

As noted, Crown prosecutors may still engage in vigorous advocacy. While maintaining judicial authority over the trial process,[23] and the right to check prosecutorial conduct that constitutes an abuse of process,[24] courts will not interfere with prosecutorial decisions that can be understood as a matter of ordinary trial tactics. Prosecutors may, for example, decide which witnesses to call,[25] and which jurors to select,[26] without judicial interference.

The unique prosecutorial role also requires that Crown counsel remain open to the possibility that they may be wrong, that the defence may have a point, and be prepared to act on that information even if doing so precludes the obtaining of a conviction. The *Federal Prosecution Service Deskbook* requires that Crown counsel remain "open to alternative theories put forward by the defence" and zealously guard "against the possibility of being afflicted by 'tunnel vision'".[27] Cases in which the Crown has succumbed to tunnel vision have led to wrongful convictions, most notably in the case of Guy Paul Morin, discussed in Chapter 3.[28]

The decision of the Nova Scotia Court of Appeal in *R. v. Aldhelm-White*[29] provides an example of a Crown prosecutor acting consistently with this understanding of the prosecutorial role. In *Aldhelm-White* the RCMP discovered that one of their own was involved in criminal activities related

---

[18] *R. v. Boucher*, [1954] S.C.J. No. 54, [1955] S.C.R. 16 (S.C.C.); *R. v. Hillier*, [1994] N.J. No. 51, 115 Nfld. & P.E.I.R. 27 (Nfld. C.A.) (Crown noted in argument that the police officer testifying against the accused had been on the force "12 years", been promoted and had "no identifiable reason to come in here and give false evidence".).

[19] *R. v. Rose*, [2001] O.J. No. 1150 at para. 11, 153 C.C.C. (3d) 225 (Ont. C.A.) (In a remarkable exchange, when the defence objected to the leading questions, the Crown responded that he was not asking leading questions, he was simply putting facts before the witness for the witness to confirm or deny.); *R. v. Paquette*, [2008] A.J. No. 133, 2008 ABCA 49 (Alta. C.A.); *R. v. Situ*, [2005] A.J. No. 998, 2005 ABCA 275 (Alta. C.A.).

[20] Department of Justice Canada, *Federal Prosecution Service Deskbook* (Ottawa: Department of Justice, 2001) s. 9.3.3.

[21] *Ibid.*

[22] *Ibid.* s. 9.3.3.1.

[23] *R. v. Felderhof*, [2003] O.J. No. 4819, 68 O.R. (3d) 481 (Ont. C.A.).

[24] *R. v. Power*, [1994] S.C.J. No. 29, [1994] 1 S.C.R. 601 (S.C.C.).

[25] *R. v. Cook*, [1997] S.C.J. No. 22, [1997] 1 S.C.R. 1113 (S.C.C.).

[26] *R. v. Gayle*, [2001] O.J. No. 1559, 154 C.C.C. (3d) 221 (Ont. C.A.).

[27] Department of Justice Canada, *The Federal Prosecution Service Deskbook* (Ottawa: Department of Justice, 2000) s. 9.3.3.

[28] Report from the Ontario Attorney General of the Kaufman Commission on Proceedings Involving Guy Paul Morin, "Chapter I: The Scope and Nature of the Inquiry" at 35, online: Ontario. Ministry of the Attorney General <http://www.attorneygeneral.jus.gov.on.ca/english/about/pubs/morin/morin_ch1.pdf>.

[29] [2008] N.S.J. No. 433, 2008 NSCA 86 (N.S.C.A.).

to illegal drugs. The RCMP reviewed all of the officer's files and discovered that he had obtained search warrants based on fabricated and unreliable information. On being provided with the results of the RCMP review, Crown counsel contacted the parties affected and assisted them in having the convictions quashed. As the Court noted, the Crown asserted to the Court that "had it been aware of Ryan's misdeeds, it would not have even pursued charges in such circumstances".[30] The Crown urged the Court to "quash [the convictions] and stay the proceedings in each case".[31]

A further feature of the prosecutorial function is the need for prosecutorial independence from political or other influences that may push prosecutors toward conviction seeking. Prosecutors and the police are required, for example, to act independently of each other in fulfilling their roles within the judicial system. The police decide whether a charge should be laid, but it is the prosecutor acting independently who decides whether that charge should be prosecuted.[32]

Judicial protection of prosecutorial independence occurs mostly in the context of judicial review of prosecutorial discretion, discussed in the following section; however, even in the context of a trial, courts are sensitive to the need for prosecutorial decisions to be free from outside influence. In *R. v. Cook*[33] the Supreme Court justified its refusal to review Crown decisions on the calling of witnesses in part because such a review "would be a clear interference with the broad discretionary powers which are said to be within the purview of the Crown attorney".[34]

In *R. v. J.(G.P.)*,[35] the Manitoba Court of Appeal held that it was improper for the trial counsel for the complainant in a sexual assault case to appear as counsel of record for the Crown on an appeal of an order requiring the production of the complainant's counselling records. The Court noted that allowing a lawyer to act for the complainant and the Crown "ignores the unique role of counsel for the Crown in the criminal justice system"[36] and, in particular, creates the impression that the Crown and complainant are working together to obtain conviction. "That may well be the purpose of the

---

[30] *Ibid.* at para. 18.
[31] *Ibid.* at para. 5.
[32] This relationship is more complicated in jurisdictions that have pre-charge Crown screening. In British Columbia, for example, the Crown has a role in determining whether charges should be laid.
[33] [1997] S.C.J. No. 22, [1997] 1 S.C.R. 1113 (S.C.C.).
[34] *Ibid.* at para. 19. See also *R. v. Jackson*, [2005] B.C.J. No. 2439 (B.C.C.A.). As discussed in the following section, it is not entirely clear whether a decision about which witnesses to call falls within the ambit of "prosecutorial discretion" or is simply an exercise of ordinary discretion by a person who occupies the role of a prosecutor. See in general *Krieger v. Law Society of Alberta*, [2002] S.C.J. No. 45 at para. 46, 2002 SCC 65, [2002] 3 S.C.R. 372 (S.C.C.), in which the Court defined the "core elements of prosecutorial discretion" and noted that Crown discretion over document disclosure was not an exercise of "prosecutorial discretion" in that sense.
[35] [2001] M.J. No. 53, 151 C.C.C. (3d) 382 (Man. C.A.).
[36] *Ibid.* at 399.

complainant, but it is no part of the public duty of a prosecutor exercising his quasi-judicial functions."[37]

Finally, the prosecutorial function requires scrupulous observation of the ethical obligations imposed on all lawyers in the adjudicative process. This is consistent with the explanation of the idea of "controlled zeal" above; while all lawyers must refrain from abusive conduct in cross-examination, the unique function of Crown prosecutors makes abusive cross-examination by them more likely to undermine the functioning of the legal system, and more worthy of condemnation. It is bad practice for any lawyer; it is egregious practice for a Crown.

The idea of controlled zeal has particular weight in the context of the obligation to correct misapprehensions to the court, as was emphasized by the Ontario Court of Appeal in *R. v. Ahluwaia*.[38] In *Ahluwaia* a Crown witness was asked about his criminal record during cross-examination. He admitted only to one offence when, in fact, he had an extensive criminal record. The witness was an FBI informant and the FBI had not informed the Canadian Crown of the criminal record. The Crown could not explain why the record was not disclosed but nonetheless refused to produce the witness for further cross-examination. In ordering a new trial on the specific issue of entrapment (the accused had otherwise admitted guilt), the Ontario Court of Appeal condemned the Crown's approach:

> These concerns remain unanswered largely because of the position taken by the Crown when confronted with the perjury of its own witness. Once the Crown had verified the information provided to it by the defence, it knew that Makdesion had committed perjury. It must also have been obvious to the Crown that Makdesion's perjured testimony was consistent with the incomplete disclosure that the Crown says came from the F.B.I. I would think that the Crown would have recognized that the information provided to them by the defence raised serious questions about the integrity of the prosecution, and would have launched a thorough investigation aimed at finding out exactly what had happened.
>
> For reasons not shared with this Court, the Crown does not appear to have regarded itself as under any obligation to get to the bottom of this matter. It contented itself with inquiries of counsel involved in the case and some of the Canadian police officers ...
>
> The Crown has obligations to the administration of justice that do not burden other litigants. Faced with its own witness's perjury and the fact that the perjured evidence coincided with the incomplete disclosure that the Crown says it innocently passed to the defence, the Crown was obliged to take all reasonable steps to find out what had happened and to share the results of those inquiries with the defence. In my view, the Crown did not fulfill its obligations to the administration of justice by acknowledging the incomplete disclosure discovered by the defence, and after making limited inquiries, professing neither a responsibility for

---

[37] *Ibid.* at 400.
[38] [2000] O.J. No. 4544, 149 C.C.C. (3d) 193 (Ont. C.A.).

the incomplete disclosure nor an ability to provide any explanation for it. The Crown owed both the appellant and the Court a fuller explanation than it chose to provide.[39]

Law societies have also disciplined Crown prosecutors who have failed to correct misleading information provided to the Court. In *Law Society of Alberta v. Piragoff*,[40] the Law Society of Alberta suspended Arnold Piragoff for six months following his failure to disclose information to the court and to the accused, and the making of misleading statements to the court.

Piragoff was acting as prosecutor on a murder case. The accused, J.D., was in prison and the police sent J.D. a letter, supposedly from S., with the hope that J.D. would write a reply incriminating himself. Before sending the letter, the police consulted with Piragoff, who gave them some advice with respect to the ability to use S. as an informant without turning S. into an agent of the state. The letter "from S." was sent but instead of responding, J.D. took the letter to his own lawyer. Both J.D. and his lawyer thought the letter had been sent by S., and his lawyer sought to use the fact that J.D. had provided the letter to his lawyer in support of J.D.'s bail application. While Piragoff surmised that the letter had in fact been sent by the RCMP, he did not disclose that to the court or to the defence. Instead, he made statements that "would clearly lead a listener to believe that S. was the author of the letter. This was not true and it is acknowledged that this misstatement did in fact mislead [the lawyer for the accused] Mr. Royal and the Court".[41]

The Law Society of Alberta found that it was not Piragoff's "intention to consciously provide false information";[42] however, he was "extremely careless" and "reckless" in making the statements that he did, and in failing to correct the misapprehension that had been created. After he had made the statements, the RCMP had raised with him the possibility that his statements might mislead the Court, but Piragoff "did not judge that the source of the letter was material to the Court's conclusions".[43] Further, once the truth of the letter's origins came out at the preliminary inquiry, Piragoff's "explanation was far from candid".[44]

The Law Society noted in particular the problematic nature of Piragoff's conduct given the context within which it occurred:

> Mr. Piragoff's role in the administration of justice is one that brings with it great power and great discretion. When that discretion is abused, through recklessness or gross errors in judgment by a senior Crown prosecutor in whom the public has a right to expect exemplary conducted [sic], the administration of justice and the legal profession as a whole is all the more hurt ...

---

[39] *Ibid.* at paras. 70-74.
[40] [2005] L.S.D.D. No. 47.
[41] *Ibid.* at para. 21.
[42] *Ibid.* at para. 26.
[43] *Ibid.* at para. 32.
[44] *Ibid.* at para. 37.

The potential injury of Mr. Piragoff's conduct was extreme. Misstatements occurred during the course of an application that affected an individual's liberty. Misstatements in such circumstances must draw a special attention.[45]

Being a Crown prosecutor requires, then, a commitment to fairness in the conduct of the trial reflected by controlled zeal, an open mind, independence from external forces that might create pressure in the Crown to seek conviction rather than fairness, and scrupulous observance of the ethical obligations imposed on all lawyers. Prosecuting criminal cases is consistent with vigorous advocacy, and courts should not interfere with the Crown's conduct of its case because it has acted consistently with adversarial norms;[46] however, that vigorous advocacy must be coupled with, as the rhetoric suggests, fairness, dignity, moderation and the pursuit of justice.

B. Prosecutorial Discretion

i. What is Prosecutorial Discretion?

The most significant aspect of the Crown prosecutor's unique ethical duties is the exercise of prosecutorial discretion. Prosecutorial discretion "does not simply refer to any discretionary decision made by a Crown prosecutor".[47] Rather, it refers to the Crown prosecutor's exercise of the "delegated sovereign authority peculiar to the office of the Attorney General",[48] pursuant to which the Attorney General decides whether to proceed with, continue, or stay a criminal prosecution, and in what way. As stated by the decision of the Supreme Court in *Krieger v. Law Society of Alberta*:

> Without being exhaustive, we believe the core elements of prosecutorial discretion encompass the following: (a) the discretion whether to bring the prosecution of a charge laid by police; (b) the discretion to enter a stay of proceedings in either a private or public prosecution, as codified in the *Criminal Code*, R.S.C. 1985, c. C-46, ss. 579 and 579.1; (c) the discretion to accept a guilty plea to a lesser charge; (d) the discretion to withdraw from criminal proceedings altogether: ...; and (e) the discretion to take control of a private prosecution.[49]

The Court in *Krieger* went on to hold that a decision about disclosure, while requiring the exercise of discretionary judgment, was not an exercise of prosecutorial discretion.

---

[45] *Ibid.* at paras. 45 and 47. The Law Society noted that, on the facts, it did not appear that a miscarriage of justice had resulted from Piragoff's actions.
[46] See in general, Michael Code, "Judicial Review of Prosecutorial Decisions: A Short History of Costs and Benefits, in Response to Justice Rosenberg" (2009) 34 Queen's L.J. 863.
[47] *Krieger v. Law Society of Alberta*, [2002] S.C.J. No. 45, 2002 SCC 65, [2002] 3 S.C.R. 372 at 393-94 (S.C.C.).
[48] *Ibid.* at 395.
[49] *Ibid.* at 394.

Prosecutorial discretion has been described as an aspect of the "rule of law",[50] as a means of ensuring that prosecutions are based only on the fair and equal application of the law, rather than on politics, power or other extraneous concerns. Through the combination of prosecutorial discretion and prosecutorial independence, decisions about when prosecutions should be initiated, continued or ceased can be made fairly and impartially.

In other cases the courts have confirmed, consistent with *Krieger*, that prosecutorial discretion includes decisions about whether to proceed by way of summary conviction or indictable offence,[51] to stay a proceeding,[52] to consent to a re-election for trial by judge alone,[53] or to seek a higher level of sanction available for the offence.[54]

Prior to its decision in *Krieger*, the Supreme Court had treated other discretionary decisions by the Crown — such as whether to call witnesses or whether to present evidence — as within the Crown's authority, and subject to the deference appropriate in reviewing an exercise of prosecutorial discretion.[55] The invocation of prosecutorial discretion in these earlier decisions cannot easily be reconciled with *Krieger*. The decisions about which evidence to call, or whether to call evidence, are arguably more analogous to a decision about disclosure than to a decision about whether to proceed with a prosecution.

It is true that the Crown has a legal obligation to disclose all relevant documents, and that the failure to call a witness, or evidence, may be linked to a decision to stay a proceeding, since potentially bringing proceedings to a close.[56] Indeed, in some circumstances — such as where a Crown does not call evidence because recognizing that the case should not have been brought, and an acquittal is appropriate — the decision not to call evidence *is* properly considered an exercise of prosecutorial discretion. However, in an ordinary case, the mere fact that discretion is part of the Crown's decisions about witnesses and evidence does not make those decisions an exercise of prosecutorial discretion. The Court has recognized that discretionary judgment applies to disclosure (What is relevant? When should it be disclosed?) but has also clearly stated that disclosure is not an instance of prosecutorial discretion. Ordinary course decisions about witnesses and evidence seem to

---

[50] Marc Rosenberg, "The Attorney General and the Administraton of Justice" (2009) 34 Queen's L.J. 813 at para. 23.
[51] *R. v. Smythe*, [1971] O.J. No. 1520, 3 C.C.C. (2d) 97 (Ont. C.A.), affd [1971] S.C.J. No. 62, 3 C.C.C. (2d) 366 (S.C.C.); *R. v. Randell*, [2001] N.J. No. 77 (Nfld. Prov. Ct.).
[52] *R. v. D.N.*, [2004] N.J. No. 271, 2004 NLCA 44 (Nfld. C.A.); *Kostuch v. Alberta*, [1995] A.J. No. 866, 101 C.C.C. (3d) 321 (Alta. C.A.); *Werring v. British Columbia*, [1997] B.C.J. No. 2952, 122 C.C.C. (3d) 343 (B.C.C.A.).
[53] *R. v. Ng*, [2003] A.J. No. 489, 173 C.C.C. (3d) 349 (Alta. C.A.).
[54] *R. v. Haneveld*, [2008] A.J. No. 1487, 2008 ABPC 382 (Alta. Prov. Ct.).
[55] *R. v. Power*, [1994] S.C.J. No. 29, [1994] 1 S.C.R. 601 (S.C.C.) and *R. v. Cook*, [1997] S.C.J. No. 22, [1997] 1 S.C.R. 1113 (S.C.C.). See also *R. v. Jolivet*, [2000] S.C.J. No. 28 at para. 18, [2000] 1 S.C.R. 751 (S.C.C.).
[56] In *R. v. Power*, *ibid.*, the Crown did not call any evidence in order to terminate the trial and allow it to bring an appeal of an interlocutory decision on the admissibility of evidence.

be similarly matters of trial tactics with a discretionary component rather than an exercise of "delegated sovereign authority". Prosecutors who do not call witnesses make decisions much like any other litigation lawyer, whether representing the Crown or a corporation. By contrast, Crown prosecutors who decide that a legal violation that can be proved should nonetheless not be prosecuted, exercise an authority no private sector lawyer enjoys.

Lower court decisions subsequent to *Krieger* have suggested that the earlier Supreme Court cases must be read in light of *Krieger*, and that matters of trial tactics are not within prosecutorial discretion. How a Crown conducts its case is subject to the usual authority of the court to manage its own processes.

Most notably, in *R. v. Felderhof*,[57] the Crown appealed to the Ontario Court of Appeal in part on the basis that the trial judge made rulings in relation to the order in which the Crown presented its witnesses and other matters. It argued that doing so was an improper interference with the Crown's presentation of its case. The Court of Appeal held that the trial judge may make decisions about the conduct of the proceeding, even if affecting the Crown's approach to the trial; doing so does not interfere with prosecutorial discretion:

> Finally, the broad statements by Justice L'Heureux-Dubé J. in *Power* and *Cook* must now be read in light of the recent decision of the Supreme Court in *Krieger v. Law Society of Alberta* ... Iacobucci and Major JJ. speaking for the court at para. 43 held that "prosecutorial discretion" is a term of art. It does not simply refer to any discretionary decision made by a Crown prosecutor. ...
>
> In my view, the trial judge's power to manage the trial, including the power to review the order in which certain evidence may be called, properly falls within the area of the prosecutor's "tactics or conduct before the court" and thus does not implicate prosecutorial discretion that is reviewable only on the standard of abuse of process, bad faith or improper purpose. I do not think the appellant's separation of powers rationale stands in the way of recognizing a trial management power.[58]

The Court's position in *Felderhof* makes sense in light of *Krieger*. The exercise of sovereign authority, and discretionary decisions about how to manage a trial, are conceptually distinct, and should be approached that way by courts. How a Crown decides to proceed with a trial is a different type of decision than the exercise of prosecutorial discretion, and should not be confused with it.

This does not mean, of course, that courts may routinely interfere with Crown decisions about trial tactics, any more than they may routinely

---

[57] [2003] O.J. No. 4819, 68 O.R. (3d) 481 (Ont. C.A.).
[58] *Ibid.* at paras. 53-54. See also *R. v. Riley*, [2008] O.J. No. 880 at para. 33 (Ont. S.C.J.): "[T]he trial judge has a broad discretion to make orders designed to ensure that a trial is fair and manageable, including orders that the Crown provide reasonable assistance to the defence about the way that a prosecution will be conducted."

interfere with the decisions of private litigants about such matters.[59] Interference with trial tactics may be justified where any litigant violates the rules of procedure or evidence, or abuses the process of the court, or where necessary for the effective management of the trial. Such interference is not warranted, however, simply because the court does not approve of decisions that are within the discretion of that counsel. Apart from the general requirement that it restrict itself to "the lawful exercise of adversarial rights",[60] a Crown has no obligation to conduct a trial in a particular way; rather, it has an obligation to prove its case. If it fails to do so then the accused will be acquitted, but no other result need follow.

One final area of uncertainty with respect to the scope of prosecutorial discretion arises in relation to Crown withdrawal of a plea agreement. In *R. v. Nixon*,[61] the Alberta Crown entered into a plea agreement under which Nixon would plead guilty to the traffic violation of careless driving. Nixon had driven her RV through a stop sign, collided with another vehicle, killed the husband and wife driving the vehicle, and seriously injured the couple's seven-year-old child. She was charged with various offences related to impaired and dangerous driving. Before the plea agreement was entered in Court, the Attorney General withdrew it on the basis that it was not in the "best interests of the administration of justice".[62]

The Alberta Court of Appeal held that resiling from a plea agreement was a matter of prosecutorial discretion and "must be reviewed with that in mind".[63] It should only be rejected if it constituted an abuse of process. On April 22, 2010 the Supreme Court of Canada granted leave to appeal *Nixon*. Given the clarity of the Alberta Court of Appeal's reasons, and the nature of the decision, it is not entirely clear why the Court would have done so. Prior to a matter being presented to court, a decision about whether to proceed with a particular resolution of the case seems to be at the heart of the prosecutorial discretion as set out in *Krieger*. The issue that the court needs to address may be that, as discussed below, plea bargaining raises distinct issues of fairness that require consideration. There may be a risk that in circumstances like *Nixon*, where the plea agreement was viewed as likely to be disapproved of by the general public, permitting higher levels of the Attorney General's office to resile from a plea agreement increases the risk of improper political interference with prosecutorial discretion. Nonetheless,

---

[59] See in this respect Michael Code, "Judical Review of Prosecutorial Decisions: A Short History of Costs and Benefits, in Response to Justice Rosenberg" (2009) 34 Queen's L.J. 863. Code suggests that *Krieger* is problematic insofar as it "implied that any discretionary decision by the Crown relating to its conduct of a case before the court can be judicially reviewed on some unspecified relaxed standard" (para. 54). I think this overstates the holding in *Krieger*. A court may control its own process, and that control extends to Crown prosecutors, but that does not grant the court an unspecified review power.

[60] *Ibid.* at para. 56.

[61] [2009] A.J. No. 871, 2009 ABCA 269 (Alta. C.A.).

[62] *Ibid.* at para. 2.

[63] *Ibid.* at para. 5.

withdrawal of a plea prior to its being entered seems similar to an exercise of sovereign authority akin to those identified in *Krieger*.

ii. How is Prosecutorial Discretion to be Exercised?

The scope of prosecutorial discretion matters because when something is a matter of prosecutorial discretion, it is at once almost entirely shielded from review, yet is also subject to distinct obligations with respect to the basis on which it is made. Like any discretionary decision made by a state authority, the exercise of prosecutorial discretion must not be arbitrary and capricious,[64] and must be made consistently with the prosecutor's overarching role as "minister of justice".

The best articulation of how prosecutorial discretion should be exercised is found in the *Federal Prosecution Service Deskbook*[65] and its provincial counterparts.[66] The Deskbook states that decisions on whether to prosecute must be based, first, on whether there is sufficient evidence to justify "the institution or continuation of proceedings" and, second, on whether the "public interest require[s] a prosecution to be pursued".[67]

Whether there is a sufficient basis to proceed depends on whether the evidence reveals a "reasonable prospect of conviction", taking into account the "availability, competence and credibility of witnesses".[68]

Identification of the public interest should be based on:

a. the seriousness or triviality of the alleged offence;
b. significant mitigating or aggravating circumstances;
c. the age, intelligence, physical or mental health or infirmity of the accused;
d. the accused's background;
e. the degree of staleness of the alleged offence;
f. the accused's alleged degree of responsibility for the offence;
g. the prosecution's likely effect on public order and morale or on public confidence in the administration of justice;

---

[64] *Baker v. Canada (Minister of Citizenship and Immigration)*, [1999] S.C.J. No. 39 at para. 53, [1999] 2 S.C.R. 817 (S.C.C.). *Baker* stands for the administrative law proposition that exercises of discretion must occur within the bounds of the statutory authority given to the administrative decision-maker. This is not a real analogy to prosecutorial discretion, which is an exercise of inherent executive power not statutory authority. However, the shift in *Baker* away from granting absolute deference to all discretionary decisions reflects, I think, a broader recognition that discretionary power does not obviate the need for respect for rule of law — *i.e.*, the need to make decisions that are not arbitrary and capricious.

[65] Department of Justice, *Federal Prosecution Service Deskbook* (Ottawa: Department of Justice, 2000).

[66] Graeme Mitchell, "'No joy in this for anyone' Reflections on the Exercise of Prosecutorial Discretion in *R. v. Latimer*" (2001), 64 Sask. L. Rev. 491 at para. 13.

[67] Department of Justice, *Federal Prosecution Service Deskbook* (Ottawa: Department of Justice, 2000) s. 15.

[68] *Federal Prosecution Service Deskbook*, ibid.

h. whether prosecuting would be perceived as counter-productive, for example, by bringing the administration of justice into disrepute;
i. the availability and appropriateness of alternatives to prosecution;
j. the prevalence of the alleged offence in the community and the need for general and specific deterrence;
k. whether the consequences of a prosecution or conviction would be disproportionately harsh or oppressive;
l. whether the alleged offence is of considerable public concern;
m. the entitlement of any person or body to criminal compensation, reparation or forfeiture if prosecution occurs;
n. the attitude of the victim of the alleged offence to a prosecution;
o. the likely length and expense of a trial, and the resources available to conduct the proceedings;
p. whether the accused agrees to co-operate in the investigation or prosecution of others, or the extent to which the accused has already done so;
q. the likely sentence in the event of a conviction; and
r. whether prosecuting would require or cause the disclosure of information that would be injurious to international relations, national defence, national security or that should not be disclosed in the public interest.

Because, as discussed in the next section, courts will not review prosecutorial discretion absent egregious circumstances, Canadian courts have given relatively little in the way of useful guidance as to how prosecutorial discretion should be exercised in an ordinary case.

Courts have, though, occasionally been very critical of specific decisions made by prosecutors to pursue charges that the police have laid. In particular, courts have been critical in cases where they view the conduct of the accused as insufficiently morally blameworthy to warrant the prosecution of the charge by the Crown. Thus, in *R. v. K.(M.)*,[69] the Manitoba Court of Appeal was critical of the Crown for prosecuting a case involving parental discipline of a child. In that case MK had been charged with, and convicted of, simple assault after kicking his child with his stocking foot. The conviction was reversed on appeal as an improper exercise of prosecutorial discretion. The Court stated that "Instead of going after real criminals, men and women who wantonly attack innocent neighbours, the whole engine of the state has been concentrated in this case on the prosecution of a citizen who has been accused of using excessive force in the disciplining of his children."[70]

---

[69] [1992] M.J. No. 334, 74 C.C.C. (3d) 108 (Man. C.A.).
[70] *Ibid.* at 108.

In *R. v. Latimer*,[71] Robert Latimer was charged with second degree murder after deliberately killing his disabled daughter, which meant that upon conviction he faced a mandatory minimum sentence of life imprisonment without chance of parole for 10 years. At the appeal of his conviction to the Saskatchewan Court of Appeal, Chief Justice Bayda in his dissent criticized the Crown for bringing a charge against Latimer which precluded the possibility of judicial discretion in sentencing. Had the prosecution charged Latimer with manslaughter, the sentence could have been variable. Others also criticized the Crown's exercise of its prosecutorial discretion in this case because of Latimer's belief that he had acted in a spirit of mercy.[72]

This judicial condemnation does not, however, provide much in the way of useful direction to Crown prosecutors in future cases; ultimately, the guidelines set out by the *Federal Prosecution Service Deskbook* and its provincial counterparts dictate Crown conduct in this respect.

Given those guidelines, could a prosecutor ethically proceed with a case where conviction is likely to result not because conviction is warranted on the facts, but because of imperfections in the system of justice? Could a prosecutor proceed with charges where an eyewitness identifies the accused, but the eyewitness appears evidently unreliable? Where, for example, the witness is the elderly white victim of an assault by an aboriginal man, who now claims to have identified the accused walking by on the street? Could the prosecutor simply take the position that even on this scant and not very reliable evidence there is, in fact, a reasonable chance of conviction, and none of the public interest factors listed in the Deskbook speak to the reliability and credibility of witnesses? In my view the prosecutor could not. To do so would mean that a prosecutor could assess whether there is a reasonable chance of conviction on the basis of a posited failure of the system — that the jurors will irrationally and unfairly assess credibility. The assessment of whether there is a reasonable chance of conviction must include consideration of whether there is a reasonable chance of conviction *assuming that the system functions as it ought to*, not whether there is a chance of conviction because the system is flawed. Any other result is inconsistent with the role of the prosecutor as a minister of justice, and not a mere zealous advocate.

---

[71] [1995] S.J. No. 402 (Sask. C.A.).

[72] See Graeme Mitchell, "'No joy in this for anyone' Reflections on the Exercise of Prosecutorial Discretion in *R. v. Latimer*" (2001), 64 Sask. L. Rev. 491. Like Mitchell, I think prosecutorial discretion was exercised reasonably in the *Latimer* case. Latimer was legally guilty of second degree murder — he deliberately ended his daughter's life. And as for the public interest, as said by the trial judge in Latimer's first trial:
> There is no joy in this for anyone. I know you believe you did the right thing and many people will agree with it; however, the criminal law is unremitting when it comes to the taking of human life for whatever reason. Life was not kind to Tracy but it was a life that was hers to make of what she could.

(Cited by Mitchell, at para. 1).

iii. Oversight of Prosecutorial Discretion

In March, 1981, Susan Nelles was charged with the murder of four babies at the Toronto General Hospital. A number of babies had died at the Hospital in circumstances that were considered suspicious. Nelles had not, however, been at work when several of the babies had died, including one of the babies she was accused of murdering. Moreover, one of the reasons why Nelles had fallen under suspicion was that she had exercised her right to speak to legal counsel when the police came to interview her.

At the preliminary inquiry, in response to the Crown suggestion that asking to speak to a lawyer tended to indicate guilt, the Judge stated that:

> In my opinion, the alleged statement in substance merely reflects the exercise by Susan Nelles of two of the most elementary and fundamental civil rights of a citizen when charged by police officers with an offence: the right to speak to a lawyer and the right to remain silent, which is the well-known right against self-incrimination. No inference of guilt may be drawn from the opening manoeuvre of the officers when, after misleading her about coming from the coroner's office, they cautioned her and then virtually told her she had poisoned Justin Cook and asked her if she wished to explain, upon which she replied: "I think I want to speak to a lawyer."[73]

Ultimately, in an unusual decision, the preliminary inquiry judge refused to allow the matter to proceed to trial and discharged Nelles:

> Upon the whole of the evidence, it is my conclusion that there is no evidence to go before a jury on the count of murder in connection with Janice Estrella; that on each of the remaining counts, the evidence against the accused is at least equally consistent with the rational conclusion, grounded in the evidence, that the accused is innocent of the offence charged as it is that the accused is the guilty person. The evidence viewed in its entirety is either of too dubious a nature or amounts to no evidence at all to go before a jury; in either case, a reasonable jury, properly instructed, could not find beyond a reasonable doubt that the guilt of the accused is the only reasonable inference to be drawn from the proven facts.[74]

The judge's decision leads inexorably to the conclusion that the decision to prosecute Nelles was at best in error, almost certainly was made without sufficient attention to the prosecutor's duty to ensure that there was a factual basis for proceeding, and was at worst an abuse of the prosecutor's discretionary authority.

What follows from that? What *should* follow from that? Should prosecutors be held accountable when they make mistakes in proceeding to trial with a charge? Should they be prevented from making mistakes through some mechanism for review of prosecutorial discretion before trial? And, if accountability is appropriate, through what mechanism should it be imposed?

---

[73] *R. v. Nelles*, [1982] O.J. No. 3654 at para. 67, 16 C.C.C. (3d) 97 (Ont. Prov. Ct.).
[74] *Ibid.* at para. 97.

Because of the centrality of independence to prosecutorial discretion, the notion of review of that discretion, and of accountability for perceived "mistakes", presents a difficult problem. If the courts, legislatures or law societies review prosecutorial decisions, it may be perceived as an interference with the independence of the prosecutor. On the other hand, if Crown prosecutors are given absolute immunity from any sort of scrutiny, it means that few clear incentives exist to encourage prosecutors to exercise their considerable power with due care and attention.

The resolution of this dilemma by the Supreme Court has been to permit review of prosecutorial discretion by courts, law societies and the executive, but only in highly limited circumstances.

The courts themselves will only interfere with prosecutorial discretion where it constitutes an abuse of process or where the tort of malicious prosecution is made out. The power to regulate abuses of process is normally used as a mechanism to review and regulate prosecutorial discretion prior to a trial of a case; the tort of malicious prosecution operates after the criminal case has been resolved.

To be an abuse of process, the prosecutor must have acted wrongfully in exercising her discretion:

> Where there is conspicuous evidence of improper motives or of bad faith or of an act so wrong that it violates the conscience of the community, such that it would genuinely be unfair and indecent to proceed, then, and only then, should courts intervene to prevent an abuse of process which could bring the administration of justice into disrepute. Cases of this nature will be extremely rare.[75]

Establishing malicious prosecution is equally onerous.[76] In its decision in *Miazga v. Kvello Estate*,[77] the Court held that the plaintiff must demonstrate (a) that the defendant was responsible for the prosecution; (b) that the legal proceedings ultimately resolved in favour of the plaintiff; (c) that the defendant did not have reasonable and probable grounds for a prosecution, objectively speaking (that is, that the defendant's professional judgment should have indicated that it was not possible that "proof beyond a reasonable doubt could be made out in a court of law");[78] and, (d) that the defendant acted for some improper purpose in bringing forward the prosecution — that the defendant "deliberately intended to subvert or abuse

---

[75] *R. v. Power*, [1994] S.C.J. No. 29 at para. 12, [1994] 1 S.C.R. 601 (S.C.C.). See also: *R. v. Jewitt*, [1985] S.C.J. No. 53, [1985] 2 S.C.R. 128 (S.C.C.); *R. v. T.(V.)*, [1992] S.C.J. No. 29, [1992] 1 S.C.R. 749 (S.C.C.); *R. v. O'Connor*, [1995] S.C.J. No. 98, [1995] 4 S.C.R. 411 (S.C.C.). An interesting lower court decision is *Stucky v. Canada*, [2004] F.C.J. No. 2155 at para. 63 (F.C.). The applicant on judicial review was seeking disclosure of information relevant to the Crown's decision to proceed by way of indictment. The prothonotary held that disclosure could not be granted unless there was "some evidentiary basis or threshold of impropriety" established by the applicant.
[76] See *Nelles v. Ontario*, [1989] S.C.J. No. 86, [1989] 2 S.C.R. 170 (S.C.C.); *Miazga v. Kvello Estate*, [2009] S.C.J. No. 51, 2009 SCC 51 (S.C.C.).
[77] [2009] S.C.J. No. 51, 2009 SCC 51 (S.C.C.).
[78] *Ibid.* at para. 63.

the office of the Attorney General or the process of criminal justice".[79] It is not enough that the prosecutor is guilty of "incompetence, inexperience, poor judgment, lack of professionalism, laziness, recklessness, honest mistake, negligence, or even gross negligence".[80] Actual malfeasance must be demonstrated.

Miazga involved notorious and ultimately unfounded allegations of child abuse, including elements of ritualistic and satanic activities, made against the Kvello family in Saskatchewan by three children under their care. After being exonerated in part through the recantation of the children when they were older, the family brought an action against the Crown for malicious prosecution, based largely on the unbelievable nature of the allegations that had been made. The action ultimately floundered, however, in part on the fact that at least one party had been convicted of the offences charged, albeit wrongfully, and in part on the fact that there was no real evidence that the Crown did not believe in the validity of the charges. In those circumstances, the Supreme Court held that malicious prosecution could not be established.

Law societies may also discipline Crown prosecutors for wrongful exercise of prosecutorial discretion. As was the case with abuse of process and malicious prosecution, there must be evidence of wrongful conduct by the Crown to warrant law society discipline. In rejecting the Attorney General's challenge of law society jurisdiction in *Krieger v. Law Society of Alberta*,[81] the Supreme Court held that the statutory authority given to law societies over the professional conduct of their members, including Crown prosecutors, was sufficient to allow the law societies to sanction prosecutors who have violated in an egregious fashion their ethical obligations with respect to the exercise of prosecutorial discretion. Law societies may discipline prosecutors who, for example, "laid charges as a result of bribery or racism or revenge".[82]

Finally, prosecutors may be accountable to the executive branch of government in some circumstances. In *British Columbia (Ministry of Attorney General, Criminal Justice Branch) v. British Columbia (Commission of Inquiry into the Death of Frank Paul – Davies Commission)*,[83] the Attorney General for British Columbia sought judicial review of the scope of a Commission of Inquiry established by Order-in-Council. The Commission had been established "to explore issues surrounding the exercise of the Crown's prosecutorial discretion" [84] in connection with the death of Frank Paul-Davies. On December 5, 1998 Paul-Davies had been taken into police custody and put into the drunk tank. The police decided not to keep him

---

[79] *Ibid.* at para. 89.
[80] *Ibid.* at para. 81.
[81] [2002] S.C.J. No. 45, 2002 SCC 65 (S.C.C.).
[82] *Ibid.* at para. 52.
[83] [2009] B.C.J. No. 1469, 2009 BCCA 337 (B.C.C.A.).
[84] *Ibid.* at para. 1.

there, drove him to an alleyway and left him. He died of hypothermia caused in party by his "acute alcohol intoxication".[85] The police investigated the death and gave the Crown a neutral report — that is, one that made no recommendation as to charging.[86] The "Crown counsel concluded that no charges should be laid";[87] the police took internal disciplinary measures against the two officers. A purpose of the Commission was to inquire into the charging decision.

The Court of Appeal held that the Commission could do so. Ultimately this was an exploration by the executive of how an executive function had been exercised; the Attorney General is a member of the Cabinet which issued the Order-in-Council establishing the Commission, and this "gives us an assurance that he must not have considered the mandate of the Commission to be an unlawful incursion on prosecutorial independence".[88] The Attorney General has the authority to review the delegated exercises of his prosecutorial discretion:

> The role of the Attorney General in the establishment and continuation of the Commission of Inquiry is of great importance. Prosecutorial discretion, ultimately, rests with the Attorney General. As the Attorney General concedes on this appeal, he is entitled to establish a system to review exercises of prosecutorial discretion, and for improving the policies that govern its exercise. He is also entitled to take steps to satisfy the public that prosecutorial discretion is being exercised in a principled way. The Attorney General is in a unique position to gauge the necessity for a public airing of issues surrounding prosecutorial discretion, and to balance the need for prosecutorial independence with public accountability. Thus, it will be a rare case where a commission of inquiry that is established with the specific mandate of inquiring into an exercise of prosecutorial discretion, and which is established with the apparent approval of the Attorney General, will be found by a court to constitute an unlawful interference with prosecutorial independence.[89]

The Supreme Court of Canada denied leave to appeal in *Paul-Davies*.[90]

It is not entirely clear how the approach of the British Columbia Court of Appeal in *Paul-Davies* can be reconciled with the general tenor of the case law regarding review of prosecutorial discretion. The position that the Attorney General authorized the review through membership in Cabinet is strained given that the Attorney General subsequently brought an application to prevent the Commission from undertaking the review. And while a Commission of Inquiry may not have the ability to sanction similar to a court or law society's, it also has the capacity to make statements and

---

[85] *Ibid.* at para. 4.
[86] It should be noted that British Columbia does have pre-charge screening, where the Crown always has some role in determining whether charges should be laid at all.
[87] *Ibid.* at para. 5.
[88] *Ibid.* at para. 74.
[89] *Ibid.* at para. 77.
[90] [2009] S.C.C.A. No. 421 (S.C.C.).

recommendations about prosecutorial discretion that could not unreasonably be perceived as an intrusion on that discretion.

That being said, the British Columbia Court of Appeal's decision seems correct. The need for prosecutorial independence should not shield prosecutors from responding to an inquiry into why prosecutorial discretion was exercised as it was, and into whether it should have been so exercised. Not every inquiry is legitimate — as the British Columbia Court itself recognized in its concurrently released judgment denying a Coroner the ability to *subpoena* Crown prosecutors about their decision not to oppose an application for judicial interim release (bail).[91] However, carefully tailored inquiries into prosecutorial action should not be suppressed by an undue concern for prosecutorial independence.

In sum, then, prosecutorial discretion may be reviewed by the Attorney General internally, or even through a Commission of Inquiry, but will only be reviewed by external bodies, such as courts or law societies, in circumstances of malfeasance. Does this strike the right balance?

In my view, the Supreme Court's very limited use of the doctrine of abuse of process to control prosecutorial discretion is sensible. Granting a stay of proceedings because of an abuse of process prevents legal adjudication of the merits of a case; yet, absent some evidence of prosecutorial malfeasance, it is through legal adjudication that the legitimacy of the prosecutor's decision to charge can be tested. For example, in *R. v. K.(M.)*,[92] a decision noted earlier with respect to how discretion should be exercised, the Manitoba Court of Appeal granted a stay in a case where the accused was accused of using excessive force in disciplining a child, and was convicted of assault. The Court of Appeal stayed the proceedings on the basis that proceeding was a waste of judicial resources, and the force used did not warrant a charge being brought:

> I shudder to think what would have happened to my father or mother if they had got caught in the toils of the law enforcement authorities as administered by the current Department of Justice. The discipline administered to the boy in question in these proceedings was mild indeed compared to the discipline I received in my home. There were times when I thought my parents were too strict, but in retrospect I am glad that my parents were not subjected to prosecution or persecution for attempting to keep the children in my family in line.[93]

With all due respect to the Manitoba Court of Appeal, surely the question of whether the force was excessive was the very matter to be tried, and was the very matter that was tried and resolved at the court below, based on an evaluation of the facts and applicable law. The style in which a judge of the Court of Appeal was parented has no relevance to the question of whether, in law, what this parent did was a criminal offence. The Court of

---

[91] *Picha v. Lee Inquest (Coroner of)*, [2009] B.C.J. No. 1461, 2009 BCCA 336 (B.C.C.A.).
[92] [1992] M.J. No. 334, 74 C.C.C. (3d) 108 (Man. C.A.).
[93] *Ibid.* at 109.

Appeal's decision subverts the ordinary operation of the legal process, and the exercise of prosecutorial discretion, in favour of the *ad hoc* and unsubstantiated discretion of the Court of Appeal.[94]

On the other hand, the Supreme Court's confining of the tort of malicious prosecution to extraordinary cases seems unduly restrictive. Once the legal process has run its course, the plaintiff will have been shown to be innocent, and will have suffered a loss as a result of the decision to prosecute. At that point the only question is, who is properly responsible for the loss?

While it may be reasonable to require something more than mere carelessness or negligence before imposing that loss on the Crown, the position of the Supreme Court that *recklessness* is not sufficient to attract civil liability appears to shield the exercise of authority by Crown prosecutors to the point where it seems less to protect the rule of law than to undermine it. A person is innocent. He suffers at minimum the loss associated with the cost of running a criminal trial, and being publicly accused of a crime. The prosecutor acted recklessly in bringing the charge. To shield the Crown from accountability in order to protect prosecutorial independence seems to posit an extraordinarily timorous prosecutor, while requiring a plaintiff to bear a loss for which he has no responsibility. It may be that individual prosecutors should not bear the loss, and that the loss should be borne by the government as a whole.[95] But to leave the loss with the person wrongfully convicted is wrong, and unfair.

Consider again the case of Susan Nelles. Although Nelles was permitted to pursue a legal action against the Attorney General,[96] and ultimately obtained payment from the Ontario government of the legal fees she had incurred, it is almost certain that, had *Miazga*[97] been decided then, her case could not have succeeded. It was right that it did succeed. I remember the Nelles prosecution: the nation-wide publicity it received, the apparent certainty of her guilt at the outset, the shocking and sick nature of the allegations made against her. I had no sophisticated understanding of the issues at the time, but I know I assumed that she must be both guilty and insane. I am sure most Canadians assumed the same. And, as an additional tragedy, before she had been exonerated her father died of a heart attack. The ordeal she and her family went through was appalling.

From this vantage point I cannot judge whether the prosecutors in the *Nelles* case acted carelessly or recklessly. But I will suggest this: ensuring that prosecutors are independent from judicial or political interference does

---

[94] The Supreme Court granted leave to appeal in *K.(M.)*; however the appeal was "quashed" on June 16, 1993 — that is, without any decision being made on the merits. It seems unlikely that the decision could have withstood Supreme Court review.
[95] Although even there, if prosecutors were required to carry insurance, as are lawyers in private practice, the fear of liability might be mitigated.
[96] *Nelles v. Ontario*, [1989] S.C.J. No. 86, [1989] 2 S.C.R. 170 (S.C.C.).
[97] [2009] S.C.J. No. 51, 2009 SCC 51 (S.C.C.).

not require that the Crown be unaccountable if it wrongs someone in the way Susan Nelles was wronged. Given the significance of prosecutorial independence, a standard of mere negligence is too low to justify the imposition of liability on the Crown; however, where the wrong is caused by gross negligence, or recklessness, then the loss should be born by the Attorney General, not by the wrongfully prosecuted.[98]

C. Disclosure

Crown prosecutors must disclose to the accused all relevant information in their possession or control, whether inculpatory or exculpatory, and whether the Crown intends to rely on the evidence in prosecuting its case.[99] The duty to disclose does not extend to information that is privileged, "clearly irrelevant"[100] or where the disclosure of the information "is otherwise governed by law".[101] While the Crown cannot be required to produce information that it no longer has, it must provide a satisfactory explanation for the loss or destruction of otherwise producible material.[102]

In fulfilling this duty the Crown prosecutor may rely on the corollary duty of the police "to disclose to the Crown all relevant material in their possession";[103] however Crown prosecutors are not simply passive parties awaiting information from others. They have a duty to "make reasonable inquiries of other Crown agencies or departments that could reasonably be considered to be in possession of evidence" relevant to the case.[104] The Crown's duty to disclose "survives the trial" of the matter.[105]

The Crown's duty to disclose is both a constitutional requirement[106] and an ethical duty.[107]

---

[98] For similar reasons, I would argue that law societies should also be permitted to discipline Crown prosecutors who exercise their discretion in a way that is reckless or grossly negligent.

[99] *R. v. Stinchcombe*, [1991] S.C.J. No. 83 at para. 29, [1991] 3 S.C.R. 326 (S.C.C.). Under the *Federal Prosecution Service Deskbook*, Crown are directed to provide "as soon as reasonably practical", the charging document, particulars of the offence, witness statements (or notes of an interview or will say statements), audio or video evidence of statements by witnesses, statements by the accused, the accused's criminal record, expert witness reports, documentary or other evidence, exhibits, search warrants, search authorizations, similar fact evidence intended to be relied upon at trial, identification evidence, witnesses' criminal records where relevant to credibility, material relevant to the case-in-chief, impeachment material, information obtained during witness interviews and "other material".

[100] *Ibid.* at para. 20.

[101] *R. v. McNeil*, [2009] S.C.J. No. 3 at para. 18 (S.C.C.).

[102] *R. v. La*, [1997] S.C.J. No. 30 at para. 1, [1997] 2 S.C.R. 680 (S.C.C.).

[103] *R. v. McNeil*, [2009] S.C.J. No. 3 at para. 23 (S.C.C.).

[104] *Ibid.* at para. 49, citing *R. v. Arsenault*, [1994] N.B.J. No. 417, 153 N.B.R. (2d) 81 (N.B.C.A.). See in general, Department of Justice, *Federal Prosecution Service Deskbook* (Ottawa: Department of Justice, 2000) s. 18.2.

[105] *Ibid.* at para. 17.

[106] *R. v. La*, [1997] S.C.J. No. 30, [1997] 2 S.C.R. 680 (S.C.C.).

[107] CBC MC Chapter 9, Commentary 9; FLS MC Rule 4.01(3), commentary; LSUC RPC Rule 4.01(3); AB CPC Chapter 10, Rule 28(d); BC PCH Chapter 8, Rule 18 and Canon 1(2).

If the Crown does not fulfill its duty to disclose, the accused may be entitled to a legal remedy. If the failure to disclose affected the fairness of the trial, either in the sense of affecting the reliability of the verdict, or in the sense of affecting the overall fairness of the trial, the accused will be entitled to remedies varying from an adjournment to deal with the newly disclosed material, a new trial[108] or, even, a stay of proceedings.[109] Stays have been granted in exceptional cases, such as where the appellant was already eligible for parole, with the result that requiring a new trial would simply "contribute to perpetuating an injustice and would tarnish the integrity of our judicial system".[110] Stays have also been granted where the evidence was important to the defence and had been lost for reasons that were not satisfactorily explained in the view of the trial judge,[111] and where the non-disclosure resulted in trial conduct that tarnished the administration of justice.[112]

In the latter case, *R. v. Nome*,[113] the accused was charged with assaulting a corrections officer in prison. The accused had refused to leave his cell when directed and had attempted to prevent corrections officers from entering his cell. The corrections officers forced their way into the accused's cell, struck him ten times with a baton, and handcuffed him on the bed. During their entry, it was alleged that the accused had thrown a soup can at the officers, and had struck one of them on the helmet. The charges against the accused arose out of this allegation. During the trial of the matter photographs of the accused's cell were produced as evidence. However, at the end of the trial the Crown produced further evidence that indicated that the contents of the accused's cell had been "removed and later put back prior to the photographs of the cell being taken".[114] Although the Crown had not been aware of this additional evidence, the fact that the "investigating body in this case, disassembled the crime scene and then reconstructed it to use as evidence in this trial",[115] tainted "this prosecution to such a degree that to proceed would tarnish the integrity of this court".[116]

---

[108] *E.g., R. v. Illes*, [2008] S.C.J. No. 59, 2008 SCC 57 (S.C.C.); *R. v. O'Grady*, [1995] B.C.J. No. 2041, 64 B.C.A.C. 111 (B.C.C.A.).

[109] *R. v. Dixon*, [1998] S.C.J. No. 17 at para. 34, [1998] 1 S.C.R. 244 (S.C.C.). For examples of cases in which relief but not a stay was granted for non-disclosure see: *R. v. Illes*, [2008] S.C.J. No. 59, 2008 SCC 57 (S.C.C.); *R. v. Taillefer*, [2003] S.C.J. No. 75, 2003 SCC 70 (S.C.C.); *R. v. La*, [1997] S.C.J. No. 30, [1997] 2 S.C.R. 680 (S.C.C.); *R. v. O'Grady*, [1995] B.C.J. No. 2041, 64 B.C.A.C. 111 (B.C.C.A.); *R. v. MacInnis*, [2007] O.J. No. 2930 (Ont. S.C.J.); *R. v. Wood*, [2006] A.J. No. 1457, 2006 ABCA 343 (Alta. C.A.); and *R. v. Bain*, [2005] O.J. No. 1237, 196 O.A.C. 81 (Ont. C.A.). For a case in which no relief was granted because trial fairness was not affected see *R. v. Nguyen*, [2006] S.J. No. 436 (Sask. C.A.).

[110] *R. v. Taillefer*, [2003] S.C.J. No. 75 at para. 128, 2003 SCC 70 (S.C.C.) (there were co-accused, one of whom had not pled guilty, and who was given a new trial).

[111] *R. v. Grabowski*, [2009] O.J. No. 5497 (Ont. C.J.).

[112] *R. v. Nome*, [2009] S.J. No. 671, 2009 SKQB 103 (Sask. Q.B.).

[113] *Ibid.*

[114] *Ibid.* at para. 10.

[115] *Ibid.* at para. 23.

[116] *Ibid.* at para. 30.

Crown non-disclosure can, in some circumstances, also lead to professional discipline for the lawyer in question. The point at issue in the case of *Krieger v. Law Society of Alberta*[117] was the jurisdiction of the Law Society to discipline a prosecutor alleged to have deliberately failed to provide adequate disclosure. Specifically, it was alleged that on May 24, 1994, prior to a preliminary inquiry in a murder case, Krieger had been provided with biological and DNA testing results from the crime scene that implicated someone other than the accused. One week later, on June 1, he advised counsel for the accused that the test results would not be available in time for the preliminary inquiry. At the preliminary inquiry, counsel for the accused learned for the first time about the existence and results of the test. He complained to the Attorney General who reprimanded Krieger and removed Krieger from the case; he also complained to the Law Society of Alberta about Krieger's conduct.

Like other Canadian codes of conduct, the Law Society of Alberta Code requires that Crown prosecutors make timely disclosure of all relevant evidence, whether inculpatory or exculpatory.[118] The Law Society sought to proceed against Krieger. Krieger challenged the Law Society's jurisdiction to do so. As already noted, however, the Supreme Court of Canada held that while the Crown exercises discretionary judgment with respect to the timing of disclosure, disclosure itself does not fall within the scope of prosecutorial discretion. Therefore, while the law society may only investigate the Crown's exercise of prosecutorial discretion where the Crown has acted with bad faith or dishonesty, a failure to disclose can be investigated by the Law Society in accordance with its ordinary regulatory practice.

Subsequent to *Krieger*, law societies have been prepared to proceed against Crown prosecutors who do not provide proper disclosure, especially when coupled with other wrongful conduct. In *Law Society of Saskatchewan v. Kirkham*,[119] the Law Society proceeded against Randy Kirkham as a result of his failure to disclose information to the court and to the accused. Kirkham was the Crown prosecutor on the first trial of Robert Latimer. As noted earlier, Latimer was charged with deliberately killing his disabled daughter.

Kirkham was concerned about whether potential jurors in the Latimer case would have strongly held views on euthanasia or mercy killing. Since "prosecutors in the area often routinely asked local RCMP to provide any background information they had available concerning prospective jurors",[120]

---

[117] [2002] S.C.J. No. 45, 2002 SCC 65 (S.C.C.).
[118] AB CPC, Chapter 10, Rule 28(d). See similarly: CBC MC Chapter 9, Commentary 9; FLS MC Rule 4.01(3), commentary; LSUC RPC Rule 4.01(3); BC PCH Chapter 8, Rule 18 and Canon 1(2).
[119] [1999] L.S.D.D. No. 19.
[120] *Ibid.*, Appendix C, Agreed Statement of Facts, para. 8. The ethics of this practice seem highly doubtful to me, unless the resulting information is routinely disclosed to the defence. It seems to give the state an advantage in the proceedings, when the whole point of prosecutorial ethics is to ensure that the state has no improper advantage relative to the accused.

Kirkham sent a "background form" to various RCMP detachments. His intention was that, based on their existing knowledge, the RCMP would fill out the form and provide it to Kirkham. He discovered, however, that some RCMP had been contacting potential jurors to ask them the questions on the background form. Kirkham directed the RCMP not to do so.

At that point Kirkham chose not to advise the court, Latimer, or Latimer's counsel, of what had happened. He instead decided that he would use his preemptory challenges to keep contacted jurors off the panel. Unfortunately, two of the jurors who had been contacted nonetheless ended up on the panel, resulting in Latimer having to be tried a second time.

Kirkham was charged with obstruction of justice, but acquitted because the Court was not convinced that the conduct met the *actus reus* for obstruction and that, in any event, "Kirkham had neither objective nor subjective foresight that his conduct could result in an obstruction of justice."[121] In the subsequent Law Society proceedings, Kirkham acknowledged that he had breached his duty to disclose information to the Court, and the Law Society agreed to withdraw the charge relating to his failure to give timely disclosure to the accused. He was suspended from practice for six months.

In *Law Society of Alberta v. Piragoff*,[122] noted earlier with respect to the Crown's duty to fulfill its ethical obligations, the Law Society suspended Piragoff in part for misleading the Court about the letter that had been sent to the accused, JD, by the police, but also for failing to disclose the origins of the letter to JD or his counsel.

In both *Piragoff* and *Kirkham*, the motivation behind the discipline was the non-disclosure or misrepresentation in relation to the Court, as much or more than non-disclosure to the accused. Even so, the Crown's ethical duty of disclosure to the accused is a potential reason to justify law society discipline. The Crown's duty of disclosure can be understood as the nexus between the Crown's role as minister of justice and its role as vigorous advocate;[123] through providing timely and full disclosure to the accused, the Crown helps to make the vigorous advocacy between the parties more of a contest of equals. Where, by contrast, the Crown fails to provide full and timely disclosure, the Crown's vigorous advocacy occurs within a context in which the Crown has an information advantage, and makes that advocacy hard to reconcile with the Crown's fundamental duty to ensure that justice is done.

This is not to suggest that providing full and timely disclosure exhausts the Crown's ethical obligations, but rather that providing such disclosure

---

[121] *R. v. Kirkham*, [1998] S.J. No. 458 at para. 29 (Sask. Q.B.).
[122] [2005] L.S.D.D. No. 47.
[123] This was the point made by L'Heureux-Dubé in *R. v. Cook*, [1997] S.C.J. No. 22, [1997] 1 S.C.R. 1113 (S.C.C.) where she emphasized that Crown disclosure prevented trial by ambush, and made it unnecessary to require the Crown to take specific steps such as calling particular witnesses.

fulfills a significant portion of those obligations. And, *eo ipso*, that failing to disclose is a significant and important ethical violation.

3. DEFENCE COUNSEL ETHICS

A. Defending the Guilty

Representing "guilty" clients presents no inherent ethical problem for lawyers. Yet a lawyer's representation may mean that a person who is morally culpable escapes legal sanction. It may even mean that a person who is also legally culpable, in the sense of having committed both the physical and mental elements of a crime, escapes legal sanction. So how can I suggest that such representation presents no ethical problem?

It presents no ethical problem for the same reason that zealous advocacy generally presents no ethical problem: the lawyer's role as zealous advocate, in whatever context, and for whatever client, permits the system of laws to fulfill its social function. As explained in Chapter 2, a system of laws allows each of us to be self-determining through and within the law. By acting as zealous advocates for individuals who cannot themselves fully access or maneuver through the legal system, lawyers ensure that those individuals are able to be self-determining in the way the law allows. This involves taking into account both the substantive content of the law — defining what constitutes unlawful action — and its procedural content — defining the procedure through which a person may be found to have acted in a manner that is unlawful. The role of a criminal defence lawyer is to ensure that it is only in accordance with the law's substantive content, *and* in accordance with the procedure that the law requires, that the sanctions of criminal law will be brought to bear on a client.

Observers generally perceive there to be an ethical problem with the representation of guilty clients when they view procedural requirements and values of the system of law as unimportant — as "loopholes" or "technicalities" — that do not speak to the moral or ethical point of importance, namely, whether the client "did" or "did not do" the acts of which he is accused. Yet the essence of legality is both procedural and substantive; what the law permits or requires is not simply that certain things be done, but that they be done in a particular way. Indeed, a significant part of the moral settlement legality accomplishes is the choice of the process that will be used to establish the content of law, to adjudicate disputes, and to determine the proper application of any particular legal requirement or entitlement. Criminal defence lawyers, whether representing the "guilty" or the "innocent", make sure that the adjudicative process we have chosen functions properly, and that it is only through that process that the sanctions of criminal law are brought to bear on a client.

One way to articulate this point is to suggest that a client is not "guilty" in a sense that creates an ethical issue for the lawyer until the law has both substantively and procedurally established that the client is guilty.

That determination can only be made after the legal process has functioned, not by the lawyer (or anyone else) looking at the client and his actions prior to the functioning of that process.

This perspective is reflected in the various codes of conduct, which direct defence counsel to seek to prevent conviction of a client

> except by a court of competent jurisdiction and upon legal evidence sufficient to support a conviction for the offence charged. Accordingly, and notwithstanding the lawyer's private opinion as to credibility or merits, the lawyer may properly rely upon all available evidence or defences including so-called technicalities not known to be false or fraudulent.[124]

This is not to say, however, that representing a guilty client does not create some ethical issues for the lawyer. That something is ethically justified does not mean that it is ethically straightforward. This section considers two ethical issues in relation to the representation of a "guilty" client: the temptation to judge the client's guilt or innocence, and the restrictions on representation that arise where a client has admitted the physical and mental elements of an offence.

Michael Code has said that "the most important ethical principal, when 'defending the guilty client', is to avoid forming any opinions on the subject of guilt or innocence in the first place".[125] Where lawyers judge their clients' culpability they run the risk of undermining their advocacy by diminishing their zeal.

In *R. v. Delisle*,[126] Delisle was accused of assault. He maintained his innocence, expressed his desire to testify, and identified Kevin Carl as one of the people who had attacked the victim. His lawyer, who was very inexperienced, did not believe Delisle's account of what happened, did not contact Carl, and decided that Delisle should not testify at the trial. Delisle was convicted. After Delisle's conviction, Carl contacted Delisle's lawyer and confirmed Delisle's account that it was he, Carl, who had committed the acts attributed to Delisle. Delisle's lawyer then attempted to re-open the trial, but was unsuccessful. Delisle appealed his conviction and produced an affidavit from Carl in support; Carl could not be reached to testify. The Crown conceded that the appeal had to be granted.

In its reasons the Québec Court of Appeal emphasized the importance of the lawyer refraining from judgment of his client: "The lawyer's explanation that he did not believe his client's story is also totally unacceptable. *The lawyer cannot set himself up as the judge of his client.*"[127]

---

[124] CBC MC Chapter 9, Commentary 10. See similarly FLS MC Rule 4.01(1), commentary; NB CC Chapter 8, Rule 14(b); LSUC RPC 4.01(1), commentary; BC PCH Canon 3(6).
[125] Michael Code, "Ethics and Criminal Law Practice", in Alice Woolley *et al.*, eds., *Lawyers' Ethics and Professional Regulation* (Toronto: LexisNexis Canada, 2008) ch. 8 at 374.
[126] [1999] J.Q. no 18, 133 C.C.C. (3d) 541 (Que. C.A.).
[127] *Ibid.* at 555 [emphasis in original].

The Court emphasized that a lawyer must not rely on his impressions of the client in deciding how to conduct a case, and that, always, the lawyer must fulfill her function in the legal system, which is to advocate for the client, not to judge him.[128] The Court quashed Delisle's conviction and ordered a new trial.

Competent criminal defence lawyers will mount a zealous defence of a client even where they suspect the client's guilt — that is, "notwithstanding the lawyer's private opinion as to credibility or merits".[129] At the same time, however, reserving judgment of a client is, as Michael Code emphasizes, part of how this result is achieved; the defence lawyer's open mind helps motivate her to investigate her client's case, identify available defences, and present the case in the most cogent and persuasive way possible.

What if the lawyer cannot escape knowledge of the client's guilt? Specifically, what if the client has voluntarily admitted the physical and mental elements of the offence with which he is charged?

Under the Canadian law governing lawyers, a client's admission of guilt constrains the lawyer's advocacy. If the lawyer is "convinced that the admissions are true and voluntary" the lawyer may object to jurisdiction or to the indictment, and may challenge the "admissibility or sufficiency of the evidence", but "should go no further than that".[130] The lawyer may not suggest that someone else committed the offence, call evidence that must be false if the client's admissions are true, or set up

> an affirmative case inconsistent with such admissions, for example, by calling evidence in support of an alibi intended to show that the accused could not have done, or in fact had not done, the act.[131]

The questions raised by these constraints on the lawyer's advocacy are, first, at what point are these obligations triggered? And, second, how far do these restrictions go? Do they prevent counsel from presenting true and accurate evidence that may result in an incorrect inference of the client's innocence? Or do they simply reinforce the general restriction against presenting false and misleading evidence to the court?

Michel Proulx and David Layton suggest that these obligations are triggered when counsel has "an unequivocal and reasonable subjective belief in the client's guilt".[132] This may result from a true and voluntary confession,[133] whether to the lawyer or to another,[134] but may also result from something such as DNA evidence that has been otherwise excluded

---

[128] *Ibid.* at 557-58, citing Daniel Soulez Larivière, *L'avocature* (Éditions du Seuil, 1995).
[129] CBC MC Chapter 9, Commentary 10.
[130] CBC MC Chapter 9, Commentary 11.
[131] *Ibid.* See also: FLS MC Rule 4.01(1), commentary; NB CC Chapter 8, footnote 33; LSUC RPC Rule 4.01(1), commentary; AB CPC Chapter 10, Rule 14.
[132] Michel Proulx & David Layton, *Ethics and Canadian Criminal Law* (Toronto: Irwin Law, 2001) at 41.
[133] *Ibid.* at 47.
[134] *Ibid.* at 44.

from the trial of the matter.[135] Any admission or evidence of guilt must establish both the mental and factual elements of the offence.[136] The question is whether "counsel reasonably draws an irresistible conclusion of guilt from available information".[137]

This interpretation of when the rule is triggered is reasonable so long as counsel emphasize the high standard required before determining that the client is guilty, and so long as counsel recognize that it is not the obligation of counsel to enter into such judgments unnecessarily. The lawyer has no obligation to make an assessment of guilt in each case. Indeed, as noted, lawyers should aim to be open-minded and non-judgmental about clients. The obligation to restrict the lawyer's defence of a client only arises where the lawyer cannot help but conclude that the client is guilty based on the information that the lawyer has.

Proulx and Layton further argue that the heart of the rule is to prevent defence counsel from knowingly misleading the court. This leads, though, to the second question to which the rule gives rise: at what point does a counsel cross from legitimately challenging the sufficiency of the Crown's case, to improperly establishing an affirmative case inconsistent with the client's admission?

Consider a fact scenario presented in order to obtain an ethics opinion from the Michigan State Bar:[138] a lawyer represents a client who has admitted to a violent robbery. The victim has testified during a preliminary examination that the robbery occurred at a particular time. The client has friends who can testify that, at that time, the client was with them. The client advises the lawyer that the friends' testimony is truthful, and that the victim has identified the time of the robbery incorrectly, in part because the client "stole the victim's watch and rendered him unconscious".[139] The lawyer asked for guidance from the Michigan State Bar about whether he could present the testimony of the friends.

The Michigan State Bar advised the lawyer that he could present the evidence. The evidence was truthful, and to refuse to present the evidence "would mean that a defendant who confessed guilt to counsel would never be able to have an active defense at trial".[140] They noted that confessions may not be accurate or reliable, and that "[o]ur society has made the decision to permit a person charged with a crime to make full disclosure to his counsel without fear that, absent the threat of some future conduct (such as a threat to kill a witness), the lawyer will not disclose the information so provided."[141]

---

[135] *Ibid.* at 42.
[136] *Ibid.* at 45.
[137] *Ibid.* at 42.
[138] Michigan Bar Opinion, January 23, 1987, CI-1164, online: <http://www.michbar.org/opinions/ethics/numbered_opinions/ci-1164.html>.
[139] *Ibid.*
[140] *Ibid.*
[141] *Ibid.*

Could the same opinion be provided under Canadian law? It is arguable that it could not. The point of the testimony is to do exactly what the codes of conduct forbid, namely, to establish an alibi that is inconsistent with the client's admission that, in fact, he committed the robbery and assault.

Yet to forbid counsel to present the evidence is to subvert the operation of the legal system. If counsel does not present the alibi evidence, the state will be facilitated in obtaining a conviction based on false evidence — that the assault occurred at a time of day when it could not have taken place. The conviction would occur based on misleading evidence — that is, by means of the very procedural error that the rule restricting defence advocacy is intended to avoid.

I would argue that this cannot be the intended result of the restriction arising from the client admissions rule, even if apparently necessitated by the broad language in which the restriction is stated. The one Canadian case that deals with this rule provides some support for this position. In *R. v. Li*,[142] the accused had confessed his participation in robberies to his lawyer. The evidence of guilt was primarily eye witness identification of the accused. At trial, the lawyer presented evidence about the accused's hairstyle and fluency in English so as to challenge the identification evidence offered by the Crown. The accused was convicted. On appeal he relied primarily on the argument that it was improper for his lawyer to refuse to permit him to testify. His counsel submitted an affidavit indicating that the client had confessed to the crime in order to explain the decision not to call the client as a witness. The Court agreed that counsel was not required to put forward false evidence for the accused.[143] It also, in the course of its reasons, considered the legitimacy of the introduction of the hairstyle and fluency evidence given the client's admissions.

The Court held that the lawyer could not call the accused as a witness to offer testimony inconsistent with the confession. The lawyer also could not set up "any inconsistent defence".[144] The lawyer could, however, call witnesses to give "uncontroversial evidence about the hairstyle of the accused, and about his fluency in English" which "might have raised a doubt about the reliability of the identification evidence given by the jewellery store clerks".[145]

Li suggests that lawyers may introduce truthful evidence, even if it leads to a misleading impression of innocence. *Li* may, though, be distinguishable from the Michigan case. In *Li*, the evidence did not establish an affirmative defence; it only challenged the Crown's identification evidence. In the Michigan case the evidence not only challenged the state's

---

[142] [1993] B.C.J. No. 2312 (B.C.C.A.).
[143] With respect to the distinct issue of the presentation of false evidence by a criminal accused, see Chapter 6.
[144] *R. v. Li*, [1993] B.C.J. No. 2312 at para. 66 (B.C.C.A.).
[145] *Ibid.*

evidence about the time of the crime, but also established an alibi to the commission of the crime. Nonetheless, the unifying aspect of the cases is that, in both instances, the evidence offered was true, and without it the conviction would have been based on a false premise, even if in some sense warranted.

Under the Alberta Code of Professional Conduct, the restriction on the conduct of the defence where the client has admitted guilt is found as a commentary to the rule against misleading the court. This placement indicates the true purpose of the rule; the specific prohibition on the conduct of a defence in the face of a client's admission of guilt bolsters the rule against providing false evidence to the court. It is not — it cannot — be intended to permit the Crown to achieve convictions based on false or unreliable assertions. The distinction between an affirmative defence and the challenging of the Crown's case confuses this fundamental purpose, and is unhelpful.

Unless narrowly interpreted in this way, the rule also has the potential to undermine the lawyer's duty of confidentiality, as noted by the Michigan State Bar. If broadly interpreted, this rule would mean that if a client provided full disclosure to his lawyer then the lawyer's representation would be restricted to the point that truthful exculpatory evidence could not be presented in his defence. The client in that instance may choose not to provide full disclosure; however, the absence of full disclosure may also undermine the quality of the representation the client receives, as was discussed with respect to lawyers who adopt "intentional ignorance" in order to avoid knowledge of a client's perjury.[146]

Further, as discussed in Chapter 5, the duty of confidentiality should ensure that the client is no worse off by retaining counsel than he would be if he could defend himself. Since he could legally present the Court with any truthful evidence, the lawyer should be permitted to do so as well, even if the lawyer knows that that evidence might lead to a result inconsistent with the client's admissions.

Assuming that this position is correct, and that a lawyer may present the court with any evidence that the lawyer does not know to be false, how far can the lawyer go in inviting the trier of fact to draw inferences that, while based on accurate and truthful evidence, are themselves incorrect? Can the lawyer not only present the accurate evidence that suggests an alibi, but also argue that the evidence establishes an alibi?

In a well-known legal ethics hypothetical, a client is charged with possession of stolen property after he is discovered with stolen goods in the backseat of the car. The client admits the crime to his lawyer, and also tells the lawyer that the reason that the goods were in the backseat is because the

---

[146] Recall from Chapter 6, Section 5.D., the example of *R. v. I.B.B.*, [2009] S.J. No. 378, 2009 SKPC 76 (Sask. Prov. Ct.), in which counsel refused to obtain information from the client and, as a result, did not obtain knowledge of the client's innocence, or identify the significant weaknesses in the Crown's case against the client.

client did not have keys to the trunk.[147] Under the Canadian rules, can the lawyer not only present the evidence that the goods were in the backseat, but also invite the trier of fact to draw the inference that the client cannot have known the goods were stolen, since if he had, he would not have placed them in plain view?

Proulx and Layton argue with respect to this scenario that the lawyer can "put the possibility to the jury, despite knowing it to be false, but in so doing cannot assert that the possibility is in fact true".[148] While this draws a fine distinction — it is not entirely obvious at what point a lawyer will have progressed from putting a possibility to the jury to asserting that the possibility is true — it is consistent with my general thesis. The restrictions on advocacy where the client has admitted guilt prohibit the presentation of false evidence to the court, or the assertion of the truth of false inferences, but should not inhibit the lawyer's forceful presentation of all available accurate evidence to advocate the client's innocence.

It should also be noted that the burden of proof in a criminal case lies with the Crown, and this extends to inferences that can be drawn from the evidence. The obligation is not on the defence to prove that the inference they invite is true; the burden is on the Crown to *disprove* inferences favouring the defence, beyond a reasonable doubt. It is therefore arguable that in pointing out the possibility of a favourable inference, the defence is simply pointing out the Crown's failure to discharge its burden.

The problem with Proulx and Layton's interpretation, and with mine, is that, if interpreted in this way, it is not clear that the rule restricting criminal defence advocacy contributes anything to the law governing lawyers. Other provisions of the codes of conduct prohibit the presentation of false evidence; the client's admission gives the lawyer knowledge of falsity which, under those rules, will restrict the lawyer's presentation of evidence. On Proulx and Layton's interpretation of the additional restriction on criminal defence advocacy, and on mine, the restriction does nothing more than to emphasize that the existing rule against presenting false evidence applies in the criminal defence context.

This may support the argument that the broader interpretation of the rule is correct, and that a criminal defence lawyer may not present the evidence raised in the Michigan State Bar opinion, and may not invite the inference about the client's knowledge in the stolen goods hypothetical. This argument, based on an assumption that a code would not be deliberately redundant, is, however, outweighed by the need for a code to be coherent with the structure of adversarial justice, and the presumption of innocence. A rule that would permit an accused to be convicted in part because his lawyer

---

[147] Obviously this hypothetical is now somewhat technologically dated.
[148] Michel Proulx & David Layton, *Ethics and Canadian Criminal Law* (Toronto: Irwin Law, 2001) at 72.

does not present truthful evidence to the court would violate that broader structure. The narrower interpretation is, on this basis, justified.

Thus, even where a client admits guilt, his lawyer should present to the court all available evidence, and truthful testimony, and invite the drawing of exculpatory inferences from that evidence. The lawyer should not present evidence that, given the admission, the lawyer knows to be false. The lawyer should not assert that the exculpatory inferences are true when the client's admission demonstrates that they are false. But the lawyer should make the best case for the client that the evidence allows, regardless of the client's admissions.

B. Plea Bargaining

The majority of criminal trials are resolved after an accused pleads guilty to an offence.[149] Assisting clients to determine when and whether to enter a guilty plea is, therefore, an essential aspect of the criminal defence lawyer's role, one that both creates ethical obligations and imposes ethical duties.

Most significantly, because a guilty plea eliminates the adjudication of guilt or innocence, the trial lawyer must ensure that a client only enters the plea where warranted on the facts and law. Most codes of conduct provide that a lawyer has a duty to investigate;[150] the lawyer must assess whether the client has any available defences before recommending that the client enter a guilty plea.

A failure to take such steps is unethical, as indicated by the case, *Law Society of Alberta v. Syed*,[151] discussed in Chapter 4. In *Syed* the lawyer proposed a plea for a client in a sexual assault case where he had not determined whether his client was guilty and, in particular, whether the complainants were minors, or whether the client thought that the complainants had consented. He had not interviewed the accused or explored potential defences. The lawyer did not look at the witness statements in a detailed fashion. The lawyer suggested a plea because he was unprepared. Doing so was unethical.

A significant aspect of the lawyer's pre-plea investigation and preparation is ensuring that the client is voluntarily prepared to admit the necessary factual and mental elements of the offence charged. Under Canadian law, an accused may not enter a plea of convenience; a client who maintains his innocence cannot enter a plea of "no contest". Further, a lawyer's ethical obligation not to mislead the court prohibits a lawyer from assisting a client who maintains his innocence to enter a plea under which that client admits to

---

[149] *Ibid.*
[150] FLS MC Rule 4.01(8); NB CC Chapter 8, Commentary 15(a); LSUC RPC Rule 4.01(9); AB CPC Chapter 10, Rule 27; BC PCH Chapter 8, Rule 20.
[151] [1994] L.S.D.D. No. 211.

the factual and mental elements of the offence;[152] since the client maintains his innocence those admissions would be misleading and improper.

In considering whether an accused has maintained innocence so as to invalidate a plea, the courts will consider the totality of the facts in relation to the lawyer's representation of the accused. Where the client's maintenance of innocence is implausible, and the lawyer has fully explored the meaning of the plea with the client, the court will not overturn the verdict that resulted from the plea, even if the client maintained his innocence.

Thus in *R. v. Hector*[153] a plea was upheld despite the accused's maintenance of innocence: the accused was an "experienced criminal", the evidence against the accused was extensive, his denials were equivocal and vague, his trial counsel was experienced, and he had signed a written acknowledgement with regard to the effect of the plea and his right to be tried. As his counsel stated:

> It is not unusual in my experience for a seasoned criminal charged with a serious offence, to profess their [sic] innocence even when the evidence indicates otherwise and they enter pleas of guilty. In my experience this has happened in every murder case I have handled. It's not uncommon for an accused to still profess their [sic] innocence even after they've had a trial by jury and been convicted.
>
> What struck me as odd with the appellant was that he did not profess his innocence when initially charged with the murders. It wasn't until after a number of meetings with him that he just casually threw out the statement that he was innocent to see how I would react to it. Once the appellant said he was innocent, my strategy was to explain why he was in possession of the gun that killed three people and to explain why he locked the bag containing the gun in the truck. He never explained that in any interview that I had with him.[154]

In those circumstances, it was neither improper nor unethical for his lawyer to participate in Hector's guilty plea.[155]

Conversely, where the client maintained his innocence to his lawyer and his lawyer simply forgot what the client had said;[156] where the client has maintained his innocence consistently both with his lawyer and in statements to others;[157] or where the client's apparent willingness to enter a plea is coupled with equivocations and denials, and there is reason to question the

---

[152] FLS MC Rule 4.01(8); NB CC Chapter 8, Commentary 15(a); LSUC RPC Rule 4.01(9); AB CPC Chapter 10, Rule 27; BC PCH Chapter 8, Rule 20.
[153] [2000] O.J. No. 1597, 146 C.C.C. (3d) 81 (Ont. C.A.).
[154] *Ibid.* at para. 11.
[155] For other cases in which an attempt to reverse a plea was rejected, see *R. v. Messervey*, [2010] N.S.J. No. 341, 2010 NSCA 55 (N.S.C.A.); *R. v. Stockley*, [2009] N.J. No. 239, 2009 NLCA 38 (Nfld. C.A.); *R. v. Joseph*, [2000] B.C.J. No. 2850 (B.C.S.C.), affd [2003] B.C.J. No. 1526, 2003 BCCA 369 (B.C.C.A.); *R. v. Pivonka*, [2007] O.J. No. 3138 (Ont. S.C.J.).
[156] *R. v. J.P.B.*, [2007] B.C.J. No. 1871, 2007 BCPC 270 (B.C. Prov. Ct.).
[157] *R. v. Scotney*, [2005] O.J. No. 2034 (Ont. S.C.J.); *R. v. Malone*, [1997] B.C.J. No. 835 (B.C.S.C.); *R. v. M.(G.O.)*, [1989] S.J. No. 482, 51 C.C.C. (3d) 171 (Sask. CA); *R. v. Yarlasky*, [1999] O.J. No. 4313, 140 C.C.C. (3d) 281 (Ont. C.A.); *R. v. K.(S.)*, [1995] O.J. No. 1627, 24 O.R. (3d) 199 (Ont. C.A.).

client's capacity and understanding of the plea,[158] the Court will vacate the plea that was entered.

This case law indicates that in deciding whether the circumstances warrant entering a guilty plea, a lawyer does not need to have a direct admission from the client, and may even have a client who in some way maintains his innocence; however, the circumstances must be such as to be equivalent to such an admission. Any reasonable question about the client's guilt, whether based on the client's maintenance of innocence or other evidence, will make entering into a plea agreement improper.

A lawyer must also not pressure the accused to enter a guilty plea because of the lawyer's own concerns or motivations. These include such obviously improper grounds as trying to protect the lawyer herself from criminal prosecution[159] but also include concerns about work pressures, the effort involved in preparing for a trial or being on good terms with the Crown.[160]

In addition to ensuring that the plea is voluntarily given, and that the client can properly admit the physical and mental elements of the offence, the lawyer must ensure that the client fully understands the implications of entering a guilty plea. The lawyer must ensure that the client understands the general effects of a conviction on the accused (with respect to, for example, deportation), the fact that the court is not bound by the Crown's sentencing recommendation; that once a guilty plea has been entered issues such as the constitutionality of Crown conduct cannot be argued; and, the advantages of a plea such as achieving a final resolution quickly and ameliorating the potential sentence.[161]

Can a lawyer push a client to accept a plea? A lawyer can (and should) indicate the benefits and costs of a plea relative to going to trial, and that may include making a recommendation to the client as to which approach would be better. Where a client appears to be acting irrationally and imprudently in proceeding to trial, the lawyer may advise against that decision in strong terms. The lawyer must, though, "fully respect the client's freedom of choice"[162] about how to proceed, and should not use withdrawal as a threat to pressure the client to take a course of action, unless withdrawal would be mandated on other grounds.

This last point — about the client's freedom of choice — brings the conversation back to the question of the client who maintains innocence but nonetheless wants to plead guilty. As noted, the law is clear that, in Canada, a lawyer may not assist that client to enter a plea. What if, though, the lawyer recognizes the client's reason for wanting to accept a plea; in

---

[158] *R. v. J.M.*, [2001] N.J. No. 232, 204 Nfld. & P.E.I.R. 318 (Nfld. Prov. Ct.).
[159] *R. v. Laperrière*, [1995] J.Q. no 635, 101 C.C.C. (3d) 462 (Que. C.A.), affd [1996] S.C.J. No. 66, [1996] 2 S.C.R. 284, 109 C.C.C. (3d) 347 (S.C.C.).
[160] Michel Proulx & David Layton, *Ethics and Canadian Criminal Law* (Toronto: Irwin Law, 2001) at 421.
[161] *Ibid.* at 432-34. See also: FLS MC Rule 4.01(8); NB CC Chapter 8, Commentary 15(a); LSUC RPC Rule 4.01(9); AB CPC Chapter 10, Rule 27.
[162] *Ibid.* at 435.

particular, what if the lawyer thinks that conviction is highly probable, that the Crown has offered an attractive resolution, and that the client is fundamentally correct in his assessment that the best course of action is to take the plea? Or what if the client wants to enter a plea in order to protect a third party — his child, or his wife?

For the reasons set out in discussion of the perjury trilemma in Chapter 6, in my view a lawyer should not withdraw from representing a client who, after full information, careful deliberation and proper investigation, wants to enter a guilty plea. A lawyer must never pressure a client to accept a plea bargain. But in this instance, just as in the perjury trilemma, the importance of the client's right to counsel and right to confidentiality should outweigh the importance of preventing the client from misleading the court by falsely admitting the physical and mental elements of the crime. Even where a client who proclaims his innocence is contemplating pleading guilty, his lawyer can still be of assistance by helping that client to weigh, in an informed and careful manner, the prospect and possible consequences of a conviction. Would it be ethical to allow a person who maintains his innocence but has decided to plead guilty to be without counsel at so existential a moment? This is not to say that pleas of convenience should be permitted, or that Canadian criminal accused should be subjected to the unconscionable pressure to plead faced by American criminal accused due to high minimum sentences and aggressive charging decisions, which together create an enormous incentive for an American accused to take a plea bargain to a lesser offence, whether guilty or not. But it is to say that, like in other cases where clients have admitted something to their lawyers that they do not want to admit in court, the duty of the lawyer to the client should be paramount.

This is, again, not an accurate statement of the law in Canada. Canadian criminal defence lawyers may not lawfully assist a client to enter a plea where the client maintains his factual or legal innocence. And, in general, it is more appropriate that lawyers do what they can to make a plea of convenience unnecessary, through diligent and competent representation of the client's interests, than that they help an innocent client to plead guilty.

4. CONCLUSION

For the most part being a prosecutor or criminal defence lawyer heightens the significance of the lawyer's ethical duties rather than changing the nature of those duties. Competent zealous representation, in which client confidences are maintained, and conflicts are avoided, primarily constitutes the ethical obligations with which lawyers working in the criminal law context must comply. Having said that, for prosecutors there is a material shift in the usual understanding of what zealous advocacy should accomplish, and for defence lawyers there are unique challenges to ensuring that zealous advocacy operates effectively within the bounds of legality. And that is why — as popular culture can attest — lawyers who practice in the context of criminal law will always be the zeitgeist of the legal profession.

Chapter 10

ZEALOUS ADVOCACY AND ACCESS TO JUSTICE

1. INTRODUCTION

This book's justification and explanation of lawyers' various professional responsibilities asserts the importance of lawyers in a civil society. Through the system of laws we resolve our disagreements over the right way to live, settling the "rules" for our interactions with each other, and what we will require, permit or enable each member of our society to do. Lawyers facilitate the achievement of the social compromise of legality at every point, helping to write the law, to advise people on the law's content, and to enable people to resolve their disputes through the framework law provides. In order to do so lawyers must defer to clients' assessment of the goals they want to achieve through the law, and act zealously within the bounds of legality to help clients achieve those goals; hence the lawyer's professional responsibilities.

This analysis leads, though, to another significant conclusion: the social compromise of legality will not operate fairly — and may not operate at all — if people cannot access lawyers. If people do not know when they need a lawyer, the help that lawyers can provide or, most significantly, simply cannot afford to pay a lawyer's fees, then the social compromise of law may exist, but it will not apply fairly, and may be wholly denied.

From this conclusion follow issues of public policy — of how much funding we give to legal aid, and for what sorts of matters — but also issues about lawyers' professional responsibilities. Namely, if access to justice requires access to lawyers, then what responsibilities do lawyers have to ensure that access?

This chapter considers lawyers' professional responsibilities in relation to access to justice. It begins with an analysis of the barriers to access to lawyers — why people may not have a lawyer, even though they need one. It then considers some of the ways in which lawyers can facilitate access to legal services, focusing in particular on advertising and solicitation, *pro bono* and regulatory initiatives to increase consumer information and reduce the economic barriers to purchasing legal services.

2. BARRIERS TO ACCESS TO LAWYERS

A. Do I Need A Lawyer?

In 1874 Canada began funding residential schools for First Nations' children. The schools were operated by churches, and were intended to ensure the assimilation of aboriginal children into the English or French communities. In addition to being removed from their communities, children were taught English or French, and were punished for speaking their native languages. They were inculcated with Christian beliefs. Many students were also abused, sexually and physically, and, during one 14-year period, 24% of the students died from tuberculosis.[1]

In the official apology to residential school survivors Prime Minister Harper acknowledged the wrongs that the schools had done:

> To the approximately 80,000 living former students, and all family members and communities, the government of Canada now recognizes that it was wrong to forcibly remove children from their homes and we apologize for having done this.
>
> We now recognize that it was wrong to separate children from rich and vibrant cultures and traditions, that it created a void in many lives and communities, and we apologize for having done this.
>
> We now recognize that, in separating children from their families, we undermined the ability of many to adequately parent their own children and sowed the seeds for generations to follow, and we apologize for having done this.
>
> We now recognize that, far too often, these institutions gave rise to abuse or neglect and were inadequately controlled, and we apologize for failing to protect you.
>
> Not only did you suffer these abuses as children, but as you became parents, you were powerless to protect your own children from suffering the same experience, and for this we are sorry.
>
> The burden of this experience has been on your shoulders for far too long. The burden is properly ours as a government, and as a country.
>
> There is no place in Canada for the attitudes that inspired the Indian residential schools system to ever again prevail.[2]

The governmental acknowledgement of the wrongs done to residential school survivors was not self-generated. It followed from many years of advocacy and litigation, driven by aboriginal groups and leaders but also in part by lawyers who identified that these wrongs were legally cognizable

---

[1] Bill Curry & Karen Howlett, "Natives died in droves as Ottawa ignored warnings" *The Globe and Mail* (24 April 2007), online: <http://www.theglobeandmail.com/news/politics/article754798.ece>. See also Cigdem Iltan, "Truths about the truth commission" *The Globe and Mail* (15 June 2010), online: <http://www.theglobeandmail.com/news/national/truths-about-the-truth-commission/article1604264/?cmpid=tgc>.

[2] Statement of Apology of Prime Minister Stephen Harper, online: <http://www.cbc.ca/canada/story/2008/06/11/pm-statement.html>.

and warranted compensation. The lawyers identified not just the physical and sexual abuse that took place in the schools as wrongful, but also the cultural destruction and alienation from community that affected the survivors and their families.

Those lawyers came too late to prevent the wrongs that were done, and even had they arrived earlier the structure and prejudice in the legal system at the time would almost certainly have precluded successful advocacy on the students' behalf.[3] However, the lawyers were not incidental to the final settlement and apology; they were central and necessary, and without the information they provided to survivors about what constitutes a wrong in law, and their persistence in filing and pursuing claims, it is not obvious that the settlement and apology would have occurred.

How was that information provided? It came in part from lawyers approaching prospective clients. For example, Tony Merchant, a lawyer in Saskatchewan, actively solicited residential school survivors to participate in litigation, informing them that they had a claim, of what the recovery associated with that claim might be, and as to how they could take steps to realize that recovery.

Merchant was disciplined by the Law Society of Saskatchewan for the fact that his letters were misleading about the costs and risks associated with bringing the litigation.[4] However, sending the letters to potential claimants nonetheless did something important: it told residential school survivors that they had legal rights, and it gave those survivors the opportunity to retain a lawyer who could, and did, help enforce those rights.

As discussed by Monroe Freedman and Abbe Smith, five-year-old Ernest Gene Gunn was not so well-informed. Ernest was seriously injured when he was hit by a car driven by John J. Washek. Shortly after the accident, Ernest's mother was visited at home by an adjuster from Washek's insurance company. The adjuster told Ms. Gunn that there was no need for her to hire a lawyer, because the company would make a settlement as soon as Ernest was out of his doctor's care. If Ms. Gunn was not satisfied then, he explained, she could get a lawyer and file suit.

Ernest's injuries were severe enough to require medical treatment for twenty-three months. During that time, the insurance adjuster was regularly in touch with Ms. Gunn. At the end of Ernest's medical treatment, however, despite several efforts on her part to reach him, the adjuster was unavailable. Finally, she retained a lawyer, who promptly filed suit for her. Ernest never

---

[3] As discovered by Mark O'Meara. See Chapter 2, Section 2.
[4] Merchant is also a controversial figure within the residential schools settlement, in part because of the fees that he was awarded as a condition of that settlement, and in part because of concerns with aspects of his conduct, such as the misleading nature of his solicitation. While I share those concerns, I am nonetheless suggesting that he should be given some credit for the positive aspects of the part he played, in particular with respect to raising awareness of the existence and legitimacy in law of the claims of the residential school survivors.

had his day in court, however, because the insurance company successfully pled a two-year statute of limitations.[5]

One difference in these cases is apparent: the residential school survivors were told that they needed a lawyer. Ms. Gunn was told that she didn't.

As noted, access to a lawyer will not cure injustices that inhere in the legal system — had the residential school survivors had a lawyer in 1930 it would not have helped, and when the Gunns retained a lawyer it was too late. But where the law provides justice, knowing that you need a lawyer is the first and crucial step to seeing that justice done.

This leads to the identification of the first barrier to access to lawyers and justice: ignorance about when a lawyer is necessary, or what a lawyer can accomplish. Unless people know when they have a problem that will be resolved better with the help of a lawyer, they will not seek out legal advice and, like the Gunns, will suffer the consequences.

Do people know when they need a lawyer? Certainly they know sometimes, but not always. Not only do people not always realize when their legal rights are affected — like the residential school survivors or the Gunns — but they also do not always realize what exactly it is that a lawyer can accomplish in navigating the entitlements and prohibitions of the law. Lawyers do not just litigate in courts, they advocate with government agencies. They ensure that information is presented in the best way possible to get a result. They negotiate. All of these services help ensure that the law is applied properly and fairly. Yet if people do not know what a difference having a lawyer will make, they will not seek a lawyer out.

When I was in practice I represented a family to assist them in obtaining residential care for their adult disabled son. The family was in crisis because their adult son's needs did not permit them to also meet the needs of their younger children. Their circumstances were such that they were entitled to support under the government's law and policy. The family was nonetheless denied support by the government workers they dealt with; the family had functioned well for a long time, the disabled son was well cared for, and the family was not draining other governmental resources. The workers had no motivation to help, had numerous other claims on their resources and pressure to keep costs down, and so nothing was done.

The family did not need information about their legal entitlements. They knew what was happening was wrong. But what they did need was to know that it would make a difference to have a lawyer who could persistently and assertively advocate for them with the government and, with the threat of litigation in the background, ensure that the advocacy was given due attention. That information was available to the family because that

---

[5] Monroe Freedman & Abbe Smith, *Understanding Lawyers' Ethics*, 4th ed. (New Providence, NJ: LexisNexis, 2010) at 323-24, discussing *Gunn v. Washek*, 405 Pa. 521, 187 A.2d 635 (1961).

disabled man is my nephew, and his parents my sister and brother-in-law. I represented them because I knew it would make a difference, and I told them so. But otherwise they would not have known; all they would have known is that no one was listening, and the crisis would have evolved in due course.

B. How Do I Pay For One?

The second barrier to legal services is that most often cited in explaining the access to justice problem: lawyers cost more than most people can afford when faced with a legal problem. Employees who are wrongfully dismissed, tenants abused by landlords, landlords abused by tenants, divorcing parents and parents of disabled children wrongfully denied service, may know that they will benefit from the services of a lawyer, but hiring a lawyer costs too much.

What does it mean to say that hiring a lawyer costs too much? A number of ideas are incorporated in that statement. A lawyer may cost too much relative to the amount of money at issue. An employee who is fired without cause or notice might be entitled to two weeks or a month's pay in lieu of notice; hiring a lawyer to enforce that payment will leave the employee with only a few dollars remaining if any. A lawyer may cost too much relative to other things of importance to the consumer — goods, clothes or housing. At the margins, it might simply be irrational to choose to retain a lawyer rather than to purchase other things of more immediate value.

The costs of legal services may also be too uncertain to be worth incurring. The costs are uncertain in three senses. First, especially with hourly billing, it may be hard to predict up front what the actual cost of legal services will be; taking on that uncertainty is too high risk and may not be worthwhile relative to the benefit that the consumer will receive. Second, it may be difficult to know whether retaining a lawyer will in fact lead to a benefit; even the most competent lawyers do not always achieve their clients' goals. Third, it may not be clear whether, in retaining a particular lawyer, the consumer will be receiving good value for money. The consumer may not know whether a particular lawyer is diligent, intelligent or effective.

When a consumer purchases a loaf of bread she can make a precise determination of the relationship between the cost of the bread and the benefit of having the bread. When a consumer purchases legal services, making that cost-benefit determination is difficult or impossible. It would be as if, to continue the bread analogy, the purchaser did not know what the bread costs; did not know whether in fact she would be permitted to eat the bread; and did not know whether the bread she was buying was delicious or nasty. In that situation a rational consumer may simply decline to buy the bread.

Why do lawyers cost too much in the various ways I've identified? The first reason is income distribution. In Canada in 2007, 75% of the population had income under $50,000.[6] Median family income in 2007 was $66,550.[7] Canadians are, by world standards, wealthy. However, it is still the case that for most Canadians, paying for a lawyer requires sacrificing something else of importance, or going into debt.

Second, there is likely a floor below which legal costs will not fall. Becoming a lawyer is expensive. Taking into account only lost income for a university graduate (assume $35,000 per year), and the average cost of tuition and associated costs at a Canadian law school ($15,000 per year), becoming a lawyer requires an investment of $50,000 per year. Given that investment, and the costs associated with running a legal practice, lawyers are unlikely to be willing to work for low cost unless they can leverage through using paralegals or law clerks to do most of the work on files (as some real estate practitioners do, for example).

Third, the demand for legal services is both corporate and individual. Personal consumers of legal services must therefore compete for the supply of service providers with corporations who can pay a much higher price, both because they have more money, and because legal fees for a corporation are tax deductible, whereas those for an individual normally are not.[8] While this may not directly increase price, since lawyers tend to work either for corporations or for individuals, rather than doing both types of work, it shrinks the quantity and quality (as defined by success in law school) of the supply of lawyers working for individual clients, which is likely both to indirectly increase price and to increase the consumer's uncertainty as to quality.

Finally, the market for legal services is imperfect, and those imperfections both make the market difficult for consumers to participate in effectively, and make it likely that legal services cost more than they would in a perfectly functioning market.[9]

In order to be perfectly competitive an economic market must have five central attributes: (1) numerous buyers and sellers, so that no part of the market can exercise market power to distort price; (2) complete information held by all economic actors in the market so that people can make choices that reflect what they actually want; (3) product homogeneity (one product is essentially the same as another) so that producers are meaningfully competitive with each other on the basis of price; (4) free entry and exit, so that there is supply and demand responsiveness; and (5) an absence of "externalities" (costs and benefits of the economic relationship between buyers and sellers that do not get included in the price paid for a particular

---

[6] Statistics Canada Table, "Individuals by total income level, by province and territory (Canada)", online: <http://www40.statcan.gc.ca/l01/cst01/famil105a-eng.htm>.

[7] Statistics Canada Table, "Median total income, by family type, by province and territory", online: <http://www40.statcan.gc.ca/l01/cst01/famil08a-eng.htm>.

[8] The test being whether the expense is used for the purpose of earning income.

[9] This discussion is drawn in part from Alice Woolley, "Imperfect Duty: Lawyers' Obligation to Foster Access to Justice" (2007) 45(5) Alta. L. Rev. 107.

product, such as environmental pollution caused by an economic activity) so that producers bear the full costs of production and consumers bear the full costs of consumption.[10]

With the exception of the first criterion (there are numerous buyers and sellers of legal services), the market for legal services satisfies none of these criteria. However, to understand why legal services cost so much, in the ways I've identified, only two imperfections really matter: the absence of complete information for market participants, and the absence of product homogeneity.

The market for legal services is notable for the total absence — and actual impossibility — of informational sufficiency and symmetry with and between participants in the market. This arises most obviously from the fact that any person who needs a lawyer — who does not have himself the relevant qualifications and abilities — self-evidently lacks knowledge about what needs to be done to solve his problem. He must rely on the lawyer not only to do the work, but also to tell him what it is that needs to be done and how best to do it. A client often does not know, for example, whether writing a will should take one hour or five; he depends on the lawyer to provide an honest answer as to which it is, and to do no more work than is necessary to get the job done. Clients are both relatively and deeply uninformed relative to the lawyer they are retaining: clients know less than their lawyers, and what they do not know is significant, going to the essence of the commodity which they are purchasing.[11]

The client's lack of sufficient information is absolute as well as relative. Because legal outcomes are significantly determined by factors outside the control of either the lawyer *or* the client, it may be impossible for anyone to determine how much work will be required to resolve a particular problem, or whether even with a great deal of work the problem will be

---

[10] Michael J. Trebilcock, Carolyn J. Tuohy & Alan D. Wolfson, *Professional Regulation: A Staff Study of Accountancy, Architecture, Engineering and Law in Ontario prepared for the Professional Organizations Committee* (Toronto: Ontario Law Reform Commission, 1979) at 47.

[11] For discussions of the informational asymmetry/credence good problem see Gillian Hadfield, "The Price of Law: How the Market for Lawyers Distorts the Justice System" (2000) 98 Mich. L. Rev. 953; David Barnhizer, "Profession Deleted: Using Market and Liability Forces to Regulate the Very Ordinary Business of Law Practice for Profit" (2004) 17 Geo. J. Legal Ethics; Michael J. Trebilcock, Carolyn J. Tuohy & Alan D. Wolfson, *Professional Regulation: A Staff Study of Accountancy, Architecture, Engineering and Law in Ontario prepared for the Professional Organizations Committee* (Toronto: Ontario Law Reform Commission, 1979); Michael J. Trebilcock, "The Profession and public policy: the nature of the agenda" in *The Professions and Public Policy*, Phillip Slayton & Michael Trebilcock, eds. (Toronto: University of Toronto Press, 1978); Michael Trebilcock & Lilla Csorgo, "Multi-Disciplinary Professional Practices: A Consumer Welfare Perspective" (2001) 24 Dal. L.J. 1 at 15-16; Larry E. Ribstein, "Ethical Rules, Agency Costs, and Law Firm Structure" (1998) 84 Va. L. Rev. 1707 at 1709 (Jack Ladinsky, "The Traffic in Legal Services: Lawyer-Seeking Behavior and the Channeling of Clients" (1976) 11(2) Law & Soc'y Rev. 207 at 215; Paul Fenn & Alistair McGuire, "The assessment: the economics of legal reform" (1994) 10 *Oxford Review of Economic Policy* 1 at 4-5; Roger Bowles, "The structure of the legal profession in England and Wales" (1994) 10 *Oxford Review of Economic Policy* 18.

capable of successful resolution. In addition, even after the fact it may be difficult to determine whether an unsuccessful outcome arose from a lack of effort of counsel or from bad luck with respect to the judge, other relevant third parties (a regulator or financial institution), the conduct of other counsel, or a myriad of other factors. As one commentator asked rhetorically, "If the intrinsic quality of the service does remain unobservable, as there are factors outside the lawyers' control which contribute to the outcome, how does the consumer react? In other words is a good reputation consistent with a long run of bad luck?"[12] Or, conversely, should a long run of good luck warrant a good reputation?

As well as suffering from information problems, legal services are inherently non-homogeneous. The services offered by the most intelligent, practical, diligent and experienced counsel in closing a corporate transaction are not the same as those offered by his less qualified counterpart. The differences relate to the time that is put into a matter; the quality of the legal reasoning brought to bear upon a problem; the prior experience of the lawyer in resolving similar difficulties in the past, perhaps to the point of specialization in the area; the inter-personal skills of the lawyer in dealing with other individuals involved in the issue; and a myriad of other relevant skills and qualities. An hour of one lawyer's time may have radically different value than an hour of another lawyer's time. The organizational structures within which lawyers practice may differ as well, and in a way that is relevant for the services a lawyer provides. There is a vast difference between a sole practitioner or small partnership and a large "full service" firm. Such a firm will comprise several layers of legal professionals, specialized practice groups, "hired guns" (*i.e.*, prominent rain makers and star litigators), support staff and resources.

Further, even were one lawyer much like another, the demands placed on lawyers by their clients are not. The needs of a client litigating a contractual dispute are entirely different from the needs of a client doing an initial public offering for a company. And even the needs of a client litigating a contractual dispute may not be the same of those of another client who is also litigating a contractual dispute. While not all demands are highly variable — one residential house closing is generally much like another — more often than not what one client needs from her lawyer is quite different from what another client needs.[13]

These imperfections in the market for legal services lead directly to the cost issues I identified earlier and, in particular, to the problem that buying legal services is too uncertain. Clients do not have enough information to gauge whether the product they are buying is appropriate for their legal

---

[12] Paul Fenn & Alistair McGuire, "The assessment: the economics of legal reform" (1994) 10 *Oxford Review of Economic Policy* 1 at 7.
[13] R.E. Olley, "The future of self-regulation: a consumer economist's viewpoint" in *The Professions and Public Policy*, Phillip Slayton & Michael Trebilcock, eds. (Toronto: University of Toronto Press, 1978) at 79.

needs, whether the price they are paying is fair, or whether it will achieve what they need it to achieve. Any rational consumer of legal services will recognize that, to some extent, participating in the legal services market is a gamble, and gambling is rarely a rational economic proposition.

3. REDUCING THE BARRIERS TO ACCESS

The barriers to access to justice are thus significant. People do not necessarily know whether or to what extent they need a lawyer, and even if they know they may not be able to afford to pay for one. These barriers are reflected in statistics about access to justice in Canada. According to the federal Justice Department, 13% of criminal accused appear in court without a lawyer. Not surprisingly, although disturbingly, those accused are more likely to be convicted.[14] The Report of the Ontario Civil Legal Needs Project in May 2010 stated:

> Low and middle-income Ontarians experience many barriers to access to civil justice, including the real and perceived cost of legal services, lack of access to legal aid and lack of access to information and self-help resources. Once again, the poorest and most vulnerable Ontarians experience the greatest barriers.[15]

A variety of studies indicate that the number of litigants who are unrepresented by counsel is growing, particularly in family law matters.[16]

To a significant extent reducing the barriers which result in these access issues is beyond the control or professional obligations of lawyers; questions of income inequality, or the capital investment required to become a lawyer, are matters of social and economic policy for the country as a whole, not matters of lawyer responsibility or regulation.

Lawyer's professional responsibilities and regulation cannot, though, ignore these barriers to justice. Further, to the extent their mandate and jurisdiction permits, they should respond to them. In this section I will focus on appropriate responses by lawyers to barriers to legal services, including advertising and solicitation, *pro bono*, and regulatory initiatives to increase consumer information and reduce the economic barriers to participation in the legal services market.

---

[14] Jeremy Hainsworth, "Government budget-slashing cuts into Legal Aid" *The Lawyers Weekly* 30:24 (29 October 2010) 14.

[15] Ontario Civil Legal Needs Project, *Listening to Ontarians: Report of the Ontario Civil Legal Needs Project*, at p. 46, online: <http://www.lsuc.on.ca/media/may3110_oclnreport_final.pdf>.

[16] Minister of Justice and Attorney General Saskatchewan, *Unrepresented Litigants Access to Justice Committee, Final Report*, November 2007, summarizing various Canadian studies on the issue, at 26-27, online: <http://www.justice.gov.sk.ca/Final-Report-Unrepresented-Litigants.pdf>. The Report notes that the extent of the unrepresented litigants problem varies regionally and across groups, and is somewhat difficult to measure. See also Alberta Law Reform Institute, *Self-Represented Litigants*, March 2005, online: <http://www.law.ualberta.ca/alri/docs/cm01218.pdf>.

A. Advertising and Solicitation

Historically, Canadian lawyers were prohibited from advertising and soliciting. As stated by the Law Society of Upper Canada, advertising "was regarded as unprofessional conduct" which lowered "the tone of the lawyer's high calling and should not be tolerated".[17]

In 1980 Donald Jabour, a lawyer in North Vancouver, advertised the provision of "legal services at prices middle income families can afford".[18] He provided information on "sample fees"[19] for various services, such as a simple will or incorporation. He put a sign outside his building that said "The North Shore Neighbourhood Legal Clinic".[20] For these activities Jabour was suspended from practice for six months. The Law Society of British Columbia's rules prohibited fee advertising, restricted the type of signs a lawyer could use, and only permitted advertising through activities such as the occasional publication of announcements in a local newspaper. Jabour had violated all these rules.

Jabour unsuccessfully challenged the Law Society of British Columbia's regulations to the Supreme Court of Canada. Despite the almost total prohibition on commercial speech imposed by the regulations, the pre-*Charter* Court was unwilling to see any illegitimate constraint on Jabour's freedom of expression, and identified the law society as having clear jurisdiction over the definition of conduct unbecoming a barrister and solicitor. The Court concluded that "[i]t can hardly be contended that the province by proper legislation could not regulate the ethical, moral and financial aspects of a trade or profession";[21] the restriction on misleading advertising "is just such a lawful regulatory restriction on freedom of expression or freedom of economic speech".[22]

After Jabour's case the attitude towards professional advertising gradually relaxed until, in 1990, the Supreme Court of Canada made it clear that blanket prohibitions on professional advertising are not constitutional. In *Rocket v. Royal College of Dental Surgeons*,[23] a unanimous court held that professional advertising serves "an important public interest by enhancing the ability of patients to make informed choices".[24] Thus, professional bodies may regulate advertising, but only for the purpose of protecting the public and maintaining professionalism. Specifically, regulation may prohibit "unverifiable",[25] "misleading, deceptive and unprofessional

---

[17] *Law Society of Upper Canada v. Barnett*, [1997] L.S.D.D. No. 94, discussing the historical attitude towards lawyer advertising.
[18] *Canada (Attorney General) v. Law Society of British Columbia*, [1982] S.C.J. No. 70, [1982] 2 S.C.R. 307 at 318 (S.C.C.).
[19] *Ibid.* at 319.
[20] *Ibid.*
[21] *Ibid.* at 364.
[22] *Ibid.* at 365.
[23] [1990] S.C.J. No. 65, [1990] 2 S.C.R. 232 (S.C.C.).
[24] *Ibid.* at para. 30.
[25] *Ibid.* at para. 49.

advertising while permitting legitimate advertising"[26] that speaks to "objective facts"[27] about the services that the professional provides.

Law society codes of conduct reflect the direction given by the Court in *Rocket*. Generally the codes begin by recognizing the relationship between advertising and the obligation of lawyers "to make legal services available to the public".[28] The codes prohibit all misleading, deceptive and inaccurate advertising,[29] in some cases requiring further that ads be "demonstrably true, accurate and verifiable".[30] The codes identify improper advertising as advertising that creates unjustified expectations,[31] that suggests the lawyer is a "specialist" when the lawyer has not been certified as such,[32] or that is coercive or exploitative.[33] Fee advertising must not use terms such as "from", "minimum", or "and up", must be precise about how disbursements are treated, and must not be comparative.[34] Some codes also prohibit lawyers from giving fees or items of value to others for referring clients.[35]

The codes of conduct also regulate advertising to protect professionalism. Codes require generally that advertisements be "consistent with a high standard of professionalism"[36] and many further require that marketing be in "good taste".[37] The Alberta code goes on to specify that

> The prohibition includes the use of inflammatory statements, undignified comments, or similar material unrelated to the selection of counsel. It also applies to the use of photographs or other depictions of: dramatic scenes, accidents or injury victims, as well as dramatizations, emotional appeals, sound effects, hawkish spokespersons, celebrity endorsements, or slapstick routines.[38]

The codes also prohibit lawyers from approaching individuals who are vulnerable, with the Alberta code expressly prohibiting a lawyer from

---

[26] *Ibid.*
[27] *Ibid.* at para. 41.
[28] CBA MC Chapter XIV, Rule; NB CC Chapter 16, Principle 1; AB CPC Chapter 5, Statement of Principle. Both the FLS MC and LSUC RPC advertising rules follow Rule 3.01, which requires that lawyers make "legal services available to the public in an efficient and convenient way that commands respect and confidence and is compatible with the integrity and independence of the profession".
[29] CBA MC Chapter XIV, Commentary 3; FLS MC Rule 3.02(1)(b); NB CC Chapter 16, Commentary 3; Que. CEA Rules 3.02.03 and 5.01; LSUC RPC Rule 3.04(1)(a); AB CPC Chapter 5, Rule 1(b).
[30] FLS MC Rule 3.01(a); AB CPC Chapter 5, Rule 1(a).
[31] BC PCH Chapter 14, Rule 5(b); AB CPC Chapter 5, Rule 1(b), commentary.
[32] FLS MC Rule 3.03(1); Que. CEA Rule 5.02; LSUC RPC Rule 3.05; AB CPC Chapter 5, Rule 5; BC PCH Chapter 14, Rule 18.
[33] CBA MC Chapter XIV, Commentary 7; FLS MC Rule 3.01(2).
[34] FLS MC Rule 3.02(2); Que. CEA Rule 5.03 (re lump-sum fee advertising); LSUC RPC Rule 3.04(1) and (2); AB CPC Chapter 5, Rule 6.
[35] AB CPC Chapter 5, Rule 7; BC PCH Chapter 9, Rule 2(a).
[36] FLS MC Rule 3.01(1)(c); CBA MC Chapter XIV, Commentary 3; NB CC Chapter 16, Rule (a); LSUC RPC Rule 3.04(1)(b); AB CPC Chapter 5, Rule 1(c).
[37] LSUC RPC Rule 3.04(1)(b); AB CPC Chapter 5, Rule 1(c), commentary.
[38] AB CPC Chapter 5, Rule 1(c), Commentary C.1(c).

soliciting "professional employment from a person who is believed to be in need of legal services, arising out of traumatic circumstances".[39] The Law Society of Upper Canada commentary notes, however, that this rule is not intended to "prevent a lawyer from offering his or her assistance" to someone who has suffered a traumatic experience, but is only intended to prohibit "the lawyer from using unconscionable or exploitative means" in so doing.[40]

The Supreme Court's decision in *Rocket*, and the approach taken by the codes, have materially altered the regulatory landscape for lawyer advertising. However, the codes still place significant barriers in the way of lawyers communicating information to prospective clients about their legal rights, and about what lawyers can do.

For example, Donald Jabour was suspended for indicating "sample fees" for various services in his advertisement. In those jurisdictions that prohibit lawyers from using words such as "from …" or "minimum" or "… and up",[41] that sort of advertisement would still be prohibited. And that suggests, I think, that almost all fee advertising will be prohibited in practice. Lawyers cannot precisely indicate in an ad what the legal fees will be for every transaction under the heading "will" or even "real estate transaction". As noted, legal services are a non-homogenous product, and prices will be non-homogeneous.

This blanket prohibition is undesirable. Without these rules, advertisements could indicate typical fees, and give thereby information of value to potential consumers. Consumers are unlikely to be duped or mislead by language that is entirely normal in modern consumer culture. Consumers know what is meant by "minimum" or "… and up". But they also know that, if one lawyer's fees start at $850 for a residential real estate transaction, and another lawyer's fees start at $650, that they have information that they can take into account in deciding which lawyer to use.[42] The restriction in the rules on providing this information means that clients are deprived of that information, while being "protected" from a confusion that they are unlikely to fall prey to.

The prohibition on comparing one lawyer to another similarly inhibits the provision of useful information to consumers, while not obviously protecting consumers from a meaningful harm. Consider this hypothetical

---

[39] AB CPC Chapter 5, Rule 3. See CBA MC Chapter XIV, Commentary 7; FLS MC Rule 3.01(2)(c); Que. CEA Rule 5.05; NB CC Chapter 16, Commentary 3; LSUC RPC Rule 3.06(2)(c); BC PCH Chapter 14, Rule 5(a).
[40] LSUC RPC Rule 3.06(2)(c), commentary.
[41] LSUC RPC Rule 3.04(2)(c).
[42] Interestingly, the choice they might make, because of the inability to judge which lawyer is better, is to retain the lawyer whose prices are higher. Since in general price signifies quality, consumers with no better information will often use price as a heuristic to determine quality. This is one factor that can lead to price escalation in a market with poor information.

ad:[43] a beautiful well dressed woman stands in front of an expensive car. Underneath runs a caption: "my ex's lawyer was in general practice" and the name of a law firm, "Smith, Jones: practicing only family law since 1990". This ad would not run contrary to the specialist rules, since the law firm does not say it specializes in family law, but only that its practice is restricted to that area. It also does not compare the firm to another lawyer or firm specifically. It does, however, compare the services that Smith, Jones would offer to "other lawyers" in general and, as a consequence, seems *prima facie* to violate the requirements of the codes of professional conduct.[44]

Yet I would argue that an ad of this sort provides important information to consumers that they would not otherwise have. It tells them that some lawyers practise only in one area of law. It tells them — I think accurately — that lawyers who practise only within an area are likely to know more about that area than lawyers who practise in diverse areas. It tells them that having a lawyer who knows something about an area is important for obtaining good results in litigation. It may imply that this law firm can obtain good results, and that may of course not be true — the law firm of Smith, Jones may be peopled by lazy incompetents — but only a blanket prohibition on advertising could eliminate that particular form of inaccuracy. Further, consumers know that even a fancy picture does not turn a fast food burger into haute cuisine.

This ad also arguably violates the "good taste" rules, rules that are perhaps the most problematic of all. In order to communicate information effectively to consumers an ad has to be more than accurate and complete; it also has to be memorable, capture the attention of consumers and in a short and straightforward way tell them what they need to know. The picture of the beautiful woman and the expensive car is vulgar and sexist,[45] but it is effective; in one small image it communicates extensive and important information about legal services that consumers should know.

A well known Canadian ad campaign by the DioGuardi firm, "The Taxman is Watching",[46] is even more informative, if in equally dubious taste. In the Taxman ad, people (presumably taxpayers) engage in everyday activities like driving or working on the computer, when up pops a vaguely sinister looking man in a suit and sunglasses. Against a song proclaiming "you can run ... but you can't hide ... Taxman!" the narrator asks whether the "taxman is on your case" and identifies reasons why that might be so — that you have not filed in a few years, that you are being audited, or reassessed. It then says that in those circumstances a tax lawyer can help

---

[43] This ad is based on an ad described to me by a student, but which I have never seen and could not track down.
[44] LSUC RPC Rule 3.04(1)(c), for example.
[45] It invokes the stereotype — repeated incessantly online — that women on divorce are avaricious gold diggers who bleed their husbands dry.
[46] Online: <http://www.youtube.com/user/dioguarditax#p/u/4/5qLx71n3siA>. See also "Taxman Games", online: <http://www.youtube.com/watch?v=UqGbOfoV5mk&feature=related>, which describes the risks to clients of being unrepresented when dealing with the CRA.

you. The tax lawyer can "stand between" you and the tax man, protect you from criminal prosecution and penalties, while negotiating a settlement. It notes the existence of lawyer-client confidentiality, and that the "sooner you call us, the more we can do to help".

The amount of information contained in this one minute ad about what constitutes a legal issue in a tax context, and about what a lawyer can do to help someone with that sort of issue, is remarkable. And the cheesy lyrics, and visual of the looming taxman, make it likely that someone watching the ad — especially someone getting letters from the Canada Revenue Agency — will remember what the ad communicates. And that is a good thing.

If an ad is not misleading, if it communicates information of importance, then the fact that it does so in a way that is memorable is something to be supported, even if it might be in dubious taste.

Issues also arise with respect to the rules that impose broad restrictions against contacting vulnerable people, or those who have suffered an injury in traumatic circumstances. The Law Society of Upper Canada articulated this requirement correctly. It is proper to require that lawyers approach people who are vulnerable in a manner that is not unconscionable or exploitative. It would also be proper to require that lawyers not persist if they are told not to contact the person a second time. And it would even be appropriate to highlight in the rules the need for sensitivity and empathy in making contact with individuals in traumatic circumstances.

However, people — like Ernest Gunn and his mother — who have suffered injury in traumatic circumstances are often the very people who need legal counsel the most and who, if they do not receive it, will suffer an adverse legal consequence. Others — insurance companies, lawyers for affected parties — are not prohibited from contacting the victims of such injuries to negotiate a settlement, and the limitation period does not cease to run while personal injury lawyers maintain a respectful distance. Every day that passes from the time of the traumatic event may be significant for the gathering of evidence, the recording of useful facts or otherwise; the absence of a lawyer at that critical time may have a detrimental effect on the prosecution of the case. A lawyer who approaches a client in those circumstances, and who does so respectfully and sensitively, should be encouraged as acting with professional virtue, not condemned as acting improperly.

Fortunately, based on a review of the few disciplinary decisions on lawyer advertising, it appears that law societies are taking a hands-off approach to the question of advertising and, as the Canadian Bar Association ("CBA") rules suggest, do not enforce the rules against lawyers who have "acted in good faith in trying to make legal services available more efficiently, economically and conveniently than they would otherwise have been".[47] The few disciplinary cases have arisen where lawyers paid third

---

[47] CBA MC Chapter XIV, Commentary 8.

parties for referrals[48] or where the advertisements were misleading.[49] Further, in at least two of the misleading cases the lawyer in question — Tony Merchant — had sent a direct solicitation letter to vulnerable clients, clients injured by a traumatic experience. Yet the Law Society of Saskatchewan, which was the regulator involved in both cases, took no exception to the use of solicitation letters in that context; its only concern was with whether the letters were misleading.

This is not to suggest that the rules in their current form are acceptable, but simply that in practice it appears that lawyers are free to advertise in a way that is effective even if tasteless, and that solicitation of clients who need legal services, even if that need arises from vulnerability or injury in traumatic circumstances, is acceptable.

One final point on advertising should be noted. In my view part of the discomfort with advertising is that lawyers do not advertise for the purpose of benefiting clients; advertising may benefit clients, but the motivation for advertising is the economic interests of lawyers. It seems awkward to praise as a professional virtue something that is motivated by economic self-interest. The happy accident of capitalism is, however, that rational self-interest can maximize social welfare. This happy accident may not always be realized, but, in the context of lawyer advertising, it often is. For that reason, within the constraints on misleading or abusive advertising, the regulation of lawyer advertising should continue to be applied as it is, and law societies should amend their rules to reflect the apparent disciplinary practice.[50]

B. *Pro Bono*

Law society codes of conduct state that lawyers have an obligation to foster access to justice, and to contribute to the availability of legal services. Typical is the commentary to Chapter 1, Rule 4 of the Law Society of Alberta's Code of Professional Conduct:

> The right of every person to legal counsel creates a corresponding obligation on the part of society and the profession to supply legal representation. Such representation must be available in fact, and not merely in theory, or the right to counsel is meaningless.

---

[48] *Law Society of Upper Canada v. Barnett*, [1997] L.S.D.D. No. 94; *Law Society of British Columbia v. Siebenga*, [1993] L.S.D.D. No. 181; *Law Society of Alberta v. Stemp*, [1996] L.S.D.D. No. 297.

[49] *Law Society of British Columbia v. Pierce*, [1995] L.S.D.D. No. 267; *Merchant v. Law Society of Saskatchewan*, [2000] L.S.D.D. No. 24, affd [2002] S.J. No. 288, 2002 SKCA 60 (Sask. C.A.); *Merchant v. Law Society of Saskatchewan*, [2009] S.J. No. 145, 2009 SKCA 33 (Sask. C.A.) (misleading advertising was not sanctionable because sent out inadvertently).

[50] It may be the case that law societies deal with inappropriate advertising informally — by contacting the lawyer and simply requesting that the advertisement be removed. I hope that that is not the case; if it is, then it is not a practice that should continue unless the ad in question is misleading.

Members of society with the most pressing need for legal services often encounter difficulty in obtaining representation because of economic or social disadvantages. Lawyers should be willing to assist such persons through participating in legal aid programs, accommodating requests by the court to represent parties appearing before the court, and reducing or waiving fees in appropriate circumstances. A lawyer should be slow to decline to act for a disadvantaged client unless the refusal has substantial ethical justification.[51]

Most codes direct lawyers that it is in "the best traditions of the legal profession" to participate in *pro bono* activities or to otherwise offer legal services at a reduced price in order to ensure that representation is available.[52] Law societies have taken steps to encourage *pro bono* activities by lawyers.[53] In no Canadian jurisdiction, however, is the provision of *pro bono* required, nor are lawyers required any longer to fund legal aid or other programs through a levy included in the price of bar membership.[54]

The justification for the lawyer's role grounded in the authority of law also justifies strong public funding for legal aid, and for funding that applies to civil and administrative matters, not simply criminal matters. If legality only applies fairly to those who can afford to retain counsel, legality ceases to be a meaningful compromise to social disagreement, and instead risks becoming a vehicle for the assertion of power by the well off.

This does not necessarily mean, however, that lawyers themselves have a particular duty to ensure that legal services are broadly accessible. They have such a duty as members of a civil society, but being the lawyers whose services are required does not oblige them to provide those services for free, any more than it does doctors or others who provide important public services. Indeed, when government regulates the provision of public services — such as utilities — it operates on the regulatory principle that the provider of such services should receive fair and reasonable compensation, not that they should provide services without pay. Working for free is a professional virtue, and one that can be used to meaningfully address the tension that can arise from the competition between professional and

---

[51] FLS MC Rule 3.01(1), commentary; CBA MC Chapter XIV, Commentary 1; NB CC Chapter 16, Commentary 1; LSUC RPC Rule 3.01 and commentary; AB CPC Chapter 1, Commentary 4; BC PCH, Canon 3.

[52] AB CPC Chapter 1, Commentary 1; CBA MC Chapter XIV, Commentary 5; FLS MC Rule 3.01(1), commentary; LSUC RPC Rule 3.01, commentary.

[53] *Pro Bono Publico* – For the Public Good, Report of the *Pro Bono* Committee of the Law Society of Alberta, April 2003 and *Pro Bono* Law Alberta (www.pbla.org); *Pro Bono Publico* – Lawyers Serving the Public Good in British Columbia, Report of the *Pro Bono* Initiative Committee, a joint committee of the Law Society of British Columbia and the Canadian Bar Association (B.C. branch), June 2002 and Access *Pro Bono* Society of British Columbia at (<http://probononet.bc.ca/>); *Pro Bono* Law Ontario (www.pblo.org); *Pro Bono* (www.pbls.org).

[54] Such a levy used to be applied to Ontario lawyers, but was abolished in 1998. See "LSUC votes for independent administration of legal aid", online: <http://www.lsuc.on.ca/news/b/olg/marchapril-1998-vol2-no2/>.

personal moral values,[55] but holding the professional role does not transform that virtue into a moral requirement.

As I have argued elsewhere,[56] the argument that lawyers have a mandatory obligation to provide *pro bono* services, or to otherwise fund the availability of legal aid, can be best justified through identification and analysis of the imperfections in the market for legal services as set out above. When markets are imperfect, the expected outcome of those imperfections will be that some market participants will extract "rents" — economic returns that would not arise from the operation of a perfect market. In the case of the market for legal services, because the imperfections tend to empower lawyers relative to their clients, it is probable that if rents are being extracted from the market, they are being extracted by lawyers, not clients. If the imperfections in the market cannot otherwise be addressed, it is legitimate to require that those rents be returned in some way to redress the problems associated with the market imperfections.

The difficulty, however, is that while it is theoretically likely that lawyers enjoy rents as a result of the imperfections in the market for legal services, the nature and amount of those rents cannot be easily identified. Analysis of the earnings of lawyers over time does not clearly demonstrate that such rents exist. Lawyers' incomes have remained relatively constant when assessed against those of other professionals over time, and fluctuations in lawyer incomes tend to reflect overall economic trends.[57] As a consequence, while the imperfections in the market provide a modest (theoretical) justification for the imposition of a levy on lawyers to fund legal services, they do not provide a justification sufficient to warrant a mandatory *pro bono* requirement.

C. Other Regulatory Measures

This is not to say that lawyers can ignore the barriers to justice that arise from the cost of legal services. As a self-regulating profession charged with protecting the public interest in relation to the provision of legal services, lawyers have a clear regulatory obligation to address barriers to justice. Regulation of the legal profession should increase the availability of information to consumers about when legal services would be beneficial. They should also, where possible, take measures that will reduce the cost barriers to legal services, addressing in particular imperfections in the market for legal services where the benefits of doing so outweigh the costs.

To a significant extent, Canadian law societies have discharged this obligation well. In cooperation with the law foundations that manage interest

---

[55] See Tim Dare, *The Counsel of Rogues? A Defence of the Standard Conception of the Lawyer's Role* (Burlington: Ashgate Publishing Company, 2009) at 151-52.

[56] Alice Woolley, "Imperfect Duty: Lawyers' Obligation to Foster Access to Justice" (2007) 45(5) Alta. L. Rev. 107.

[57] *Ibid.*

from trust accounts, law societies are involved in activities in relation to public education. They operate lawyer referral services through which prospective clients receive a half hour of free legal advice to determine whether, and to what extent, they require legal services. They support the operation of community legal clinics, run by volunteer lawyers, law students or some combination thereof. They, along with the CBA, also play an important role in advocating for the continued funding of legal aid, and in explaining the meaning and importance of the lawyer's role in a civil society.[58]

There are, though, further measures that could be taken, a few of which are noted here. First, relatively little attention has been paid to attempting to create minimum competency obligations in relation to the performance of legal services.[59] Identification of the standards that need to be fulfilled when, for example, writing a will or prosecuting a claim, helps to increase the homogeneity of the product for legal services, and to reduce the uncertainty for consumers participating in the legal services market.

Second, concerns with professionalism have, as was the case with advertising, tended to orientate regulators away from concerns with market function, and towards protection of professional interests. Professional interest protection has the tendency to exacerbate, rather than to eliminate, imperfections in the market for legal services, since it often discourages activities because they are vulgar or in bad taste, even if they promote access to justice. Regulators should de-emphasize professionalism initiatives.

Third, where consistent with the provision of an appropriate level of service, lawyers should be encouraged to work with law clerks and paralegals in order to reduce the cost of legal services. A service delivery model which couples lawyer expertise with the cost savings of using law clerks and paralegals to implement that expertise, can protect the public interest while meaningfully reducing costs.

Fourth, more attention should be paid to billing practices, and to the standards and requirements to be met by lawyers when billing clients. Lawyers should be required to give clear *ex ante* information about what services are included, the risks and rewards associated with proceeding, and about the most efficient way of achieving a legal outcome.[60] At the same time, the use of alternative billing methods, such as contingency fees, should continue to be encouraged by the profession as a legitimate way of expanding the availability of justice.

Fifth, in a world of dwindling public financial support for legal aid, law societies need to provide real guidance to lawyers practising in the new

---

[58] See, for example, Luis Millan, "Barreau's appeal for broader access to legal aid snubbed" *The Lawyers Weekly* 30:24 (29 October 2010) 1.
[59] Michael J. Trebilcock, "Regulating the Market for Legal Services" (2008) 45(5) Alta. L. Rev. 215.
[60] See Alice Woolley, "Time for Change: Unethical Hourly Billing in the Canadian Profession and How to Fix It" (2004), 83(3) Can. Bar Rev. 859.

legal clinics as to what constitutes competent legal services, and how those lawyers can meet their ethical obligations in constrained circumstances, particularly when acting under a limited scope retainer. Law societies need to be involved in articulating what competent service looks like for a lawyer providing limited scope retainer services to consumers in a legal clinic setting.

Finally, all lawyers, the CBA and the law societies must continue to be tireless and unflinching advocates for continued and meaningful funding for legal aid which, in the end, is almost certain to be the difference between access to justice and not for the majority of low- and middle-income Canadians.

4. CONCLUSION

The legal profession's poor reputation troubles lawyers. It should. Within a free and democratic society lawyers play a crucial role, ensuring that the compromise of legality works. To view the lawyers who do so as liars, cheats and thieves is wrong and unfair. In a world of compromise it may also be unsurprising — the success of the moral position one rejects is easy to blame on the person instrumental in the accomplishment of that success.

Addressing this poor reputation cannot be done directly, and may well be impossible. What lawyers can do — and should do — is fulfill the role they are called on to play to the best of their ability, and work hard to ensure that lawyers are available to those who need them.

INDEX

ABORIGINALS
First Nations' residential schools, 314-315

ACCESS TO JUSTICE
advertising and solicitation, 322-327
- codes of conduct regulation of professionalism, 323-324
- comparison shopping, 324-325
- generally, 322
- "good taste" rules re marketing, 323-326
- solicitation, 326

barriers to, 314-321
- expense, 317-321
- legal services issues. *See* legal services
- need for lawyer, consciousness of, 314-317

First Nations' residential schools case, 314-315
generally, 313, 331
lawyers
- expense of education, 318
- role in procuring justice, 314-317

legal services
- competence, 320
- costs of, 318
- demand for, competition re, 318
- imperfect market re, 318
- information, lack of, 319
- expense, 317-321

need for lawyer, consciousness of, 314-317
pro bono work, 327-329
reduction of barriers to, 321-331
- advertising. *See* advertising and solicitation
- generally, 321
- pro bono work, 327-329

- *self-regulation*. *See* self-regulation measures

self-regulation measures, 329-331
- billing practices, 330
- generally, 329-330
- legal clinics, participation in, 330
- minimum competency standards, 330
- paralegals, use of, 330
- professional interest protection, 330

ADVERTISING AND MARKETING. *See* **ACCESS TO JUSTICE**

ADVOCACY. *See also* **WITNESS PREPARATION**
adversarial role. *See* ZEALOUS ADVOCACY
codes of conduct re, 69, 71
competence, 71-75
- administration of justice and, 73
- client, effect on, 73
- codes of conduct re, 71
- examples, 72
- professional discipline re, 72
- solicitor negligence, 74

criminal action, threat of, 79-81
discovery, examinations for, 87-88
duty, limits of zeal, 69-70
ex parte applications, full and frank disclosure requirement, 88-90
frivolous arguments, 75-81
- advice, 79
- codes of conduct re, 76
- costs against lawyer, 76-77
- courts' attitude re, 76-77
- non-litigation context, 78-79

frivolous litigation, prohibition re, 79-81

ADVOCACY — *cont'd*
generally, 69-71, 104-105
investigation of client's case, 90-93
- corporate representatives, 93
- covert investigation, 91
- potential witnesses, dealing with, 92
- scope of, 90
- unlawful activity, 91

lawyer speech, 93-104
- criticism of judges and legal system, 101-104
- • codes of conduct re, 101
- • discipline for, 102
- • "scandalizing the court" contempt offence, 103
- criticism of other lawyers, 96-101
- • discipline for, 97-99
- • justified discipline, 101
- • legal remedies re, 101
- • profession's reputation, principle of, 99
- • unjustified discipline, 100
- generally, 93-94
- public statements, 94-96
- • client's interest, 94
- • defamation, 95
- • *sub judice* rule, 95-96

negligence law and, 74
relevant adverse authority, obligations re, 85-87
resolute advocacy, 71-75
sharp practice, rule against, 81-85
- codes of conduct re, 81
- elements of, 82
- mistakes in law by opposing counsel, correction of, 83-84
- settlement enforcement and, 82

zeal, *see also* ZEALOUS ADVOCACY
- restraints on, 75-87
- scope of, 69-71

BARRIERS TO JUSTICE. *See* **ACCESS TO JUSTICE**

CANADIAN CHARTER OF RIGHTS AND FREEDOMS
"prescribed by law" requirement, 27-28
procedural fairness provisions, 28
right to counsel, 29
testimonial immunity, 207

CLIENT
confidentiality, rights of. *See* CONFIDENTIALITY
conflicts of interest with. *See* CONFLICTS OF INTEREST
counselling. *See* LAWYER-CLIENT RELATIONSHIP
corporate. *See* CORPORATE CLIENT
criminal. *See* CRIMINAL CLIENT
decision making and. *See* LAWYER-CLIENT RELATIONSHIP
defined. *See* CONFLICTS OF INTEREST
firing. *See* LAWYER-CLIENT RELATIONSHIP
guilty. *See* GUILTY CLIENT
investigation of case. *See* ADVOCACY
relationship with. *See* LAWYER-CLIENT RELATIONSHIP
selection. *See* LAWYER-CLIENT RELATIONSHIP
solicitor-client privilege. *See* CONFIDENTIALITY

COACHING. *See* **WITNESS PREPARATION**

CODES OF CONDUCT. *See* **ETHICS**

COMPETENCE, 71-75, 320, 330

CONFIDENTIALITY
client's right to, lawyer's duty to protect, 142
disclosure, duty of/permission, *see also* non-disclosure, duty of

CONFIDENTIALITY — *cont'd*
- confidential but not privileged information, 125-127
- generally, 124
- innocence of accused, to establish, 133-136
- joint retainer, as between clients vs. third parties, 129
- law society discipline proceedings, 130-131
- legal advice from another lawyer, obtaining, 132
- legal order, duty to comply with valid, 127
- non-confidential/privileged information, 125-127
- physical/real evidence of crime, 139-142
- self-defence of lawyer in litigation, 132, 156
- threats, *etc.*, to safety of person/group, to prevent serious, 136-139, 155-156
- waiver of rights by client, 127-129

foundations of duty re, 107-109
generally, 107-109
justification of general duty, 145-157
- Bentham's argument, 147-148
- contextual approach, 152-155
- corporations/organizations, 157
- critics of utilitarian argument, 148-149
- Frankel's utilitarian argument, 146, 150
- full and frank disclosure issue, 148-151
- generally, 145-146
- human dignity argument, 147, 151
- lawyer's self-interest exception, 156
- Luban non-consequentialist argument, 151-155
- protection function analysis, 152-155

- public safety exception, 155-156
- Supreme Court of Canada's utilitarian argument, 146-147
- utilitarian argument, 146-151

non-clients, duty to protect confidentiality claims of, 143-145
- improper receipt and review of opposing party's information, 143
- improper use of inadvertently disclosed information, 143-145

non-disclosure, duty of, *see also* disclosure, duty of/permission
- absolute secrecy requirement, 119
- breach of, 121-124
  - benefit of current clients, for, 122
  - discipline, 121-124
  - examples, 122-123
  - lawsuits, 121
- colleagues and staff, extension to, 120
- corporate/organization client, 119, 157
- criminal communications exclusion, 112-115
- general rule, 109
- identity of client, 117-118
- implied undertaking rule, 124
- indefinite life of, 120
- information not from client, 118
- lawyer-client relationship, requirement of, 109
- legal advice element, 110-112
- privilege vs. confidentiality, 110
- property, 119
- solicitor-client privilege and. *See* solicitor-client privilege
- third party, information re, 124
- third party knowledge of information, 115-117

solicitor-client privilege, *see also* disclosure, duty of
- absolute secrecy requirement, 119
- colleagues and staff, extension to, 120
- confidentiality and, 107

CONFIDENTIALITY — *cont'd*
- criminal communications exclusion, 112-115
- indefinite life of, 120
- identity of client, 117-118
- information not from client, 118
- legal advice element, 110-112
- property, 119
- third party knowledge of information, 115-117

CONFLICTS OF INTEREST
appearances rationale for rule re, 241
client, definition of, 223
- conversation, mere, 225
- "near client" concept, 225-227
- non-retainer context, 223-224
- retainer context, 223
- trust, establishment of, 224
current clients, duties to, 233-235, 257-272
- concurrent representation of clients, 265-272
- • adverse interests, consent and best interests requirements, 266-268
- • breach of fiduciary duties, 268
- • "bright line rule", 266, 268, 269-272
- • case law applying "bright line", 270-272
- • conflict, potential for, 265
- • lawyer's personal interests, 268
- generally, 257-258
- simultaneous representation of clients in conflict, 259-264
- • best interests requirement, 262
- • conflict, identification of actual/potential, 260
- • dispute, occurrence of, 263
- • high risk joint retainers, 263-264
- • information required to be provided clients, 261
- simultaneous representation of clients in dispute, 258-259
definition, 216-223, 276

former clients, duties to, 232-233, 243-257
- case law, 244-245
- CBA Guidelines, 244
- codes of conduct, 244
- confidential information
- • degree issue, 249-251
- • misuse of, scope of restriction, 251
- • no use of, where, 255-257
- • presumption re, 245
- general principles, 243-246
- law firm conflicts, 243
- new matters, prior retainer and, 246-248
- screening devices, sufficiency of, 254
- tactical disqualification, 253-254
- transfers of lawyers between firms, 252
generally, 215-216, 276
informed consent, 227-231
- codes of conduct re, 227-228
- independent legal advice requirement, 231
- inference of, 228
- information/ignorance, 229
- prior to conflict arising, 230
- writing requirement, 228
lawyer-client conflicts, 272-276
- business dealings, 231-232, 274-275
- case law examples, 272-276
- principles re, 272
- sexual relationships, 273-276
loyalty, duty of, 236-238
- lawyer-client relationship and, 236-237
- scope of, 238
misuse of confidential information, 220-221
obtaining improper advantage, 221-223
- breach of confidence, as, 222
- damages for breach of loyalty, 222
- sexual advantages, 223

CONFLICTS OF INTEREST — *cont'd*
preventative rationale of law re, 238
prohibitions, justification for, 236-238
rationale for rules re, 238-241
regulatory function of law re, 239-241
substantial risk of material and adverse effect on representation, 217-220
- actual adverse effect, 218
- lawyer-client relationship, nature of, 219
- possibility of adverse effect, 218
- retainer, relevance of, 219-220
types of, 231-236
- current clients, between, 233-235
- former vs. new clients, 232-233
- lawyer's own interests, 231-232
- third party and multiple role conflicts, 235-236

CONSENT. *See* **CONFLICTS OF INTEREST**

CORPORATE CLIENT, 93, 119, 157

CRIMINAL CLIENT, 56, 67-68, 165, 167

CRIMINAL COMMUNICATIONS, 112-115

CRIMINAL LAW CONTEXT
defence counsel. *See* DEFENCE COUNSEL ETHICS
generally, 277, 311
prosecutors. *See* PROSECUTORIAL ETHICS

CRIMINAL RECORD, 207

CROSS-EXAMINATION
codes of conduct, constraints imposed by, 205
credibility, 203
distorting effects of, 203
ethical issues, 207-213
- adjudication system and, 212
- character and credibility, 208
- ethical requirements, 207-208
- false inferences, creating, 209
- judgment calls, 208
- lawyer's knowledge re truth of testimony, 209-212
- relevance issues, 209
- truthful witness
- • creating false impression re, 210
- • lawyer's knowledge re, 209-212
evidence law, constraints imposed by, 205-206
- character issue, 206
- *Charter*, testimonial immunity, 207
- criminal record, 207
- good faith basis for question, 206
- prejudicial effects, 206
- relevance and admissibility, 206
- sexual assault cases, 207
generally, 201-204
importance of, 204
law re, 204-207
lie-detector, as, 203
misled triers of fact, factors re, 202
process cross-examination, 204, 205
substantive cross-examination, 204-205
truth vs. untruth, difficulty of determining, 202-203
types of, 204
wide latitude of courts, 204

CROWN COUNSEL. *See* **PROSECUTORIAL ETHICS**

DEFENCE COUNSEL ETHICS
guilty clients, defending, 301-308
- "guilty", meaning of, 301-302
- opinion, suspension of judgment, 302-303
- specific knowledge of guilt, 303-308
- technicalities, use of, 301

DEFENCE COUNSEL ETHICS
— cont'd
- truthful evidence, presenting, 303-308

plea bargaining, 308-311
- client who maintains his innocence, 308-310
- establishing basis for guilty plea, 308, 310
- freedom of choice, 310-311
- influencing guilty plea, 310
- voluntariness of guilty plea, 310

DISCIPLINE, 12, 72, 97-102, 121-124, 130-131, 293, 298-301

DISCLOSURE. *See* **CONFIDENTIALITY**

DISCOVERY, 87-88

ETHICS. *See also* **DEFENCE COUNSEL ETHICS; PROSECUTORIAL ETHICS; WITNESS PREPARATION**
codes of conduct as source of
- legality and, 16
- limited influence of, 13-14
- loyalty and, 16
- 1987 CBA Code, 12
- 1920 CBA Canons of Legal Ethics, 10-11
- opposition to, 9-10

defined, 2
democracy, relation to, 2-3
generally, 1-3
integrity challenge, 17-19
law society discipline as source of, 12
legal profession, regulatory structure of, 4-9
- *B.C. Legal Profession Act*, 5-6
- Canada vs. common law world, 4
- Canadian Bar Association, 7
- Federal of Law Societies, 6
- provincial law societies
- • disciplinary function, 8
- • purpose and mandate of, 4-6
- self-regulation, arguments re, 7-9

meaning and purpose, as source of, 3
miscellaneous sources of, 14
purposes of regulation, 15-17
rationale for studying, 1-3
self-regulation. *See* legal profession, regulatory structure of
socio-economic critiques, 15-16
sources of duties, 3-4

EVIDENCE LAW. *See* **CROSS-EXAMINATION**

EX PARTE **APPLICATIONS,** 88-90

EXAMINATION. *See* **WITNESS CROSS-EXAMINATION**

FEES. *See* **LAWYER-CLIENT RELATIONSHIP**

FRIVOLOUS ARGUMENTS. *See* **ADVOCACY**

GUILTY CLIENTS. *See* **DEFENCE COUNSEL ETHICS; PERJURY**

INVESTIGATION BY LAWYER. *See* **ADVOCACY**

LAW SOCIETIES. *See* **ADVOCACY**

LAW SOCIETIES
described. *See* ETHICS
discipline proceedings, 12, 130

LAWYER-CLIENT RELATIONSHIP
client counselling, 52-54, 59-63
- codes of conduct re, 59
- morality, 60-61
- unlawful activity, prohibition re, 61-63

client selection, 46-52
- access to justice principle, 47
- "cab rank rule", 51
- choice vs. discrimination, 46
- conflicts, prohibition re, 47
- discretion, exercise of, 50

LAWYER-CLIENT RELATIONSHIP — *cont'd*
- discrimination, rule against, 47-50
- general right to decline representation, 50
- personal moral commitments, 49
- rules re, 46

fees, 64-65
- codes of conduct re, 64
- contingency fees, 65

generally, 45-46, 68

lawyer-client decision making, 52-59
- codes of conduct re, 54-55
- cooperation, principle of, 58
- criminal context, 56
- litigation context, 55-57
- *Morin* case, 52-54, 58
- pleas and defences, 54-55
- raising defence absent proper instruction, 52-54
- range of decisions made, 54
- witnesses, calling of, 56

withdrawal, 65-68
- cause for, 65-66
- criminal context, 67-68
- expense and prejudice to client, 66
- non-payment of fees, 67
- required, 66
- required continued representation, 68
- timing issue, 67

LAWYER-CLIENT TRUST. *See* **CONFIDENTIALITY**

LAWYER'S ETHICS. *See* **ETHICS**

LEGAL PROFESSION. *See* **ACCESS TO JUSTICE; ADVOCACY; ETHCS**

LEGAL SERVICES. *See* **ACCESS TO JUSTICE**

LOYALTY. *See* **CONFLICTS OF INTEREST**

MALICIOUS PROSECUTION, 292, 296

NEGLIGENCE, 74

PERJURY

assisting client to deceive court, prohibition re, 163-165
- civil context, 164
- criminal context, 165

candour, obligation of to court, 163

certainty re deceptive testimony, degree/standard re, 165-167

civil litigation context, 171-172

codes of conduct re, 160, 169

confidentiality, duty of, 162, 169

contextual factors, 159

counsel, right to, 162

criminal context
- accused, evidence of, 173-183
  - withdrawal and limited disclosure, 174
  - withdrawal and non-disclosure, 173-174
- American practice, 175
- candour to court principle, 175
- disclosure, 176
- intentional ignorance approach, 177-179
- narrative testimony approach, 179
- non-accused, evidence of, 172
- present evidence as truthful approach, 180-182

dilemma re, approaches to. *See* criminal context

disclosure of, 169-170, 176

duty re
- generally, 159-160
- obligation to withdraw, 168-171, 173-174

generally, 159-163, 182-183

judge's question re, 161

New Brunswick rules, 169, 176

principles around, 162

qualified/non-duty re, 160

solicitor-client privilege and, 170

PERJURY — *cont'd*
statement of intention to deceive
• circumstance re, 159
• information to be given civil client, 168
• information to be given criminal client, 167
• lawyer's duty, 167-173
statement of past deception
• circumstance re, 160
• lawyer's duty, 167-173
withdrawal, obligation re, 168-171, 173-174

PLEA BARGAINING. *See* **DEFENCE COUNSEL ETHICS; LAWYER-CLIENT RELATIONSHIP, lawyer-client decision-making**

PREPARATION. *See* **WITNESS PREPARATION**

PRIVILEGE. *See* **CONFIDENTIALITY**

PROSECUTORIAL DISCRETION
abuse of process, 292, 295
Attorney General, review of, 293
described, 284-288
disclosure decisions, 284-285
exercise of, manner of, 288-290
factual basis for prosecuting, 291
malicious prosecution, 292, 296
manner of proceeding decisions, 285
"mistakes", consequences of, 292
oversight of, 291-297
plea agreement, withdrawal of, 287
recklessness, 296
trial tactics, 286-287
wrongful exercise of, discipline re, 293

PROSECUTORIAL ETHICS
complainant, acting for, 281
constraints, 279-280
controlled zeal requirements, 277-284

discipline
• discretion, abuse of. *See* **PROSECUTORIAL DISCRETION**
• non-disclosure, 298-301
disclosure, 297-301
• constitution and ethical duty, as, 297-298
• non-disclosure, consequences of, 298-301
discretion. *See* **PROSECUTORIAL DISCRETION**
generally, 277
inappropriate behaviour, examples of, 279
integrity and fairness, duties of, 278, 284
misapprehensions of court, correction of, 282-284
political independence, 281
prosecutorial function, balance required, 278-281
vigorous advocacy, role of, 280

RESOLUTE ADVOCACY. *See* **ADVOCACY; ZEALOUS ADVOCACY**

SELF-REGULATION. *See* **ACCESS TO JUSTICE; ETHICS**

SEXUAL RELATIONSHIPS, 223, 273-276

SHARP PRACTICE. *See* **ADVOCACY**

SOLICITATION. *See* **ACCESS TO JUSTICE**

SOLICITOR-CLIENT PRIVILEGE. *See* **CONFIDENTIALITY**

SPEECH, LIMITATIONS ON. *See* **ADVOCACY**

TRUST. *See* **CONFIDENTIALITY**

WITNESS CROSS-EXAMINATION. *See* **CROSS-EXAMINATION**

WITNESS PREPARATION
Adair, Geoffrey, analysis by. *See* stages of
avoidance of coaching, challenges, 190-197, 200
- facts vs. legal concepts, problem of, 191-192
- generally, 190-191, 197
- inexperience of witness, 193
- memory problems/distortions, 193-196
- witness variability factor, 192

coaching
- challenges of avoiding. *See* avoidance of coaching, challenges
- rules re, 187-189

codes of conduct re, 187
constraints on, 190
contemporaneous information, reliance on, 197, 200
copies of evidence, giving to witnesses, 189
duties re, 187
ethical and effective approach to, 199-201
generally, 185-187, 201
independent investigation by lawyer, 200
information, techniques for eliciting, 197-198
law re, 187-190
leading questions, use of, 200
memory
- distortions of, 193-196
- unrealistic expectations of, 200

perception problem, 186
personality issues, 185
pre-meeting prep, 197, 200
prohibitions, 190, 199
skills re, 197-199
stages of, 197-199
- cross-examination, re, 198
- meeting, 197
- polishing, 198
- preliminary preparation, 197

talking between cross and re-examination, 188

ZEALOUS ADVOCACY. *See also* **ADVOCACY**
adversarial role, 21
arguments against, 33-40
- morality-of-law objection, 38-40
- personal morality objection, 36-38
- postmodern theory, 34-36
- sustainable professionalism, 34-36

arguments for, 40-43
- central features of resolute advocacy, 40-41
- complexity of law factor, 41
- meaning and purpose, 42
- moral obligation vs. professional role, 42

Canadian legal culture, 22-24
- nonconformist resolute advocates, examples, 23-24
- principles behind, 22-23

generally, 21-22
substantive legal norms, 25-33
- access to legal redress, state facilitation of, 30
- *Charter* "prescribed by law" requirement, 27-28
- general principles, 25
- interpretation and law, 31-32
- lawyers as resolute advocates, 32-33
- procedural fairness, *Charter* provisions, 28
- restricting vs. mandating state action, court tendency, 31
- right to counsel, *Charter* provisions, 29
- *Roncarelli v. Duplessis*, 26
- rule of law, principle of, 26-27
- self-determination, principle of, 26, 28
- substantive judicial review, 32

"sustainable professionalism" vs., 34-36